D0176090

WineTrails

OF WASHINGTON, 2nd Edition

A guide for uncorking your memorable wine tour

Happy WineTrails!
Steve Roberts

by Steve Roberts

MORE WINE ▶

South Slope
Productions

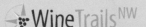
WineTrails NW

WineTrails of Washington, 2nd Edition
A guide for uncorking your memorable wine tour

Published by
South Slope Productions (Imprint, WineTrails Northwest)
6150 West Mercer Way, Mercer Island, WA 98040
800-533-6165
www.winetrailsnw.com

Readers should also be aware that winery locations as well as tasting room particulars (e.g., hours of operation, tasting fees) may have changed since this book was printed. Readers are advised to contact the winery in advance to verify the information. Remember to drink responsibly.

Note that no wineries paid to be included in this book.

Library of Congress Cataloging in Publication record available.

 Original WineTrails Northwest logo by Beth Hayes, King Salmon Creative Communications; modified by Lisa J. Pettit, Lisa Pettit Designs

Edited by Sunny Parsons

Cover and interior design by Lisa J. Pettit, Lisa Pettit Designs, Seattle, Washington

Photos by Steve Roberts, South Slope Productions, unless otherwise indicated

Production by Seattle Publishing Inc.

Second Edition

ISBN 978-0-9792698-5-1

Printed in China by C&C Offset Printing Company

Acknowledgements & Dedication

I am hugely indebted to the WineTrails Northwest production team, and to my friends and family for their support. I would be particularly remiss in not mentioning the patience and loving support of my wife, Kathleen Roberts, who has endured a husband who was often missing in action as he spent enumerable weekends in wine country researching this book. Hey, someone had to do it!

The inimitable design talent and artwork of Lisa Pettit grace this guide from cover to cover. I may have written this book, but Lisa designed it. Every little navigation icon you see, every color chosen, and every design element demonstrate Lisa's unwavering attention to detail.

An essential member of the production team is Sunny Parsons, editor extraordinaire. I remain in awe that anyone can understand what a dangling modifier is, let alone fix it. She has this amazing ability to preserve my voice, and as in the previous edition, has loaned her signature editing prowess throughout.

Speaking of production, the crew of Seattle Publishing once again rose to the WineTrail challenge in preparing the manuscript for printing. It's no small task and requires a mixed bag of skill sets and experience. The axiom "It takes a village" is especially true when it comes to the production of a book.

Washington's position as the second-leading producer of premium wine in America would not have happened without the hard work and dogged determination of select pioneers who came before us. Washington's foray into growing wine grapes goes back to 1825, when grape seeds were first planted at Fort Vancouver. At the turn of the century, William B. Bridgman saw the potential for premium wine production and played a vital role in bringing irrigation to the Yakima Valley, in addition to establishing one of Washington's preeminent vineyards at Harrison Hill, outside Sunnyside. By 1934, Bridgman had more than 165 acres of wine grapes under contract with more than 70 growers.

This set the stage for Washington State University (WSU) researcher Dr. Walter J. Clore to demonstrate that Washington was the perfect place to cultivate vinifera. Through 40 years of research at the WSU research center in Prosser, Clore pursued his passion and established the foundation for Washington's wine industry. Upon his death in 2003, the Washington State Legislature officially recognized Clore as the "Father of the Washington Wine Industry."

I dedicate this book to these pioneers of the Washington wine industry, whose toil and perseverance bore such rich fruit, which, in turn, has resulted in the emergence of a thriving wine-tour industry. To them I am eternally grateful.

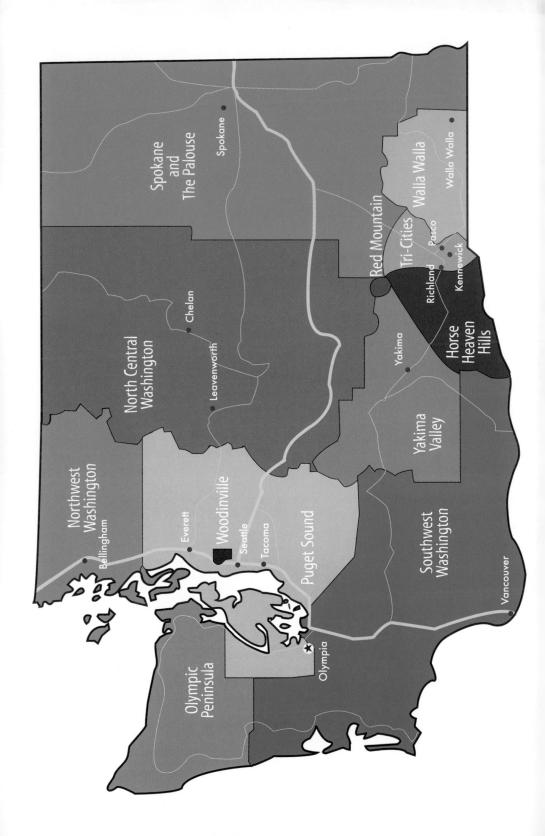

Contents at a Glance

Detailed Table of Contents

Woodinville Wine Country

Southwest Washington Wine Country

Yakima Valley Wine Country

Spokane Wine Country

Practical Stuff

About the Author

A Great Wine Region of the World — Washington

Listening to My Tongue — Part Two

Welcome to *WineTrails of Washington*, the second edition. More than an update, it's a complete overhaul. You see, since the release of the original *WineTrails of Washington* guide in 2007, Washington's wine world has undergone many changes and this is especially true with the wine industry.

During that time, I was aware that there were new wineries sprouting up as well as wineries dying on the vine, casualties of the recession, but I was focused on WineTrails guidebooks for Oregon, Idaho, and Walla Walla. While I was busy tending to those endeavors, the state's wine industry changed: It grew much bigger and became even better. Today, people from all over the world come to Washington to experience our wines and to immerse themselves in all the creature comforts that wine tourists enjoy, from the expected — fall crush — to the surprising — wine-centric spa services (no kidding).

To put this changing industry into perspective, here are some interesting facts from the Washington Wine Commission:

- Washington is the second-largest producer of premium wines in the U.S.
- There are more than 750 wineries in the state.
- More than 45,000 acres of premium wine grapes are under production.
- The state has more than 30 different wine grape varieties, produced in 13 different American Viticultural Areas (AVAs).
- The Washington wine industry contributes more than $3 billion to the state's economy and employs more than 19,000 full-time jobs.

However, the numbers provided above don't tell the full story. The details await those visitors who venture to Washington's storied wine country destinations — such as Yakima, Walla Walla, and Lake Chelan — to sip and swirl. These individuals will find friendly tasting room staff, generous pours, and welcoming winery dogs. And you needn't be rich to savor Washington's wines; just be a willing trekker who's open to discovering why Washington wines continue to rack up awards and high praise from the world's wine critics.

How to Use This Guidebook

Please know that the basic premise of this guide is to be "inclusive." That is, I've made every attempt to include wineries open to the public, rather than just those wineries that earn high scores from my palate. After all, my choices in wine may not be yours, and frankly, my wine preferences change depending upon the season, or what dish I'm pairing it with, or a particu- lar wine varietal that I'm enamored with at the moment. (Lately, I've developed a crush on tempranillo-based wines, perhaps because they seem so food-friendly or maybe it's because I have a hankering to visit Spain's Rioja region.) The point is, the second edition of *Wine Trails of Washington* is all about providing you, dear reader, with the information you need to get out there and explore Washington's wine with ease, and to find the winery, or the varietal, or the region that most appeals to your tastes.

Tamarack Cellars

To accomplish that, I've organized this book into 12 wine country regions (which roughly follow Washington's AVAs) and within these AVAs, I have identified a total of 32 WineTrails and profiled more than 400 wineries. These are wineries that are open to the public and have regular tasting room hours. For easy trekking, I've organized the wineries within each WineTrail geographically rather than alphabetically. In addition, within each wine region, I have listed "Other Wineries to Visit," which typically are establishments that are open by appointment only.

This guide includes maps and tasting-room hours, with WineTrail tips sprinkled throughout. Because the Washington wine scene is forever changing, please consult *WineTrailsNW.com* for updates regarding hours, tasting fees, and other important details (such as event information and wine releases).

In addition, mobile device users can download two WineTrails apps (available for iPhone/iPad or Android smartphones) for current winery-related information. The first app released focuses on Walla Walla, hence its title: *Wine Trails of Walla Walla*. I subsequently published the *Wine Trails of*

Washington app, which covers the entire state, but provides cursory information on Walla Walla wineries. I'm really proud of these apps, both of which essentially mirror the information found in their namesake guidebooks, although I do my best to keep them updated as Washington's wine industry continues to transform itself.

Winery Amenities

Wine tourists do not live by wine alone. They eventually will need places to stay, food to eat, and a place to park the RV. They may want to bicycle, play bocce, or enjoy other outdoor activities. Throughout this second edition of WineTrails of Washington, I've identified specific amenities that each winery offers in

Comforts of Whidbey

order for WineTrail tourists to get the most out of their visit. In addition, tourists often have other family members in tow, whether they are of the two-legged variety (kids) or the four-legged, tail-wagging type (dogs). Most wineries offer an assortment of amenities to make everyone's experience a pleasurable one. These may include:

- Art galleries
- Gift shops
- Live music
- Lodging
- Pet friendliness
- Picnic areas
- Private events
- Restaurant/food pairings
- RV/bus parking
- Tours
- Vineyards on premise
- Wedding venues
- Wines by the glass

A word of caution is called for with respect to "restaurant/food pairings," lest you think that means a sit-down, order-off-the-menu type of restaurant. In many cases, the winery may provide a selection of small-plate offerings to pair with your wine. You might have a choice of charcuterie or sliced cheeses with gourmet crackers and fresh fruit — that sort of thing. So depending upon your culinary desires, you will want to call ahead to get a better idea of what the winery offers in the way of sustenance.

In addition to the amenities above, most wineries reach out to tourists and consumers via social media, which may include Facebook, Twitter, YouTube, e-mail lists, blogs, online stores, as well as wine clubs. These attributes have also been identified for each winery profiled in this book.

The following chart highlights select amenities for all the wineries included in the 32 WineTrails. In addition, the Practical Stuff section at the end of this guide provides useful information concerning wheelchair access, visiting wineries with kids and/or dogs, bicycling in wine country, and planning a perfect wedding. Phone numbers, along with website and e-mail addresses, are also provided in that section.

Waters Winery

Some wineries go above and beyond in providing exceptional service, be it a stellar dining experience, luxurious overnight lodging, a well-stocked gift shop, a dedicated picnic area, or jaw-dropping views. I have bestowed on these wineries a "Best" award, which is denoted by a star icon within the winery profile. For those wineries that are over the top in the quality of service and amenities they offer, I have awarded them a "Best Destination" distinction. These wineries also are indicated by a star; be sure to budget a generous amount of time to spend at these wineries.

Ready, Set, Swirl!

My hope is that you will experience the same joys that I've discovered in Washington's tasting rooms. From Woodinville to Walla Walla (and everywhere in between), I personally visited each winery and met with as many of their winemakers as possible. No winery paid to be included in the book; and I've done my utmost to show no favoritism.

Winemakers are a passionate lot, strongly committed to producing the best wine possible that expresses the varietal character of the grape and its particular terroir). Most winemakers still have their day jobs and work their "hobbies that got out of control" at night and on the weekends. They are not rich — many are just getting by — and they're not snooty. In fact, most wine folks I visit are down-to-earth, average people who just happen to be driven by a passion to make great wine.

It's a cardinal rule of mine to be flexible and open-minded, and I advise WineTrail trekkers to follow that same maxim. Don't rule out visiting a winery because it's housed in a former Army barracks, or features unusual varietals, or requires driving a few miles down a dusty road. Often, those places can be the most interesting and fun. If the tasting fee is nominal, spring for it. You have traveled a good distance to get there, and a $10 tasting fee allows your taste buds to experience a full range of wines. Besides, tasting fees are usually waived with the purchase of wine.

Be open to different styles of winemaking. There is no one right way to make wine, and over the course of a few thousand years, myriad winemaking styles have emerged. It is amazing how the same wine varietal can vary depending upon the winemaker's choice of oak barrels or how long the wine has been aged. Again, jettison any preconceived notions and allow yourself to discover something out of the ordinary. With just one sip, you may become a convert.

In addition to my advice to call ahead, I also strongly recommend having the following four essentials on hand before venturing out on a wine tour:

1. Cash for tasting fees
2. A cooler in your vehicle to transport wine in hot weather
3. Drinking water
4. A local map or GPS device in your vehicle

Perhaps the most important advice I can give any winery tourist is to designate a driver before hitting the WineTrail, or at least take the trail at a leisurely pace   those ounces add up. Know that it is absolutely acceptable to spit or dump after sampling a wine. That's what those receptacles on top of the tasting room bar are for. Drink responsibly. Drive responsibly.

Take along this guidebook on your wine adventures and read aloud as you swirl and sip your way along these WineTrails! Oh, and make a point of asking the winemaker for his or her autograph. They get a big kick out of it and take great pleasure in signing their winery's page in this book.

Happy WineTrails!

Steve Roberts,
The WineTrails Guy

Winery Amenities

Wine Trail	Winery	Gift Shop	Live Music	Lodging	Pet Friendly	Picnic Area	Restaurant	Weddings	Wine Club	By the Glass	Pg #
	21 Cellars								●		108
	509 Wine Company										77
	Adamant Cellars				●				●		532
	Adytum Cellars										149
	Agate Field Vineyard	●			●						358
	Airfield Estates Winery	●			●				●	●	386
	Alexandria Nicole Cellars				●	●			●	●	375
	Almquist Family Vintners					●				●	78
	Alta Cellars Winery									●	177
	àMaurice Cellars			●	●				●		524
	Amavi Cellars			●	●				●		501
	Amelia Bleu										188
	AniChe Cellars				●				●		244
	Anton Ville Winery										186
	Arbor Crest Wine Cellars	●			●			●	●		567
	Ash Hollow Winery	●		●					●		543
	Aspenwood Cellars										213
	Atam Winery				●		●				286
	Auclair Winery								●		214
	Badger Mtn./Powers Winery	●			●			●	●		440
	Baer Winery								●		196
	Balboa Winery				●				●		503
	Barnard Griffin Winery	●	●		●	●			●		436
	Baroness, Bergdorf										304
	Barons Winery										219
	Barrage Cellars								●		195
	Barrel Springs Winery				●						381
	Barrister Winery							●	●		554
	Bartholomew Winery	●							●		84
	Basalt Cellars								●		577
	Basel Cellars Estate Winery	●		●				●	●		498
	Bella Terrazza Vineyards				●				●		319
	Benson Vineyards Estate				●						277
	Beresan Winery				●				●		502
	Bergevin Lane Vineyards	●							●		463
	Bethany Vineyard & Winery	●			●			●	●		235
	Black Diamond Winery				●						65

WineTrail	Winery	Gift Shop	Live Music	Lodging	Pet Friendly	Picnic Area	Restaurant	Weddings	Wine Club	By the Glass	Pg #
	Blooms Winery	●		●					●	●	49
	Bonair Winery	●			●			●	●		352
	Boudreaux Cellars				●				●		301
	Brian Carter Cellars				●				●		164
	Bunchgrass Winery				●				●		457
	Buty Winery								●		533
	C.R. Sandidge Wines				●				●		282
	Cairdeas Winery				●				●		283
	Camaraderie Cellars				●				●		66
	Canoe Ridge Vineyard	●		●					●		460
	Canon de Sol Winery								●		166
	Canyon's Edge Winery										393
	Carpenter Creek Winery	●			●				●		39
	Cascade Cliffs Winery				●				●		253
	Cascadia Winery	●									310
	Castillo de Feliciana				●			●	●		517
	Caterina & Lone Canary								●	●	558
	Cave B Estate Winery	●		●	●	●	●		●		328
	CAVU Cellars				●						542
	Celaeno Winery			●							138
	Challenger Ridge	●			●				●		41
	Chandler Reach Vineyard		●		●	●			●		418
	Charles Smith Wines		●							●	489
	Chateau Faire Le Pont	●	●		●	●	●	●			321
	Chateau Rollat Winery										483
	Chateau Ste. Michelle	●	●		●				●	●	132
	Chatter Creek Winery								●		215
	Chelan Estate Winery								●		293
	Chelan Ridge Winery				●	●				●	278
	China Bend Winery	●		●	●	●			●		571
	Chinook Wines				●						372
	Claar Cellars	●			●				●		364
	Clearwater Canyon Cellars										576
	Cloudlift Cellars										85
	Col Solare				●					●	426
	College Cellars Walla Walla			●				●			522
	Columbia Crest Winery	●	●		●	●			●	●	408

Winery Amenities

WineTrail	Winery	Gift Shop	Live Music	Lodging	Pet Friendly	Picnic Area	Restaurant	Weddings	Wine Club	By the Glass	Pg #
	Columbia Winery	●			●	●	●	●		●	135
	Comforts of Whidbey				●						46
	Confluence Winery							●	●		239
	Convergence Zone Cellars										211
	Cooper								●		420
	Copper Mountain Vineyards	●	●		●						266
	Cor Cellars				●				●	●	248
	Corvus Cellars								●		540
	Cougar Crest Estate Winery	●		●	●				●	●	454
	Covington Cellars					●			●		218
	Cowan Vineyards	●		●		●					376
	Crayelle Cellars								●		313
	Cuillin Hills Winery								●		198
	Cultura Wine			●	●						361
	Dakota Creek Winery				●				●	●	25
	DaMa Wines								●		484
	Darby Winery								●		168
	Davenport Cellars								●		181
	DeLille Cellars							●	●		163
	Des Voigne Cellars										180
	Desert Wind Winery	●		●		●	●		●		396
	DiStefano Winery								●		144
	Domaine Pouillon				●				●		249
	Domanico Cellars										76
	Don Carlo Vineyard								●		472
	Dunham Cellars	●			●	●			●		528
	Dusted Valley Vintners				●				●		510
	Dusty Cellars Winery										51
	Dutch John's Wines										315
	Dynasty Cellars									●	29
	Eagle Creek Winery	●		●		●			●		306
	Eagle Harbor Wine Co.										98
	Eagle Haven Winery	●	●			●			●	●	40
	Eaglemount Wine & Cider					●					62
	East Fork Cellars		●								237
	Efesté	●							●		176
	Eight Bells Winery								●		81

WineTrail	Winery	Gift Shop	Live Music	Lodging	Pet Friendly	Picnic Area	Restaurant	Weddings	Wine Club	By the Glass	Pg #
	El Corazon Winery			●					●	●	488
	Eleganté Cellars								●		538
	Elevation Cellars								●		199
	Eleven Winery								●		99
	Elsom Cellars										139
	English Estate Winery				●				●		241
	Esther Bricques Winery		●		●					●	269
	Eye of the Needle Winery										191
	Facelli Winery										143
	FairWinds Winery	●			●				●		61
	Fidelitas Wines				●				●		422
	Finn Hill Winery								●		210
	Finnriver Farm & Cidery			●	●	●			●		60
	Five Star Cellars	●		●					●		537
	Fjellene Cellars						●				514
	Flying Dreams Winery								●		201
	Flying Trout Wines								●		470
	Forgeron Cellars	●		●					●		492
	Fort Walla Walla Cellars	●			●				●		486
	Foundry Vineyards			●	●				●		462
	Four Lakes Winery				●				●		284
	Gamache Vintners				●				●		391
	Gârd Vintners						●		●		329
	Gifford Hirlinger Winery			●	●				●		516
	Gilbert Cellars		●				●		●	●	342
	Glacial Lake Missoula										24
	Glacier Peak Winery				●						42
	Glencorrie Tasting Room								●		453
	Goose Ridge Winery				●				●	●	439
	Gordon Brothers Cellars								●		178
	Gorman Winery						●		●		156
	Gougér Cellars Winery		●							●	240
	Gramercy Cellars								●		461
	Grande Ronde Cellars	●	●				●			●	563
	Grantwood Winery				●						458
	Guardian Cellars								●		193
	Hamilton Cellars		●		●	●			●	●	438

Winery Amenities

Winery	Gift Shop	Live Music	Lodging	Pet Friendly	Picnic Area	Restaurant	Weddings	Wine Club	By the Glass	Pg #
Harbinger Winery	•							•		67
Hard Row to Hoe Vineyards				•				•		279
Heaven's Cave Cellars				•				•		373
Hedges Family Estate				•				•		423
Hestia Cellars								•		183
Heymann Whinery	•									233
Hightower Cellars				•						425
Hollywood Hill Vineyards								•		169
Holmes Harbor Cellars				•				•		50
Hoodsport Winery	•									116
Horan Estates Winery										314
Horizon's Edge Winery				•			•	•		366
Hyatt Vineyards	•			•		•				357
Icicle Ridge Winery	•	•		•				•		309
Illusion Winery				•						251
Isenhower Cellars	•							•		511
Island Vintners					•				•	97
J. Bookwalter Winery		•		•				•		435
Jacob Williams Winery				•				•	•	254
Januik Winery	•			•	•	•		•	•	136
JM Cellars				•			•	•		134
Jones of Washington Estate	•							•		327
K Vintners				•						523
Kaella Winery		•								212
Kalamar Winery		•	•					•		106
Kana Winery	•	•						•	•	343
Karma Vineyards					•	•		•		294
Kerloo Cellars								•		476
Kestrel Vintners	•			•				•		377
Kiona Vineyards & Winery	•			•						421
Knight Hill Winery	•			•						355
Knipprath Cellars	•			•				•		568
Kontos Cellars			•	•				•		539
L'Ecole No 41	•			•				•		451
Lachini Vineyards	•			•						162
Lake Chelan Winery	•			•		•	•	•		276
Latah Creek Wine Cellars	•			•				•		570

Wine Trail	Winery	Gift Shop	Live Music	Lodging	Pet Friendly	Picnic Area	Restaurant	Weddings	Wine Club	By the Glass	Pg #
	Laurelhurst Cellars								●		86
	Locati Cellars	●							●		468
	Lodmell Cellars			●	●				●		471
	Lopez Island Winery	●			●			●	●		32
	Lost River Winery				●	●			●	●	270
	Madsen Family Cellars	●							●		113
	Maison Bleue Family Winery								●		474
	Maison de Padgett Winery				●			●	●		359
	Malaga Springs Winery				●						325
	Mannina Cellars			●					●		536
	Mansion Creek Cellars								●		490
	Mark Ryan Winery								●		151
	Market Place Wine Bar	●	●				●			●	561
	Marshal's Winery				●						252
	Martin-Scott Winery				●		●	●	●	●	323
	Maryhill Winery	●	●		●		●	●	●	●	255
	Masset Winery								●		347
	Matthews Estate			●				●	●		148
	McCrea Cellars								●		114
	McKinley Springs Winery	●			●				●		410
	Medicine Creek Winery		●						●	●	110
	Memaloose McCormick				●				●		250
	Mercer Estates	●			●				●		378
	Merry Cellars		●		●				●		574
	Michael Florentino Cellars				●				●		185
	Milbrandt Vineyards	●			●	●			●		390
	Morrison Lane Winery										494
	Mount Baker Winery	●			●					●	27
	Naches Heights Vineyard	●				●	●	●			340
	Napeequa Vintners	●		●	●				●	●	307
	Nefarious Cellars				●				●		292
	Nodland Cellars		●								569
	Northstar Winery	●		●	●	●			●		508
	Northwest Cellars								●		95
	Northwest Mountain Winery	●	●								112
	Northwest Totem Cellars								●		173
	Northwest Wine Academy										90

Winery Amenities

WineTrail	Winery	Gift Shop	Live Music	Lodging	Pet Friendly	Picnic Area	Restaurant	Weddings	Wine Club	By the Glass	Pg
	:Nota Bene Cellars								●		88
	O·S Winery								●		87
	Obelisco Estate								●		204
	Okanogan Estate	●			●				●		267
	Olympic Cellars	●			●				●	●	64
	Otis Kenyon Wine								●		479
	Ott & Murphy Wines	●							●	●	48
	Overbluff Cellars								●		564
	Page Cellars								●		202
	Palouse Winery								●		102
	Paradisos del Sol	●			●						360
	Pasek Cellars Winery	●			●						38
	Patit Creek Cellars	●			●		●		●		530
	Patterson Cellars								●		157
	Pepper Bridge Winery				●				●		509
	Piccola Cellars										190
	Piety Flats Winery	●			●					●	248
	Plumb Cellars										491
	Pomum Cellars										220
	Pondera Winery							●			179
	Pontin del Roza Winery	●			●				●		379
	Portteus Vineyards & Winery				●						363
	Preston Premium Wines	●	●		●		●		●		442
	Red Sky Winery								●		203
	Reininger Winery	●			●				●	●	455
	Revelry Vintners										535
	Rio Vista Wines				●		●		●	●	274
	Robert Karl Cellars								●		560
	Robert Ramsay Cellars								●		205
	RockWall Cellars		●		●		●		●		269
	Rolling Bay Winery										100
	Ross Andrew Winery								●		152
	Rotie Cellars								●		482
	Rulo Winery										512
	Russell Creek Winery								●		526
	Rusty Grape Vineyard	●	●		●		●		●		238
	Ryan Patrick Vineyards								●		299

WineTrail	Winery	Gift Shop	Live Music	Lodging	Pet Friendly	Picnic Area	Restaurant	Weddings	Wine Club	By the Glass	Pg #
	Saint Laurent Winery	•			•			•	•	•	324
	Samson Estates Winery				•		•	•			26
	San Juan Vineyards	•			•				•	•	33
	Sapolil Cellars		•			•		•	•		478
	Saviah Cellars				•				•		504
	Seven Hills Winery			•					•		466
	Severino Cellars	•			•				•		365
	Sheridan Vineyard								•		216
	Silvara Vineyards				•			•		•	308
	Silver Lake Winery	•			•			•	•		362
	Sinclair Estate Vineyard		•	•					•	•	485
	Sky River Meadery	•			•				•		172
	Skylite Cellars			•					•		459
	Sleight of Hand Cellars								•		505
	Smasne Cellars	•	•				•				441
	Snoqualmie Vineyards	•			•						395
	Sparkman Cellars								•		159
	Spofford Station				•				•		518
	Spring Valley Vineyard	•									475
	Stemilt Creek Winery								•		322
	Steppe Cellars				•				•		368
	Stevens Winery										221
	Stina's Cellars									•	109
	Stomani Cellars Falling Rain				•			•			79
	Stottle Winery							•	•	•	111
	Swakane Winery	•					•		•		320
	Sweet Valley Wines			•					•		477
	Swiftwater Cellars	•	•		•	•	•		•		318
	Syncline Wine Cellars				•				•		247
	SYZYGY				•				•	•	531
	Tagaris Winery & Taverna		•			•		•	•	•	437
	Tamarack Cellars			•					•		534
	Tanjuli Winery	•		•							353
	Tapteil Vineyard & Winery	•		•	•				•		424
	Tefft Cellars Winery	•		•	•			•	•	•	367
	Tempus Cellars								•		529
	Tero Estates								•		469

Winery Amenities

WineTrail	Winery	Gift Shop	Live Music	Lodging	Pet Friendly	Picnic Area	Restaurant	Weddings	Wine Club	By the Glass	Pg
	Terra Blanca Winery	•			•	•	•	•			419
	Tertulia Cellars				•				•	•	513
	The Blending Room		•		•	•	•		•	•	281
	The Bunnell Family Cellar						•		•	•	389
	The Chocolate Shop	•									481
	The Hogue Cellars	•			•				•		374
	The Tasting Room — Seattle						•		•	•	83
	The Tasting Room — Yakima	•			•		•		•	•	341
	The Woodhouse Wine Estates								•		141
	Thomas O'Neil Cellars		•		•	•			•		434
	Three Brothers Winery	•			•			•	•	•	236
	Three Rivers Winery	•			•			•	•		456
	Thurston Wolfe Winery	•			•				•		388
	Tildio Winery	•			•				•		285
	Townshend Cellar	•			•				•		565
	Treveri Cellars				•				•		345
	Trillium Creek Winery				•						107
	Trio Vintners	•			•				•		467
	Trust Cellars				•				•		527
	Tsillan Cellars	•	•		•	•		•	•		290
	Tucker Cellars	•			•						382
	Tunnel Hill Winery			•	•			•	•		291
	Two Mountain Winery	•			•				•		356
	Two Vintners Winery				•				•	•	217
	Va Piano Vineyards	•			•				•		507
	Vartanyan Estate Winery		•		•			•	•		28
	Vashon Winery		•		•				•		103
	Vin du Lac Winery	•	•		•		•		•	•	275
	VineHeart Winery				•			•	•		380
	Vintage Hill Cellars	•									562
	Vortex Cellars				•						197
	Walla Faces			•					•		487
	Walla Walla Village Winery	•	•		•				•	•	493
	Walla Walla Vintners			•	•				•		525
	Walter Dacon Wines	•			•				•		115
	Wapato Point Cellars	•			•		•		•	•	280
	Ward Johnson Winery								•		80

Winery Amenities

Winery	Gift Shop	Live Music	Lodging	Pet Friendly	Picnic Area	Restaurant	Weddings	Wine Club	By the Glass	Pg #
Waterbrook Winery	●				●		●	●		452
Watermill & Blue Mountain					●			●		500
Waters Winery					●			●		506
Waterville Winery										312
Waving Tree Winery					●			●		256
Wawawai Canyon		●			●			●		575
Wedge Mountain Winery					●			●		311
Westport Winery			●		●	●	●	●		232
Whidbey Island Winery	●	●			●				●	47
White Heron Cellars					●		●	●		326
Whitestone Winery		●						●		556
Widgeon Hill Winery					●					234
William Church Winery					●			●	●	161
Willow Crest Winery	●				●	●		●		387
Wind River Cellars					●		●	●		245
Wind Rose Cellars		●			●					63
Windy Point Vineyards	●				●		●	●		346
Wineglass Cellars	●				●			●		354
Winemakers Loft	●				●					392
Woodinville Wine Cellars					●			●	●	145
Woodward Canyon Winery	●					●				450
XSV Wines										182
Yakima River Winery					●					394
Zerba Cellars				●	●			●		499

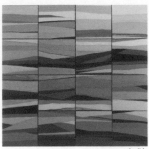

Artist Series #16

WOODWARD CANYON
2007
Washington State Cabernet Sauvignon

DUSTED
VALLEY

MALBEC
Columbia Valley 2007

ALC. 14.6% BY VOL.

WINERY

2005 Semillon

WALLA WALLA VALLEY
ALC. 13.7% BY VOL

SAPOLIL CELLARS
2006 SYRAH · Patina Vineyard, Walla Walla Valley

isenhower
Snapdragon
White Wine
2008 · Red Mountain

Forgeron Cellars

2006 Roussane
Columbia Valley
Alc. 13.8% by vol.

RED
SKY

WINERY

Washington State

2008
MERLOT

Dunham Cellars

THREE
LEGGED
RED

2004

Red Table
Wine

Alc. 13.8% by Vol.

COLUMBIA VALLEY

ROSÉ *columbia valley* 2008
cabernet franc

TRUST

SLEIGHT OF HAND CELLARS

Simply Magical Wines

THE SPELLBINDER

2008

Columbia Valley Red Wine

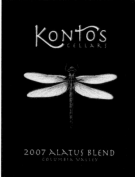

KONTOS CELLARS

2007 ALATUS BLEND
COLUMBIA VALLEY

Waters

2007

PEPPER BRIDGE

SYRAH

Walla Walla Valley

ALCOHOL 14.1% BY VOLUME

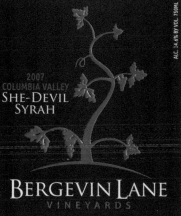

ALC. 14.6% BY VOL. 750ML

2007
COLUMBIA VALLEY
SHE-DEVIL
SYRAH

BERGEVIN LANE
VINEYARDS

NORTHSTAR

CABERNET
SAUVIGNON

COLUMBIA VALLEY

2006

ALC. 14.9% BY VOL.

tertulia cellars

2006 cabernet sauvignon

HORSE HEAVEN HILLS

ALC. 14% BY VOL.

CHINOOK®

2008

CABERNET FRANC

YAKIMA VALLEY

PRODUCED AND BOTTLED BY
CHINOOK WINES OF PROSSER WA

ALCOHOL 13% BY VOLUME

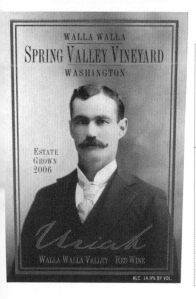

WALLA WALLA
SPRING VALLEY VINEYARD
WASHINGTON

ESTATE
GROWN
2006

Uriah

WALLA WALLA VALLEY   RED WINE

ALC. 14.9% BY VOL.

SEVEN HILLS

Merlot

SEVEN HILLS VINEYARD

WALLA WALLA VALLEY

2006

ALCOHOL 13.7% BY VOLUME

LEGENDS

Four Horsemen

Northwest Washington
WINE COUNTRY

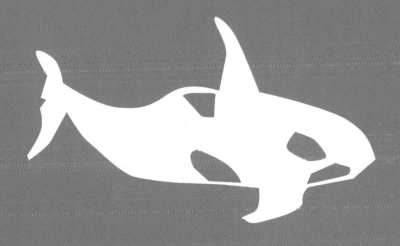

SAN JUAN

VINEYARDS

San Juan Island, Washington

2010 Merlot
Horse Heaven Hills

CARPENTER
CREEK

Cabernet Sauvignon

Yakima Valley Red Wine
Alcohol 13.8% by Volume

20 06

whidbey island
WINERY

Island White

PUGET SOUND WHITE WINE

ALC 10.5% BY VOL

CARPENTER
CREEK

2008
Washington State

Signature Series
RIESLING
ALCOHOL 11.2% BY VOLUME - 750 ML

2008 Syrah
EAGLE
HAVEN
Winery   WASHINGTON STATE • YAKIMA VALLEY
Alcohol 13.5% By Volume

Pasek
CELLARS

Chardonnay
Semi Dry
2005 Yakima Valley
ALCOHOL 12% BY VOLUME

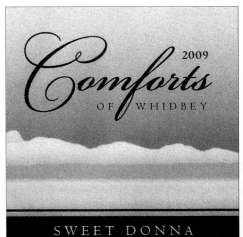

2009
Comforts
OF WHIDBEY

SWEET DONNA
PUGET SOUND • WHITE WINE

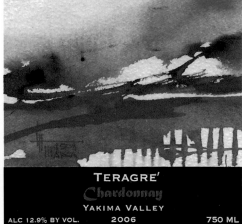

TERAGRE'
Chardonnay
YAKIMA VALLEY
ALC 12.9% BY VOL.   2006   750 ML

MOUNT BAKER
VINEYARDS & WINERY
ESTABLISHED 1982

2008
YAKIMA VALLEY
MERLOT
Reserve

Alc. 13.6% by vol.

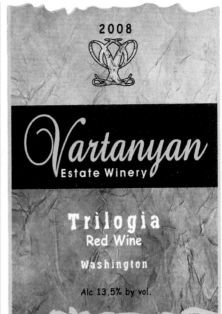

2008

Vartanyan
Estate Winery

Trilogia
Red Wine

Washington

Alc 13.5% by vol.

2007
DYNASTY
CELLARS

DC3

MERITAGE
RED WINE
WALLA WALLA
VALLEY
14.6% ALC. BY VOL.

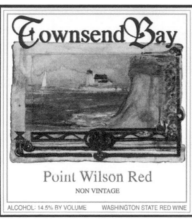

Townsend Bay

Point Wilson Red

NON VINTAGE

ALCOHOL: 14.5% BY VOLUME   WASHINGTON STATE RED WINE

HOT MESS

Riesling
WASHINGTON
STATE

Double
Bluff Red

2008
Columbia Valley
Red Wine

Ott & Murphy

Alc. 15.4% by Vol

750ml

Whatcom County
Wine Trail

Our visit to Washington's northwest corner takes us to the state's fifth-largest city: Bellingham, whose rather underwhelming nickname is "The City of Subdued Excitement." It's where commercial fishermen and white-collar professionals mingle easily with students and "sustainers" who produce locally and buy locally. With easy access to Whatcom County's farmland, meandering seacoast and the rugged foothills of the North Cascades, a diversity of outdoor activities abound. And speaking of diversity, this WineTrail offers an array of wines to sample, from traditional still wines to wines made from honey and berries.

Although Bellingham is your base camp for exploring this rich environment, you'll need a car to zigzag your way around. It's possible to experience most of the wineries in one day, but we recommend at least two days to savor this land (and wine). You will find elegant Bordeaux-style wines made from eastern Washington grapes as well as delicious fruit wine made from locally grown raspberries. I can hardly contain my subdued excitement!

Whatcom County WineTrail

1. Glacial Lake Missoula
2. Dakota Creek Winery
3. Samson Estates Winery
4. Mount Baker Vineyards & Winery
5. Vartanyan Estate Winery
6. Dynasty Cellars

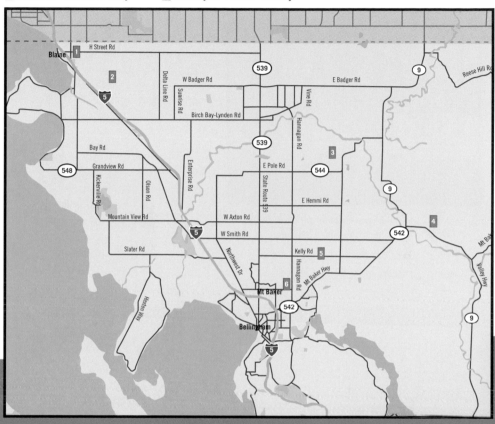

Region:	**Northwest Washington Wine Country**
# of tasting rooms on tour:	**6**
Estimate # of days for tour:	**2**
Getting around:	**Car**
Key Events:	❑ **Red Wine and Chocolate in February**
Tips:	❑ **See Whatcom Winery Association at www.whatcomwineries.com for event information**
	❑ **Visit all Whatcom Winery Association wineries and get 20% discount off case price**
	❑ **Bellingham offers a variety of places to eat and stay**
	❑ **Village Books in Fairhaven is a must-stop for book lovers**
	❑ **Rather than I-5 drive the 21-mile Chuckanut Drive that winds its way along the seacoast. Bring camera.**

Glacial Lake Missoula

Such a curious name deserves an explanation, and those geeky wine lovers who get into soil types will appreciate the fact that the so-called Missoula Floods that occurred 12,000 years ago resulted in the soil profile of today's Columbia Valley. For more about the end-of-the-ice-age floods, visit the website GlacialLakeMissoula.org.

Glacial Lake Missoula Wine Company (GLM) is the northernmost of Washington's wineries, located in Blaine, with Canada just across the border. GLM winemaker/co-owner Tom Davis and his spouse, Tracey DeGraff, commute from downtown Vancouver, British Columbia, to make and sell their wine.

GLM is best known for its red blend, Deluge, a Bordeaux blend of luscious cabernet sauvignon and cabernet franc. Its bold flavors are a result in large part to the bleeding off (called saignée) of the initial extraction, thus leaving a more concentrated wine.

The label on the Deluge bottle is a Photoshop-ped fantasy interpretation of the humongous floods from Lake Missoula and a reflection of the power of the wine inside the bottle. Tom's graphic arts background — and his vivid imagination — are at play here.

WineTrail Note: The Blaine tasting room is open on Saturday afternoons only. Time your visit accordingly.

GLACIAL LAKE MISSOULA
opened: 2002
winemaker(s): Tom Davis
location: 1678 Boblett Street, Blaine, WA 98230-9260
phone: 360-332-2097
web: www.glmwine.com
e-mail: sales@lakemissoulawine.com
fee: Complimentary wine tasting
hours: Saturday 12–6 or by appointment
amenities: RV/Bus Parking, Wheelchair Accessible
connect: 🐦 f

Dakota Creek Winery ❷

After a few decades of working for U.S. Customs and Border Protection, Ken Peck retired to pursue his ultimate passion — making wine. Actually, he's one-half of the equation in this winemaking venture, with his wife, Jill, being a partner/winemaker in Dakota Creek Winery. Together they make a wide range of wines, sourcing grapes from Washington Columbia Valley American Viticultural Area.

When asked about their portfolio of wines of nearly twenty wines, Ken's response is simply that he likes to dabble with all varieties. It's the challenge of bringing out the expression of each variety, of working with the fruit.

In addition to the truly relaxing tasting room (a great place to make new friends), one eye-catching feature of Dakota Creek Winery is the metal arch building serving as the cellar. Hard to believe, but this cellar is home to more than 100 French and American oak barrels resting comfortably in a constant temperature between 50 and 65 degrees Fahrenheit. If Ken isn't too busy pouring and making guests comfortable, ask him to show you the barrel room and get the story behind the construction of this half-buried steel building, which resembles a Quonset hut. The imposing doors are marvelous, but of equal pleasure is how, with its covering of native soil and bark, this building harmoniously integrates with its environment.

DAKOTA CREEK WINERY
winemaker(s): Ken and Jill Peck
location: 3575 Haynie Road, Blaine, WA 98230-9741
phone: 360-820-4752
web: www.dakotacreekwinery.com
e-mail: ken@dakotacreekwinery.com
fee: Tasting fee
hours: Thursday through Saturday 1–5
amenities: Picnic Area, RV/Bus Parking, Wheelchair Accessible, Wines by the Glass, Wine Club
connect: f

Samson Estates Winery 🔳

Samson Estates Winery brings a fresh face and displays a willingness to think outside the traditional barrel. Besides traditional wines, Samson Estates is perhaps best known for its incredible raspberry estate wine.

With a family history of farming, winemaker Rob Dhaliwal crafts fruit, traditional and dessert wines. His brother, Dhar, handles the marketing/administrative chores.

The quaint tasting room/production area is housed on a former dairy barn. Here you can look around the property and take in 200 acres of raspberries – the source of their delicious fruit wine. It's also plenty big for hosting weddings and other events, which it does with regularity during the warmer months.

For the numbers crunchers among us, let the record show that an astounding 3 pounds of raspberries go into producing one bottle of raspberry wine. No wonder it tastes like biting into a big handful of fresh raspberries picked at their zenith. By the way, the brothers' father, Sam, still tends to the more than 200 acres of fruit, and they honor their dad in the winery's name: Sam-son.

Bring a friend and split a carafe of wine near the cozy fireplace or, weather permitting, sit outside on the comfortable deck chairs and enjoy stunning views of the Twin Sisters Mountain in the distance. Blissing there, I felt moved to paraphrase the Beatles, "Raspberry fields forever."

SAMSON ESTATES WINERY
opened: 2002
winemaker(s): Rob Dhaliwal
location: 1861 Van Dyk Road, Everson, WA 98199
phone: 360-966-7787
web: www.samsonestates.com
e-mail: info@samsonestates.com
fee: Tasting fee
hours: Friday through Sunday 11–5
amenities: Mailing List, Picnic Area, Private Events, RV/Bus Parking, Weddings, Wheelchair Accessible, Wine Club
connect: 🐦 📘

Mount Baker Vineyards & Winery

Randy Finley, owner of Mount Baker Vineyards, purchased the winery and vineyard in 1989. Prior to that, he had gained fame as the creator of Seattle's Seven Gables Theatre in the U District. However, a year's sojourn in France gave him the wine bug, and upon his return, he purchased Mount Baker Vineyards.

Having a sense of humor is a prerequisite for a grape grower in northwest Washington near Mount Baker. Most years, the Nooksack Valley provides a long, mild growing season for the production of varietals favored by Mount Baker Vineyards. Randy's 6 acres produce cool-weather grapes, including Chasselas, Madeleine Angevine, Müller-Thurgau, pinot noir, pinot gris, and siegerrebe. But Mother Nature can be unreliable, and in some years there isn't enough heat for the grapes to produce sufficient sugars.

2009
YAKIMA VALLEY
Chardonnay
Barrel Select
Alc. 13.7% by vol.   CONTAINS SULFITES

To mitigate that risk, Randy imports eastern Washington grapes, such as cabernet sauvignon, merlot, and syrah. Including his estate wines, Randy is able to produce about 12,000 cases per year, which requires a small army of helpers for crushing, fermenting, and bottling.

The other key partner to this endeavor is Randy's spouse, Patricia Clark Finley. Her distinctive artwork adorns the walls of the tasting room and graces the wine labels of many of their releases. This convergence of land, wine, art, friends, and family defines Mount Baker Vineyards.

My eyes settled on one of Patricia's paintings as I smelled some nice earthy mushroom notes in my just-swirled merlot. Taking in the sights and the aromas around me reinforced my impression that Mount Baker Vineyards is a nexus of art and mist-shrouded forest.

MOUNT BAKER VINEYARDS & WINERY
opened: 1989
winemaker(s): Randy Finley
location: 4298 Mount Baker Highway, Everson, WA 98247
phone: 360-592-2300
web: www.mountbakervineyards.com
e-mail: mountbakervineyards@verizon.net
fee: Tasting fee
hours: Thursday through Monday 12–5
amenities: Art Gallery, Gift Shop, Newsletter/Blog, Picnic Area, RV/Bus Parking, Tours, Vineyard on Premise, Wheelchair Accessible, Wines by the Glass

Vartanyan Estate Winery 5

The view of Mount Baker from this winery — on a clear day, anyway — is spectacular. But equally entrancing is the owner/winemaker of Vartanyan Estate Winery, Margarita Vartanyan.

Her Russian accent hints at an interesting background. She amazes guests not just with her wine, but also with her warmth and passion for the vine.

The Vartanyan family tradition of winemaking began centuries ago in Armenia. During Stalin's regime, some members of the Vartanyan family were sent to Siberia. That's where Margarita was born, and where she met her husband.

Thanks to Mikhail Gorbachev and perestroika, the family was allowed to move back to Armenia, where Margarita learned from the family winemaking heritage. From Armenia, Margarita immigrated to the U.S., where she's poured her heart and soul into this spot of earth, where the biggest issue you will face is what to pack in the picnic basket.

Vartanyan Estate Winery makes a full sleight of red and white wines with a pronounced bias toward French-derived varieties. I found them all to be easily quaffable but I must admit to asking for an extra pour of the red-blend Trilogia (Russian for Trilogy) comprised of 50% cabernet franc, 25% merlot and 25% syrah. This one danced on my tongue a la Baryshnikov to which I say, "Spasiba Margarita."

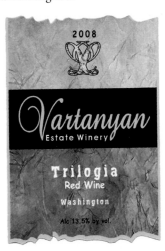

VARTANYAN ESTATE WINERY
opened: 2008
winemaker(s): Margarita Vartanyan
location: 1628 Huntley Road, Bellingham, WA 98226
phone: 360-756-6770
web: www.vewinery.com
e-mail: info@vewinery.com
fee: Tasting fee refunded with purchase
hours: Thursday through Sunday 1–5 from April through October; Friday through Sunday 1–5 from November through March
amenities: Live Music, Picnic Area, Private Events, Tours, Weddings, Wheelchair Accessible, Wine Club
connect: f

Dynasty Cellars 6

Prepare for the unexpected.

It's rare that a winery can burst on the scene with top accolades. But this is the case with Dynasty Cellars. Opened in 2010, this unknown jewel of a winery is located next to the Salish Sea north of Bellingham. Relying on fruit exclusively from the Walla Walla Valley (Les Collines, Seven Hills and Pepper Bridge vineyards), winemaker Peter Osvaldik has hit home runs with his first two vintages.

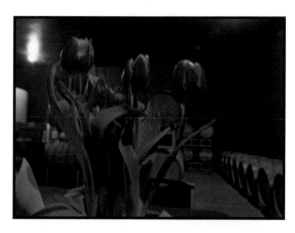

As my eyes adjusted to Dynasty Cellars tasting room, I took in the warm greeting of Peter's wife, Olga. Both possess charming accents from their native Czechoslovakia and friendly smiles. Peter's family has more than 200 years of winemaking experience, and this would explain his passion for the juice. But the tasting room reveals another talent of Peter's, namely the crafting of exquisite cabinetry, the type reserved for luxury homes. The pieces you'll see in the tasting room provide insight into Peter's meticulous nature, both as an artisan woodworker and as a winemaker.

Peter Osvaldik

If your palate prefers the big, bold Walla Walla varieties, the kind with flavors that tingle on the tongue and last on the finish, try the DC3 Meritage red blend, packed with dark cherry, cocoa and licorice notes. This would pair very nicely with beef goulash, a popular dish in the Czech Republic.

DYNASTY CELLARS
winemaker(s): Peter Osvaldik
location: 2169 East Bakerview Road, Bellingham, WA 98226
phone: 360-758-2958
web: www.dynastycellarswine.com
fee: Tasting fee
hours: Thursday, Friday and Saturday 1–6:30; Sunday 1–5
amenities: RV/Bus Parking, Wheelchair Accessible, Wines by the Glass
connect:

San Juan County
WineTrail

The San Juan County WineTrail includes only two wineries, but you will need to budget time for getting to and from the islands via the Washington State Ferries service. Actually, for most of us mainlanders, that's a good thing. The ride is spectacular and it's a short hop from Friday Harbor to Lopez Island. Along the way, you will discover the charm of Friday Harbor and the quaintness of Roche Harbor.

While in Friday Harbor, be sure to visit Island Wine Company at Cannery Landing, next to the ferry terminal. The wine shop features select wines from around the world as well as wine bearing its own label: Island Wine Company. Owners David Baughn and Kathryn Lawson Kerr rely on the talents of renowned winemaker Rob Griffin (Barnard Griffin Winery) to craft wines of exceptional value. Check it out and discover why others keep coming back for more.

San Juan County WineTrail

1 Lopez Island Vineyard & Winery

2 San Juan Vineyards

3 San Juan Vineyards' Friday Harbor Tasting Room

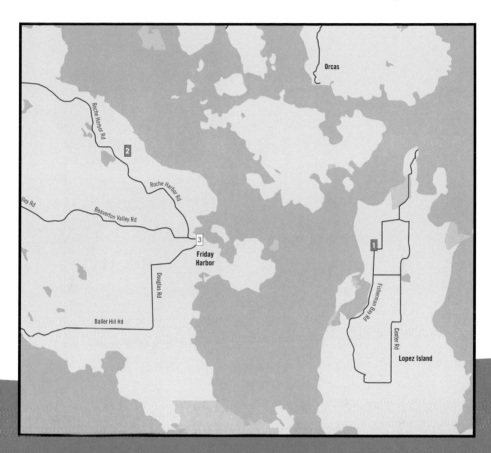

Region:	**Northwest Washington Wine Country**
# of tasting rooms on tour:	**3**
# of satellite tasting rooms:	**1**
Estimate # of days for tour:	**1 or 2**
Getting around:	**Car, ferry and bike**
Tips:	❑ **Friday Harbor offers a variety of places to eat.**
	❑ **A side trip to Roche Harbor is recommended; close by is Westcott Bay Orchards for hard cider wine — appointment only.**
	❑ **American Camp is great for picnicking, beach combing, and views of the Straits of Juan de Fuca.**
	❑ **Lopez Island's town village offers shopping and a variety of restaurants.**

 Best: ❑ **Picnicking: Lopez Island Vineyard & Winery**

❑ **Gift shop and picnicking: San Juan Vineyards**

Lopez Island Vineyard & Winery

A short 10-minute drive from the Lopez Island ferry dock takes you to the small stone-and-timber winery that is Lopez Island Vineyards. The grapes in its vineyards are cool-weather grapes suitable for the Puget Sound viticultural area, and include Madeleine Angevine and siegerrebe.

These grapes go into Lopez Island's estate white wines. For better-known wines, such as merlot and cabernet sauvignon, winemaker Brent Charnley uses grapes from Washington's Columbia Valley. In addition, Lopez Island Vineyards makes fruit wine using berries and stone fruit from nearby organic farms.

First and foremost, this winery is about using organic farming techniques and natural winemaking practices to produce food (i.e., wine) that is "clean and healthy." This has been its focus since its beginning back in 1987. The goal is sustainability.

Plop down on an Adirondack chair and relax with a glass of wine. Breathe slowly, really taste the wine, observe the vineyard's canopy growing skyward, listen to the birds, and notice how the sunlight plays on the glass window. Heck, the ferry won't depart for another four hours. Just chill and enjoy.

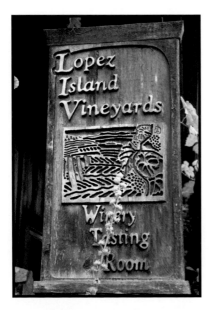

LOPEZ ISLAND VINEYARD & WINERY
opened: 1987
winemaker(s): Brent Charnley
location: 265 Lopez Road, Lopez Village, Lopez Island, WA 98261
phone: 360-468-4888
web: www.lopezislandvineyards.com
e-mail: winery@lopezislandvineyards.com
fee: Tasting fee refunded with purchase of 6 or more bottles
hours: Seasonal hours; call ahead or see website
amenities: Gift Shop, Picnic Area, Private Events, Tours, Weddings, Wheelchair Accessible, Wine Club
connect: 🐦 📘

⭐ **BEST Picnicking**

San Juan Vineyards

Owned by Yvonne Swanberg, Tim Judkins and his daughter, Madison, San Juan Vineyards is a mere 10-minute drive from the ferry landing on San Juan Island. Once off the ferry, head three miles north toward Roche Harbor and look for the diminutive white church on the right. (Note: The church is a replica of a church found on the Hawaiian island of Molokai.)

You'll find that the San Juan Vineyards compound has some rather unusual features. A turn-of-the-19th-century, one-room schoolhouse is home to the tasting room and a well-stocked gift shop. The 1896 schoolhouse features original hardwood floors, a blackboard, and plenty of chalk to write: "I will not throw wine corks at Jimmy anymore." From the deck, you can look across the road and see a camel lazily grazing. Did we say camel? Yep. Her name is Mona, and there's a white wine blend named in her honor.

San Juan Vineyards' estate wines feature siegerrebe, pinot noir, and Madeleine Angevine grapes, both grown in the winery's 7-acre vineyard. The grapes used to produce the winery's Bordeaux- and Rhône-style wines hail from the Columbia Valley. Be sure to try the rosé with the rather suggestive name of Afterglow Blush. Hmmm.

Mona the camel, near San Juan Vineyards

SAN JUAN VINEYARDS
opened: 1996
winemaker(s): Chris Primus
location: 3136 Roche Harbor Road, Friday Harbor, WA 98250
phone: 360-378-9463
web: www.sanjuanvineyards.com
e-mail: sjvineyards@rockisland.com
fee: Tasting fee
hours: Daily 11–5 in summer; Wednesday through Sunday in fall and spring 11–5; January and February by appointment
amenities: Gift Shop, Picnic Area, RV/Bus Parking, Vineyard on Premise, Wheelchair Accessible, Wine Club, Wines by the Glass
connect: 🐦 📘

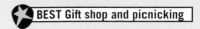 **BEST Gift shop and picnicking**

San Juan Vineyards' Friday Harbor Tasting Room ③

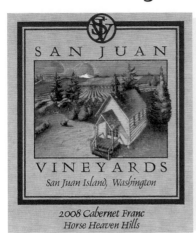

2008 Cabernet Franc
Horse Heaven Hills

SAN JUAN VINEYARDS' FRIDAY HARBOR TASTING ROOM
opened: 1996
winemaker(s): Chris Primus
location: 55 Spring Street, Piano and Wine Tasting Room, Friday Harbor, WA 98250
phone: 360-378-9462
web: www.sanjuanvineyards.com
e-mail: sjvineyards@rockisland.com
fee: Tasting fee
hours: Friday through Tuesday 11-5
amenities: Gift Shop, Live Music, Wheelchair Accessible, Wine Club, Wines by the Glass
connect: 🐦 f

www.winetrailsnw.com/wineries/san_juan_vineyards'_friday_harbor_tasting_room

Skagit County
WineTrail

Crush

Skagit County WineTrail includes five wineries that offer a cornucopia of flavors set in a rich tapestry of farmland. Here, diversity rules, and our palates celebrate. One of the best times to visit these wineries is in April during the annual Skagit Tulip Festival, when more than 300 acres of colorful tulips leave visitors slack-jawed. Seriously.

With a little imagination, you can see the amber hue of dessert wine in those yellow tulips, and the red tulips begin to resemble the merlot you've been swirling. In between visiting Skagit County wineries, be sure to visit the towns of La Conner (my favorite), Anacortes, and Mount Vernon, each with loads of shops, restaurants and quaint inns to experience. Cheers!

Skagit County WineTrail

1 Pasek Cellars Winery
2 Carpenter Creek Winery

3 Eagle Haven Winery
4 Challenger Ridge Vineyard
& Cellars

5 Glacier Peak Winery

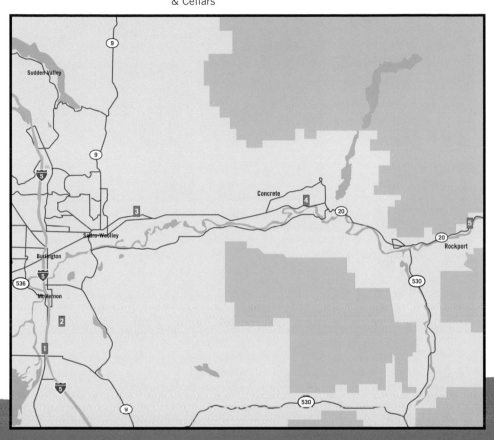

Region: **Northwest Washington Wine Country**
# of tasting rooms on tour: **5**
Estimate # of days for tour: **2**
Getting around: **Car**
Key Events: ❏ **Skagit Valley Tulip Festival in April —**
see www.tulipfestival.org for details.
Many wineries participate in the Tulip Festival
with special offerings.
Tips: ❏ **Take in the North Cascade Highway (US-20), from**
Burlington to Winthrop and explore wineries along
the way.
❏ **Pasek Cellars Winery is co-located with a deli and also**
has a second tasting room in Leavenworth.
Best: ❏ **Music venue: Eagle Haven Winery**
❏ **Views: Glacier Peak Winery**

Pasek Cellars Winery

Cork dorks might make the mistake of passing by Pasek's Mount Vernon tasting room, located right off I-5's exit 221, because this winery's focus is on the creation of fruit wine. But that would be their loss. While Pasek Cellars makes several traditional wines, including syrah and merlot, it is renowned for its exceptional fruit wines.

Its list of fruit wines reads more like a fruit smoothie menu board: blackberry, cranberry, raspberry, loganberry, guava, pineapple, and passion fruit. Incidentally, the raspberry, loganberry, and blackberry also come as dessert-style port wines, to be enjoyed on their own, or drizzled on vanilla ice cream or (my favorite) pound cake.

A visit to Pasek Winery puts you smack dab in the middle of Skagit Valley's famous tulip area. Come April, the fields are painted with reds, yellows, and other tulip colors, stretching for miles, with an occasional red barn popping up in the distance. Each year an original painting is selected to represent the Tulip Festival, and the chosen image adorns the label on Pasek's Tulip Red merlot-cabernet blend. Folks come from all over to purchase the Tulip Red, and many feel as though they're getting a "twofer," a great wine and a terrific label.

According to owner/winemaker Gene Pasek, the winery had a "tiger by the tail" from the start, and demand for its fruit wines often exceeds supply. Which wine do you think is Pasek's most popular? If you guessed cranberry, you are correct. And when asked which food pairs the best with cranberry wine, you may be surprised by Gene's answer: everything.

PASEK CELLARS WINERY
opened: 1995
winemaker(s): Gene Pasek
location: 18729 Fir Island Road, Mount Vernon, WA 98273
phone: 888-350-9463
web: www.pasekcellars.com
e-mail: pasekwinery@hotmail.com
fee: Complimentary wine tasting
hours: Daily 11–5
amenities: Gift Shop, Picnic Area, RV/ Bus Parking, Mailing List, Online Store, Wheelchair Accessible
connect: f

Carpenter Creek Winery 2

When you think of Skagit County, perhaps your mind doesn't conjure up images of wine tasting, but instead visualizes tulips blooming in April across the valley. But there is more to experience in the county than those admittedly stunning fields of brilliant color. Mount Vernon is also home to Carpenter Creek Winery, where winemaker/owner Jeffrey Hammer specializes in handcrafted, premium wines.

The approach to Carpenter Creek Winery is a nice surprise in itself. The winery is nestled amongst tall fir and cedar trees, just far enough off the beaten path that you can hear Carpenter Creek gurgling in the background. Awaiting you is a robust portfolio of wines that includes riesling, pinot noir, sauvignon blanc, chardonnay, semillon, syrah, and cabernet sauvignon. Make a point of sampling the estate siegerrebe and the pinot noir. The awards draping many of the wine bottles are a promising sign that you have arrived at the right place for tasting. But you be the judge. After all, that's why you're here.

WineTrail Tip: Pack a picnic for this winery. The picnic area, down by Carpenter Creek, will feel like your own private reserve. Enjoy!

CARPENTER CREEK WINERY
opened: 2001
winemaker(s): Jeffrey W. Hammer
location: 20376 East Hickox Road, Mount Vernon, WA 98274-7730
phone: 360-848-6673
web: www.carpentercreek.com
e-mail: wwcinfo@carpentercreek.com
fee: Complimentary wine tasting
hours: Thursday through Sunday 11–6
amenities: Gift Shop, Picnic Area, Tours, Wheelchair Accessible, Wine Club
connect: f

Eagle Haven Winery 🔳

Located four miles east of Sedro-Woolley, tucked into the foothills of the North Cascade Mountains, in a setting straight out of an Eddie Bauer catalog (including the eponymous eagle haven!), is Eagle Haven Winery. Surrounded by 40 acres of orchards (containing 50 apple varieties), berry fields, and vineyards, this winery is a celebration of Northwest fruit.

Eagle Haven is the collaboration of owners Tom and Jim Perkins (father and son), Fred Vochatzer, and winemaker Chuck Jackson. These guys are hard-working, salt-of-the-earth types who haven't forgotten how to have a good time after a good day's work. Their chosen motif for the winery is "Old West," and the large tasting room boasts an expansive tasting bar that surely took much of the Northern Hemisphere's forests of knotty pine to construct. The result is a welcoming environment most suitable for tasting wine and striking up a conversation with other WineTrail enthusiasts. Next to the winery is a charming garden area with outdoor furniture, the perfect place to uncork a bottle of Eagle Haven's blend of Madeleine Angevine and siegerrebe, which is especially delicious when paired with Gouda cheese and nutty crackers.

Be sure to check the event schedule at the winery, in particular, the summer concert series, with performances taking place in the new outdoor pavilion. In my humble opinion, the rockin' tunes of Gertrude's Hearse and 10-napkin barbecue go great with sangiovese.

EAGLE HAVEN WINERY
opened: 2004
winemaker(s): Chuck Jackson
location: 8243 Sims Road, Sedro-Woolley, WA 98284-7990
phone: 360-856-6248
web: www.eaglehavenwinery.com
e-mail: info@eaglehavenwinery.com
fee: Complimentary wine tasting
hours: Friday through Sunday 11–5
amenities: Gift Shop, Live Music, Picnic Area, Tours, Vineyard on Premise, Wheelchair Accessible, Wine Club, Wines by the Glass
connect: 🐦 f

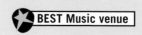
BEST Music venue

www.winetrailsnw.com/wineries/eagle_haven_winery

Challenger Ridge Vineyard & Cellars 4

From high in the Cascades, melted snow becomes part of the Skagit River, which flows by the lovely burg of Concrete (a good, solid name!) on its way to Puget Sound. It's quiet here, lush green and not where you would expect more than 13 acres of pinot noir to be growing. This happy surprise will cause many a traveler along the North Cascade Highway to make an unexpected detour to check out Challenger Ridge Vineyard & Cellars, located just north of Highway 20 on Challenger Road.

In the grape-growing world, "growing degree days" (GDD) are a measure of heat accumulation, and with an average of 2,050 GDDs, Challenger Ridge's south-facing slope provides perfect conditions for growing pinot noir (clones 777, 667, 115, and 828 for devout pinot fans). That's plenty of fruit for winemaker Randy Bonaventura to craft into award-winning pinot, which he does at the relatively new production facility on the property. Grapes sourced from the Columbia Valley become part of the remaining red and white portfolio of 3,000 cases produced annually by Randy and his team.

Challenger Ridge's tasting room is a charmingly restored early-1900s farmhouse where visitors can enjoy a glass of wine ensconced in leather chairs. Throughout the year, the winery sponsors special events, such as celebrations of the release of red wines in the fall and white wines in the spring; a Corvette car rally; pumpkin carving; and more. The bocce court and sprawling grounds, including the vineyards, invite a visitor to stay a while and explore.

CHALLENGER RIDGE VINEYARD & CELLARS
opened: 2000
winemaker(s): Randy Bonaventura
location: 43095 Challenger Road, Concrete, WA 98237-9416
phone: 360-853-7360
web: www.challengerridge.com
e-mail: info@challengerridge.com
fee: Complimentary wine tasting
hours: Friday through Sunday 12–6; Monday 12–5
amenities: Gift Shop, Mailing List, Picnic Area, Tours, Vineyard on Premise, Wheelchair Accessible, Wine Club
connect: 🐦 f

Glacier Peak Winery 5

The sight of vineyards along Washington's Cascade Loop Highway may give you pause. In the upper Skagit Valley you anticipate dramatic mountain views, an occasional bald eagle, endless tree-populated hillsides and a fast-flowing river named Skagit. But rows of pinot noir? I think not.

However, that's exactly what you'll see along State Route 20 near Rockport, where 3 acres of vineyards grow next to Glacier Peak Winery.

Original owners Steve and Susan Olson opened the tasting room in 2002, selecting a location featuring mountain peaks in the distance. Among those peaks is Glacier Peak — one of five active volcanoes in Washington. Fortunately for WineTrail trekkers and everyone else, Glacier Peak has not stirred for nearly 200 years.

In 2011, Gary Outzen and his partner, Jackie Schneider, purchased the winery lock, stock and barrels. And within those barrels are wines produced from their own vineyard, composed of pinot noir, siegerrebe, and a unique Hungarian varietal called Agria. By itself, Agria offers a robust flavor that pairs nicely with Northwest seafood. However, when it's blended with siegerrebe, you get a pretty pinkish sunrise hue that dances on the palate. Apropos to the blend, the wine is called Glacier Sunrise.

In addition to estate wines, Glacier Peak Winery creates big reds from cabernet, syrah, and merlot varieties grown in the Yakima Valley. In total, Glacier Peak Winery produces 750 cases of wine per year, using the winemaking talent of Louis Dailly (the original owner of nearby Challenger Ridge Vineyard & Cellars). Born and raised in France's Burgundy region, Louis has considerable experience working with a wide range of grapes, but given his Burgundian roots, it will be interesting to see what he does with the estate pinot noir.

GLACIER PEAK WINERY
opened: 2002
winemaker(s): Louis Dailly
location: 58575 SR-20, Rockport, WA 98283
phone: 360-873-4074
web: www.glacierpeakwinery.com
e-mail: glacierpeakwinery@yahoo.com
fee: Tasting fee
hours: Monday through Friday 12–6; Saturday and Sunday 11–5
amenities: Picnic Area, RV/Bus Parking, Vineyard on Premise, Wheelchair Accessible

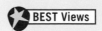 BEST Views

Island County
Wine Trail

On the Island County WineTrail, you will become familiar with the two main islands that comprise this county: Whidbey and Camano. In doing so, you will experience a Washington state ferry or two, perhaps spot an orca pod cruising by in Saratoga Passage along the way, and learn that loganberry wine and vanilla ice cream make a heavenly pairing.

Although most wineries featured here are on Whidbey Island, don't neglect Dusty Cellars Winery on Camano Island on your tasting sojourn. Please note that there is no direct route between Whidbey and Camano. To get to Camano, you cross the Camano Gateway Bridge via car near the mainland town of Stanwood.

Whichever island you explore, you may also want to bring along a bicycle — there are plenty of gentle hills and spectacular views to experience by bike.

Island County WineTrail

1 Comforts of Whidbey   **3** Ott & Murphy Wines   **5** Holmes Harbor Cellars
2 Whidbey Island Winery   **4** Blooms Winery   **6** Dusty Cellars Winery

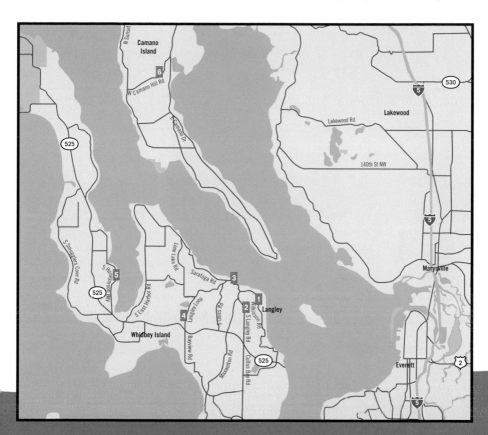

Region: **Northwest Washington Wine Country**
\# of tasting rooms on tour: **6**
Estimate # of days for tour: **2**
Getting around: **Car, ferry and bike**
Tips: ❑ **Greenbank Farm on Whidbey Island offers local and regional wines from a variety of local producers as part of their commitment to right-sized commerce.**
❑ **Get to know Washington State Ferry schedule — see www.wsdot.wa.gov/ferries.**
❑ **Budget time to explore the waterside village of Langley offering up a variety of restaurants and places to stay.**
❑ **For walking on the beach and picnicking explore Fort Casey Park near the ferry terminal to Port Townsend.**
Best: ❑ **Views and picnicking: Comforts of Whidbey**
❑ **Views: Ott & Murphy Wines**

Comforts of Whidbey

An excursion to Comforts of Whidbey feels like a field trip, only for grown-ups. With a view of Puget Sound that will have you snapping pictures like a paparazzo, this 22-acre parcel of land makes you feel like a sixth-grader on a class trip to farm country.

However, this farm is a little different. Here you will discover "cool weather" grapes, varieties that happen to thrive in the Puget Sound American Viticultural Area. These grape varieties have intimidating names like siegerrebe, Madeleine Angevine, and Madeleine Sylvaner. Carl and Rita Comfort lovingly tend these estate grapes, grown on property the Comforts purchased in 2006; at that time, its existing rows of vines were in serious need of attention.

The Comforts' goal is to produce estate wines that you would also find in other northern climes such as Alsace, France, and Germany. But the reality is, the winery is on an island wrapped in the protective embrace of Puget Sound, which provides a mild climate and a long growing season.

If the weather permits, pack a picnic and commandeer an outside picnic table with a bottle of Comforts wine. I'd recommend John Folly, a pinot noir rosé that has wonderful strawberry notes and nice acidity. Cross your fingers that it's not sold out!

Carl Comfort

COMFORTS OF WHIDBEY
opened: 2010
winemaker(s): Carl Comfort
location: 4361 Witter Road, Langley, WA 98260
phone: 360-969-2961
web: www.comfortsofwhidbey.com
e-mail: comfortsofwhidbey@gmail.com
fee: Tasting fee refunded with purchase
hours: Friday 1-5; Saturday and Sunday 11–5 or by appointment
amenities: Picnic Area, Vineyard on Premise, Wheelchair Accessible

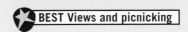
BEST Views and picnicking

Whidbey Island Winery [2]

Whereas a winery dog seems almost ubiquitous at most wineries these days, at Whidbey Island Winery you'll instead find a winery cat, who goes by the name of Sangiovese. He's not an average cat, however. Weighing in at what's got to be about 30 pounds, he could easily be mistaken for one of those winery dogs at first glance!

Although you may be under the impression that it rains continuously on Whidbey Island, the fact is that the growing season is relatively long and dry. In our northern latitude, it means long summer days with cool nights. Add to the equation the proximity of Puget Sound and the result is mild winters, creating unique conditions for growing grapes.

Owners Greg and Elizabeth Osenbach planted their vineyards' first grapes in 1986, and today, the winery produces unique white wines, such as Madeleine Angevine and siegerrebe, that are a perfect complement to Northwest seafood. My favorite: The Island White blend, perfect for a picnic on one of Whidbey Island's splendid beaches. However, for those with a palate for more traditional wines, fret not. Greg crafts a wide assortment of red and white wines using grapes from the Yakima Valley.

Winery cat Sangiovese

WHIDBEY ISLAND WINERY
opened: 1992
winemaker(s): Greg and Elizabeth Osenbach
location: 5237 South Langley Road, Langley, WA 98260
phone: 360-221-2040
web: www.whidbeyislandwinery.com
e-mail: winery@whidbey.com
fee: Tasting fee may apply
hours: Wednesday through Sunday 11–5
amenities: Gift Shop, Live Music, Mailing List, Picnic Area, Tours, Vineyard on Premise, Wheelchair Accessible, Wine Club, Wines by the Glass
connect:

Ott & Murphy Wines 3

The name Ott & Murphy derives from the surnames of winemakers David Ott and Eric Murphy. Back in the '80s, they were focusing their fermentation skills on making beer. In time, however, they tried their hand at making wine — and met with success.

The scene of their winemaking is David Ott's Swede Hill Farm, where fellow "cellar rat" Diane Kaufman lends a hand managing the garden and immersing herself in a laundry list of winemaking chores, along with tasting-room duty. In fact, on our visit to their comfy offsite tasting room, located right on the waterfront in beautiful Langley on Whidbey Island, we found Diane working alongside David, greeting visitors and pouring Bordeaux- and Rhône-style wines of layered complexity. Chances are, Eric Murphy won't be present during your visit to the tasting room. His job with Seattle-based Alpine Ascents International takes him to far-flung mountain destinations to guide roped-up heavy breathers. Among the peaks he's climbed is Mount Everest, and I'm guessing that after the descent from its 29,029-foot peak, he arrived in base camp and promptly uncorked a bottle of Ott & Murphy L'Entente Bordeaux red blend in celebration.

Be sure to budget time to enjoy a glass of wine at a table overlooking the waters of Puget Sound. Who knows, maybe an orca whale or a Trident class submarine will cruise by in this shipping lane.

OTT & MURPHY WINES
opened: 2007
winemaker(s): David Ott and Eric Murphy
location: 204 First Street, Langley, WA 98260
phone: 360-221-7131
web: www.swedehillcellars.com
e-mail: sales@swedehillcellars.com
fee: Tasting fee
hours: Thursday 5–10; Friday and Saturday 1–10; Sunday and Monday 1–6
amenities: Gift Shop, Wheelchair Accessible, Wine Club, Wines by the Glass

★ BEST Views

Blooms Winery 4

At their Bayview Cash Store location Blooms Winery provides a well appointed tasting room and a full slate of red and white wines to sample. They refer to their establishment as "Taste for Wine." Makes sense but, more than wine to sample, there's plenty of art to sample as well as wine pairing with select cheeses.

Although it's not like Baskin & Robbins with 31 flavors, visitors have the enviable task of selecting among a robust line-up of wines to sample.

My visit brought me up close and personal with Bloom's Poetry — a rich blend of malbec, syrah and cabernet sauvignon that just happened to win a double gold at the 2010 San Francisco Chronicle wine competition. Winemaker Ken Bloom and his wife Virginia noted that they got the wine bug back in 1998 when they helped in the harvest at a California vineyard owned by Ken's brother.

WineTrail Note: Don't miss out on live music every Sunday at Taste for Wine.

Kenneth Bloom

Virginia Bloom

BLOOMS WINERY
opened: 2003
winemaker(s): Kenneth M. & Virginia A. Bloom
location: 5603 Bayview Road,
Bayview Cash Store — Time For Wine,
Langley, WA 98260
phone: 360-331-4084
web: www.bloomswinery.com
e-mail: tasteforwine@whidbey.com
fee: Tasting fee
hours: Monday, Thursday and Saturday 12–6;
Friday 12–7; and Sunday 12–6
amenities: Art Gallery, Gift Shop, Pet Friendly,
Wheelchair Accessible, Wine Club, Wines by
the Glass
connect: f

Holmes Harbor Cellars

Imagine for a moment that one of the clichés about wine is true — that it really is a blend of art and science. But *clichés* exist for a reason; primarily because they are based in truth. When it comes to wine, if you don't have the palate, you can forget about blending. If you don't have a science background, what will you do when the wine lacks acidity?

Holmes Harbor Cellars is a case in point. Here, science and art come together in a beautiful spot on Whidbey Island. Named for the nearby harbor, Holmes Harbor Cellars is the home of Theresa and Greg Martinez. By day, Theresa applies her science as a chemist, and Greg is a pilot instructor for the Naval Reserve. Both, however, share a common background that includes growing up in California, graduating from Cal Poly San Luis Obispo, and taking coursework at University of California-Davis' school of enology.

Pack a picnic for this slice of paradise and have a corkscrew handy. You'll likely want it for their Etude, a bold red blend of cabernet sauvignon, merlot and syrah created with grapes from Les Collines Vineyard.

And who knows, maybe their pet cockapoo, Vino de Wine Stane, will join you seeking a belly rub!

HOLMES HARBOR CELLARS
opened: 2009
winemaker(s): Greg and Theresa Martinez
location: 4591 South Honeymoon Bay Road, Greenbank, WA 98253
phone: 360-331-3544
web: www.holmesharborcellars.com
e-mail: winemaster@holmesharborcellars.com
fee: Tasting fee
hours: Saturday and Sunday 11–5 and by appointment
amenities: Picnic Area, Private Events, Wheelchair Accessible, Wine Club
connect: f

Dusty Cellars Winery 6

Ryan, Dusty and Kramer kids

Many Seattle residents are surprised to learn that Camano Island is less than a two-hour drive away, and with no ferry ride involved. Going through the mainland town of Stanwood takes you to a bridge that connects to Camano. Once you've arrived, don't be surprised to feel your blood pressure easing down. This bucolic setting is ideal for picturesque views, friendly locals, organic gardens, and beaches where dogs can romp freely. But is it known for wine? Not really, at least not until residents Dusty and Ryan Kramer started Dusty Cellars Winery back in 2006.

Producing only 700 cases per year, Dusty Cellars may be a surprise to even the most ardent WineTrail trekkers. Only open the first weekend of the month, Dusty Cellars offers free tastings to those making the trip to Camano Island. Provided the Kramers still have wine in stock, you can expect to sip riesling, chardonnay, gewürztraminer, syrah, cabernet franc, rosé, and some red blends. Like most winemakers in western Washington, Dusty and Ryan source their grapes from eastern Washington's Columbia Valley. (At least that is the plan as they wait for their own backyard vineyard to mature, which is planted with grape varieties suitable to the mild Puget Sound weather.)

With Camano Island's permanent population of approximately 16,500 residents, those 700 cases go quickly. Factor in winemaker dinners, loyal fans, and year-round events, you would be wise to plan a visit in the spring, when they release their new vintage. As you sip and swirl, keep in mind that each bottle of wine is filled, corked, and boxed one by one. It's a labor of love for all to enjoy — on the first weekend of each month anyway.

DUSTY CELLARS WINERY
opened: 2008
winemaker(s): Ryan and Dusty Kramer
location: 529 Michael Way, Camano Island, WA 98282
phone: 360-387-2171
web: www.dustycellars.net
e-mail: via website
fee: Tasting fee may apply
hours: Open first weekend per month — call for hours
amenities: RV/Bus Parking, Wheelchair Accessible
connect: f

Other Wineries to Visit

CAMANO CELLARS
winemaker(s): Geno Genovese
and Tom Tazer
location: 7420 300th Street NW,
Stanwood, WA 98292
phone: 360-333-4899
web: www.camanocellars.com
hours: By appointment only

HONEY MOON
winemaker(s): Honey Moon, LLC
location: 1053 North State Street,
Bellingham, WA 98225-5097
phone: 360-734-0728
web: www.honeymoonmead.net
hours: Monday through Saturday 5–11

LEGOE BAY WINERY
winemaker(s): Larry L. Smith
location: 4232 Legoe Bay Road,
Lummi Island, WA 98262
phone: 360-758-9959
web: www.legoebaywinery.com
hours: By appointment only

COACH HOUSE CELLARS
location: 5012 Samish Way,
Bellingham, WA 98229
phone: 360-389-0884
web: www.coachhousecellars.com
hours: By appointment only

INYO VINEYARD AND WINERY
location: 3337 Agate Heights Road,
Bellingham, WA 98226
phone: 360-647-0441
hours: By appointment only

MASQUERADE WINE COMPANY
winemaker(s): Jennifer Kimmerly
location: 2001 Iowa Street, Suite F,
Bellingham, WA 98229
phone: 360-220-7072
web: www.masqueradewines.com
hours: Wednesday through Sunday
11–6 April through December; Friday
through Sunday 12–5 January through
March, or by appointment

SILVER BELL WINERY
location: 106 South First Street, La Conner, WA 98257
phone: 360-757-9463
web: www.silverbellwinery.com
hours: 12–6 Saturday & Sunday

TULIP VALLEY VINEYARD & ORCHARD
winemaker(s): Drew Zimmerman
location: 16163 State Route 536, Mt. Vernon, WA 98042
phone: 360-428-6894
web: www.redbarncider.com
hours: Friday through Sunday 11–5 and special events (call for details)

WESTCOTT BAY CIDER
winemaker(s): Richard Anderson
location: 43 Anderson Lane, Friday Harbor, WA 98250
phone: 360-378-3880
web: www.westcottbaycider.com
hours: Saturday 3–5 Memorial Day to Labor Day

SPOILED DOG WINERY
winemaker(s): Jack and Karen Krug
location: 5881 Maxwelton Road, Langley, WA
phone: 360-321-6226
web: www. spoileddogwinery.com
hours: Friday 12–6, Saturday 11–6 and Sunday 12–6 (summer only) and by appointment

USELESS BAY WINES
location: 220 First Street, Langley, WA 98260
phone: 360-632-4976
web: www.uselessbaywines.com
hours: Monday through Thursday 1-7:30, Friday and Saturday 1–10 and Sunday 1–6

WILLOW TREE VINEYARD
winemaker(s): Don Anderson
location: 5551 Finsrud Road, Everson, WA 98247
phone: 360-592-4505
web: www.willowtreevineyard.com
hours: Friday through Sunday 11:30–5

Olympic Peninsula
WINE COUNTRY

eaglemount

eaglemount red

2006
red wine from washington state

ALCOHOL 13.8% BY VOLUME

finn river

SPARKLING APPLE WINE

WITH BLUEBERRY JUICE

Appleblueberry

Olympic Peninsula
Wine Trail

From Bordeaux-style blends to wines that rely on rhubarb and plums, variety defines the Olympic Peninsula WineTrail. Along the way, you will discover that Port Angeles offers the perfect climate to ferment hot-weather eastern Washington grapes. You also can find a wonderful beach on which to uncork a cabernet franc, or a fine restaurant that features local wines. From Port Townsend to Port Angeles there are plenty of places to stay and eat (especially seafood), not to mention easy access to Olympic National Park via Hurricane Ridge.

Olympic Peninsula WineTrail

1 Finnriver Farm & Cidery
2 FairWinds Winery
3 Eaglemount Wine and Cider

4 Wind Rose Cellars
5 Olympic Cellars
6 Black Diamond Winery

7 Camaraderie Cellars
8 Harbinger Winery

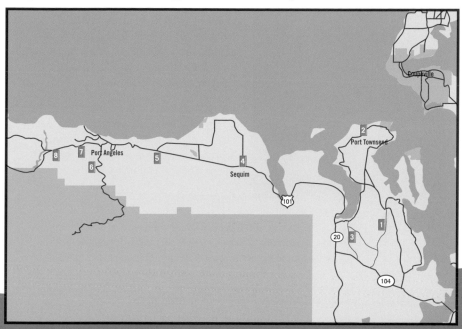

Region:	**Olympic Peninsula Wine Country**
# of tasting rooms on tour:	**8**
Estimate # of days for tour:	**2**
Getting around:	**Car**
Key Events:	❑ **Wineries are part of the Olympic Peninsula Wineries Association — select annual events: Red Wine & Chocolate (February), Northwest Wine & Cheese Tour (May), Sequim Lavender Farm Faire (July) and Dungeness Crab Festival (October) See www.olympicpeninsulawineries.org for event times and tickets.**
Tips:	❑ **Budget time to walk along the beach and visit Olympic National Park.**
	❑ **Ferry service twice a day to Victoria, BC. See www.cohoferry.com/schedules.htm.**
	❑ **Many restaurants feature local wines.**
	❑ **Harbinger Winery also features kayaking excursions and gear.**
Best:	❑ **Destination: Finnriver Farm & Cidery**
	❑ **Gift shop: Olympic Cellars**
	❑ **Picnicking: Camaraderie Cellars**

Finnriver Farm & Cidery

Crystie Kisler

The fact that Finnriver Farm & Cidery took home the Double Gold medal from the prestigious 2011 Seattle Wine Awards in the sparkling wine competition got my attention. Being a huge fan of the sparklers, I figured I had better check this place out.

Little did I know that Finnriver is a certified organic and Salmon Safe farm, complete with berries (raspberries, strawberries, blackberries, blueberries), a vegetable garden, and heirloom apple orchards. There's even a farm walk on which you can visit the egg-laying chickens and friendly honeybees.

The farm is central to the charm of a visit and reflects the authenticity of its owners, Crystie and Keith Kisler (winemaker). Naturally, I had to sample their award-winning Artisan Sparkling Cider. As the bubbles danced on my tongue, I delighted in the cider's refreshing, crisp and dry character. But that was just the start of our tasting adventure, which continued with a sparkling apple-blueberry wine that had me reaching for my wallet. Also to sample are several fruit infused brandy cordial wines. Sweet, high in alcohol (due to the use of apple brandy spirits to arrest fermentation) and warm on the finish, these cordials may have you guessing whether to imbibe before dinner as an aperitif or after dinner as a dessert wine.

Lately it seems that we're surrounded by agritourism opportunities that offer a chance to engage with an active farm without having to wake at 4 a.m. to milk the cows. Well, Finnriver is that sort of bucolic place, where city slickers can roam among the row crops, smell freshly picked apples, and hear clucking chickens.

Keith Kisler

FINNRIVER FARM & CIDERY
opened: 2008
winemaker(s): Keith Kisler
location: 62 Barn Swallow Road, Chimacum, WA 98325
phone: 360-732-6822
web: www.finnriver.com
e-mail: info@finnriverfarm.com
fee: Tasting fee refunded with purchase
hours: Daily 12–5
amenities: Lodging, Online Store, Pet Friendly, Picnic Area, Tours, Wheelchair Accessible, Wine Club
connect: ⓕ

★ BEST Destination

FairWinds Winery 2

Sure, we all love those mainstream merlots and chardonnays, but for a delightful change of pace check out a little gem of a winery located on the outskirts of Port Townsend: FairWinds Winery.

Michael Cavett

Its owners, Michael and Judy Cavett, are committed to producing unusual varietals, in addition to more well-known wines, and pricing them within most folks' reach. To this end, FairWinds is the only Washington winery to produce aligoté (a white Burgundy). And while aligoté's color will remind you of chardonnay, it has its own unique taste and aroma. (Note to WineTrail enthusiasts: Aligoté makes a harmonious accompaniment to chicken Marsala or a summer salad.)

One of the treats of visiting FairWinds is the winery tour routinely given by Michael. As you take in the sights, you can easily imagine all his volunteers assisting during crush or squeezing corks into skinny necks bottle by bottle.

FairWinds Winery was established in 1993 by two retired Coast Guard couples, and the tasting room was opened in 1996. Eventually Michael and Judy took sole possession of the winery. The FairWinds name and label are nods to Michael's Coast Guard past. Here's wishing them smooth sailing!

FAIRWINDS WINERY
opened: 1993
winemaker(s): Michael Cavett
location: 1984 Hastings Avenue West, Port Townsend, WA 98368-9638
phone: 360-385-6899
web: www.fairwindswinery.com
e-mail: info@fairwindswinery.com
fee: Complimentary wine tasting
hours: Daily 12–5 from Memorial Day to Labor Day; 12–5 Monday through Friday from September through May
amenities: Gift Shop, Picnic Area, Tours, Wheelchair Accessible, Wine Club
connect: f

Eaglemount Wine and Cider ❸

The word "harvest" takes on more meaning at Eaglemount Wine and Cider. Here the concern is not just for the ripeness of grapes (which it gets from a small vineyard in the Wahluke Slope AVA), but also for the crop of apples and pears that grow in the homestead orchard on the property. If you think worrying about the growing season and all the calamities that can befall your grape crop is bad, think what it must be like to fret over the apple and pear crops in the Puget Sound region's brief growing season. It's enough to make you reach for the hard cider — which wouldn't be far at Eaglemount.

Co-owner Jim Davis is usually staffing the tasting room. At age 70, he doesn't look a day older than 60. Between sips of some surprisingly dry and crisp ginger cider, he mentioned that his neighbors are very much alive and kicking in their 90s. If you thought "blue zones" were confined to places like Costa Rica, think again.

Jim's wife, Trudy Davis, is the winemaker extraordinaire responsible for both the ciders and fine wines. The wines and ciders — and ultimately, their drinkers — benefit from her rich background in science. Her analytical prowess is routinely exercised in the matter of fermentation science. If all one had to do was stomp grapes and let them ferment, we'd all be winemakers!

EAGLEMOUNT WINE AND CIDER
opened: 2006
winemaker(s): Trudy Davis
location: 2350 Eaglemount Road, Port Townsend, WA 98368
phone: 360-732-4084
web: www.eaglemountwinery.com
e-mail: info@eaglemountwinery.com
fee: Tasting fee
hours: Friday through Sunday 12–5 and by appointment
amenities: Online Store, Picnic Area, Wheelchair Accessible
connect:

Wind Rose Cellars

Midwest transplants David Volmut and spouse Jennifer States moved to Washington in 2007 when Jennifer took a job at science-driven Battelle in Richland. With Jennifer working on geeky science projects "for the greater good" (Battelle's mantra), David needed an outlet to exercise his brain. Realizing that they were living in the heart of wine country, David took a job in the tasting room of Barnard Griffin. He thrived there.

Living in Richland and working on the production side of the wine industry brought David in close contact with Washington grape growers. He discovered that the Wahluke Slope and Red Mountain AVAs were the perfect setting for Italian varieties, including the likes of dolcetto, barbera, and nebbiolo. These Italian varieties resonated with David, because, as a member of an Italian family growing up in Kansas, he understood that wine was an everyday beverage at the dinner table.

However, in 2011, life intervened and Jennifer took a position with Battelle's Marine Sciences Laboratory, headquartered in Sequim, Washington. This could have been the end of David's budding winemaking career, but a little move to the Olympic Peninsula wasn't going to quash the wine bug he'd come down with. Sequim gave David the perfect opportunity to launch his own label, in particular, making wine from grapes grown in the Columbia Valley and on Wahluke Slope.

Needing a name for their winery, David and Jennifer drew upon Jennifer's background in the study of wind energy, selecting the name Wind Rose Cellars. The winery's logo is a natural offshoot of the name, featuring a wind rose compass with its needle pointing to the northwest — so apropos. Reflecting on this, I took another sip of my barbera and thought to myself, David's inner compass is pointed in the right direction.

WIND ROSE CELLARS
opened: 2011
winemaker(s): David Volmut
location: 143 West Washington Street, Sequim, WA 98382
phone: 360-681-0690
web: www.windrosecellars.com
e-mail: wine@windrosecellars.com
fee: Tasting fee waived for $20 purchase
hours: Saturday 1–7; Sunday 1–4; November and December Saturday only 1–7
amenities: Art Gallery, Live Music, Online Store, Picnic Area, Wheelchair Accessible
connect: f

Olympic Cellars

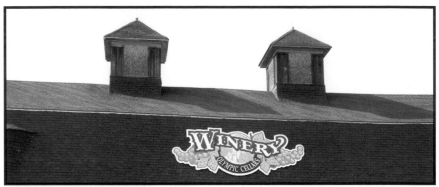
Olympic Cellars' distinctive red barn tasting room

Located in a huge old barn on U.S. Highway 101, nine miles west of Sequim, Olympic Cellars produces "Wines for women who want it all." The owners of Olympic Cellars — Kathy Charlton, Molly Rivard, and Lisa Martin — comprise the "Olympic Women in Wine." With this mantra, it was only natural that they geared their marketing to women and produced the Working Girl wine series.

Although it's not a wise strategy to buy wine based on the label alone, it is hard to resist a bottle of Olympic Cellars' Rosé the Riveter. This affordable wine pairs nicely with coworkers after a long day in pantyhose and pumps. Depending upon availability, check out its premium La Dolce Vida line of wine, which includes varietals produced in small lots.

Their Dungeness series of wine includes the heritage and artist series of labels, which were first made in 1980. The Dungeness white is a semisweet riesling; the Dungeness red is a Beaujolais-style lemberger; and their newest member of the series is a refreshing rosé. The well-stocked gift shop features a world of wine-related items guaranteed to satisfy that hard-to-buy-for aunt. You go, girl!

OLYMPIC CELLARS
opened: 1979
winemaker(s): Benoit Murat
location: 255410 Highway 101, Port Angeles, WA 98362
phone: 360-452-0160
web: www.olympiccellars.com
e-mail: wines@olympiccellars.com
fee: Tasting fee
hours: Daily 11–6 from April through October; Daily 11–5 from November through March
amenities: Gift Shop, Mailing List, Online Store, Picnic Area, RV/Bus Parking, Tours, Wheelchair Accessible, Wine Club, Wines by the Glass
connect: 🐦 f

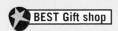
BEST Gift shop

Olympic Cellars gift shop

Black Diamond Winery 6

Located in the foothills of the Olympic Mountains southwest of Port Angeles, Black Diamond Winery specializes in making fruit wines, the kind of wine that some may call back-porch wines. Lance and Sharon Adams began perfecting fruit wines 20 years ago and haven't deviated from their specialty, despite the proliferation of Bordeaux-style wineries around the state.

Black Diamond barn

Leaving the road, you make the 200-yard drive up to the winery to lay eyes on the Adams' orchard and small 2-acre vineyard. In the summer, you can see the plums, raspberries, and rhubarb ripening for harvest. Lance or Sharon will greet you in the small tasting room situated in the end of the building, which houses the winery, just above Tumwater Creek. A small tasting fee gives you access to their Ridge white wine, a Müller-Thurgau wine (the Müller-Thurgau grapes are from Whidbey Island Vineyard), and Sharon's Blush, a blend of red and white wines from the Adams' vineyard; and shiro plum, rhubarb, loganberry, cranberry, and raspberry fruit wines.

Their passion for making specialized fruit wines comes through in every sip you take. Each berry picked, each pressing made, each vintage bottled translates into a lot of work to produce 800 cases a year. To get a sense of the task, check out the photos on the tasting room wall showing the ripened shiro plums, ready to be picked, and the huge stalks rhubarb pulled during harvest. One can almost feel the sore arm muscles after a day of picking those babies. Instead, let's opt for some mental exercise: Imagine raspberry wine poured over French vanilla ice cream. That should get those salivary glands pumping.

Black Diamond vineyard — early spring

BLACK DIAMOND WINERY
opened: 2000
winemaker(s): Lance and Sharon Adams
location: 2976 Black Diamond Road, Port Angeles, WA 98363-9443
phone: 360-457-0748
web: www.blackdiamondwinery.com
e-mail: bdwinery@prodigy.net
fee: Tasting fee
hours: Summer hours: June through September, Friday through Sunday 12–5. Winter hours: October, November, December, April and May, Saturday and Sunday 12–5; Closed January, February and March and major holidays
amenities: Picnic Area, Tours, Vineyard on Premise, Wheelchair Accessible

Camaraderie Cellars 7

In 1992 Don Corson and his wife Vicki formed Camaraderie Cellars with a "combination of hope, a small new building, great vineyard connections and a family philosophy that the best things in life are meant to be shared." OK, they had me at "hope" but what distinguishes Camaraderie is this sense of community and sharing the good things of life. You see it in the beautiful gardens that greet you when you arrive, the handcrafted outdoor furniture, and their recently completed new tasting room with the beautiful weathervane on top. This, my fellow WineTrails lover is one winery you need to have your camera nearby.

Camaraderie Cellars wines are made to complement a wide range of cuisine. You find yourself wondering how Steak au Poivre would taste with Camaraderie's hearty merlot blend or how Beethoven might sound as one of Don's Bordeaux-style red blends is swishing around your palate. It's no wonder that you find Camaraderie Cellar Wines at select restaurants and wine bars.

One question that Don routinely gets is "why is your winery in Port Angeles?" He responds that the cool marine air and mild summers are the perfect spot for grapes to ferment in their French barrels. But he also adds that great wine only begins with the best fruit and to that end, Camaraderie is fortunate to source their grapes from Artz Vineyards from Red Mountain and Champoux Vineyards in the Horse Heaven Hills. It is the combination of a dry hot climate in Eastern Washington and the mild wet climate of Western Washington that completes the process. Ying and yang. Hearty stew and Cabernet Sauvignon. Beethoven and a white Bordeaux blend. It don't get no better than that.

CAMARADERIE CELLARS
opened: 1992
winemaker(s): Don Corson
location: 334 Benson Road, Port Angeles, WA 98363-8492
phone: 360-417-3564
web: www.camaraderiecellars.com
e-mail: info@camaraderiecellars.com or corson4@tenforward.com
fee: Complimentary wine tasting
hours: Saturday and Sunday 11–5 May through October, or by appointment; also available at The Tasting Room in Seattle
amenities: Online Store, Picnic Area, RV/Bus Parking, Tours, Wheelchair Accessible, Wine Club
connect: f

BEST Picnicking

Harbinger Winery 8

Harbinger, *n.* — one that indicates or foreshadows what is to come; a forerunner.

In 2004, Sara Gagnon and Tammi Hinkle experienced a traumatic event that proved to be life altering: They survived a plane crash. Tragically, the pilot of the small plane died, but Sara and Tammi managed to get out of the crash with their lives. The accident proved to be the impetus for living each day as if it were their last. Indeed, emblazoned across the Harbinger sign inside the winery is their mantra, "Step forth and be the harbinger of your dreams."

And after that close call, harbingers of their dreams they became! Sara had been the chief winemaker at nearby Olympic Cellars, which gave her considerable exposure to the commercial side of the business. Her dream was to have her own winery. Tammi had been a kayaking guide and harbored notions of owning her own kayaking business. After the plane crash, both women decided to act on their dreams and together they launched Harbinger Winery.

As winemaker, Sara spends most days tending to myriad winery duties. Tammi, on the other hand, invests most of her time in her "baby": Adventures Through Kayaking guide service.

Harbinger's winery and tasting room are located just west of Port Angeles on the south side of Highway 101 in a large blue metal building that looks "suspiciously like an old logging-truck shop." Inside the winery, the atmosphere is "Northwest comfort," with Buddha statues serving as decoration, a huge gold couch, and kayaks hanging on the wall. The concrete floors provide cool comfort even on the hottest days of the summer. It's a decidedly relaxed atmosphere and a perfect place to contemplate your life's ambitions while sampling Harbinger's treasures.

HARBINGER WINERY
opened: 2006
winemaker(s): Sara Gagnon
location: 2358 West Highway 101, Port Angeles, WA 98363-9420
phone: 360-452-4262
web: www.harbingerwinery.com
e-mail: info@harbingerwinery.com
fee: Tasting fee
hours: Monday through Saturday 11–6; Sunday 11–5. Closed Christmas Day
amenities: Gift Shop, Online Store, RV/Bus Parking, Wheelchair Accessible, Wine Club
connect: f

Other Wineries to Visit

ALPENFIRE CIDER
location: 220 Pocket Lane, Port Townsend, WA 98368
phone: 360-379-8915
web: www.alpenfirecider.com
hours: Friday through Sunday 1-5 May through September; Call for hours October through April

CHRISTINA JAMES WINERY
winemaker(s): Christina Pivarnik
location: 205 St. James Place, Port Townsend, WA 99368
phone: 360-531-0127
web: www.facebook.com/pages/Christina-James-Winery/269864140810?fref=ts
hours: By appointment only

LULLABY WINERY
location: 274 South Otto Street, Port Townsend, WA 98368
phone: 509-386-1324
web: www.lullabywinery.com
hours: By appointment only

Puget Sound
WINE COUNTRY

EIGHT BELLS

2011
Sangiovese

Red Willow Vineyard
Yakima Valley

ALC. 13.1% BY VOL

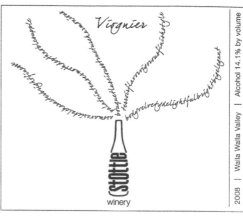

Viognier

stottle
winery

2008 | Walla Walla Valley | Alcohol 14.1% by volume

509

SYRAH
2007
WALLA WALLA VALLEY

14.3% VOL.

Palouse
winery

2009
WASHINGTON

ECLIPSE
Blend

MEDICINE CREEK WINERY

LIMITED EDITION
RED DESSERT WINE

Fini

375 ML - ALC. 12.6% BY VOL

Perennial
Vintners

Ichigo

STRAWBERRY
DESSERT WINE

Made from Bainbridge
Island strawberries.

500mL
Alcohol 19% by volume
Contains sulfites

eleven

PORT
PINOT GRIS
OREGON

ALCOHOL 18.0% BY VOLUME

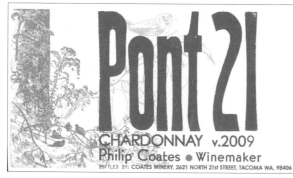

Pont 21

CHARDONNAY v.2009
Philip Coates ⊛ Winemaker

BOTTLED BY: COATES WINERY, 2621 NORTH 21st STREET, TACOMA WA, 98406

VINTAGE: 2009
VARIETAL DESIGNATION: Chardonnay
ALCOHOL CONTENT: Alc. 13.7% by Vol.
APELLATION OF ORIGIN: Columbia Valley
NET CONTENTS: 750 ml

ROLLING BAY
winery

2008

Syrah
Snipes Mountain

FallingRain

2008
ARC-EN-CIEL

COLUMBIA VALLEY RED WINE

Alc 14.8% by Vol

Kalamar

2007

SANGIOVESE
Yakima Valley

ALCOHOL 14.6% BY VOLUME

BSH
2006

O • S WINERY
CABERNET SAUVIGNON 67%
CABERNET FRANC 17%
MERLOT 12%
PETIT VERDOT 4%

COLUMBIA
VALLEY

WASHINGTON
STATE

14.6% ALC./VOL.

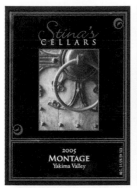

Stina's
CELLARS

2005
MONTAGE
Yakima Valley

ALC. 14.5% BY VOL.

GOVERNMENT WARNING: (1) ACCORDING TO THE SURGEON GENERAL, WOMEN SHOULD NOT DRINK ALCOHOLIC BEVERAGES DURING PREGNANCY BECAUSE OF THE RISK OF BIRTH DEFECTS. (2) CONSUMPTION OF ALCOHOLIC BEVERAGES IMPAIRS YOUR ABILITY TO DRIVE A CAR OR OPERATE MACHINERY, AND MAY CAUSE HEALTH PROBLEMS.

750 ML   CONTAINS SULFITES

Stomani
CELLARS

cabernet sauvignon

2007

Columbia Valley

ALC. 13.8% BY VOL.

Our Cabernet Sauvignon is full bodied and bold, dark fruit shows best, with hints of Bing cherry. The complexity and layers within show through the supple mid-palate remains. The finesse of the nice long finish, teases you into taking that next sip. Barrel aged 16 months.

Produced and Bottled by Stomani Cellars & Winery, LLC
85 S. Atlantic, Suite 110, Seattle, Washington
www.StomaniCellars.com   206-601-1833

NORTHWEST MOUNTAIN WINERY

FIRE BREATHING MEAD

HONEY WINE FERMENTED WITH JALAPEÑOS
375 MLS   ALC 13% BY VOLUME

Madsen Family Cellars

Riesling
Rattlesnake Hills 2008

cloudlift

PANORAMA
2010 · COLUMBIA VALLEY

Perennial Vintners

Madeleine Angevine
2007

Estate Grown
Dry White Wine

Puget Sound Appellation
ALCOHOL 11% BY VOLUME

Seattle
WineTrail

One need not venture to Woodinville or points east to experience delectable Washington wine. Seattleites and visitors can go on an urban wine-tasting spree from Everett to south Seattle and discover commercial winemaking ventures that, more often than not, started in someone's garage or basement. Many of the winemakers on this trail are former Boeing Wine Club members, who learned from each other while attempting to find a cure for the wine bug. However, once members go commercial, they can no longer participate in the Boeing Wine Club or take advantage of its collective buying power (it purchases more than 50 tons of grapes annually). Yep, the former member who goes pro is on their own — well, them and the cloud of drunken fruit flies that fills their production area in the fall.

Seattle WineTrail

1. Domanico Cellars
2. 509 Wine Company
3. Almquist Family Vintners
4. Stomani Cellars & Falling Rain Wines
5. Ward Johnson Winery
6. Eight Bells Winery
7. Lost River Winery Seattle Tasting Room
8. The Tasting Room — Seattle
9. Bartholomew Winery
10. Cloudlift Cellars
11. Laurelhurst Cellars
12. O·S Winery
13. :Nota Bene Cellars
14. Stottle Winery Seattle Tasting Room
15. Northwest Wine Academy

Region:	**Puget Sound Wine Country**
# of tasting rooms on tour:	**15**
# of satellite tasting rooms:	**2**
Estimate # of days for tour:	**3**
Getting around:	**Car, bus, light rail**
Key Events:	❏ **Seattle is home to the annual Taste Washington! event at the Century Link Event Center in late March. See www.tastewashington.org for tickets and times.**
Tips:	❏ **Most Seattle WineTrail wineries participate in the Seattle Urban Winery scene with doors open every second Saturday. See www.seattleurbanwineries.com for more information.**
	❏ **Wineries of the South Seattle Artisan Wineries Association are collectively open the second Saturday of each month from February through August. See www.ssaw.info for times and locations.**
	❏ **A number of Seattle area Farmers Markets include wine tasting.**

Domanico Cellars

Jason Domanico

Some wineries sprout signs of their organic leanings right and left. By that I mean smells, textures, sights, and sounds that have evolved randomly but form a cohesive front. Call it "accidental branding" or just call it smart, but such is the case at Seattle's urban winery Domanico Cellars.

Tucked into one of Ballard's working neighborhoods, the unobtrusive winery could easily be overlooked as another machine shop, woodworking space, or boat supplier. However, the smells of wine resting in the barrel and perhaps a staccato laugh of a patron inside lead you to the promised land.

The interior stretches vertically with plenty of space for stacking barrels, but it's the bar itself that draws your attention. Thick planks of light wood form the bar's countertop, which rests on used wine barrels, and behind the bar, owner/winemaker Jason Domanico greets visitors with a friendly smile. Jason's shining pate reflected the light from above, and the look works for Jason as much as it does Andre Agassi — both good-looking guys. As Jason poured a sample of Domanico's Lewis Vineyard riesling, a patron at the end of the bar jokingly noted, "Too bad his wife [Jill Domanico] isn't here; she's much easier on the eyes." I thought to myself that they must be a handsome couple.

Recently, the couple acquired an existing vineyard in the booming wine center of Prosser, complete with an old farmhouse and views of Horse Heaven Hills in the distance. I could easily imagine the Domanico family (including their winemaker in training, daughter Anna) escaping the gray skies of Seattle to happily work the harvest at their Yakima Valley vineyard.

DOMANICO CELLARS
opened: 2006
winemaker(s): Jason and Jill Domanico
location: 825 NW 49th Street, Seattle, WA 98107
phone: 206-465-9406
web: www.domanicocellars.com
e-mail: info@domanicocellars.com
fee: Tasting fee may apply
hours: Friday 5–9; Saturday 12–6 or by appointment
amenities: Mailing List, Newsletter/Blog, Private Events, Wheelchair Accessible
connect: 🐦 📘

509 Wine Company

Here's a tip: On the first Friday of each month, Seattle's quirky Fremont neighborhood opens its doors for Art Walk, an event that features paintings, photography, live music, sculpture, ray guns, jewelry, bicycles, wine and a whole lot more. Open every Friday night, 509 Wine Company's Fremont tasting room is the place for tasting some enological works of art right out of the bottle. In addition to the wine, you can enjoy small bites and music.

As most locals know, the area code in the wine country east of the Cascades is 509. This is the region from which 509 Wine Company sources its grapes (hence the winery's name), specifically, from Les Collines Vineyard in the Walla Walla Valley. Nestled against the foothills of the Blue Mountains, this land is a grape's idea of heaven — volcanic soil, a relatively dry climate, and plenty of heat units.

509 Wine Company is the brainchild of Kevin Conroy and Mike Blom. Kevin's internet-based marketing firm shares an address with the building housing 509's tasting room, making it convenient to go from his executive office to the wine bar — about a 22-second commute. Winemaker Mike is originally from California, where he cut his teeth producing wine from northern California grapes. Now, he's calling on that experience to turn Northwest fruit into syrah, merlot, cabernet sauvignon, viognier, and rosé. Speaking of rosé, 509's Côtes du Fremont syrah rosé is a must, especially during Summer Solstice when Fremont gets a little bizarre — in a good way.

509 WINE COMPANY
winemaker(s): Mike Blom
location: 1300 North Northlake Way, Seattle, WA 98103
phone: 206-632-7516
web: www.509Wines.com
fee: Tasting fee
hours: Friday 3–8
amenities: Online Store, Private Events, Wheelchair Accessible

Almquist Family Vintners ③

Harvest came late in 2011, and the drunken fruit flies and the smell of fermenting grapes didn't surprise me as I entered Almquist Family Vintners. I was a first-time visitor to the winery, two blocks west of the Fremont Bridge on the Queen Anne side, and hadn't a clue what awaited me. I spied a lone figure toward the back of a very spacious building punching down the cap of fermenting grapes. That solitary figure was none other than owner/winemaker Mike Almquist.

Mike Almquist

I discovered that to appreciate Almquist Family Vintners, one must experience the mind of Mike Almquist. He's brilliant, with no shortage of opinions on various subjects, and with swagger to match. Leaving the comfortable confines of his East Coast home, Mike ventured to Seattle to take a job with the University of Washington. Somewhere along the line, he began making wine, but rather than hanging out the shingle and releasing his first batch of 300 cases, he did the unheard thing of putting together a business plan. Essentially, the plan informed him that to be successful, he needed to think big. And "big" he thought, with a winery that can readily serve as a hangar for a small commercial airplane, a barrel room that easily accommodates 15 rows of barrels stacked eight barrels high, and an adjacent restaurant, The Book Bindery, which has become all the rage with Seattle's ever-buzzing foodies.

Mike explained that Almquist Family Vintners is a BYOB custom-crush facility, which means that he's making wine for lots of folks who want to get into the wine business without investing in the latest Italian destemmer-crusher. He's also embraced the craft distilled spirits world and pointed to the distilling equipment in back. I figure Mike must keep a small army of Washington's Liquor Control Board employees busy with licensure issues.

ALMQUIST FAMILY VINTNERS
opened: 2008
winemaker(s): Mike Almquist
location: 198 Nickerson Street, Seattle, WA 98109
phone: 206-352-9262
web: www.almquistfamilyvintners.com
e-mail: contact@almquistfamilyvintners.com
fee: Tasting fee refunded with purchase or eating at the Book Bindery
hours: Monday through Saturday 5–10
amenities: Private Events, Restaurant/Food Pairings, RV/Bus Parking, Wheelchair Accessible, Wines by the Glass
connect: 🐦 f

Stomani Cellars & Falling Rain Wines ④

Judith Papesh and Alex Manoni must get along. Judith (owner/winemaker of Falling Rain Wines) and Alex (owner/winemaker of Stomani Cellars) have been making wine under the same roof for years — sharing equipment, advice and rent.

Making wine in their Lower Queen Anne/South Lake Union location, they continue their small lot pursuit with Alex brewing wines of the Italian persuasion and Judith focusing on rich Bordeaux blends. You don't need to lay Stomani Cellars wines down — they are ready to serve with anything pasta. Take for example, Stomani Cellar's Aglianico, a red grape variety from Italy that you rarely find outside of central Italy (which makes me realize rather randomly that is where Pliny the Elder died in Pompeii's Mount Vesuvius eruption in 79AD). Also check out Alex's Super Tuscan style blend of sangiovese, merlot and cabernet sauvignon named Insieme — an Italian word meaning "together."

Artisan winemaker Judith Papesh wines lean toward the meatier side. Chewy. Layered and loads of complexity. Her 2007 Bordeaux-blend Mischief garnered a 92+ rating from Jay Miller of the Wine Advocate. In part, here's what Miller wrote about the 2007 Mischief, "It exhibits a splendid bouquet of sandalwood, incense, herbs, lavender, cassis, and blackberry. Already complex on the palate, this is a mouth-coating, layered, spicy, and impeccably balanced blend that will reward 4-5 years of cellaring and which will effortlessly see its 20th birthday." Nevertheless, knowing a cassoulet recipe I'm anxious to try, I paid the $25 for a bottle knowing there's no way that I will let this sit in my measly cellar for 20 years.

STOMANI CELLARS & FALLING RAIN WINES
opened: 2008
winemaker(s): Judith Papesh (Falling Rain) and Alex Manoni (Stomani Cellars)
location: 1403 Dexter Avenue North, Seattle, WA 98109
phone: 206-340-6137
web: www.stomanicellars.com & www.fallingrainwines.com
e-mail: info@stomanicellars.com & judy@fallingrainwines.com
fee: Tasting fee refunded with purchase
hours: Wednesday 5–8; Friday 4–8; Saturday and Sunday 12–5 or by appointment
amenities: Picnic Area, Private Events, Wheelchair Accessible, Wine Club
connect: 🐦 📘

Ward Johnson Winery 5

"We aim to please," remarked Charlie Johnson, co-owner of Ward Johnson Winery. "When you walk in, we want you to have a pleasant experience throughout your visit," he added as I dipped a strawberry into their chocolate fountain.

If you didn't know you were close to Queen Anne Hill, a quick survey of the wine menu would provide a clue. Longtime Seattle residents would catch on once they read a name like Counterbalance Chardonnay. The Counterbalance refers to the steep stretch of Queen Anne Avenue along which electric trolley cars once ran up and down. For Charlie, having a sense of place is important, after spending the better part of his life in the U.S. Air Force and teaching in Europe.

After retiring, Charlie, along with his wife, Sherri Johnson, joined forces with his brother Kurt and his wife, Tammara Johnson, to launch Ward Johnson. The "Ward" half of the name comes from Sherri's and Tammara's maiden names, which happen to be the same — Ward — although they are not related. Strange but true.

Kurt is the primary winemaker for Ward Johnson, and he has a penchant for making single varietal red wines. He relies on fruit from the Red Mountain AVA, using Kiona Vineyards (cabernet), Hedges (merlot), and Ranch at the End of the Road (syrah) vineyards. The chardonnay is sourced from Columbia Valley's Sun River Vineyard.

Charlie recalls that, as young men, he and his brother would drive to a nearby vineyard from their Richland home with empty apple boxes to gather grapes for their home winemaking. One can only imagine how the grape grower laughed at the sight of those apple boxes; small potatoes — or grapes — compared to his portion of the harvest, which is sold by the ton. However, from those naïve beginnings, Ward Johnson Winery has established a solid reputation for fine wines.

WARD JOHNSON WINERY
opened: 2006
winemaker(s): Kurt Johnson
location: 1405 Elliott Avenue West, Suite F2, Seattle, WA 98119
phone: 206-229-3421
web: www.wardjohnsonwinery.com
e-mail: info@wardjohnsonwinery.com
fee: Tasting fee refunded with purchase
hours: Saturday and Sunday 1–5 or by appointment
amenities: Newsletter/Blog, Wheelchair Accessible, Wine Club
connect: 🐦 📘

Eight Bells Winery 6

Their Facebook page states, "Eight Bells Winery is a small urban winery in the Ravenna/Roosevelt neighborhood of North Seattle producing hand-crafted red and white wines." However, this is just the preface to what is otherwise a remarkable story of three men who weren't ready to retire. Owners Tim Bates, Andy Shepherd, and Frank Michiels, possessing inquisitive minds and a deep desire to make something with their hands, were having none of the "R" word.

They present their establishment as a small artisan winery, but truth be told, the space they use for crushing, fermenting, barreling, and bottling is quite large at least vertically, with enough vertical room to fully test a forklift.

With crush in full swing, I was fortunate to catch all three winemakers on a well-earned break and was treated to samples of their full portfolio of wines. While quaffing their refreshing pinot gris (whose grapes came from the Methven Family Vineyard in Oregon's Eola-Amity Hills near Dayton), I learned that Tim and Andy still have day jobs with the National Oceanic and Atmospheric Administration (NOAA), and that scientific background served them well in completing Washington State University's viticulture and enology coursework. Later, while savoring their delicious 2009 Red Willow Vineyard syrah, I discovered that Frank had a legal background that had leveraged his fluency in the Japanese language. But what struck me most was how different each man was in terms of personalities, skill sets, and interests. It's a fine blend of talent.

For those who are curious, "eight bells" is a nautical term referring to a seaman's four-hour watch, during which the bell strikes on the half-hour. By the eighth bell, his shift is over and it's time for a changing of the watch. Tim, Andy, and Frank all heard that eighth bell ring, and this exceptional winery is the result.

EIGHT ☸ BELLS

2011
Sangiovese
Red Willow Vineyard
Yakima Valley

ALC. 13.1% BY VOL.

EIGHT BELLS WINERY
opened: 2010
winemaker(s): Tim Bates, Andy Shepherd and Frank Michiels
location: 6213 B Roosevelt Way NE, Seattle, WA 98115
phone: 206-947-9692
web: www.8bellswinery.com
e-mail: info@8bellswinery.com
fee: Complimentary wine tasting
hours: Saturday 11–4
amenities: Mailing List, Online Store, Wheelchair Accessible, Wine Club
connect: 🐦 f

Lost River Winery Seattle Tasting Room 7

LOST RIVER WINERY SEATTLE TASTING ROOM
opened: 2002
winemaker(s): John Morgan
location: 2003 Western Avenue, Suite 100, Seattle, WA 98121
phone: 206-448-2124
web: www.lostriverwinery.com
e-mail: info@lostriverwinery.com
fee: Tasting fee refunded with purchase
hours: Wednesday through Sunday from 11–7
amenities: Wine Club, Mailing List, Wines by the Glass, Online Store, Wheelchair Accessible
connect: 🐦 f

www.winetrailsnw.com/wineries/lost_river_winery_seattle_tasting_room

The Tasting Room — Seattle

Take a number of outstanding Washington wineries, put them in a historic building in the heart of Seattle's Pike Place Market, and you have The Tasting Room Seattle. Now, if

you did the same thing but placed it in a completely different venue, say, outside Yakima, you would have The Tasting Room Yakima.

And that's just what owner/winemaker Paul Beveridge of Wilridge Winery has done. To feature his wines, he embraced an open concept, for which he invited other wineries to join him at a Pike Place tasting salon that he named The Tasting Room Seattle, Wines of Washington.

Located in Post Alley, next to Kells Irish Pub and across from the Pink Door Restaurant, The Tasting Room Seattle, Wines of Washington invites everyone to come in and experience a wide assortment of wines. Visitors can sample a plethora of wines from several wineries, which at press time included Naches Heights Vineyards, Camaraderie Cellars, Harlequin Wine Cellars, Mountain Dome, Latitude 46 North, Wineglass Cellars, and Wilridge Winery.

In 2007, Paul purchased a parcel of land outside Yakima to grow grapes and make wine. The setting, called The Tasting Room Yakima, features many of the same wineries you find at the Pike Place location. However, visitors can go beyond the early-1900 Craftsman-style house turned tasting room to tiptoe through the 10-acre estate vineyard, drink a glass (or two) on the expansive patio or hike the nearby Cowiche Canyon Nature

Preserve. It's beautiful. It's relaxing. And it goes beyond drive-by tasting. You will want to budget a generous amount of time for this sport of heaven on earth.

THE TASTING ROOM — SEATTLE
winemaker(s): Various Winemakers
location: 1924 Post Alley, Pike Place Market, Seattle, WA 98101
phone: 206-770-9463
web: www.winesofwashington.com
e-mail: info@thetastingroomseattle
fee: Tasting fee
hours: Daily 12–8 with extended hours Friday and Saturday until late
amenities: Newsletter/Blog, Online Store, Private Events, Restaurant/Food Pairings, Wheelchair Accessible, Wines by the Glass
connect: 🐦 📘

Bartholomew Winery 9

Have you ever experienced "friendly" wines? You know, the type of wine that is approachable, easy to drink; good with burgers or with nothing but a summer day. Crisp, clean, tail-wagging refreshment. Well, that describes the kind of wine you'll experience at

Bartholomew Winery, one of Seattle's newest urban wineries, located in the Tully's building (the former Old Rainier Brewery building, an iconic sight you can't miss cruising south from downtown on Interstate 5).

You know how dogs often look like their owners. That observation also can hold true when it comes to winemakers and their creations. Bart Fawbush just happens to be one of the nicest, most unassuming vintners around, and his wines reflect that friendly demeanor.

Bart Fawbush

Now, lest you think I have gone off the deep end, find out for yourself. Budget some time on a Saturday or Sunday to do a little urban reconnaissance at Bartholomew Winery; check out his southern Rhône blend dubbed Orsa, or his equally approachable Reciprocity, an intriguing blend of cabernet sauvignon and carménère.

Discover for yourself how an average guy makes above-average wine. I'm not the only one to think so; check out *Sunset* magazine's nod to Bartholomew Winery when it spotlighted the winery at the no. 17 spot — "Urban wineries" — in its 2011 "Top 100 cultural trends shaping the West." Or, hear it from Bart himself on YouTube; go to youtube.com and search "Winery Words, Bartholomew Winery."

BARTHOLOMEW WINERY
opened: 2010
winemaker(s): Bart Fawbush
location: 3100 Airport Way South, Seattle, WA 98134
phone: 206-395-8460
web: www.bartholomewwinery.com
e-mail: bart@bartholomewwinery.com
fee: Complimentary wine tasting
hours: Saturday and Sunday 12–5
amenities: Gift Shop
connect: 🐦 f

Cloudlift Cellars 🔟

My ignorance was showing when I asked proprietor/winemaker
Tom Stangeland if he named his winery "Cloudlift" because
of its proximity to Puget Sound. I figured that even with our
marine air, blue skies do occasionally appear when the fog
lifts. "No," said Tom, "the cloud lift is a design feature used in
furniture. It's the rise you see on the back of a chair or other fine
pieces made by a woodworker." "Oh, I see," I said in response,
and chocked it up as my first lesson in furniture making.

Tom Stangeland

Tom was giving me a $2 tour of his South Seattle wine
production facility and woodworking studio. Unfinished chairs,
C-clamps, and band saws were scattered among fermentation
tanks and barrels. It's not unusual for winemakers to have other
jobs and hobbies they're passionate about, but I had never met
someone who is both master woodworker and winemaker; it
makes for an interesting blend. Yet, when you think about it, the detail work that goes
into producing fine furniture reflects the same level of exacting detail needed to produce
fine wine.

Tom's first vintage was in 2009, and if the 2010 Cloudlift Cellars chardonnay that I enjoyed
is evidence of his skill, we have lots to look forward to. Take a gander at what *Wine Press
Northwest* had to say about his 2009 Ascent: "It's easy to tell that this blend of Bordeaux
varieties leads with Cabernet Franc (72%) from Alder Ridge Vineyard in the Horse Heaven
Hills, which creates a spicy and tobacco leaf theme behind the cassis, Marionberry, smoky
black cherry, moist earth, crushed nutmeg, green tea, and
cocoa powder. The racy acidity and medium body screams
for pork loin or a puttanesca." Such verbiage makes me want
to sit in one of Tom's cloudlift-adorned chairs and enjoy a
good pour of his Ascent. No puttanesca necessary.

CLOUDLIFT CELLARS
opened: 2011
winemaker(s): Tom Stangeland
location: 312 South Lucile Street,
Seattle, WA 98018
phone: 206-622-2004
web: cloudlift.net
e-mail: tom@cloudlift.net
fee: Tasting fee refunded with purchase
hours: Saturday 1–5
amenities: Mailing List, Newsletter/Blog,
Wheelchair Accessible
connect:

Laurelhurst Cellars

Located in Seattle's Georgetown neighborhood, Laurelhurst Cellars is the reflection of owners/winemakers Greg Smallwood and Dave Halbgewachs love affair with wine. It's a big step up from their garage-days in Laurelhurst. It's urban-assault wine tasting at its finest, with free parking to boot.

Laurelhurst Cellars also happens to be a member of the South Seattle Artisan Wineries, which means that WineTrail trekkers can look forward to a fun day of wine tasting at Bartholomew Cellars, OS Winery, Fall Line Winery, Cadence and :Nota Bene, which are open collectively on the second Saturday of every month from February through August.

Laurelhurst produces elegant wines, to be sure, and there's no secret to its formula — they start with grapes purchased from renowned vineyards in the Columbia Valley. With fruit from the likes of Klipsun, Kiona, Songbird, Burgess, and Boushey vineyards, you know your palate is in for a real treat.

My favorite happens to be the Laurus Nobilis Bordeaux-style blend, in part because I like to pronounce the name (which is the Latin moniker for the bay laurel tree). — it's a pleasure on the tongue just as the wine itself is.

LAURELHURST CELLARS
opened: 2004
winemaker(s): Gabe Warner, Greg Smallwood and Dave Halbgewachs
location: 5608 7th Avenue South, Seattle, WA 98108
phone: 206-992-2875
web: www.laurelhurstcellars.com
e-mail: wine@laurelhurstcellars.com
fee: Tasting fee refunded with purchase
hours: Second Saturday, from February through August, and for special events around the holidays.
amenities: Mailing List, Online Store, Wheelchair Accessible, Wine Club
connect: [f]

O·S Winery 12

When conservative banker Rob Sullivan joined forces with liberal winemaker Bill Owen in 1997 to create Owen Sullivan Winery, you would have put money on a short-lived partnership. But you would have been wrong. Now, more than 10 years later, the renamed O•S Winery is clearly a success story. But don't take my word for it.

Instead, take the words of *Wine Spectator*'s Harvey Steiman regarding O•S: "From their jury-rigged winery in a nondescript business park, Bill Owen and Rob Sullivan are making some of Washington's plushest and headiest reds.... They make small lots that just keep getting better with each vintage." Heady indeed. And the words "sold out" that commonly accompany O•S wines is further proof.

When it comes to naming wines, O•S Winery takes the cake. With cryptic names like BSH, R3, and M, the monikers appear simple — but actually may require a secret decoder ring. Take "BSH," which Bill, a lover of big, full-flavored wines, accidentally coined when he exclaimed that a still-in-the-barrel red wine was built like a "Brick Shit House." Love it!

Rob and Bill may seem like the yin and the yang in this venture. But as one Sydney J. Harris once noted, "Opposites attract because they are not really opposites, but complementaries."

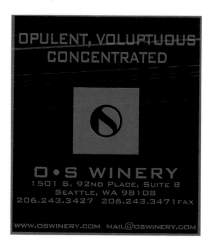

O·S WINERY
opened: 1997
winemaker(s): Bill Owen
location: 1501 South 92nd Place, Suite B, Seattle, WA 98108
phone: 206-243-3427
web: www.oswinery.com
e-mail: mail@oswinery.com
fee: Tasting fee refunded with purchase
hours: Second Saturday 1–5 from February through August; open select Saturdays in November and December: consult www.ssaw.info for details
amenities: Online Store, Wheelchair Accessible, Wine Club
connect: 🐦 📘

:Nota Bene Cellars

Being meticulous doesn't guarantee great results, but clearly, gold medal winners and sloppy winemaking don't mix. The best winemakers are painstakingly fussy: They monitor fermentation like a hawk and religiously keep detailed records. The production facility itself is clean and well organized, comparable to what you would find in a top-notch Lexus or Cadillac dealer service center.

To such perfectionists, winemaking is more science than art. Count owner/winemaker Tim Narby among those exacting types.

Nota bene is Latin for "note well" and happens to be associated with the first letter of :Nota Bene owners' respective surnames: "N" for Narby and "B" for Tim's wife, Carol Bryant.

Tim, a Boeing systems analyst for more than 30 years, joined the Boeing Employees Wine and Beer Makers Club years ago to learn first-hand the ingredients necessary for creating premium wines. He became a club member fresh out of the University of Washington with a degree in zoology.

Tim Narby (r) and assistant winemaker

That zoology training serves him well when it comes to understanding the microbiology of what Saccharomyces cerevisiae (a species of yeast) does to sugar. Although it was Louis Pasteur who figured out the role of yeast in converting sugar to alcohol, we suggest that you leave the discussion about fermentation science for another day and just enjoy the treasures of Tim's craft.

:NOTA BENE CELLARS
opened: 2001
winemaker(s): Tim Narby
location: 9320 15th Avenue South, Unit CC, Seattle, WA 98108
phone: 206-459-2785
web: www.notabenecellars.com
e-mail: info@notabenecellars.com
fee: Tasting fee refunded with purchase
hours: Second Saturday 1–5 from February through August; open selected other Saturdays in November and December: consult www.ssaw.info for details
amenities: Online Store, RV/Bus Parking, Wheelchair Accessible, Wine Club
connect: ▪

www.winetrailsnw.com/wineries/_nota_bene_cellars

Stottle Winery Seattle Tasting Room ⒁

STOTTLE WINERY SEATTLE TASTING ROOM
opened: 2010
winemaker(s): Josh Stottlemyer
location: 3400 Harbor Avenue SW, Suite 113, Seattle, WA 98126
phone: 360-515-0356
web: www.stottlewinery.com
e-mail: info@stottlewinery.com
fee: Tasting fee
hours: Saturday and Sunday 12–6
amenities: Wine Club, Wines by the Glass, Online Store, Wheelchair Accessible
connect: ☐f

www.winetrailsnw.com/wineries/stottle_winery_seattle_tasting_room

Northwest Wine Academy 15

As you bebop around the tasting rooms of Washington, you'll discover a fair number of winemakers who got their start at South Seattle Community College's distinguished Northwest Wine Academy. It's the first of its kind in the area, offering three different tracks toward attaining a certificate: wine production; wine sales and marketing; and food and wine pairing.

I can personally testify that it is a rigorous program, since I am a graduate of the program. Admittedly however one never really "graduates" from learning about wine. It's a lifelong endeavor and just when you think you have it fairly well understood somebody slips you a bottle from some unknown wine region!

What makes the program shine is its stellar staff, with the likes of renowned industry professionals Regina Daigneault, Peter Bos, and Leonard Rede. Because classes fill up all too quickly, students are wise to register early, a point underscored in a report by Seattle KOMO-TV on the wine academy's popularity.

The winner of several awards in the prestigious 2011 Seattle Wine Awards, including a gold medal for its 2010 Mourvèdre, the Northwest Wine Academy holds its own against established wineries. However, my favorite among prize winners is the Wine Library TV's Gary Vaynerchuk for winning the "Best of the Best" for college-made wine; see the "March Madness" episode at tv.winelibrary.com/category/college.

NORTHWEST WINE ACADEMY
opened: 2005
winemaker(s): Peter Bos
location: 6000 16th Avenue SW, Seattle, WA 98106-1499
phone: 206-934-7955
web: www.nwwineacademy.southseattle.edu
e-mail: mmay@sccd.ctc.edu
fee: Complimentary wine tasting
hours: Open during regular school hours and special events
amenities: RV/Bus Parking, Wheelchair Accessible
connect: ⓕ

Around the Sound
WineTrail

The islands to the west of Seattle are home to a number of select wineries that make island hopping a fun getaway. Residents of Vashon Island and Bainbridge Island already know the fine wines produced by local vintners. And now, WineTrail enthusiasts, too, are hearing the buzz surrounding these award-winning wines. With plenty of restaurants, boutique shops, and mist-shrouded beaches to explore, this WineTrail is a sensory explosion. And knowing that your vehicle's weight doesn't factor into your ferry expense, you might as well stock up on several cases of wine from these artisan winemakers.

Around the Sound WineTrail

1. Skylite Cellars Kirkland Tasting Room
2. Northwest Cellars
3. Waving Tree Winery Kirkland Tasting Room
4. Island Vintners
5. Eagle Harbor Wine Company
6. Eleven Winery
7. Rolling Bay Winery
8. Eleven Winery Poulsbo Tasting Room
9. Palouse Winery
10. Vashon Winery

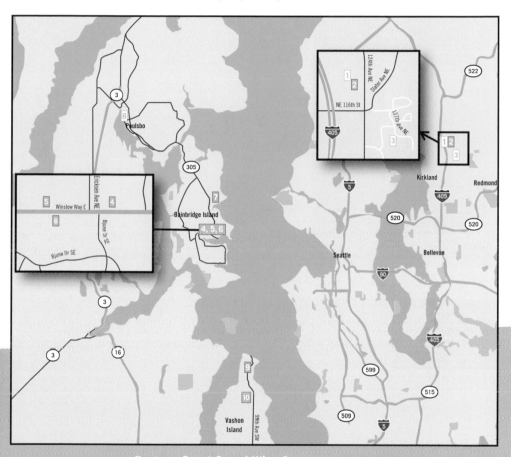

Region:	**Puget Sound Wine Country**
# of tasting rooms on tour:	**10**
# of satellite tasting rooms:	**3**
Estimate # of days for tour:	**3**
Getting around:	**Car and ferry**
Tips:	❏ **Check out Winery Alliance of Bainbridge Island at www.bainbridgewineries.com.**
	❏ **Walk off the Bainbridge Island ferry dock and visit several winery tasting rooms in downtown Winslow.**
	❏ **Pack a picnic for Vashon Island and discover award-winning wineries and Puget Sound vineyards.**
	❏ **Vashon's Farmers Market provides wine tasting**

Skylite Cellars Kirkland Tasting Room

SKYLITE CELLARS KIRKLAND TASTING ROOM
opened: 2005
winemaker(s): Robert Smasne
location: 11901 124th Avenue NE,
Kirkland, WA 99362
phone: 509-529-8000
web: www.skylitecellars.com
e-mail: info@skylitecellars.com
fee: Tasting fee refunded with purchase
hours: Friday 3–7, Saturday 12–6 and Sunday 12–5
amenities: Online Store, Private Events,
RV/Bus Parking, Wheelchair Accessible
connect: 🐦 f

www.winetrailsnw.com/wineries/skylite_cellars_kirkland_tasting_room

Northwest Cellars

I was in search of some wine as a gift for friends of WineTrails Northwest. With my diminutive budget, however, I couldn't exactly spring for a couple of cases of Château Lafite Rothschild, yet I still wanted a quality wine. And while I was dreaming, wouldn't it be great if this wine sported a WineTrails Northwest label? (After all, one can never have too much branding.) Unfortunately, all the private-label wines that I have tasted bring to mind leftover bath water (not that I have actually tasted such, but one can imagine). That's when I heard from a friend about Kirkland's Northwest Cellars, a winery that offers affordable wine that you can personalize with a custom label.

Tucked behind a strip mall, Northwest Cellars in Kirkland was a bit of a challenge to find, but fortunately, the sandwich boards steered me to the right place. Once there, I met former software CEO turned winery owner Bob Delf. Unassuming and friendly to boot, Bob made me feel welcome. The small tasting room (which includes a variety of wine-related gifties) opened into an adjacent production area, where there was a table with plates of bite-size treats to enjoy with the wine.

And enjoy the wine I did, at least according to my notes, which I reviewed later. Those scribbles included the word "delish" followed by an exclamation point in describing Northwest Cellars' affordable white blend wine dubbed Adagio — very light yellow, slight oakiness, crisp with loads of grapefruit and lemon notes. At $18 a bottle, a perfect match for grilled skewered shrimp and dipping sauce. The showstopper for me, however, was Bob's red wine blend labeled Intrigue, which possesses a cabernet sauvignon backbone.

NORTHWEST CELLARS
winemaker(s): Robert Smasne, Dave Moore, Bob and Kathleen Delf
location: 11909 124th Avenue NE, Kirkland, WA 98034
phone: 425-825-9463
web: www.northwestcellars.com
e-mail: info@northwestcellars.com
fee: Tasting fee refunded with purchase
hours: Friday 3–7, Saturday 12–6 and Sunday 12–5, or by appointment for groups of 10 or more
amenities: Newsletter/Blog, Online Store, Private Events, RV/Bus Parking, Wheelchair Accessible, Wine Club
connect: 🐦 📘

Waving Tree Winery Kirkland Tasting Room 3

WAVING TREE WINERY KIRKLAND TASTING ROOM
opened: 2002
winemaker(s): Terrence Atkins
location: 11901 SE 124th Avenue, Kirkland, WA 98034
phone: 425-820-0102
web: www.wavingtreewinery.com
e-mail: atkins@gorge.net
fee: Tasting fee refunded with purchase
hours: Friday 3–7, Saturday 12–6, Sunday 12–5 and by appointment
amenities: Online Store, RV/Bus Parking, Wheelchair Accessible
connect: f

www.winetrailsnw.com/wineries/waving_tree_winery_kirkland_tasting_room

Island Vintners

Which excites you more, wine and cheese or wine and smoked salmon? How about wine paired with good friends? Or perhaps you'd choose all of the above in a setting that invites you to kick back and relax. Such is the quaint ambiance that welcomes wine lovers to the Island Vintners' tasting establishment in downtown Winslow on pedestrian-friendly Winslow Way.

Island Vinters co-owner Jim Wilford of Fletcher Bay Winery focuses on delivering full-palate pleasures at his winery, which happens to be accessible by land and by sea. However, getting to Fletcher Bay Winery on the occasional weekend that it's open is problematic, so Jim has done the next best thing. He has teamed up with two other Bainbridge Island vintners to create a space convenient to locals and ferry trekkers alike. Each of the winemakers brings their own unique libations. Jim provides a full complement of Bordeaux-focused wines with Spanish tempranillo and Italian sangiovese to spice up his collection.

Another in the Island Vintners trio is Victor Alexander Winery, which, like Fletcher Bay Winery, is a small-lot winery. It uses grapes from the Columbia Valley to create fewer than 1,000 cases of food-friendly merlot and semillon. Located close to Bainbridge Island's Gazzman Lake, Charlie Merrill's Victor Alexander Winery also is off the beaten path for most Bainbridge Island visitors. It makes good business sense to give people a chance to sample your wares in downtown Bainbridge, rather than leave them to search you out with a GPS device.

Paul Bianchi's Amelia Wynn Winery is the third player to this unique setting. A winner of many wine awards, Paul produces a full slate of European red wines for the consuming public. Dominated by Bordeaux blends, Paul's wines are bold but soft and oh so ready for tonight's meal. In other words, you don't need to cellar these babies.

A plethora of wines — enough to satisfy most palate preferences, from refreshing whites to tannin-rich reds — paired with platters of breads, cheeses, and smoked salmon, make for an afternoon of joy. Just remember to check the ferry schedule before you order another bottle.

ISLAND VINTNERS
winemaker(s): Charlie Merrill, Paul Bianchi and Jim Wilford
location: 450 Winslow Way East, Bainbridge Island, WA 98110
phone: 206-451-4344
web: www.islandvintners.com
fee: Tasting fee
hours: Monday through Wednesday 1–7; Thursday 1–8; Friday and Saturday 12–9; and Sunday 12–7
amenities: Restaurant/Food Pairings, Wheelchair Accessible, Wines by the Glass
connect: ▪️

Eagle Harbor Wine Company ⑤

One look at Hugh Remash and you know he's a lover of French wine. What gives it away? The beret on his head. His Bordeaux-style wines have subtle fruit-forward flavors devoid of the astringent feeling that you get with young wines possessing to much tannin. In fact, his wines reflect a decided bent toward Old World style with a judicious use of oak. Exhibit A is his cabernet sauvignon, with its layered flavors of dark fruit, tobacco, cedar, and oh so subtle chocolate. Although the label indicates that the grapes come from the Walla Walla Valley, the wine tastes as though their source is Bordeaux's "left bank."

Hugh Remash

Located in a contemporary business park on Bainbridge Island, Eagle Harbor Wine Company is open on select weekends, along with other Bainbridge Island wineries. Be sure to consult Eagle Harbor's Facebook page or the Bainbridge Island wineries website for its hours.

Originally hailing from Pennsylvania, Hugh somehow made it west, creating a lifetime of experiences along the way before finding his passion making wine. Unfortunately, just when I was about to dig into his past, a busload of women — celebrating a big occasion in a big way — converged on the winery, diverting Hugh's attention. Oh well, I'll don my beret and return to visit Bainbridge another time.

EAGLE HARBOR WINE COMPANY
opened: 2008
winemaker(s): Hugh Remash
location: 278 Winslow Way East, Winslow Wine Shop & Tasting Room, Bainbridge Island, WA 98110
phone: 206-227-4310
web: www.eagleharborwinecompany.com
e-mail: via website
fee: Tasting fee
hours: Wednesday through Friday 11–7; Saturday 12–6; Sunday 12–5
amenities: Online Store, Wheelchair Accessible
connect: ◼

Eleven Winery

Main Street U.S.A. That's what it feels like when entering Eleven Winery's comfy tasting room in downtown Winslow. It's a charming place and one of the first pit stops made by most wine tourists hopping a ferry to Bainbridge Island from Seattle.

The owners of the winery, Matt (winemaker) and Sarah Albee, have never sought to create a big winery with mega-case production. Rather, with the "small is beautiful" mantra, their plans call for small-lot production of approximately 1,000 cases per year.

Once inside the tasting room, kick back and experience a nice portfolio of reds, whites, a dry rosé, and port-style dessert wines. I proceeded to taste out of sequence and went with an unusual Mourvèdre with bright cherry fruit flavors and a nice finish to boot.

The name Eleven Winery derives from Matt's former bike-racing career. Within the cluster of gears on a racing bike's back wheel is the smallest cog, with only 11 teeth. The bike racer turns to that cog when he really needs extra power to finish strong. It's the winning gear.

BTW, Eleven Winery has a second tasting room in nearby Poulsbo at 18827 Front Street. Its tasting room hours are the same as the Bainbridge location. It's a nice pit stop on the way to the Olympic Peninsula.

ELEVEN WINERY
opened: 2003
winemaker(s): Matt Albee
location: 287 Winslow Way East, Winslow Wine Shop & Tasting Room, Bainbridge Island, WA 98110
phone: 206-780-0905
web: www.ElevenWinery.com
e-mail: matt@elevenwinery.com
fee: Tasting fee
hours: Wednesday through Sunday 1–7 from October through May; open seven days June through September.
amenities: Art Gallery, Online Store, Private Events, Tours, Wheelchair Accessible, Wine Club

Rolling Bay Winery 🔢

Alphonse de Klerk is his name, and wine is his game — a game he plays on beautiful Bainbridge Island, where you find a half-dozen other wineries in close proximity to visit, should you have the time. But don't count on that. You may just find yourself spending most of the day in Rolling Bay Winery's intimate tasting room, where Alphonse could keep you charmed for hours.

Alphonse de Klerk

Alphonse is not one of those Puget Sound-centric winemakers who insists on producing wines from only cool-climate grapes, ones with tongue-twisting names like siegerrebe and Müller-Thurgau. He eschews such notions and goes with the best cabernet sauvignon and syrah grapes he can find, which, for Rolling Bay, come from Snipes Mountain Viticultural Area in eastern Washington.

If you're as fortunate as I was on my visit, you'll experience a sort of golden glow bathing the tasting room. Maybe it was the lovely afternoon light in combination with the glass of stellar syrah, but the atmosphere had my Nikon working overtime. Discover it for yourself — and don't forget your camera.

ROLLING BAY WINERY
opened: 2009
winemaker(s): Alphonse DeKlerk
location: NE 10334 Beach Crest Drive, Bainbridge Island, WA 98110
phone: 206-419-3355
web: www.rollingbaywinery.com
e-mail: contact@rollingbaywinery.com
fee: Tasting fee
hours: Select weekends — see www.bainbridgewineries.com
amenities: Newsletter/Blog, Online Store, Wheelchair Accessible
connect: 🐦 📘

Eleven Winery Poulsbo Tasting Room ⑧

ELEVEN WINERY POULSBO TASTING ROOM
opened: 2003
winemaker(s): Matt Albee
location: 18827 Front Street,
Poulsbo, WA 98370
phone: 206-780-0905
web: www.ElevenWinery.com
e-mail: matt@elevenwinery.com
fee: Tasting fee
hours: Wednesday through Sunday 1–7 from February
through December; open seven days June - September
amenities: Wine Club, Art Gallery, RV/Bus Parking,
Wheelchair Accessible
connect: 🐦 📘

www.winetrailsnw.com/wineries/eleven_winery_poulsbo_tasting_room

Palouse Winery

For owners George and Linda Kirkish, coming up with a moniker for their winery was a head scratcher. However, a trip to Walla Walla crystallized the name when they turned on to Palouse Street and George recalled that his grandmother was born in the Palouse. Besides that, they liked the way the word "Palouse" rolled off the tongue. Their winery motto, "Smooth, round and voluptuous," naturally followed, inspired by the iconic imagery of the Palouse's rolling hills — layered and textured with colors of golden yellow, earth brown and chartreuse, and domed by a cloudless blue.

A short five-minute car trip from the Vashon Island ferry dock takes you to Palouse Winery, which is housed in a supersize shed next to the Kirkishs' home. It's an intimate space, perfect for a couple of dozen friends to gather and sample wine; it's also the production site of 1,000 cases of wine per year. A small tasting fee entitles visitors to grab a table and have George and Linda pour samples of Palouse Winery's riesling, viognier, cabernet franc, merlot, cabernet sauvignon, petit verdot, petite syrah, zinfandel, and a red blend called Eclipse.

In developing a wine style that emphasizes single varietal wines, the couple has relied on assistance from the likes of Paul Portteus (Zillah's Portteus Vineyards & Winery), Vashon neighbor Bill Owen (co-owner/winemaker for O•S Winery), and Jim and Barbara Richards (creators of Napa's famed Paloma Vineyard). Fortunately for the Kirkishs, it's not difficult to get around wine country in the western U.S. Turns out that George is a pilot and owner of three airplanes. For George and Linda, doing a flyover of the Rattlesnake Hills AVA vineyards from which they source their fruit is an afternoon adventure. It gives them a chance to see the smooth, round, rolling hills from up high.

PALOUSE WINERY
opened: 2005
winemaker(s): George P. Kirkish
location: 12431 Vashon Highway SW, Vashon, WA 98070
phone: 206-567-4994
web: www.palousewinery.com
e-mail: info@palousewinery.com
fee: Tasting fee
hours: Saturday and Sunday 2–5; May through September, Friday 12–5 or by appointment
amenities: Newsletter/Blog, Online Store, Wheelchair Accessible, Wine Club
connect:

Vashon Winery 🔟

Although you don't need an excuse to take the short ferry ride to picturesque Vashon Island, if you're looking for one, try Vashon Winery. Ron Irvine is the proprietor and winemaker for this gem of a winery, which he himself describes as "boutique" and he's happy to keep it that way.

Students of the Washington wine industry will likely recognize Ron Irvine as the co-author of The Wine Project, which traces the history of the state's wine industry, from pioneer grape growers to today's movers and shakers. The other author of The Wine Project was none other than Walter J. Clore, who is generally credited as being the father of Washington's modern-day wine industry.

Included on Ron's résumé is the little fact that he was a wine retailer for many years as the owner of Pike & Western Wine Shop at Pike Place Market. Working in the trade no doubt reinforced his winemaking style, which uses neutral oak to create smooth (i.e., soft) wines.

Ron makes a full portfolio of wines. For a real treat, check out his wonderfully named Isletage (rhymes with Meritage), which is a blend of Puget Sound–area grapes: Madeleine Angevine, siegerrebe, and Müller-Thurgau. He also makes wine from a relatively obscure island-grown varietal called Chasselas, best known in Switzerland.

Ron Irvine (r)

Ron is an amazingly approachable, fun individual. He's an educator at heart. Even inexperienced wine tasters feel at ease with him. In Vashon Winery's barn-like tasting room, a chandelier hangs from the rafters, a basketball hoop graces the wall, and the sign above the tasting bar reads "Ron Irvine, owner, winemaker, janitor." A whimsical guy, but one serious winemaker.

VASHON WINERY
opened: 1995
winemaker(s): Ron Irvine
location: 10317 SW 156th Street, Vashon, WA 98070
phone: 206-567-0055
web: www.vashonwinery.com
e-mail: vashonwinery@yahoo.com
fee: Complimentary wine tasting
hours: Saturday 2–5 from April through September, or by appointment; Call ahead
amenities: Picnic Area, Wine Club, Live Music, Wheelchair Accessible
connect: 📘

South Sound
WineTrail

The South Sound WineTrail is a hot bed of winemaking activity. With a dozen wineries to visit, from Tacoma south to Olympia and then north to Hoodsport, you'll need to budget several days to explore this WineTrail. And you might as well mix in a tour of a world-class glass museum or an amazing vintage-car museum along the way. Besides the wine, what many a WineTrail trekker takes away is the sincere friendliness of the staffs working the tasting rooms. Chances are that affable fellow pouring the wine is actually the winemaker. Without the crowds you find in Woodinville or the Willamette Valley, you now have the chance to learn about his winemaking style, his favorite wine, and why he named his dog Rhône Ranger.

South Sound WineTrail

1 Kalamar Winery
2 Trillium Creek Winery
3 21 Cellars
4 Stina's Cellars
5 Medicine Creek Winery
6 Stottle Winery
7 Northwest Mountain Winery
8 Madsen Family Cellars
9 McCrea Cellars
10 Walter Dacon Wines
11 Hoodsport Winery
12 Stottle Winery Hoodsport Tasting Room

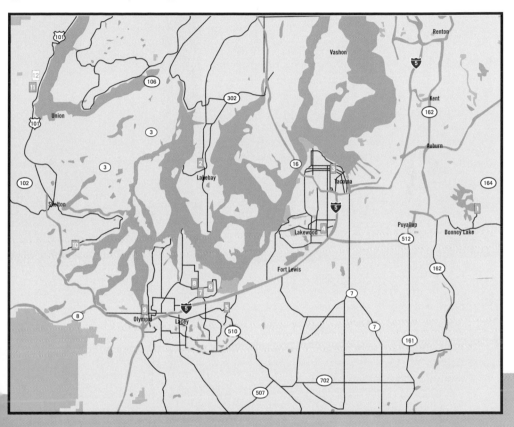

Region: **Puget Sound Wine Country**
# of tasting rooms on tour: **12**
# of satellite tasting rooms: **1**
Estimate # of days for tour: **3**
Getting around: **Car**
Tips: ❑ **Budget time to check out Tacoma's thriving Museum District including Tacoma Art Museum, Museum of Glass, Washington State History Museum and Lemay — America's Car Museum. See www.traveltacoma.com for more information.**
❑ **Proctor Farmers Market offers wine tasting**
 Best: ❑ **Picnicking: Trillium Creek Winery**

Kalamar Winery [1]

Stop by on any Friday night at Kalamar Winery between late November and spring release and enjoy the wines of Mark Kalamar. Using Columbia Valley grapes, Mark focuses on producing lush, full-bodied reds. If you are a white zinfandel fan, this may not be your cup of tea.

My personal favorites are his sangiovese-dominant wines, which have a dose of merlot to give them some muscle on the palate. Aged for four years in neutral French oak, these wines are reminiscent of Tuscany's Brunello di Montalcino, which also is aged for long periods in oak, resulting in wine less austere than traditional sangiovese wines. Translation: lip-smacking good with a hint of vanilla and a perfect complement to anything meaty and fatty.

Mark's vino-making aspirations come from his great-uncle Fred Terrile. Prior to Washington's own grape production kicking into gear, Uncle Fred, along with other Italian farming families of King and Pierce counties, made a trip down to Seattle's Georgetown neighborhood to buy their grapes each year. That's where the trains from California would stop to deliver freshly harvested grapes. Once the families returned home, they vinified the grapes, typically in someone's basement or garage, and later used the end result for personal consumption.

Similar to Pend d'Oreille Winery's "Think green, drink red" refillable bottle campaign, Kalamar Winery offers a bottle-swap program. With a $20 bottle deposit, you become a member of the Kalamar wine club and receive a 3-liter bottle of red wine for an additional $50. Three liters translates into four 750-milliliter bottles of wine, which breaks down to a recession-busting $12.50 a bottle. Who thought that going green could be both economical and delicious at the same time?

KALAMAR WINERY
winemaker(s): Mark Kalamar
location: 5906 218th Avenue East, Bonney Lake, WA 98391
phone: 253-862-9844
web: www.kalamarwinery.com
e-mail: la-mark@msn.com
fee: Tasting fee
hours: Friday 4–8 during winter, and two weekends a year: First weekend before Thanksgiving and third weekend in April for Spring release
amenities: Live Music, Mailing List, Pet Friendly, Wheelchair Accessible, Wine Club
connect: 🐦 f

Trillium Creek Winery 2

Claude Gahard

"I'm not a believer in malolactic fermentation. I like the crispness and freshness you get with malic acid remaining in the wine," stated Trillium Creek Winery's owner/winemaker, Claude Gahard. He was sporting a French beret and a mustache that paired nicely with his soft eyes and friendly demeanor. As I glanced at the wine still swirling in my glass, I realized he was referring to the tart, green-apple-like crispness that malic acid gives before converting to its softer cousin, lactic acid.

Most wine we taste has gone through malolactic fermentation (or MLF, for short), because most winemakers desire a rounder, more full-bodied feel on the palate. However, a minority of winemakers (count Claude among them) prefer a crisper wine, one that complements foods especially rich in fat, such as cheese and cream sauces. Quaffs of such crisp wine have a palate-cleansing effect.

I detected a slight accent as Claude talked about his winemaking style, which prompted me to inquire about his origins. Turns out, Claude's family immigrated to New York from his native France when he was 11. Although his French is a little rusty these days, he remembers well how wine is a part of everyday life in France, especially around the dinner table.

As we worked our way through the assortment of wine (including Claude's wonderfully delectable syrah), I noted signs posted on the wall informing visitors that Trillium Creek wines are low in sulfites. It was yet another reminder that Claude has a distinct wine style, one that eschews the use of sulfur dioxide, a chemical winemakers have used since ancient Roman times to maintain wine's freshness. Claude's mission is to retain the natural qualities of wine without additional chemicals. For those wine drinkers who have a sensitivity to sulfites, Trillium Creek Winery is an oasis.

TRILLIUM CREEK WINERY
opened: 2006
winemaker(s): Claude F. Gahard
location: 17812 18th Street, Lakebay, WA 98349
phone: 253-884-5746
web: www.trilliumcreekwinery.com
e-mail: trilliumcreekwines@msn.com
fee: Complimentary wine tasting
hours: Tuesday through Sunday 11–6
amenities: Picnic Area, RV/Bus Parking, Tours, Vineyard on Premise, Wheelchair Accessible
connect: ◼

⭐ BEST Picnicking

21 Cellars ³

Tucked away in a little brick building on North 21st Street in Tacoma, 21 Cellars can be a little hard to find for first-time visitors. Once they locate the building, they should be on the lookout for a red wine bottle sign set outside the winery entrance, as this indicates that the winery is open for business. But don't let any of this deter you; often the best wine-tasting

experiences occur in the smallest production places. And that's precisely what you will discover for yourself with a trip to 21 Cellars, where winemaker/owner Philip Coates often is on hand to explain the process he uses to craft his award-winning wines. This presents a great opportunity to ask questions and learn about Coates' winemaking background and style.

Generous pours of chardonnay, sauvignon blanc and cabernet sauvignon await your palate's pleasure. A sauvignon blanc bearing the name "OmRikki" got my attention with its crisp acidity and lasting flavors of pear and apple. Although it was a cold, wet day outside when I visited, I could easily imagine this wine pairing perfectly with a warm summer day.

21 Cellars splashed onto the scene in 2011 when its 2006 Pont 21 Cabernet Sauvignon was named one of the "Top 10 New Washington Wines" by *Seattle* magazine. The word pont is French for "bridge" (as in the Pont Neuf in Paris), so we can only surmise that Pont 21 is a bridge to a great tasting experience. Surprisingly, considering its small production, 21 Cellars produces another cabernet sauvignon dominant wine, called Promesse 21, using grapes from the Wahluke Slope. Be sure to taste both Pont 21 and Promesse 21 to experience the distinctive characters of two different cabernets created by the same winemaker.

21 CELLARS
opened: 2003
winemaker(s): Philip Coates
location: 2621 North 21st Street, Tacoma, WA 98406
phone: 253-220-7752
web: www.21cellars.com
e-mail: info@21cellars.com
fee: Tasting fee
hours: Saturday 12–4 or by appointment
amenities: Mailing List, Online Store, Private Events, Tours, Wheelchair Accessible, Wine Club
connect: 🐦 f

Stina's Cellars

Penny Preston, the wife of winemaker Perry Preston, explained that her husband earned the nickname "Prestina" while working for United Airlines' baggage service at Seattle-Tacoma International Airport. Such a name would seem to belie his 6-foot-4-inch frame, but because he is exceptionally precise — down to the crease of his pants — the work crew began calling him "Prestina," as in precise to the nth degree. Eventually, a fellow employee shortened the name to "Stina," and it stuck. Thus, it came to be that when Perry and Penny launched their winery, it was only natural to call it Stina's Cellars.

Tucked inside an industrial warehouse park in Lakewood, Stina's Cellars invites WineTrail trekkers to come and taste a smorgasbord of wines. From riesling to cabernet, visitors can sip and swirl reds and whites to their hearts' content. However, if you're seeking an unusual tasting experience, be sure to sample the Baco noir. This hybrid grape variety is a cross of the French white wine grape Folle Blanche and an indigenous American red grape of unknown Vitis riparia origin. This variety is a favorite of many, who enjoy its fruit-forward, rather acidic composition, and tantalizing spicy notes on the finish. Unlike Stina's Cellars' other varietal wines, which rely on eastern Washington grapes, Perry's Baco noir is sourced from a western Washington grape grower. That's unusual.

Incidentally, hats off to Perry and Penny for coming up with a terrific wine label, which features the image of an Old World–style door handle. The picture echoes the care and attention that Stina's Cellars imparts in each bottle of Old World–style wine it produces.

STINA'S CELLARS
winemaker(s): Perry Preston
location: 9316 Lakeview Avenue SW, Lakewood, WA 98499
phone: 253-227-9748
web: www.stinascellars.com
e-mail: stina@stinascellar.com
fee: Tasting fee
hours: Friday and Saturday 12–6
amenities: Online Store, Wheelchair Accessible, Wines by the Glass
connect: f

Medicine Creek Winery

Winemaker Jim Myers likes to tinker in woodworking. Residing on a farmstead in the Nisqually Valley, Jim transformed an old barn house to its present-day incarnation of tasting room, production facility, and storage space. Aside from his wine (more on that to come), the centerpiece of the winery is a restored 1865 Abbot & Downing passenger stagecoach reminiscent of the old Wells Fargo wagons. Jim picked it up in 2000 and spent years restoring the coach to its pristine condition today. Clearly, this restoration required woodworking skill to achieve, but perhaps equally important is a deep appreciation of the history associated with these 19th-century vehicles.

Located in the wetlands of the Nisqually Valley, on land once inhabited by the Nisqually Indian Tribe, the winery has a wrought iron gate entrance that provides a clue of what's to come: The gate's iron work includes Medicine Creek Winery's stagecoach logo. Once you've come through the double doors of the restored barn, your eyes adjust to the sight of what looks like a classy saloon of the Old West. The Western furnishings, the bright red wallpaper, and oversized mirror give you a sense of those bygone days; the only thing missing is the player piano music. You'll be tempted to belly up to the bar and order a sarsaparilla.

But we'd encourage you to try the cabernet instead.

Working with Columbia Valley growers, Jim makes the annual trek to the valley to obtain his freshly harvested grapes, as do many western Washington winemakers. His artisan-crafted wines include syrah, cabernet franc, cabernet sauvignon, merlot, and a Bordeaux blend with the unsurprising name of Stage Coach Red; in fact, each of Medicine Creek's bottles bears a stagecoach on its label.

MEDICINE CREEK WINERY
winemaker(s): Jim Myers
location: 947 Old Pacific Highway SE, Olympia, WA 98513
phone: 360-701-6284
web: www.medicinecreekwines.com
e-mail: jmeyers@medicinecreekwinery.com
fee: Tasting fee
hours: Saturday and Sunday 12–5
amenities: Live Music, Newsletter/Blog, Online Store, Wheelchair Accessible, Wine Club, Wines by the Glass
connect: f

Stottle Winery ⑥

Josh and Amy Stottlemyer knew the secret of making great wine right from the get-go: It all starts in the vineyard. With famed Elerding Vineyard in the Horse Heaven Hills AVA providing most of the fruit for their initial releases, the Stottlemyers probably paid a premium per ton, but you get what you pay for.

A fine example of their winemaking efforts is a tempranillo, so fine that it makes you wonder if Washington's grape reputation will expand to include this Spanish grape in the years to come. The nice spice in this wine mirrors (or perhaps emphasizes) the spice you find in dishes such as paella or tomato-based sauces.

Located in Lacey, just north of Washington's state capital, Olympia, the winery's business-park setting seems an unexpected spot for a winery. Inside the winery's light-filled tasting room, there are plenty of tables to park at and enjoy a glass of Stottle wine. For such a young winery, the tasting list is ambitious, with a choice of the aforementioned tempranillo, plus Malbec, cabernet sauvignon, sangiovese, viognier (from Walla Walla), a red blend, nebbiolo, and barbera (from Sagemoor Vineyards). It's a United Nations of varietals, with France, Spain and Italy well represented.

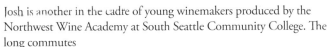

Josh is another in the cadre of young winemakers produced by the Northwest Wine Academy at South Seattle Community College. The long commutes — an hour on a good day — gave Josh ample time to think of the label design for their wine bottles. Featuring a white on black label, the image of a Stottle bottle of wine has "vines" composed of words describing the wine growing out of the bottle. Imaginative, fun and approachable, the labels invite loyal fans of Stottle Winery and newbies alike to uncork and imbibe.

STOTTLE WINERY
opened: 2010
winemaker(s): Josh Stottlemyer
location: 2641 Willamette Drive NE, Suite C, Lacey, WA 98516
phone: 360-515-0356
web: www.stottlewinery.com
e-mail: info@stottlewinery.com
fee: Tasting fee
hours: Wednesday through Sunday 11–6
amenities: Online Store, RV/Bus Parking, Wheelchair Accessible, Wine Club, Wines by the Glass
connect:

Northwest Mountain Winery

Kristi Curtis

The Firebreathing Mead got my attention. Kristi Curtis, co-owner of Northwest Mountain Winery and wife of winemaker Ray Curtis, asked if I would like to try it. "Sure," I replied. After all, what could be the harm in sampling something that just took home the bronze medal at the 2011 Seattle Wine Awards? "Wow!" I exclaimed as the sweet honey taste gave way to the fire of the jalapeños. Sweet and spicy converging in one sip confirms that opposites do attract — to fiery yet excellent effect. I figure any winemaker daring to think outside the proverbial barrel has a future in this industry.

New to the south Puget Sound–area wine scene, Northwest Mountain Winery opened in 2010 with a host of dessert, fruit and traditional wines. The winery may be new, but Ray isn't a newbie to winemaking, having dabbled in it when he worked for a winery as a teenager back in his native Ohio. Typically sporting a Seahawks sweatshirt (Ray and Kristi got married on the field at a Seahawks game), this burly and genial man believes in making a variety of libations. Grapes aren't the only thing with sugar for fermentation; people have been making honey wine (mead) since ancient times.

Located in the same business park complex as Madsen Family Cellars, Northwest Mountain Winery offers a cozy interior, with cushy chairs to relax in while enjoying their wines. The décor is Kristi's signature and has a homey feel. Unpretentious and inviting, it reflects the couple's attitude toward wine as a drink to share with friends and family, to be woven into the culture of life. This is the perfect environment for uncorking a bottle of their Firebreathing Mead and savoring the moment. My only suggestion would be to bring a hankie for mopping that brow.

NORTHWEST MOUNTAIN WINERY
opened: 2010
winemaker(s): Ray Curtis
location: 2825 Marvin Road NE, Suite Q, Olympia, WA 98516
phone: 360-464-7125
web: www.nwmountainwine.com
e-mail: raycurtis@nwmountainwine.com
fee: Tasting fee
hours: Friday through Sunday 10–5
amenities: Gift Shop, Live Music, RV/Bus Parking, Wheelchair Accessible

Madsen Family Cellars

Sandi Madsen, co-owner of Madsen Family Cellars, asked local artist Andrew Wood to create a label for their wine incorporating the image of a lotus flower. Not only did he execute the drawing, he nailed it. These are gorgeous labels that pop when you see them from a distance. The lotus is a perennial tropical plant indigenous to Asia, and also happens to be the national flower of both Vietnam and India. You won't find a lotus blossoming in the wilds of the Pacific Northwest, but you can find one blooming on a bottle in a South Sound wine shop.

Riesling
Rattlesnake Hills 2008

Winemaker Dana Madsen relies on fruit from eastern Washington to produce small lots of chardonnay (both unoaked and oaked), gewürztraminer, riesling, rosé, sangiovese, a port-style dessert wine, and their flagship cabernet sauvignon. Here's what *Wine Press Northwest* (spring 2010 issue) had to say about Madsen Family Cellars 2007 cabernet sauvignon: "Here marks the first sizable vintage for this couple in Lacey, Washington, and the primary fruit source for this release — Destiny Ridge Vineyard — shows they mean business. A dense profile of black cherries, prunes, allspice, cigar box, green tea, and eucalyptus makes for a mouth-filling wine, but the finish of youthful tannins and baker's chocolate should reward patience." At $30 a bottle, the cabernet makes a nice addition to a wine lover's cellar.

Dana Madsen

With their Australian shepherd under foot, Dana poured a sample of the orange muscat dessert wine. How he knew that I have a raging sweet tooth is anyone's guess. With the sweet nectar of the wine still on my palate, I ate a slice of Beecher's Flagship cheese and had one of those harmonic moments when the semihard, salty-nutty flavor of this cheese paired perfectly with the sweet wine.

MADSEN FAMILY CELLARS
opened: 2007
winemaker(s): Dana Madsen
location: 2825 Marvin Road NE, Unit D, Olympia, WA 98516
phone: 360-438-1286
web: www.madsenfamilycellars.com
e-mail: info@madsenfamilycellars.com
fee: Tasting fee
hours: Wednesday through Sunday 10–4
amenities: Gift Shop, Wheelchair Accessible

McCrea Cellars 9

When it comes to creating Rhône-style wines in Washington, few can match the achievements of Doug McCrea. With at least 25 crushes under his belt, Doug makes other Washington winemakers with a reputation for Rhône wines (such as those of Syncline Wine Cellars and Rotie Cellars) seem like relative newcomers. Raised in New Orleans, where food is king, Doug learned first-hand that grenache and syrah wines are incredibly food friendly. The big cabernet-dominant Bordeaux wines are fine for all things roasted or dishes with rich sauces, but he feels white and red blends of the Rhône meet the needs of the full spectrum of food-and-wine pairings.

Beginning with his first crush in 1998, Doug relied on grenache from the Columbia River Gorge, and soon thereafter began a long-term vineyard relationship with Dick Boushey of Boushey Vineyard, in the Yakima Valley, and Jim Holmes of Ciel du Cheval, on Red Mountain. At the time, Washington had a paltry 5 acres of syrah under production. However, with the growing popularity of this grape, the number of acres devoted to syrah has mushroomed to more than 4,000 acres. Despite the increasing number of growers producing syrah, Doug stays with the "old vines" of Boushey and Ciel du Cheval, preferring their flavor profiles to the newer growers. (Syrah can be rather "chameleon," taking on the characteristics of the site where it grows, which is cause for concern among Washington wine leaders.)

Believing that wine is made in the vineyard, Doug spends many days away from his Rainier, Washington, home and in eastern Washington, visiting with grape growers. It gives him an opportunity to anticipate what this year's weather will mean to the wine's taste years from now.

MCCREA CELLARS
opened: 1996
winemaker(s): Doug McCrea
location: 116 5th Avenue East, Olympia Wine Tasting Bar, Olympia, WA 98501
phone: 800-378-6212
web: www.mccreacellars.com
e-mail: mccreawine@aol.com
fee: Tasting fee
hours: Thursday through Saturday 1–6; Sunday 1–4
amenities: Mailing List, Wheelchair Accessible, Wine Club
connect:

Walter Dacon Wines 🔟

WineTrail enthusiasts who enjoy syrah will want to plan a visit to Walter Dacon Winery. But this doesn't entail a trip to Walla Walla or even Woodinville. We're talking Shelton. "Shelton?" you ask. Yep, Shelton, Washington. Set in the heart of Mason County, Walter Dacon Winery produces about 1,000 cases of syrah per year, as well as small lots of sangiovese, viognier, and lip-smacking-good port-style wine.

Lloyd Anderson

Upon starting his winery in 2003, owner/winemaker Lloyd Anderson named it after his grandfather Walter Dacon. Lloyd's background is in forestry, having had a career at Weyerhaeuser and owning his own logging-related enterprises. But after the logging industry took a downturn, Lloyd took a turn of his own — to his passion for making wine. Together with his wife, Ann, the Andersons have managed to distinguish their winery from the slew of other wineries, and received awards and feel-good accolades to prove it.

Before launching Walter Dacon Winery, Lloyd learned his winemaking skills from the best with a stint at McCrea Cellars as well as coursework at University of California-Davis. But ever the tinkerer and do-it-yourselfer, Lloyd has taken his skills much further, employing European winemaking techniques not practiced elsewhere in the state. For example, following destemming, Lloyd uses frozen carbon dioxide to cold-stabilize the syrah grapes. And, remaining true to Rhône-style wines, he makes liberal use of blending — typically blending syrah from different vineyards in the Columbia Valley to create a syrah cuvée. However, Lloyd defers to Ann's sensitive palate for the taste test.

All Walter Dacon wines exhibit tamed tannins and are much smoother than many of the syrahs associated with Washington. These wines pair wonderfully with lamb, duck, or salmon, yet are delicious sans food. *C'est fantastique!*

WALTER DACON WINES
opened: 2003
winemaker(s): Lloyd Anderson
location: 50 SE Skookum Inlet Road, Shelton, WA 98584
phone: 360-426-5913
web: www.walterdaconwines.com
e-mail: winemaker@walterdaconwines.com
fee: Complimentary wine tasting
hours: Wednesday through Sunday 12–6, or by appointment
amenities: Gift Shop, Newsletter/Blog, Picnic Area, Tours, Wheelchair Accessible, Wine Club
connect: 🐦 📘

Hoodsport Winery 11

Now with its distinctive "Orca" series of wine labels, Hoodsport Winery has evolved in its 30-plus years of existence, but the great views, friendly staff and a tasting room packed with delectable treats remain constant.

Founded by Montana transplants Dick and Peggy Patterson in 1978, Hoodsport is among only about a dozen wineries in the state to be situated with magnificent views of the Olympic Mountains and Hood Canal. The Patterson family, with daughter Ann, continues its involvement with the winery in partnership with Washington Wine & Beverage Company (parent company of Silver Lake Winery and Glen Fiona). Perhaps this strategic relationship has updated the winery's image, but its core character remains the same.

Hoodsport produces a unique red wine called Island Belle (part *Vitis labrusca*, a native grape species of the northeastern U.S., and part *Vitis vinifera*, the common European wine grape species). These particular labrusca vines are found on Stretch Island, near the town of Grapeview (no kidding), and are about 100 years old, as noted in the book The Wine Project by Ron Irvine and Walter J. Clore. It's worth asking if Hoodsport has this wine available for tasting, because you will not find it anywhere else.

After you sample some of the vinifera varietals (e.g., syrah, cabernet franc, cabernet sauvignon, chardonnay, gewürztraminer, riesling, syrah, pinot gris, and merlot), you might want to end your tasting experience on a "sweet" note with a sample of Hoodsport's fruit wine. Hoodsport specializes in fruit wines, and offers a wide selection: raspberry, cranberry, loganberry, apple, pear, rhubarb, and blackberry. The raspberry wine has made off with some top honors and can be enjoyed by itself or soaked up in some pound cake accompanied by fresh raspberries. Yumm!

HOODSPORT WINERY
opened: 1978
winemaker(s): Dick Patterson
location: North 23501 Highway 101, Hoodsport, WA 98548
phone: 360-877-9894
web: www.hoodsport.com
e-mail: wine@hoodsport.com
fee: Complimentary wine tasting
hours: Daily 10–6
amenities: Gift Shop, Tours, Wheelchair Accessible

Stottle Winery Hoodsport
Tasting Room 12

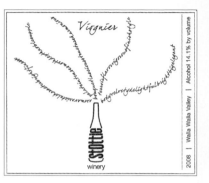

STOTTLE WINERY HOODSPORT TASTING ROOM
opened: 2010
winemaker(s): Josh Stottlemyer
location: 24180 Highway 101, Suite B, Hoodsport, WA 98548
phone: 360-877-2247
web: www.stottlewinery.com
e-mail: info@stottlewinery.com
fee: Tasting fee
hours: Saturday 11–5
amenities: Wine Club, Wines by the Glass, Online Store, Wheelchair Accessible
connect: f

www.winetrailsnw.com/wineries/stottle_winery_hoodsport_tasting_room

ALIA WINES
winemaker(s): John Olsen
location: 23732 Bothell Everett Highway,
Suite B, Mercantile Wine & Goods,
Bothell, WA 98021
phone: 360-794-0421
web: www.aliawines.com
hours: Friday 4–9, Saturday and
Sunday 12–7

ANDREW WILL WINERY
winemaker(s): Chris Camarda
location: 12526 SW Bank Road,
Vashon, WA 98070-4519
phone: 206-463-9227
web: www.andrewwill.com
hours: By appointment only

BLACKTHORN MOUNTAIN WINERY
winemaker(s): Alistair (Alex) Sloley
location: 25318 Kanaskat Drive,
Black Diamond, WA 98010
phone: 360-886-2308
web:
www.blackthornmountainwinery.com
hours: First Saturday of each
month 1–4

CADENCE WINERY
winemaker(s): Benjamin Smith and
Gaye McNutt
location: 9320 15th Avenue South;
Unit CF, Seattle, WA 98108
phone: 206-381-9507
web: www.cadencewinery.com
hours: By appointment only

CAVATAPPI WINERY
winemaker(s): Peter Dow
location: 9702 NE 120th Place,
Kirkland, WA 98034-4206
phone: 206-282-5226
web: www.cavatappi.com
hours: By appointment only

CEDAR RIDGE WINERY
winemaker(s): Richard Fairfield
location: 101 2nd Street,
Snohomish, WA 98290
phone: 425-377-8538
web: www.cedarridgewinery.com
hours: Friday 2–6, Saturday 11–7
and Sunday 12–4

CEDAR RIVER CELLARS
location: 23732 Bothell Everett
Highway, Suite B, Mercantile Wine &
Goods, Bothell, WA 98012
phone: 206-229-2104
web: www.cedarrivercellars.com
hours: Friday 4–9, Saturday and
Sunday 12–7

DEVORAH CREEK VINEYARDS
winemaker(s): Joshua and Christine
location: 37901 183rd Avenue SE,
Auburn, WA 98092
phone: 206-579-8906
web: www.devorahcreek.com
hours: By appointment only

DONEDEI WINES
winemaker(s): Carolyn Lakewold
location: 12035 Gibbons Lane SE,
Tenino, WA 98589
phone: 360-264-8466
web: www.donedei.com
hours: By appointment only

DUBINDIL WINERY
location: 1311 Bonneville Avenue,
Suite 105, Snohomish, WA 98290
phone: 360-453-7352
web: www.dubindilwinery.com
hours: By appointment only

ESTRIN ESTATES
location: 830 Big Tree Drive NW,
Issaquah, WA 98027
phone: 425-392-1131
web: www.estrinestates.com
hours: By appointment only

Estrin
E S T A T E S

FALL LINE WINERY
winemaker(s): Tim Sorenson
location: 6122 Sixth Avenue South,
Seattle, WA 98108-3308
phone: 206-768-9463
web: www.falllinewinery.com
hours: By appointment only

FORCE MAJEURE VINEYARDS
winemaker(s): Various winemakers
location: 12514 130th Lane NE,
Kirkland, WA 98034
phone: 425-998-REVE
web: www.forcemajeurevineyards.com
hours: By appointment only

GRACE CELLARS
location: 23732 Bothell Everett
Highway, Suite B, Mercantile Wine &
Goods, Bothell, WA 98012
phone: 425-787-4163
web: www.gracecellars.com
hours: Friday 4–9, Saturday and
Sunday 12–7

FELICITY WINES
location: 120 McRae Road NW,
Arlington, WA 98223
phone: 425-232-8264
web: www.felicitywines.com
hours: By appointment only

FIVASH CELLARS
location: 602 234th Avenue SE,
Sammamish, WA 98074
phone: 425-224-2455
web: www.fivashcellars.com
hours: By appointment only

ISABELLA GRACE WINERY
winemaker(s): Thomas Hornberg
location: 28611 SE 204th Street,
Hobart, WA 98025
phone: 425-941-6364
web: www.isabellagracewines.com
hours: By appointment only

Other Wineries to Visit

LANTZ CELLARS
winemaker(s): Kevin Lantz
location: 3001 South Lake Stevens Road, Everett, WA 98205
phone: 425-770-2599
web: www.lantzcellars.com
hours: By appointment only or check website

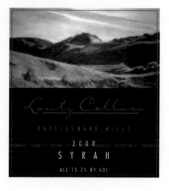

LIBERTY BAY CELLARS
winemaker(s): Dave Prigmore
location: 4250 NE Emerald Lane, Poulsbo, WA 98370
phone: 206-910-2588
web: www.libertybaycellars.com
hours: By appointment only

MARCUS SOPHIA WINERY
winemaker(s): Leala Cramer
location: 21825 161st Avenue East, Graham, WA 98338
phone: 425-591-2346
web: www.marcussophiawinery.com
hours: By appointment only

MAYFLY WINE
winemaker(s): Mitch
location: 198 Nickerson Street, Seattle, WA 98109
phone: 206-920-9322
web: www.mayflywine.com
hours: Monday through Saturday 5–10 and by appointment

MOSQUITO FLEET WINERY
winemaker(s): Brian Petersen
location: NE 21 Old Belfair Highway, Belfair, WA 98528
phone: 360-710-0855
web: www.mosquitofleetwinery.com
hours: By appointment only

OLALLA VALLEY VINEYARDS
winemaker(s): Joe Serka
location: 13176 Olalla Valley Road, Olalla, WA 98359
phone: 253-851-4949
web: www.olallavalleyvineyard.com
hours: Call ahead

Other Wineries to Visit

OPEN ROAD WINE COMPANY
location: 23732 Bothell Everett
Highway, Suite B, Mercantile Wine &
Goods, Bothell, WA 98012
phone: 425-243-9463
web: www.openroadwine.com
hours: Friday 4–9, Saturday and
Sunday 12–7

PANDORA CELLARS
location: 32305 NE 8th Street,
Carnation, WA 98014
phone: 206-227-5929
web: www.pandoracellars.com
hours: By appointment only

PASSION VINEYARDS
winemaker(s): Chuck Laird
location: 13228 202nd Avenue NE,
Issaquah, WA 98027
phone: 206-334-0178
web: www.passionvineyard.com
hours: See website for dates

PERENNIAL VINTNERS
winemaker(s): Mike Lempriere
location: 8840 Lovgreen Road,
Bainbridge Island, WA 98110
phone: 206-780-2146
web: www.PerennialVintners.com
hours: See website or make an
appointment

PLEASANT HILL CELLARS
winemaker(s): Larry Lindvig
location: 32305 8th Street NE,
Carnation, WA 98014
phone: 425-333-6770
web: www.pleasanthillcellars.com
hours: By appointment only

QUILCEDA CREEK VINTNERS
winemaker(s): Alex Golitzen &
Paul Golitzen
location: 11306 52nd Street SE,
Snohomish, WA 98290
phone: 360-568-2389
web: www.quilcedacreek.com
hours: By appointment only

Other Wineries to Visit

ROCKRIDGE ORCHARDS & CIDERY
location: 41127 212th Avenue SE,
Enumclaw, WA 98022
phone: 360-825-1962
web: www.rockridgeorchards.com
hours: Daily 10–7, seasonally

ROCKWELL BROWN WINES
location: 10106 422nd Lane SE,
North Bend, WA 98045-8265
phone: 425-985-1363
web: www.rockwellbrownwines.com
hours: By appointment only

SAINTPAULIA VINTNERS
winemaker(s): Paul Shinoda Jr.
location: 18302 83rd Avenue, SE,
Snohomish, WA 98296
phone: 425-922-8985
web: www.saintpauliavintners.com
hours: By appointment only

SCARBOROUGH WINERY
winemaker(s): Travis Scarborough
location: 808 Industry Drive,
Tukwila, WA 98188
phone: 206-575-2554
web: www.scarboroughwines.com
hours: Tuesday through Saturday by
appointment only

SCATTER CREEK WINERY
winemaker(s): Terril Keary
location: 291 Sussex Avenue West,
Tenino, WA 98589
phone: 360-264-9463
web: www.scattercreekwinery.com
hours: Wednesday through Friday
12–6; Saturday 12–8; Sunday 12–6

SIREN SONG WINES
location: 1613 46th Avenue SW,
Seattle, WA 98116
phone: 206-465-0147
web: www.sirensongwines.com
hours: By appointment only

Other Wineries to Visit

SOJEN CELLARS
winemaker(s): Max & Jennifer Jensen
location: 2818 Hewitt Avenue,
Everett, WA 98201
phone: 425-876-2396
web: www.sojencellars.com
hours: Wednesday and Thursday 5–8,
Friday and Saturday 5–10

SOOS CREEK WINE CELLARS
winemaker(s): David and Cecile Larsen
location: 20404 140th Avenue SE,
Kent, WA 98042
phone: 253-631-8775
web: www.sooscreekwine.com
hours: Annual open house only

SOVEREIGN CELLARS
winemaker(s): Dennis W. Gross
location: 7408 Manzanita NW Drive,
Olympia, WA 98502
phone: 360-866-7991
web: www.sovereigncellars.com
hours: By appointment only

STRINGTOWN CELLARS
winemaker(s): John Adams
location: 39610 Eatonville Cutoff
Road, Eatonville, WA 98328
phone: 360-832-4743
web: www.stringtownfarms.com
hours: Friday through Sunday 10–5
or by appointment

TIGER MOUNTAIN WINERY
winemaker(s): John Girt
location: 4629 191st Avenue SE,
Issaquah, WA 98027
phone: 425-562-4205
web: www.TigerMountainWinery.com
hours: By appointment only

TWIN CEDARS WINERY
location: 26504 SE 146th Street,
Issaquah, WA 98027
phone: 425-392-0453
web: www.twincedarswinery.com
hours: Saturday and Sunday 12–5

VAN CAMP CELLARS
winemaker(s): Jim Van Camp
location: 1311 Bonneville Avenue,
Suite 104, Snohomish, WA 98290
phone: 425-330-0338
web: www.vancampcellars.com
hours: Saturday 12–5

WHITE CELLARS
winemaker(s): Gus White
location: 1307 240th Way SE,
Sammamish, WA 98075
phone: 425-246-1419
web: www.whitecellars.com
hours: By appointment only

WILRIDGE WINERY
winemaker(s): Paul Beveridge
location: 250 Ehler Road , The Tasting
Room Yakima, Yakima, WA 98908
phone: 206-325-3051
web: www.wilridgewinery.com
hours: Thursday through Monday
11–7, or by appointment

VINO AQUINO WINERY
winemaker(s): Rich Aquino
location: 4417 6th Avenue,
Suite 1, Tacoma, WA 98406
phone: 253-272-5511
web: www.vinoaquino.com
hours: Tuesday through
Saturday 12–6

WILLIS HALL WINERY
winemaker(s): John Bell
location: 4715 126th Street NE,
Marysville, WA 98271
phone: 360-653-1247
web: www.willishall.com
hours: By appointment only

ZERO ONE VINTNERS
location: 131 Lake Street South,
Kirkland, WA 98033
phone: 425-242-0735
web: www.zeroonevintners.com
hours: Friday and Saturday 2–7,
Sunday 12–3 and by appointment

Woodinville

WINE COUNTRY

the BUNNELL

Family Cellar
vin de l'esprit

2006 **vif**

COLUMBIA VALLEY

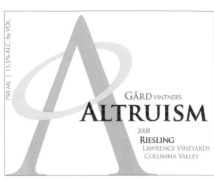

750 ML | 13.5% ALC. by VOL.

GÂRD VINTNERS

ALTRUISM

2008
RIESLING
LAWRENCE VINEYARDS
COLUMBIA VALLEY

COLUMBIA VALLEY
RED WINE 2007

SPARKMAN

STEVENSDIVIO
2009 Yakima Valley Viognier

Kindred
2008

Columbia Valley
Red Wine

CONVERGENCE
ZONE
CELLARS

sigaro
Washington Red Wine

distefano winery

2007

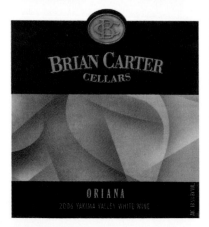

BRIAN CARTER
CELLARS

ORIANA
2006 YAKIMA VALLEY WHITE WINE

C
Z

SUNBREAK

MICHAEL

FLORENTINO

VINTAGE 2009
SYRAH

COLUMBIA VALLEY
ALC 15.4% BY VOL

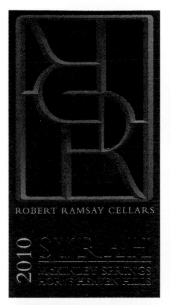

ROBERT RAMSAY CELLARS

2010 SYRAH
MCKINLEY SPRINGS
HORSE HEAVEN HILLS

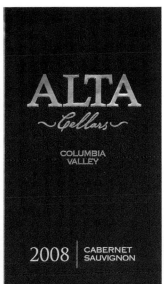

ALTA
Cellars

COLUMBIA
VALLEY

2008 | CABERNET
SAUVIGNON

Aspenwood Cellars

2009
Proprietor's Choice Matt's Merlot
MERLOT
YAKIMA VALLEY

SHERIDAN
VINEYARD
Cabernet Franc
2008

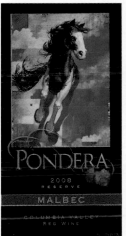

PONDERA

2008
RESERVE

MALBEC

COLUMBIA VALLEY
RED WINE

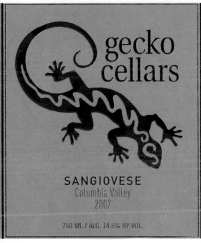

gecko
cellars

SANGIOVESE
Columbia Valley
2007

750 ML / ALC. 14.5% BY VOL.

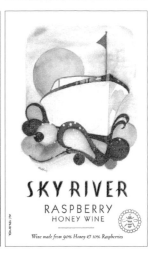

SKY RIVER

RASPBERRY
HONEY WINE

Wine made from 90% Honey & 10% Raspberries

ALC 14.5% BY VOL

CAÑON
DE SOL

2006

Columbia Valley
RED TABLE WINE

Page
Cellars

2007
THE NORSEMAN
RED MOUNTAIN MERLOT

ALC. 14.4% BY VOL.

EFESTE

LOLA

Tourist District West
Wine Trail

This is the heart and soul of Washington's wine industry. I could easily have named it the "Heritage WineTrail" because, in a real sense, this is where it all began.

Chateau Ste. Michelle Winery, Woodinville's grande dame (and still its centerpiece), gave birth to Washington's modern-day wine industry, and the resulting tourist trade. Many of the winemakers throughout the state and beyond cut their purple-stained teeth at Chateau Ste. Michele. It's this history that led the way for others to follow their passion to create premium wine.

Although Tourist District WineTrail West is home to some relatively major producers — Ste. Michelle, Januik, and Columbia wineries — it also harbors small artisan wineries tucked away in converted homes and industrial buildings. Indeed, if you enjoy a diversity of tasting rooms, this is your kind of WineTrail.

Tourist District WineTrail West

1. Chateau Ste. Michelle
2. Col Solare Bottega
3. JM Cellars
4. Columbia Winery
5. Januik Winery
6. Isenhower Cellars Tasting Room
7. Celaeno Winery
8. Elsom Cellars
9. Silver Lake Winery
10. The Woodhouse Wine Estates
11. Tefft Cellars Winery
12. Facelli Winery
13. DiStefano Winery
14. Woodinville Wine Cellars

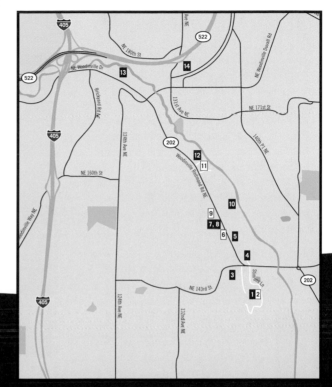

Region: **Woodinville Wine Country**

\# of tasting rooms on tour: **14**

\# of satellite tasting rooms: **4**

Estimate # of days for tour: **3**

Getting around: **Car**

Key Events: ❏ **St. Nicholas Day Open House (December) and Passport to Woodinville (April) — both sponsored by Woodinville Wine Country.**
See www.woodinvillewinecountry.com for details and ticket information.

Tips: ❏ **Woodinville offers a variety of restaurants: Some popular places include the Barking Frog, Pasta Nova, Garden Café in Mobaks, The Herbfarm at Willows Lodge, Italianissimo Ristorante, and Purple Café & Wine Bar.**

❏ **Consider hiring a limousine service.**

Best: ❏ **Destination, gift shop, picnicking and music venue: Chateau Ste. Michelle**

❏ **Destination, eats, gift shop and wedding venue: Columbia Winery**

❏ **Eats and picnicking: Januik Winery**

Chateau Ste. Michelle ❶

This is the granddaddy of them all. Chateau Ste. Michelle put Washington wine on the map. Not only does Chateau Ste. Michelle produce award winning wine, it also produces a large number of winemakers who often end up launching their own winery (Mike Januik at Januik Winery, Brennon Leighton at Efestē, Bob Betz of Betz Family Winery, to name a few). It's no exaggeration to say that without Chateau Ste. Michelle, the Washington wine industry as we know it today would likely have been a mere footnote in the story of North American wines.

A visit to Chateau Ste. Michelle usually entails a walk around its well-manicured grounds, a visit to the fish ponds, and a stroll by the old Stimson family residence. During the summer, pack a picnic and a blanket and sprawl on the spacious lawn (with a bottle or two of wine, of course).

However, the main reason you're here is for the wine. But before you start tasting, we suggest that you take a complimentary guided tour through the facility. On the tour, you learn about Ste. Michelle's estate vineyards, and discover that the reds are made in eastern Washington and the whites are made in Woodinville. Armed with that background information, you're now ready to explore the world of Ste. Michelle wines at its upscale tasting pavilion and grand gift shop.

For a special treat, plan ahead and make an appointment to experience Ste. Michelle's plexiglass-enclosed winery within a winery, Col Solare Bottega. It's a bit of a splurge, but worth it.

CHATEAU STE. MICHELLE
opened: 1934
winemaker(s): Bob Bertheau (Red) and Wendy Stuckey (White)
location: 14111 NE 145th Street, Woodinville, WA 98072
phone: 425-488-1133
web: www.ste-michelle.com
e-mail: info@ste-michelle.com
fee: Tasting fee refunded with purchase
hours: Daily 10–5, except New Year's Day, Easter, Thanksgiving, and Christmas Day
amenities: Gift Shop, Live Music, Picnic Area, Private Events, Tours, Wheelchair Accessible, Wine Club, Wines by the Glass
connect: 🐦 📘

⭐ **BEST Destination, gift shop, picnicking and music venue**

 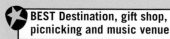

Col Solare Bottega

COL SOLARE BOTTEGA
opened: 2006
winemaker(s): Marcus Notaro
location: 14111 NE 145th Street,
Woodinville, WA 98072
phone: 800-267-6793
web: www.colsolare.com and www.ste-michelle.com
e-mail: info@colsolare.com
fee: Tasting fee
hours: By appiontment
amenities: Gift Shop, Live Music, Mailing List,
Online Store, Picnic Area, RV/Bus Parking,
Wheelchair Accessible
connect: ⓕ

www.winetrailsnw.com/wineries/col_solare_bottega

JM Cellars 🖪

John Bigelow

Leave the crowds behind at the big wineries, drive up the hill near Chateau Ste. Michelle, and look for the sandwich board on the left. After leaving your vehicle with a valet parking attendant, you follow the shrub-lined path to the tasting room. For some, the tasting fee may be a bit steep for some ($10), but you get it back with a purchase of wine (and generous pours, not to mention a cheese bar, select meats, and crackers). And odds are you won't be able to resist these treasures.

John and Peggy Bigelow began JM Cellars in 1998 in the basement of their Laurelhurst home. In 2001, the Bigelows moved their operation and home to Woodinville. Like so many other "artisan" winery owners just starting out, John Bigelow kept his high-tech job and found time at night and on the weekends to produce some lovely blends of red wines. Lucky for us, John decided to jettison his day job in 2006 and now devotes all of his time to the winery.

While enjoying your visit with John and Peggy, check out these red beauties: their flagship wine Tre Fanciulli (tray-fan-CHEW-lee), Longevity, and Bramble Bump Red (named after the location of their home/winery). All of these wines are breathtakingly gorgeous and equally deserving of your Visa.

Bramble Bump, with its acres of trees and quietude, is a rejuvenating wine-tasting experience. You feel refreshed in a special way — especially if John is on hand to give you a guided tour of the barrel room, which he often does. Here's what Robert Parker's Wine Advocate had to say about JM Cellars: "John and Peggy Bigelow's JM Cellars is a required visit for wine tourists in the Seattle/Woodinville area. The winery's landscaping is breath-taking and, most important, the wines are first-class and reasonably priced."

JM CELLARS
opened: 1998
winemaker(s): John Bigelow
location: 14404 137th Place NE, Woodinville, WA 98072
phone: 206-321-0052
web: www.jmcellars.com
e-mail: info@jmcellars.com
fee: Tasting fee refunded with purchase
hours: Friday through Sunday 12–5
amenities: Picnic Area, Private Events, Weddings, Wheelchair Accessible, Wine Club
connect: 🐦 f

Columbia Winery

Founded in 1962, Columbia Winery is one of the most prestigious wineries in the state. Now under the ownership of California giant E&J Gallo Winery, from banquet rooms to a

well-stocked gift shop, Columbia Winery offers the whole package. Here you'd be thrilled to host a wedding and you wouldn't have to worry about a thing: the parking lot is huge and the garden will be in blossomed glory.

From humble beginnings in a garage in Seattle's Laurelhurst neighborhood, Columbia Winery was the creation of Dr. Lloyd Woodburne and nine other wine enthusiasts. They were Washington's original "garagistes" making their first wines with grapes from what would become Washington's Columbia Valley viticulture region. This pioneering spirit showed the world that Washington's location, soil, and climate could create superlative grapes similar to those of the Bordeaux region of France.

The late David Lake, Columbia Winery's master of wine, joined the winery in 1979. His close working relationship with the premium grapes growers of Washington spearheaded the production of many award-winning wines and introduced a number of varietals and blends new to consumers' palates.

COLUMBIA WINERY
opened: 1962
winemaker(s): Kerry Norton
location: 14030 NE 145th Street, Woodinville, WA 98072-6994
phone: 425-488-2776
web: www.columbiawinery.com
e-mail: contact@columbiawinery.com
fee: Tasting fee applies
hours: Daily 10–6 excluding major holidays
amenities: Food Pairings, Gift Shop, Online Store, Picnic Area, Private Events, Restaurant/Tours, Weddings, Wheelchair Accessible, Wine Club, Wines by the Glass
connect: 🐦 f

★ **BEST Destination, eats, gift shop and wedding venue**

 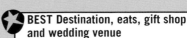

Januik Winery 5

I would like to ask everyone to clear out of the Novelty Hill and Januik Winery. The reason? I want to live there. I fantasize about living in such a contemporary, stylish fusion of glass, wood, and concrete. Opened in the spring of 2007, this winery occupies more than 33,000 square feet on 3.1 acres in Woodinville.

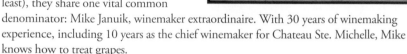

Although Novelty Hill and Januik Winery are two separate wineries (on paper at least), they share one vital common denominator: Mike Januik, winemaker extraordinaire. With 30 years of winemaking experience, including 10 years as the chief winemaker for Chateau Ste. Michelle, Mike knows how to treat grapes.

With its modern Spartan-like feel, this is a relaxed setting where visitors are encouraged to sample wine, order from a small plate menu (featuring among other tummy pleasers, brick-oven pizza served 12 to 4 Friday through Sunday), meander around the grounds and play a round of bocce ball on the outside court.

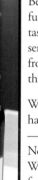

Beyond the inviting structure, visitors have a number of "touch points" to further experience their wines. There are several meeting rooms for private tasting and events varying in size to fit a range of needs. The full-size kitchen serves up delicious fare for corporate and family retreats. They host weddings from rehearsal dinners to the reception.

With each event, visitors have one thing in common — the fine wines of Novelty Hill and Januik Winery. Many become fans and spread the word to friends and family. Not surprisingly, others end up joining their popular Cellar Circle wine club with all its membership advantages, including discounts on wine shipments, seminars and private wine tastings. Excellent wine, the thoughtful insights of Mike Januik, and savings to boot — membership does have its privileges!

JANUIK WINERY
opened: 2000
winemaker(s): Mike Januik
location: 14710 Woodinville Redmond Rd NE, Woodinville, WA 98072
phone: 425-481-5502
web: www.januikwinery.com
e-mail: contact@januikwinery.com
fee: Tasting fee
hours: Daily 11–5
amenities: Food Pairings, Gift Shop, Online Store, Picnic Area, Private Events, Restaurant/Tours, RV/Bus Parking, Weddings, Wheelchair Accessible, Wine Club, Wines by the Glass
connect: 🐦

⭐ **BEST Eats and picnicking**

Isenhower Cellars Tasting Room ⑥

ISENHOWER CELLARS TASTING ROOM
opened: 1998
winemaker(s): Brett Isenhower
location: 15007 Woodinville Redmond Road NE, Woodinville, WA 98072
phone: 425-488-2299
web: www.isenhowercellars.com
e-mail: info@isenhowercellars.com
fee: Tasting fee refunded with purchase
hours: Friday through Sunday 12–5
amenities: Mailing List, Online Store, Wheelchair Accessible, Wine Club, Wines by the Glass, YouTube
connect: 🐦 📷 f

www.winetrailsnw.com/wineries/isenhower_cellars_tasting_room

Celaeno Winery 7

Brian Countryman, co-owner and winemaker of Woodinville's Celæno Winery likes to do things a little differently. For starters, he chooses to use American oak, and not just your garden-variety Wisconsin or Minnesota oak. Rather, Brian has opted for Kentucky oak, harvested from Daniel Boone National Forest. So if you detect a bit of bourbon-like quality in his syrah, don't be surprised.

The winery is named for Celæno, a star in the constellation Taurus, whose name has roots in Greek mythology. Whatever the name on their labels, Brian Countryman's wines reflect his passion for the vine. His career with Microsoft is now in the rearview mirror, allowing Brian to craft small-lot wines with fellow tenant Jody Elsom of Elsom Cellars.

Don't leave without sampling Brian's Road to Hell viognier, and be sure to check out the back label, where he explains the derivation of the word "viognier." According to Brian, "viognier" evolved from the Latin phrase "via Gehennae," which means "road to hell." This refers to the scored-earth policy of Roman emperor Vespasian, who became miffed at the peasantry for raiding Roman barges along the Rhône River. Just goes to show that trivia and wine often make a fine pairing in Washington's tasting rooms!

Brian Countryman

Trixie, winery dog of Celæno & Elsom

CELAENO WINERY
opened: 2010
winemaker(s): Brian Countryman
location: 15007 Woodinville Redmond Road NE, Suite A-100, Woodinville, WA 98072
phone: 425-417-9725
web: www.celaenowinery.com
e-mail: celaeno@celaenowinery.com
fee: Tasting fee
hours: Wednesday 2–6; Saturday and Sunday 12–5 or by appointment
amenities: Pet Friendly, Wheelchair Accessible
connect: ￼

Elsom Cellars 8

Do you love Malbec? If so, this is your kind of place. Supple, complex, full of fruit, black pepper, brown sugar and hints of tobacco all come together to distinguish Jody Elsom's signature wine. A bit on the pricey side at $38 a bottle, Elsom Cellars' Malbec is worth every penny, as long as you don't have to share it with your uncle Fred who can't — nor cares to — tell the difference between jug and premium wine. But since I had a New York sirloin waiting at home to be grilled, I didn't have to be convinced to purchase this beauty. It would make a good steak a glorious steak, I figured.

Sharing a space with Celaeno Winery, Elsom Cellars is no mere one-trick pony. At Elsom, your tasting fee entitles you to savor Jody's rosé, cabernet sauvignon, and a red Bordeaux-

blend with the lovely name of Isabella. The tasting room is a relaxing space to pet the winery dog (Trixie) and experience the fruit of Jody's labor of love. If you like what you taste, be sure to friend her on the winery's Facebook page.

ELSOM CELLARS
opened: 2008
winemaker(s): Jody Elsom
location: 15007 Woodinville Redmond Road NE, Suite A, Woodinville, WA 98072
phone: 425-298-308
web: www.elsomcellars.com
e-mail: jody@elsomcellars.com
fee: Tasting fee
hours: Wednesday 2–6; Saturday and Sunday 12–5 or by appointment
amenities: Wheelchair Accessible
connect:

Silver Lake Winery 9

SILVER LAKE WINERY
opened: 1988
winemaker(s): William Ammons
location: 15029 Woodinville Redmond Road NE, Woodinville, WA 98072
phone: 425-485-2437
web: www.silverlakewinery.com
e-mail: info@washingtonwine.com
fee: Complimentary except $5 charge for reserve wines
hours: Saturday 11–5; Sunday 12–5
amenities: Gift Shop, Online Store, Picnic Area, Private Events, RV/Bus Parking, Wheelchair Accessible, Wine Club
connect: 🐦 📘

www.winetrailsnw.com/wineries/silver_lake_winery

The Woodhouse Wine Estates 🔟

Question: What do Darighe, Dussek, Kennedy Shah, Maghee, and Hudson Shah have in common (besides being great names)? Answer: They all are wine labels produced by Woodhouse Wine Estates, and as you may surmise from these names, this is a family affair.

Woodhouse Wine Estates is a partnership between husband and wife, Bijal and Sinead Shah, and Bijal's uncle and winemaker, Tom Campbell (owner/winemaker for Yakima Valley's Tanjuli Winery). The winery debuted with 100 cases of its 1998 vintage of Darighe, a Bordeaux-style blend that sold out three months after its release in 2001. Darighe, meaning "red" in Gaelic, is an homage to Sinead's Irish roots and is their flagship wine. The Dussek and Maghee labels are named after family friends.

The Kennedy Shah and Hudson Shah labels bear the names of the Shahs' daughter and son respectively and reinforce the tagline "From our family to yours ... " With a price tag of $12, the Hudson Shah cab is a favorite for many, including this WineTrail trekker. It surely is one of the best values in the stores. For a few bucks more, the Kennedy Shah La Vie en Rouge, produced by winemaker Jean Claude Beck, delivers a surprisingly complex experience.

Unlike many tasting rooms where you need to keep your wineglass close to your chest when the throngs arrive, at Woodhouse Wine Estates there is plenty of space to mill around and explore. You can check out the barrel room, enjoy wine in the intimate banquet area, and note those many chandeliers when you gaze upward. As you might expect, this is a space often reserved for private events and winery-sponsored events, including cooking classes. A full-size kitchen comes in handy when a pastry chef is teaching a class on pie making — from crust to fruit filling.

THE WOODHOUSE WINE ESTATES
opened: 2001
winemaker(s): Tom Campbell and Jean Claude Beck
location: 15500 Woodinville Redmond Road NE, Suite C600, Woodinville, WA 98072
phone: 425-527-0608
web: www.woodhousefamilycellars.com
e-mail: Victoria@woodhouse-usa.com
fee: Tasting fee refunded with purchase
hours: Daily 12–5 or by appointment
amenities: Mailing List, Private Events, RV/Bus Parking, Wheelchair Accessible, Wine Club

Tefft Cellars Winery [11]

TEFFT CELLARS WINERY
opened: 1991
winemaker(s): Brian Wavernek
location: 16110 Woodinville Redmond Road NE,
Woodinville, WA 98072
phone: 425-481-4081
web: www.tefftcellars.com
e-mail: ptollner@gmail.com
fee: Tasting fee refunded with purchase
hours: Daily 11–7
amenities: Online Store, RV/Bus Parking, Wheelchair
Accessible, Wine Club, Wines by the Glass
connect: 🐦 f

www.winetrailsnw.com/wineries/tefft_cellars_winery

Facelli Winery 12

Located in one of Woodinville's many business parks is a gem of a winery: Facelli Winery. This family-owned and operated winery prides itself on producing outstanding reds and offering an especially friendly welcome to the many visitors who frequent the winery. Its varietals include cabernet sauvignon, merlot, syrah, sangiovese, cabernet franc, lemberger, chardonnay, and fumé blanc. Some wines are only available at the winery. All grapes come from renowned Columbia Valley growers and are handpicked, hand-sorted, and processed with gravity flow.

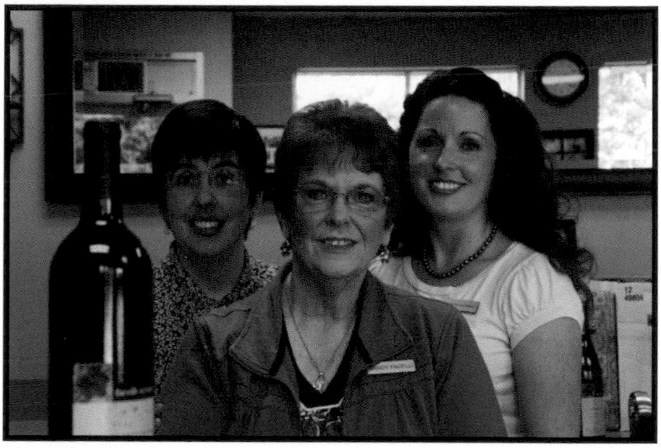

Mama Facelli and daughters

Winemaker Louis Facelli celebrates more than 20 years of experience with Washington grapes, and often Lou himself is there to autograph your purchased bottle of wine. With an annual production of around 4,000 cases, Louis Facelli has gone through a lot of Sharpies.

Especially unusual is Facelli's late-harvest syrah. This after-dinner treat contains 4 percent residual sugar, yet it doesn't seem overly sweet, which only enhances the syrah's rich flavors and overall tasting experience. Also, a warning to the hungry wine sampler: Lou's sangiovese pairs wonderfully with all things Italiano and conjures up images of fresh mozzarella and basil drizzled with extra virgin olive oil, as well as other Italian fare. Drool cups are optional.

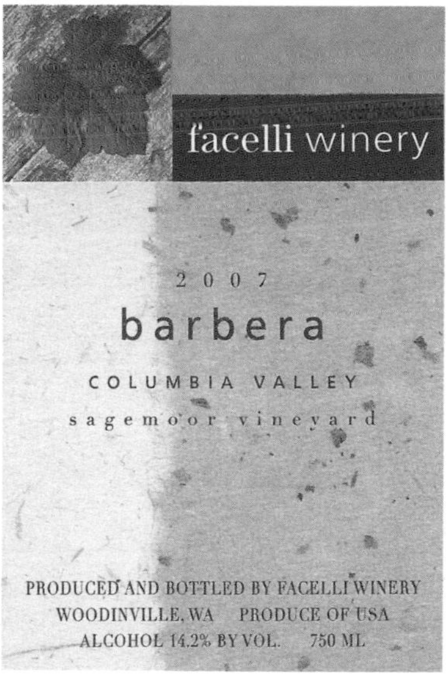

FACELLI WINERY
opened: 1988
winemaker(s): Lou Facelli
location: 16120 Woodinville Redmond Road NE, Suite 1, Woodinville, WA 98072-9090
phone: 425-488-1020
web: www.facelliwinery.com
e-mail: facelliwinery@msn.com
fee: Complimentary wine tasting
hours: Saturday and Sunday 12–4, groups by appointment only
amenities: Mailing List, Tours, Wheelchair Accessible
connect:

DiStefano Winery 🔟

As Mark Newton, owner and winemaker of DiStefano Winery states, "The DiStefano wines are a gift to my wife, Donna, and offered in tribute to her family — a family combining great personal and business integrity with a strong sense of tradition." And what a tribute it is. This surprising find is located within a small industrial park in Woodinville. It's not the wines that are surprising; DiStefano Winery already enjoys an outstanding reputation. It's the inviting ambiance of the tasting room, with its warm colors and view of the barrel room, that's an unexpected treat in such a locale. Equally welcoming is the tasting-room staff, which includes Mark's wife, Donna.

Be sure you try the Sogno, a cabernet-franc-dominant blend that displays all the flavors of this varietal while keeping its smooth, supple finish. There's a reason *Wine Spectator* gave this wine 90 points. Also sample the sauterne-style Saint John. and in mid-sip, ask yourself "How good would this be with caramel-drizzled pound cake?" Heavenly, of course!

WineTrail Note: DiStefano opened a second tasting room location in the summer of 2012 in Woodinville's popular Hollywood Schoolhouse neighborhood. It's where SoHo (i.e., South Hollywood) meets Sogno.

DISTEFANO WINERY
winemaker(s): Mark Newton
location: 12280 NE Woodinville Drive, Woodinville, WA 98072
phone: 425-487-1648
web: www.distefanowinery.com
e-mail: info@distefanowinery.com
fee: Complimentary wine tasting except $5 for reserve wines
hours: Saturday and Sunday 12–5, or by appointment
amenities: Online Store, Private Events, Tours, Wheelchair Accessible, Wine Club
connect: 🐦 📘

Woodinville Wine Cellars 🏠 14

Situated by Little Bear Creek near downtown Woodinville, Woodinville Wine Cellars is a little off the beaten path. To WineTrail trekkers, that translates into an oasis from the crowds. Woodinville Wine Cellars possesses none of the business-park feel. Rather, it has an elegant, showroom-like quality that just happens to feature a great place to enjoy a picnic. The warm colors of the tasting room help to create a perfect environment for sampling the winery's Bordeaux-dominant reds and winemaker Sean Boyd's beautifully balanced sauvignon blanc. He produces an unusual blend called Odd Man Out, featuring two Bordeaux grapes varieties you simply don't see blended: Malbec and petit verdot.

Sean seems to have been destined to make wine from an early age. His father was key in launching *Wine Spectator* magazine, and as a small boy, Sean was exposed to many great wine-growing regions of the world. Later, he worked at wineries in Australia, Spain, Portugal, and New Zealand before signing on as Woodinville Wine Cellars' assistant wine maker and lead salesperson. It wasn't long before Sean became its chief winemaker with the goal of creating small lots of ultrapremium wine displaying the *terroir* of the Columbia Valley. All of these factors have made him into the epitome of an artisan winemaker, and a superb one at that.

The green space adjoining the winery — with its sprawling lawn, mature trees, and Little Bear Creek gurgling in the background — is the perfect venue for summertime parties for wine club members and friends of Woodinville Wine Cellars. Imagine pairing WWC syrah with a pulled pork slider while soft rock music plays in the background. Now bring Sean into the scene, pouring wine as he smiles his contagious smile and you have life at its finest, Northwest style.

WOODINVILLE WINE CELLARS
opened: 1999
winemaker(s): Sean Boyd
location: 17721 132nd NE Avenue, Woodinville, WA 98072
phone: 425-481-8860
web: www.woodinvillewinecellars.com
e-mail: winesales@woodinvillewinecellars.com
fee: Tasting fee refunded with purchase
hours: Saturday 12–5 or by appointment on Fridays
amenities: Picnic Area, RV/Bus Parking, Tours, Wheelchair Accessible, Wine Club, Wines by the Glass
connect: 📘

Tourist District East
WineTrail

Also known as the Hollywood Schoolhouse District, this is home to nearly three dozen tasting rooms, several exciting restaurants, limited parking on weekends and an occasional wedding party at the schoolhouse. It's an area in transition, reflecting changes that have Woodinville's citizens debating its future. From an area originally zoned for agriculture and light industry to a wine lover's destination (with requisite accommodations and amenities) with the emergence of the wine industry, this area is still morphing. Indeed, though it may be evolving into a wine-tasting mecca, don't call it the "Napa of the north" — this area will define its own identity and future.

Tourist District WineTrail East

1. Matthews Estate
2. Adytum Cellars
3. J. Bookwalter Winery Tasting Studio
4. Mark Ryan Winery
5. Ross Andrew Winery
6. Amavi Cellars
7. Pepper Bridge Winery
8. Alexandria Nicole Cellars
9. Otis Kenyon Wine
10. Zerba Cellars
11. Cougar Crest Estate Winery
12. Gorman Winery
13. Patterson Cellars
14. Mark Ryan Winery
15. Sparkman Cellars
16. Trust Cellars
17. Dusted Valley Vintners
18. William Church Winery
19. Lachini Vineyards
20. DeLille Cellars
21. Brian Carter Cellars
22. Apex at Alder Ridge
23. The Library
24. Canon de Sol Winery and Vineyard
25. Goose Ridge Winery
26. Airfield Estates Winery
27. Darby Winery
28. Hollywood Hill Vineyards
29. DiStefano Winery
30. Patit Creek Cellars
31. Forgeron Cellars
32. Sky River Meadery
33. Northwest Totem Cellars

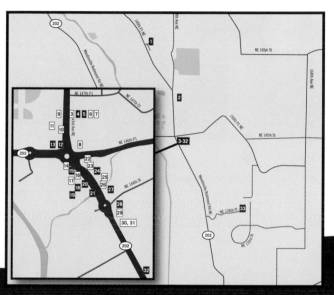

Region:	**Woodinville Wine Country**
# of tasting rooms on tour:	**33**
# of satellite tasting rooms:	**17**
Estimate # of days for tour:	**6**
Getting around:	**Car and foot**
Key Events:	❑ **St. Nicholas Day Open House (December) and Passport to Woodinville (April) — both sponsored by Woodinville Wine Country. See www.woodinvillewinecountry.com for details and ticket information.**
Tips:	❑ **Experience the 1st Thursday Wine Walk.**
	❑ **Woodinville offers a variety of restaurants: Some popular places include the Barking Frog, Mazatlan Restaurant, Pasta Nova, Garden Café in Mobaks, The Herbfarm at Willows Lodge, Italianissimo Ristorante, and Purple Café & Wine Bar.**
	❑ **For take out or delivery, check out Le Petit Terroir — see www.lepetitterroir.com**
	❑ **Consider hiring a limousine service.**
Best:	❑ **Music venue: Matthews Estate**

Matthews Estate

Cliff Otis-owned Matthews Estate is located on 8+ acres in the heart of Woodinville — a rarity in this wine tourist mecca. The winery's diminutive tasting room opens onto a spacious production facility and if your visit happens to fall on a Friday evening you're lucky to enjoy the sounds of a live band. At $10, the tasting fee is a bit steep, but you can recoup it with any purchase. And, if you are like this WineTrail enthusiast, you won't leave empty-handed.

Although it takes a number of people behind the scenes to make a successful winery, the public face of the winery often makes the biggest impression. Although we heap praise on the owners and the winemakers, often it is the role of the tasting-room manager that matters most. In the case of Matthews Estate, visitors are made to feel at home right away with a sincerely friendly greeting followed by quaffable pours. In between sips, learn first-hand what distinguishes Matthews Estate from rival Woodinville wineries. One of those distinguishing factors is having winemaker Aryn Morrell at Matthews Estate's helm. (Note: Aryn is also the winemaker for Gård Vintners.) Get ready for some spectacular red blends, as well as delicious cabernet sauvignon, sauvignon blanc, late harvest viognier, and cabernet franc. Cheers!

P.S. For those seeking overnight accommodations, Matthews Estate runs a bed and breakfast called The Estate House. Located near the winery in the heart of Woodinville wine country, The Estate House features two tastefully appointed bedrooms with king-size beds, deluxe bathrooms, full-size kitchens, a break-out-the-popcorn theater room, private decks, and free WiFi. It's a perfect getaway for those exploring the great wines of Woodinville.

MATTHEWS ESTATE
opened: 1993
winemaker(s): Aryn Morell
location: 16116 140th Place NE, Woodinville, WA 98072
phone: 425-487-9810
web: www.matthewscellars.com
e-mail: wine@matthewscellars.com
fee: Tasting fee refunded with purchase
hours: Daily 1–6; until 9 on Friday
amenities: Lodging, Mailing List, Online Store, Private Events, Tours, Weddings, Wheelchair Accessible, Wine Club
connect:

⭐ **BEST Music venue**

Adytum Cellars ❷

In ancient Greece, an "adytum" was a temple's most sacred place of worship, an inner sanctum laypeople were prohibited from entering. What clandestine activity was going on in the adytum that caused the priests to turn away normal folks? Perhaps they were fermenting mead from honey — and testing the results. Who knows?

Someone whom we do know is making mead is Adytum Cellars owner Vince Carlson, a real farmer at heart. He's a dirt guy — no, make that a soil guy — who has a deep appreciation of Mother Earth and the bounty she provides. He understands that any plant with enough sugar can be fermented and transformed into a beverage, and he's particularly well educated in the conversion of honey into a potent libation, one not reserved for ancient priests, but for everyone who calls Mother Earth home.

As a maker of mead and a beekeeper, Vince appreciates how the taste of honey wine (i.e., mead) bears the signature of the environment in which the bees reside. The weather, the flowers, and the bees themselves help shape the "vintage" of each season's honey crop. As the year's honey crop varies, so does the honey wine.

Dubbing them with alluring names such as Harvest Moon, Perry, Vintis, Melissaios, Oränj, Red Rain, Bingo, and Vango, Vince crafts meads of various fruits and degrees of sweetness. His Perry mead includes a healthy dose of pear, and for cherry lovers, such as myself, his Red Rain, Bingo, and Vango all possess various levels of cherry flavor that satisfy the craving.

Visiting Adytum Cellars is like stepping into the past. It brings to mind ancient lore and earthly pleasures as you imbibe the most basic of agrarian wines. You half expect a Norse king to enter, mutton shank in hand, to stake his claim on this intoxicating liquor.

Vince Carlson

ADYTUM CELLARS
winemaker(s): Vince Carlson
location: 15132 148th Avenue NE, Woodinville, WA 98072-6927
phone: 425-482-9030
web: www.adytumcellars.com
e-mail: mead@adytumcellars.com
hours: Saturday 11–4
amenities: Wheelchair Accessible
connect:

J. Bookwalter Winery Tasting Studio ③

J. BOOKWALTER WINERY TASTING STUDIO
opened: 1983
winemaker(s): John Bookwalter and Zelma Long
location: 14810 NE 145th Street, Building B, Woodinville, WA 98072
phone: 425-488-1983
web: www.bookwalterwines.com
e-mail: info@bookwalterwines.com
fee: Tasting fee refunded with purchase
hours: Sunday through Thursday 12–6; Friday and Saturday 12–8
amenities: Live Music, Online Store, Private Events, RV/Bus Parking, Wheelchair Accessible, Wine Club
connect: 🐦 f

www.winetrailsnw.com/wineries/j_bookwalter_winery_tasting_studio

Mark Ryan Winery ④

Mark Ryan McNeilly

What's in a name? By any other name, a wine would taste just as sweet, to paraphrase a guy in England a few centuries back. Nevertheless, to WineTrail enthusiasts, a name is very important, because it can represent a certain attention to detail. Thus, we suspect that when you read the names of Mark Ryan wines, you will want to sample the whole lot. And what titles they are! With designations such as Wild-Eyed Syrah, Long Haul, Dead Horse, and (our favorite) The Dissident, you know that owner Mark Ryan McNeilly has given great thought and care to what's in the bottle.

He obviously has a sense of humor, with the Dead Horse wine being a prime example. "Dead Horse" is a play on words associated with its grapes, which are harvested from the famed Ciel du Cheval Vineyard; "ciel du cheval" loosely translates to "horse heaven" in English. But as Mark points out, "No horses were hurt during the production of this wine, and it was tested on humans." What a relief!

Mark, chief winemaker and New Zealander Mike MacMorran, and consultant Erica Orr (with her University of California-Davis cred) may have the names of the wines down, but each vintage is a test of their skills. Although these three may rely on new yeast variants or perhaps correct for high acidity, each vintage of The Dissident will differ. Whatever Mother Nature serves up — and anyone living in the Pacific Northwest for the last few years knows about changing weather patterns — this team stands ready to respond.

At Mark Ryan's ideally located, light-filled tasting studio just north of the Hollywood Schoolhouse, you can hitch your horse and sample wine. Perhaps it will bring out the wild-eyed dissident wine lover in you, causing you to "commandeer" a case or two for the long haul home.

MARK RYAN WINERY
opened: 1999
winemaker(s): Mark Ryan McNeilly, Mike MacMorran, Erica Orr (Enologist/Consultant)
location: 14810 NE 145th Street, Hollywood Schoolhouse; Building A-1, Woodinville, WA 98072
phone: 206-910-7967
web: www.markryanwinery.com
e-mail: mark@markryanwinery.com
fee: Tasting fee
hours: Daily 12–5
amenities: Mailing List, Online Store, RV/Bus Parking, Wheelchair Accessible
connect: f

Ross Andrew Winery

Ross Andrew Mickel

Ross Andrew Mickel must have learned a thing or two as an assistant winemaker for Betz Family Winery. This thought was front and center as I tasted his utterly juicy, oh-so-delicious Boushey syrah. With its penetrating black fruits and hints of smoke, plus a dash of tar to make it even more interesting, this little syrah had legs. As I was contemplating a splurge and buying both the Ross Andrew syrah and his lovely white blend called Meadow, it dawned on me that I was the only one in the tasting room. How could this be? If wine quality was indicated by the number of bodies in a tasting room, this place should have been packed.

Perhaps this low turnout has something to do with the fact that Ross Andrew's tasting room is sandwiched between those of Mark Ryan Cellars and Pepper Bridge, two prominent names in Washington wine biz. Whether overshadowed or just low-key, Ross Andrew warrants more attention. On the other hand, being far from the madding crowd provided me a quiet respite and the opportunity to schmooze with the tasting room pourer while savoring those wines.

This eponymous winery has everything going for it but a cult following. Perhaps Ross isn't actively involved in the Twitter-sphere or maybe he lacks the egocentricity exuded by certain winemakers who shall go unnamed here. However, if you like nice, unpretentious, modest winemakers who opine such self-effacing phrases as "It all starts in the vineyard" and their job is not to screw it up, then I suggest without reservation that you give Ross Andrew wines a swirl.

ROSS ANDREW WINERY
winemaker(s): Ross Andrew Mickel
location: 14810 NE 145th Street, Suite A-2, Hollywood Schoolhouse, Woodinville, WA 98072
phone: 425-485-2720
web: www.rossandrewwinery.com
e-mail: info@rossandrewwinery.com
fee: Tasting fee
hours: Thursday through Monday 12–5; Closed major holidays
amenities: RV/Bus Parking, Wheelchair Accessible
connect:

Amavi Cellars 6

AMAVI CELLARS
opened: 2001
winemaker(s): Jean-François Pellet
location: 14810 NE 145th Street; Building A-3,
Woodinville, WA 98072
phone: 425-483-7026
web: www.amavicellars.com
e-mail: info@amavicellars.com
fee: Tasting fee
hours: Sunday through Thursday 11–5; Friday and
Saturday 12–6
amenities: Mailing List, Online Store, Private Events,
RV/Bus Parking, Wheelchair Accessible, Wine Club
connect: 🐦 📘

www.winetrailsnw.com/wineries/amavi_cellars

Pepper Bridge Winery 7

PEPPER BRIDGE WINERY
opened: 2000
winemaker(s): Jean-Francois Pellet
location: 14810 NE 145th Street; Building A-3,
Hollywood Schoolhouse,
Woodinville, WA 98072
phone: 425-483-7026
web: www.pepperbridge.com
e-mail: info@pepperbridge.com
fee: Tasting fee refunded with purchase
hours: Sunday through Thursday 11–5; Friday and
Saturday 12–6
amenities: Mailing List, Online Store, Private Events,
RV/Bus Parking, Wheelchair Accessible, Wine Club
connect: 🐦 📘

www.winetrailsnw.com/wineries/pepper_bridge_winery

Alexandria Nicole Cellars ⑧

ALEXANDRIA NICOLE CELLARS
opened: 1998
winemaker(s): Jarrod Boyle
location: 14810 NE 145th Street,
Hollywood Schoolhouse,
Woodinville, WA 98072
phone: 425-487-9463
web: www.alexandrianicolecellars.com
e-mail: info@alexandrianicolecellars.com
fee: Tasting fee refunded with purchase
hours: Thursday through Monday 12–5, or by private
appointment (Friday night happy hour 5–8)
amenities: Restaurant/Food Pairings, Wine Club,
Private Events, Online Store, Newsletter/Blog,
Wheelchair Accessible
connect: ■f

www.winetrailsnw.com/wineries/alexandria_nicole_cellars

Otis Kenyon Wine ⑨

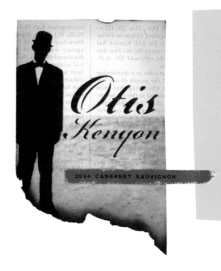

OTIS KENYON WINE
opened: 2004
winemaker(s): Dave Stephenson
location: 14525 148th Avenue NE, Suite 111,
Woodinville, WA 98072
phone: 425-949-7865
web: www.otiskenyonwine.com
e-mail: info@otiskenyonwine.com
fee: Tasting fee refunded with purchase
hours: Thursday through Saturday 12–6, Sunday 12–5
amenities: Mailing List, Online Store, Wheelchair
Accessible, Wine Club
connect: ✆ ■f

www.winetrailsnw.com/wineries/otis_kenyon_wine

Zerba Cellars 🔟

ZERBA CELLARS
opened: 2004
winemaker(s): Cecil Zerba
location: 14525 148th Avenue NE, Suite 114, Woodinville, WA 98072
phone: 425-806-2749
web: www.zerbacellars.com
e-mail: info@zerbacellars.com
fee: Tasting fee refunded with purchase
hours: Thursday through Sunday 12–6
amenities: Mailing List, Online Store, RV/Bus Parking, Wheelchair Accessible, Wine Club
connect: f

www.winetrailsnw.com/wineries/zerba_cellars

Cougar Crest Estate Winery 🔟🔟

COUGAR CREST ESTATE WINERY
opened: 2001
winemaker(s): Deborah Hansen
location: 14545 148th Avenue NE, Woodinville, WA 98072
phone: 425-806-1700
web: www.cougarcrestwinery.com
e-mail: info@cougarcrestwinery.com
fee: Tasting fee refunded with purchase
hours: Thursday through Saturday 11–6; Sunday 12–6
amenities: Newsletter/Blog, Online Store, RV/Bus Parking, Wheelchair Accessible, Wine Club, Wines by the Glass
connect: 🐦 f

www.winetrailsnw.com/wineries/cougar_crest_estate_winery

Gorman Winery

In the past, you could only sample Chris Gorman's wines at irregular times of the year. These events were typically associated with the release of a new wine and accompanied by head-banging rock music and good food. Now, you needn't worry if you missed a tweet announcing such an event. With Gorman Winery's expansive Hollywood Schoolhouse tasting room, which flows to an outdoor seating area (where you can order gourmet pizza from nearby pizzeria The Station), and a delightful staff to boot, you can experience Chris' Red Mountain-derived "vibrant blackberry" creations yourself.

Chris cut his teeth in the wine-import trade fresh out of college, and during that formative period, learned that to make exceptional wine you don't compromise. From the finest grapes to the use of high-quality French oak (think really tight grain), Chris empties the bank account to produce wines that *Wine Spectator* has scored in the 90s. You won't find synthetic cork here or cheapo glassware for tasting. Instead, quality reigns supreme as you discern the difference between a Saturday-night wine versus a Wednesday-night wine.

For my wood-fired pizza, I opted for Gorman's 100 percent syrah — The Pixie — and came to a personal understanding of Harvey Steiman's wine notes on The Pixie for *Wine Spectator*, "Firm in texture and explosive in flavor, with plenty of vibrant blackberry, black cherry and black pepper flavors to push through the layer of fine-grained tannins." Sure, at $45 a bottle, The Pixie is a bit pricey, but to borrow L'Oréal's slogan, I figured I'd splurge "because I'm worth it."

Loyal fans of Gorman Winery

GORMAN WINERY
opened: 2006
winemaker(s): Chris Gorman
location: 14505 148th Avenue NE, Woodinville, WA 98072
phone: 206-351-0719
web: www.gormanwinery.com
e-mail: Chris@gormanwinery.com
fee: Tasting fee refunded with purchase
hours: Thursday through Sunday 1–5
amenities: Restaurant/Food Pairings, Wheelchair Accessible, Wine Club
connect: 🐦 f

www.winetrailsnw.com/wineries/gorman_winery

Patterson Cellars 🅱

It seems as though John Patterson has been making wine longer than his youthful looks belie. As a young cellar rat, John helped his dad, Jack Patterson, at crush during the early '80s. They began making wine on a commercial basis in 2000, initially in Monroe and eventually moving to Woodinville's Warehouse District in 2007. It was at that time that John's spouse, Stephanie Patterson, joined the team and began focusing on the marketing side of the business, along with working the tasting room.

John has fine-tuned his winemaking craft through numerous vintages. However, he's not one to rest on his laurels; not one to be satisfied with working with the same vineyard, cranking out the same wine year after year. Ever on a quest to expand his knowledge in the

science of wine, he's a graduate of South Seattle Community College's distinguished Northwest Wine Academy. John's years of experience and willingness to try new winemaking styles have resulted in a tasty portfolio of wines, including single varietal wines, red and white blends, non-vintage wines and late-harvest dessert wines.

Thinking outside the proverbial barrel, the Pattersons demonstrate a deep understanding that half the battle of a successful winery is making good wine. The other half involves the business side of the enterprise, i.e., cash flow. In this regard, the spacious Woodinville location is available to rent for private events, and there is plenty of room for guests to mingle in the barrel room. In addition, they opened a secondary tasting room in the well-trafficked Hollywood Schoolhouse traffic circle.

Having gushed about Patterson Cellars' many attributes, the one that stands out in my mind is the oft repeated refrain heard from visitors to the Woodinville winery; namely, "We had the most fun at Patterson Cellars." Hey, the smell of success often includes an appealing bouquet of fun.

PATTERSON CELLARS
opened: 2007
winemaker(s): John Patterson
location: 14505 148th Avenue NE, Woodinville, WA 98072
phone: 425-483-8600
web: www.pattersoncellars.com
e-mail: info@pattersoncellars.com
fee: Tasting fee refunded with purchase
hours: Daily 12–5
amenities: Online Store, Private Events, RV/Bus Parking, Wheelchair Accessible, Wine Club
connect: 🐦 f

Mark Ryan Winery ⑭

MARK RYAN WINERY
opened: 1999
winemaker(s): Mark Ryan McNeilly, Mike MacMorran, Erica Orr (Enologist/Consultant)
location: 14475 Woodinville Redmond Road NE, Hollywood Vineyard Complex, Woodinville, WA 98072
phone: 206-910-7967
web: www.markryanwinery.com
e-mail: mark@markryanwinery.com
fee: Tasting fee
hours: Daily 12–5
amenities: Mailing List, Online Store, RV/Bus Parking, Wheelchair Accessible
connect:

www.winetrailsnw.com/wineries/mark_ryan_winery

Sparkman Cellars 🗓15

Noted wine writer Paul Gregutt classifies Woodinville's Sparkman Cellars among his "Rising Stars" of Washington wineries. That is not quite "second-growth" classification à la Bordeaux, but it's getting close. In Gregutt's taxonomy, Sparkman Cellars joins other cult-status wineries such as Efestē, Rulo, Buty, Syncline, and Mark Ryan as part of the new guard of Washington wineries.

Chris Sparkman, a Tennessean with a restaurateur background (which reads like a who's who of famous American restaurants), must pinch himself mightily when he reads heady praise from Gregutt. After all, it was only back in 2004 that he launched Sparkman Cellars — with zero background in making wine. However, Chris had a few things going for him, most notably a hugely supportive family, with his wife, Kelly Sparkman, the primary cog in this family enterprise. In addition, as the general manager for Seattle's renowned Waterfront

Seafood Grill, Chris orchestrated innumerable winemaker dinners and tasting events, and, in the process, got to know the Washington wine scene intimately, through the best winemakers, the best Columbia Valley vineyards, and the best mentors who could advise him on how to succeed in the wine industry.

Early on, amiable Chris turned to winemaker Mark McNeilly of Mark Ryan Winery to be his vintner/ mentor. Since then, Chris continues to rely on consultant winemakers, including Erica Orr, who also assists with William Church, Baer and other Woodinville wineries, causing one to wonder, does she sleep during crush? Chris' friendly demeanor likely had something to do with his ability to contract for fruit from the likes of Ciel du Cheval, Boushey, Stillwater Creek, Klipsun, and Hedges vineyards, and, interestingly, one vineyard in Oregon's Eola Hills called Temperance Hill (pinot noir!). In fact, rare among Woodinville wineries is his L'Autre pinot noir, which explodes blossoms on the palate with a silky finesse, rich in earthy mushrooms and cherries. *Bon appetit!*

SPARKMAN CELLARS
opened: 2006
winemaker(s): Chris Sparkman
location: 14473 Woodinville Redmond Rd NE, By Purple Cafe, Woodinville, WA 98072
phone: 425-398-1045
web: www.sparkmancellars.com
e-mail: wine@sparkmancellars.com
fee: Tasting fee
hours: Thursday through Monday 1–6
amenities: Mailing List, Online Store, Private Events, RV/Bus Parking, Wheelchair Accessible, Wine Club, Winemaker Dinners
connect: 🐦 📘

Trust Cellars

TRUST CELLARS
opened: 2007
winemaker(s): Steve Brooks
location: 14469 Woodinville Redmond Road NE,
Woodinville, WA 98072
phone: 509-529-4511
web: www.trustcellars.com
e-mail: Trust.Cellars@facebook.com
fee: Tasting fee
hours: Friday and Saturday 1–6; Sunday 1–5
amenities: Mailing List, Online Store, RV/Bus Parking,
Wheelchair Accessible, Wine Club
connect:

www.winetrailsnw.com/wineries/trust_cellars

Dusted Valley Vintners

DUSTED VALLEY VINTNERS
opened: 2003
winemaker(s): Chad Johnson and Corey Braunel
location: 14465 Woodinville Redmond Road NE,
Woodinville, WA 98072
phone: 425-488-7373
web: www.dustedvalley.com
e-mail: jmayer@dustedvalley.com
fee: Tasting fee refunded with purchase
hours: Wednesday through Sunday 12–5
amenities: Online Store, Private Events,
Wheelchair Accessible, Wine Club, YouTube
connect:

www.winetrailsnw.com/wineries/dusted_valley_vintners

William Church Winery

Evidently, the "R" word wasn't in Rod and Leslie Balsley's vocabulary when they were faced the prospect of retirement. They simply weren't ready; they had too much energy and too many miles to go before settling into a doublewide in Arizona. They already knew they had a passion for wine, but a trip to Italy sealed the deal when they discovered how wine was intricately woven into the fabric of Italian life; wine as a complement to good food, friends, family, and perhaps a little opera. With that epiphany, they returned home and worked with consultant winemaker Matthew Loso to launch William Church Winery in 2005.

The production facility and tasting room of William Church resides in Woodinville's Warehouse District. For weekend tasters, the Warehouse District location is perfect for experiencing a half-dozen or so wineries. For many WineTrail trekkers, though, the drawback is the rest of the week, when the winery is closed. To address that, the Balsleys opened a second William Church tasting room in 2011 in the well-trafficked Hollywood Schoolhouse area of Woodinville.

Although Italy might have been the place that ignited the Balsleys' passion for wine, the wine list at William Church is of a decidedly French persuasion, with cabernet, syrah, viognier, and Malbec leading the charge. It's a sangiovese-free zone, with big Bordeaux and Rhône varieties dominating. This is a reflection of these two WSU graduates' palates.

The name "William Church" pays homage to the first name of Rod's father and the middle name of Leslie's father, and signifies the importance of legacy to the family. It's fitting then that a French Gothic rose window design decorates the William Church label. The rose window embodies beauty and precision, as does the contents of the bottle adorned with its image.

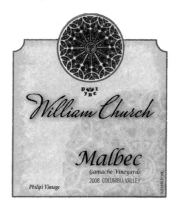

WILLIAM CHURCH WINERY
opened: 2005
winemaker(s): Leslie & Rod Balsley
location: 14455 Woodinville Redmond Road NE, Woodinville, WA 98072
phone: 425-427-0764
web: www.williamchurchwinery.com
e-mail: info@williamchurchwinery.com
fee: Tasting fee
hours: Sunday through Tuesday and Thursday 12–6, Friday and Saturday 12–8
amenities: Mailing List, Picnic Area, Private Events, Wheelchair Accessible, Wine Club, Wines by the Glass
connect:

Lachini Vineyards 🔟

Pinot noir requires a climate warm enough to ripen the grapes, yet cool enough to develop its delicacy and firm acidity. Thus, with its hot climate for much of the year, you can pretty much rule out the Columbia Valley's 11,000,000 acres for growing pinot. The Puget Sound region has pockets that show promise for growing pinot noir, but so far that area hasn't produced anything approaching the great pinots of Oregon's Willamette Valley. Consequently, if you have a burning desire to grow it, possible sites include Oregon, France's Burgundy region, northern California and New Zealand's South Island.

Fortunately for us, Seattle-area residents Ron and Marianne Lachini didn't travel far to establish their vineyard. They went south on Interstate 5 to the Willamette Valley and established 45-acre Lachini Vineyards outside Newberg, Oregon. With more than 30 acres under production — with a vast majority given to Pommard, Dijon and Wadenswil clones — the Lachinis' belief that the vineyard makes the wine bears fruit.

In Oregon, growing grapes requires a big dose of organic principles, more so than in Washington. To that end, Lachini Vineyards is LIVE (Low Impact Viticulture & Enology) certified, and follows biodynamic farming practices to the letter. As a consumer, you know you are ingesting the best ingredients Mother Nature has to offer.

With the opening of their light-filled tasting room in the Hollywood Schoolhouse District in 2011, the Lachinis have brought something different to the wine scene in Woodinville. Whereas the vast majority of other wineries serve up wine made from the big reds of the Columbia Valley — primarily Bordeaux and Rhône varieties — Lachini Vineyards gives us luscious, supple, sexy pinot noirs. These are food-friendly wines born for Pacific Northwest seafood, chicken and lamb dishes, and blue-veined cheeses. Complex, silky and oh so rewarding, this wine compels you to raise your glass and blurt "Santé!"

LACHINI VINEYARDS
opened: 2001
winemaker(s): Laurent Montalieu and Peter Rosback
location: 14455 Woodinville Redmond Road NE, Suite A, Woodinville, WA 98072
phone: 503-864-4553
web: www.lachinivineyards.com
e-mail: info@lachinivineyards.com
fee: Tasting fee
hours: Monday and Thursday 2–6, Friday and Saturday 12–6:30, Sunday 12–5; Closed Tuesday and Wednesday
amenities: Gift Shop, Picnic Area, Private Events, Wheelchair Accessible, Winemaker Dinners
connect: ▪

DeLille Cellars 🔟

In the past, you may have passed by the DeLille Cellars estate on Woodinville-Redmond Road and thought about taking a field trip there. Unfortunately, unless you were a guest of a corporate event or a wedding, the chateau-like facility was off limits. However, all that recently changed with the opening of DeLille's Carriage House Tasting Room, located farther down the road near the Hollywood Schoolhouse traffic circle.

At the Carriage House, visitors experience Chris Upchurch's distinctive wines, which exhibit his predilection for Bordeaux- and Rhône-style wines. He's all about creating wines in which the sum is greater than the parts. He'd rather hear drinkers of his wine use terms like opulence, mouthfeel, structure, balance, and finish, than identifying individual tastes, such as licorice, tobacco, cassis, and chocolate.

Sourcing grapes from renowned vineyards, primarily in the Yakima Valley, DeLille Cellars produces a variety of wines under various labels: DeLille Cellars, Doyenne, and Grand Ciel. The price tags definitely will assist you in reaching your air-mileage point goal, and for that reason, you may want to get chummy with any wine distributor who has the DeLille portfolio.

DELILLE CELLARS
opened: 1992
winemaker(s): Chris Upchurch
location: 14421 Woodinville Redmond Road NE, Redmond, WA 98072
phone: 425-877-9472
web: www.delillecellars.com
e-mail: contact@delillecellars.com
fee: Tasting fee
hours: Sunday through Thursday 12–4:30, Friday 12–7, Saturday 11–4:30 (last tasting poured 30 minutes prior to closing time)
amenities: Mailing List, Newsletter/Blog, Online Store, Weddings, Wheelchair Accessible
connect: 🐦 f

Brian Carter Cellars 🔲

"A passion for the art of blending": With that tagline, Brian Carter Cellars stakes its claim on European-style blends. With more than 30 years of winemaking experience, noted vintner Brian Carter blends wines that have great names, great labels and, even more important, great awards.

An afternoon of wine tasting at Brian Carter's tasting room, located in a bright yellow house near the Hollywood Schoolhouse, offers a multitude of magical blends. You'll be introduced to wines with names like Oriana, a white blend of three varietals; Tuttorosso, a sangiovese-based, Tuscan-style blend; Byzance, a southern Rhône–style blend of grenache and syrah; and Solesce, the winery's signature Bordeaux-style blend.

While sampling, you can engage the knowledgeable pouring staff and perhaps Brian Carter himself. Mike Stevens, managing partner, is often around and, with an engaging smile, speaks eloquently about Brian Carter's vision and history.

Note: While at Brian Carter, you also can find yet another fine example of wine complementing art. As you sample the Tuttorosso, examine Stephen Black's stunning wine label; I think you'll agree, they make a perfect blend.

BRIAN CARTER CELLARS
opened: 2006
winemaker(s): Brian Carter
location: 14419 Woodinville Redmond Road NE, Woodinville, WA 98072
phone: 425-806-WINE
web: www.briancartercellars.com
e-mail: info@briancartercellars.com
fee: Tasting fee refunded with purchase
hours: Thursday through Monday 12–5
amenities: Picnic Area, Wheelchair Accessible, Wine Club
connect: 🐦

Apex at Alder Ridge 22

APEX AT ALDER RIDGE
winemaker(s): Peter Devison
location: 14450 Woodinville Redmond Road NE,
Suite 105, Woodinville, WA 98072
phone: 425-408-1796
web: www.alderridge.com
e-mail: info@apex-at-alderridge.com
fee: Tasting fee
hours: Monday 12–6, Thursday 12–6, Friday 12–7,
Saturday 11–7, Sunday 11–6; Closed Thanksgiving,
Christmas, and New Years Day. Happy Hour starts
everyday at 3 until close.
amenities: Mailing List, Online Store, Wheelchair
Accessible, Wine Club, Wines by the Glass

www.winetrailsnw.com/wineries/apex_at_alder_ridge

The Library 23

THE LIBRARY
winemaker(s): Boudreaux, Long Shadow, Den Hoed
location: 14450 Woodinville Redmond Road NE,
Suite 105, Woodinville, WA 98072
phone: 425-408-1608
web: www.thelibrarywines.com
fee: Tasting fee applies
hours: Thursday through Sunday 11–6 by reservation
amenities: Private Events, Wheelchair Accessible
connect:

www.winetrailsnw.com/wineries/the_library

Cañon de Sol Winery and Vineyard

Cañon de Sol is a 45-acre winery in the heart of Washington's wine country. Located outside of Benton City, the winery makes its home in Badger Canyon. Its owner, Victor Cruz, left his comfortable career as an engineer to reinvent himself as a winemaker — alas, another victim of the notoriously infectious wine bug.

Cañon de Sol is one of only two Latino-owned wineries in the state; the other being Prosser-based Martinez & Martinez. In his 10-plus years of winemaking, Victor's accomplishments speak for themselves; one fine example is Cañon de Sol's "Best in Show" award at the prestigious Northwest Wine Summit in 2004. There is also the fact that he's the winemaker for Irlandés Limited Reserve Winery (which shares his Woodinville tasting room) and Kennewick's Anelare, which tells us he's in demand. Interestingly, Victor attended middle school with Washington's renowned winemaker Charlie Hoppes (Fidelitas). One wonders if they discussed the nuances and flavor profile of Mountain Dew during PE.

Victor's 2,300-square-foot tasting room in Woodinville provides ample space for a vanload of WineTrail fans to experience both the Cañon de Sol and Irlandés labels. It's a managable portfolio of wines to sample; don't pass up the chance to try his Meritage label, featuring a delicious blend of cabernet sauvignon, merlot, Malbec, and cabernet franc. If that swirling and sipping works up an appetite, check out nearby Mazatlan Mexican Restaurant and imagine its chile relleno paired with with Victor's viognier. ¡Muy delicioso!

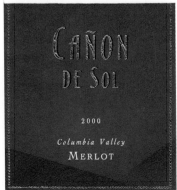

CANON DE SOL WINERY AND VINEYARD
opened: 1999
winemaker(s): Victor Cruz
location: 14450 Woodinville Redmond Road NE Suite 107, Woodinville, WA 98072
phone: 509-588-6311
web: www.canondesol.com
e-mail: wine@canondesol.com
fee: NA
hours: Thursday through Monday 12–6
amenities: Mailing List, Wheelchair Accessible
connect: 🐦

Goose Ridge Winery

GOOSE RIDGE WINERY
opened: 1999
winemaker(s): Kendall Mix
location: 14450 Woodinville Redmond Road NE, Suite 108, Woodinville, WA 98072
phone: 425-488-0200
web: www.gooseridge.com
e-mail: info@gooseridge.com
fee: Complimentary wine tasting
hours: Monday through Saturday 11–6; Sunday 12–6 or by appointment
amenities: Mailing List, Online Store, Private Events, Wheelchair Accessible, Wine Club, Wines by the Glass
connect:

www.winetrailsnw.com/wineries/goose_ridge_winery

Airfield Estates Winery 26

AIRFIELD ESTATES WINERY
opened: 2007
winemaker(s): Marcus Miller
location: 14450 Woodinville Redmond Road NE, Suite 109, Woodinville, WA 98072
phone: 425-877-1006
web: www.airfieldwines.com
e-mail: info@airfieldwines.com
fee: Tasting fee refunded with purchase
hours: Monday through Thursday 12–5, Friday through Sunday 11–6; Winter hours vary; call ahead
amenities: Newsletter/Blog, Online Store, Wheelchair Accessible, Wine Club, Wines by the Glass
connect:

www.winetrailsnw.com/wineries/airfield_estates_winery

Darby Winery 27

Darby English is a member of a pack of young guns shaping the Washington wine industry. Like other Woodinville wineries, Darby Winery's grapes come from select vineyards in the Columbia Valley. And, like other Woodinville wineries, Darby produces limited lots of premium wine (3,500 cases annually). However, most other wineries lack the accolades Darby Winery has received from *Wine Spectator* or been named *Seattle* magazine's "2010 Winemaker to Watch" award.

Piqued your curiosity?

Not yet? Well then, imagine a viognier/rousanne blend called Le Deuce, which combines a great balance of citrus-leaning fruit and acid with a long finish that leaves you grinning. For those with a red predilection, Darby's layered syrah proves an irresistible seduction for the palate. In short, if you like the wine of Gorman Winery, Guardian Cellars or Baer Winery, then Darby Winery is a required stop along the Woodinville WineTrail. (Besides that, Darby's Hollywood Schoolhouse District tasting room is an inviting space any time of the year — there's just something about the atmospherics that traps me like a spider's web.)

DARBY WINERY
opened: 2007
winemaker(s): Darby English
location: 14450 Woodinville Redmond Road NE Suite 110, Woodinville, WA 98072
phone: 425-482-7999
web: www.darbywinery.com
e-mail: darby@darbywinery.com
fee: Tasting fee may apply
hours: Thursday and Friday 12–5; Saturday and Sunday 12–6
amenities: Mailing List, Private Events, Wheelchair Accessible, Wine Club
connect: 🐦 f

Hollywood Hill Vineyards 28

Steve and Becky Snyder are out to show that the cool marine air of Puget Sound is a great place to grow certain varieties of wine grapes. In fact, their Hollywood Hill Vineyards is more than an ornamental vineyard; the fruit of their labor is producing around 200 cases per year. Because the Snyders are adherents of sustainable practices, the vines (70 percent pinot noir clones 667 and 777 and Pommard; 30 percent chardonnay) receive only small doses of sulfur as needed.

While they do use their own grapes for some of the production, the majority of fruit comes from Columbia Valley vineyards, such as Gilbert Vineyards (certified organic) and Portteus Vineyards. Steve and Becky make wines true to their own palate with a decided bias toward Rhône-style wines, using varieties such as viognier, roussanne (which an anonymous source once said is really a syrah in drag), grenache, Mourvèdre, and syrah. Moreover, true to a French-style wine, the wines are aged in 70 percent neutral oak, with lower alcohol levels as a result.

Given Steve's passion for cool-climate grapes, you can look for more Puget Sound AVA varieties bottled by Hollywood Hill Vineyards. His active role with the Puget Sound Wine Growers Association provides a rich breeding ground for experimenting with a large number of grape varieties that thrive in cool climates. Such varieties abound, including Zweigelt, St. Laurent, Dornfelder, regent, Auxerrois, pinot gris, pinot blanc, and pinot meunier. The Puget Sound viticultural area is huge, spanning north to the Canadian border and south to Olympia, with growing days averaging 210 days per year, and rainfall averaging 15 to 60 inches. Consequently, there are many locations ideal for grape growing, as Washington State University researchers have been demonstrating for several decades.

HOLLYWOOD HILL VINEYARDS
opened: 2007
winemaker(s): Steve Snyder
location: 14366 Woodinville Redmond Road NE, Woodinville, WA 98072
phone: 425-753-0093
web: www.hollywoodhillvineyards.com
e-mail: info@hollywoodhillvineyards.com
fee: Complimentary wine tasting
hours: Friday through Sunday 12–5, or by appointment
amenities: Mailing List, Newsletter/Blog, Wheelchair Accessible, Wine Club
connect:

DiStefano Winery 29

2009
SAUVIGNON BLANC
TRADITIONALLY PRODUCED HAND CRAFTED WINES
COLUMBIA VALLEY

PRODUCED AND BOTTLED BY
DISTEFANO WINERY, LTD. WOODINVILLE, WA.
750 ML ALC. 14.2% BY VOL.

DISTEFANO WINERY
winemaker(s): Mark Newton
location: 14356 Woodinville Redmond Road NE, Woodinville, WA 98072
phone: 425-487-1648
web: www.distefanowinery.com
e-mail: info@distefanowinery.com
fee: Complimentary wine tasting except $5 for reserve wines
hours: Friday through Sunday 12–7
amenities: Online Store, Private Events, Wheelchair Accessible, Wine Club
connect: 🐦 📘

www.winetrailsnw.com/wineries/distefano_winery

Patit Creek Cellars 30

PATIT CREEK CELLARS
opened: 1999
winemaker(s): Joe Forest
location: 14344 Woodinville Redmond Road NE, Woodinville, WA 98052
phone: 425-354-0015
web: www.patitcreekcellars.com
e-mail: info@patitcreekcellars.com
fee: Complimentary wine tasting
hours: Friday and Saturday 11–6; Sunday and Monday 11–5
amenities: Online Store, Private Events, RV/Bus Parking, Wheelchair Accessible, Wine Club
connect: 🐦 📘

www.winetrailsnw.com/wineries/patit_creek_cellars

Forgeron Cellars 〚31〛

FORGERON CELLARS
opened: 2001
winemaker(s): Marie-Eve Gilla
location: 14344 Woodinville Redmond Road NE, Woodinville, WA 98052
phone: 425-242-8872
web: www.forgeroncellars.com
e-mail: WoodinvilleTR@forgeroncellars.com
fee: Tasting fee refunded with purchase
hours: Summer: Thursday, Sunday and Monday 12–5, Friday and Saturday 12–6; Winter: Thursday, Sunday and Monday 12–5; Friday and Saturday 12–6
amenities: Mailing List, Online Store, RV/Bus Parking, Wheelchair Accessible, Wine Club, YouTube
connect: 🐦 📘

www.winetrailsnw.com/wineries/forgeron_cellars

Sky River Meadery

Denice Ingalls, owner of and winemaker for Sky River Meadery, has a sweet thing going. Using select honeys from Washington (most of them from Skagit County), she employs advanced techniques to create mead (aka honey wine). This is a grape-free zone: You won't find traditional still wines here. Instead, at Sky River, what you will find are three different premium honey wines: sweet mead (6 percent residual sugar), semi-sweet mead (3 percent residual sugar), and dry mead (less than 1 percent residual sugar). Each mead sells for around $15 a bottle.

But that's not all.

You can also indulge in raspberry honey wine and blackberry honey wine. One sip of the lush blackberry honey wine and I was imagining a nice pork tenderloin with a balsamic berry sauce to pair with this drink.

Working with a variety of honey suppliers, Denice chooses honeys for their colors, flavors, aromatics, and sugars, not unlike traditional winemakers working closely with grape growers. However, her "farmers" are bees, rather than growers from the Columbia Valley. At wine-tasting events, she is surrounded by traditional grape wine vintners who go to great lengths to explain why their merlot is different from their neighbor's. Denice, however, has no explaining to do. Honey wine is unique, and her product sets her apart.

Mead also has a uniquely rich lore from ancient Europe. For example, Greeks called mead "ambrosia," or nectar of the gods, and believed that the gods drank mead. Consequently, the Greeks thought that mead had magical and sacred properties. The term "honeymoon" comes from the ancient tradition of giving bridal couples a month's (one cycle of the moon) worth of honey wine. For a quick and interesting read, there are a number of other mead-related tales and anecdotes noted on the Sky River Meadery website.

SKY RIVER MEADERY
opened: 1999
winemaker(s): Denice Ingalls
location: 14270 Woodinville Redmond Road NE, Redmond, WA 98052
phone: 425-242-3815
web: www.skyriverbrewing.com
e-mail: denice@skyriverbrewing.com
fee: Tasting fee refunded with purchase
hours: Thursday through Saturday 1–6; Sunday 12–4 and by appointment
amenities: Art Gallery, Gift Shop, Picnic Area, Tours, RV/Bus Parking, Wheelchair Accessible
connect: 🐦 📘

Northwest Totem Cellars 33

Your first inclination is to knock on the door when you approach Northwest Totem Cellars. Nestled among tall fir trees in this suburban location on the edge of Redmond is the home of Mike and Kate Sharadin. It's also the home of their winemaking venture. Unlike tasting rooms located in strip malls, warehouse districts and buildings devoted solely to winemaking, the Sharadins' home serves the dual purpose of home and winery, where even the backyard sport court becomes a crush pad at harvest time.

Mike greets visitors in the kitchen area, where he pours and chats about wine and other subjects. His outgoing personality is a plus when it comes to distributing his own wine. He's also a very caring person, involved in his neighborhood and the larger community. During stints as a swimming coach in Quebec and Peru, he learned to speak both French and Spanish. Perhaps it was that exposure to the French culture and his extensive travels that helped define his style of winemaking, which he describes as being "Old World, food friendly, and relatively low in alcohol." He relies on gravity, rather than pumps, in the winemaking process, and dispenses with fining additives and filters. The results are pure, clean, and oh so delicious.

Mike Sharadin

The use of the word "Totem" and the iconic images of Northwest native Indian tribes in the winery's branding are intended to give a sense of place when you taste these wines. You know the wine is Northwest in origin and taste, and you aren't distracted by cute pictures of dogs on the label or the use of "chateau" in the name.

Northwest Totem's Low Man Red wine (a Bordeaux blend) acknowledges the leader of the tribe, and who's image is depicted as the base image of the totem pole, shouldering the weight of others. Delectable wines with a story behind the label have a special ring for me.

NORTHWEST TOTEM CELLARS
opened: 2006
winemaker(s): Mike Sharadin
location: 15810 NE 136th Place, Redmond, WA 98052
phone: 425-869-9778
web: www.nwtotemcellars.com
e-mail: info@nwtotemcellars.com
fee: Tasting fee refunded with purchase
hours: Saturday 12–4
amenities: Mailing List, Wine Club
connect:

Warehouse District
North
WineTrail

Along Woodinville's Warehouse District WineTrail North, you will discover that business parks are not what they used to be. This is the suburban equivalent to urban garage winemakers, or garagistes. These boutique wineries transform grapes from eastern Washington into award-winning wines that continually receive accolades from connoisseurs. Don't look for any vineyards or *faux-chateau* wineries. There aren't any — there's just gorgeous wine to relish.

Other than the short drive to nearby Efestē Winery, you can simply park your car and follow the signs. **WineTrail Note:** More than any of the other WineTrails featured in this book, this one wins the prize for being in a continuous state of flux; new wineries come and go. The best advice I can give is to download the WineTrails of Washington app from Google Play or Apple's app store. I regularly update the app to keep up with the changes.

Warehouse District WineTrail North

1 Efestē
2 Alta Cellars Winery
3 Gordon Brothers Cellars
4 Pondera Winery
5 Des Voigne Cellars
6 Davenport Cellars
7 XSV Wines
8 Hestia Cellars
9 Bunnell Family Cellars
10 Kestrel Vintners Tasting Room
11 Michael Florentino Cellars
12 Anton Ville Winery
13 Vortex Cellars
14 Amelia Bleu
15 Patterson Cellars Warehouse District
16 Piccola Cellars
17 Eye of the Needle Winery
18 Sparkman Cellars Warehouse District

19 Guardian Cellars
20 Darby Winery & Live Wire
21 Barrage Cellars
22 Baer Winery
23 William Church Winery
24 Cuillin Hills Winery
25 Elevation Cellars

26 Tenor Wines
27 Flying Dreams Winery
28 Page Cellars
29 Red Sky Winery
30 Obelisco Estate
31 Robert Ramsay Cellars
32 Gård Vintners
33 Smasne Cellars

Region:	**Woodinville Wine Country**
# of tasting rooms on tour:	**33**
# of satellite tasting rooms:	**9**
Estimate # of days for tour:	**8**
Getting around:	**Car and foot (mostly)**
Key Events:	❏ **St. Nicholas Day Open House (December) and Passport to Woodinville (April) — both sponsored by Woodinville Wine Country. See www.woodinvillewinecountry.com for details and ticket information.**
Tips:	❏ **Experience the 3rd Thursday Wine Walk — see www.woodwarewine.com for details.**
	❏ **Woodinville offers a variety of restaurants: Some popular places include the Barking Frog, Pasta Nova, Garden Café in Mobaks, The Herbfarm at Willows Lodge, Italianissimo Ristorante, and Purple Café & Wine Bar.**
	❏ **Consider hiring a limousine service.**
Best:	❏ **Destination: Efeste**

Efestē

Although Efestē is part of the collection of wineries in the Warehouse District, it stands out — and apart. First off, the setting itself is huge. At Efestē, you won't be sipping wine in a warehouse bay, but rather in an industrial building that can comfortably store a Boeing 737. There's plenty of space under this one roof for winemaking, barrel storage and wine tasting. However, along with the grand square footage allotted for the actual winemaking process, Efestē features a generously sized kitchen spacious enough for cooking classes and private parties.

Indeed, at the winery's swirl and sip events, guests learn new cooking techniques and prepare dishes such as ahi tuna tartar in toasted won ton cups, mini gyros with grilled lamb and tzatzki sauce, crostini of homemade ricotta and roasted red bell pepper jam, and lots of other luscious recipes. Of course, all these delightful dishes demand fine wine, and Efestē accommodates with such wines as Feral sauvignon blanc and (my favorite) Big Papa cabernet sauvignon.

All this is happening in Woodinville while Efeste's 60 acres of estate grapes continues to mature in eastern Washington.

Former winemaker Brennon Leighton's background as winemaker for Ste. Michelle's Winery's renowned Eroica riesling and his degree in viticulture and enology from the University of California-Davis, led the way to award-winning wines. However, in 2012 Brennon departed for Walla Walla to work on Charles Smith's "chardonnay project" leaving the winemaking tasks in the very capable hands of Nova Scotia bred Peter Devison.

Peter is particularly adept at "reductive winemaking" where oxygen and wine are kept separate to minimize the harmful impact of O_2 on the vino. Until the wine is opened and encouraged to breathe through a good swirl or two, oxygen is our enemy. Peter knows this and he does something about it through his reductive technique.

EFESTE
opened: 2008
winemaker(s): Peter Devison
location: 19730 144th Avenue NE, Woodinville, WA 98072
phone: 425-398-7200
web: www.efeste.com
e-mail: info@efeste.com
fee: Tasting fee
hours: Friday through Sunday 12–4
amenities: Gift Shop, Private Events, Wheelchair Accessible, Wine Club
connect:

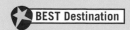 **BEST Destination**

Alta Cellars Winery **2**

The rose compass embellishing the wall in the Alta Cellars tasting room hints at the story behind the winery. It turns out that co-owner/winemaker Jay Pedersen is the captain of The Ocean Leader in the Bering Sea. For two months in winter and two months in summer, Jay roams the Bering Sea hauling in pollock.

However, the public face of the winery, is Jay's spouse, Karen Wagner, who, with an engaging smile and an obvious passion for wine, informs you that the name "Alta" comes from Lake Alta in north-central Washington, about five miles from the sleepy burg of Pateros. That little patch of paradise is where the couple retreats whenever possible to renew themselves and entertain the very real possibility that one day they will call Lake Alta their permanent home.

Karen Wagner

In the meantime, Woodinville's Warehouse District serves as the locus for selling and making their Bordeaux-inspired wines. (Current production is at 500 cases per year.) It was while assisting Karen's brother Derek DesVoignes at nearby Cuillin Hills Winery that the notion occurred to Jay that he, too, could make wine. And that's precisely what he did, beginning in 2007 with his first batch of cabernet, and he succeeded in quadrupling his production the following year. Good stuff does that.

Relying on grapes from eastern Washington vineyards such as Sagemoor, Weinbau, Meek Family Estate, and Seven Hills, Jay has a preference for using new French oak, which brings an important element to the winemaking process — especially when you employ a schedule of two years in the barrel, an aging process reminiscent of that employed to produce world-class Bordeaux.

My taste of Alta Cellars 2008 cabernet sauvignon, from initial sip to lingering finish, had me smacking my lips as I experiencing its blackberry-infused flavors. With that finish still on my tongue, I noticed that Alta Cellars sold wines by the glass, so I obliged by ordering up a full pour — and cautioned myself not to tell any fish tales during my visit.

ALTA CELLARS WINERY
winemaker(s): Jay Pedersen
location: 19501 144th Avenue NE, Suite A-500, Woodinville, WA 98072
phone: 425-424-9218
web: www.altacellarswinery.com
e-mail: info@altacellars.com
fee: Tasting fee refunded with purchase
hours: Saturday and Sunday 12–4; Third Thursday Wine Walk 4–8
amenities: Mailing List, Wheelchair Accessible, Wines by the Glass
connect: 🐦 📘

Gordon Brothers Cellars

Get in your way-back machine to visit this winery. Started in 1982, Gordon Brothers Family Vineyards originated with two brothers, Jeff and Bill Gordon, after they consulted with Walter Clore, whom many consider to be the "father of the Washington wine industry." Now approaching their 30th year of production, the Gordon brothers truly can claim to be Washington's oldest estate winery (i.e., their wines are made only from grapes grown in their vineyard). Today, they produce chardonnay, cabernet sauvignon, merlot, syrah, sauvignon blanc, gewürztraminer ice wine, and their flagship red blend, Tradition.

It's the Tradition, a blend of cabernet and syrah, that brings many people to the brothers' tasting room in Woodinville's Warehouse District. (The actual estate winery is in Pasco.) The reward for this trek is a wine that bursts with fruit on the palate, particularly berry fruits: raspberries, blueberries, and strawberries. When you add a long finish of cedar and spice notes, your tasting just got turbo-charged. Tradition's $40 price tag may be a bit steep, but for those who have a special steak to grill or an event to celebrate (e.g., you're alive), it's well worth the splurge. Their other wines are more wallet friendly, to be sure, with the merlot, syrah, and cabernet sauvignon going for half that price.

Incidentally, if you happen to walk among the rows of vineyards at their Pasco location when the ripened fruit clusters are hanging from the vine, feel free to munch on a few grapes. Their vineyard is certified organic, which means zippo in the way of pesticides and herbicides. It's all good.

GORDON BROTHERS CELLARS
opened: 1985
winemaker(s): John J. Gabriel
location: 19501 144th Avenue NE, Suite A-800, Woodinville, WA 98072
phone: 425-398-9323
web: www.gordonwines.com
e-mail: tastingroom@gordonwines.com
fee: Tasting fee may apply
hours: Friday and Saturday 12–7; Sunday 12–5
amenities: Wheelchair Accessible, Wine Club
connect: 🐦

Pondera Winery  ❹

Winemaker Shane Howard had me with his statement that Pondera will always focus on Bordeaux varieties. Yes, I'm a decidedly Bordeaux kind of guy, with my tastes running toward cabernet sauvignon, merlot, and Malbec. Pondera Winery owner Melvin Howard is a man after my own heart, and palate, and for that we celebrate.

The happy truth is, Bordeaux-derived grapes grow wonderfully in Washington.

For a taste of Washington *terroir*, park the car in the Woodinville Warehouse District and do a winery walk. There are lots of sampling ops; among them, Pondera Winery, for all the "big red" lovers among you. This family-owned boutique winery specializes in the production of high-quality, well-balanced red varietals and Bordeaux-style blends. Select

Columbia Valley vineyards provide the grapes for the wine, with production limited to fewer than 2,000 cases annually. These are small-lot grapes, punched down and aged in French oak barrels, and individually nurtured for your tasting pleasure. Be sure to sample the red blend Melvado, which *Wine Press Northwest* noted as having "an amazing amount of fruit on the plummy palate, joined by dark chocolate and black olive."

Taste isn't the only sense to get a treat in this tasting room. To please the eye, there is the rotating exhibit of fine art supplied by Dan and Pat Howard of Kirkland's Howard/Mandville Gallery. These works are from leading Northwest artists and they are testament to the notion that good wine pairs with the finer things in life, including art. Check out howardmandville.com. On the subject of fine art, we all know that the beauty of a wine's label shouldn't sway us in deciding what to drink, but Pondera Winery's labels are works of art that entice you to uncork the bottle and enjoy. Be swayed.

PONDERA WINERY
opened: 2007
winemaker(s): Shane Howard
location: 19501 144th Avenue NE, Suite B-400, Woodinville, WA 98072
phone: 425-825-3917
web: www.ponderawinery.com
e-mail: shane@ponderawinery.com
fee: Tasting fee may apply
hours: Saturday and Sunday 1–5
amenities: Art Gallery, Private Events, Wheelchair Accessible, Wine Club
connect:

Des Voigne Cellars 5

Get ready for another one of those Warehouse District wineries — but with a twist. Owner/winemaker Darren Des Voigne (twin brother of Cuillin Hills' Derek Des Voigne) eschews wine snobbery in favor of fun. Rather than hit you with Francophile names and high price tags, he wants you to relax and enjoy your time at the winery.

Rather than taking the staid approach of pairing wine with Bach or Beethoven, Darren matches up his wine with jazz artists, as reflected on his bold wine labels. Exhibit A is his red blend Solea, which he suggests harmonizes very well with Jimmy McGriff's "Electric Funk."

Solea is a blend of cabernet sauvignon, merlot, cabernet franc, Malbec, and petit verdot, all from Washington's prized Red Mountain AVA. This would be great wine for a summertime barbecue or on a wet winter Seattle night as a complement to red beans and rice, smoked sausage, and the strains of jazz in the background.

DES VOIGNE CELLARS
opened: 2005
winemaker(s): Darren DesVoigne
location: 19501 144th Avenue NE, Suite B-500
Woodinville, WA 98072-4409
phone: 425-415-8466
web: www.desvoignecellars.com
e-mail: info@desvoignecellars.com
fee: Tasting fee refunded with purchase
hours: Saturday 1–5
amenities: Mailing List, Wheelchair Accessible
connect:

Davenport Cellars

Following total immersion in South Seattle Community College's wine program, as well as a good dunking in coursework at University of California-Davis and Washington State University, Jeff and Sheila Jirka opened their tasting room in 2009. Located in Woodinville's Warehouse District, where they compete with dozens of other wineries, their challenge is to distinguish Davenport Cellars from the masses.

However, by choosing to source the highest-quality grapes available, using a minimalist approach, paying attention to detail, handling the fruit and wine as gently as possible, and maintaining traditional practices, they hope to create wines that are a cut above. After all, the *crème de la crème* does rise to the top.

Davenport's labels are plain, and its portfolio small, but that's what is so endearing about this winery. The Jirkas aren't trying to overwhelm you with a dozen wines in the hope that one of them will speak to your palate. In fact, they offer but three wines: Snowflake (a sauvignon blanc/semillon blend); R.H.D. (a merlot-dominant Bordeaux red blend); and Continuity (more of a "Right Bank" Bordeaux blend with a cab backbone). Yet it is precisely this focus that makes these wines appealing.

Well, that focus and their affordability: At $24 a bottle, both the R.H.D. and Continuity are a steal; this quality of wine easily would go for three times that price if born in Napa.

DAVENPORT CELLARS
opened: 2009
winemaker(s): Jeff and Sheila Jirka
location: 19501 144th Avenue NE, Suite B-600, Woodinville, WA 98072
phone: 425-457-4957
web: www.davenportcellars.com
e-mail: jeff@davenportcellars.com
fee: Tasting fee refunded with purchase
hours: Saturday 1–5 or or by appointment
amenities: Wheelchair Accessible, Wine Club

XSV Wines ⑦

My communications teacher in college once said, "Tell it by the numbers!" With that in mind, here are three compelling reasons for you to experience this Woodinville Warehouse District gem.

First, XSV (as in "eXceSsiVe") is rather remarkable in that its winemaker/owner, Michael LeMieux, makes wine from grapes sourced from his family vineyard in Pasco. More than 50 years ago, Michael's parents bought vineyard property in the city of Pasco, and the family continues to manage the vineyard, which is composed of cabernet, merlot, chardonnay, syrah, and zinfandel grapes. Unlike most Woodinville wineries, XSV Wines has the distinction of relying on estate fruit.

Second, most wines you find on the grocery shelf are actually blends. That is, the label may say "merlot," but that simply means that at least 75 percent of the grapes used to make the wine come from the merlot grape variety. However, in the case of XSV Wines, consumers have no need to wonder what's in the bottle. Michael uses 100 percent grape varietals in crafting his wines. When you buy a bottle of XSV chardonnay, you know you're getting 100 percent chardonnay.

Third, check out the vintage on the bottle and note the age. For example, it's not unusual that a cabernet he's pouring in the tasting room is four or five years old. Like the famous 1970s television ads for Paul Masson wine in which Orson Welles declares, "We will sell no wine before its time," Michael believes in plenty of time in the barrel and bottle before a wine is released.

There are other reasons for you to visit XSV Wines (including that fact that Michael happens to be one of the nicest winemakers in the state) but following my communications teacher's directive, I'm sticking to the promised three reasons; you will discover the others for yourself.

Michael LeMieux

XSV WINES
opened: 2000
winemaker(s): Michael LeMieux
location: 19501 144th Avenue NE, Suite C-300, Woodinville, WA 98072
phone: 425-210-1554
web: www.xsvwines.com
e-mail: info@xsvwines.com
fee: Tasting fee may apply
hours: Saturday 12–5, Sunday 12–4
amenities: Wheelchair Accessible

Hestia Cellars 🔲

The next time you're at a party and want to show off your gift for trivia, mention the name Hestia and explain that in Greek mythology, Hestia is the virgin goddess of hearth or fireside, architecture, and the right ordering of domesticity and the family. In other words, she's all about family and the coming together of family by the fireside — perhaps with a glass of wine.

Given the winery's name, then, it's no surprise to learn that Hestia Cellars is a family-owned enterprise, located in Western Washington's Snoqualmie River Valley. Family member Shannon Jones is responsible for crafting a limited number of voluptuous red wines. As he states on the Hestia website, "Remaining a small family winery allows us to be intimate with each and every barrel of wine in our cellar. All of our red wines are gently moved by gravity flow, and are bottled unfined and unfiltered." The proof is in the tasting, and the intense taste of the 2008 Hestia cabernet sauvignon, with its tamed tannins, good acidity, and long finish, demonstrated why *Wine Enthusiast* gave this vintage a 92. Lovely.

If it's a white you desire (assuming there is any inventory left), try Hestia's lively, citrus-packed chenin blanc. Perhaps you'll wonder, as I did, why we don't see this French derived grape more often in Washington.

Incidentally, we're sure Dionysus (the Greek god of wine) would suggest that Hestia cook up some lamb to go with Hestia Cellars' syrah. That was the opinion of the folks at Seattle's 2011 Lamb Jam when they tasted chef Wayne Johnson's rioja-braised lamb shank paired with Hestia Cellars 2008 syrah. Both are rich and flavorful on their own, but when paired, take the tasting experience to a whole new level of flavor.

2008 SYRAH

HESTIA

HESTIA CELLARS
opened: 2004
winemaker(s): Shannon Thomas Jones
location: 19501 144th Avenue NE, Suite C-700, Woodinville, WA 98072
phone: 425-333-4270
web: www.hestiacellars.com
e-mail: info@hestiacellars.com
fee: Tasting fee refunded with purchase
hours: Friday 3–7, Saturday 1–5, Sunday 1–5, or by appointment
amenities: Mailing List, Wheelchair Accessible, Wine Club
connect: 🐦 f

Bunnell Family Cellars ⑨

Ron Bunnell

BUNNELL FAMILY CELLARS
opened: 2004
winemaker(s): Ron Bunnell
location: 19501 144th Avenue NE, Woodinville, WA 98072
phone: 425-286-2964
web: www.bunnellfamilycellar.com
e-mail: info@bunnellfamilycellar.com
fee: Tasting fee refunded with purchase
hours: Saturday and Sunday 12–5 Third Thursday Wine Walks 4–8
amenities: RV/Bus Parking, Wheelchair Accessible, Wine Club
connect: ▪️

www.winetrailsnw.com/wineries/bunnell_family_cellars

Kestrel Vintners Tasting Room ⑩

KESTREL VINTNERS TASTING ROOM
opened: 1995
winemaker(s): Flint Nelson
location: 19501 144th Avenue NE, Suite C-900, Woodinville, WA 98072
phone: 425-398-1199
web: www.kestrelwines.com
e-mail: woodinville@kestrelwines.com
fee: Tasting fee
hours: Thursday through Monday 12–5 or by appointment
amenities: Newsletter/Blog, Online Store, Picnic Area, Private Events, RV/Bus Parking, Wheelchair Accessible, Wine Club, Winemaker Dinners
connect: 🐦 ▪️

www.winetrailsnw.com/wineries/kestrel_vintners_tasting_room

Michael Florentino Cellars

Another graduate from the Boeing Employees Wine & Beer Club has gone commercial and found a home in the Woodinville Warehouse District. Brad Sherman began his grape-fermentation career back in college, and expanded his amateur skills during his career with Boeing via the wine club and extensive travel to other great wine-growing regions in the world.

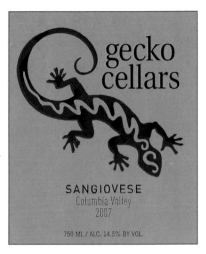

This exposure to the wines other countries explains why Michael Florentino Cellars (MFC) offers some unusual grape varieties, such as primitivo, Counoise and Monastrell (aka Mourvèdre). If your palate happens to be jonesing to explore the wines of Spain, such as tempranillo and garnacha (aka grenache), head for MFC's tasting room. If Italy is your thing and you have a hankering for sangiovese or pinot grigio, then MFC has something to quench those cravings. And for the classic Bordeaux-style wines (because you can never tire of cabernet), I suggest you make a beeline for MFC.

Another fine feature of MFC is its Gecko wine label, which offers moderately priced wines. For $20 or less, you can cart away delectable wines such as Malbec, sangiovese, rosé, and a selection of red blends. These are everyday wines ready to enjoy tonight.

However, if you're looking for a Saturday-night wine, the wines under the Michael Florentino label still provide excellent value, priced in the mid-$20s. My personal favorite is the MFC Monastrell, a rich and supple wine featuring plenty of cherry and black currant flavors, soft tannins, and a lingering finish. Brad's 2008 vintage of Monastrell took home the Double Gold at the Seattle Wine Awards, a Silver Medal at the Tri-Cities Wine Festival, and 91 points (count them!) from The *Wine Enthusiast*. Being the carnivore that I am, I envision a lamb shank dish paired with Brad's Monastrell.

MICHAEL FLORENTINO CELLARS
opened: 2008
winemaker(s): Brad Sherman
location: 19501 144th Avenue NE, Suite C-1200, Woodinville, WA 98072
phone: 425-281-2323
web: www.michaelflorentinocellars.com
e-mail: geckowinecompany@comcast.net
fee: Tasting fee refunded with purchase
hours: Friday 3–7, Saturday and Sunday 12–5 and Third Thursday Wine Walks 4–8
amenities: Newsletter/Blog, Online Store, Picnic Area, Wheelchair Accessible, Wine Club
connect: 🐦 f

Brad Sherman

Anton Ville Winery 🄬

The winery was the brainchild of Andrew and Janiece Haug, who honored Andrew's Norwegian grandfather Tony by referencing his name in the winery's name — Anton Ville. Grandfather Tony was a meticulous carpenter, and it's this same attention to detail that Andrew brought to the creation of his wines. Unfortunately, Andrew's premature death soon after the launch of Anton Ville Winery left the challenge of running a winery to Janiece.

However, a visit to the tasting room indicates that, by all accounts, Janiece has embraced this test.

Anton Ville Winery differs from every tasting room you will visit in the Warehouse District. First, each serving of its wines — starting with its blend of riesling/viognier dubbed Harmony (love the name) and concluding with its cabernet sauvignon — features a wine and food pairing. Not to worry if you have dinner plans; the tiny morsels of crackers and chocolates won't fill you up. Rather, they complement the wine by bringing out its flavor, mouthfeel or finish.

A second unusual feature of this tasting room is the fact that it's a storefront for Janiece's other passion: imported items from Southeast Asia, pieces that make a home decorator's mind swirl with ideas. From woodcarvings to unusual baskets, visitors gawk in wonderment at the artisan craftsmanship on display.

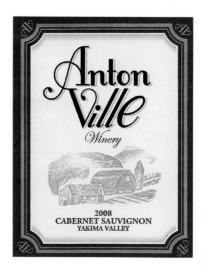

ANTON VILLE WINERY
opened: 2008
winemaker(s): Janiece Haug and consultant
location: 19501 144th Avenue NE, Suite D-300, Woodinville, WA 98072
phone: 206-683-3393
web: www.antonvillewinery.com
e-mail: info@antonvillewinery.com
fee: Tasting fee
hours: Saturday and Sunday 12–4
amenities: Wheelchair Accessible

Vortex Cellars 🔟

Vortex — *n.* A spiral motion of fluid within a limited area, especially a whirling mass of water or air that sucks everything near it toward its center.

Nichole and Ed Wicklein

It only seems natural that, as both a hydraulic engineer by profession and a passionate winemaker, co-owner/winemaker Ed Wicklein named his winery Vortex Cellars. After all, the twirling motion you see in a whirlpool is reminiscent of the whirlpool created when you swirl your glass of wine before tasting. And perhaps taking his cue from the quiet eye of a hurricane, another whirling vortex of liquid, Ed exudes a calm demeanor and ease while pouring samples and introducing you to his varied portfolio of wine. He's at the center of a new enterprise, a powerful, tempestuous force called the wine business.

His partner in this venture is his equally unruffled spouse, Nichole, who, between raising their dimpled and adorable son, Keaton, and working as a mental health therapist with a concentration in addiction therapy (there's some irony for you), is busy performing myriad chores at their new tasting room in Woodinville's Warehouse District. It's a partnership of affirmation: At the winery she says, "Yes, dear," but at home it's Ed who replies, "Yes, dear."

Although relatively new to the commercial wine scene, Ed has been dabbling in fermentation science for more than a decade, with educational stints at the University of California-Davis, Washington State University, and South Seattle Community College.

Perhaps it was the hot August day outside, but the viognier, with floral notes, honey, and a touch of lemon zest, held true to its northern Rhône heritage and refreshed the palate. However, the Rioja-derived tempranillo, a deep ruby red, cherry-infused delight, had me thirsting for more. I knew then that leaving Vortex Cellars anytime soon would be impossible. I had been sucked in.

VORTEX CELLARS
opened: 2010
winemaker(s): Ed Wicklein
location: 19501 144th Avenue NE, Suite D-500A, Woodinville, WA 98072
phone: 206-383-1235
web: www.vortexcellars.com
e-mail: info@vortexcellars.com
fee: Tasting fee refunded with purchase
hours: Saturday 12–5, most Sundays — call or check Facebook
amenities: Art Gallery, Picnic Area, Private Events, Tours, Wheelchair Accessible
connect: 🐦 📘

Amelia Bleu 🔢14

Doug Roberts

Unlike most Woodinville wineries, Amelia Bleu has a rather unique feature — Doug and Heather Roberts have their own vineyard. Situated outside Chelan, their six acres of heaven resides on a hilltop overlooking the mighty Columbia River. Their vineyard's name is Ashlyn and it is the source of grapes for most of their wines including a red blend christened Riverenza as well as a delightful barbera. You could safely say that winemaker Doug is a true vigneron, as the French say to describe someone who plants and maintains the vineyard and derives wine from his fruit. It's a term that connotes prestige to the person involved from bud break to bottling.

Interestingly enough Ashlyn Vineyard lies just outside the border of the federally designated Lake Chelan American Viticulture Area (AVA). Thus, you will note on the bottle's label that the Riverenza and barbera wines are from Chelan County.

While it is doubtful that most mortal palates can discern the difference between Amelia Bleu's barbera and the barbera grown in the Lake Chelan AVA, the impact is perhaps felt more with the marketing of the product than anything.

I'm not saying that Lake Chelan AVA is equivalent to Châteauneuf-du-Pape but I am saying that only for marketing purposes does it matter. But sometimes in a strange twist of fate, a renegade winery outside the demarcated wine district can break through. Heck, Chateau Le Pin is simply a regional Bordeaux wine but happens to be one of the most expensive wines in the world. At around $2,000 a bottle, Le Pin is way more expensive than it's first-growth neighbors such as Chateau La Tour! Perhaps the Roberts will command the pricing that Le Pin achieves. It just takes a stellar review by *Wine Spectator* and you've hit the big time.

AMELIA BLEU
opened: 2012
winemaker(s): Doug Roberts
location: 19501 144th Avenue NE, Suite D-500, Woodinville, WA 98072
phone: 425-444-1559
web: www.ameliableu.highwire.com
e-mail: heather@ameliableu.com
fee: Tasting fee refunded with purchase
hours: Saturday and Sunday 12–5 and Third Thursday Wine Walks 4–8
amenities: Wheelchair Accessible
connect: ⓕ

Patterson Cellars Warehouse District ⑮

PATTERSON CELLARS WAREHOUSE DISTRICT
opened: 2007
winemaker(s): John Patterson
location: 19501 144th Avenue NE, Suite D-600, Woodinville, WA 98072
phone: 425-483-8600
web: www.pattersoncellars.com
e-mail: info@pattersoncellars.com
fee: Tasting fee refunded with purchase
hours: Saturday and Sunday 12–5; call ahead during winter
amenities: Online Store, Private Events, RV/Bus Parking, Wheelchair Accessible, Wine Club
connect: 🐦 📘

www.winetrailsnw.com/wineries/patterson_cellars_warehouse_district

Piccola Cellars 🔟

Looking for a unique wine tasting experience? Check out Piccola Cellars in Woodinville's Warehouse District. Here, samples of wine are poured from a stand-up piano bar. Yes, you read that right. The piano has a half-dozen taps tethered to kegs within, each containing a premium Washington state wine. These are 19.5- liter stainless steel kegs holding the equivalent of 26 bottles of wine and delivering 131 5-ounce-glass pours.

The keg idea is the brainchild of founder Diana Kaspic, who evolved the idea while attending Central Washington University's World Wine Program. The benefits of tap wine, as noted on the Piccola website, include no packaging waste (100 percent reusable), no product waste, and less expended energy, because the keg weighs less than bottles. All this translates into economy for the consumer since the cost is less per volume when purchased.

While it is easy to imagine how a restaurant/bar would benefit from a wine tap system (see it in action at Seattle's Four Seasons Hotel near Pike Place Market), it's a little harder to see how consumers access this new packaging system. For that, Diana and her partners have created the "Tapped In" program, in which members buy their own dispensing tap for home use and, in return, receive 15 percent discounts on wine purchases.

We tend to think that wine should only come in a bottle or a box, but, historically, wine came to consumers via clay amphorae and then wooden barrels. For centuries, wine from Bordeaux came to merry ol' England in 60-gallon barrels, and patrons at bars and restaurants were served from the barrel. (Think of the oxidation issue!) The invention of mass-produced quality glass for containing wine didn't come about until the 17th century, and even then, it took a generation or so to figure out how to seal it. Thank goodness for cork!

PICCOLA CELLARS
winemaker(s): Doug Petersen
location: 19501 144th Avenue NE, Suite D-700, Woodinville, WA 98072
phone: 206-406-2123
web: www.piccolawine.com
e-mail: piccola@piccolawine.com
hours: Friday 5–7, Saturday 12–6 and Sunday 12–5
amenities: RV/Bus Parking, Wheelchair Accessible
connect: ⨍

Eye of the Needle Winery

For those of you who like a great value in wine and aren't already a fan of "Ten-Buck Bob," I've got a suggestion for you! Try Eye of the Needle wine. No, I don't mean "try"; I mean make a beeline to your nearby bottle shop and get a case of this elixir. At $9.99 a bottle for Eye of the Needle merlot, what have you got to lose?

The wizards behind the creation of Eye of the Needle wines are Bob and Lauren Bullock, who surprisingly are négociants. I say "surprisingly" because in France, négociants are held in high esteem — many of them, anyway — for their ability to create wine that's better than the sum of its parts. But in the Northwest, successful négociants are a rare find (with the fabulous success story of Oregon's A to Z Wineworks being an example). That is, with an abundance of unsold wine resting comfortably in wineries throughout the state, winemaker Bob comes along and purchases the excess wine and then blends the wine to create wines that cost less than $10.

Bob's most popular wine is his sangiovese-based Little Red Italy wine, which makes even the most ardent Chianti lover take notice with flavors that stay true to this variety, including strawberry, cherry, rhubarb, and raspberry. This is a true everyday wine and pairs equally well with pizza, spaghetti, burgers, and brats. It's sangio for the blue-collar set as well as for folks whose collars are of the Ralph Lauren turned-up polo variety.

Bob and Lauren Bullock

If I sound like an unabashed devotee of Eye of the Needle, I plead guilty. Great wine at insane prices — what's not to love?

EYE OF THE NEEDLE WINERY
opened: 2008
winemaker(s): Bob Bullock
location: 19501 144th Avenue NE, Suite D-1200, Woodinville, WA 98072
web: www.facebook.com/pages/Haystack-Needle-Winery/124675424252919
e-mail: info@hsnwinery.com
fee: Complimentary wine tasting
hours: Saturdays and Sundays 12–5
amenities: Wheelchair Accessible

Sparkman Cellars Warehouse District 18

SPARKMAN CELLARS WAREHOUSE DISTRICT
opened: 2006
winemaker(s): Chris Sparkman
location: 19501 144th Avenue NE, Suite E-400, Woodinville, WA 98072
phone: 425-398-1045
web: www.sparkmancellars.com
e-mail: wine@sparkmancellars.com
fee: Tasting fee may apply
hours: Saturday and Sunday 1–5
amenities: Mailing List, Online Store, Private Events, RV/Bus Parking, Wheelchair Accessible, Wine Club, Winemaker Dinners
connect: f

www.winetrailsnw.com/wineries/sparkman_cellars_warehouse_district

Guardian Cellars 19

Police officer Jerry Riener is owner/winemaker at Guardian Cellars. When he's not arresting people, he's making wine — really good wine. His wines reinforce the law-enforcement theme with names such as Chalk Line, The Alibi and my favorite, Gun Metal, a Bordeaux red blend that I can attest is lip-smacking good.

Sean Sullivan of the *Washington Wine Report* gave some great insights into Jerry Riener in an article he wrote on Guardian Cellars on March 16, 2010: "Riener was driving down the highway in the late 1990s when he saw something suspicious. Stopping for a closer inspection, Riener looked past the barrels and grapes and went straight to the object that drew his attention — the shiny new forklift. Growing up, Riener had spent summers on his uncle's farm in the Midwest, and machinery had always held a fascination to him. After interrogating Matthew Loso (then of Matthews Cellars) about the nature of his business, Riener was hooked. He began spending forty hours a week volunteering at the winery, working harvest, crush, and racking barrels. With a degree from the University of Washington in chemistry, it was the science of winemaking that most interested Riener. As payment for his service, Loso let him make a barrel of his own wine at the winery each year."

In 2001, Jerry met Mark Ryan McNeilly, who was starting Mark Ryan Winery at the time. Mark encouraged Jerry to make wine under his own label, and two barrels later, Guardian Cellars emerged. Jerry's love of "all things winemaking," including the paraphernalia, the fruit, the racking, and the bottling, is the secret to his success. His command of the process goes a long way toward a good outcome, but he also knows that along the way, one has to step back and let Mother Nature express herself.

GUARDIAN CELLARS
opened: 2008
winemaker(s): Jerry Riener
location: 19501 144th Avenue NE, Suite E-600, Woodinville, WA 98072
phone: 206-661-6733
web: www.guardiancellars.com
e-mail: jerry@guardiancellars.com
fee: Tasting fee refunded with purchase
hours: Saturday and Sunday 12:30–4:30
amenities: Mailing List, Wheelchair Accessible
connect: f

Darby Winery & Live Wire [20]

DARBY WINERY & LIVE WIRE
opened: 2007
winemaker(s): Darby English
location: 19501 144th Avenue NE,
Woodinville, WA 98072
phone: 425-482-7999
web: www.darbywinery.com
e-mail: darby@darbywinery.com
fee: Tasting fee may apply
hours: Saturday and Sunday 12–5
amenities: Mailing List, Online Store, Private Events,
RV/Bus Parking, Wheelchair Accessible, Wine Club
connect: 🐦 📘

www.winetrailsnw.com/wineries/darby_winery_and_live_wire

Barrage Cellars 21

Get this, *Seattle* magazine voted Kevin Correll's 2007 cabernet franc the best in the state for 2011. Not bad for a guy who started making wine in his garage, worked crushes in eastern Washington, and in between, found time to take a class or two at the University of California-Davis. But with the "best in the state" accolade, this Warehouse District winery is now on the map and deserves your palate's attention.

The word "barrage" has many synonyms, including "bombard," "pepper," and "shower," to name a few. And perhaps a barrage of flavor is what you would have experienced when you tasted its 2007 Outcast cabernet franc. Unfortunately, we'll never know. You see, by the time this WineTrail trekker arrived at Barrage, this wine had sold out. Alas, I had to content myself with sampling Kevin's riesling, syrah, and cabernet sauvignon — no hardship there! All were eminently quaffable and available to take home that evening.

The story goes that Kevin, while mulling over a name for his winery, came up with idea of fusing "barn" and "garage" — the two settings for his first winemaking efforts. The result was "Barrage," and thus the winery was named. And if that garage had been roomy enough for two vehicles? Well, you have to admit, "Two-Car Barrage" has a certain ring to it.

BARRAGE CELLARS
opened: 2008
winemaker(s): Kevin Correll
location: 19501 144th Avenue NE, Suite E-800, Woodinville, WA 98072
phone: 425-772-0384
web: www.barragecellars.com
e-mail: info@barragecellars.com
fee: Tasting fee refunded with purchase
hours: Saturday and Sunday 1–5
amenities: Wheelchair Accessible, Wine Club
connect: 🐦 📘

Baer Winery 22

Here's what noted wine critic Sean Sullivan had to say about Baer Winery's 2004 Ursa: "Blueberry and other blue fruit with traces of spice, chocolate, and espresso. Spice becomes bolder as the wine opens up. Very well balanced on the palate with silky tannins and a good finish." Reading his commentary of this Bordeaux blend makes me want to bolt for the car and make a beeline to the closest wine shop.

Lisa Baer

Following a stint as the assistant winemaker for DeLille Cellars, Lance Baer founded Baer Winery in 2000. Lance's meticulous standards led to the emergence of Baer Winery and the well-deserved accolades he received for Ursa. (FYI, "ursa" is Latin for bear.) It came as a shock to everyone when Lance passed away in 2007, leaving his sister, Lisa, and his father, Les, to take over the reins of the winery. When they took over, they did so not with the intent of selling out the inventory, but rather to keep Lance's legacy alive. And the two have succeeded, under the direction of winemaker consultant Erica Orr, although Lisa remains the public face of the winery. In fact, Lisa can drive a forklift with the best of them and is involved in all the workings of the winery.

Sourcing fruit exclusively from the renowned Stillwater Creek Vineyard, located in the Frenchman Hills of Columbia Valley, Baer Winery limits its production to 2,000 cases per year. Its proprietors wish it to remain small — it's that familial "attention to detail" thing.

BAER WINERY
winemaker(s): Baer Winery, LLC
location: 19501 144th Avenue NE, Suite F-100, Woodinville, WA 98072
phone: 425-483-7060
web: www.baerwinery.com
e-mail: info@baerwinery.com
fee: Tasting fee
hours: Open most Saturdays, call ahead
amenities: Mailing List, Online Store, Wheelchair Accessible
connect: 🐦

William Church Winery ⃞23

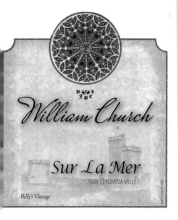

WILLIAM CHURCH WINERY
opened: 2005
winemaker(s): Leslie & Rod Balsley
location: 19495 144th Avenue NE, Suite A-100, Woodinville, WA 98072
phone: 425-427-0764
web: www.williamchurchwinery.com
e-mail: info@williamchurchwinery.com
fee: Tasting fee
hours: Saturday 12–4 Sunday 1–4 or by appointment
amenities: Mailing List, Pet Friendly, Private Events, RV/Bus Parking, Tours, Wheelchair Accessible, Wine Club
connect: 🐦 📘

www.winetrailsnw.com/winerles/william_church_winery

Cuillin Hills Winery 24

According to the Cuillin Hills Winery's website, the winery "is a family-owned and -operated boutique winery located in Woodinville's Warehouse District. Derek DesVoigne and Shannon McLeod began this journey with a commitment to produce small lots of distinct wines, which display balance, depth and intensity of character." Sprinkled in with that balance, depth and intensity is a wee bit of Scotland.

Located in Woodinville's Warehouse District, Cuillin Hills provides an interesting array of wines with unforgettable names that are bound to give you pause: Shackled (a southern Rhône blend), The Dungeon (a syrah-based wine), and my favorite, Riff-Raff (a red blend priced at only $19 a bottle). The winery's tasting room is Warehouse chic; wearing a kilt is optional.

We suggest that you uncork a bottle of Cuillin Hills' The Dungeon, settle in to watch Braveheart, and be glad drawing and quartering is a thing of the past.

Derek DesVoigne

CUILLIN HILLS WINERY
opened: 2005
winemaker(s): Derek DesVoigne
location: 19495 144th Avenue NE, Suite A-110, Woodinville, WA 98072-4409
phone: 425-402-1907
web: www.cuillinhills.com
e-mail: info@cuillinhills.com
fee: Tasting fee refunded with wine purchase
hours: Saturday 12–4
amenities: Mailing List, Newsletter/Blog, Wheelchair Accessible
connect: 🐦 📘

Elevation Cellars 25

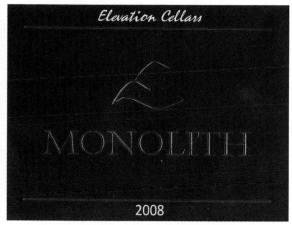

If you've been on the hunt for some Arlington Road Cellars inventory, but come up empty-handed, your search is over. A few years back when Arlington Road Cellars suddenly exited the wine business, it created a sweet opportunity for someone hankering to launch their own winery. Enter Steve Stuart.

Along with winemaking equipment, Steve acquired the remaining inventory of the big, bold, stellar Monolith red blend. Celebrated winemaker Matthew Loso, who had previously consulted with Arlington Road Cellars, made the transition to consultant winemaker for Steve. Even the Warehouse District location is the same, and that means the sparkling barrel room remains, with its French oak barrels resting comfortably for the next vintage.

Boatbuilder by day, winemaker at night (and weekends), Steve now has a tiger by the tail with Elevation Cellars. He's a busy guy, but you can't detect any stress behind his smile as he pours that nectar-of-the-gods Monolith, along with a lip-smacking dry riesling named Imperium and a straight cabernet sauvignon. Steve's ship has come in.

Steve Stuart

ELEVATION CELLARS
opened: 2010
winemaker(s): Steve Stuart
location: 19495 144th Avenue NE, Suite A-115, Woodinville, WA 98072
phone: 425-483-2800
web: www.elevationcellars.com
e-mail: wine@elevationcellars.com
fee: Tasting fee refunded with purchase
hours: Saturday 12–5:30 or by appointment
amenities: Mailing List, Wheelchair Accessible
connect: f

Tenor Wines 26

TENOR WINES
winemaker(s): Aryn Morell
location: 19495 144th Ave NE, Suite A-120,
Woodinville, WA 98072
phone: 425-974-9515
web: www.tenorwines.com
e-mail: eric@tenorwines.com
fee: Tasting fee refunded with purchase
hours: Saturday 12–6 and by appointment
amenities: Mailing List, Online Store, RV/Bus Parking,
Wheelchair Accessible, Wine Club
connect: 🐦 📘

www.winetrailsnw.com/wineries/tenor_wines

Flying Dreams Winery 27

I love the name, but must confess that I thought it had to do with the phenomenon of "flying winemakers." Such winemakers follow the harvest. In North America, our harvest is September to November, whereas in South America it is the opposite — March through May.

But I discovered, however, that energetic Leroy Radford of Flying Dreams Winery named his winery in reference to taking a leap of faith, or "leap and find your wings on the way down," which requires major intestinal fortitude rather than competence in speaking Spanish. Note: speaking of leaping, Leroy was a former dancer with NYC-based Twyla Tharp Dance in the early 80s.

Leroy Radford

Speaking of Spanish, it's noteworthy that Leroy has a predilection for grape varieties of Spanish origin, including tempranillo, garnacha and Monastrell (aka grenache and Mourvèdre, respectively, in France). His recently released 2011 tempranillo relies on grapes from Stone Tree, Hedges, and Stillwater Creek vineyards to create a wine with raspberry and tobacco flavors, soft tannins, and a lingering finish. **Suggestion**: Try a side-by-side tasting with Oregon's Abacela Vineyard & Winery's tempranillo — same grape variety, but distinctly different *terroirs*.

Also noteworthy during my visit was the sauvignon blanc, which I have been drinking much of lately. Nicely crisp with lots of pear on the palate, this wine really highlights the characteristics of Washington's version of sauvignon blanc. Note: I say "Washington's version" not with negative connotations, but rather to distinguish it from the grassy, tart-like sauvignon blanc of New Zealand. I felt that Flying Dreams' take on sauvignon blanc would pair with all things summer, especially a fresh, bright green salad with grilled chicken and Gorgonzola cheese. At $19 a bottle, I scribbled the following entry in my notebook, "Get before they run out!"

FLYING DREAMS WINERY
opened: 2008
winemaker(s): Leroy Radford
location: 19495 144th Avenue NE, Suite A-140, Woodinville, WA 98072
phone: 425-402-6300
web: www.flyingdreamswine.com
e-mail: leroy@flyingdreamswine.com
fee: Tasting fee refunded with purchase
hours: Saturday and Sunday 1–5 or by appointment
amenities: Mailing List, RV/Bus Parking, Wheelchair Accessible, Wine Club
connect: 🐦 f

Page Cellars 28

2007
THE NORSEMAN
RED MOUNTAIN MERLOT

ALC. 14.4% BY VOL.

Jim and Rothelle Page launched Page Cellars from the garage of their Gig Harbor house back in 2000. Jim, a corporate pilot, had the pleasure of transporting Eric Dunham (Dunham Cellars) and Matt Loso (winemaker for Matthews Cellar at the time) to a wine event in Florida. They struck up a conversation about winemaking and not long thereafter, Jim hired Matt as a consultant winemaker. You could say that Jim caught the wine bug at 30,000 feet.

A few vintages later, Jim and Rothelle transplanted their winemaking operations to the Warehouse District in Woodinville, and have been pouring (and winning awards) ever since. Many fans come to Page Cellars to stock up on its signature cabernet dubbed Preface. Here's what The Pour Fool of the *Seattle P-I* had to say about Jim's '07 Preface: "The Preface Cabernet Sauvignon Red Mountain 2007 shows the lovely balance of all its predecessors, but does it in a deeper, less ebullient way, expressing a canoe-load of black fruit flavors, dried fig, caramel, coffee, something faintly like grilled meat, and a fine, fleeting note of pomegranate on the finish." He had me at "canoe-load."

Primarily relying on fruit from the Red Mountain AVA, Page Cellars also offers red blends, cabernet franc, and sauvignon blanc. And as for its syrah, the Pages say, "The 'Lick My Lips Syrah' speaks for itself!"

This is a working winery, complete with production area, barrel storage and tasting room all packed into a relatively small space. Don't be surprised to find Jim operating a forklift, while Rothelle greets people with bottle in hand. She's a natural at making people feel at home. Even with other tasters in the room, she talks to you as if no one else was there. Simply said, this is a must-see hidden gem in the Woodinville wine scene.

PAGE CELLARS
opened: 2000
winemaker(s): Jim Page
location: 19495 144th Avenue NE, Suite B-205, Woodinville, WA 98072
phone: 253-232-9463
web: www.pagecellars.com
e-mail: info@pagecellars.com
fee: Tasting fee
hours: Saturday 12–4; Sunday 1–5
amenities: Online Store, Wheelchair Accessible, Wine Club

Jim Page

Red Sky Winery

One evening, while enjoying a glass of wine under a red-sky sunset in eastern Washington, Jim and Carol Parsons made the decision to start a winery. They clinked glasses in a toast to their dreams on that night in 1999, and Red Sky Winery was born.

The Parsons' love affair with wine began back in 1982 when they opened a retail wine and cheese shop in Seattle. Eventually they collaborated with friends to produce 50 cases of Red Sky wine in their Bellevue basement in 1999. It must have tasted pretty darned good, because they haven't looked back.

WineTrail lovers will appreciate the fact that Red Sky's grapes come from such vineyards as Boushey, Conner Lee, Dineen, Klipsun, Chelle den Pleasant, Pepper Bridge, Rosebud, and Sheridan vineyards. To coax the best flavors from these grapes, the Parsons needed a great winemaker, which they found in John Ogburn, Boeing's master chef for its ship. (That's right, Boeing apparently takes every part of the word "aeronautical" to heart, with a seagoing corporate yacht.) John helped them get the winemaking ball rolling, but soon Carol took over the vintner's reins for the winery. Today, she and a host of volunteers produce 1,000 cases of rich and elegant Red Sky wines with a definite leaning toward Bordeaux varietals.

RED SKY WINERY
opened: 1999
winemaker(s): Carol Parsons
location: 19495 144th Avenue NE, Suite B-210, Woodinville, WA 98072
phone: 425-481-9864
web: www.redskywinery.com
e-mail: contact@redskywinery.com
fee: Tasting fee refunded with purchase
hours: Saturday 12–4 (Open Sunday during summer)
amenities: Wine Club, Online Store, Wheelchair Accessible
connect: 🐦 f

Obelisco Estate 30

Doug Long gets it. He understands that it all starts in the vineyard. Yes, you can make bad wine from terrific grapes, but you can't make good wine from bad grapes. Even the Romans understood the importance of the vineyard when they called their renowned Falernian wine "first growth." This "cult wine" was the precursor of the future premier cru in France. So when Doug retired from his retirement, he knew what he was looking for, and the place he chose to begin his new venture was 30 acres of premium wine-grape land smack dab in the Red Mountain appellation.

The vineyard was planted in 2004, and by third leaf (depending on how you're counting), Obelisco had its first vintage. As proof positive that it all starts in the vineyard, that first vintage took home the double gold from the Seattle Wine Awards. Not bad.

However, to create prized wine from prized grapes you need a winemaker to bring out the grape's true expression, or *terroir*. For this, Doug turned to Pete Hedges (Hedges Family Estate) and Sarah Goedhart (Goedhart Family winery). As winemakers for Hedges Family Estate, Pete and Sarah already have a proven track record for creating award-winning wines. Of equal importance is their intimate understanding of the Red Mountain AVA and its "*terroir*-ocity."

Be sure to check out the local artwork that graces the walls of Obelisco's Woodinville tasting room. But do so with a sample of its decadent Electrum cabernet-based wine. Swirl while you take in the art, allowing the wine open up a bit before indulging your palate.

OBELISCO ESTATE
opened: 2010
winemaker(s): Doug Long
location: 19495 144th Avenue NE, Suite B-220, Woodinville, WA 98072
phone: 425-485-2472
web: www.obelisco-estate.com
e-mail: Via website
fee: Tasting fee
hours: Saturday and Sunday 1–4 or by appointment
amenities: Newsletter/Blog, Online Store, Wheelchair Accessible, Wine Club
connect: 🐦 📘

Robert Ramsay Cellars

Bob Harris named the winery after his great-uncle Mason Ramsay, a teacher, mentor, and nurturer of creative talents — and Scottish, to boot. This is a small-lot winery with limited production of syrah, cabernet sauvignon, and Mourvèdre. It's a Scottish-American twist with a decidedly French accent.

Definitely go for the syrah and, in particular, experience the syrah from Horse Heaven Hills' McKinley Springs vineyard. Bob's fermented blend of syrah and viognier relies on Old World winemaking techniques from the northern Rhône region of France. When you think about Washington wine, what varietal best represents the state industry? Oregon has pinot noir, Argentina produces Malbec, and Italy grows its sangiovese. The question for many is what variety emerges as Washington's premier grape. Why not syrah? It grows crazy wild in eastern Washington, and people snap it up. Moreover, it goes great with Northwest cuisine.

Where does Bob Harris want to take his winery? How big? How will he distinguish his winery? There are gazillion small-lot wineries that create wine using Columbia Valley grapes. What will Bob want to do from a marketing perspective to rise above the fray? Perhaps a

distinguished label, a novel way to bottle his juice, high scores from Robert Parker. Bob has these questions and many more to mull over going forward. That's the next phase in the life cycle of Robert Ramsay Cellars, and for this observer, it's going to be fun watching the evolution unfold.

ROBERT RAMSAY CELLARS
winemaker(s): Robert Ramsay
location: 19495 144th Avenue NE, Suite C-235, Woodinville, WA 98072
phone: 425-686-9463
web: www.robertramsaycellars.com
e-mail: sales@robertramsaycellars.com
fee: Tasting fee refunded with purchase
hours: Friday 3–7, Saturday 12–5, Sunday 1–4
amenities: Wheelchair Accessible
connect: ⑤

Gård Vintners

32

GÅRD

LAWRENCE VINEYARDS

2007
CABERNET SAUVIGNON
COLUMBIA VALLEY

750ML   13.9% ALC. BY VOL.

GÅRD VINTNERS
opened: 2006
winemaker(s): Aryn Morell
location: 19151 144th Avenue NE, Unit D,
Woodinville, WA 98072
phone: 509-346-2585
web: www.gardvintners.com
e-mail: josh@gardvintners.com
fee: Tasting fee refunded with purchase
hours: Fridays 2–7; Saturdays and Sundays 12–6
amenities: Mailing List, Online Store, Private Events,
RV/Bus Parking, Wheelchair Accessible, Wine Club
connect: f

www.winetrailsnw.com/wineries/gård_vintners

Smasne Cellars

33

SMASNE CELLARS
opened: 2010
winemaker(s): Robert O. Smasne
location: 19151 144th Avenue NE, Unit D,
Woodinville, WA 98072
phone: 425-485-9461
web: www.smasnecellars.com
e-mail: via website
fee: Tasting fee
hours: Friday 2–7, Saturday and Sunday 12–6
amenities: Mailing List, Online Store, Private Events,
RV/Bus Parking, Wheelchair Accessible, Wine Club
connect: 🐦 f

www.winetrailsnw.com/wineries/smasne_cellars

Warehouse District
South
WineTrail

Sometimes referred to as the Warehouse District "annex," this group of wineries features a number of outstanding wines to explore. If suburban industrial ever becomes chic, this WineTrail will be high on the "glamour scale." Prepare to see lots of bay doors opening to small production areas containing wine barrels stacked to the ceiling. All of these wineries have one thing in common — they all source their grapes from Washington's Columbia Valley. However, the similarity ends there; each winery showcases the winemaker's personal style and varietal focus. For the most part, these wineries are open on weekends only, with the ubiquitous sandwich board announcing which is open.

Warehouse District WineTrail South

1. Finn Hill Winery
2. Convergence Zone Cellars
3. Kaella Winery
4. Aspenwood Cellars
5. Auclair Winery
6. Chatter Creek Winery
7. Sheridan Vineyard
8. Two Vintners Winery
9. Covington Cellars
10. Barons Winery
11. Pomum Cellars
12. Stevens Winery

Region:	**Woodinville Wine Country**
# of tasting rooms on tour:	**12**
Estimate # of days for tour:	**3**
Getting around:	**Car and foot**
Key Events:	❑ **St. Nicholas Day Open House (December) and Passport to Woodinville (April) — both sponsored by Woodinville Wine Country. See www.woodinvillewinecountry.com for details and ticket information.**
Tips:	❑ **Experience the 3rd Thursday Wine Walk — see www.woodwarewine.com for details.**
	❑ **Woodinville offers a variety of restaurants: Some popular places include the Barking Frog, Pasta Nova, Garden Café in Mobaks, The Herbfarm at Willows Lodge, Italianissimo Ristorante, and Purple Café & Wine Bar.**
	❑ **Consider hiring a limousine service, such as, Bon Vivant 206-437-1298, Bayview Limo Service 206-223-6200, Butler Seattle 206-233-9233 or 425-883-0850, EverGreen Escapes 206-650-5796 or 866-203-7603, and Winery Bus 425-481-8860.**

Finn Hill Winery

Visitors to the Finn Hill tasting room are welcomed by a red-hatted greeter of sorts. It's a gnome statue, the kind made famous in the Travelocity ads featuring the roaming gnome.

"What's with the gnome?" I asked the man working behind the wine bar. "It references the winery's namesake — Finn Hill. The winery began in the Finn Hill area of Kirkland, where the original settlers were from Finland. In Finland, gnomes protect owners' homes. It's part of their mythical lore."

The man expanding my education was Rob Entrekin, co-owner (along with his wife, Karen) and winemaker for Finn Hill Winery, now in Woodinville. He wanted to pay homage to the place where he began his winery, which happened to be a two-car garage turned production area/barrel room/crush pad in Kirkland's Finn Hill neighborhood. That sounds about right. In the wine world, many a winery takes its name from its original stomping ground.

Rob has a biomedical engineering background and keeps his day job at Phillips Healthcare so that he's not completely dependent upon the winery for a livable income. His objective is to make wine that pleases his palate, with an emphasis on Bordeaux varietal wines minus the heavy oak monster. Translation: lighter, food-friendly wines.

Now comfortably ensconced in his 1,800-square-foot winery/tasting room, Rob continues his quest to produce wine from a wide array of grape varieties. Although Finn Hill Winery produces fewer than 500 cases annually, visitors will discover a nice portfolio of wines to sample, including chardonnay, petit verdot, cabernet sauvignon, merlot, and a Bordeaux blend appropriately named Le Rouge.

Speaking of, as I sipped my 1-ounce pour of Le Rouge, I could have sworn that the grinning garden gnome was keeping a protective eye on me.

FINN HILL WINERY
opened: 2012
winemaker(s): Rob Entrekin
location: 18899 142nd Avenue NE, Suite 5A, Woodinville, WA 98072
phone: 206-409-4378
web: www.finnhillwinery.com
e-mail: finnhillwinery@gmail.com
fee: Tasting fee refunded with purchase
hours: Saturday 12–5
amenities: Art Gallery, Mailing List, Wheelchair Accessible
connect: 🐦 📘

Convergence Zone Cellars ②

As Wikipedia explains it, "The Puget Sound Convergence Zone occurs when winds in the upper atmosphere are split by the Olympic Mountains. The winds then converge beyond the mountains, producing convection uplift that results in the development of clouds and even stormy weather." That's the long version of the bumper sticker message "Weather Happens."

In the case of owner/winemaker Scott Greenberg, we suspect that there are several converging factors: a meeting of his western Washington winemaking skills and eastern Washington fruit; the combining of grapes from different viticultural areas in the Columbia Valley; a melding of art and science; and a convergence of Old World winemaking techniques involving a wine press, oak barrels, 750-milliliter bottles and Portuguese cork; and in-depth understanding of fermentation science. What all of this ferments to is this: Scott's wines are a blend of his extensive background and Mother Nature's gifts.

Scott's full-time job as a planner for the City of Burien precludes him from being at the winery full-time. In fact, his Warehouse District tasting room is open only on Saturdays, and that's contingent on having wine to sell. That's right, when you produce fewer than 500 cases per year (of mostly red wines) there's a good chance your stock will sell out. But the location of his winery in the Warehouse District among a couple of dozen other small-lot wineries has distinct advantages. For instance, you can share in the cost of a forklift or lend another winemaker your wine cap punch-down tool; you can exchange ideas, such as where best to buy next year's bottles, and get advice for problems such as restarting a stuck fermentation. It's a convergence of like-minded souls sharing a common challenge: how to make really great wine.

Scott Greenberg

CONVERGENCE ZONE CELLARS
opened: 2010
winemaker(s): Scott Greenberg
location: 18800 142nd Avenue NE, Suite 5B, Woodinville, WA 98072
phone: 425-233-5638
web: www.czcellars.com
e-mail: scott@czcellars.com
fee: Tasting fee refunded with purchase
hours: Saturday 12–5; 3rd Thursday of each month 4–8 and by appointment
amenities: Live Music, RV/Bus Parking, Wheelchair Accessible
connect: 🐦 📘

Kaella Winery ❸

"Look here, at the label, what do you see?" asked co-owner/winemaker Dave Butner. I stared at what appeared to be a wine goblet on the Kaella label and thought that it was either a trick question or some sort of Rorschach test that would expose my inner child. At last, I said rather sheepishly, "I just see a wine goblet." To which he responded, "There's that,

too, but the 'wine glass' you see are the profiles of our two youngest daughters, Katelyn and Ellen." He went on to explain that the winery's name is a contraction of sorts of their two youngest daughters' names.

Despite Kaella having won a gold medal from the Seattle Wine Awards for its 2011 Rosé of Sangiovese, I was fortunate that some cases of it were still in stock when I visited. As Dave poured, my eyes were transfixed by the wine's beautiful strawberry color, and a sip of this crisp, refreshing drink prompted me to respond, "Delicious!" to Dave's question "What do you think?"

When visiting small-lot wineries, WineTrail trekkers should expect the possibility of depleted inventory — it's the nature of the business.

Dave Butner

And with Kaella's production of only 500 cases a year, you can expect these wines to disappear quickly, especially when they are collecting medals from the likes of Seattle Wine Awards as they did with their 2009 Cabernet Franc.

Dave is quick to point out that it all starts in the vineyard, specifically Columbia Valley vineyards. He and Nancy, his spouse and winery co-owner, make numerous forays during the year to esteemed vineyards — such as Conner Lee, Ciel du Cheval, and Ambassador to choose their grapes. It truly is a collaborative relationship between winemaker and grape grower, and the trust that the winemakers have for their grape-growing partners is fundamental to their success.

KAELLA WINERY
opened: 2010
winemaker(s): Dave Butner
location: 18800 142nd Avenue NE, Suite 5B, Woodinville, WA 98072
phone: 425-241-8585
web: www.kaellawinery.com
e-mail: info@kaellawinery.com
fee: Tasting fee refunded with purchase
hours: Saturday 1–5
amenities: Live Music, Mailing List, Wheelchair Accessible
connect: 🐦 f

Aspenwood Cellars

I surveyed the tasting sheet and noted that one of the wines had the name "Bubba's Best." Naturally, that prompted me to ask winemaker/owner Jim Petty how that moniker came about.

"There's a story there" was Jim's response. I grabbed my pen, knowing that I'd need to write furiously. "A few years back, my Boeing friend Wayne and I went to eastern Washington to get some grapes at harvest. I bought 40 small bins [called lugs]

Jim Petty

of grapes, and we filled my van with all these lugs. We got back home to my Aspenwood neighborhood and crushed all the bins of grapes, and then I spent a lot of time cleaning the crusher/destemmer. I was pretty much done when Wayne came from the van bearing one more lug of grapes. Somewhat dismayed, I told him it was too late. I had just spent a lot of time cleaning the equipment, and we might as well toss the grapes. Well, Wayne would not have any of that. He started crushing the grapes by hand and seeing that, I joined in. Together we crushed the last bin of grapes by hand and added them to the batch. I realized then just what a dear friend Wayne was to me. He became my 'Bubba,' and I mean that in an endearing way."

Jim had other stories to tell in his own inimitable Brooklyn way, but there's not enough space here to share them. Let's just say that visitors to the Warehouse District "annex" (as Jim refers to it) are in for a real treat. Yes, there are plenty of luscious wines to explore, but equally important are the tales that Jim tells, each of them shaping the winery and adding texture to the juice inside the bottles.

ASPENWOOD CELLARS
winemaker(s): Jim Petty
location: 18642 142nd Avenue NE, Woodinville, WA 98072
phone: 425-844-2233
web: www.aspenwoodcellars.com
e-mail: woodinvilleman@hotmail.com
fee: Tasting fee refunded with purchase
hours: Saturday 12–5
amenities: Wheelchair Accessible

Auclair Winery 🖲

Charlie Auclair is his name, and wine is his game. This rather unassuming 40-something winemaker caught the proverbial wine bug in 1988 during a visit to Napa. Fortunately for WineTrail trekkers, he elected to move to western Washington in 1992. Thereafter ensued a multitude of visits to many of the world's great wine-growing regions, including Australia's

Charlie Auclair

Barossa and Yarra valleys, and South Africa's Stellenbosch and Constantia appellations. He also ventured to Spain and France, but didn't make it to Bordeaux.

At least not yet.

Auclair Winery's focus on Bordeaux varietals, such as merlot, cabernet sauvignon, cabernet franc, and sauvignon blanc, demonstrate Charlie's palate preference. It also reflects his easy access to Columbia Valley's prime vineyards, with most fruit derived from Red Mountain's Artz Vineyard, a vineyard many wine critics believe produces Washington's finest cabernet sauvignon and merlot.

I tasted Charlie's pleasingly refreshing Auclair sauvignon blanc, which possesses some notable grapefruit and honey notes, and prompted visions of pairing it with ceviche. Next up was his delectable Auclair Right Blend Bordeaux (as in "right bank"), oh so chewy, with loads of dark berry flavors showcasing Artz Vineyard's merlot. There followed an equally bold Left Blend Bordeaux, with a layered complexity of black currant and noticeable anise. (He must have sensed that I'm a sucker for anything licorice.) Priced in the mid-$40 range, these red blends might be a bit steep for most mortals, especially those seeking an everyday wine.

To meet the demand for a more wallet-friendly wine, Charlie vinifies a second label, dubbed 96 Cedars — so called because he planted 100 cedar saplings on his property, and 96 managed to grow. At $25 a bottle, the 96 Cedars merlot proves to have just as much muscle as the higher-priced version and is as packed with fruit as the more expensive Right version.

AUCLAIR WINERY
opened: 2008
winemaker(s): Charlie Auclair
location: 18654 142nd Avenue NE, Woodinville, WA 98072
phone: 425-501-8099
web: www.auclairwinery.com
e-mail: Auclairwinery@comcast.net
fee: Tasting fee refunded with purchase
hours: Most Saturdays 12–5 or by appointment
amenities: Wheelchair Accessible, Wine Club
connect: 🐦 f

Chatter Creek Winery 🖸

A self-described "terroirist" and curmudgeon, Gordon "Gordy" Rawson isn't your typical winemaker. His personality is reflected in his distinctive single-vineyard wines, his eye-catching labels, and his anything-goes manner of speech.

As a Seattle boy, Gordy would seem ill suited to toil among the chardonnay-and-Brie crowd in suburban Woodinville. But he has managed to make the State Route 520 commute for many years, which included

Gordon Rawson

driving to a stint as the cellar master at Columbia Winery, where he worked with David Lake (now deceased) and company.

Chatter Creek produces about 2,000 cases of wine each year, and if all 2,000 cases were suddenly to appear in my backyard — along with the mandatory corkscrew — I would indeed be a happy man!

Gordy's portfolio of wines includes orange muscat, viognier, grenache, syrah, cabernet franc, and cabernet sauvignon, and several others, from vineyards such as Lonesome Spring Ranch and Clifton Hill in the Columbia Valley. These wines exhibit the true *terroir* of the different viticultural areas of Washington.

Chatter Creek "Wine Diva" visitors

CHATTER CREEK WINERY
opened: 2000
winemaker(s): Gordon Rawson
location: 18658 142nd Avenue NE, Building East, Woodinville, WA 98072-8521
phone: 206-985-2816
web: www.chattercreek.com
e-mail: gordy@chattercreek.com
fee: Complimentary wine tasting
hours: Saturday 11–5
amenities: Tours, Wheelchair Accessible
connect: 🐦 📘

Sheridan Vineyard 7

Sheridan Vineyard Winery

There are many reasons why someone would start a winery, but sometimes it can be as simple as a philosophy. In the case of Sheridan Vineyard, it's a philosophy that wine should be shaped by the vineyard that surrounds the winery, and Sheridan Vineyard happens to produce excellent grapes.

In 1996, owner and winemaker Scott Greer acquired 76 acres of land in the Yakima Valley known as Sheridan Vineyard. Thus began his quest to exhibit the surprisingly intense flavors of the grapes grown in this part of the upper Yakima Valley by making wine under the Sheridan Vineyard label. Low yields of grapes on a per-acre basis result in fruit that is deeply red — almost black — and harboring huge flavors.

Scott Greer is a self-taught winemaker, but after more than 15 years of making wine, his former life in finance must be a distant memory. Fortunately, Scott's winemaking skills have been honed by drawing upon the experience of a number of industry leaders. We're sure, for example, that Scott has drawn from his friendship with fellow vintner Tim Stevens of Stevens Winery fame. In fact, a look at Sheridan's wine label reveals two children stomping grapes. The two kids are a depiction of Scott's children, an image taken from a sculpture executed by Tim.

Scott's spirit and strength are embodied in his wine L'Orage (French for "The Storm), the end result of a small harvest following a major hail storm in 2001 that essentially wiped out his vineyard. Rather than being deterred by the storm, Scott was bound and determined to make wine that year, and in subsequent years. L'Orage, a blend of cabernet sauvignon and cabernet franc, is the product of that determination.

With every sip of Scott's wines, the words power, beauty, and balance come to mind. A poetic drink.

SHERIDAN VINEYARD
opened: 2005
winemaker(s): Scott Greer
location: 18564 142nd Avenue NE, Woodinville, WA 98072
phone: 425-401-0167
web: www.sheridanvineyard.com
e-mail: info@sheridanvineyard.com
fee: Tasting fee may apply
hours: Saturday 1–5
amenities: Wheelchair Accessible, Wine Club

Two Vintners Winery

How's this for a company overview: "Two guys making wine, livin' the dream." Simple and to the point, the two guys in this case are Morgan Lee and Donavon Claflin. Morgan is the chief vintner, and the two men met and continue to work at Covington Cellars, just next-door.

The main greeter for the winery deserves special acknowledgment since one of the wines is named for her — Lola, the black Lab. Lola quietly goes about her business of making young and old feel at ease and accepting all belly rubs with gratitude. Not coincidentally, the aforementioned wine, affectionately named Lola (a half cab/half syrah blend), is one of Two Vintners' most popular. One sip led to a full glass pour, and now I'm a big fan — of the wine and the dog.

Morgan Lee

Inside this spacious tasting room/storage site in the Warehouse District are tables for enjoying a glass of wine; a large TV screen for watching sports events, rock concerts or whatever; and, in the back of the tasting room behind a curtain, a playground for children. It's a rare thing to find a winery that's kid friendly, but Two Vintners fits the bill.

Morgan Lee, a graduate of Purdue University, worked at Columbia Crest before joining Covington Cellars as its winemaker. Now as the vintner for Two Vintners, Morgan relies on fruit from eight different Columbia Valley vineyards, including StoneTree Vineyard — a renowned vineyard in the Wahluke Slope that is noticeably hotter than most vineyards.

Be sure to bring your wallet to pick up a few (or more) bottles of their $13 Make Haste red blend. This is a mystery wine; Morgan won't reveal what grape variety he used to make the wine, but he does confess that the image of the leaping suit-clad man on the bottle is from his wedding invitation. Make Haste my man!

Lola

TWO VINTNERS WINERY
winemaker(s): Morgan Lee
location: 18572 142nd Avenue NE, Woodinville, WA 98072
phone: 425-361-9746
web: www.twovintners.com
e-mail: morgan@twovintners.com
fee: Tasting fee refunded with purchase
hours: Saturday 12–5
amenities: Picnic Area, RV/Bus Parking, Wheelchair Accessible, Wine Club, Wines by the Glass
connect:

Covington Cellars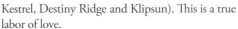

David Lawson

Covington Cellars is a family affair and a true labor of love. Founded in 2002 by David and Cindy Lawson, this is the story of a beer guy who meets a wine woman and falls in love with both her and the wine. Ever the tinkerer that he is, David began experimenting at the house in Covington and one good success lead to another and a few UC Davis courses later Covington Cellars was born.

Cindy is usually working the Tuscan-inspired tasting room while David and David Junior are handling the ongoing stream of winemaking chores in the back. The warm colors of the tasting room are a pleasant switch from the asphalt parking lot at the 142nd Avenue business park. And while David's job as an elevator mechanic during the day is up-and-down, his winemaking duties are often back-and-forth as he travels to Walla Walla and Yakima Valley to collaborate with their growers (e.g., Seven Hills, Les Collines, Kestrel, Destiny Ridge and Klipsun). This is a true labor of love.

David explains that Covington Cellars is a "hobby gone mad" and is quick to point out that Cindy is the business brains behind the operation and that his winemaking efforts are also an opportunity to give back. For example, mindful of his Naval Reserve involvement, David produces a Rough House Red as a tribute to US Armed Forces. This wine is dedicated to the men, women, and families who have served or who are serving in the Armed Forces.

David's loyalty to family and the US has in turn spawned a loyal following of Covington Cellars buyers. At Passport to Woodinville, the line to sample his reds snakes out the tasting room to the outside parking lot. They must be doing something right. Check it out. That's an order!

COVINGTON CELLARS
opened: 2002
winemaker(s): David Lawson and Morgan Lee
location: 18580 142nd Avenue NE, Woodinville, WA 98072-8520
phone: 425-806-8636
web: www.covingtoncellars.com
e-mail: cindy@covingtoncellars.com
fee: Tasting fee refunded with purchase
hours: Friday 1–5, Saturday: 12–5, and Sunday 1–5 or by appointment
amenities: Mailing List, Restaurant/Food Pairings, Wheelchair Accessible, Wine Club
connect: 🐦 📘

Barons Winery 🔟

Imagine having the coin to create your own private winery for your personal consumption as well as that of others, and then having the good fortune to find some passionate partners, ones with deep pockets, and hiring one of Washington's top winemakers to make premium cabernet. For this fantasy wine, you would need a label and name to slap on the bottle, something that has a rather regal ring to it — Barons, perhaps.

That's precisely what Washington wine advocate Gary McLean did back in 2001 when he spearheaded the creation of Barons V — the "V" representing five partners whom he assembled to create their private label. He also secured the services of renowned winemaker Matthew Loso.

The Warehouse District location of Barons Winery includes more than an intimate tasting room; it also serves as the winemaking facility, with plenty of stainless steel tanks and stacked barrels occupying the production area. Of course any field trip to this winery must also include a gander at Barons' cement egg for fermenting wine, a tool that is used in France but rarely seen in America.

The egg is unusual in itself, but a closer inspection of the stored barrels reveals that most of them are of American origin. For his cabernet, Matthew relies on a recipe that calls for two years in the barrel, followed by one year in the bottle, but in this case he eschews French oak in favor of American oak for his cabernet sauvignon.

For $45 a bottle, you can take home a 750-milliliter bottle of Barons V Columbia Valley cabernet sauvignon to accompany your meat-studded cassoulet. While you savor the pairing, you can dream of starting a winery with Matthew as your winemaker. All you need is that winning lottery number and you'll be set!

BARONS WINERY
opened: 2001
winemaker(s): Matthew Loso
location: 18506 142nd Avenue NE, Woodinville, WA 98072
phone: 425-398-7147
web: www.baronsv.com
e-mail: info@baronsv.com
fee: Tasting fee refunded with purchase
hours: Saturday and Sunday 12–5
amenities: Online Store, RV/Bus Parking, Wheelchair Accessible
connect: 🐦 f

Pomum Cellars 🗓

"As a kid in Spain, I hated going to our family vineyard. It meant hours of work, and I dreaded going there," noted Javier Alfonso of Pomum Cellars. So who would have guessed at the time that decades later, Javier would be in little ol' Woodinville, Washington, making

Javier Alfonso

premium wine that reflects his Spanish heritage. Indeed, Spain's Ribera del Duero, from where Javier hails, has a rich heritage of growing tempranillo — Spain's noble grape.

Pursuing a degree in mechanical engineering from the University of Washington, Javier met his future wife, Shylah, and both found a common interest in Washington wines. From a garage operation to a commercial winery, Pomum Cellars has always relied on Yakima Valley vineyards, including Upland, DuBrul, and Dineen.

It's this dry, desert-like land that reminds Javier of the high desert terrain of the Ribera del Duero; both are defined by hot daytime summer temperatures giving way to cool nights, and both are conductive to growing tempranillo.

With access to a variety of premium grapes, Pomum Cellars is not an exclusive "Iberian Peninsula varietal zone," as you might have thought. Indeed, Javier makes a delightful off-dry riesling, with a balance of acidity and sweetness to provide a refreshing drink. His lush and decadent (imagine cherry-infused chocolate with soft tannins) Shya Red is viewed by many as his signature wine. And no, "Shya" is not a typo — Shyla's nickname as a child was Shya.

But this WineTrail trekker must confess to falling in love with Pomum Cellars' tempranillo. I'm so infatuated that I have revised my bucket list to place Spain in my top three great wine regions of the world to visit. But while I'm stateside, I'll fulfill my Spanish dining fantasy by devouring *mucho paella* accompanied by a generous pour of Pomum Cellars' gorgeous tempranillo.

POMUM CELLARS
opened: 2008
winemaker(s): Javier Alfonso
location: 18512 142nd Avenue NE, Woodinville, WA 98072
phone: 206-362-9203
web: www.pomumcellars.com
e-mail: info@pomumcellars.com
fee: Tasting fee refunded with purchase
hours: Saturday 12–5 or by appointment
amenities: Mailing List, RV/Bus Parking, Wheelchair Accessible
connect: 🐦 📘

Stevens Winery

WineTrail trekkers know two tendencies that are common among most Washington wineries: First, the vast majority of winemakers/owners are friendly people with a healthy dose of passion. Second, winemakers have divergent backgrounds and often arrive at winemaking from different paths. Such is the case with Stevens Winery, where owners Tim and Paige Stevens welcome each visitor to their Woodinville tasting room with a friendly, "glad to see you" smile.

Tim and Paige Stevens

Prior to launching Stevens Winery, Tim had been a commercial artist, dabbled in the restaurant business, earned an English degree, and got his fingers dirty at Sheridan Vineyards in Zillah. It was at Sheridan Vineyards, under the tutelage of Scott Greer, that Tim caught a bad case of the wine bug.

Stevens Winery focuses on big reds. Using grapes from the Yakima Valley, Tim crafts premium syrahs, cabernet sauvignons, merlots, and cabernet francs. In particular, Stevens Winery has gained a reputation for its Stevens424 red blend (named for the fact that Stevens Winery is the 424th bonded winery in Washington). In terms of names, though, their Black Tongue syrah takes the prize!

Incidentally, for each wine produced, Tim creates original artwork for the label of each. It's just one more role for Tim the winemaker/artist/grower/English major/father/husband/waiter — a true renaissance man.

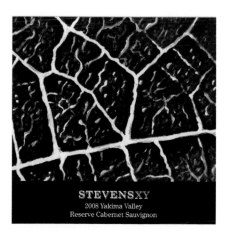

STEVENSXY
2008 Yakima Valley
Reserve Cabernet Sauvignon

STEVENS WINERY
opened: 2002
winemaker(s): Tim Stevens
location: 18510 142nd Avenue NE, Woodinville, WA 98072
phone: 425-424-9463
web: www.stevenswinery.com
e-mail: info@stevenswinery.com
fee: Complimentary wine tasting
hours: Saturday 12–4
amenities: Mailing List, RV/Bus Parking, Wheelchair Accessible
connect: f

Other Wineries to Visit

ADAMS BENCH
winemaker(s): Tim and Erica Blue
location: 14360 160th Place NE,
Woodinville, WA 98072
phone: 425-408-1969
web: www.adamsbench.com
hours: By appointment and 12–4
most Saturdays

Photo courtesy of Adams Bench

AVENNIA
winemaker(s): Chris Peterson
location: 18808 142nd Avenue NE,
Suite 2B, Woodinville, WA 98072
phone: 425-877-1639
web: www.avennia.com
hours: By appointment only

BETZ FAMILY WINERY
winemaker(s): Bob Betz
location: 13244 Woodinville Redmond
Road NE, Redmond, WA 98052
phone: 425-861-9823
web: www.betzfamilywinery.com
hours: Open twice yearly on mailing
list Release Weekends

DOMAINE STE. MICHELLE
winemaker(s): Rick Casqueiro
location: 14111 NE 145th Street,
Woodinville, WA 98072
phone: 866-701-3187
web: www.domainestemichelle.com
hours: Daily 10–5

Bob Betz

EROICA
winemaker(s): Ernst Loosen and
Bob Bertheau
location: 14111 NE 145th Street,
Woodinville, WA 98072
phone: 425-488-1133
web: www.ste-michelle.com
hours: Daily 10–5

Other Wineries to Visit

GIRLY GIRL WINES

location: 15029 Woodinville-Redmond Road NE, Woodinville, WA 98072
hours: Monday through Saturday 11–5, Sunday 12–5

GLEN FIONA

winemaker(s): William Ammons
location: 15029 Woodinville Redmond Road NE, Woodinville, WA 98072
phone: 509-522-2566
web: www.glenfiona.com
hours: 11–4 Saturday and Sunday; first weekend in May is Spring Release; Holiday Barrel Tasting in December; or by appointment

KEVIN WHITE WINERY

winemaker(s): Kevin White
location: 19501 144th Avenue NE, Suite F-100, Woodinville, WA 98072
phone: 206-992-5746
web: www.kevinwhitewinery.com
hours: By appointment only

Other Wineries to Visit

LAUREN ASHTON CELLARS
winemaker(s): Kit Singh
location: 19510 144th Avenue NE,
Suite D-12, Woodinville, WA 98072
phone: 206-504-8546
web: www.laurenashtoncellars.com
hours: Saturday through Sunday 12–5
or by appointment

NOVELTY HILL
winemaker(s): Mike Januik
location: 14710 Woodinville Redmond
Road NE, Woodinville, WA 98072
phone: 425-481-5502
web: www.noveltyhillwines.com
hours: Daily 11–5

LEONE ITALIAN CELLARS
location: 15029 Woodinville Redmond
Road NE,
Woodinville, WA 98072
phone: 425-485-2437 ext 109
web: www.leonecellars.com
hours: Monday through Saturday 11–5,
Sunday 12–5

TROUVAILLE WINERY
winemaker(s): Attila Kovacs-Szabo
location: 16735 NE 139th Place,
Woodinville, WA 98072
phone: 425-861-8020
web: www.trouvaillewinery.com
hours: By appointment only for
groups of 6+

Southwest Washington

WINE COUNTRY

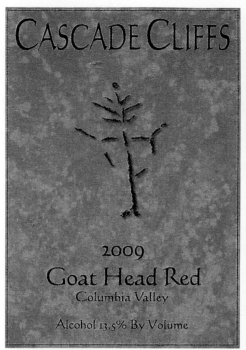

CASCADE CLIFFS

2009
Goat Head Red
Columbia Valley

Alcohol 13.5% By Volume

2010

AniChe
cellars

ATTICUS

97% Syrah, 3% Viognier
Co-fermented • Rattlesnake Hills

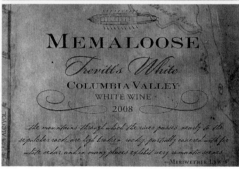

MEMALOOSE
Trevitt's White
COLUMBIA VALLEY
WHITE WINE
2008

the mountains through which the river passes nearly to the
sepulcher rock, are high broken, rocky, partially covered with fir
white cedar and in many places exhibit very romantic scenes

—MERIWETHER LEWIS

ILLUSION®

2005 Apparition®
Red table wine
Columbia Valley

Contains sulfites   Alcohol 13.5% by volume

COR
CELLARS

2009

MOMENTUM

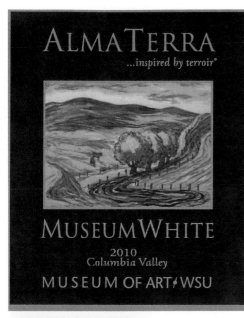

ALMATERRA
...inspired by terroir®

MUSEUMWHITE

2010
Columbia Valley

MUSEUM OF ART⁄WSU

Klickitat Canyon

Organic
Ruby Red
Wine

Columbia Gorge

Cypripedium montanum

Where the grapes speak for themselves

Alcohol 12% By Vol.

ALMATERRA
...inspired by terroir

2008 COEO
Three-Vineyard Syrah
COLUMBIA VALLEY
13.9% Alcohol by Volume

Jacob Williams

SYRAH
2009 Hi-Valley Vineyard
Alc 13.5% by Vol   Columbia Valley   750 ml

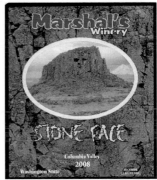

Marshal's
Winery

STONE FACE

Columbia Valley
2008

Washington State

domaine

Pouillon

KATYDID

2009

55% GRENACHE   35% SYRAH 10% MOURVEDRE

HORSE HEAVEN HILLS

PRODUCED AND BOTTLED BY DOMAINE POUILLON LYLE, WA POP. 511

CONTAINS SULFITES   750ML   ALC. 14.5% BY VOL.

WWW.DOMAINEPOUILLON.COM

Southwest
Washington
WineTrail

Photo courtesy of Westport Winery

For those adventurous souls checking out the Southwest Washington WineTrail, you're in for a real treat — especially if you combine your wine tasting with an overnight stay in the Vancouver/Portland area. There are plenty of wineries to experience but surprisingly little pinot noir to sample. I say surprisingly, since these wineries are within a couple of hours of Oregon's Willamette Valley. You'd think pinot to be the wine of choice but *au contraire, mon ami*. Most of these wineries rely on grapes harvested from the Columbia Valley. People still love their Bordeaux varieties, and these winemakers know it. Given the distance from Clark County to Lewis County, budget two or three days to soak in this WineTrail.

Southwest Washington WineTrail

1 Westport Winery
2 Heymann Whinery
3 Widgeon Hill Winery
4 Bethany Vineyard & Winery

5 Three Brothers Vineyard and Winery
6 East Fork Cellars
7 Rusty Grape Vineyard

8 Confluence Winery
9 Gouger Cellars Winery
10 English Estate Winery

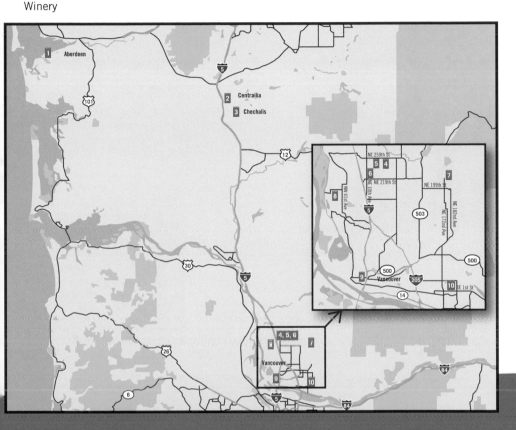

Region:	**Southwest Washington Wine Country**
# of tasting rooms on tour:	**10**
Estimate # of days for tour:	**3**
Getting around:	**Car**
Key Events:	❑ **Consult individual winery websites for events.**
Tips:	❑ **Portland metro area (including Vancouver) offers an abundance of places to stay and eat.**
	❑ **Vancouver Farmers Market offers wine tasting.**
Best:	❑ **Destination, eats: Westport Winery**
	❑ **Gift shop: Heymann Whinery**
	❑ **Weddings and picnicking: Bethany Vineyard & Winery**
	❑ **Music venue, weddings and picnicking: Three Brothers Vineyard and Winery**
	❑ **Music venue: East Fork Cellars**

Westport Winery

Westport Winery celebrates community, a seafaring history and coastal culture.

Washington's only coastal winery, Westport Winery is relatively easy to find, thanks to its 40-foot lighthouse acting as a beacon. But for travelers, discovering a vineyard and winery on Washington's coast is a bit peculiar. Indeed, most people would consider Kim and Blain Roberts certifiably cuckoo for purchasing 22 acres of overgrown land off Highway 105 in Aberdeen, Washington. After all, growing grapes in the maritime climate seems like an exercise in futility. However, Washington State University Extension agent Don Tapio encouraged them, saying, "Plant a vineyard and open a winery. It will be historic."

The grapes grown in the Roberts' Vineyards By-the-Sea are among the same varieties grown in the Loire Valley

Photos courtesy of Westport Winery

of France, such as pinot noir, riesling, chardonnay, cabernet franc, gewürztraminer, pinot gris, and Melon de Bourgogne. Fruit from their vineyard, along with Bordeaux varieties sourced from eastern Washington, are made into the wines of Westport Winery. Kim and Blain's son, Dana (a graduate of WSU's professional winemaking program) produces more than 30 different wines, which his sister Carrie pours as the manager of the tasting room. It's a true family affair, with everyone bringing a unique skill set to the mix, blending perfectly.

Despite no overnight lodging, this is a destination winery, not only for the award-winning wines, but also for the restaurant (lunch and dinner) and bakery on the premises. Hanky at the ready, imagine amaretto-coconut-chocolate-chip cookies. If that doesn't get you salivating, there are also picnic baskets of gourmet cheese, meat, crackers, chocolates and other munchies available to nosh on in the Gathering Room or to purchase to take to the beach. The food, wine and down-home country charm of Westport Winery explains why it won the title of the Best Northwest Escapes: Best Wine Tour for 2010.

WESTPORT WINERY
opened: 2007
winemaker(s): Blain and Kim Roberts
location: 1 South Arbor Road, Aberdeen, WA 98520
phone: 360-648-2224
web: www.westportwines.com
e-mail: info@westportwines.com
fee: Tasting fee refunded with purchase
hours: Daily 11–6; Extended hours Friday and Saturday from 11–8
amenities: Lodging, Picnic Area, Private Events, Restaurant/Food Pairings, RV/Bus Parking, Weddings, Wheelchair Accessible, Wine Club
connect: 🐦 📘

⭐ **BEST Destination, eats**

Heymann Whinery ❷

With the slogan "We can help you whine!" Bob and Flossie Heymann clearly convey their vision for Heymann Whinery: Don't take things — including wine — too seriously. Heymann Whinery's new tasting room location is in downtown Centralia, on North Tower Avenue. As you will discover, it is much more than a tasting room. Yes, you can sample winemaker Bob's many berry and Bordeaux-style wines, but you also can purchase a wide

variety of wine- and beer-related merchandise. Heymann has everything you need to become the neighborhood winemaker or brewmaster.

From refrigerator magnets (the type with quotations like "I love to cook with wine. Sometimes I even put it in the food.") to Betty Boop wine stoppers, Scorned Woman's Fudge, wine jelly, and sweet 'n' hot mustard, it's easy to shop for your favorite wine- or beer-loving uncle. But many visitors

come to Heymann Whinery for Bob's fruit wines, which include cranberry, raspberry, cherry, apricot, and blackberry wines, all made from Washington state fruit. However, for those WineTrail trekkers who want to stick with grape wines, Bob offers his chardonnay, cabernet sauvignon, merlot, sauvignon blanc, and riesling — all made with grapes from the Yakima Valley.

Warning: Cork dorks will need to check their attitude at the door; you're entering a "No Whining Zone."

HEYMANN WHINERY
opened: 2004
winemaker(s): Bob Heymann
location: 212 North Tower Avenue, Centralia, WA 98531
phone: 360-623-1106
web: www.heymannwinery.com
e-mail: sales@heymannwhinery.com
fee: Complimentary wine tasting
hours: Monday through Friday 11–5:30, Saturday 10–5:30, Sunday 11–4
amenities: Gift Shop, Wheelchair Accessible
connect: 🇫

⭐ **BEST Gift shop**

Widgeon Hill Winery 3

Wid-geon, *n* — a freshwater duck (Anas americana of North America) having a grayish or brownish back, and a white belly and wing coverts.

Established in 1991 by Joel Mills, Widgeon Hill Winery is located about four miles east of I-5 via exit 81, between Chehalis and Centralia. It's a little off the beaten path, but a short 10-minute drive brings you to a cozy tasting room/winery surrounded by forest. From small beginnings as an amateur winemaker to attaining a more commercial presence, Joel (and his

apprentice son, Rhett) established Widgeon Hill Winery, winning awards along the way. Sadly, Joel passed away in 2005, leaving the winery solely in the hands of Rhett to manage. While maintaining a day job as a real estate appraiser, Rhett has gone on to enhance the winery's already good reputation.

With annual production at nearly 1,000 barrels of wine, Rhett gets his grapes primarily from the Yakima Valley. For a small winery, Widgeon Hill offers an impressive array of wines, including chenin blanc, unoaked chardonnay, viognier, syrah, merlot, cabernet sauvignon, cabernet franc, zinfandel, and a red blend named Tunupa Red.

Legend has it that the old-timers feasted on the widgeon duck that populated the Salzer Valley watershed, where Widgeon Hill is located. Now, the new-timers can feast on wine at Widgeon Hill Winery. Come to think of it, a bottle of Widgeon Hill merlot would pair nicely with roasted duck!

WIDGEON HILL WINERY
opened: 1996
winemaker(s): Rhett Mills
location: 121 Widgeon Hill Road, Chehalis, WA 98532
phone: 360-520-2919
web: www.widgeonhill.com
e-mail: widgeonhillwinery@yahoo.com
fee: Complimentary wine tasting
hours: Daily 11–5
amenities: Picnic Area, Tours, Wheelchair Accessible
connect: f

Bethany Vineyard & Winery  4

Walt Houser named his vineyard and winery after the love of his life: his wife, Bethany. Another great love of his is wine, which he makes not with the aim of winning awards,

Walter Jay Houser

mind you, but for the sheer joy of it. In his younger years, Walt focused on berry wines, but he quickly moved to making premium grape wines. Nevertheless, he keeps his hand in the creation of berry wines, including a strawberry-watermelon wine that grabbed my palate's attention during a recent visit.

But it is Walt's vinifera wines that steer WineTrail lovers off Interstate 5 at Exit 14 and head them east to Bethany Vineyard & Winery. Bethany Vineyard grows 15 different varieties of wine grape, all of

them suited to southwestern Washington's cool climate. Walt is proud of the fact that all Bethany Vineyard wines include some grapes from his vineyard, which wraps around his winery and tasting room. The other grapes he uses come from Eastern Washington and go into the making of cabernet sauvignon, Malbec, merlot, and syrah. Preferring to emphasize the taste of the grape, Walt transfers his wine, after just seven months in new oak, to older, neutral oak barrels. He then allows the wine to remain in the barrels for an additional two years or longer, depending upon the varietal. The result is handcrafted, premium wines, and his no. 1 seller is his pinot noir.

Walt and Bethany present a meticulously kept winery and tasting room worthy of a navy admiral's inspection. Inside the tasting room, visitors can see the barrels in the backroom, resting comfortably between racking. During the summer, music and wine lovers alike flock to the winery to enjoy "Music in the Vines" summer concerts featuring local artists. The performances take place next to the winery's private lake, which is also the setting for many outdoor weddings, held with regularity on weekends.

BETHANY VINEYARD & WINERY
opened: 2002
winemaker(s): Walter Jay Houser
location: 4115 NE 259th Street, Ridgefield, WA 98642-9749
phone: 360-887-3525
web: www.bethanyvineyard.com
e-mail: beth@bethanyvineyards.com
fee: Complimentary wine tasting
hours: Saturday 11–6, Sunday 12–5, or by appointment
amenities: Gift Shop, Picnic Area, Private Events, Tours, Weddings, Wheelchair Accessible, Wine Club

⭐ **BEST Weddings and picnicking**

Three Brothers Vineyard and Winery 5

Dan Anderson, owner and winemaker of Three Brothers Vineyard & Winery in Ridgefield, Washington, operates with a moral compass of a decidedly Christian bent. Inside the tasting room on the wall, a plaque reads, "I am the vine; you are the branches. If a man remains in me and I in him, he will bear much fruit; apart from me you can do nothing" (John 15:5).

The relationship between wine and Christianity entwines through the ages. Indeed, Jesus' first miracle involved turning water into wine at the marriage at Cana reported in the Gospel of John. There are more than 200 references to wine in the Bible — most of them positive. Wine is a part of the Christian fabric, although, ironically, the word "alcohol" is Arabic in origin.

Named in reference to Dan's three sons, this relatively new winery includes 15 acres of grapes, several event venues, a wine production building and a tasting room. When the winery invites you to "stroll through our grounds," you might want to pack a comfortable pair of sneakers. The property is expansive; in fact, it's big enough to sponsor a popular summer concert series, with stage and advanced sound system located in the amphitheater. It can also accommodate large-scale weddings by the pond.

But if you're not there to attend an event, packing a picnic is highly recommended. There's loads of space to throw down a blanket or sponsor your own private function. Late summer, in particular, is a good time to explore the winery's vineyards and snap pictures of maturing pinot noir, cabernet, syrah, merlot, chardonnay, gewürztraminer, tempranillo, and chenin blanc. The interesting fact about these vines is that they will go dormant in the winter and resurrect in the spring. You might say that the clusters of grapes you see are born again.

THREE BROTHERS VINEYARD AND WINERY
winemaker(s): Dan Anderson
location: 2411 NE 244th Street, Ridgefield, WA 98642
phone: 360-887-2085
web: www.threebrotherswinery.com
e-mail: threebrotherswinery@yahoo.com
fee: Complimentary wine tasting
hours: Saturday 11–6 and Sunday 12–5
amenities: Gift Shop, Picnic Area, Private Events, Vineyard on Premise, Weddings, Wheelchair Accessible, Wine Club, Wines by the Glass

★ **BEST Music venue, weddings and picnicking**

East Fork Cellars

Cellar rat — one who labors in the cellar (or barrel room) of a winery never seeing the light of day. Quite like a rat. UrbanDictionary.com

Ridgefield's East Fork Cellars specializes in red blends, including its well-known Cellar Rat Red. But why keep all that mixing fun to themselves? Owners Jeff and Stacie Waddell decided to take it a step further with a "Blend Your Own" program, in which guests can concoct their own special blend, with their own private label. That's right, you can reserve the barrel room for a private event and blend to your heart's content. It provides hours of fun, and there is no right or wrong results. At the end, you can put your name on the label and share the fruit (ahem) of your labors with your duly impressed friends and family. For other private events, there's the Pacific Northwest Best Fish Co. restaurant next door, which caters such occasions for the winery.

Jeff and Stacie not only exercise their passion for wine; their winery also provides an outlet for their other passion — music. Jeff is the musician in the family, and every Friday night the tasting room makes room for a live band, along with dancing and plenty of wine. Not surprisingly, one of the favorite bands for everyone to rock out to is called Les Cellar Rats.

East Fork Cellars obtains grapes from surrounding wine regions as well as its own backyard, and features pinot noir, pinot gris, and chardonnay. The Waddells like to compare East Fork's growing conditions to those of the Burgundy region in France. Well, Burgundy has its Yonne River, which flows into the Seine; north Clark County has its East Fork River, which flows into the Lewis River. In addition, both regions produce cool-weather grapes, with pinot noir leading the charge. However, that is about the extent of the Burgundian resemblance.

EAST FORK CELLARS
location: 24415 NE 10th Avenue, Ridgefield, WA 98642
phone: 360-727-3055
web: www.eastforkcellars.com
e-mail: via website
fee: Tasting fee may apply
hours: Spring hours: Thursday 12–9, Friday 12–10, Saturday and Sunday 12–6
amenities: Live Music, Wheelchair Accessible, Wine Club

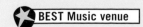 **BEST Music venue**

Rusty Grape Vineyard

Jeremy and Heather Brown had a problem. With a 2-year-old baby and another "bun in the oven," they were running out of space in their small house. In dire need of a larger house to raise a family, they purchased a fixer-upper one mile east of downtown Battle Ground. The sloping property of 5 acres provided plenty of extra space, and with the wine business burgeoning in southwest Washington and nearby Willamette Valley, the couple decided to plant a vineyard. Mulling over a name for their new enterprise, they decided on Rusty Grape Vineyard, because "they liked the sound of it." As good a reason as any, I'd say.

This is a fun, unpretentious winery. It reflects the easygoing personalities of the owners. But don't be fooled; that relaxed demeanor belies Jeremy and Heather's hard work and ambition. Not only have they planted a vineyard and learned to make wine with little training;

they've also opened an on-site restaurant featuring wood-fired pizza, and host live music performances and screen movies on the lawn. This would explain why they were voted Best Winery in Clark County by readers of the local The Columbian newspaper in 2011. Indeed, this "laid-back" winery has worked hard to earn its nearly 2,500 friends on Facebook.

Winery dog

Rusty Grape makes cabernet sauvignon, merlot, syrah, sangiovese, and pinot noir, as well as strawberry and blackberry wines. While pinot noir enjoys a stellar reputation in Oregon, it has not achieved such acclaim in Washington, due in large part to that little thing called "climate." Still, that doesn't keep Washington winemakers from trying to create this most supple of food-friendly wines.

This family is in it to win it, and with such determination, their odds are good.

RUSTY GRAPE VINEYARD
opened: 2007
winemaker(s): Jeremy Brown
location: 16712 NE 219th Street, Battle Ground, WA 98604
phone: 360-513-9338
web: www.rustygrape.com
e-mail: info@rustygrapevineyard.com
fee: Complimentary wine tasting
hours: Friday 12–varies, Saturday 12–8, Sunday 12–6
amenities: Gift Shop, Live Music, Picnic Area, Private Events, Weddings, Wheelchair Accessible
connect: 🐦 f

Confluence Winery

There are some surprising finds in southwest Washington, especially as you travel east along the Columbia Gorge. For this WineTrail trekker, discovering the wines of Confluence Winery was indeed an eye-opener. I didn't see it coming.

Located in rural Clark County a good 20 minutes from Vancouver, Washington, Confluence Winery derives its name from the confluence of rivers (e.g., the nearby Cowlitz and Columbia Rivers) and the convergence of eastern Washington grapes and western Washington winemaking. However, as owners Jae and Greg Weber will tell you, the name reflects the gathering of friends to share great wine.

Winemaker Norm Banks (with input from Walla Walla vintner Marie Eve Gilla of famed Forgeron Cellars) employs prefermentation cold maceration to extract colors and flavors from the grapes. The resulting wine is both softer and more intense in color. The voluptuous mouthfeel and fruit-forward tastes had me offering up my glass for a refill. In particular, the Confluence Equilibrium, a blend of merlot, cabernet, and petit verdot, had me imagining a velvet hammer, with its smooth texture and full-bodied finish. Perhaps the 20 months of aging in oak had something to do with it, I suggested to Norm, to which he only smiled.

Confluence Winery's setting, with its cozy tasting room and outdoor seating area, is wonderful in itself. But just as agreeable is the friendly staff, led by co-owner Jae. Confluence adds to that sense of comfort with a little sustenance, laying out a spread of gourmet cheeses and crackers. How often does a WineTrail traveler encounter that? It's just one of the nicer touches visitors experience at Confluence Winery.

CONFLUENCE WINERY
winemaker(s): Norm Banks and Marie Eve Gilla
location: 19111 NW 67th Avenue, Ridgefield, WA 98642
phone: 360-887-2343
web: www.confluencewinery.net
e-mail: confluencewinery@aol.com
fee: Tasting fee refunded with purchase
hours: Saturday 12–5 and by appointment
amenities: Weddings, Wheelchair Accessible, Wine Club

Gougér Cellars Winery

Winemaker Gary Gougér's bio reads like a man in pursuit of some pretty eclectic passions. His professional career and education comprise pharmacy, optometry, and winemaking. At first glance, these may appear as unrelated interests, but the winemaking community has many a practitioner with a health science background. In fact, when I was writing the WineTrails of Washington book in 2006–2007, there were a half-dozen pharmacists engaged in winemaking in the Walla Walla Valley. Yes, there is an art to winemaking but there is also a heavy dose of science.

Speaking of science, it was none other than Louis Pasteur who explained the process of fermentation and the role of yeast in converting sugar to alcohol. For scientists at the time, the belief was that alcoholic beverages resulted from a chemical reaction rather than a biological reaction. Those little yeast critters just weren't appreciated. It may have been Gary's penchant for science that led him to make wine at the turn of the millennium, but it was his drive for excellence that compelled him to move to

Australia and complete a degree in enology (or is it "oenology" there?) from the University of Adelaide in 2005.

Interestingly, Gary focuses on the art of blending to create award-winning wines. Rather than single varietal wines, Gougér Cellars Winery blends syrah, Malbec, cabernet sauvignon, cabernet franc, zinfandel, petite syrah, viognier, pinot gris, and muscat ottonel. Because of the winery's location in southwest Washington, he sources grapes from eastern Washington, Oregon, and California. Once blended, each wine is named using numbers. For example, his bold No. 128 is a blend of syrah and cabernet sauvignon; No. 522 is a blend of old and new zinfandel vines; and No. 903 — which took home the Platinum Award from the 2011 San Diego International Wine Competition — is a blend of cabernet, petite syrah, zinfandel, and syrah.

GOUGER CELLARS WINERY
opened: 2010
winemaker(s): Gary Gougér
location: 1812 Washington Street, Vancouver, WA 98660
phone: 360-909-4707
web: www.gcwinery.com
e-mail: info@gcwinery.com
fee: Tasting fee
hours: Friday 2–8 (Happy Hour 5–8), Saturday 10–6, Sunday 12–5
amenities: Live Music, Wheelchair Accessible, Wines by the Glass
connect: ■

www.winetrailsnw.com/wineries/gouger_cellars_winery

English Estate Winery 🔟

English Estate's founder Carl English rolled the dice and decided to offer premium wines in a box. That's right, that same box that got a bad rap 20 or 30 years ago. Cheap wine in a box translates into bad taste in the mouth. However, imagine if you could have premium cabernet sauvignon or pinot noir one glass at a time over a period of months and the taste would never change. How? Because, thanks to a bag within the box, those nasty little oxygen molecules don't touch the wine. For those wine drinkers who enjoy a glass of wine a day, the bag in a box just might be the right solution.

At age 70 Carl English passed away however, the tradition continues with English Estate Winery's Loafing Shed providing an inviting space to relax and enjoy wine as a sample or by the glass. By reputation, this east Vancouver winery is a popular nightspot on Friday evening where live music accompanies their estate wines.

Housed in 1913 dairy barn, Vancouver, Washington–based English Estate Winery is the closest vineyard and winery to Portland. Many of the wines are estate made using pinot noir from their own 20-acre vineyard, Gravel Mine Vineyards. Other grapes come from nearby vineyards that enjoy the confluence of the Columbia and Willamette rivers and the special *terroir* of the Columbia River Gorge.

At his death, Carl did not want a traditional funeral. Instead, he wanted a party to celebrate his achievements. He wanted a potluck for friends and family to "cry a little, laugh a lot, and dance all night." That tells you something about Carl English, a remarkable man with a zest for life.

ENGLISH ESTATE WINERY
opened: 2001
location: 17806 SE 1st Street, Vancouver, WA 98684
phone: 360-772-5141
web: www.englishestatewinery.com
e-mail: sales@englishestatewinery.com
fee: Tasting fee applies
hours: Friday through Sunday 12–6; (Live music Friday 6–9); Monday 4:30–7 or by appointment
amenities: Mailing List, Picnic Area, Tours, Wheelchair Accessible, Wine Club
connect: 🐦 📘

Columbia River
Gorge
WineTrail

Going east from Vancouver, Washington, the Columbia River Gorge WineTrail takes you through the territory made famous by Lewis and Clark. However, the Columbia River is far tamer now than what those explorers experienced in the fall of 1805. Today, you have plenty of windsurfing opportunities, destination resorts, vineyards and wineries to check out during your expedition. You'll discover wineries with names like Wind River, Marshal's, Syncline, Maryhill, and Waving Tree. In between wine tasting, you can find several places to catch 40, such as the Skamania Lodge or across the Columbia in Hood River, Oregon, where there are many choices. For sightseeing, check out the Stonehenge replica or the Maryhill Museum, or go white-water rafting on the White Salmon River. Pack your camera, too — there are photo ops galore.

Columbia River Gorge WineTrail

1. AniChe Cellars
2. Wind River Cellars
3. AlmaTerra Wines
4. Syncline Wine Cellars
5. Cor Cellars
6. Domaine Pouillon
7. Memaloose McCormick Family Vineyards
8. Illusion Winery
9. Marshal's Winery
10. Cascade Cliffs Winery & Vineyard
11. Jacob Williams Winery
12. Maryhill Winery
13. Waving Tree Winery

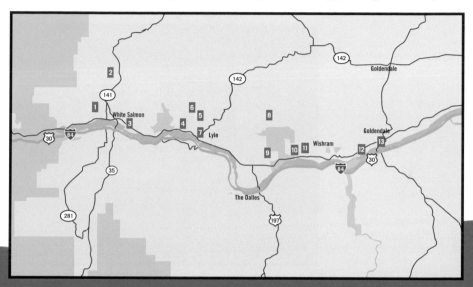

Region: **Southwest Washington Wine Country**

\# of tasting rooms on tour: **13**

Estimate # of days for tour: **2**

Getting around: **Car**

Key Events:
❑ **Columbia Gorge Winery Association features a number of annual events (in both Washington and Oregon) including Passport Weekend (April), Memorial Day Weekend, Labor Day Weekend and Thanksgiving Weekend. See www.columbiagorgewine.com for details.**

Tips:
❑ **Maryhill Winery sponsors a summer concert series at their outdoor amphitheater — see www.maryhillwinery.com for schedule and tickets.**
❑ **Cross over to Oregon to wine and dine in Hood River.**

 Best:
❑ **Views: AniChe Cellars**
❑ **Views and picnicking: Wind River Cellars**
❑ **Picnicking: Syncline Wine Cellars**
❑ **Views: Memaloose McCormick Family Vineyards**
❑ **Views: Cascade Cliffs Winery & Vineyard**
❑ **Views: Jacob Williams Winery**
❑ **Destination, views, music venue, gift shop and picnicking: Maryhill Winery**

AniChe Cellars ❶

Oregon has claim on pinot noir; New Zealand, on sauvignon blanc; and South Africa is known for its pinotage. Yet Washington seems to lack a rep for producing the *crème de la crème* of a particular varietal. Perhaps that's OK; some believe that Washington may eventually become known for its "mutt wines," or blends. And it would be in good standing. After all, Bordeaux's winemakers blend cabernet and merlot into world-renowned wines; and when thinking of the Rhône, many a wine lover salivates at the memory of a blend of grenache, syrah, and Mourvèdre.

And indeed, Washington's AniChe Cellars excels when it comes to blends. Winemaker/co-owner Rachael Horn exercises her discerning palate to derive whites composed of gewürztraminer with a backbone of riesling, or a Left Bank style of Bordeaux composed of cabernet sauvignon and merlot. And by focusing on blends, Rachel has editorial license to christen her wines with great monikers such as Goat Boy, Moth Love, and Lizzy.

The name "AniChe" is a clever blend of the names of Rachel and husband Todd Mera's two offspring: Anais (Ani) Mera and Che Horn. The name is as harmonious as the wonderful wines created at this family-owned winery in the Columbia River Gorge.

ANICHE CELLARS
opened: 2009
winemaker(s): Rachael Horn
location: 71 Little Buck Creek Road, Underwood, WA 98651
phone: 360-624-6531
web: www.AniCheCellars.com
e-mail: info@anichecellars.com
fee: Tasting fee
hours: Wednesday through Sunday 11–5; Appointment only December 23rd to February 14th
amenities: Picnic Area, RV/Bus Parking, Wheelchair Accessible, Wine Club
connect:

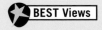 **BEST Views**

Wind River Cellars

The views are stunning. The wine is magnificent. The hospitality is first-rate. Wind River Cellars has it all.

With magnificent views of Mount Hood to the south and Mount Adams to the east, visitors to Wind River Cellars have license to use the word "stunning." This is the perfect setting in which to get married (which many couples do) or to enjoy a catered lunch on the deck after a day of white water rafting (which visitors also do). Wind River Cellars' vintner, Joel Goodwillie, loves living in the Columbia River Gorge. He makes the perfect ambassador for the tiny town of Husum. A visit there might have you packing your bags and taking up windsurfing.

Joel Goodwillie

Joel handcrafts 12 varietal wines using grapes from his own and other local vineyards (including Celilo Vineyard) in the Columbia River Gorge. He says that Columbia Gorge grapes have more acid than grapes from other wine-growing areas of Washington, and therefore that the wines have a clean, crisp, lively finish on the tongue. But it was the word "velvety" that sprang to mind when we sampled our way through a fairly ambitious list of Wind River wines: riesling, chardonnay, gewürztraminer, pinot gris, merlot, pinot noir, syrah, lemberger, pinot noir, cabernet franc, tempranillo, a "save room for dessert" Port of Celilo, and a beguiling white port. Phew! By the time this WineTrail adventurer got to the tempranillo, Joel was starting to bear a strong resemblance to Hollywood celebrity Kiefer Sutherland. Joel assured me, however, that they had not been separated at birth.

If you happen to be there with your sweetie, make it a point to kiss on the deck. There's good reason that Wind River Cellars was voted one of the "Best Places to Kiss in the Northwest"!

WIND RIVER CELLARS
opened: 1995
winemaker(s): Joel Goodwillie
location: 196 Spring Creek Road, Husum, WA 98623
phone: 509-493-2324
web: www.windrivercellars.com
e-mail: info@windrivercellars.com
fee: Tasting fee refunded with purchase
hours: Daily 10–6
amenities: Newsletter/Blog, Picnic Area, Private Events, Weddings, Wheelchair Accessible, Wine Club
connect: 🐦 f

⭐ **BEST Views and picnicking**

AlmaTerra Wines

Inspired by *terroir*, owner Dr. Alan Busacca's AlmaTerra Wines is all about expressing the fruit of Washington's vineyards. Since it's the soil, the climate and man's caring touch that conspire to grow the grape, it stands to reason that even the same grape variety should be different from one *terroir* to another.

Take syrah for example. Now here's a grape that you'd expect to hold its own no matter the soil profile or the heat units experienced by the vineyard. However, to the palate of Dr. Busacca the syrah grape grown in one appellation differs considerably from the same variety grown in another appellation.

Dr. Busacca knows a thing or two about Washington viticulture areas having spent 25 years at Washington State University working as a research professor in geology, agriculture and soil science. Given his extensive resume as a research scientist and more recently as a viticulture consultant, it is little wonder that Dr. Busacca has earned the nicknames, Doctor Dirt and Savant of Soils.

Now retired from WSU, Dr. Busacca selected the Columbia Gorge AVA to start his own winery which he fittingly called AlamTerra Wines in the small town of Bingen, WA.

Relying on the talents of celebrated winemaker Robert Smasne, AltmaTerra offers a manageable assortment of wines for tasting. However, it's the aforementioned syrahs from AlmaTerra that leads many visitors to stop at its Bingen tasting room to taste the *terroir*. AlmaTerra produces three different syrahs from three different Washington vineyards — Ciel du Cheval (Red Mountain AVA), Coyote Canyon (Horse Heaven Hills AVA) and Minick Vineyards (Yakima Valley AVA). A fourth syrah labeled Coéo is a cuvée blend of all three vineyards. Four syrahs; four distinct tastes. Why does he do this? Duh. He's inspired by the *terroir*!

ALMATERRA WINES
opened: 2010
winemaker(s): Robert O. Smasne
location: 208 West Steuben Street, Bingen, WA 98605
phone: 509-592-0756
web: www.almaterrawines.com
e-mail: alan@almaterrawines.com
fee: Tasting fee
hours: Thursday 12–6; Friday 12–9:30; Saturday and Sunday 12–6
amenities: Live Music, Mailing List, Online Store, Restaurant/Food Pairings, RV/Bus Parking, Wheelchair Accessible, Wine Club, Wines by the Glass
connect:

Syncline Wine Cellars

Vintners James and Poppie Mantone are transplants from other parts of the country. They met and fell in love at LaVelle Vineyards in the Willamette Valley. Settling on the Washington side of the Columbia River Gorge, they started Syncline in 1999. (Note: A syncline is a type of rock formation seen in the Columbia River Gorge.)

James' background as a microbiologist and organic chemist has ingrained in him an exceptional attention to detail. In his mind, the gaseous, bubbly, seemingly out-of-control fermentation process makes perfect scientific sense. Syncline Wine Cellars' focus is on Rhône-style wines, and that aforementioned attention to detail may help explain why a growing number of wine lovers call Syncline their favorite wine.

If your taste buds have a predilection for the supple, food-friendly flavors of grenache, Mourvèdre, roussanne, or viognier, this is the place for you. Plus, if you're like me and enjoy wineries located in an old barn with rows of manicured vineyards in the background, Syncline makes for a beautiful afternoon and an ideal setting for a picnic. And keep in mind that its southern Rhône blend makes a great companion for the picnic fare you've packed.

SYNCLINE WINE CELLARS
opened: 1998
winemaker(s): James and Poppie Mantone
location: 111 Balch Road, Lyle, WA 98635
phone: 509-365-4361
web: www.synclinewine.com
e-mail: info@synclinewine.com
fee: Tasting fee refunded with purchase
hours: Thursday through Sunday 11–6 from February through November; Saturday and Sunday 11–5 during December and January; Closed December 24th through January 11th
amenities: Newsletter/Blog, Online Store, Picnic Area, RV/Bus Parking, Vineyard on Premise, Wheelchair Accessible, Wine Club
connect: 🐦 📘

BEST Picnicking

Cor Cellars

## 5

If a stranger turns to you and says, "Bonum vinum laetificat cor hominis," don't throw a punch at him. He's simply exercising his Latin by saying, "Good wine gladdens a person's heart." Such are the words that Luke Bradford embraced when he started COR Cellars in

2005. Luke is one of a growing number of young winemakers who have splashed onto the Washington wine scene.

Still young and wearing a carefree smile, this graduate of The Evergreen State College honed his winemaking skills before launching COR Cellars. Luke worked at a relative's winery in Italy (which helps to explain the Latin connection) as well as doing stints with Wind River Cellars and Syncline Winery. He gives particular credit to James Mantone at Syncline for mentoring him in the chemical and microbiological aspects of making wine. In addition, Luke is grateful to the many growers with whom he collaborates, including McKinley Springs Vineyard in Horse Heaven Hills, Underwood Mountain Vineyards, Celilo Vineyard, Columbia View, and Alder Ridge.

Samples of Luke's wines include cabernet sauvignon, chardonnay, sauvignon blanc and riesling. However, his aptly named red table wine Momentum reflects Luke's "movement, impulse, and effort" to make great wine. Everything about COR Cellars reflects the promise of youth: an up-and-coming winery with a maturing vineyard nearby.

COR CELLARS
opened: 2005
winemaker(s): Luke Bradford
location: 151 Old Highway 8, Lyle, WA 98635-9308
phone: 509-365-2744
web: www.corcellars.com
e-mail: info@corcellars.com
fee: Tasting fee refunded with purchase
hours: Thursday through Sunday 11–6 Valentine's Day through Thanksgiving weekend or by appointment
amenities: Picnic Area, RV/Bus Parking, Vineyard on Premise, Wheelchair Accessible, Wine Club, Wines by the Glass
connect:

Domaine Pouillon

With labels graced with such names as Black Dot, Deux, Pierre, Blanc du Moulin and Katydid, a potential imbiber is drawn in; the titles are simple, poetic, intriguing. And so are the wines of Domaine Pouillon winery, located outside of Lyle, Washington. They are imbued with authenticity — no pretension here.

At Domaine Pouillon, owners/ winemakers Alexis (a soil scientist) and Juliet Pouillon celebrate their heritage in the form of juice in a bottle. Exhibit A is Pierre, a blend of syrah and cabernet sauvignon. The moniker Pierre pays homage to Alexis' father, Papa Pierre. Sadly, the two words that are the bane of wine tourists, "Sold Out," were posted with the Pierre. Still, not all was lost. I tipped my glass to a picture of Pierre on the wall as I swirled and sipped my sample of Black Dot. As I experienced its lingering finish, it struck a chord as I relished one of my favorite flavors — licorice. (Isn't it great that wine somehow never develops the flavor of lima beans, sweaty socks, or seawater?) As the Pouillons say on their website, "Sorry: Offers of first borns, mineral rights, and oceanfront property no longer accepted in trade for Black Dot." I get it. Instead, I opted to exchange my Visa digits for two bottles of Black Dot beauty.

Rarely does the WineTrail Guy gush about a particular winery. However, I'm unabashedly giddy about Domaine Pouillon. The tasting room and friendly staff (including their dog, T-Bone) are decidedly of Columbia Gorge, yet everything about the property and wine is French. As a case in point, I present Exhibit B: Katydid, a blend of southern Rhône varieties that had me fondly recalling Châteauneuf-du-Pape. *Ooh-la-la, mon ami.*

DOMAINE POUILLON
opened: 2008
winemaker(s): Alexis and Juliet Pouillon
location: 170 Lyle Snowden Road, Lyle, WA 98635
phone: 509-365-2795
web: www.domainepouillon.com
e-mail: dpnwine@gmail.com
fee: Tasting fee refunded with purchase
hours: Friday through Sunday 11–6 (Call ahead for winter hours)
amenities: Picnic Area, Wheelchair Accessible
connect:

Memaloose McCormick Family Vineyards 7

Rob McCormick

Close to other stellar wineries — Domaine Pouillon, Cor Cellars, and Syncline Wine Cellars, to name a few — Memaloose Wines/McCormick Family Vineyards offers fine examples of the *terroir* of the Columbia Gorge AVA. That's no happy accident. Father Rob McCormick and winemaking son Brian McCormick have five estate vineyards to provide fruit. What's interesting and unique is the fact that their vineyards straddle the Columbia River, with three vineyards on the Washington side and two vineyards on the Oregon side. There is an island in the middle of the river that the native Indians called Memaloose — hence the name of the winery.

The distinctive Memaloose wine labels pay homage to Lewis and Clark and the 1806 stay of their "Corps of Discovery" on the banks of the Columbia River overlooking Memaloose Island. The antiqued parchment label includes sketches from the explorers' journal and a quotation.

A graduate of the distinguished University of California-Davis School of Viticulture and Enology, Brian succeeds in creating food-friendly wines that don't fall victim to the dreaded oak monster and have a mellow, won't-burn-your-throat alcohol level. My personal favorite is the 2008 Idiot's Grace label cabernet franc at $25 a bottle. With a lamb shank recipe waiting at home, I left with a bottle of this lovely gem tucked under my arm.

Conveniently located along Highway 14 in Lyle, the Memaloose tasting room offers commanding views of the Columbia River below, an inviting deck to uncork a bottle of wine, Rob's friendly demeanor responding to outstretched hands with empty wine glasses and one yellow Lab equipped with a wagging tail.

MEMALOOSE MCCORMICK FAMILY VINEYARDS
opened: 2007
winemaker(s): Brian McCormick
location: 34 State Street, Highway 14, Lyle, WA 98635
phone: 360-635-2887
web: www.winesofthegorge.com
e-mail: mistralranch@gmail.com
fee: Tasting fee refunded with purchase; waived for club members
hours: Thursday through Sunday 11–5, April through November; Daily during summer
amenities: Newsletter/Blog, Online Store, Picnic Area, Vineyard on Premise, Wheelchair Accessible, Wine Club

BEST Views

Illusion Winery

The winery's back porch is the perfect place to throw the ball to winery dog Siena. Armed with a glass of David Guest's Bordeaux-blend Apparition, I think I could have tossed the ball to Siena for much of the afternoon before my arm gave out. Surrounded by stop-in-your-tracks views of sparsely populated canyons, Mount Hood, Mount Adams, and a sliver of the Columbia River, this little slice of heaven is miles away from the past life of owners David and wife Dina.

David Guest

It's a curvy 11 miles from Highway 14 in Lyle to the hilltop abode of Illusion Winery. During the journey, you wonder what the heck you're doing but, not to worry, you're on the right track. And when you finally pull up and are greeted by a tail-wagging Siena, you know for sure you're there. Illusion is no illusion.

Since 2007, David and Dina have gone back and forth between their home in Black Diamond, Washington, to their new digs outside Lyle. During this time, they've built the winery/tasting room from scratch. But it's a work in progress, and now includes a concrete pool/spa and a diminutive golf course perfect for a trusty 9-iron and putter. David continues to work the garden and patio creating additions (he's definitely a "project guy"), so don't be surprised if he has dirt mixed with the purple of a new vintage on his hands.

WineTrail Note: Make a point of sampling Illusion Winery's port-style wine. It's lip-smacking good!

ILLUSION WINERY
opened: 2002
winemaker(s): David Guest
location: 31 Schilling Road, Lyle, WA 98635
phone: 206-261-1682
web: www.illusionwine.com
e-mail: illusion@sprintmail.com
fee: Complimentary wine tasting
hours: Most summer weekends 11–5 from May through September; call ahead or check website for details
amenities: Picnic Area, Wheelchair Accessible
connect: 🐦 ⓕ

Marshal's Winery

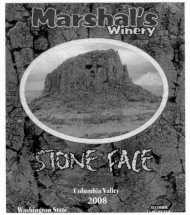

Just past The Dalles Bridge on Highway 14, watch for the signs that will lead you to Marshal's Winery. As you wind your way up to Marshal's, check out the jutting rock formations; with a little imagination, you might see a stone face on one.

Ron Johnson, known as "RonJohn," named the winery after his son Marshal upon its launch in 2001. RonJohn is what you call a "vigneron," meaning that he produces wines from bud to bottle, and he has the good fortune of owning a south-facing vineyard to help him in that task.

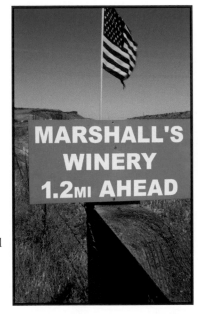

RonJohn's diminutive wife, Lilie, originally from the Philippines, manages the tasting room. From the Filipino culture, she has brought rich traditions, including the hosting of big parties at which a farm animal of some type ends up on the barbecue. This cultural tradition is observed every summer when they host and roast at the annual "Swine and Wine" event.

RonJohn makes some of the more traditional wines, such as riesling, cabernet sauvignon, and cabernet franc along with a red table wine blend called "Stone Face Red," named for those unusual rock formations you will see as you drive in. However, RonJohn is also known for other, more remarkable creations, including a "hot tub wine" called Black Homberg, made from the fruit of 100-year-old vines and very appealing to those with a sweet tooth; and Sweet Anna Marie, a port-like wine made without brandy, resulting in a restrained alcohol level of 13.5 percent.

As you sample Marshal's wines, check out the lantern-adorned labels on its bottles. Created by RonJohn, the lantern drawing includes the words "Put a little light in your life." RonJohn and family live by those words every day.

MARSHAL'S WINERY
opened: 2001
winemaker(s): Ron Johnson
location: 150 Oak Creek Road, Dallesport, WA 98617
phone: 509-767-4633
web: www.marshalsvineyard.com
e-mail: marshalswinery@gorge.net
fee: Tasting fee refunded with purchase
hours: Daily 9–6
amenities: Picnic Area, Wheelchair Accessible

Cascade Cliffs Winery & Vineyard

At mile marker 88.5 on Highway 14, you'll find the entrance to Cascade Cliffs Vineyard & Winery. We know, it looks like a fruit-packing shed, but that's part of Cascade Cliffs' charm. Named for the basalt cliffs rising 400 feet on the north side of the vineyard, Cascade Cliffs is the creation of owner/winemaker Bob Lorkowski. The geography, which includes the Columbia River and surrounding cliffs, creates a climate well suited to the 23-acre vineyard juxtaposed with the winery. Lots of heat units, combined with a long growing season, translate into the perfect climate for grapes of Mediterranean origin.

So, how is your Italian? You may be speaking it with a Piedmont accent by the time you depart Cascade Cliffs. This is the home to outstanding barbera, nebbiolo, and dolcetto. Bob also produces a red blend called Goat Head Red (GHR), with cabernet sauvignon, barbera and nebbiolo, but sans the oak. In the process of making a number of his wines, Bob does use American, French, and Hungarian oak to create a kaleidoscope of flavors that he blends to create his award-winning wines. However, Bob gives a nod to non-Italian varieties by producing small quantities of zinfandel, merlot, syrah, and cabernet sauvignon, along with a lovely Bordeaux blend called Horsethief Red (HTR).

Buon gusto!

Author's daughter, Meg Roberts

CASCADE CLIFFS WINERY & VINEYARD
opened: 1985
winemaker(s): Robert Lorkowski
location: 8866 Highway 14, Wishram, WA 98673
phone: 509-767-1100
web: www.cascadecliffs.com
e-mail: cascadecliffs@gorge.net
fee: Complimentary wine tasting
hours: Daily 10–6
amenities: Mailing List, Picnic Area, Tours, Wheelchair Accessible, Wine Club
connect: f

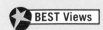 BEST Views

Jacob Williams Winery

I first became aware of Jacob Williams Winery with a glass of syrah I ordered at Hood River's Cielo Restaurant. That was way back in early 2010 but ironically it wasn't until late 2012 that I ventured to the actual winery on the Washington side of the Gorge. It's not my fault it took so long to visit proprietor Brad Gearhart's labor of love. After all he moved his winery and tasting room from various locations before settling on a piece of prime real estate perched on a bluff above the mighty Columbia.

It's here in the hamlet of Wishram, where even a stop sign might be difficult to find, that Jacob Williams Winery resides. Actually it's better to say "evolves" more than "resides" because as the architectural rendering on the wall suggests, the winery will eventually morph to a full-fledged destination of sorts, complete with production facility, tasting room, peach and apple orchards and plenty of deck space to camp out and watch eagles circling in the distance above the Columbia.

Often you will find Brad's father, Len Gearhart, working the tasting room. In a demure way, Len lets visitors know, "let me know if you wish more" as he pours a small sample. To which this visitor wishes to opine, "oh sure, let er' rip" but my Spokane middle-class roots place a governor on my voice. That's until got I got Brad's zinfandel. That's when I extended my empty wineglass toward Len and exclaimed "I better try that wine one more time." I left with two freshly purchased bottles.

Named for his two sons, Jacob and William, this winery stands ready to assume its rightful spot as one of Washington's up-and-coming artisan wineries producing oh-so-ultra-premium wine. Check it out for yourself; just remember to pack binoculars for the view.

JACOB WILLIAMS WINERY
opened: 2009
winemaker(s): Brad Gearhart and consulting winemaker John Haw
location: 3 Avery Road, Avery Park on Highway 14, Wishram, WA 98635
phone: 541-645-0462
web: www.jacobwilliamswinery.com
e-mail: info@jacobwilliamswinery.com
fee: Tasting fee refunded with purchase
hours: Daily 10–6
amenities: Picnic Area, Vineyard on Premise, Wheelchair Accessible, Wine Club, Wines by the Glass
connect: ❡

⭐ **BEST Views**

Maryhill Winery

There are many reasons to make a journey to Maryhill Winery. Many visitors stop for the view, and why not? With stupendous views of Mount Hood to the west and the

Columbia River Gorge below, visitors are so entranced they might forget to sample Maryhill Wine. Then too, many trekkers come here for the summer concert series at Maryhill's outdoor amphitheater.

Maryhill may be the wine-event capital of the world. Throughout the year, Maryhill Winery hosts such events, from crush to bottling and everything in between. It even takes time in

August to celebrate "veraison," when the white grape varieties turn from opaque to translucent, and when the red grape varieties turn from green to deep red. However, many tourists are here simply because they love the wine. They note the view, browse the well-stocked gift shop, but make a quick beeline for the tasting bar.

The tasting bar is the centerpiece of the spacious tasting room. Built in the early 1900s, the massive Brunswick bar is 20 feet long and 12 feet high, with inset mirrors and wood carvings. The same crew responsible for the Egyptian pyramids must have moved this wine bar into position. Behind the bar, the well-trained staff pours and educates. The fee for sampling reserve wines is well worth it, especially if you are thinking of purchasing a bottle or two; the fee applies to purchases of $20 or more.

Owners Craig and Vicki Leuthold and family members Donald Leuthold and Cherie Brooks launched the winery in 2000. With an annual production of 35,000 cases, Maryhill Winery is one of the largest family-owned wineries in the state. Their slogan is "Passion, Patience, and Balance." However, they could easily switch it for the motto, "Fun, Celebrate, Drink," and WineTrail enthusiasts would understand.

MARYHILL WINERY
opened: 1999
winemaker(s): Richard Batchelor
location: 9774 Highway 14, Goldendale, WA 98620
phone: 877-627-9445
web: www.maryhillwinery.com
e-mail: Submit via website
fee: Tasting fee for reserved wines waived for purchase of $20 or more on wine
hours: Daily 10–6
amenities: Gift Shop, Live Music, Online Store, Picnic Area, RV/Bus Parking, Tours, Weddings, Wheelchair Accessible, Wine Club, Wines by the Glass
connect: 🐦 📘

⭐ **BEST Destination, views, music venue, gift shop and picnicking**

Waving Tree Winery  13

If you are looking for a wine-tasting experience that's a little out of the ordinary, check out the Waving Tree Winery tasting room. The room is in a log cabin located across from Maryhill State Park. From the outside, it looks like a visitor information center, and, indeed, once inside you'll find rows of colorful tourist brochures touting Columbia River Gorge attractions, of which there are many.

For Waving Tree wines, owner/winemaker Terrence Atkins chose a unique blue-and-green label with the phrase "The wind was once created by the trees waving back and forth to one another" printed in big block letters on the bottle. There's plenty of wind in the Gorge, after all, and someone had to explain it.

Terrence is usually in the Goldendale tasting room, where he pours reds primarily, made from the grapes in his 60-acre vineyard. If available, be sure to sample his sangiovese; it's a hearty libation and perfect for Italian cuisine.

Now armed with this information, and perhaps a bottle or two of Waving Tree wine, you're ready to take on the Stonehenge Memorial. It's just four miles east of the Maryhill Museum of Art, according to the brochure.

WAVING TREE WINERY
opened: 2002
winemaker(s): Terrence Atkins
location: 123 Maryhill Highway, Goldendale, WA 98620
phone: 509-773-6552
web: www.wavingtreewinery.com
e-mail: atkins@gorge.net
fee: Complimentary wine tasting
hours: Daily 9–5 from Memorial Day through Labor Day; 9–5 Friday through Sunday from April through May and September through November
amenities: Online Store, Picnic Area, RV/Bus Parking, Wheelchair Accessible
connect: ▯

Other Wineries to Visit

AGATE CREEK CELLARS
winemaker(s): John Petaja and Gayle Willis
location: 105 Agate Creek Lane, Chehalis, WA 98532
phone: 360-740-1692
web: www.agatecreekcellars.com
hours: Saturday 12–5, March through October

BENKE CELLARS
winemaker(s): Rob Benke
location: 1804 NW 119th Street, Vancouver, WA 98685-3714
phone: 360-907-9525
web: www.benkecellars.com
hours: By appointment only

BURNT BRIDGE CELLARS
winemaker(s): David Smith
location: 1500 Broadway, Vancouver, WA 98663
phone: 360-600-0120
web: www.burntbridgecellars.com
hours: Saturday and Sunday 11–5; First Friday of the month 5–9

BATEAUX CELLARS
winemaker(s): Marcus Miller
location: 288 Smokey Valley Road, Toledo, WA 98591
phone: 360-921-9594
web: www.bateauxcellars.com
hours: Open Saturdays during summer 12–5 or special event weekends

BIRCHFIELD WINERY
winemaker(s): Virgil Fox, Craig Steepy and Gary Fox
location: 921 B Middle Fork Road, Onalaska, WA 98570-9710
phone: 360-864 5500
web: www.birchfieldwinery.com
hours: By appointment only

CAPSTONE CELLARS
winemaker(s): Roy Bays
location: 4305 Pacific Way, Longview, WA 98632-5340
phone: 360-749-1034
web: www.capstonecellars.com
hours: By appointment only

Other Wineries to Visit

HEISEN HOUSE VINEYARDS
winemaker(s): Michael Bloomquist
location: 28005 NE 172nd Avenue,
Battle Ground, WA 98604
phone: 360-713-2359
web: www.heisenhousevineyards.com
hours: Saturday and Sunday 12–6

MAJOR CREEK CELLARS
winemaker(s): Steve Mason
location: 306 Bates Road,
White Salmon, WA 98672
phone: 503-860-8712
web: www.majorcreekcellars.com
hours: By appointment only

MAJOR CREEK
CELLARS

2009
OREGON PINOT NOIR

14.7% ALC. BY VOL

KLICKITAT CANYON &
COLUMBIA GORGE WINERY
winemaker(s): Robin Dobson
location: 350 Highway 14,
Stevenson, WA 98648
phone: 509-365-2543
web: www.klickitatcanyonwinery.com
hours: Wednesday through Saturday
12–6 (March through October);
See website for winter hours

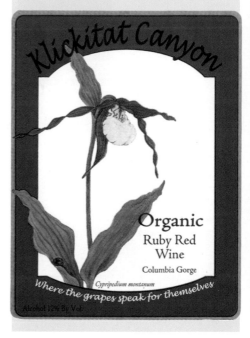

Klickitat Canyon

Organic
Ruby Red
Wine
Columbia Gorge

Cypripedium montanum

Where the grapes speak for themselves

Alcohol 12% By Vol

MT ST HELENS CELLARS
winemaker(s): Gary Dunbar
location: 2846 Spirit Lake Hwy,
Blue Heron Inn,
Castle Rock, WA 98611
phone: 360-967-2257
web: www.mtsthelenscellars.com
hours: Friday through Sunday 12–5

OLEQUA CELLARS
winemaker(s): Olequa Farms, LLC
location: 24218 NE 142nd Avenue,
Battle Ground, WA 98604
phone: 360-666-8012
web: www.olequa.com
hours: Saturday 12–5 and event
weekends, or by appointment

Other Wineries to Visit

ROLAND WINES
winemaker(s): Marc Roland
location: 2556 Cascade Way,
Longview, WA 98632
phone: 360-846-7304
web: www.rolanwines.com
hours: By appointment only

WELLS WINERY
winemaker(s): Carol Wells
location: 140 Eschaton Road,
Onalaska, WA 98570
phone: 360-978-6254
web: www.wellswinery.com
hours: By appointment only

WHITE SALMON VINEYARD
winemaker(s): Peter Brehm
location: 391 Newell Road,
Underwood, WA 98651
phone: 509-493-4640
web: www.WhiteSalmonVineyard.com
hours: Friday through Sunday
12:30–5:30 (April through October)
or by appointment

North Central Washington

WINE COUNTRY

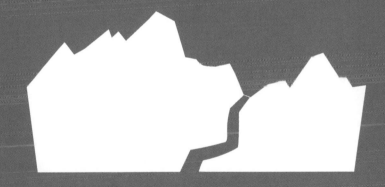

'37 Cellars

Petit Verdot
2009

SAGEMOOR FARMS DIONYSUS VINEYARD
COLUMBIA VALLEY

Frank Dechaine and Chuck Egner
Vintners

14.4% Alc. by Vol.

CERTAVI ET VICI

Ryan Patrick
Vineyards

RESERVE
CHARDONNAY
Columbia Valley
2008

ALC. 13.3% BY VOL

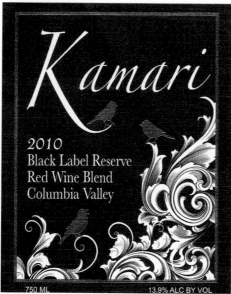

Kamari

2010
Black Label Reserve
Red Wine Blend
Columbia Valley

750 ML   13.9% ALC BY VOL

2009

WINERY
MARTIN-SCOTT

COLE'S COLLAGE
RED WINE
COLUMBIA VALLEY

ALC. 5.1% BY VOL.

Bergdorf

CELLARS
LEAVENWORTH

2006
WASHINGTON
Lemberger
ALC. 13.4% BY VOL.
750 mL.

Malaga Springs Winery
Al y Kat
RED WINE
WASHINGTON STATE
ALC. 13% BY VOL.

2008

SILVARA
VINEYARDS

Syrah

CHÂTEAU FAIRE
LE PONT

"MILBRANDT VINEYARDS"
Viognier
~2009~
WASHINGTON STATE WINE

ALC. 13.7% BY VOL.

CAIRDEAS
WINERY

SYRAH
LEWIS VINEYARD

20
08

COLUMBIA VALLEY

14.4% ALC./VOL. 750 ML

Firá
2011 COLUMBIA VALLEY

CHARDONNAY

750 mL
13.4% ALC BY VOL

FOUR LAKES
CHELAN

★
2007
Cabernet Sauvignon
COLUMBIA VALLEY

ALC. 13.6% BY VOL.   750 ML

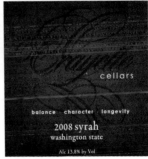

cellars

balance   character   longevity

2008 syrah
washington state

Alc 13.8% by Vol

Icicle Ridge
Winery
WASHINGTON STATE WINES
ALC. 12% BY VOL.

MERLOT
2003

The Blending Room

nano - WINERY

Okanogan Valley
Wine Trail

I still remember the surprise I felt when I first visited this Wine Trail. Who knew that *Vitis vinifera* could grow so well this far north? But in actuality, this is high desert terrain. With long summer days coupled with cool nights, the grapes grown here thrive. Traditionally, this is apple and pear country, but economic reality has made the region ripe for growing cabernet sauvignon and other noble grape varieties.

This land has no equal. I'm sure the early settlers on their way to the Puget Sound area paused here for a few days just to take in the valley's rugged landforms, the result of transformational geologic upheavals. With the influence of Canada's Okanagan winemaking region just to the north and the assistance of expert Washington State University viticulture researchers, this nascent wine region is destined to blossom.

Okanogan Valley WineTrail

1 Copper Mountain Vineyards

2 Okanogan Estate and Vineyards

3 Esther Bricques Winery & Vineyard

4 RockWall Cellars

5 Lost River Winery

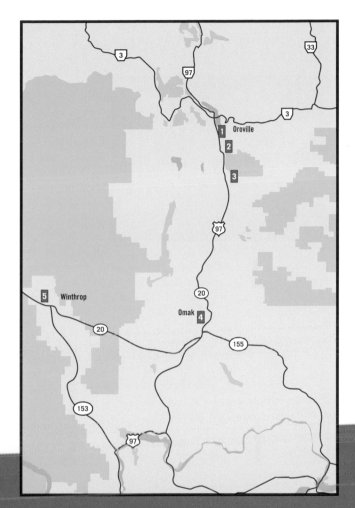

Region: **North Central Washington Wine Country**

# of tasting rooms on tour: **5**

Estimate # of days for tour: **2**

Getting around: **Car**

Tips:
- ❏ **Experience Esther Bricques Winery & Vineyard Thursday evenings after 6 for "social hour" during warm weather months. Includes food and music.**
- ❏ **Visit Copper Mountain Vineyard on Wednesday Wine Nights for food and music on the deck.**
- ❏ **During summer months, check out Wine Down Wednesday during the evening at RockWall Cellars.**
- ❏ **Food and wine pairing are nobly presented at Lost River Winery.**

 Best:
- ❏ **Music venue and views: Copper Mountain Vineyards**
- ❏ **Picnicking: Esther Bricques Winery & Vineyard**

Copper Mountain Vineyards

David Taber with daughter Angela Taber

In my Northwest travels, I've run across a few fruit stands that have wine for the tasting. It's great; you can pack away the berries and the corn and a bottle or two of wine. Such is the case at Taber's Taste of Summer Fruit Stand just two miles from the Canadian border on Highway 97. From approximately mid-April to mid-October, visitors to the fruit stand enjoy fresh produce, a generously sized gift shop, an onsite greenhouse and flower shop, as well as estate-grown cabernet and chardonnay. But more than that, you will take with you memories of a down-to-earth oh-so-friendly family. The Tabers make you feel right at home; especially if your visit coincides with one of their weekly Wednesday Nite Wine nights including live music on the deck overlooking Lake Osoyoos.

David and Judi Taber have been part of the agriculture scene in this idyllic spot for decades, but it wasn't until 1996 that they began planting premium wine grapes. Today, 10 different grape varieties reside at Copper Mountain Vineyards, which is surrounded by mountain and unforgettable lake views.

First-time visitors to the area are surprised to find a wine-growing region this far north. However, its "growing degree days," or GDDs, are similar to other viticultural areas in Washington. Vines happen to like the area's glacial soils and arid desert-like conditions (annual precipitation at 11.5 inches), with the marked difference between day and nighttime temperatures giving balance to sugars and acids. Embrace your diurnal rhythms, I always say.

With these conditions, it's no surprise that there are a few other wineries thriving here, such as Okanogan Estate & Vineyards and Esther Bricques Winery & Vineyard. Be sure to budget a full day to enjoy these local wines.

COPPER MOUNTAIN VINEYARDS
opened: 2008
winemaker(s): David Taber
location: 33345 Highway 97, Oroville, WA 98844
phone: 509-476-0202
web: www.coppermountainvinyards.com
e-mail: info@coppermountainvineyards.com
fee: Tasting fee may apply
hours: Daily 9–5
amenities: Gift Shop, Live Music, Newsletter/Blog, Picnic Area, RV/Bus Parking, Wheelchair Accessible

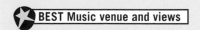

★ **BEST Music venue and views**

Okanogan Estate and Vineyards [2]

Most visitors experience Okanogan Winery at its wine and gift shop (located below Starbucks) in Leavenworth on Highway 2. Okanogan Estate's wines come from its vineyards

in the Okanogan Valley, which are located — along with its winery and one of its tasting room — north on Highway 97 just this side of the Canadian border. On the other side of that border is Canada's premier wine-growing region, British Columbia's Okanagan. (No, that's not a typo: On the American side, it's spelled "Okanogan," but on the Canadian side, it's spelled "Okanagan.") In its brochure, Okanogan Winery describes the terrain thusly: "The vineyards are located on the valley's sandy, desert sage benches and on the sunny slopes amongst the orchards of this fruitful valley that sits at the edges of beautiful Lake Osoyoos." Seriously, a desert-like climate in the northern reaches of Washington? Yep.

However, it's at Okanogan Winery's Wine & Gift Shoppe that many a lucky Leavenworth tourist gets to experience Okanogan in a glass. Here you can sample a full slate of dry and sweet white wines, such as pinot grigio, riesling, gewürztraminer, and late harvest sauvignon blanc, as well as some classic reds: merlot, pinot noir, and the Bench Rock blend. Formerly known as Gold Digger Cellars, after the name of its fruit orchards, the rechristened Okanogan Winery is proud of the fact that its wines don't rely on grapes trucked in from Yakima Valley or other points south.

If, however, your wine-related travels take you north on Highway 97, Okanogan Winery's downtown Oroville location is a fun pit stop. Oroville is an old mining town, and you will want to budget time to poke around and experience Oroville's charm. You won't have to dig very deep to find it.

OKANOGAN ESTATE AND VINEYARDS
opened: 2000
winemaker(s): Michael P. Buckmiller
location: 1205 Main Street, Oroville, WA 98844
phone: 509-476-2736
web: www.okanoganwine.com
e-mail: winery@okanoganwine.com
fee: Complimentary wine tasting
hours: Daily 11–5 (may vary off season)
amenities: Gift Shop, Online Store, Picnic Area, RV/Bus Parking, Tours, Wheelchair Accessible, Wine Club
connect: ⓕ

Esther Bricques Winery & Vineyard

Steve and Linda Colvin probably get a kick out of the surprised looks they often see on visitors' faces. After all, as you drive north from Tonasket along the Okanogan River, toward Oroville and the Canadian border, you don't anticipate the sight of vineyards.

As the Colvins are quick to point out, it's all about choosing the right site for your vineyard. The soil in this location reflects the remains of the last ice age and offers good drainage, but even more important is the strategic positioning of their vineyard, which butts up against the slope of Mount Hull. Having that gradient allows cool air to flow down at night during the growing season, and the mountain itself provides protection from winter storms. Grape clusters get long hang time here before Mother Nature ushers in the cold.

Steve and Linda share a common professional background. They both teach science at Oroville High School, and it's this science background that gives them an in-depth appreciation of the chemistry involved in fermenting sugar into alcohol. Another byproduct of fermentation are the more than 200 esters — fragrant organic compounds — that add to the wine's ultimate flavor. Grapes have trace amounts of esters, but during fermentation those compounds change and give rise to the aromas you smell, such as raspberry and tobacco. Likewise, sugar — or glucose — is converted into alcohol during fermentation. Knowing when to pick the grapes is based in large part on the grapes' sugar content, which is measured in brix.

To make wine, the winemaker must understand the role of esters and keep their finger on the pulse of the brix at harvest. Putting these terms together, you get "ester brix" or in the Colvins' variation of the spelling, "Esther Bricques." A clever name for a most remarkable winery!

ESTHER BRICQUES WINERY & VINEYARD
opened: 2008
winemaker(s): Linda and Steve Colvin
location: 38 Swanson Mill Road, Oroville, WA 98844
phone: 509-476-2861
web: www.estherbricques.com
e-mail: info@estherbricques.com
fee: Tasting fee refunded with purchase
hours: Summer hours: Thursday through Monday 1–6 or by appointment
amenities: Live Music, Picnic Area, RV/Bus Parking, Vineyard on Premise, Wheelchair Accessible, Wines by the Glass
connect: 🐦 ⬛

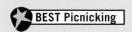 ⭐ **BEST Picnicking**

RockWall Cellars

Visitors to this spot in the Okanogan Valley may need to bring one of those family-tree forms to fill in, just to keep these familial ties untangled. You see, RockWall Cellars is truly a family affair involving several generations and a brother and sister (who actually get along) at the center of the enterprise. Their farming past actually began decades ago when their great grandma and grandpa Swallom moved from Iowa in the 1920s to farm in Washington's agricultural fruit basket. Apples were their core crop and that worked fine for generations — until the apple industry hit the skids around the millennium.

Doug Sheets

The decades marched on, and the time came when Greg and Diana "Di" Mock said adios to their medical practices in Oregon, bought the aforementioned family property in Omak, and converted it to vineyards. Di's brother Doug Sheets, with more than 25 years of experience as an orchardist and in marketing, got involved with tending the vines and knows every grape variety, every row, and darned near every vine that goes into making RockWall Cellars' lineup of reds, whites, and port.

Should you find yourself on some warm summer Wednesday looking for some respite, perhaps after a hard day working the 9 to 5, or tracking your Dow Jones stocks, or getting trounced in solitaire, you're in luck. It's Wine Down Wednesday at RockWall Cellars, where, from 7 to 9 p.m., you can enjoy a glass (or two) and listen to live music. All 21-year olds and older welcomed!

ROCKWALL CELLARS
opened: 2008
winemaker(s): Greg Rahn and Doug Sheets
location: 110 Nichols Road,
Omak, WA 98841
phone: 509-826-0201
web: www.rockwallcellars.com
e-mail: winemaker@rockwallcellars.com
fee: Complimentary wine tasting
hours: May through December, Daily 11–6; January through April, Thursday, Friday and Saturday 11–5
amenities: Live Music, Picnic Area, Private Events, RV/Bus Parking, Vineyard on Premise, Weddings, Wheelchair Accessible, Wine Club

Lost River Winery 🔒

Tucked into the northern tip of the state's north-central wine region, Lost River Winery is where John Morgan, his spouse, Barbara House, and Liam Doyle "produce fine wine at a fair price."

John and Barbara moved from Bellingham to the Methow Valley in 2001 on a mission to create fine wines. With no vineyards nearby, they source fruit from about a dozen vineyards in the Columbia Valley.

Interestingly, the Methow Valley has embraced the "slow food" movement, which advocates the growth and consumption of local produce and beef. Consequently, Lost River wines are often part and parcel in the enjoyment of locally sourced meals at many of the region's tables. Speaking of food, try your hand at the recipe for smoky grilled lamb and figs Moroccan style on Lost River's website. Pair the finished dish with the Lost River syrah and you'll have yourself one delectable, unforgettable meal.

Lost River Winery is located in the town of Winthrop, which is close to the wine cornucopia of the famed Okanagan Valley in British Columbia. It is also just an hour's drive north of the Chelan Valley wine region. Being the only winery in this funky frontier town has its distinct advantages. After you park your horse and mosey around the town, sit a spell and enjoy Lost River's delicious cabernet or syrah.

For those that just can't find the time to venture to Winthrop, they also offer a secondary tasting room in Seattle at the Pike Place Market. In between dodging flying fish and listening to the street performers, you can relish Lost River's treasures.

LOST RIVER WINERY
opened: 2002
winemaker(s): John Morgan
location: 26 Highway 20, Winthrop, WA 98622
phone: 509-996-2888
web: www.lostriverwinery.com
e-mail: info@lostriverwinery.com
fee: Tasting fee refunded with purchase
hours: Thursday through Monday 11–5, or by appointment
amenities: Mailing List, Online Store, Picnic Area, Restaurant/Food Pairings, RV/Bus Parking, Wheelchair Accessible, Wine Club, Wines by the Glass
connect: 🐦 📘

Lake Chelan North
WineTrail

Few places in Washington can boast of offering great places to eat, stay, and sample wine, but Lake Chelan easily meets such requirements. The North Shore is the perfect place to recreate and check out outstanding wines from more than a dozen wineries. Your WineTrail excursion can start with outdoor bistro fare and a white blend at Vin du Lac, and end at Wapato Point Cellars with a hearty steak and cabernet sauvignon. In between, you will experience award-winning wines and spectacular views; check out Benson Vineyards Estate Winery, Four Lakes Winery, or Atam Winery for proof positive that scenic views pair wonderfully with wine.

Lake Chelan WineTrail North

1 Rio Vista Wines
2 Vin du Lac Winery
3 Lake Chelan Winery
4 Benson Vineyards
   Estate Winery
5 Chelan Ridge Winery
6 Hard Row to Hoe Vineyards
7 Wapato Point Cellars
8 The Blending Room by
   WineGirl Wines
9 C.R. Sandidge Wines
10 Cairdeas Winery
11 Four Lakes Winery
12 Tildio Winery
13 Atam Winery

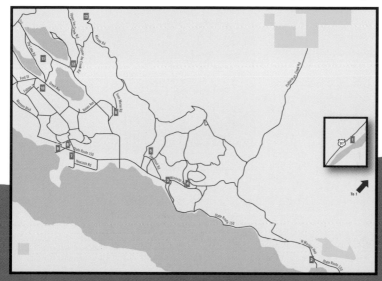

Region:	**North Central Washington Wine Country**
# of tasting rooms on tour:	**13**
Estimate # of days for tour:	**3**
Getting around:	**Car**
Key Events:	❏ **Lake Chelan Wine Valley association sponsors a number of annual events including Fall Barrel Tasting, Red Wine and Chocolate, Spring Barrel, Lake Chelan Crush and Chelan Nouveau. See www.lakechelanwinevalley.com for details.**
Tips:	❏ **Vin du Lac Winery, Lake Chelan Winery and Wapato Point Cellars offer food service.**
	❏ **Take Lady of the Lake to Stehekin for a great escape.**
Best:	❏ **Views and picnicking: Rio Vista Wines**
	❏ **Views and eats: Vin du Lac Winery**
	❏ **Eats and gift shop: Lake Chelan Winery**
	❏ **Views and picnicking: Benson Vineyards Estate Winery**
	❏ **Views and picnicking: Chelan Ridge Winery**
	❏ **Picnicking: Hard Row to Hoe Vineyards**
	❏ **Eats: Wapato Point Cellars**
	❏ **Views and picnicking: Four Lakes Winery**
	❏ **Views and picnicking: Tildio Winery**
	❏ **Picnicking: Atam Winery**

Rio Vista Wines

Fun. Unpretentious. Relaxing. These words come to mind when reflecting on my visit to Rio Vista Wines. Located along the banks of the mighty Columbia River, this is one winery where you can arrive by car, boat or float plane. In fact, coming upriver from Wenatchee via powerboat is the transportation of choice for many would-be sippers and picnickers.

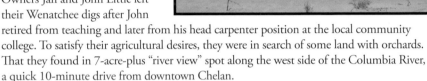

Owners Jan and John Little left their Wenatchee digs after John retired from teaching and later from his head carpenter position at the local community college. To satisfy their agricultural desires, they were in search of some land with orchards. That they found in 7-acre-plus "river view" spot along the west side of the Columbia River, a quick 10-minute drive from downtown Chelan.

With vineyard on premise, John works the 3 acres of red and white grape varieties like a true vigneron, managing the production from planting, pruning, harvesting, and bottling. With current production at around 600 cases, don't be surprised to find a plentitude of "sold out" signs. Do be sure to sample Rio Vista's crisp off-dry riesling, which shows nice stone fruit and refreshing acidity. If the riesling is sold out, no worries — go with the chardonnay, a nice choice to pair with your salami and cheese.

John and Jan Little

RIO VISTA WINES
opened: 2009
winemaker(s): John and Jan Little
location: 24415 SR 97, Chelan, WA 98816
phone: 509-682-9713
web: www.riovistawines.com
e-mail: info@riovistawines.com
fee: Complimentary wine tasting
hours: Summer hours: Wednesday through Sunday 11–6; Winter hours: Friday through Sunday 12–5; December and January weekend winter events only
amenities: Art Gallery, Online Store, Picnic Area, RV/Bus Parking, Vineyard on Premise, Weddings, Wheelchair Accessible, Wines by the Glass
connect: f

⭐ **BEST Views and picnicking**

Vin du Lac Winery

Vin du Lac, which is French for "wine of the lake," is the creation of Larry Lehmbecker and Michaela (Micki) Markusson. After visiting Paris and the French countryside, and venturing to Lake Chelan innumerable times, they decided to take the plunge and launch Vin du Lac Winery in 1998.

With its eye-pleasing yellow exterior and striped awning, the Vin du Lac tasting room, an old orchard farmhouse in its past life, has the look and feel of a French countryside bistro. It offers a relaxed space in which to enjoy Vin du Lac's lineup of delectable wines. When the weather's warm, visitors can enjoy the outdoor patio and order from a menu for both lunch and dinner. A certain *joie de vivre* is likely to come over you as you stroll through the surrounding orchards and vineyards — especially if you're toting a glass of one of Larry's critically acclaimed reds or whites.

Speaking of that acclaim, in 2010, *Wine Press Northwest* awarded Vin du Lac its Northwest Winery of the Year title.

Be sure to sample the affordable Cuvée Rouge red table wine — a bottle of this will go so nicely with that bistro meal.

VIN DU LAC WINERY
opened: 1998
winemaker(s): Larry Lehmbecker
location: 105 Hwy 150, Chelan, WA 98816-9505
phone: 509-682-2882
web: www.vindulac.com
e-mail: info@vindulac.com
fee: Complimentary wine tasting
hours: Thursday Friday and Sunday 12–5; Saturday 12–6; Bistro hours differ from tasting room
amenities: Gift Shop, Live Music, Picnic Area, Restaurant/Food Pairings, Tours, Vineyard on Premise, Wheelchair Accessible, Wine Club, Wines by the Glass
connect:

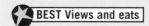 **BEST Views and eats**

Lake Chelan Winery

Lake Chelan Winery distinguishes itself on many fronts. First, WineTrail enthusiasts might be interested to know that Lake Chelan Winery was the first of its kind in the Lake Chelan area, having planted the first commercial vineyard in the Chelan Valley. Since 2001, Lake Chelan Winery has been serving premium wines from its Chelan-Manson Highway location. Second, its tasting room is located in what was the last privately owned apple-packing operation in Chelan. You might find this hard to believe when you visit the 3,000-square-foot tasting room with its generously sized gift shop. The transformation from packing shed to tasting room is nothing short of spectacular. Third, Lake Chelan Winery is in the top 10 in the gift shop category. We're not talking about the sheer number of items for sale (there are plenty), but the good quality of the merchandise.

The winery also distinguishes itself with a wine garden situated next to the winery. During the summer, the winery features a nightly "BBQ in the Vineyard." You can pick up a bottle of Lake Chelan wine and order up baby back pork ribs, chicken breasts, salmon, Bratwurst, or hot dogs (for the kids) and side of corn on the cob, coleslaw, or baked beans. Get ready to go through a pile of napkins devouring this barbecue, or simply jump into the lake afterward to wash off.

Bobbi and Steve Kludt are co-owners of Lake Chelan Winery, along with Spencer Bell, and John and Dawn Abbott. To assist with winemaking, Ray Sandidge (of C.R. Sandidge Winery fame) acts as consultant winemaker. Complimentary wine tasting gives visitors a taste-bud tour of the winery's chardonnay, muscat, pinot noir, syrah, gewürztraminer, cabernet sauvignon, and a luscious red blend called Stormy Mountain Red, composed of pinot noir, syrah, and small doses of cabernet franc and cabernet sauvignon.

LAKE CHELAN WINERY
opened: 2001
winemaker(s): Ray Sandidge
location: 3519 SR 150, Chelan, WA 98816
phone: 509-687-9463
web: www.lakechelanwinery.com
e-mail: lakechelanwinery@verizon.net
fee: Complimentary wine tasting
hours: Monday through Thursday 11–5; Friday and Sunday 11–7; BBQ from May through October 4–8 in the Wine Garden
amenities: Food Pairings, Gift Shop, Mailing List, Online Store, Picnic Area, Restaurant/Tours, Vineyard on Premise, Weddings, Wheelchair Accessible, Wine Club

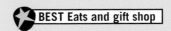
★ BEST Eats and gift shop

Benson Vineyards Estate Winery

Benson Vineyards Estate Winery can boast that 100 percent of its wines are estate wines — the grapes sourced right from its own vineyards, situated on the same property as the winery.

Located on Lake Chelan's north shore, the 30-acre Benson vineyard is reminiscent of northern Italy, with its hills, tall, spindly trees, terra-cotta homes, and the deep blues of the pristine lake below. OK, it's a cliché, I know, but these are truly stunning, breath-taking views from the winery's terrace. See for yourself. But the Benson family encourages visitors to "come for the view, but stay for the wine."

Although the winery is relatively new (established in 2005), the vineyards began much earlier. The Bensons knew that to be true vintners, they needed to know the land first. To this day, they require that all their staff — tasting room personnel included — work the vineyard during the year, pruning, picking, and getting dirt under their fingernails.

When the Bensons note on their website that their wine is "from our family to yours," they mean that literally. The entire family gets in on the act, with Paul and Kathy Benson managing the tasting room and other day-to-day operations, and son Scott at the helm as winemaker.

BENSON VINEYARDS ESTATE WINERY
opened: 2005
winemaker(s): Scott Benson
location: 754 Winesap Avenue, Manson, WA 98831-9581
phone: 509-687-0313
web: www.bensonvineyards.com
e-mail: info@bensonvineyards.com
fee: Complimentary wine tasting
hours: Daily 11–5
amenities: Online Store, Picnic Area, Private Events, Tours, Vineyard on Premise, Wheelchair Accessible
connect: 🐦 f

★ **BEST Views and picnicking**

Chelan Ridge Winery 5

"I like to be out in the vineyard pruning. I find it relaxing," noted Lynn Munneke, referring to the 13 acres of grapes growing next to Chelan Ridge Winery. One of the newest wineries in the Lake Chelan appellation, Chelan Ridge is perhaps the AVA's best, because of its incredible views of the surrounding area, the facility itself and the quality of its wine, which

belies the fact that this is a new winery. Vineyard manager, winemaker, and adept at making visitors feel at home, Lynn is a big part of the success story behind this infant winery.

However, don't plan on visiting in the winter when Lynn and her retired pilot husband, Henry, escape the cold to their home in Arizona. Not to give the impression that Henry is a passive co-owner of the

winery. This renaissance man designed the facility down to the last detail, including a barrel room that remains at a constant 56–57 degrees Fahrenheit and an inviting fireplace for relaxing next to with a glass of wine. Henry is often at the winery greeting visitors and making them feel welcome with his magnetic smile and, if time permits, a tour of the underground barrel room.

To educate herself on managing the vineyard — planted with eight different grape varieties — as well as the winemaking process, Lynn immersed herself in the Washington State University online viticulture and enology programs. It's given her a healthy dose of the science behind winemaking and the latest in grape-growing practices from WSU researchers. It's also shaped her style of winemaking, which leans toward "letting the fruit express itself" and includes the use of gravity for bottling their wine. Here, grapes get the primo spa treatment as she gently coaxes the fruit through the conversion process to wine. P.S. don't leave without trying her sinfully rich Rouge de Moraine red blend. Lovely.

CHELAN RIDGE WINERY
opened: 2010
winemaker(s): Lynn Munneke
location: 900 Swartout Road, Manson, WA 98831
phone: 509-668-0593
web: www.chelanridgewinery.com
e-mail: chelanridge@msn.com
fee: Tasting fee refunded with purchase
hours: Summer: Daily 12–6; Winter: Friday through Sunday 12–6
amenities: Picnic Area, Restaurant/Food Pairings, RV/Bus Parking, Vineyard on Premise, Wheelchair Accessible, Wines by the Glass
connect: 🐦 📘

⭐ **BEST Views and picnicking**

 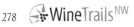

Hard Row to Hoe Vineyards ⑥

As you drive by Mill Bay Casino and turn up Ivan Morse Road in Manson, you have the beauty of Lake Chelan behind you and the promise of an established winery before you.

A 2006 startup, Hard Row to Hoe Vineyard is the creation of Don and Judy Phelps. Don's background as an engineer comes in handy nurturing their vineyard. Judy's mathematical mind (she's a biostatistician) is often exercised in the science of winemaking. She can readily tell you that 30 tons of grapes translate into 2,000 cases of wine.

The winery's name is a stroke of marketing genius and celebrates the fact that Lake Chelan had a thriving brothel in the 1930s. Miners were ferried via rowboat to the brothel at Point Lovely, and the name "Hard Row to Hoe" recognizes those sex-starved lads. Even the name of their wine club, "The Oar House," is a play on the enterprising business. Note: When at the winery, check out the Kama Sutra wallpaper in the restroom. With branding following such a randy theme, this WineTrail trekker was hot to try their wines.

Be sure to sample the Bear Mountain syrah, made from grapes harvested from their south shore vineyard — the finish on this wine is positively climactic.

HARD ROW TO HOE VINEYARDS
opened: 2006
winemaker(s): Judy Phelps
location: 300 Ivan Morse Road, Manson, WA 98831
phone: 509-687-3000
web: www.hardrow.com
e-mail: jumpintheboat@hardrow.com
fee: Tasting fee refunded with purchase
hours: Tuesday through Sunday 12–5
amenities: Online Store, Picnic Area, Vineyard on Premise, Wheelchair Accessible, Wine Club
connect: 🐦 📘

★ **BEST Picnicking**

Wapato Point Cellars 7

Many WineTrail trekkers time their visit to Wapato Point Cellars for the evening, so that they can dine at the casually elegant restaurant and enjoy live music from local talent. For a great evening meal, try the New York strip steak with the estate merlot. Delish. Family owned and operated, Wapato Point Cellars is a destination winery featuring premium wine and the aforementioned restaurant, Winemakers Grill, which offers an ever-changing fresh sheet, local beef, and seasonal seafood. But before venturing to the restaurant, be sure you sip and savor Wapato Point Cellars wines in the spacious tasting room — it's complimentary.

Jonathon Kludt is a mature young man. His youth may explain the unbridled energy he channeled to create a destination where visitors can enjoy great cuisine and great wine. Yet even at his young age, his résumé includes extensive experience in the wine industry. He is the son of Steve and Bobbi Kludt of Lake Chelan Winery fame. Jonathon also spent time in Santa Barbara working at Fess Parker Winery and Vineyards while taking courses at the University of California-Davis and Washington State University.

Located in the heart of Wapato Point Resort, the winery is family friendly, with a huge yard that includes playground equipment for kids — or adults who act like kids. There's also plenty of space for picnicking and tossing a Frisbee.

Jonathon Kludt

WAPATO POINT CELLARS
opened: 2003
winemaker(s): Jonathon Kludt
location: 200 Quetilquasoon Road, Manson, WA 98831
phone: 509-687-4000
web: www.wapatopointcellars.com
e-mail: jkludt@wapatopointcellars.com
fee: Complimentary wine tasting
hours: Daily starting at 12; Dinner served beginning at 5
amenities: Gift Shop, Online Store, Picnic Area, Private Events, Restaurant/Food Pairings, Tours, Wheelchair Accessible, Wine Club, Wines by the Glass
connect: 🐦 f

BEST Eats

The Blending Room by WineGirl Wines 🎱

This winery is all about fun. And why not? Someone with owner and entrepreneur Angela Jacobs' *joie de vivre*, especially with the beautiful surroundings of Lake Chelan to inspire, can't help but celebrate her love of wine, dogs, and John Deere tractors.

Exhibit A is Yappy! Hour every Thursday evening, when dog owners can mingle with their four-legged friends while sipping WineGirl Wines. The $5 fee goes toward a great cause: the Wenatchee Valley Humane Society. A word of warning: Those treats are meant for the dogs and are not to be paired with the cabernet. This event, and others, takes place at the winery, which Angela has dubbed The Blending Room and describes as a "nano-winery." In other words, it's teeny-tiny.

With a mind that's always running in overdrive, Angela isn't one to be satisfied with just one label. Check out her original Firá wines, My Derby Wife wines (the sassy roller-derby chick on the label is a nod to Angela's previous involvement in the sport), and Karmari Black Label. There's a reason behind each of the labels, and your mission, dear WineTrail trekker, is to discover what's driving Angela to produce multiple labels. Don't forget to check out the wine-and-food pairings; I found myself drooling over the food pairing suggestion with her Derby Wife cabernet-merlot blend: thinly sliced beef over a bed of red lettuce with sliced tomatoes and avocado. I'll take mine medium-rare, please!

THE BLENDING ROOM BY WINEGIRL WINES
opened: 2004
winemaker(s): Angela K. Jacobs
location: 222 East Wapato Way, Manson, WA 98831
phone: 509-293-9679
web: www.winegirlwines.com
e-mail: winegirl@winegirlwines.com
fee: Tasting fee refunded with purchase
hours: Daily 11–8 but call ahead in winter
amenities: Live Music, Online Store, Pet Friendly, Picnic Area, Restaurant/Food Pairings, Tours, Wheelchair Accessible, Wine Club, Wines by the Glass
connect: 🐦 📘

C.R. Sandidge Wines

The story behind C.R. Sandidge Winery centers on Ray Sandidge himself. Considered one of the state's top winemakers, Ray consults with a number of Chelan-area wineries and is also the winemaker for nearby Lake Chelan Winery. Some wineries come off more like business entities, and their survival doesn't seem to depend on their winemakers. However, Ray is the heart of C.R. Sandidge. We can only hope that he doesn't win the lottery and move to Australia to start "C.R. Sandidge Down Under."

At the C.R. Sandidge tasting room, on Wapato Way in Manson, visitors have the opportunity to experience Ray's exceptional reds, including a syrah, his Triumph red blend, and Stone Tree Red. However, don't neglect Ray's white wines, which showcase wine grapes from the Lake Chelan Valley AVA and parts north toward Oroville. My personal favorite is the Triumph, which carries a hefty price tag of $50 a bottle. (Note: You can save 10 of those smackaroos on Triumph's retail price by joining the wine club.) If you're pinching those pennies, The Whistle Punk Red is a more wallet-friendly $18 a bottle.

The way I see it, C.R. Sandidge wines enhance the Lake Chelan experience. How do you figure that, you ask; how does a wine improve on this 55-mile lake and recreational playground. Well, when you visit Lake Chelan, you experience a paradise where you relax, have some outdoor fun and soak in the natural beauty. Ray's wines also take us to a wonderful place, one where we can pause and experience the simple, pure pleasure of a delectable drink. But discover this for yourself: Find a spot with a view of the lake and open a bottle of Ray's Stone Tree Red; see if the dapples of sunlight on the water don't sparkle just a tad more.

C.R. SANDIDGE WINES
opened: 2004
winemaker(s): Ray Sandidge III
location: 145 East Wapato Way, Suite 1, Manson, WA 98831
phone: 509-682-3704
web: www.crsandidgewines.com
e-mail: tastingroom@crsandidgewines.com
fee: Tasting fee refunded with purchase
hours: Summer: Wednesday through Saturday 11–7; Winter: Friday and Saturday 11–7
amenities: Picnic Area, Wheelchair Accessible, Wine Club
connect: f

Cairdeas Winery ⑩

Cairdeas (pronounced "car-dess") is an ancient Gaelic word meaning friendship, goodwill or alliance. It embodies the vision young owners Charlie and Lacey Lybecker have for their start-up winery — to create lasting friendships, spread goodwill and form alliances with others who share a passion for fine wine.

Charlie Lybecker

As Charlie poured a sample of his white Rhône blend (a delicious fusion of viognier and roussanne), he noted that they named the wine after his grandmother Nellie Mae, who, in her mid-80s, decided to help out with crush to learn "what all these grapes were about." As the bright fruit notes of Nellie Mae took hold of my palate, Charlie mentioned that Lacey was in Seattle attending a wine event and that I really needed to meet her because she's a vital part of the winery. Referring fondly to Lacey as the "palate diva," Charlie explained that the two of them are 100 percent a team and that without her, the venture would never have sprouted wings.

Most people would lack the intestinal fortitude required to break the bonds of Seattle and plant new roots in Manson. The fear of the unknown and the need to pay little things such as college debt and home mortgages keep most of us entrenched. But Charlie and Lacey fell in love with Lake Chelan and its burgeoning wine industry. Fortunately, their work allows them to pursue their passion on the eastern side of the mountains near the Wahluke Slope and Yakima Valley, where they have partnered with a select group of grape growers. They traded a postage-stamp-size tasting room in West Seattle for an expansive facility and tasting room in Manson. It's the perfect space to escape summer's heat or winter's cold, make new friends, and swap stories at the wine bar. It can truly be called the embodiment of cairdeas.

CAIRDEAS WINERY
opened: 2012
winemaker(s): Charlie Lybecker
location: 2480 Totem Pole Road, Manson, WA 98831
phone: 509-687-0555
web: www.cairdeaswinery.com
e-mail: info@cairdeaswinery.com
fee: Complimentary wine tasting
hours: Summer: Daily 12–7; Winter: Saturday 12–5
amenities: Mailing List, Online Store, RV/Bus Parking, Wheelchair Accessible, Wine Club
connect: 🐦 f

Four Lakes Winery

Did you know that Chelan has four lakes? I'm sure that you are familiar with 55-mile-long Lake Chelan. However, there are three other lakes, although they are mere ponds compared to the size of Lake Chelan. Yes, indeed, Wapato, Roses and Dry lakes are a little string of pearls waiting for picture snapping.

This is a small-lot family winery, with owner Don Koester investing in the passion of his life, and son Karl Koester doing the honors as winemaker. Lake Chelan was Don's boyhood retreat where he went every summer with his family to recreate. It was only natural that he would satisfy his love of the vine by planting a vineyard and nursery on the Manson side of the lake.

From the deck of the Four Lakes Chelan Winery, you can swirl and sip while taking in the view of the nearby lake. The usual suspects of reds (cabernet, merlot, syrah) and whites (gewürztraminer, riesling, chardonnay) make for a nice afternoon (or evening, for that matter). To say that this is an inviting space to break bread — and slice some salami — doesn't begin to do it justice. In fact, it is one of the state's top wineries to visit for unpacking a picnic basket and uncorking some wine.

FOUR LAKES WINERY
opened: 2009
winemaker(s): Karl Koester
location: 4491 Wapato Lake Road, Manson, WA 98816
phone: 509-687-0726
web: www.fourlakeschelanwinery.com
e-mail: karl@fourlakeswinery.com
fee: Tasting fee
hours: Daily 12–6 with extended hours in summer, call ahead
amenities: Online Store, Picnic Area, Vineyard on Premise, Wheelchair Accessible, Wine Club
connect: 🐦 📘

⭐ **BEST Views and picnicking**

These people like to party!

Tildio Winery

It's not unusual for friends and neighbors to stop by and spend the afternoon drinking wine, munching on cheese and assorted fruit, and yakking with Tildio Winery owners Milum and Katy Perry. The shaded patio offers an inviting place to relax and enjoy the view of nearby Roses Lake.

The fact is, the couple pays as much loving attention to their guests as they do their vintages. Both Milum and Katy cut their winemaking teeth in California before they ventured north in 2001 to stake a claim in the burgeoning Washington wine industry. They named their winery Tildio, which is the Spanish word for killdeer, a shorebird that breeds in large numbers in the Perrys' 8-acre vineyard.

The couple's estate vineyard is planted with cabernet franc, tempranillo, syrah, grenache, and sauvignon blanc. Having the vineyard gives them control, from vine bud to bottling, and allows Katy to exercise her degree in enology and viticulture from University of California-Davis. Before opening Tildio with Milum, she gained hands-on experience at some well-established wineries, including Robert Mondavi, Benzinger, Geyser Peak, Stag's Leap Wine Cellars, and even did a stint Down Under, at the Yalumba Winery in Australia.

The art of winemaking is crucial, but its science spells the difference between acceptable and outstanding. Katy's scientific knowledge proves this time and again, in Tildio's varietals. Exhibit A for me was her 2008 Estate Tempranillo packing a boatload of fruit and notes of licorice — clearly she has done justice to Spain's most noble grape. With a view of dappled sparkling Roses Lake from the outdoor patio I retreated with my glass of Tempranillo to reflect on how life's ingredients come together to create a perfect moment.

TILDIO WINERY
opened: 2000
winemaker(s): Milum and Katy Perry
location: 70 East Wapato Lake Road, Manson, WA 98831
phone: 509-687-8463
web: www.tildio.com
e-mail: milum@tildio.com
fee: Tasting fee refunded with purchase
hours: Summer: Daily 12–7; Winter: Saturday 12–5; Spring and fall, call ahead or check web
amenities: Gift Shop, Picnic Area, RV/Bus Parking, Tours, Vineyard on Premise, Wheelchair Accessible, Wine Club
connect:

★ **BEST Views and picnicking**

 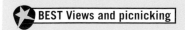

Atam Winery 🔟

Come for the view, but stay for the wine. Atam Winery offers a picture-perfect elevated location and a friendly space to sample estate wine from German transplants Denis and Irmi Atam. With their German heritage as a compass, the Atams were quick to plant a vineyard in 2002. Not surprisingly, the vineyard is composed primarily of riesling and gewürztraminer plantings, but there also are barbera and syrah vines.

The hard-working couple has created a beautiful timber-beamed home (the place is spotless), with a downstairs tasting room that offers respite from the hot summer sun and a patio populated with inviting outdoor furniture. The whole place cajoles, "Kick back, relax, and enjoy some wine." Which I most willingly did as I watched Denis attack a leaking irrigation sprinkler with a post hole digger. Perhaps I should have offered to help, but the refreshing riesling kept me planted in the chair.

Denis Atam

The riesling itself is Washington's version of this most noble white grape. Whereas Germany produces breathtaking rieslings that border on the edge of tartness, with crystal clear notes of apple and pear wrapped in a slate minerality, Washington's riesling is much fruitier, with a noticeable lack of minerality. It just goes to show you that *terroir* matters. You can start with the same grape variety, but without the steep slopes of Germany's Mosel Valley and devoid of that country's slate and cooler climate, the fruit ripens differently in Washington's hotter weather. Benefiting from more "growing degree days," Washington's grapes possess more sugars, less acid, and plenty of fruit notes. Not better, not worse, just different — and true to the place from which it grows and to the bounty of Lake Chelan.

ATAM WINERY
opened: 2009
winemaker(s): Denis Atam
location: 750 Kinsey Road, Manson, WA 98831
phone: 509-687-4421
web: www.atam-winery.com
e-mail: contact@atam-winery.com
fee: Tasting fee
hours: Summer: Friday through Sunday 2–6; Winter: Saturday 1–5
amenities: Picnic Area, RV/Bus Parking, Vineyard on Premise, Weddings, Wheelchair Accessible
connect: 📘

⭐ **BEST Picnicking**

Lake Chelan South
WineTrail

Summer concert at Tsillan Cellars

Most visitors come to Lake Chelan via Highway 97-Alt and are surprised to find rows of vineyards climbing up the hillside from the Lake. From Karma Vineyards to Tsillan Cellars, visitors may have a hard time getting to their hotel. Budget time to have dinner (and wine) at Tsillan (pronounced "Chelan") Cellars, where the Italian-style architecture and distinct clock tower host a steady flow of WineTrail enthusiasts. However, to find your inner peace, be sure and retreat to an outdoor Adirondack chair at Nefarious Cellars. The wines coupled with the view defines decadence in a great way.

Lake Chelan WineTrail South

1 Tsillan Cellars   **3** Nefarious Cellars   **5** Karma Vineyards

2 Tunnel Hill Winery   **4** Chelan Estate Winery and Vineyard

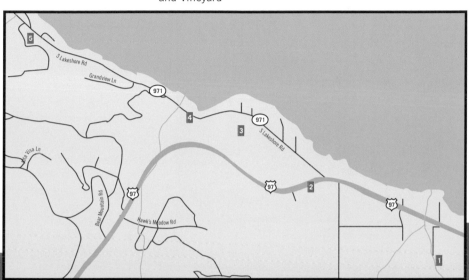

Region: **North Central Washington Wine Country**

# of tasting rooms on tour: **5**

Estimate # of days for tour: **1 to 2**

Getting around: **Car**

Key Events: ❏ **Lake Chelan Wine Valley association sponsors a number of annual events including Fall Barrel Tasting (first weekend following Thanksgiving), Red Wine and Chocolate (February), Spring Barrel (May), Lake Chelan Crush (October) and Chelan Novueau (April). See www.lakechelanwinevalley.com for details.**

Tips: ❏ **Tsillan Cellars provides a full service restaurant (Sorrento's) for outdoor dining by the waterfalls.**

❏ **Consider hiring a limousine service (e.g., Lakeside Limousine Tours 509-470-0333 or Northwest Limousine 509-670-4952 or Chelan Valley Tours 509-682-2FUN to name a few).**

❏ **Pack a camera.**

Best: ❏ **Destination, eats, views, weddings and gift shop: Tsillan Cellars**

❏ **Views and picnicking: Tunnel Hill Winery**

❏ **Views and picnicking: Nefarious Cellars**

❏ **Views and picnicking: Chelan Estate Winery and Vineyard**

❏ **Views, eats: Karma Vineyards**

Tsillan Cellars ❶

With spectacular views of Lake Chelan, a huge tasting room, and an Italian restaurant on the premises, there is little doubt that Tsillan (pronounced "Chelan") Cellars is the destination winery.

Dr. Robert Jankelson, a retired dentist and the owner of Tsillan Cellars, has a special love for Italy, having enjoyed more than 40 separate sojourns in that country over the years. As you turn off the highway and make your way up the gentle hill to Tsillan's 135-acre estate, you spy the Tuscan-inspired architecture of the winery and tasting room. The majestic 35-foot bell tower houses a 650-pound, cast-bronze bell. The surrounding vineyard is composed of more than 40 acres of syrah, merlot, Malbec, chardonnay, pinot grigio, riesling, and gewürztraminer.

Not far from the tasting room is a fabulous amphitheater, where live musical performances are hosted during the summer. Three waterfalls surround the island stage, creating a sense of harmony and offering a spectacular backdrop for the performers.

Top off your visit by uncorking that bottle of freshly purchased Tsillan Cellars' Bellissima Rossa to accompany Sorrento's Ristorante's spaghetti and meatballs. *Mamma mia!*

TSILLAN CELLARS
opened: 2004
winemaker(s): Shane Collins
location: 3875 Highway 97 Alt, Chelan, WA 98816
phone: 509-682-9643
web: www.tsillancellars.com
e-mail: info@tsillancellars.com
fee: Tasting fee
hours: Summer: Daily 11–7; Winter: Daily 12–5; tours of winery and tasting room conducted twice daily at 1 and 3
amenities: Gift Shop, Live Music, Mailing List, Online Store, Picnic Area, Private Events, Restaurant/Food Pairings, Tours, Vineyard on Premise, Weddings, Wheelchair Accessible, Wine Club

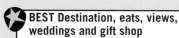
★ BEST Destination, eats, views, weddings and gift shop

Tunnel Hill Winery 2

For generations, the slopes above this winery had produced award-winning apples, but now those same hills are home to the estate vineyards of Tunnel Hill. Rows of pinot noir, riesling, and syrah grapes stripe the hillside.

Tunnel Hill's owner, Denny Evans, together with his winemaking son, Guy Evans, is producing small lots of wine. Being a small operation, requires Denny and Guy to wear many hats: grape grower, winemaker, production manager, head of marketing, and chief bottle washer. However, understanding Tunnel Hill Winery is to know the road that brought them here.

If you have been lucky enough to have seen the Emmy-nominated documentary Broken Limbs, you may recognize that one of the "stars" of the show is Denny himself. Denny's son Guy made Broken Limbs to explain the sudden demise of Washington's apple industry and to highlight how this downturn has affected families in the Chelan-Wenatchee area. Denny's orchard was once one of the largest apple-producing farms in the state. Overnight, it fell on hard times, but Denny has taken advantage of Washington's rich educational resources as well as its community of supportive winemakers and viticulturists. From the ashes of burning applewood, Tunnel Hill Winery has risen.

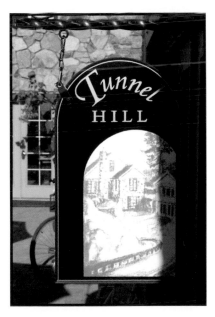

TUNNEL HILL WINERY
opened: 2003
winemaker(s): Guy Evans
location: 37 Highway 97A, Chelan, WA 98816
phone: 509-682-5695
web: www.tunnelhillwinery.com
e-mail: info@tunnelhillwinery.com
fee: Tasting fee refunded with purchase
hours: Summer: Daily 11–6; Winter: Saturday and Sunday 12–5
amenities: Lodging, Online Store, Picnic Area, RV/Bus Parking, Vineyard on Premise, Weddings, Wheelchair Accessible, Wine Club
connect: f

BEST Views and picnicking

Nefarious Cellars ❸

This ranks as one of my top 10 wineries to visit in the state, for a host of reasons. It begins with the wine, of course, and in this regard, both whites and reds excel. The friendliness of owners Dean and Heather Neff certainly adds to the charm and relaxed feel of the place. When you add the "OMG!" views from the deck of the winery, overlooking rows of vineyards and Lake Chelan in the distance, you have the makings of a fun-filled afternoon.

A visit to the winery reveals that Heather creates the white wines, and Dean is in charge of the reds. In Heather's world, fruit is separated quickly from the skins and bathed in stainless steel. In Dean's realm of reds, skins and pulp, touched by oak, commingle for long periods. A sample of Heather's Consequence (a blend of sauvignon blanc and riesling) will encourage you to head outside to the patio with your glass and enjoy the magnificent view of the lake. However, as you progress to the reds, Dean's jammy and hedonistic Defiance Vineyard syrah will have you hankering for something substantial, such as a New York strip steak, to pair with this wine.

Patio view of Lake Chelan from Nefarious Winery

As you know, the WineTrails Guy attempts to be somewhat neutral about the wines and the wineries. After all, the premise of the WineTrail guides is to give you the reader the information to go and experience the wine and ambience yourself letting you to be the judge. But all that aside, let me gush briefly here because Nefarious Cellars is one of my favorite places to visit and imbibe anywhere in the Northwest. It has it all and it all starts with their remarkable wines. Wines of distinction. Neff said.

NEFARIOUS CELLARS
opened: 2005
winemaker(s): Dean and Heather Neff
location: 495 South Lakeshore Road, Chelan, WA 98816
phone: 509-682-9505
web: www.nefariouscellars.com
e-mail: getsome@nefariouscellars.com
fee: Tasting fee
hours: Saturday 11–5, Sunday 11–4
amenities: Online Store, Picnic Area, Vineyard on Premise, Wheelchair Accessible, Wine Club
connect: 🐦 f

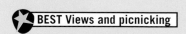

⭐ **BEST Views and picnicking**

Chelan Estate Winery and Vineyard

The popular belief is that it is simply too hot to grow pinot noir in eastern Washington, particularly in the area around Lake Chelan. However, because of an interesting meteorological phenomenon known as a microclimate, Bob and Mary Broderick, owners of Chelan Estate Vineyards & Winery, have discovered fertile ground for pinot noir on the south shore of Lake Chelan. The lake provides cooler summers and warmer winters. Thus, of the 8 acres of grapes the Brodericks cultivate, the majority is devoted to pinot noir.

Winemaker Bob must be doing something right. The estate-grown pinot noir is elegant and stylish — a rich reward for these growers/winemakers, considering this grape demands more time and attention than most.

From the deck of the tasting room, you enjoy a stunning view of Lake Chelan. Pack a picnic, because you'll want to make a leisurely day of it. Your most difficult decision may be whether to uncork the chardonnay-viognier blend, a cabernet from Stillwater Creek Vineyard, or the estate pinot noir. Decisions, decisions. For me, I struck a balance, going with the merlot. Cheers!

CHELAN ESTATE WINERY AND VINEYARD
opened: 2004
winemaker(s): Bob Broderick
location: 755 South Lakeshore Road, Chelan, WA 98816
phone: 509-682-5454
web: www.chelanestatewinery.com
e-mail: chelanestatewinery@nwi.net
fee: Tasting fee refunded with purchase
hours: Summer: Daily 11–6; Non-summer, call ahead
amenities: Online Store, Tours, Vineyard on Premise, Wheelchair Accessible, Wine Club
connect: f

⭐ **BEST Views and picnicking**

Karma Vineyards 5

This winery admits it right on its website home page for the whole world to see: "Our passion is bubbling…" — in the literal sense, that is, with its production of sparkling wines.

Only a handful of Washington wineries use the *méthode champenoise* to make sparkling wine, and Lake Chelan WineTrail trekkers have the opportunity to experience the end results of this method at Karma Vineyards. Although a bottle of Karma Vineyards' bubbly sports a hefty price tag of $46.99 a bottle, the truth is that much labor and love goes into each bottle. From secondary fermentation in the bottle to the riddling that follows, each batch is subject to singular care and attention.

The surrounding vineyards of this south-shore winery add beauty to the landscape, but there's also a manmade cave underneath the winery that's quite a sight to behold. Here, you can peruse the sparkling wines resting comfortably in their riddling racks and glance longingly at the banquet room where candelabra bathe private parties in warm light.

If your tummy groans with hunger, you're at the right place. Karma Vineyards' 18 Brix Restaurant will quiet those pangs. Hint: Assuming your Weight Watchers counselor isn't around, check out the TBBC sandwich: a delicious concoction of tomato, hickory bacon, fresh basil and chicken. Delish!

KARMA VINEYARDS
opened: 2007
winemaker(s): Craig Mitrakul
location: 1681 South Lakeshore Road, Chelan, WA 98816
phone: 509-682-5538
web: www.goodkarmawines.com
e-mail: info@goodkarmawines.com
fee: Tasting fee for wine, cheese and bread; $1 of fee donated to local cause
hours: Wednesday and Thursday 12–5; Friday and Saturday 12–8; Sunday 12–3
amenities: Online Store, Private Events, Restaurant/Food Pairings, Vineyard on Premise, Weddings, Wheelchair Accessible, Wine Club
connect: 🐦 f

⭐ **BEST Views, eats**

Leavenworth–
Cashmere
Wine Trail

Pack your lederhosen for this Wine Trail and toss in your beer stein. There will be chances to use both in Leavenworth. A few years back, the town's business community saw an opportunity to attract tourists by creating a Bavarian-themed village. It was the right decision. Today, Leavenworth is one of the most visited places in Washington state.

This is arguably the most majestic location in Washington. Here, on Front Street, you'll discover friendly pouring staff and tasting rooms within walking distance of each other. Then, head east on Highway 2 and discover more great wineries in Peshastin and Cashmere. Home to wineries with evocative names like Ryan Patrick, Eagle Creek, Napeequa, Icicle Ridge, and Wedge Mountain, the Leavenworth-Cashmere Wine Trail takes the cake for great names and good times.

Leavenworth-Cashmere WineTrail

1. Stemilt Creek Winery
2. d'Vinery - Eagle Creek Winery
3. Ryan Patrick Vineyards
4. Okanogan Estate and Vineyards
5. Swakane Winery
6. Boudreaux Cellars
7. A Taste of Icicle Ridge Winery
8. Dusty Cellars Winery
9. Bella Terrazza Vineyards
10. Kestrel Vintners
11. Baroness, Bergdorf and Mannina Cellars
12. Willow Crest Winery
13. Pasek Cellars Winery
14. Eagle Creek Winery & Cottage
15. Napeequa Vintners
16. Silvara Vineyards
17. Icicle Ridge Winery
18. Cascadia Winery
19. Wedge Mountain Winery
20. Waterville Winery
21. Crayelle Cellars
22. Horan Estates Winery
23. Dutch John's Wines

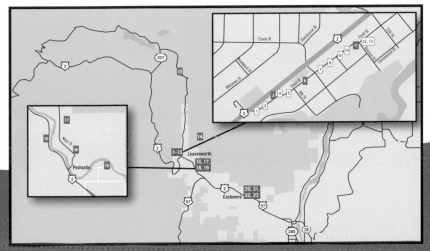

Region:	**North Central Washington Wine Country**
# of tasting rooms on tour:	**23**
# of satellite tasting rooms:	**10**
Estimate # of days for tour:	**5**
Getting around:	**Car and foot**
Key Events:	❑ **The Great Leavenworth Wine and Food Festival — late June. See www.columbiacascadewines.com.**
	❑ **Christmas Lighting Festival during December weekends in Leavenworth.**
Tips:	❑ **Leavenworth offers a variety of places to eat and sleep although for a true vineyard experience plan to stay at Eagle Creek Winery and Cottage.**
	❑ **Consider hiring a limousine service.**
	❑ **Plan visit to the area by clicking on www.leavenworth.org or call 509-548-5807.**
Best:	❑ **Gift shop: Okanogan Estate and Vineyards**
	❑ **Lodging: Eagle Creek Winery & Cottage**
	❑ **Music venue, picnicking and weddings: Icicle Ridge Winery**
	❑ **Views: Wedge Mountain Winery**

Stemilt Creek Winery [1]

STEMILT CREEK WINERY
opened: 2007
winemaker(s): Jan Mathison
location: 617 Front Street,
Leavenworth, WA 98826
phone: 509-888-5357
web: www.stemiltcreekwinery.com
e-mail: winery@stemiltcreekwinery.com
fee: Tasting fee refunded with purchase
hours: Monday through Thursday 12–6; Friday and
Saturday 12–7; Sunday 11–5
amenities: Mailing List, Online Store, Wheelchair
Accessible, Wine Club, YouTube
connect: 🐦 f

www.winetrailsnw.com/wineries/stemilt_creek_winery

d'Vinery — Eagle Creek Winery [2]

D'VINERY - EAGLE CREEK WINERY
opened: 2002
winemaker(s): Ed Rutledge
location: 617 Front Street, Suite 4A,
Leavenworth, WA 98826
phone: 509-548-7059
web: www.eaglecreekwinery.com
e-mail: info@eaglecreekwinery.com
fee: Complimentary wine tasting
hours: Monday through Friday 12–7; Saturday 12–8;
and Sunday 11–6
amenities: Gift Shop, Online Store, Wheelchair
Accessible, Wine Club
connect: f

www.winetrailsnw.com/wineries/d'vinery_-_eagle_creek_winery

Ryan Patrick Vineyards

Ryan Patrick Vineyards' tasting room is in the heart of Bavarian-inspired Leavenworth. When not at the tasting room, owner Terry Flanagan is often tending to his vineyards or marketing his wines. His charming wife, Vivian, manages the tasting room with aplomb.

The winery is the namesake of the couple's two sons, Ryan and Patrick.

Their estate wines use fruit grown in two family-owned vineyards: The Bishop's Vineyard, containing 20 acres of chardonnay, cabernet sauvignon, merlot, and cabernet franc; and The Homestead Vineyard, with its 25 acres of exquisite chardonnay. Low yields in the vineyard, combined with prime locations for heat and sunlight, produce concentrated fruit.

The Leavenworth tasting room is ideally located on Front Street, below Visconti's Italian Restaurant.

The Flanagans recently sold their winery to the Milbrandt brothers. However, lest you think that the brand will disappear with the Milbrandt acquisition, think again. Ryan Patrick will continue live on with its new owners. Hey, if it ain't broke, don't fix it!

RYAN PATRICK VINEYARDS
opened: 1996
winemaker(s): Jeremy Santo
location: 636 Front Street, Leavenworth, WA 98826
phone: 509-888-2236
web: www.ryanpatrickvineyards.com
e-mail: via website
fee: Complimentary wine tasting
hours: Daily 11–6, extended summer hours
amenities: Tours, Wheelchair Accessible, Wine Club
connect: 🐦 📘

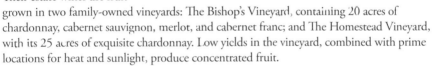

Okanogan Estate and Vineyards ④

OKANOGAN ESTATE AND VINEYARDS
opened: 2000
winemaker(s): Michael P. Buckmiller
location: 1205 Main Street on US Highway 97, Oroville, WA 98844
phone: 509-476-2736
web: www.okanoganwine.com
e-mail: winery@golddiggerscellars.com
fee: Complimentary wine tasting
hours: Daily 11–5 (may vary off season)
amenities: Gift Shop, Online Store, Wheelchair Accessible, Wine Club
connect: 🇫

www.winetrailsnw.com/wineries/okanogan_estate_and_vineyards

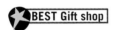
BEST Gift shop

Swakane Winery ⑤

SWAKANE WINERY
opened: 2009
winemaker(s): Mike Franks
location: 725 Front Street, Leavenworth, WA 98826
phone: 509-888-7225
web: www.swakanewinery.com
e-mail: donna@swakanewinery.com
fee: Tasting fee
hours: Sunday through Thursday 11–6; Friday and Saturday 11–7ish
amenities: Art Gallery, Gift Shop, Wine Club
connect: 🇫

www.winetrailsnw.com/wineries/swakane_winery

Boudreaux Cellars

I could listen to Rob Newsom all day. His voice has that Louisiana Cajun accent going on. Nevertheless, despite his Southern heritage, he's been here long enough to embrace certain Northwest trappings, including ice climbing, the charming town of Leavenworth, and, of course, Washington wines. Still, you half expect Rob to offer you a cup of chicory coffee rather than a taste of his cabernet sauvignon.

Although Rob opened a downtown Leavenworth tasting room (New Orleans' French Quarter style with gaslights), the actual winery is located 7.7 miles from Leavenworth off Icicle Creek Road, just a few miles past the Sleeping Lady Conference Center. The winery is open by appointment only, but if you do happen to go there, get ready for an off-the-grid tasting experience, literally. Four miles off the power grid, Boudreaux is the only winery in Washington state to be completely self-powered. Four miles off the power grid, Boudreaux is the only winery in Washington state to be completely self-powered. As you cross the wooden bridge to Boudreaux Cellars, taking in the majestic mountain views, look for Rob's smiling face to greet you. It's all homespun magic, but then again, so are his wines.

Discover why Robert M. Parker consistently gives scores in the 90s for Rob's voluptuous wines and why, in 2007, *Seattle* magazine named Boudreaux Cellars the "Best New Winery of the Year" and Rob Newsom as the "Best New Winemaker of the Year."

BOUDREAUX CELLARS
opened: 2001
winemaker(s): Rob Newsom
location: 821 Front Street, Leavenworth, WA 98826
phone: 509-548-4848
web: www.boudreauxcellars.com
e-mail: rob@boudreauxcellars.com
fee: Complimentary wine tasting
hours: Daily
amenities: Online Store, Picnic Area, Tours, Winemaker Dinners
connect: f

A Taste of Icicle Ridge Winery ⑦

A TASTE OF ICICLE RIDGE WINERY
opened: 2002
winemaker(s): Don Wood
location: 821 Front Street,
Leavenworth, WA 98826
phone: 509-548-6156 Tasting room in Leavenworth
web: www.icicleridgewinery.com
e-mail: info@icicleridgewinery.com
fee: Tasting fee
hours: Sunday through Thursday 11–6
amenities: Gift Shop, Wine Club
connect: 🐦 ⓕ

www.winetrailsnw.com/wineries/a_taste_of_icicle_ridge_winery

Dusty Cellars Winery ⑧

DUSTY CELLARS WINERY
opened: 2008
winemaker(s): Ryan and Dusty Kramer
location: 827 Front Street,
Leavenworth, WA 98826
phone: 360-387-2171
web: www.dustycellars.net
e-mail: via website
fee: Tasting fee may apply
hours: Daily 12–5
connect: ⓕ

www.winetrailsnw.com/wineries/dusty_cellars_winery

Bella Terrazza Vineyards ⑨

BELLA TERRAZZA VINEYARDS
opened: 2008
winemaker(s): Bob Richards
location: 837 Front Street, Suite A,
Leavenworth, WA 98826
phone: 509-662-9141
web: www.bellaterrazzavineyards.com
e-mail: info@bellaterrazzavineyards.com
fee: Tasting fee
hours: Thursday through Sunday 12–5;
Call ahead during off-peak season
amenities: Mailing List, Newsletter/Blog, Wine Club
connect: f

www.winetrailsnw.com/wineries/bella_terrazza_vineyards

Kestrel Vintners ⑩

KESTREL VINTNERS
opened: 1995
winemaker(s): Flint Nelson
location: 843 Front Street, Suite B,
Leavenworth, WA 98826
phone: 509-548-7348
web: www.kestrelwines.com
e-mail: Leavenworth@kestrelwines.com
fee: Tasting fee
hours: Daily 11–5
amenities: Newsletter/Blog, Online Store, Private
Events, Wine Club, Winemaker Dinners
connect: 🐦 f

www.winetrailsnw.com/wineries/kestrel_vintners

Baroness, Bergdorf and Mannina Cellars 11

At Leavenworth's 10,000-square-foot 939 Front Street building, visitors get a three-in-one treat with Bergdorf Cellars, Baroness Cellars and Mannina Cellars all housed under one roof. This two-story shopper's paradise is packed full of home décor items and artsy treasures, and the wine traveler is advised to budget plenty of time for tasting in between looking for that special pillow to adorn your new couch.

If it's cold outside, Bergdorf Cellars offers spicy Glühwein to warm people's cockles. And we all need our cockles warmed now and then. But if warmed piquant wine isn't to your liking, Austrian winemaker John Delvo's other wines will likely hit the mark. Be it his use of grapes from 20 different vineyards or the 36 months that he ages his wine in French oak, his quaffs are sure to please; there's a reason John is held in high regard among Leavenworth winemakers.

Once you've done justice to Bergdorf Cellars, head upstairs to the tasting rooms of Baroness Cellars and Mannina Cellars.

Baroness' Danielle Clements bottles 1,200 cases per year, including her signature wine, Mountain Meritage. This blend of (non-vintage) cabernet franc and merlot expresses a gorgeous red color, earthy smell, and good midpalate weight. At $6 a glass, this wine merits pulling up a chair and making yourself comfortable to enjoy it. If the weather is warm outside, be sure to step out to the balcony and show off your new lederhosen.

The satellite tasting room of Walla Walla–based Mannina Cellars beckons wine drinkers to taste Walla Walla's *terroir*. Using fruit from the Walla Walla Valley, winemaker Don Redman creates full-bodied reds.

A triple grand tasting venue, a shopper's delight, friendly people, and even a pet-friendly policy — what's not to love?

BARONESS, BERGDORF AND MANNINA CELLARS
winemaker(s): Danielle Clements
location: 939 Front Street, Leavenworth, WA 98826
phone: 509-548-7600
web: www.baronesscellars.com
e-mail: baronesscellars@live.com
fee: Tasting fee
hours: Daily 10–6
amenities: Wheelchair Accessible

Willow Crest Winery 12

WILLOW CREST WINERY
opened: 1995
winemaker(s): David J. Minick
location: 939 Front Street,
Leavenworth, WA 98826
phone: 509-548-5166
web: www.willowcrestwinery.com
e-mail: info@willowcrestwinery.com
fee: Complimentary wine tasting
hours: Daily 10–6
amenities: Gift Shop, Mailing List, Newsletter/Blog,
Online Store, Wine Club
connect: 🐦 ⓕ

www.winetrailsnw.com/wineries/willow_crest_winery

Pasek Cellars Winery 13

PASEK CELLARS WINERY
opened: 1995
winemaker(s): Gene Pasek
location: 939 Front Street,
Leavenworth, WA 98826
phone: 888-350-9463
web: www.pasekcellars.com
e-mail: pasekwinery@hotmail.com
fee: Complimentary wine tasting
hours: Daily 11–5
amenities: Gift Shop, Mailing List, Online Store
connect: ⓕ

www.winetrailsnw.com/wineries/pasek_cellars_winery

Eagle Creek Winery & Cottage 14

Note the name. It's not simply Eagle Creek Winery. Rather, it's Eagle Creek Winery & Cottage. Owners Ed and Pat Rutledge seem to have a penchant for the good things in life. The cottage provides a homey atmosphere in which to relax and read by the fire or play or

gaze outside at the vineyard adjacent to the property. There's also a fully equipped kitchen for those who want to cook their own meals. The cottage also serves as a home base for outdoor activities or shopping in nearby Leavenworth. No need to worry about going to town for a bottle of wine, however. As a perk of your stay, you can choose a bottle of wine from the downstairs cellar. It's one of many nice touches that cottage guests enjoy.

Winemaker Ed Rutledge produces about 4,000 cases annually of both red and white wines. Ed's chardonnay comes from grapes grown in Eagle Creek's own vineyard, but his other wines are composed of grapes from the Columbia Valley. His red wines include cabernet sauvignon, merlot, cabernet franc, and Bordeaux-style blends. Ed employs a combination of American and Hungarian oak.

To sample Eagle Creek wines, visitors enter the downstairs tasting room at the rear of the building. The tight quarters lend a "cozy" feeling to the room, making for an easy camaraderie. You soon find yourself joining other visitors on a field trip to the barrel room and cellar adjacent to the tasting room. This is where guests of the cottage come to select their bottle of wine, and if you're like this WineTrail adventurer, you find yourself turning a little green with envy.

P.S. If you can't make it to their winery/cottage, visit the Rutledges in Leavenworth at their tasting room, d'Vinery, 617 Front St.

EAGLE CREEK WINERY & COTTAGE
opened: 2002
winemaker(s): Ed Rutledge
location: 10037 Eagle Creek Road, Leavenworth, WA 98826-9113
phone: 509-548-7059
web: www.eaglecreekwinery.com
e-mail: info@eaglecreekwinery.com
fee: Complimentary wine tasting
hours: Friday through Sunday 11–5 May through October
amenities: Gift Shop, Lodging, Online Store, Picnic Area, RV/Bus Parking, Vineyard on Premise, Wine Club
connect: f

⭐ BEST Lodging

Napeequa Vintners 15

Plain, Washington — seriously? Who thinks of starting a winery in a small village situated 15 curvy miles north of Leavenworth? Sure, there are country stores, a small schoolhouse

and friendly neighbors, but it isn't exactly a major crossroads; you have to have a reason to go to Plain. But as this wine tourist discovered, winemaker/owner David Morris and partners Ann Hathaway and Michael Mann had a good reason: community. Their slogan, "Your friends, your food, our wine," isn't mere lip service; they offer a place where friends and acquaintances can mingle and enjoy great wine.

Winemaker David relies on small-lot vineyards in the Columbia and Yakima valleys to create wines that are "different and intriguing." Balancing winemaking with his Lake Stevens chiropractic practice, David talks about his goal of perfecting the best wine for food and friends. He pays homage to his volunteer experience at Quilceda Creek in 2002, which

added to his winemaking résumé. He also thanks his mentor, Ray Sandidge (of C.R. Sandidge Wines fame), whom he affectionately refers to as Master Po and to himself as Grasshopper, a bow to the hit TV show Kung Fu. David's science background lends itself to experimenting. For example, he worked with a California cooperage firm to test hybrid barrels composed of American and French oak. An interesting concept, and one you would expect from someone intent on creating wines outside the norm.

David Morris

By keeping production small (fewer than 2,000 cases), David can focus on stylish red and white wines. His current 2008-09 offerings include Randonee (viognier), two red blends dubbed Trailhead and Sexy Little Red, Malbec, chardonnay ice wine (wonderfully sweet with a long finish), and a heavenly primitivo port to pair with chocolates and cheesecake. Yummy. Bring your own friend and food to this not-so-plain paradise.

NAPEEQUA VINTNERS
opened: 2005
winemaker(s): David Morris
location: 18820 Beaver Valley Road, Plain, WA 98826
phone: 509-763-1600
web: www.napeequa.com
e-mail: via website
fee: Complimentary wine tasting
hours: Saturday 11–5 and Sunday 12–4
amenities: Gift Shop, Online Store, Pet Friendly, Picnic Area, Wheelchair Accessible, Wine Club, Wines by the Glass
connect: 🐦 f

Silvara Vineyards 16

Two miles east of Leavenworth, off Highway 2, is a delightful oasis where you can find refuge from the crowds in Leavenworth — and some good wine. Smallwood's Harvest, nearby, is the source of squealing kids on kiddy rides and adults on a mission to purchase fresh produce. This scene stands in stark contrast to the quietude of newly built Silvara, where you'll find plenty of space to imbibe and reflect either in the tasting room or out on the patio with its encircling mountains (which makes for one sweet photo op). If the weather is nippy, tuck yourself into one of two large comfortable couches inside, strategically placed in front of inviting fireplaces. Lovely.

Winemaker Gary Seidler and his pro-golfer partner Cindy Rarick produce cabernet sauvignon, chardonnay, and riesling. The manageable portfolio of wine is a reflection of the winery's youth, but it shows potential for great maturity.

The name Silvara Vineyards may give one the impression that there are vineyards to experience, but such is not the case. Gary and Cindy source their fruit from the Wahluke Slope AVA. This is very typical among Washington wineries, and in Gary's case, purchasing grapes from Columbia Valley growers allows him to exercise his degree from the prestigious University of California-Davis enology and viticulture program by crafting fine wines.

SILVARA VINEYARDS
opened: 2008
winemaker(s): Gary Seidler
location: 77 Stage Road, Leavenworth, WA 98826
phone: 509-548-1000
web: www.silvarawine.com
e-mail: info@silvarawine.com
fee: Tasting fee refunded with purchase
hours: Daily 11–5 April through December with extended hours Friday and Saturday; Friday through Monday 11–5 January to mid-February
amenities: Picnic Area, Private Events, Tours, Weddings, Wheelchair Accessible, Wines by the Glass
connect: 🐦 f

Icicle Ridge Winery 17

Most winery owners feel right at home at their wineries. But in the case of the Wagoners, the feeling is quite literal: Icicle Ridge Winery is their home. Not only do they live in it,

but Louis Wagoner actually built the log-style home, along with much of the rustic furniture that graces the winery. Situated outside Leavenworth, this jewel of a winery is a wonderful surprise for WineTrails trekkers. As you arrive, you are greeted by 40 acres of pear trees that are slowly giving way to several Bordeaux varieties. No need to ring the front doorbell — visitors can come right in and enjoy wine tasting in the kitchen.

On the way in, please note the family photo featuring the Wagoners' three daughters: They are an integral part of the winery, handling marketing, event coordinating, bottling, and myriad other jobs. The family created the art you see on the walls. You can circulate comfortably from living room to dining room to kitchen area with glass in hand while you sample premium wine. Icicle Ridge's winemaker, Don Wood, is often assisting and can explain how he went from a chemical engineering job to become the chief winemaker at Icicle Ridge Winery. (By the way, Don is married to one of the three blond daughters mentioned above.) As Don noted, "This has been the greatest experience of my life."

The family's goal is to remain a small winery devoted to the production of premium wines. For whites, check out the riesling and the Three Blondes gewürztraminer. Among the reds, the syrah and Romanze were soft and fruity.

Icicle Ridge has gained a reputation for hosting a summer event known as Jazzamatazz (see www.icicleridgewinery. com for details) as well as being a great spot for a wedding. At Icicle Ridge, it's as though Eddie Bauer met premium wine, and you'll feel right at home.

ICICLE RIDGE WINERY
opened: 2002
winemaker(s): Don Wood
location: 8977 North Road, Peshastin, WA 98847-9521
phone: 509-548-7019
web: www.icicleridgewinery.com
e-mail: info@icicleridgewinery.com
fee: Tasting fee
hours: Daily 12–5
amenities: Gift Shop, Live Music, Picnic Area, Private Events, RV/Bus Parking, Tours, Wheelchair Accessible, Wine Club, Winemaker Dinners
connect: 🐦 f

⭐ **BEST Music venue, picnicking and weddings**

Cascadia Winery 18

Owner/winemaker Alan Yanagimachi launched Cascadia Winery in 2005. This was back when Alan had just come north from California, following a stint at Monterey Wine Company, where he learned the technologies necessary to produce 1.5 million gallons

of wine annually. That's fermentation on a grand scale.

Now Alan makes small case lots and enjoys creating "artisan" wines. Among his other winemaking stints, he worked at Arbor Crest Wine Cellar in Spokane (where he met his wife, Lilith). He also traveled to the former Soviet Republic of Georgia and, for 18 months, experienced winemaking in one of the oldest winemaking areas in the world. He also worked for a winery near Angels Camp in California, made famous by Mark Twain's short story "The Celebrated Jumping Frog of Calaveras County." Alan doesn't mention if the winery's sales leapfrogged over its competitors.

His education background includes a degree in fermentation science/enology from the University of California-Davis. Alan's pursuit of this degree came about after a chance meeting with Robert Mondavi in 1985 at a dinner/jazz concert at Mondavi Cellars, during which Mondavi suggested that Alan seek such an education. With his science background, Alan has a side business providing lab services to other wineries.

In addition to its traditional whites and reds, such as chardonnay and cabernet sauvignon, be sure to sample Cascadia's apple wine. With a little sweetness remaining (2.6 percent residual sugar), this wine is the perfect accompaniment for roasted pork or sliced turkey with sage dressing. And at a mere $12 a bottle, it's a steal.

CASCADIA WINERY
opened: 2006
winemaker(s): Alan Yanagimachi
location: 10090 Main Street, Peshastin, WA 98847
phone: 509-548-7900
web: www.cascadiawinery.com
e-mail: alany@cascadiawinery.com
fee: Complimentary wine tasting
hours: Thursday through Monday 11–5, or by appointment
amenities: Gift Shop, Newsletter/Blog, Online Store, RV/Bus Parking, Wheelchair Accessible
connect:

Wedge Mountain Winery 19

The plaque at Wedge Mountain Winery's entrance says it all: "A passion for the vine; a passion for the grape; a passion for the wine."

You'll find Wedge Mountain Winery located approximately five miles east of Leavenworth off Highway 2. Upon your arrival, spend some time walking around the property, through the apple and pear trees, past the horses and cows, to the vineyard next to the meandering Wenatchee River. Towering above you is beautiful Wedge Mountain, with the Enchantments to the west. Soak it all in, then head to the tasting room for a sip.

Wedge Mountain Winery's tasting room is located in a rather unusual wine cellar. Long after your visit, you'll still recall the room built into the side of a knoll. In the fall, the top of the knoll becomes the crush pad. Winery owner Charlie McKee manages the winemaking duties, while wife Mary Ann works the tasting room. Samples of a wide variety *Vitis vinifera* wines as well as a selection of fruit wines await your swirling pleasure. Try the cabernet franc — and have your plastic on hand. Me thinks, you won't leave empty handed.

Mary Ann McKee

WEDGE MOUNTAIN WINERY
opened: 2001
winemaker(s): Charlie McKee
location: 9534 Saunders Road, Peshastin, WA 98847
phone: 509-548-7068
web: www.wedgemountainwinery.com
e-mail: charliem@nwi.net
fee: Complimentary wine tasting
hours: Friday through Monday 10–5
amenities: Newsletter/Blog, Online Store, Picnic Area, Tours, Vineyard on Premise, Wheelchair Accessible
connect: f

BEST Views

Waterville Winery 🔟

Although the town of Waterville can boast that few towns in Washington are at a higher altitude, at 2,622 feet, it's not exactly at a crossroads of the universe. In fact, few Washingtonians even know Waterville exists, let alone where it's located. A mere 1,147 Watervillians inhabit this relaxed burg, located about 30 winding miles north of Wenatchee.

Bitten by the wine bug, owners Matt and Lisa Wareham converted their garage into a winemaking production area and appropriately adopted the moniker "garagiste." Using a blue dry-erase marker, winemaker Matt inked their bottle label image of a happy stick-figure winemaker in a garage, working the basket press at crush, with the words "Vin du Garagiste" written on the front of the garage. This simple label graces the initial small-lot batches of riesling, unoaked chardonnay, and cabernet sauvignon.

Realizing that folks aren't exactly flocking to Waterville, the couple smartly located their tasting room down the street from the Aplets & Cotlets tour center in the Mission District of Cashmere. Here, in a converted fruit warehouse (also occupied by Horan Estates Winery and Crayelle Cellars), you'll find Lisa greeting folks and assuring them that the $10 price tag for their cabernet and chardonnay is for real. Talk about a steal — this might be the best value in the state!

WATERVILLE WINERY
opened: 2008
winemaker(s): Matt Wareham
location: 207 Mission Avenue, Cashmere, WA 98807
phone: 509-630-8851
web: www.watervillewinecompany.com
e-mail: wine@watervillewinery.com
fee: Tasting fee
hours: Saturday 11–5
connect: 🐦 📘

Crayelle Cellars 21

When it comes to the topic of winemaking in the Wenatchee area, the name Craig Mitrakul is very likely to pop up. As one of Washington's up-and-coming winemakers, Craig includes on his résumé the position of winemaker for both Saint Laurent Winery and Ryan Patrick Vineyards. Now, with the introduction of Crayelle Cellars, he has his own label.

Craig's youth belies the fact that he has an extensive education, which includes an advanced degree in food

Danielle Mitrakul

science, with a concentration in enology, from New York's Cornell University. While there, he studied under the renowned Thomas Henick-King, who, ironically, is now the director of enology and viticulture at Washington State University. Following a circuitous route that included stints at wineries in Oregon, Australia, and Walla Walla, Craig and his wife, Danielle, eventually made their way to north-central Washington. (The name "Crayelle" is a hybrid of sorts, created from the names Craig and Danielle.) Given Craig's background, it's little wonder that Crayelle Cellars' initial offerings are riesling (the Finger Lakes in New York state) and syrah (Australia, where it's known as shiraz).

Crayelle Cellars' tasting room is located in Cashmere's historic Mission District in a remodeled fruit warehouse it shares with Horan Estates Winery and Waterville Winery. Here, you can often find Danielle doing the pouring honors while conversing with Cashmere visitors, many of whom made the detour to experience Aplets & Cotlets only to discover that the local fruit comes in different forms.

Craig Mitrakul

CRAYELLE CELLARS
opened: 2010
winemaker(s): Craig Mitrakul
location: 207 Mission Avenue, Cashmere, WA 98807
phone: 509-393-1996
web: www.crayellecellars.com
e-mail: info@CrayelleCellars.com
fee: Tasting fee
hours: Saturday and Sunday 12–5; January through April Saturday only 12–5
amenities: Online Store, Wheelchair Accessible, Wine Club
connect: 🐦 f

Horan Estates Winery 22

Beth and Dennis Dobbs

Located in Cashmere's Mission District, just down the street from the Aplets & Cotlets visitors center, is Horan Estates Winery's tasting room. Small, intimate, and inviting, there's no combat tasting here. No siree! You can sit and visit with the tasting room staff, and learn about the family's rich history in the Wenatchee Valley and what owner/winemaker Doug McDougall's goals are.

With Horan's production at fewer than 500 cases per year, we're talking artisan winemaking. These are small-lot wines for which the winemaker controls the final product through taste and art using a modicum of science.

Horan Estates Winery shares a converted fruit warehouse with Waterville Winery and Crayelle Cellars. Bada-bing, bada-boom! You can visit several wineries within 20 feet and not have to designate a driver. Sweet.

Be sure to try the HVH red blend, a double gold medal winner of the San Francisco Chronicle's 2011 wine-tasting event. Horan's tasting notes indicate "Bing cherries and a hunk of chocolate push their way to the palate." That's something this reviewer can attest to with a smile.

Beth Dobbs

HORAN ESTATES WINERY
opened: 2003
winemaker(s): Doug McDougall
location: 207 Mission Avenue, Cashmere, WA 98815
phone: 509-860-0662
web: www.horanestateswinery.com
e-mail: bethdobbs@geneset.net
fee: Tasting fee refunded with purchase
hours: April through December, Saturday 12–5; January through March, call for hours
amenities: Online Store, RV/Bus Parking, Newsletter/Blog
connect:

Dutch John's Wines 23

The Cashmere tasting room joins several local wineries at the Mission District historic building. And speaking of history, the winery was named after "Dutch John" Galler, who is believed to have been born on December 31, 1812. Here is what the local newspaper had to say about Dutch John in his obituary:

"Dutch John" Galler, Aged 108, Dies at the Home of his son, Wm. Galler, Wednesday Night. One of Earliest Omak White Settlers.

Word was brought to town Thursday morning of the death of John Galler, who was not only one of the early white settlers in this part of the valley, but also its oldest resident in point of age.

Mr. Galler first settled near where Wenatchee now stands but later moved on to the central part of the Okanogan Valley and has been a resident of this section ever since.

As nearly as can be figured out by his children, Mr. Gallery was 108 years, 1 month and 23 days. He was of German descent, coming to this country when but a lad, and his memory of historical events of early days in both Europe and this country was remarkable as was his strength as he had always led an active life and was able to care for himself up to the time of his death."

DUTCH JOHN'S WINES
opened: 2009
winemaker(s): George Valison
location: 207 Mission Avenue, Mission District, Cashmere, WA 98815
phone: 509-782-3845
web: www.dutchjohnwines.com
e-mail: bygeorge@usa.net
fee: Complimentary wine tasting
hours: Friday through Sunday 11–5 or by appointment
amenities: RV/Bus Parking

Central Washington
WineTrail

The Central Washington WineTrail is a huge area, with the Columbia River taking center stage. The terrain is defined by ancient lava flows, the Missoula Floods of the last ice age, and wind-strewn loess, all of which create a dramatic landscape ideal for farming, planting windmills, and stomping grapes. It's laidback place, where you won't have to fight crowds in order to get a second serving of the wine that you favor. Whether you enjoy the lavish Swiftwater Cellars in Cle Elum, the picturesque Saint Laurent Winery overlooking the Columbia River, or the creature comforts of Cave B Inn & Winery, your trip (and your camera's memory card) will be filled with unique treasures.

Central Washington WineTrail

1. Swiftwater Cellars
2. Bella Terrazza Vineyards
3. Swakane Winery
4. Chateau Faire Le Pont Winery
5. Stemilt Creek Winery
6. Martin-Scott Winery
7. Saint Laurent Winery
8. Malaga Springs Winery
9. White Heron Cellars
10. Jones of Washington Estate Vineyards
11. Cave B Estate Winery
12. Gård Vintners

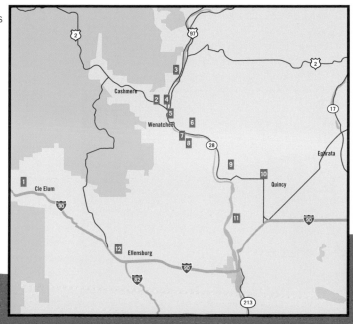

Region:	**North Central Washington Wine Country**
# of tasting rooms on tour:	**12**
Estimate # of days for tour:	**3**
Getting around:	**Car**
Key Events:	❏ **Wenatchee Wine Country sponsors a number of wine fun wine events year-round. Check out www.wenatcheewines.com for event information.**
	❏ **Red Wine and Chocolate (mid-February) sponsored by the Columbia Cascade Winery Association. See www.columbiacascadewines.com for details.**
Tips:	❏ **Sample Wenatchee wines at the Wenatchee Valley Visitors Bureau 11–5, Monday through Saturday. See www.wenatcheevalley.org.**
	❏ **Consider hiring a limousine service.**
Best:	❏ **Destination, eats, gift shop, music venue and views: Swiftwater Cellars**
	❏ **Views and picnicking: Bella Terrazza Vineyards**
	❏ **Eats: Chateau Faire Le Pont Winery**
	❏ **Views and picnicking: Martin-Scott Winery**
	❏ **Views and picnicking: Saint Laurent Winery**
	❏ **Views and picnicking: Malaga Springs Winery**
	❏ **Picnicking: White Heron Cellars**
	❏ **Destination, lodging, eats, views, picnicking and weddings: Cave B Estate Winery**

Swiftwater Cellars

Opened in September 2010, Swiftwater Cellars resides on the former site of the Roslyn No. 9 Mine. Without question, it is one of the more stunning architectural wonders in what is already a go-to destination, Suncadia Resort. Don Watts, owner of Swiftwater

Cellars, is passionate about the land, its heritage, and above all his new winery.

To appreciate Swiftwater Cellars is to realize that its tagline, "Washington's Ultimate Destination Winery" has guided everything about the design of this winery, down to the distressed-timber beams mirroring the No. 9 mineshaft and the pickaxes for door handles. It has the "wow" factor from the moment you step through its grand entrance.

Swiftwater Cellars has the rare distinction of employing two chief winemakers. Winemaker Linda Trotta is a recent transplant from California, where she was the winemaker for Sonoma's renowned Gundlach Bundschu Winery. I later learned that wine writer Dan Berger named Linda as one of California's 10 best winemakers. Tony Rynders is Swiftwater Cellars' second winemaker. Like Linda, he is also a graduate of University of California-Davis' famed enology program, but his winemaking career included a long stint at Oregon's Domaine Serene winery, where he crafted pinot noir and developed a deep love for this noble wine.

SWIFTWATER CELLARS
opened: 2010
winemaker(s): Tony Rynders and Linda Trotta
location: 301 Rope Rider Drive, Suncadia, Cle Elum, WA 98941
phone: 509-674-6555
web: www.swiftwatercellars.com
e-mail: info@swiftwatercellars.com
fee: Tasting fee
hours: Wednesday through Sunday 11:30–10
amenities: Gift Shop, Live Music, Newsletter/Blog, Online Store, Picnic Area, Private Events, Restaurant/Food Pairings, RV/Bus Parking, Weddings, Wheelchair Accessible, Wine Club, Wines by the Glass
connect: 🐦 f

Don Watts (second from right)

⭐ **BEST Destination, eats, gift shop, music venue and views**

Bella Terrazza Vineyards ²

Bob Richards, owner and winemaker of Bella Terrazza Vineyards, knows a thing or two about getting plants to grow. Equipped with an educational fruit science background from Cal Poly–San Luis Obispo as well as growing the Sleepy Hollow Nursery business (located at the Bella Terrazza Vineyards), Bob has the farmer's tan and dirt-smudged hands to prove that he's all about farming.

It's easy to understand how Bella Terrazza got its name, given the beautiful terrace, with its rows of southern-exposed vineyards, that leads down to the Wenatchee River. The setting provides lots of heat units for growing grapes, especially red grape varieties. At the top of the slope is the tasting room and patio, which gives way to a manicured lawn — the perfect setting for spreading out the proverbial picnic blanket.

Sadly, once I had found my way into the tasting room, I spotted the dreaded "sold out" message posted next to the chardonnay, but the red blend — Bella Rosso — didn't disappoint. Usually I sip and spit, but I followed my instincts on this one and swallowed, experiencing this wine's amazing, lingering finish. Impressive as the Bella Rosso was, the cabernet franc practically caused my knees to buckle. Truly magnifico. And don't miss the opportunity to sample the oh-so-rare lemberger red wine, with its fruit-forward flavors and easy drinkability.

Incidentally, this is a family-friendly winery. There's plenty of space for kids to romp on the lawn, and the U-pick blueberry patch is sure to leave everyone with big purple grins.

Note: If you're too short on time to experience Bella Terrazza Vineyards, visit its tasting room in nearby Leavenworth, conveniently located on Front Street across from the gazebo. Fantastico!

BELLA TERRAZZA VINEYARDS
opened: 2008
winemaker(s): Bob Richards
location: 1260 Lower Sunnyslope Road, Wenatchee, WA 98801
phone: 509-662-9141
web: www.bellaterrazzavineyards.com
e-mail: info@bellaterrazzavineyards.com
fee: Tasting fee
hours: Friday through Sunday 12–4; Hours may vary, call ahead
amenities: Mailing List, Newsletter/Blog, Picnic Area, RV/Bus Parking, Vineyard on Premise, Wheelchair Accessible, Wine Club
connect: ✦

⭐ **BEST Views and picnicking**

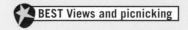

Swakane Winery 🔢

Next time you're near Wenatchee or heading to or from Lake Chelan and you have a half-hour to spare, stop at the delightful tasting room of Swakane Winery. It's delightful for two reasons: It has a great location near the banks of the Columbia River, and its owner/winemaker, Mike Franks, is usually on hand doing the pouring honors. He's a likable guy who caught a serious case of the wine bug a few years back and became a cellar rat for Tildio Winery in Manson. He's gone on to complete a degree in enology while attending college on weekends.

Mike Franks

An added treat while visiting the Wenatchee location is the vineyard next to the winery, which is planted with rows of cabernet franc, riesling, and sauvignon blanc. It's a labor of love, and no doubt Mike and his wife, Donna, know every row, if not every vine. Pruning under the hot summer sun does that. While swirling and sipping, check out the original artwork on the wall. It offers yet another example of how art and wine make a perfect pair.

Despite the winery's young age (it opened in 2007), Mike offers a robust lineup of reds, whites, and dessert wines to sample. Perhaps it was the heat outside, but the whites went down nice and crisp — especially the estate sauvignon blanc. But the strawberry-colored rosé got my palate's attention with its fresh berry flavors. Mike agreed that this makes a nice back-porch wine, but I suspect it's just as enjoyable sipped by a crackling fire.

If for some reason you can't make it to

their winery, just two miles north of Wenatchee off Highway 97A, no worries. They have a satellite tasting room in Leavenworth, where many a tourist samples Swakane's treasures.

SWAKANE WINERY
opened: 2009
winemaker(s): Mike Franks
location: 7980 State Highway 97A, Wenatchee, WA 98801
phone: 509-662-1928
web: www.swakanewinery.com
e-mail: info@swakanewinery.com
fee: Tasting fee
hours: Summer only, starting Memorial Day Weekend 11–5
amenities: Art Gallery, Gift Shop, Restaurant/Food Pairings, Tours, Vineyard on Premise, Wheelchair Accessible, Wine Club
connect: f

www.winetrailsnw.com/wineries/swakane_winery

Chateau Faire Le Pont Winery 4

Housed in a restored 1920s fruit-packing warehouse, Chateau Faire Le Pont Winery is often a day-trip destination for many Wenatchee-area residents. The restoration preserved the original hardwood-plank flooring and gently arching windows. Behind the wine bar, a mural by local artist Sarah Morgan depicts grapes growing amongst the apple and cherry orchards of Wenatchee Valley. A full-service kitchen supports its Chateau Restaurant, which serves up light and full fare. During the summer, a generously sized patio offers a great place to relax and enjoy the view.

Faire Le Pont is also a destination winery for those wishing to tie the knot. For a modest-size wedding party, the space offers outdoor/indoor seating, a full kitchen, waitstaff, plenty of photo ops and no shortage for premium wine.

Using fruit from the Columbia Valley, winemaker/owner Doug Brazil produces a full slate of dry and sweet white wines as well as classic French-style red wines. Finding the perfect complement in a bottle of its 2007 cabernet sauvignon on my visit, I retreated to the restaurant to order a steak.

Doug Brazil

CHATEAU FAIRE LE PONT WINERY
opened: 2004
winemaker(s): Doug Brazil
location: 1 Vineyard Way, Wenatchee, WA 98801-8117
phone: 509-667-9463
web: www.fairelepont.net
e-mail: DebeBrazil@nwi.net
fee: Tasting fee
hours: Daily 11–6, Wednesday through Saturday until 9; Live jazz Thursday 6–9
amenities: Gift Shop, Live Music, Newsletter/Blog, Picnic Area, Private Events, Restaurant/Food Pairings, Tours, Weddings, Wheelchair Accessible, Wine Club
connect: 🐦 f

⭐ BEST Eats

Stemilt Creek Winery

Jan and Kyle Mathison likely have the highest vineyard in the state, at more than 1,500 feet in elevation. The land bench on which the vineyard lies gets nice exposure from sunrise to sunset, when the sun disappears behind Mission Ridge. That's a good thing—those sugars need the nighttime to rise and balance out the acid.

Jan is the winemaker for Stemilt Creek Winery and, make no mistake, she's particular about her wine. From gentle crush to careful punch-down, each batch gets her minimalist attention. From there, the wine gets two years in the barrel and one year in the bottle before it's released to the public.

With two tasting rooms for their tasting pleasure, visitors can sample Stemilt Creek wines in downtown Wenatchee on North Wenatchee Avenue or in downtown Leavenworth on Front Street. If you find yourself unable to determine your fave wine at one tasting room, you can stop at the other for further research.

If labels are of interest to you, check out the wine label for their Sweet Adelaide white blend, which bears a vintage photo of Adelaide Sherwood Mathison feeding what look to be turkeys on Stemilt Hill. With her brilliant red hair and a penchant for galloping on her horse at breakneck speed, she was the heartthrob of many a young man in Wenatchee Valley.

STEMILT CREEK WINERY
opened: 2007
winemaker(s): Jan Mathison
location: 110 North Wenatchee Avenue, Wenatchee, WA 98801
phone: 509-665-3485
web: www.stemiltcreekwinery.com
e-mail: winery@stemiltcreekwinery.com
fee: Tasting fee refunded with purchase
hours: Wednesday through Sunday 11–6
amenities: Mailing List, Online Store, Wheelchair Accessible, Wine Club, YouTube
connect:

Martin-Scott Winery 6

Located above the Columbia River in east Wenatchee, Martin-Scott Winery enjoys a dazzling view, one that easily qualifies as one of the top 10 in the state. Come for the wine, uncork a bottle, and stay for the view — and some authentic hospitality.

Mike and Judi Scott host guests in their downstairs tasting room and are often behind the bar introducing visitors to Martin-Scott wines. They make a cute couple. But more than that, they make a dynamic duo, with Mike focusing on the grape-growing aspects of the venture, and Judi producing the small-batch wines.

Michael Scott

While Mike tends to their two vineyards — one of them right next to their east Wenatchee home/winery and the other farther south in Mattawa — Judi, in addition to her other tasks, manages the tasting room and coordinates events (of which there are many, including weddings). Judy's work as a laboratory technician also comes in handy with the chemistry and microbiology inherent to winemaking.

When visiting Martin-Scott, be sure to check out the banquet room, with its oversized dining table, and the room's other details. With the table's capacity to seat 20 guests, many a family and business have reserved the space for catered events.

The running of Martin-Scott Winery is a family affair. Adult sons Tim and Chris have pitched in from time to time to assist with the vineyard marketing, and daughter-in-law Becky is the winery artist responsible for the beautiful wrought-iron Martin-Scott sign at the winery's entrance. Even granddaughter Grace Scott gets in on the act: Grace's Gewürztraminer bears her name.

MARTIN-SCOTT WINERY
opened: 2003
winemaker(s): Judi Scott
location: 3400 SE 10th Street, East Wenatchee, WA 98802
phone: 509-886-4596
web: www.martinscottwinery.com
e-mail: mswines@martinscottwinery.com
fee: Complimentary wine tasting
hours: Friday through Saturday 12–5, Sunday 12–4 or by appointment
amenities: Newsletter/Blog, Picnic Area, Private Events, Tours, Vineyard on Premise, Weddings, Wheelchair Accessible, Wine Club, Wines by the Glass
connect:

⭐ **BEST Views and picnicking**

Saint Laurent Winery

Michael and Laura Laurent Mrachek grow more than 500 acres of apples, cherries, berries, and grapes. With that much fruit, it's safe to assume that agriculture is their lifeblood. About half of that acreage is dedicated to premium wine grapes, and the phrase "from vine to fine wine" is a matter of course for the Mracheks, who run a vertically integrated winery.

The Mracheks have bestowed the vinification duties on son Bryan Mrachek. His viticulture and enology degree from Washington State University, along with stints at Chateau Ste. Michelle and Snoqualmie vineyards will serve him well in his endeavor. Young, yes; inexperienced, no.

With Saint Laurent's stunning views, anytime is a great time to visit, but you may want to plan your tour to coincide with one of many events offered here. Check the event calendar for the many events the Mracheks host, including art shows, winemaker dinners and music performances. If you drop in during the warmer months, budget some time to stroll through the colorful garden (well done, Laura). Under the gazebo is a great place to uncork your wine for an afternoon respite.

Here's a tidbit of trivia to add to your mental library: Saint Laurent is the patron saint of vintners and cooks. In A.D. 25, in the blazing month of August, Saint Laurent (aka Laurence, Laurent, Laurentius, Lawrence of Rome, Lorenzo) was roasted to death on a gridiron. Since then, cooks and vintners have claimed Saint Laurent as their patron saint. A toast to Saint Laurent!

SAINT LAURENT WINERY
opened: 2004
winemaker(s): Craig Mitrakul
location: 4147 Hamlin Road, Malaga, WA 98828
phone: 509-888-9463
web: www.saintlaurent.net
e-mail: via website
fee: Tasting fee refunded with purchase
hours: Friday through Sunday 11–5
amenities: Gift Shop, Online Store, Picnic Area, Private Events, Tours, RV/Bus Parking, Vineyard on Premise, Weddings, Wheelchair Accessible, Wine Club, Wines by the Glass, Winemaker Dinners
connect: 🐦 f

⭐ **BEST Views and picnicking**

Malaga Springs Winery 🎱

Perched on a bluff above the mighty Columbia River is the Southwest-style abode of Malaga Springs Winery. The orange-hued winery and adjacent home of Al and Kathy Mathews is the perfect complement to the basalt cliffs rising in the background. Nearby is Saint Laurent Winery, and if you squint your eyes, you can see Martin-Scott Winery many miles in the distance.

Getting to Malaga Springs Winery on Cathedral Rock Drive is a bit of an adventure given that most of the journey is on gravel road. However, the destination is worth the occasional washboard bumps. As Al notes, "We are one of the smallest wineries in the state, with production well south of 1,000 cases annually." Translation: Lovingly nurtured, hand punched-down fermenting wine, for which Al has aged in oak through maturity.

When I wasn't gazing at the lemon yellow sample of viognier poured for me, I took in the pottery placed throughout the tasting room. It turns out Al throws pots when he is not busy making wine or dabbling in other things. A tour of the facilities revealed that Al built their current residence and tasting room using an ingenious straw bale technique. He also showed me the plot of land where he will build their new house, next to Kathy's well-tended gardens (she's a natural at growing things). And all these talents are sandwiched between Al's other job in Alaska, where he owns a commercial fishing business. Phew!

Be sure to note the colorful labels on Malaga Springs' bottles. That's the creation of Al's 84-year-old mother, Vera Mathews. As I packed my bottles of "Al y Kat," a big, bold red, into the car, I reflected on the pioneer spirit of this family, suffused with self-sufficiency, respect for the land, and love of family.

MALAGA SPRINGS WINERY
opened: 2010
winemaker(s): Allen R Mathews
location: 3400 Cathedral Rock Drive, Malaga, WA 98828-9601
phone: 509-679-0152
web: www.malagaspringswinery.com
e-mail: AlyKat@MalagaSpringsWinery.com
fee: Complimentary wine tasting
hours: Friday through Sunday 12–5 or by appointment
amenities: Art Gallery, Online Store, Picnic Area, RV/Bus Parking, Vineyard on Premise, Wheelchair Accessible
connect: 📘

⭐ **BEST Views and picnicking**

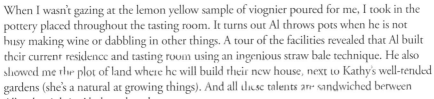

Allen Mathews and son

White Heron Cellars ⑨

Located in the ghost town of Trinidad, White Heron Cellars is the creation of Swiss-trained vintners Phyllis and Cameron Fries. The winery is about 1,000 feet above the Columbia River Gorge between Wenatchee and Quincy. Dry weather, the moderating influence of the Columbia River, the slope of the land, and the soil itself all conspire to create a unique

terroir that's perfect for growing wine grapes.

As you enter the White Heron property, you may find yourself stopping suddenly and fishing for your camera. Perched on the hillside, the White Heron Cellars winery and the Fries' contemporary-style home pop out from the rest of the scenery.

Most of White Heron's wines are estate wines and include cabernet sauvignon, cabernet franc, Malbec, petit verdot, pinot noir, gamay, syrah, roussanne, and viognier. As you sample his roussanne, Cameron notes that it is more popular than viognier in the Rhône region of France, and he characterizes it as a "syrah in drag." His wines are refreshingly honest, devoid of the puckering power of tannins. It's likely that Cameron will be there to guide you through your tasting. If so, be sure and ask about his wine-making style which includes a sur lies aging method that gives a distinctive "creaminess" feel to his wines. Decidedly different. Uniquely White Heron.

WHITE HERON CELLARS
opened: 1986
winemaker(s): Phyllis and Cameron Fries
location: 10035 Stuhlmiller Road, Quincy, WA 98848
phone: 509-797-9463
web: www.whiteheronwine.com
e-mail: info@whiteheronwine.com
fee: Complimentary although donations welcomed
hours: Thursday through Monday 11–6
amenities: Picnic Area, Tours, Vineyard on Premise, Weddings, Wheelchair Accessible, Wine Club
connect: 🐦 f

BEST Picnicking

Jones of Washington Estate Vineyards 🔟

With more than 600 acres of premium wine grapes in production, make no mistake, Jones of Washington is a true farm family affair. Although the green and orange, tractor-adorned logo may look a little too slick for this family farm operation, the truth is they are growers first and sell their grapes to a number of wineries throughout Washington.

Of course, when you own and manage several vineyards, you get to know which vineyard blocks produce the best grapes, and one can surmise that they reserve the best of the best for their own label. That would help explain the boatload of awards the Joneses have recently earned at prestigious competitions such as the San Francisco Chronicle Wine Competition, the Grand Harvest Awards, and the Monterey Wine Competition.

Two miles west of Quincy is the tasting room for Jones of Washington, which offers the opportunity to taste estate wines produced from their newly designated appellation — Ancient Lakes American Viticulture Area. (Which IMHO is the coolest name for an AVA in the state.) Jack Jones, the patriarch of this family business, is also the winemaker for Jones of Washington and may be on hand to greet you. Perhaps it is the power of suggestion, but I swear I can actually taste the heritage and closeness to the land that this farm family brings to its wines.

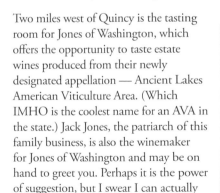

JONES OF WASHINGTON ESTATE VINEYARDS
opened: 2007
winemaker(s): Victor Palencia
location: 2101 F Street SE, Quincy, WA 98848
phone: 509-787-3537
web: www.jonesofwashington.com
e-mail: via website
fee: Tasting fee refunded with purchase
hours: Memorial Day through Labor Day, Friday through Monday 11–6; Otherwise Friday through Sunday 12–5
amenities: Gift Shop, Online Store, RV/Bus Parking, Wheelchair Accessible, Wine Club
connect: 📘

Cave B Estate Winery 11

Few Washington wineries can boast that they are a "destination winery." But Cave B Inn and Cave B Winery are in a position to brag.

Halfway between Spokane and Seattle, near the town of Vantage and next to the Gorge Amphitheatre, lies Cave B Inn and Cave B Estate Winery. The views this establishment lends of the basalt cliffs leading down to the mighty Columbia River are spectacular. However, save some room in your camera's memory card for the inn itself. The grand lobby, with its iron chandeliers hanging from the soaring ceiling will prompt you to start snapping.

The smells emanating from Tendrils Restaurant at the inn will have you grabbing for your drool cup. The menu includes suggested wine pairings for each course, always a nice touch for WineTrail travelers.

The Cave B Winery tasting room features the wonderfully rich, full-bodied wines of Cave B as well as its second label, SageCliffe. Located in the Round House, the Cave B tasting room houses a 17-foot-long tasting bar, handcrafted from used French oak wine barrel staves. It's a comfortable space in which to relax and sample Cave B's full lineup of reds and whites, including my personal favorite, Cave B's Cuvée du Soleil. This is an exquisite adventure bar none and one of the top wineries to visit in Washington. Seriously!

WineTrail Tip: Time your visit to coincide with a concert at the Gorge. See Ticketmaster.com for a concert schedule and ticket purchase.

CAVE B ESTATE WINERY
opened: 2002
winemaker(s): Alfredo "Freddy" Arredondo
location: 348 Silica Road NW, Quincy, WA 98848-9468
phone: 509-785-3500
web: www.caveb.com
e-mail: info@caveb.com
fee: Tasting fee
hours: Daily 11–5:30 from January through March; 11–5:30 Sunday through Thursday and Friday and Saturday 11–7, from April through December
amenities: Gift Shop, Lodging, Online Store, Picnic Area, Private Events, Restaurant/Food Pairings, RV/Bus Parking, Tours, Vineyard on Premise, Weddings, Wheelchair Accessible, Wine Club
connect: 🐦 📘

⭐ **BEST Destination, lodging, eats, views, picnicking and weddings**

Gård Vintners

Located in Ellensburg, Washington, Gård Vintners offers down-home charm and a relaxed setting in which to discover why its wines have taken home the double gold at the San Francisco Chronicle Wine Festival, and why *Seattle Metropolitan* magazine placed this winery in the "Top 100 Wines in the Pacific NW." Sweet accolades indeed. Now it's up to new winemaker Aryn Morell to carry on the tradition established by former winemaker Robert Smasne. Given Aryn's California pedigree at well-established wineries, Gård Vintners is in talented hands.

Gård Vintners is the product of brothers Hervey "Sandy" and John Lawrence, along with John's son Josh. Their farming roots run deep, with more than 45 years of farming in Royal City (near the Wahluke Slope AVA) in the Columbia Valley. In fact, the word gård is Swedish for "farm." After the millennium, they converted a number of acres into vineyards to grow premium wine grapes such as riesling, roussanne, syrah, viognier, grenache, pinot gris, and cabernet sauvignon.

WineTrail Note: If you can't make it to E-burg, no worries. Gård has a second tasting room located in the Woodinville Warehouse District.

GÅRD VINTNERS
opened: 2006
winemaker(s): Aryn Morell
location: 311 North Pearl Street, Ellensburg, WA 98926
phone: 509-346-2585
web: www.gardvintners.com
e-mail: josh@gardvintners.com
fee: Tasting fee refunded with purchase
hours: Tuesday through Thursday 2–7; Friday 2–9; Saturday 2–8 and Sunday 2–5
amenities: Mailing List, Online Store, Private Events, Restaurant/Food Pairings, Wheelchair Accessible, Wine Club
connect: 🐦 f

Other Wineries to Visit

'37 CELLARS
winemaker(s): Frank Dechaine and Chuck Egner
location: 8210 Dempsey Road, Leavenworth, WA 98826
phone: 509-548-8663
web: www.37cellars.com
hours: By appointment only

CAMAS COVE CELLARS
winemaker(s): Dennis Parr
location: 911 Camas Place, Moses Lake, WA 98837
phone: 509-765-9532
web: www.camascovecellars.com
hours: Saturday and Sunday 11–5

DRY FALLS CELLARS
winemaker(s): Jim Englar
location: 6828 22nd Avenue NE, Moses Lake, WA 98837
phone: 509-762-5922
web: www.dryfallscellars.com
hours: Saturday 12–5 or by appointment

BEAUMONT CELLARS
location: 8634 Road U NW, Quincy, WA 98848
phone: 509-787-5586
web: www.beaumontcellars.com
hours: Friday and Saturday 1-6 or by appointment (January and February by appointment only)

CHELANGR'LA WINERY
winemaker(s): Jim Berg
location: 3310 Manson Boulevard, Manson, WA 98831-0000
phone: 509-687-9746
web: www.chelangrla.com
hours: Daily 12–6 April through October; Closed during winter months

ELLENSBURG CANYON VISTA WINERY
location: 221 Canyon Vista Way, Ellensburg, WA 98926
phone: 509-933-3523
web: www.coxcanyon.com
hours: Special events or by appointment

Other Wineries to Visit

FIELDING HILLS WINERY
winemaker(s): Mike Wade
location: 1401 Fielding Hills Drive, East Wenatchee, WA 98802
phone: 509-884-2221
web: www.fieldinghills.com
hours: By appointment only

FOX ESTATE WINERY
winemaker(s): Jerry Fox and Consultant Winemaker
location: 24962 Highway 243 South, Mattawa, WA 99349-2009
phone: 509-932-5818
web: www.foxestatewinery.com
hours: Monday through Friday 10–5, Saturday and Sunday 12–4, summer and holidays

FOXY ROXY WINES
winemaker(s): Rhonda Davis
location: 3744 Hwy 26 East, Othello, WA 99344
phone: 509-346-2344
web: www.foxyroxywines.com
hours: Friday through Sunday 11–5, April through October, or by appointment

GINKGO FOREST WINERY
winemaker(s): Mike and Lois Thiede
location: 22561 Road T.7 SW, Mattawa, WA 99349
phone: 509-831-6432
web: www.ginkgowinery.com
hours: May through October, Wednesday through Saturday 10–5, Sunday 1–5; November through April, Friday and Saturday 10–5 or by appointment

KYRA WINES
winemaker(s): Kyra Baerlocher
location: 8029 Andrews Street NW, Moses Lake, WA 98837
phone: 509-750-8875
web: www.kyrawines.com
hours: Open for special events — call ahead

LA TOSCANA WINERY
winemaker(s): Warren Moyles
location: 9020 Foster Road, Cashmere, WA 98815-9417
phone: 509-548-5448
web: www.latoscanawinery.com
hours: By appointment only

MELLISONI VINEYARDS
winemaker(s): Rob and Donna Mellison
location: 3155 Alt Highway 97, Chelan, WA 98816
phone: 509-293-1891
web: www.mellisonivineyards.com
hours: By appointment only, Monday through Friday; Closed November through March)

METHOW VALLEY CIDERHOUSE AND WINERY
location: 13B Walter Road, Winthrop, WA 98862
phone: 509-341-4354
web: www.methowvalleyciderhouse.com
hours: By appointment only

ONE WINES, INC.
location: 526 East Woodin, Chelan, WA 98816
phone: 509-682-2646
web: www.onewinesinc.com
hours: Wednesday through Sunday 1–7

Other Wineries to Visit

SNOWDRIFT CIDER COMPANY
location: 277 South Ward Avenue, East Wenatchee, WA 98802
phone: 509-630-3507
web: www.snowdriftcider.com
hours: Friday through Sunday 12–5 or by appointment

THRALL AND DODGE WINERY
winemaker(s): Troy Goodreau
location: 111 Dodge Road, Ellensburg, WA 98926
phone: 509-925-4110
web: www.thrallwinery.com
hours: Saturday and Sunday 12–5; winter hours vary and closed during snow or ice; call ahead

SNOWGRASS WINERY
winemaker(s): Alan Moen
location: 6701 Entiat River Road, Entiat, WA 98822
phone: 509-784-5101
web: www.snowgrasswines.com
hours: By appointment only

SNOWGRASS

ENTIATQUA
CABERNET-MERLOT
60 percent Cabernet Sauvignon / 40 percent Merlot

2008

CIEL DU CHEVAL VINEYARD
RED MOUNTAIN

SNOWGRASS WINERY
ENTIAT, WASHINGTON
ALC./VOL. 13.5 %　　　　750 ML

VERANDA BEACH WINERY
winemaker(s): Katy Perry
location: 299 Eastlake Road, Oroville, WA 98844
phone: 888-476-4001
web: www.verandabeach.com/wine
hours: By appointment only

Yakima Valley

WINE COUNTRY

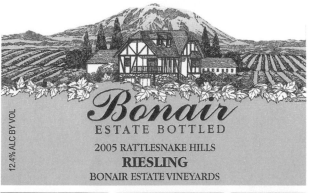

Bonair
ESTATE BOTTLED
2005 RATTLESNAKE HILLS
RIESLING
BONAIR ESTATE VINEYARDS

12.4% ALC BY VOL

milbrandt
vineyards

TRADITIONS
2006 MERLOT
COLUMBIA VALLEY
WASHINGTON

13.5% ALCOHOL BY VOLUME

★ Agate Field ★
MOON RIDER
2005
Sangiovese
Yakima Valley
Alc. 14.1% by vol.

thurston

WASHINGTON STATE
CABERNET SAUVIGNON 2002
DESTINY RIDGE VINEYARD

LATE HARVEST SYRAH
YAKIMA VALLEY
2008
ALC 12.8% BY VOL.   375 ML

SNOQUALMIE.

2007
SAUVIGNON
BLANC
COLUMBIA VALLEY
ALC 13.2% BY VOL.

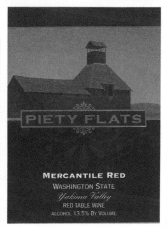

PIETY FLATS

MERCANTILE RED
WASHINGTON STATE
Yakima Valley
RED TABLE WINE
ALCOHOL 13.5% BY VOLUME

Aviator

CABERNET SAUVIGNON
MERLOT
CABERNET FRANC
PETIT VERDOT
MALBEC

YAKIMA VALLEY

08

AIRFIELD
ESTATES

SEVERINO
Cellars

2005

Cabernet Sauvignon

Yakima Valley

Alcohol 14.4% By Volume

2009
LONE BIRCH
WHITE BLEND | yakima valley

Steppe Cellars

Gewürztraminer
2007
Yakima Valley

ALC. 13.5% BY VOL.

Willow Crest

2007 **CABERNET FRANC**

YAKIMA VALLEY

AGATE FIELD
La Moisson

2006
RED WINE
YAKIMA VALLEY
alc. 14.4% by vol.

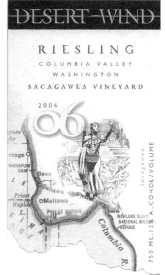

DESERT WIND

RIESLING

COLUMBIA VALLEY
WASHINGTON

SACAGAWEA VINEYARD

2006

06

750 ML. 12% ALCOHOL/VOLUME

09

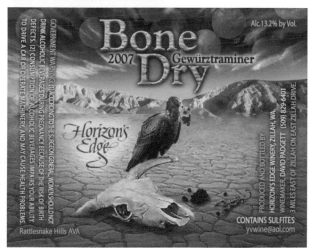

Alc. 13.2% by Vol.

Bone
2007 Gewürztraminer
Dry

Horizon's Edge

Rattlesnake Hills AVA

GOVERNMENT WARNING: (1) ACCORDING TO THE SURGEON GENERAL, WOMEN SHOULD NOT DRINK ALCOHOLIC BEVERAGES DURING PREGNANCY BECAUSE OF THE RISK OF BIRTH DEFECTS. (2) CONSUMPTION OF ALCOHOLIC BEVERAGES IMPAIRS YOUR ABILITY TO DRIVE A CAR OR OPERATE MACHINERY, AND MAY CAUSE HEALTH PROBLEMS.

PRODUCED AND BOTTLED BY
HORIZON'S EDGE WINERY, ZILLAH, WA.
WINEMAKER, DAVID PADGETT (509) 829-6401
3 MILES EAST OF ZILLAH ON EAST ZILLAH DRIVE.

CONTAINS SULFITES
yvwine@aol.com

Kestrel
Falcon Series

Estate Old Vine
CHARDONNAY
2009

WASHINGTON STATE · YAKIMA VALLEY
KESTREL VIEW ESTATE VINEYARD
ALCOHOL 13.9% BY VOLUME

Yakima
Wine Trail

Yakima WineTrail makes for a weekend getaway that comes complete with quaint lodging, hidden restaurants, and wineries that display the fruit of this prosperous valley. Several tasting rooms are located in downtown Yakima within easy walking distance of each other. A short car drive takes to you other wineries in nearby Naches Heights and Wapato. Also, with excellent restaurants like the Barrel House and Gasperetti's, it's hard to neglect any hunger pangs. All of these restaurants feature local wines from the Yakima Valley.

From Catch the Crush to Thanksgiving in Wine Country on the local calendar of wine-related happenings, don't be surprised if your visit coincides with a weekend event. These people know how to celebrate life's finer things.

Yakima WineTrail

1 Naches Heights Vineyard
2 The Tasting Room — Yakima
3 Gilbert Cellars
4 Kana Winery
5 Treveri Cellars — Downtown Yakima
6 Treveri Cellars
7 Windy Point Vineyards
8 Masset Winery
9 Piety Flats Winery

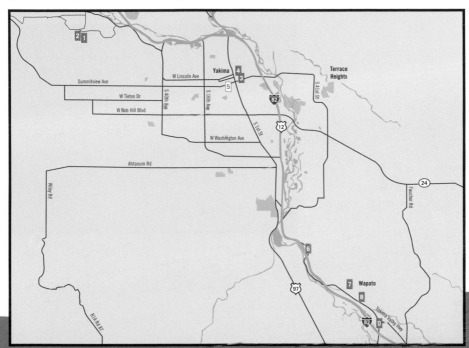

Region:	**Yakima Valley Wine Country**
# of tasting rooms on tour:	**9**
# of satellite tasting rooms:	**1**
Estimate # of days for tour:	**2**
Getting around:	**Car and foot**
Key Events:	❏ **Spring Barrel Tasting in the Yakima Valley; Red Wine and Chocolate; Catch the Crush and Thanksgiving in Wine Country sponsored by Wine Yakima Valley. See www.wineyakimavalley.org.**
Tips:	❏ **Park or stay downtown and experience several tasting rooms within easy walking distance.**
	❏ **Looking for a romantic getaway weekend? Stay at the nearby Birchfield Manor Country Inn for great food and cozy rooms.**
Best:	❏ **Views and picnicking: Naches Heights Vineyard**
	❏ **Destination, views and picnicking: The Tasting Room — Yakima**
	❏ **Picnicking: Treveri Cellars**
	❏ **Views and picnicking: Windy Point Vineyards**

Naches Heights Vineyard

According to vintner Phil Cline of Naches Heights Vineyard (NHV), wine is about fun. It's sexy, too. So why try to downplay those characteristics? NHV certainly doesn't; you can spot its bold wine labels from across the room. And what's within the bottle delivers sensual flavors that linger in your mouth, especially that Two Dancers red blend. Mmmmm....

Grape growers in the new Naches Heights American Viticultural Area (AVA), recently approved by the feds as Washington's 12th designated AVA, take advantage of the appellation's unusual soils, excellent drainage, relatively high altitude and plenitude of sunshine. It might also be the only viticultural area in the state whose vineyards are organically farmed exclusively.

Naches Heights Vineyard itself sits at one of highest elevations in the state, but the slope of the vineyard allows the excessively cold air, which can cause freeze damage, to drain off. With summer's long days, Phil's grapes see as many days of sun as anywhere else in Washington's grape-growing regions, ensuring the grapes will ripen to their full potential. The cool nights give the grapes a food-friendly acidity to balance the fruit's natural sweetness.

Phil Cline

NHV's current production focuses on riesling, pinot gris, gewürztraminer, and syrah, and makes for a truly nice lineup of wines to experience at The Naches Heights Vinyeard.

NACHES HEIGHTS VINEYARD
opened: 2007
winemaker(s): Mark Wysling (reds), Jean Claude Beck (whites)
location: 2410 Naches Heights Rd, Yakima, WA 98908
phone: 509-678-4271
web: www.nhvines.com
e-mail: info@nachesheights.com
fee: Tasting fee
hours: Thursday through Monday 11–7, extended hours Friday and Saturday until 9:30
amenities: Gift Shop, Online Store, Private Events, Restaurant/Food Pairings, RV/Bus Parking, Vineyard on Premise, Weddings, Wheelchair Accessible, Wine Club
connect: 🐦 f

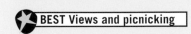

BEST Views and picnicking

The Tasting Room — Yakima [2]

Here's a concept: Invite a number of outstanding Washington wineries to join your own in an historic building in the heart of Seattle's Pike Place Market, and then welcome the wine-loving public to come in and enjoy the wide assortment of wines. That's just what owner/winemaker Paul Beveridge of Wilridge did when he launched The Tasting Room Seattle, Wines of Washington.

In 2007, Paul had purchased a parcel of land outside Yakima in the newly ordained Naches Heights AVA to grow grapes and make wine. With the great success of the Seattle Tasting Room cooperative, Paul decided to bring the concept east to his Yakima location, opening, you guessed it, The Tasting Room Yakima. The Yakima Tasting Room features many of the same wineries you find at the Pike Place location: Naches Heights Vineyards, Camaraderie Cellars, Harlequin Wine Cellars, Mountain Dome, Latitude 46 N, Wineglass Cellars and Wilridge Vineyards. Unlike its big-city cousin in Seattle, however, the Yakima experience is decidedly rural.

Visitors can go beyond the early-1900 Craftsman-style house turned tasting room to tip-toe through the 10-acre estate vineyard, drink a glass (or two) on the expansive patio or hike the nearby Cowiche Canyon Nature Preserve. It's beautiful. It's relaxing. And it goes beyond drive-by tasting. You will want to budget a generous amount of time for little spot of heaven on earth.

THE TASTING ROOM — YAKIMA
winemaker(s): Various Winemakers
location: 250 Ehler Road, The Tasting Room — Yakima, Yakima, WA 98908
phone: 509-966-0686
web: www.winesofwashington.com
e-mail: info@thetastingroomseattle
fee: Tasting fee
hours: Thursday through Monday 11–7 from May through October; Friday through Monday 11–6 November through April or by appointment
amenities: Gift Shop, Newsletter/Blog, Online Store, Picnic Area, Private Events, RV/Bus Parking, Wheelchair Accessible, Wine Club, Wines by the Glass
connect: 🐦 f

⭐ **BEST Destination, views and picnicking**

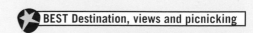

Gilbert Cellars 🄌

If you've been under the impression that downtown Yakima is Dullsville, think again. The lively wine bar/tasting room of Gilbert Cellars winery on Front Street offers live music and fine art for those adventurous people who wish to quench their souls and their thirst. If

you're short on time, take the time to sample Gilbert Cellars wines and come to understand the distinctive tastes of the different varieties from the Wahluke Slope AVA and other Columbia Valley vineyards.

The winery is a family affair involving several generations of Gilberts, with each person involved in some aspect of the business, from growing grapes to bottling to marketing. To give an example, Meg Gilbert's bio includes lots of travel and exposure to fine art. Armed with this background, Meg developed The Cave, located just outside Yakima at 2620 Draper Road, which is a venue for wine club parties and other musical events.

Curtiss Gilbert is one of the many Gilbert men involved in the grape-growing side of the business, racking up the miles traveling among the various vineyards he manages, including the Doc Stewart Estate Vineyard and 24K Vineyard in the Wahluke Slope AVA; the Sunrise Vineyard in the Columbia Valley AVA; and Chukar Vineyard in the Horse Heaven Hills.

Extended family member Justin Neufeld is the head winemaker for Gilbert Cellars. A graduate of the University of Washington with a molecular biology degree, Justin has the task of showcasing the fruit from the portfolio of Gilbert Cellars vineyards. He relishes his job, as you can discover for yourself with a hearty swirl and sip of his oh-so-velvety Doc Stewart syrah.

GILBERT CELLARS
opened: 2004
winemaker(s): Justin Neufeld
location: 5 North Front Street, Yakima, WA 98901
phone: 509-249-9049
web: www.gilbertcellars.com
e-mail: wines@gilbertcellars.com
fee: Tasting fee
hours: Monday through Thursday 11–9; Friday 12–11; Saturday 12–10; Sunday 12–5 except January to April
amenities: Live Music, Online Store, Newsletter/Blog, Private Events, Restaurant/Food Pairings, Wheelchair Accessible, Wine Club, Winemaker Dinners, Wines by the Glass
connect: 🐦 📘

Kana Winery 4

Located in the historic Larson Building on South Second Street, Kana's tasting room offers complimentary wine tasting along with rotating art on the wall. As a bonus, Kana Winery hosts happy hour between 5 and 6:30 p.m., Monday through Saturday. But wait, there's more! Downtown Yakima is a "corkage-fee-free zone," and Kana Winery is one of the wineries/tasting rooms that participate in the program. Essentially, the typical $10 corkage fee that restaurants charge is waived when you bring in a bottle of newly purchased wine (along with your receipt).

Local physician, Dr. Palmer Wright, launched Kana Winery in 2002 but not merely as a testimony for his love of wine but also get-involved and roll-up-the-sleeves involvement in wine production. Working closely with winemaker Ben Grossman they focus on Rhône-style blends, using varietals such as roussanne, viognier, Marsanne, syrah, Mourvèdre, grenache, and counoise. Kana Winery does manage to produce some non-Rhône varietal wines, including an off-dry riesling, but the real crowd pleasers are the reds. My own palate danced with the healthy sip of the Dark Star red, with its bright blueberry notes and lasting finish.

As noted on the Kana website, "Kana" is a Native American word for the spirit, or the fire, within a mountain, referring to the perceived supernatural power of volcanic activity. With the Cascade Mountains in the distance, it's not hard to imagine why the locals would have respect for Kana. Visitors are welcome at Kana Winery throughout the year; it's known to draw particularly large crowds for special events, such as Thanksgiving in Wine Country, Red Wine and Chocolate, and spring barrel tasting. No matter what their cultural backgrounds may be, visitors are likely to agree that Kana Winery is good for the spirit.

KANA WINERY
opened: 2004
winemaker(s): Ben Grossman
(Dr. Wade Wolfe consultant)
location: 10 South 2nd Street, Larson Building, Yakima, WA 98901-2646
phone: 509-453-6611
web: www.kanawinery.com
e-mail: kanawinery@aol.com
fee: Tasting fee refunded with purchase
hours: Monday through Thursday 12–6:30; Friday 12–8; Saturday 12–6:30; Sunday 12–5
amenities: Gift Shop, Live Music, Online Store, Private Events, Wheelchair Accessible, Wine Club, Wines by the Glass
connect:

Treveri Cellars — Downtown Yakima 5

TREVERI CELLARS — DOWNTOWN YAKIMA
opened: 2010
winemaker(s): Juergen Grieb
location: 225 South 2nd Avenue, Yakima, WA 98902
phone: 509-248-0200
web: www.trevericellars.com
e-mail: info@trevericellars.com
fee: Tasting fee
hours: Monday through Saturday 12–6
amenities: Online Store, RV/Bus Parking, Tours, Wheelchair Accessible, Wine Club
connect: 🐦 📘

www.winetrailsnw.com/wineries/treveri_cellars_-_downtown_yakima

Treveri Cellars 6

It's fun to discover a different type of winery, and that's exactly what Treveri Cellars is. Founded by German transplant Juergen Grieb, Treveri Cellars makes sparkling wine in the heart of Yakima.

Juergen Grieb

Although there are a variety of ways to produce bubblies, Juergen relies on the traditional *méthode champenoise* process for introducing carbon dioxide. Yes, France cranks out a lot of winemakers who understand the second fermentation process in the bottle, but what many folks don't realize is that Germany, too, has plenty of winemakers knowledgeable in the ways of sparkling wine, and it produces a vast amount of sparkling wine.

True to his German heritage, Juergen uses traditional German varieties to craft about 2,500 cases of wine per year, including riesling, Müller-Thurgau, and gewürztraminer. He also relies on chardonnay (the grape variety you would find in French champagne blended with pinot noir and pinot meunier) as well as Italian-derived pinot gris. Rather than blending these varieties, Juergen chooses to produce 100 percent varietal sparklers. Thus, his ever so crisp Treveri Cellars brut is composed of 100 percent chardonnay, and with just 1.4 percent residual sugar, you won't taste any sweetness; It's dry. But for those with a bit of a sweet tooth, including moi, his demi-sec riesling and gewürztraminers deliver a slightly sweet but nicely balanced effervescent delight.

A piece of trivia for history buffs out there: The Treveri, or Treviri, were the tribe of Gauls who inhabited the lower valley of the Moselle from around 150 years B.C. until their eventual absorption by the Franks. It's unknown if the Franks drank any bubbly to celebrate their assimilation of the Treveri.

TREVERI CELLARS
opened: 2010
winemaker(s): Juergen Grieb
location: 71 Gangl Road, Wapato, WA 98951
phone: 509-248-0200
web: www.trevericellars.com
e-mail: info@trevericellars.com
fee: Tasting fee
hours: Tuesday through Thursday 12–5; Friday and Saturday 11–7; and Sunday 12–4
amenities: Online Store, Picnic Area, RV/Bus Parking, Tours, Wheelchair Accessible, Wine Club
connect: 🐦 f

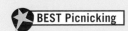
BEST Picnicking

Windy Point Vineyards **7**

Without a doubt, Windy Point Vineyards offers one of the top 10 winery views in Washington. Situated on a hilltop in Wapato, Windy Point offers a commanding view of the Yakima Valley, with mile upon mile of orchards below, and the Cascade Mountains in the distance. This is agricultural country. You can see a patchwork quilt of farms below, with Interstate 82 snaking its way southeast toward the Tri-Cities.

Featuring award-winning syrah and cabernet franc, Windy Point Vineyards is the creation of Mike and Liz Stepniewski. With three decades of farming under their belts, the Stepniewskis converted 15 acres of fruit orchards into vineyards. Plans call for adding more

grapes, with the goal of producing 100 percent estate wines. The couple is close to meeting that goal now, and is proud that all of their fruit is from the Yakima Valley. Despite a huge early success with wine critics, their goal is to remain "boutique," with total annual production of 3,000 cases.

While Mike tends the vineyards, Liz is the winemaker, focusing on "Pointless" wines, including Pointless Red, Exclamation Point, and Pointless Cabernet. In addition to these red blends, she handcrafts merlot, estate cabernet franc, syrah, estate cabernet sauvignon, gewürztraminer, and riesling.

The elegant design of the tasting room (originally Mike's tractor and repair shop) is strongly reminiscent of Frank Lloyd Wright's style, reflecting Mike's keen interest in architecture. This is especially evident in the wall facing the Yakima Valley, which incorporates plenty of glass for panoramic views. The tasting room features a full-service kitchen that clues visitors in to the Stepniewskis' devoted interest in cooking. Is there a winemaker dinner in your future? Call ahead and inquire.

Windy Point Vineyards' excellent wines, great views, and fantastic architecture add up to a highly desirable destination for a WineTrail journey.

WINDY POINT VINEYARDS
winemaker(s): Liz Stepniewski
location: 420 Windy Point Drive, Wapato, WA 98951
phone: 509-877-6824
web: www.windypointvineyards.com
e-mail: events@windypointvineyards.com
fee: Tasting fee waived for Club members
hours: Summer: Daily 10–6; Spring and Fall: Thursday through Monday 10–5; Winter: Hours vary
amenities: Gift Shop, Newsletter/Blog, Picnic Area, RV/Bus Parking, Tours, Vineyard on Premise, Weddings, Wheelchair Accessible, Wine Club
connect: 🐦 📘

⭐ **BEST Views and picnicking**

Masset Winery 8

Dripping with French country charm, the Masset Winery tasting room is located in a converted barn on the historic 1905 Angel Farmstead. We can only imagine the trepidation Greg and Michaela Masset felt when they decided to transform the dilapidated barn into an inviting tasting room. However, with considerable elbow grease and buckets of paint, Michaela succeeded—and if, heaven forbid, the winery should go south, she's got a career as an interior designer. Choosing the right mix of antiques to complement the warm yellows and earthy browns, she has created a perfect space for tasting wine and relaxing in understated elegance. A hand-hewn, 14-foot-long workbench separates the tasting-bar area from an inviting living room. This wood centerpiece invites you to go ahead and touch.

Masset Winery offers a full complement of reds, with an emphasis on syrah and petite syrah. The wallet-friendly Le Petit Rouge red blend is a favorite among fans, at $17 a bottle. However, don't miss the chance to sample the unoaked chardonnay; crisp and lively, this wine is excellent accompaniment to salads, light pastas, and Northwest seafood.

Winemaker Greg is an executive chef by day at the Yakima Country Club. He grew up in the hospitality business, with his family owning the renowned Birchfield Manor Gourmet Restaurant. He earned a degree in food science and has a background in the business, giving him the necessary skills for continuing Masset Winery's success.

Hard-working Greg is quick to give thanks to family, friends, and mentors. His quest is to create food-friendly Yakima wines while maintaining a graceful simplicity. With all these good things going for Masset Winery, it's clear that the 1905 farmstead once again bears fruit.

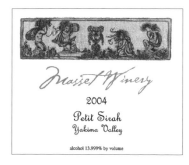

2004
Petit Sirah
Yakima Valley

alcohol 13.999% by volume

MASSET WINERY
opened: 1999
winemaker(s): Greg Masset
location: 620 East Parker Heights Road, Wapato, WA 98951
phone: 509-877-6675
web: www.massetwinery.com
e-mail: info@massetwinery.com
fee: Complimentary wine tasting
hours: Saturday and Sunday 11–5, Thursday, Friday, and Monday 2–5, from February through November by appointment
amenities: Online Store, RV/Bus Parking, Tours, Wheelchair Accessible, Wine Club
connect: f

Piety Flats Winery 🄎

Get ready for some old-country-store charm. At Piety Flats, you might even decide to forgo the wine and go straight for the Thomas Kemper root beer float! Jim and Kris Russi, proprietors of Piety Flats Winery, produce wines using Yakima Valley fruit. The tasting room/store, located in the 1911 Mercantile Building, is full of antiquated charm and famous for its peach sundaes. Conveniently located right off Interstate 82, this rustic store

still has the appearance of the past century, "complete with creaking wooden floors, old country store fixtures, and memorabilia of yesteryear." Visitors can enjoy the ambiance of another era while shopping from well-stocked shelves and sampling wine.

A very knowledgeable wine pourer proudly serves each wine. And what a lineup of wines to sample! Piety Flats produces a number of mainstay wines, including syrah, merlot, some nonvintage (NV) red table blends, and a pinot grigio/chardonnay blend. Also offered is a port-style wine called POSH (Port Out, Starboard Home), which would pair nicely with pound cake or be great on its own. By the way, as you are imbibing, check out the distinctive label and note the old hop kiln building across the way notice a resemblance?

If time permits, purchase picnic nibbles in the store, along with a bottle of Piety Flats wine, and make a beeline for one of the outside picnic tables. It's a great place to contemplate what life was like in Yakima Valley 100 years ago; tuning out the sounds of traffic from the nearby freeway, you can get a strong sense of those bygone days.

PIETY FLATS WINERY
location: 2560 Donald-Wapato Road, Wapato, WA 98951
phone: 509-877-3115
web: www.pietyflatswinery.com
e-mail: info@pietyflatswinery.com
fee: Complimentary wine tasting
hours: Daily 10–5
amenities: Gift Shop, Mailing List, Online Store, Picnic Area, Tours, Wheelchair Accessible, Wines by the Glass
connect: ⬛

Rattlesnake Hills
Wine Trail

Who would have ever guessed that one day Zillah would have stretch limousines zipping between tractors, but that's what happens when you add more than 20 wineries to the landscape. Speaking of the landscape, this is American farmland at its finest and reflects the agricultural transition from fruit orchards to vineyards. Many winemakers in this part of the Yakima Valley are "dirt guys," having farmed the land for many years. They know that great wine begins with great fruit. Take the time to walk through the vineyards when you visit and to get to the heart of grape growing.

In 2006, the Rattlesnake Hills region of Yakima Valley obtained the designation of American Viticultural Area (AVA). Winemakers with years of experience and newcomers alike banded together to obtain this prestigious federal label. With this newly won title, it didn't take long before a majority of the wineries came together to promote their products and sponsor a variety of events.

Rattlesnake Hills WineTrail

1 Bonair Winery
2 Tanjuli Winery
3 Wineglass Cellars
4 Knight Hill Winery
5 Two Mountain Winery
6 Hyatt Vineyards
7 Agate Field Vineyard
8 Maison de Padgett Winery
9 Paradisos del Sol
10 Cultura Wine
11 Silver Lake Winery
12 Portteus Vineyards & Winery
13 Claar Cellars
14 Severino Cellars
15 Horizon's Edge Winery
16 Tefft Cellars Winery
17 Steppe Cellars

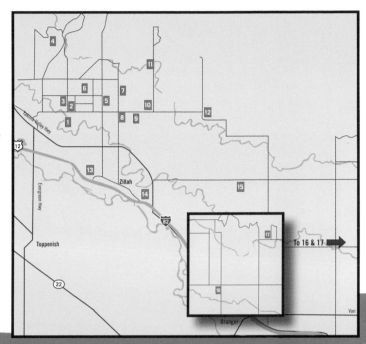

Region:	**Yakima Valley Wine Country**
# of tasting rooms on tour:	**17**
Estimate # of days for tour:	**4**
Getting around:	**Car or bike**
Key Events:	❏ **Spring Barrel Tasting in the Yakima Valley (last weekend in April); Red Wine and Chocolate (mid-February); Catch the Crush (October) and Thanksgiving in Wine Country sponsored by Wine Yakima Valley. See www.wineyakimavalley.org.**
	❏ **Rattlesnake Hills Wine Trail Association sponsors events during the year including Red Wine & Chocolate, Appellation Celebration, Spring Barrel Tasting and Snake in the Glass Passport. See www.rattlesnakehills.org for details.**
Tips:	❏ **For avid bicyclists, this WineTrail is heaven. See Wineglass Cellars website at www.wineglasscellars.com for David's 60 Miler course.**
	❏ **Purchase Rattlesnake Hills Winery Association Passport and get discounts on wine purchases and more.**
	❏ **Consider hiring a limousine service.**
Best:	❏ **Gift shop, picnicking and weddings: Hyatt Vineyards**
	❏ **Weddings: Maison de Padgett Winery**
	❏ **Picnicking and views: Silver Lake Winery**
	❏ **Views: Steppe Cellars**

Bonair Winery 1

Founded in 1985, Bonair Winery and Vineyards is located in the heart of Yakima wine country — Zillah, to be precise. With the Rattlesnake Hills to the east, this wine country region presents a constellation of images that would fill a calendar: October harvest, Fourth of July red, white and rosé tasting rooms, cases of wine under the Christmas tree, and many

more. Gail Puryear, owner and vintner of Bonair, wants visitors to experience "real wineries," for which they pass by vineyards on the way to the tasting rooms and while doing so, make the connection between the wines and their origins.

The architectural style of the Bonair Winery may remind you of an English country estate, with its turret and brown-trimmed white buildings. With a koi pond positioned in front of the winery and Yakima's typical deep blue skies as a backdrop, you're treated to another calendar-perfect image. Get ready to enjoy what Gail describes as a "hobby that got out of control." Bonair's reputation for chardonnay, quaffable reds, fruity sipping wines, and mead makes it unique. Yes, the chardonnay is aged in oak "the old-fashioned way." Bonair's flagship Chateau Puryear Reserve Chardonnay is big, soft and buttery, and as Gail puts it, is "like chardonnay used to be before self-appointed wine critics." Sample the chardonnay and imagine that paired with your wine-country turkey and cranberry sauce.

BONAIR WINERY
opened: 1985
winemaker(s): Gail Puryear
location: 500 South Bonair Road, Zillah, WA 98953-9245
phone: 509-829-6027
web: www.bonairwine.com
e-mail: winemaker@bonairwine.com
fee: Complimentary wine tasting; fee for reserves
hours: Daily 10–5 from April through November; weekends December through March, or by appointment
amenities: Gift Shop, Online Store, Picnic Area, Tours, Vineyard on Premise, Weddings, Wheelchair Accessible, Wine Club
connect: f

12.4% ALC BY VOL

Bonair
ESTATE BOTTLED
2005 RATTLESNAKE HILLS
RIESLING
BONAIR ESTATE VINEYARDS

Tanjuli Winery ②

With more than 30 years of winemaking and grape-growing experience, Tom Campbell isn't any Johnny-come-lately to the wine industry. Educated at the University of California-Davis' renowned viticulture and enology program, Tom worked in the wine regions of Sonoma Valley, Edna Valley, and Temecula, where he established vineyards and made wine. Eventually he made his way north to become the enologist for Chateau Ste. Michelle's Grandview operation, and then launched his own winery, Horizon's Edge Winery, before selling it to David Padgett in 1999.

For fans of Woodinville-based Woodhouse Wine Estates' hugely popular Darighe (Gaelic for "red") Bordeaux blend, they have Tom Campbell to thank. He's the director of wine production for Woodhouse Wine Estates.

Tanjuli Winery, located in Zillah, Washington, is constructed into the side of a hill adjacent to Tom's vineyard. Built in 2010, the spacious building offers loads of space for wine production, barrel aging and wine tasting. There's also plenty of space for picnicking outside on the patio and enough room to accommodate a big band for live music performances. While there is a full spectrum of white and red wines to taste, be sure to experience the petit verdot. Typically, winemakers blend this Bordeaux variety with other red grapes to give the wine vibrant color and midpalate strength. It's unusual to find a single varietal petit verdot, so check this one out.

Tanjuli — for a combination of the names of Tom's two children, Taj and Anjuli — epitomizes the grapes grown in the Zillah area. After spending a lifetime working the vineyards up and down the West Coast, Tom settled on the viticultural area that suits his notion of making fine wine — the unique *terroir* of the Rattlesnake Hills AVA.

TANJULI WINERY
opened: 2010
winemaker(s): Tom Campbell
location: 209 North Bonair Road, Zillah, WA 98953
phone: 509-654-9753
web: www.tanjuli.com
e-mail: tanjuli@gmail.com
fee: Tasting fee refunded with purchase
hours: Thursday through Monday 10:30–5 or by appointment
amenities: Art Gallery, Gift Shop, Newsletter/Blog, Pet Friendly, Vineyard on Premise, Wheelchair Accessible
connect: 🐦 📘

Wineglass Cellars 3

If you are looking to cycle in Yakima Valley, make a point of asking winemaker/owner David and Linda Lowe about it. As an avid cyclist, David knows the back roads of the valley well and has mapped his favorite routes. Whether you are up for a "get the heart pumping" 10-mile jaunt or a sweaty, calf-testing 60-mile trek, he can advise you.

David and Linda look forward to having you stop by and experience their wines. They will gladly point out their award winners and encourage you to linger and sample them at your leisure. For those with a picnic basket in tow, an inviting table awaits you, weather permitting.

WINEGLASS CELLARS
opened: 1994
winemaker(s): David Lowe
location: 260 North Bonair Road, Zillah, WA 98953
phone: 509-829-3011
web: www.wineglasscellars.com
e-mail: sales@wineglasscellars.com
fee: Complimentary wines except reserves
hours: Friday through Sunday 10:30–5; Closed December through March except Presidents Weekend in February
amenities: Gift Shop, Picnic Area, Tours, Wheelchair Accessible, Wine Club
connect: f

Knight Hill Winery

As they say, "A knight without wine is like a day without sunshine!" Well, at least that is what Terry and Anne Harrison, proprietors of a relatively new winery in the northern reaches of Zillah, say.

Perhaps the first thing that grabs your attention when you visit Knight Hill Winery is the view. I'd call it "breathtaking" but that's a little too hackneyed. The second thing to show up on your radar is a German shepherd, but don't be alarmed. Dixie is your friendly escort when touring the winery.

Inside the light-filled tasting room, Anne is usually doing the pouring honors of their small but respectable portfolio of wines. While their own vineyard matures, the Harrisons rely on grapes procured from other Yakima Valley grape growers, vineyards with names such as StoneTree Vineyard, Two Mountain Winery's Copeland Vineyard, and Sugarloaf Vineyards.

Terry is the keeper of the vines and also pitches in to assist with chief winemaker Anke Freimuth-Wildman who is also the winemaker for nearby Steppe Cellars. A native German who grew up in the Mosel Valley, Anke knows a thing or two about crafting riesling wines.

I suspect that for both Terry and Anne in between racking, bottling, and labeling, they look out toward the southern reaches of the Yakima Valley and realize that they wouldn't have it any other way. It's a nice space to be in.

Anne and Terry Harrison

KNIGHT HILL WINERY
opened: 2009
winemaker(s): Anke Freimuth-Wildman
location: 5330 Lombard Loop Road, Zillah, WA 98953
phone: 509-865-5654
web: www.knighthillwinery.com
e-mail: info@knighthillwinery.com
fee: Complimentary wine tasting
hours: Daily 9–6 April through December and Presidents Day Weekend; January through March by appointment only
amenities: Gift Shop, Picnic Area, Vineyard on Premise, Wheelchair Accessible
connect: 🐦 f

Two Mountain Winery 5

Brothers Matthew and Patrick Rawn are today's driving force behind Two Mountain Winery. However, they would be the first to tell you that they are but two members of a family of farmers that has been actively growing things for more than a half-century. In fact, their uncle Ron Schmidt was the initial driving force in converting part of the family's fruit orchards to *Vitis vinifera* in 2000.

Matthew and Patrick Rawn (l to r)

Today, Matthew and Patrick manage the 26-acre estate Copeland Vineyard in the Rattlesnake Hills AVA of the Yakima Valley, farming the fruit from bud break to bottling. Grape varieties include chardonnay, riesling, lemberger, merlot, syrah, cabernet sauvignon, cabernet franc and touriga nacional (a primary grape for making Portuguese port wine and one that's rarely found in Washington). From these eight grapes varieties, the brothers Rawn craft varietal reds and whites, a rosé, and a couple of lip-smacking red blends. As you sample the cabernet sauvignon, imagine how grilled tenderloin would pair with this richly layered wine.

During most years, the vineyard generates 3 to 4 tons of grapes per acre, which translates to 200 tons of grapes. It takes a lot of pruning, tendril tucking, cluster thinning, and sucker pulling to harvest a couple of hundred tons of sugar-rich grapes each year. It might be fair to say that the brothers know every vineyard row and vine.

The tasting room and winery offer a stunning view of both Mount Rainier and Mount Adams. The vista serves as a reminder that the Cascade Range is responsible for both that major rain shadow over the Yakima Valley (only about 6 inches of precipitation falls per year) as well as the water that feeds the Yakima River. Thank you, Cascades!

Matthew Rawn

TWO MOUNTAIN WINERY
opened: 2003
winemaker(s): Matthew Rawn
location: 2151 Cheyne Road, Zillah, WA 98953
phone: 509-829-3900
web: www.twomountainwinery.com
e-mail: info@twomountainwinery.com
fee: Complimentary wine tasting
hours: Daily 10–6 from Presidents Day Weekend through November, or by appointment
amenities: Gift Shop, Picnic Area, RV/Bus Parking, Tours, Vineyard on Premise, Wheelchair Accessible, Wine Club
connect:

Hyatt Vineyards

Leland and Lynda Hyatt established Hyatt Vineyards in 1985 and produced their first vintage in 1987. Since that time, they have witnessed a number of changes, including the designation of their area — Rattlesnake Hills — as an American Viticultural Area (AVA).

The Hyatt production facility and tasting room command a large footprint of real estate, with a windmill as the centerpiece of its well-manicured lawn. Upon viewing the grounds, you might think that this would be a great place for a wedding, and you'd be right. You can book the property; arrange for chairs, caterer and a preacher; and have yourself a heck of a wedding — especially if both Mount Rainier and Mount Adams decide to make an appearance. And there's certainly plenty of wine to go around.

Hyatt's winemaker, Andy Gamache, gets most of his grapes from four estate vineyards within two miles of the winery. With an annual production of approximately 30,000 cases, Hyatt wines sell for around $9 a bottle. For its more upscale, Roza Ridge label, plan to spend a wallet-friendly $15 a bottle and this clearly explains why the *Wine Enthusiast* named Hyatt's 2006 merlot and cabernet sauvignon "Best Buys."

Although you can sample the Hyatt wines free at its tasting room, there is small fee for sampling Hyatt Roza Ridge wines. It's interesting, and educational, to taste the difference between Hyatt's regular wines and its premium Roza Ridge reserves, including Roza Ridge syrah, cabernet sauvignon, and merlot.

If your trip takes you to Hyatt during fall harvest, make a point of plucking a few grapes from the vineyard. If you have never experienced the full onslaught of sugar-laden, juicy chardonnay or cabernet, here's your chance!

HYATT VINEYARDS
opened: 1985
winemaker(s): Steve Hovanes
location: 2020 Gilbert Road, Zillah, WA 98953-9766
phone: 509-829-6333
web: www.hyattvineyards.com
e-mail: info@hyattvineyards.com
fee: No tasting fee except for Roza Ridge wines—fee waived for Rattlesnake Hills Passport ticket buyers
hours: Daily 11–5 (11–4:30 during winter)
amenities: Gift Shop, Picnic Area, Private Events, RV/Bus Parking, Tours, Vineyard on Premise, Weddings, Wheelchair Accessible

⭐ **BEST Gift shop, picnicking and weddings**

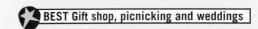

Agate Field Vineyard 🟨

In this part of the Rattlesnake Hills AVA (American Viticultural Area), the wineries serve up a mixed bag when it comes to wine quality. If you're hankering to visit a winery with a

manmade pond or an oversized white windmill, by all means, seek it out. If, however, your palate desires premium wine, then I suggest that you check out Agate Field Vineyard. Seriously.

This is a winery rich in tradition, yet young in winemaking years. Founder Ben Rashford has been growing grapes on his 10-acre Zillah-based vineyard for more than 60 years. Yet it wasn't until his wife, Ruth, suggested that they use some of the grapes to produce their own

Bob Radke

wine that Ben got the notion of Agate Field Vineyard wine. Fortunately, they decided to keep the venture in the family by turning to their daughter, Ginger, whose husband, Bob Radke, became their winemaker. Interestingly, Bob is a law enforcement officer with the Department of Agriculture by day, so WineTrail enthusiasts are advised not to be yanking any syrah plantings from the ground and making off with them.

Bob, Ginger, Ruth, and Ben often work the tasting room together, serving up elegant blends of estate cabernet sauvignon, cabernet franc, and merlot as well as syrah. But with small lot production, don't be surprised if they are sold out of a vintage or two. The tasting room itself has a rustic, cowboy-Western feel, with a second-story deck overlooking the vineyards of Whiskey Canyon. Bring a picnic, uncork a bottle of Agate Field red, and enjoy the view.

Inside, the spacious tasting room provides a comfortable environment, thanks in large part to the use of structurally insulated panels, which provide warmth during the winter, coolness in summer. It's a relaxing space reflecting the friendly demeanor of Agate Field Vineyard's familial staff.

AGATE FIELD VINEYARD
opened: 2004
winemaker(s): Bob Radke
location: 2911 Roza Drive, Zillah, WA 98953
phone: 509-930-0806
web: www.agatefieldvineyard.com
e-mail: via website
fee: Complimentary wine tasting
hours: April through November, Friday through Sunday 11–5; Also open Thursday June to September 11–5
amenities: Gift Shop, Mailing List, Newsletter/Blog, Picnic Area, Vineyard on Premise, Wheelchair Accessible

Maison de Padgett Winery

Are you game to explore one of Washington's most unusual wineries? Then check out Maison de Padgett Winery. Although owner/winemaker David Padgett concentrates on bringing you and other wine lovers fine wines, what's most important to him is that you have fun. To him, wine is bottled pleasure and it needs to be approachable. To this end, he

produces a full range of wines designed to please every palate, from that of the occasional wine taster to the informed tongue of the seasoned oenophile. Included in his arsenal are ports, for which Maison de Padgett enjoys a large following. Check out David's Smoking Gun coffee port; that's David pictured on the label.

Maison de Padgett Winery is the sister winery of nearby Horizon's Edge, which David and his wife, Lisa, also own. The winery is wonderfully spacious, with pleasing architectural touches, and includes an English-style garden large enough to host weddings and other events. In fact, the garden area includes a quaint bridal cottage for pre- and post-nuptial garment changes as well as private space for giving the caterer "what for" for bringing fruit salad rather than the ordered macaroni salad.

With 18 acres of grapes nearby, David handcrafts estate merlot and cabernet sauvignon. However, his real forte is dessert wine, be it port, late harvest, or ice wine. He has more than a dozen dessert wine labels, with names such as Singing Toad, Funky Monkey, Sleeping Giant, Lip Service, and Raging Bull.

As David states on his website, "Welcome to Washington's Most Unique Winery." He's not kidding. Adventurers beware: You are entering the fun zone. Get ready for unusual ports, succulent dessert wines, along with more traditional wines and some whimsical labels. Like other visitors, you'll leave with a smile (and, perhaps, several bottles to take home).

MAISON DE PADGETT WINERY
opened: 2002
winemaker(s): David Padgett
location: 2231 Roza Drive, Zillah, WA 98953
phone: 509-829-6412
web: www.maisondepadgettwinery.com
e-mail: yvwine@aol.com
fee: Tasting fee refunded with purchase
hours: Thursday through Monday 11–5, Tuesday and Wednesday by chance, from March through November; open Presidents Day Weekend 11–5
amenities: Picnic Area, Private Events, Weddings, Wheelchair Accessible, Wine Club

⭐ **BEST Weddings**

Paradisos del Sol 9

Paul Vandenberg, owner and winemaker for Paradisos del Sol, is mad. We're not talking "Mad Hatter" mad, but mad in the sense of being obsessed with wine.

As you approach Paradisos del Sol's tasting room outside Zillah, the colorful flags, outdoor sculpture, and chickens scampering around the backyard may have you wondering if you took a wrong turn. There may also be a strange-looking guy wearing wildly colored pants positioned by the front door welcoming visitors. The greeter is Paul himself. Like one of those free-sample stands you find at Costco, Paul sets up his table and engages wine tasters to sample a couple of his wines. He does this primarily to educate the winery's many visitors, but we suspect that he, too, is learning, about the likes and dislikes of the wine-drinking public.

Barbara Sherman, Paul's spouse, runs the tasting room as well as taking care of the winery's myriad paperwork chores. To handle weekend and event

Paul Vandenberg

crowds, the couple provides two different tasting areas featuring different wines; it's like a progressive dinner party, except that all the courses are potable. Depending on wine availability, Barbara and her team might be pouring their dry Rosé Paradiso; their mildly sweet, Thai-friendly riesling; their sangiovese-based Paradisos Red table wine; a very drinkable cabernet sauvignon to go with that wild goose in the frig; or a few dessert wines, with such beguiling names as Port Paradisos, Zort and my favorite, Angelica MRS.

To truly understand Paradisos del Sol, one needs to look beyond the tasting room to the nearby vineyard. That is where Paul spends much of his time, tending the vines, chasing critters away, and warding off powdery mildew. You can't help but notice a gleam in Paul's eye as he talks about Paradisos del Vineyard, and it's apparent that this winegrower has indeed found his paradise.

PARADISOS DEL SOL
opened: 2000
winemaker(s): Paul Vandenberg
location: 3230 Highland Drive, Zillah, WA 98953
phone: 509-829-9000
web: www.paradisosdelsol.com
e-mail: info@paradisosdelsol.com
fee: Tasting fee refunded with $20 purchase
hours: Daily 11–6; winter hours may vary — call ahead
amenities: Gift Shop, Picnic Area, RV/Bus Parking, Tours, Vineyard on Premise, Wheelchair Accessible
connect: f

Cultura Wine 🔟

Although the Cultura website compares its winery experience to those offered in France, I beg to differ. In many ways, it's like comparing a chic beret to the iconic 10-gallon cowboy hat. I doubt that the French could replicate the down-home charm you get with cowboy boots, barbecued steaks, and cabernet sauvignon from the heart of Yakima Valley.

Native Yakima Valley residents, Tad and Sarah Fewel come from families with farming backgrounds. Picture pear orchards. Add a passion for growing grapes to those agricultural histories and you have a confluence of talents, heritage, and love of wine. Cultura Wine is an expression of that love affair.

I arrived to find saddled horses tied up near the winery, munching on the tall grass. It turns out that Tad's mom is Pepper Fewel, the owner of the hugely successful Cherry Wood Bed, Breakfast and Barn. She is the trail boss, leading overnight teepee guests through vineyards and orchards before making a pit stop for lunch at Cultura Wines. It's an experience captured by the likes of *Entrepreneur* magazine and *National Geographic*.

Tad Fewel

Inside the barn-style tasting room, Sarah calls on her experience as the former tasting room manager for nearby Sheridan Vineyards. She's a natural at it. However, Tad himself is just as equal to the task, proud to pour one of his Bordeaux-based offerings. As you sip and swirl, you might ask him about his other endeavor — producing biofuel. Take a wild guess at what they call their own personal fuel mix. "Bio-Fewel," natch.

CULTURA WINE
opened: 2009
winemaker(s): Tad and Sarah Fewel
location: 3601 Highland Drive, Zillah, WA 98953
phone: 509-829-0204
web: www.CulturaWine.com
e-mail: info@culturawine.com
fee: Tasting fee waived for club members
hours: February through November, Thursday through Saturday 11–5, Sunday, 11–4
amenities: Pet Friendly, Picnic Area, RV/Bus Parking, Wheelchair Accessible
connect: ❲f❳

Silver Lake Winery 11

Get ready for Girly Girl! Silver Lakes answer to meeting the palate needs of America's women and a case study success story in marketing.

Silver Lake Winery is one of the top 10 producing wineries in Washington and relatively old in Washington-winery years. Starting in 1989, three University of Washington professors crushed their first vintage. As Silver Lake lore tells it, their "hobby got out of control" and today they produce more than 50,000 cases a year for diehard Silver Lake fans.

Silver Lake's tasting rooms are in Woodinville and Zillah. Although these locations are quite different from one another, they both offer the same lineup of exceptional wines sold at good prices.

The Woodinville tasting room is located on the main road near the Columbia Winery. It's a rather modern, glassy-pointy structure, but don't get too comfortable with this setting — there are plans to build a new tasting venue. Once completed, the new complex will dwarf the existing tasting room. Shareholders will be very proud to show off this new setting, and there's no doubt it will become a Woodinville destination.

On the other side of the mountains, in sparsely populated Zillah, is Silver Lake Winery at Roza Hills. Without a doubt, the highlight of this winery — aside from the delicious wine — is the view of the valley. One can easily imagine hosting a corporate event, a family get-together, or a wedding reception at this location. The view is overlooking the Whiskey Canyon Vineyard and the entire valley, and can be enjoyed from the "viniferanda." (What a great new term for the wine world! Doesn't everyone need a viniferanda?) Don't forget the camera, a picnic, and the bottle opener.

SILVER LAKE WINERY
opened: 1988
winemaker(s): William Ammons
location: 1500 Vintage Road, Zillah, WA 98953
phone: 509-829-6235
web: www.silverlakewinery.com
e-mail: info@washingtonwine.com
fee: Complimentary except $5 charge for reserve wines
hours: Daily 11–4 from December through March; daily 10–5 from April through November
amenities: Gift Shop, Online Store, Picnic Area, Private Events, RV/Bus Parking, Tours, Vineyard on Premise, Weddings, Wheelchair Accessible, Wine Club
connect: 🐦 📘

⭐ **BEST Picnicking and views**

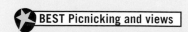

Portteus Vineyards & Winery **12**

Paul Portteus began making beer at age 19 in his houseboat on Seattle's Lake Union. Despite one unfortunate explosion of brewing beer that necessitated a remodel of the

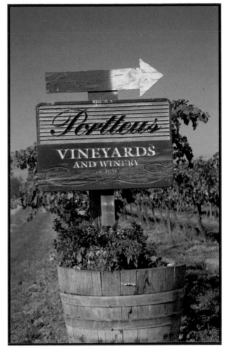

kitchen, Paul has gained a strong handle on the process of fermentation. While majoring in philosophy at the University of Washington, he took an extended tour of Europe by Norton motorcycle, discovering Europe's many wine regions and enjoying amazingly affordable wines. It was from those early beginnings and an extended visit in the Sonoma Valley, that he and his wife, Marilyn, launched Portteus Vineyards & Winery in 1981. Theirs was the 13th winery to be bonded in the state of Washington.

Among his other accomplishments, Paul championed for the designation of the Rattlesnake Hills American Viticultural Area, which obtained the official federal AVA title in early 2006. It was not an easy fight; many argued that Rattlesnake Hills' *terroir* was no different than that of Yakima Valley. But for someone who had the chutzpah to ride a motorcycle through Bordeaux in the '70s and later weather the vicissitudes of the grape industry's economy, dealing with politics surrounding the Rattlesnake Hills AVA was just another challenge to be met.

As you work your way through the lineup of Portteus' estate reds, you may be surprised when you encounter its zinfandel. In true pioneer fashion, Paul became the first grower to plant zinfandel in Washington. After you swirl and enjoy the peppery notes of this wine, you will understand why zin is Portteus' number-one seller.

PORTTEUS VINEYARDS & WINERY
opened: 1981
winemaker(s): Seth Portteus
location: 5201 Highland Drive, Zillah, WA 98953
phone: 509-829-6970
web: www.portteus.com
e-mail: info@portteus.com
fee: Complimentary wine tasting
hours: Daily 10–5
amenities: Online Store, Picnic Area, Vineyard on Premise, Wheelchair Accessible
connect: 🐦 📘

Claar Cellars 🔟

Few of us will be lucky enough to visit the Claar Cellars winery and vineyard, located in the White Bluffs area of the Columbia Valley AVA. It's certainly off the beaten path. However, getting to the Claar Cellars tasting room is way easier: Take Exit 52 off Interstate 82 and you are nearly there.

A huge, puncheon-size barrel, with Claar Cellars' distinctive red-lion logo embossed on its side, stands in front of the Zillah tasting room. Bob and Crista Claar Whitelatch have been farming in the White Bluffs area for more than 30 years. Early on, they found a market for their prized grapes, and in 1997, took the plunge and began crushing their own grapes, starting out in a 10,000-square-foot facility. The couple has expanded the winemaking facility, hired an experienced winemaker, and received a boatload of gold, silver, and bronze hardware.

John Claar Whitelatch manages the attractive tasting room and has an extensive knowledge of Claar Cellars' history and winemaking techniques. He should — he's Bob and Crista's son. With friendly aplomb and bottle in hand, John fields visitor' questions and keeps the samples coming.

CLAAR CELLARS
opened: 2000
winemaker(s): Joe Hudon
location: 1001 Vintage Valley Parkway, Zillah, WA 98953
phone: 509-829-6810
web: www.claarcellars.com
e-mail: crista@claarcellars.com
fee: Tasting fee
hours: Daily 10–6
amenities: Gift Shop, Newsletter/Blog, Online Store, Picnic Area, RV/Bus Parking, Wheelchair Accessible, Wine Club
connect: 🐦 📘

Severino Cellars 14

The first thing that grabs your attention is the remarkable Craftsman-style house serving as the home of Severino Cellars. It's old, big, and beautiful, and exudes Yakima Valley farming history and family values. You can almost smell the bread baking in the oven and hear the squeals of a laughing baby.

Lucky for us, the Spurlock and the Samaniego families have preserved the turn-of-the-century charm of the old house and added a dash of vino to the ambience. The long tasting bar gives plenty of elbow room for bellying up to the bar and visiting with the pourer. In my case, I had the pleasure of chatting with Nikki Samaniego (wife of winemaker Severino Samaniego), who provided me with shots of their refreshing whites and delicious reds. The Severino Red Lot #3 had my palate taking notice with its distinctive notes of blueberry and other dark fruit. At just $16 a bottle, it quickly gained even more appreciation.

In between sips, take time to examine the distinctive Severino wine label. If it seems to bear a strong resemblance to Northwest native art, congratulate yourself on your aesthetic acuity. It turns out that Severino Samaniego is a member of the Tlingit Nation, and the logo pays homage to this heritage. Naturally, salmon is a main staple of this Pacific Northwest coastal tribe, and I found myself thinking what a delicious match this old and venerated food source would make with native son Severino's Red Lot #3.

SEVERINO CELLARS
opened: 2008
winemaker(s): Severino Samaniego
location: 1717 First Avenue, Zillah, WA 98953
phone: 509-829-3800
web: www.severinocellars.com
e-mail: nikkispurlock@netscape.net
fee: Complimentary wine tasting
hours: March through November 10–6, Monday through Sunday 12–6; December through February, Saturday 11–5 and Sunday 12–5
amenities: Gift Shop, Newsletter/Blog, Picnic Area, RV/Bus Parking, Wheelchair Accessible, Wine Club
connect:

Horizon's Edge Winery

Got a sweet tooth? If so, Horizon's Edge Winery in the Rattlesnake Hills AVA might have just what you're craving. Try Horizon's Edge Naked Raspberry port-style wine (my favorite) or Cutting Edge chardonnay ice wine to get that sugar fix. On the other hand, if you're not in a sweet mood, winemaker/owner David Padgett has Bordeaux-style estate wines to meet your desires.

If you are familiar with the sister winery of Horizon's Edge — Maison de Padgett — you will recognize that the labels are unmistakably David Padgett's handiwork. Adjectives such as whacky, unorthodox, and whimsical might spring to mind as you gaze at the label of Brittney's Butterfly ice wine.

You will also note that this is a working winery, from vineyard to bottling. To those wine lovers who have grown used to business-park wineries, where the continuity from vineyard and winemaking is broken, Horizon's Edge will be a new experience. Adjacent to the winery are 18 acres of Yakima Valley wine grapes for Horizon's Edge use. Assuming there are 3 tons of grapes per acre, that's 108,000 pounds of grapes by our way of reckoning.

A special treat when visiting Horizon's Edge's Zillah location is the tasting room located upstairs in a loft. While you experience its wines be sure to take in those views. You just might see Mount Rainier and Mount Adams on the horizon's edge.

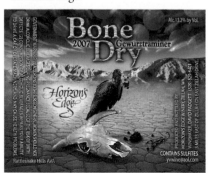

HORIZON'S EDGE WINERY
opened: 2000
winemaker(s): David Padgett
location: 4530 East Zillah Drive, Zillah, WA 98953-9326
phone: 509-829-6401
web: www.horizonsedgewinery.com
e-mail: yvwine@aol.com
fee: Tasting fee
hours: March through November, Thursday through Monday 11–5, Tuesday and Wednesday by chance; open Presidents Day Weekend 11–5
amenities: Picnic Area, RV/Bus Parking, Tours, Vineyard on Premise, Wheelchair Accessible, Wine Club
connect: 🐦 📘

Tefft Cellars Winery 16

Launched in 1991 by Joel Tefft, Tefft Cellars is one of the older wineries in Washington. Joel relied primarily on fruit from his own 12-acre vineyard in making a full range of estate and Yakima Valley reds, whites and dessert wines. Time marched on and eventually Joel sold Tefft Cellars to its current owners Paul Tollner and Rhonda Taylor.

Keeping the Tefft Cellars name and branding (such as that stately great blue heron on the label), Paul and Rhonda have given the winery a face lift of sorts. For example, using considerable elbow grease and an eye for design, they opened a tasting room studio in well-populated Woodinville in 2009, enhanced the grounds and tasting room of their flagship winery and tasting room site in Outlook, Washington, and more recently hired an experienced winemaker, Brian Wavernek.

Fans of Tefft Cellars rejoice in the fact that Tefft Cellars still maintains a fairly large collection of wines, including the traditional reds (cabernet, merlot, and syrah) and whites (chardonnay, gewürztraminer, and pinot grigio), as well as dessert wines with memorable names like Black Ice and Starboard.

But it's not all about tradition. The Tefft Cellars estate nebbiolo is noteworthy because, of the 40,000-plus acres of grapes grown in Washington, few acres are planted in nebbiolo. It's rare to see this grape outside its home base of Italy's Piedmont region. Whether or not Tefft Cellars' nebbiolo can compete with the great nebbiolo-based Barolos or Barbarescos of Piedmont is the challenge.

If you happen to visit the Outlook tasting room, pause to take a good look at its outside mural. It depicts various wine-related scenes, from crush to spring barrel tasting. Despite the bright sun, the mural's vibrant colors draw the viewer into the scene. It almost makes you wish you could shed your shoes and stomp some grapes!

TEFFT CELLARS WINERY
opened: 1991
winemaker(s): Brian Wavernek
location: 1320 Independence Road, Outlook, WA 98938
phone: 888-549-7244
web: www.tefftcellars.com
e-mail: ptollner@gmail.com
fee: Complimentary wine tasting
hours: Daily 10–5
amenities: Gift Shop, Lodging, Online Store, Picnic Area, RV/Bus Parking, Tours, Vineyard on Premise, Weddings, Wheelchair Accessible, Wine Club, Wines by the Glass
connect: 🐦 f

Paul Tollner and Rhonda Taylor

Steppe Cellars

My visit coincided with the setting sun, and the shrub-populated land was aglow in golden light. The sight had me reaching for my camera. Named after the surrounding shrub-steppe ecosystem, Steppe Cellars is a partnership between Tom and Susan Garrison and Susan's sister and brother-in-law Gabrielle and Mike Seibel.

Tom Garrison has been growing wine grapes since the early 1980s, and in 2005, despite the advice of many to either "not do it" or "do it, but keep you day job," he launched Steppe Cellars.

However, the partners knew going into it that growing premium grapes was one thing, but transforming those grapes into fine wine required the employment of an experienced winemaker. Enter Anke Freimuth-Wildman. A native of Germany's Mosel Valley, Anke comes from a long line of winemakers, and her background includes stints at German and Swiss wineries, and an advanced enology and viticulture degree from Germany's renowned Geisenheim Institute. The woman knows a thing or two about riesling.

A marriage of the Garrisons' Dalkeith Farm wine grapes and Anke's Old World winemaking style creates wines of distinction. In addition to gewürztraminer and riesling, their portfolio of wines includes merlot, syrah, cabernet sauvignon, and several red blends. However, Steppe Cellars' dry riesling grabbed my palate with its fruitiness and a lovely balance of flavors and acidity. Unlike a dry trocken riesling from the Mosel Valley, with its distinctive graphite-like taste, these wines express the fruit-forward characteristics of Washington riesling. Chicken piccata, pad Thai with shrimp, and summer salad with grilled flank steak spring to mind as great pairings for this wine.

The tasting room is Quonset-hut chic — literally — with a "swamp cooler"  providing welcome relief from the summertime heat, and patio heaters strategically placed inside for wintertime comfort. It's a perfect wine-tasting environment: cozy, unpretentious, and inviting.

STEPPE CELLARS
opened: 2006
winemaker(s): Anke Freimuth-Wildman
location: 1991 Chaffee Road, Sunnyside, WA 98944
phone: 509-837-8281
web: www.steppecellars.com
e-mail: steppecellars@steppecellars.com
fee: Complimentary wine tasting except for reserve wines
hours: Summer: April through October Friday and Sunday 11–5, Saturday 11–6; Winter: November through March by appointment only
amenities: Newsletter/Blog, Online Store, Picnic Area, RV/Bus Parking, Vineyard on Premise, Wheelchair Accessible, Wine Club
connect: 🐦 📘

⭐ BEST Views

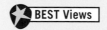

Prosser North
WineTrail

Despite the fact that there are 11 wineries on Prosser WineTrail North, you just might sample all of them in one day. How is this possible? Well, when six tasting rooms are located right off exit 82 on Interstate 82 on Lee Road, you can simply park your car and trek, like trick-or-treaters on a mission for goodies, from one winery to another: Heaven's Cave, Hogue Cellars, Alexandria Nicole Cellars, Cowan Vineyards, Kestrel Vintners, and Mercer Estates. The other wineries on this WineTrail are within easy driving distance from Lee Road, including my personal favorite, Chinook Wines. Each winery is distinctively different, each one memorable.

Prosser WineTrail North

1. Chinook Wines
2. Heaven's Cave Cellars
3. The Hogue Cellars
4. Alexandria Nicole Cellars
5. Cowan Vineyards
6. Kestrel Vintners
7. Mercer Estates
8. Pontin del Roza Winery
9. VineHeart Winery
10. Barrel Springs Winery
11. Tucker Cellars

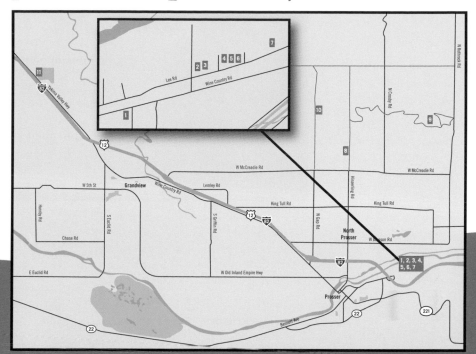

Region:	**Yakima Valley Wine Country**
# of tasting rooms on tour:	**11**
Estimate # of days for tour:	**2**
Getting around:	**Car and foot**
Key Events:	❑ **Spring Barrel Tasting in the Yakima Valley (last weekend in April); Red Wine and Chocolate (mid-February); Catch the Crush (October) and Thanksgiving in Wine Country sponsored by Wine Yakima Valley. See www.wineyakimavalley.org.**
Tips:	❑ **Park and walk to a half dozen winery-tasting rooms at the Lee Road location.**
	❑ **Alexandria Nicole Cellars restaurant features tapas menu.**
	❑ **Consider hiring a limousine service (e.g., Four Star Limos 509-521-7849, Sacco Tours 509-783-7060, Sunset Coach Tours 800-941-2941 to name a few)**
Best:	❑ **Picnicking: Chinook Wines**
	❑ **Gift shop: The Hogue Cellars**
	❑ **Eats: Alexandria Nicole Cellars**

Chinook Wines ❶

Did you know that of the five types of salmon in the Pacific Northwest, the chinook (aka king salmon) is the rarest of all? Thus, it is fitting that Chinook Wines offers up some gold-star attributes.

First is the fact that Prosser-based Chinook Wines will celebrate its 30th anniversary in 2013. Back in 1983, you could easily rattle off the names of all of Washington's wineries with nary a brain cramp — there were that few relative to today's numbers. Second, Chinook Wines is a marriage of Clay Mackey and Kay Simon — Clay manages the vineyard and Kay making the wine. It's a fusion of viticulture and enology coming together under one roof. Third, although it may not be rare today, back in the early '80s it was hard to find a woman winemaker. Kay was one of a handful of women enologists who cut their teeth at Chateau Ste. Michelle.

Chinook's renovated farmhouse houses a light-filled tasting room. Its small space is perfect for visiting with Kay or Clay and discovering the joy of balanced wine, the beauty of pink-hued rosé, and the centered lifestyle of this farming couple. Pack a picnic to enjoy in their gorgeous garden, surrounded by plum and cherry orchards, and Clay's cabernet franc vineyard.

Kay does most of the household cooking, emphasizing seasonal fruits and vegetables, which bring us back to their food-friendly wine and the desire it elicits for fennel-crusted chinook salmon paired with Chinook Wines Yakima Valley sauvignon blanc. Pop quiz: We now know that chinook is one of the five Pacific Northwest salmon, but can you name the other four?

CHINOOK WINES
opened: 1983
winemaker(s): Kay Simon
location: 220 Wittkopf Lane, Prosser, WA 99350
phone: 509-786-2725
web: www.chinookwines.com
e-mail: info@chinookwines.com
fee: Complimentary wine tasting
hours: Saturday and Sunday 12–5 May through October, or by appointment
amenities: Picnic Area, RV/Bus Parking, Tours, Vineyard on Premise

★ **BEST Picnicking**

Heaven's Cave Cellars ②

To truly appreciate Heaven's Cave Cellars one should know that proprietor Hope Moore is all about giving back to the community. In particular, she is passionate about making a difference with at-risk youth and providing them with the opportunity to live a positive life. Proceeds from the sale of Heaven's Cave wine go to cover the operating expenses associated with her 501(c)3 foundation, Make the Dash Count.

The dash in the name of her nonprofit organization refers to the dash between the date you were born and the date of your death etched on the tombstone. It reminds us to live each day in a meaningful way. Her mission is to remind us of the fact that we are the authors of our own stories, and the legacies we leave behind are important. Everyone can make a difference in the lives of others.

Relying on grapes from the famed Destiny Ridge Vineyard in the Horse Heaven Hills, Hope works with area winemakers (among them, Jarrod Boyle of Alexandria Nicole Winery) to produce small lots of white, red, and dessert wines. The big reds, reflecting the *terroir* of Horse Heaven Hills, get the most attention. However, the late harvest riesling, Nobility, and the chardonnay ice wine, Icicles, are so popular that Cave Club members can opt for "Sweets Only" shipment. In addition to discounts on wine purchases and the ability to customize their shipments, Cave Club members have access to The Cave, their new Tuscan-inspired retreat center adjacent to Destiny Ridge Vineyard.

As Hope says, "Life is not a dress rehearsal, so make the dash count!"

HEAVEN'S CAVE CELLARS
opened: 2006
winemaker(s): Various winemakers
location: 2880 Lee Road, Suite A, Prosser, WA 99350
phone: 509-788-0008
web: www.heavenscave.com
e-mail: eric@heavenscave.com
fee: Tasting fee
hours: Friday and Saturday 11–6; Sunday 11–5; Monday through Thursday by appointment only
amenities: Mailing List, Picnic Area, Wheelchair Accessible, Wine Club

The Hogue Cellars

Some tasting room experiences aren't to be rushed. The Hogue Cellars tasting room happens to be such a place.

At the Lee Road tasting room in Prosser, visitors begin by sampling wines under three different Hogue Cellars wine labels: First is Hogue Cellars wine, which includes a full lineup of fruit-forward Yakima and Columbia Valley reds and whites. Next up is Hogue's pricier Genesis label, which features varietals from select vineyards. The final offerings are Hogue Reserve wines: chardonnay, merlot, and cabernet sauvignon. Among Hogue's tasting notes is the following description about its Reserve cabernet sauvignon: "Aromas of bright cherry and an undercurrent of earth are followed by flavors of intense berry and cherry, and a pleasant hint of forest floor." The "hint of forest floor" may require deep concentration to taste, but the "intense berry and cherry" are unmistakable.

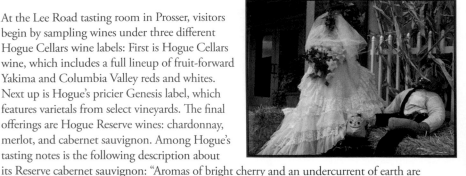

As you work your way down the list of Hogue Cellars labels, it becomes apparent why this winery produces nearly a half-million cases of wine annually. With years of experience under the ownership of Mike and Gary Hogue, access to great fruit from the Columbia and Yakima valleys, industrial-strength winemaking equipment, and top-notch winemakers, Hogue Cellars offers consistent quality throughout its product line. Also, while you are swirling and sampling, note the original museum-quality art featured behind the wine bar, as well as Hogue's specially concocted red-pepper cheese spread (which we discovered pairs wonderfully with its Reserve merlot). Assuming you don't need to dash to the next winery, check out the amply stocked gift shop. It features many unique wine-related items, including the distinctive "Washington Wine Country — Perfectly Balanced" posters.

By now, an hour has gone. My, how time flies when you're imbibing fine, fine wine!

THE HOGUE CELLARS
opened: 1982
winemaker(s): Co Dinn, Jim Mills
location: 2800 Lee Road, Prosser, WA 99350-5520
phone: 509-786-4557
web: www.hoguecellars.com
e-mail: info@hoguecellars.com
fee: Complimentary wine tasting; Tasting fee for reserve wines waived with purchase
hours: Daily 10–5
amenities: Gift Shop, Picnic Area, Wheelchair Accessible, Wine Club
connect: 🐦 f

BEST Gift shop

Alexandria Nicole Cellars

Perhaps it was the Shepherd's Mark Southern Rhône blend or the elegant Quarry Butte Red table wine — maybe it was both — that compelled me to sign up for the ANC Wine Club. Let me explain that, despite the fact that I've been to hundreds of wineries in the Northwest, I'm a member of few wine clubs.

However, Alexandria Nicole's is no ordinary wine club.

For starters, imagine a tasting room that features hidden doors leading into an exclusive "members only" space. Such is the case at both the winery's Prosser and Woodinville Hollywood Schoolhouse tasting rooms. Add to that a wine

Alexandria Nicole Cellars, Horse Heaven Hills

club that's all about fun and creating memorable experiences for its members. Throughout the year, members can participate in such unique activities as blending competitions, girls' night out and harvest parties in the vines.

Besides being the setting for some posh "glamping" (i.e., glamorous camping), the prized Destiny Ridge Estate Vineyard 263-acre vineyard, located in the Horse Heaven Hills AVA near Prosser, is the source of the 23 grape varieties Alexandria Nicole uses to create its estate wines. From budbreak to bottling, co-owner/winemaker Jarrod Boyle has control over all aspects of Alexandria Nicole Cellars' wine production. This helps explain the boatload of awards and accolades the winery has received over the years, including recognition as Washington's 2011 Winery of the Year by *Wine Press Northwest*.

Note: The name "Alexandria Nicole" is the first and maiden names of Jarrod's wife, Ali Boyle, co-owner of Alexandria Nicole Cellars.

Now, assuming that the county health department permits, let's fantasize about that vineyard glamping: a starry night, the chill kept at bay by a warm fire and down duvets, gourmet campfire grub, and, of course, excellent wine imbibed from a stemmed glass. Makes you want to check out the ANC Wine Club, doesn't it?

ALEXANDRIA NICOLE CELLARS
opened: 1998
winemaker(s): Jarrod Boyle
location: 2880 Lee Road, Suite D, Prosser, WA 99350
phone: 509-786-3497
web: www.alexandrianicolecellars.com
e-mail: info@alexandrianicolecellars.com
fee: Tasting fee refunded with purchase
hours: Daily 11–5
amenities: Newsletter/Blog, Online Store, Picnic Area, Private Events, Restaurant/Food Pairings, Tours, Wheelchair Accessible, Wine Club, Wines by the Glass
connect: ⓕ

⭐ **BEST Eats**

Cowan Vineyards 5

To be both a viticulturist and a winemaker in Washington state is unusual. Such is the case with Cowan Vineyards' David Cowan. As he puts it, "I'm a dirt guy … I'm close to the ground." The Cowans' prized land is located near Prosser in the Yakima Valley AVA, and the 65 acres of grapes they grow reflect that he's a farmer first.

David cultivates 300 acres of fruit trees (including apple, cherry, and pear) and vineyards. Grapes alone account for 200 tons of pickings, and include cabernet sauvignon, cabernet franc, merlot, gewürztraminer, and riesling. With that much fruit, David has other wineries lining up to buy his grapes. He realized that he had something very special, and the idea of starting his own winery using his choicest grapes took hold — or in this case, took root.

As David puts it, "Growing our own grapes gives us a definite advantage. We control every aspect of the grape all the way to crush. After crushing, we decide which juice goes into what barrels and then age them at least 12 to 16 months. We decide when to bottle and have our own storage, so the barrels stay at the right temperature and humidity." Sometimes it's good to be controlling.

David Cowan

The unique tartan label gracing bottles of Cowan wine reflects the family's Scottish heritage. In fact, if you happen to stop by while a Scottish festival is under way in the area (as this WineTrail trekker did), there's a good chance you'll spot David wearing his kilt. David's wife, Susan, often works the tasting room and is responsible for the wine-related merchandise available for purchase. Incidentally, if you need a place to stay, ask about their rental property, which is strategically located "in the heart of wine country."

COWAN VINEYARDS
opened: 2005
winemaker(s): David Cowan
location: 2880 Lee Road, Suite E, Prosser, WA 99350-9506
phone: 509-788-0200
web: www.cowanvineyards.com
e-mail: info@cowanvineyards.com
fee: Complimentary wine tasting
hours: Thursday through Monday 12–5 from April through November; Winter: Saturday and Sunday 11–5
amenities: Gift Shop, Lodging, Picnic Area, Wheelchair Accessible, Wine Club
connect: f

Label reads:
Cowan Vineyards
12.7% ALC. BY VOL.
Estate Grown   2005
CABERNET SAUVIGNON
YAKIMA VALLEY

Kestrel Vintners

Located on 3 acres in the Prosser Wine & Food Park (on Lee Road), Kestrel Winery occupies 15,000 square feet comprising production space, barrel area, tasting room, and gift shop. The "homey" tasting room is what draws us here.

What's not to love about a winery whose no. 1 seller is "Lady in Red"? With its distinctive label, the Lady in Red, and the Platinum white wine series, Kestrel Vintners offers food-friendly entry wines in a bottle that you won't want to throw away. Visitors also can explore a variety of winemaker Flint Nelson's other upscale wines, including the Signature Edition series or the Winemaker Select series.

If you can't make it to the Prosser tasting room, no worries. Kestrel Vintners has two other tasting rooms in the state to experience, including its Woodinville Warehouse District location as well as one in the very popular tourist destination of Leavenworth, on Front Street.

KESTREL VINTNERS
opened: 1995
winemaker(s): Flint Nelson
location: 2890 Lee Road,
Prosser, WA 99350-5520
phone: 509-786-2675
web: www.kestrelwines.com
e-mail: winery@kestrelwines.com
fee: Tasting fee
hours: Daily 12–5
amenities: Gift Shop, Newsletter/Blog, Online Store, Picnic Area, Private Events, RV/Bus Parking, Tours, Vineyard on Premise, Wheelchair Accessible, Wine Club, Winemaker Dinners
connect: 🐦 ⓕ

Mercer Estates 7

Mercer Estates reflects the coming together of two families — the Mercers and the Hogues — that have farmed the southeastern region of the Columbia Valley since the 1800s. From hops to row crops and the emergence of *Vitis vinifera* in the Horse Heaven Hills, these

are farming families, seeing themselves as stewards of the land, possessing the inherent values of hard work, and adhering to sustainable practices.

Because of this shared vision and common heritage, it was natural for the Mercer and Hogue families to unite to launch Mercer Estates. At the end of Lee Road in Prosser, the winery's new brown-stucco Southwest-style building is energy efficient with a simple yet elegance design. Clearly, every square foot of the space was planned as a first-class production facility and welcome center. Ste. Michelle trained Jessica Munnell, is the chief winemaker for Mercer Estates.

Whereas most visitors to Lee Road's string of wineries might start their touring at the first winery and work their way to the end, where Mercer Estates is located, we suggest that you start at the Mercer complex. Here you will find a spacious tasting room and gracious hosts, which translate into a sense of leisurely pleasure. Be sure to check out Mercer Estates' Columbia Valley merlot and cabernet sauvignon: Rich, meaty with midpalate harmony, these wines have loads of black fruit taste.

If you happen to be there during a quiet time, ask if you can peek into the production area, where you might see Jessica Munnell and staff moving hoses, racking barrels, or perhaps analyzing samples in the lab. A whiff of the temperature-/humidity-controlled atmosphere may take you to the Horse Heaven Hills at sunset near harvest time — it had that effect on me.

MERCER ESTATES
opened: 2007
winemaker(s): Jessica Munnell
location: 3100 Lee Road, Prosser, WA 99350
phone: 509-786-2097
web: www.mercerwine.com
e-mail: info@mercerestates.com
fee: Tasting fee refunded with purchase
hours: Wednesday through Sunday 10–5, March through December; January and February by appointment only
amenities: Gift Shop, Online Store, Picnic Area, Private Events, RV/Bus Parking, Vineyard on Premise, Wheelchair Accessible, Wine Club
connect: 🐦 📘

Pontin del Roza Winery 🔟

Scott Pontin began the Pontin Del Roza Winery as part of a Future Farmers of America project. He had yet to see his 21st birthday at the time. The Pontin (pronounced Pon-teen) family had farmed in the Yakima Valley for three generations and, with their Italian heritage, knew a thing or two about making wine. We don't know if Scott got a blue ribbon for his FFA project, but we do know that the Pontin Del Roza Winery was born in 1984.

The winery uses grapes grown only from "the Roza," an area of south-facing slopes along the north side of the Yakima Valley. Vintner Scott Pontin uses these homegrown grapes to make approximately 4,000 cases a year of white riesling, chenin blanc, cabernet, merlot, pinot gris, sangiovese, and other limited specialty wines. The newly built tasting room is a handsome complement to the 100 acres of wine grapes nearby. If you are looking for good value, make a beeline for Pontin Del Roza. Most wines sell in the teens.

The winery's north Prosser location on Hinzerling Road is a family affair that includes his parents and siblings. The newly built tasting room with a double-sided fireplace is a handsome complement to the nearby 100-acres of wine grapes. For sure, check out the old family photos adorning the walls. Picnic facilities and bocce court are available but the tasting room itself is just too darn comfortable a space to exit. That's *amore*.

PONTIN DEL ROZA WINERY
opened: 1984
winemaker(s): Scott Pontin
location: 35502 North Hinzerling Road, Prosser, WA 99350
phone: 509-786-4449
web: www.pontindelroza.com
e-mail: pontindelroza@mac.com
fee: Complimentary wine tasting
hours: Daily 10–5
amenities: Gift Shop, Picnic Area, Vineyard on Premise, Wheelchair Accessible
connect: 🐦 f

VineHeart Winery ⑨

Often, in the figurative sense of the word, there is a "marriage" between winemaker and grape grower. However, in the case of VineHeart Winery, that marriage is literal: Winemaker George Schneider and grape grower Patricia O'Brien are hitched.

George began making wine in 1987. Patricia has been growing grapes in the Yakima Valley since 1991.

Most of their wines sell for about $15 a bottle. Using estate grapes that have been handpicked and sorted, George crafts a full range of red and white wines, including a rosé named in honor of George's mother, Philomena Rose Schneider. It's a sweet homage from a winemaking couple who are the epitome of care — toward people, land, and wine.

Their tasting room, located just a few miles north of Prosser, offers a spacious and inviting space to sample wine and enjoy a picnic indoors or outside, if the weather is nice. It's a marriage of sorts between land and vintner.

VINEHEART WINERY
opened: 2000
winemaker(s): George Schneider
location: 44209 North McDonald Road, Prosser, WA 99350
phone: 509-973-2993
web: www.vineheart.com
e-mail: wineduchess@yahoo.com
fee: Complimentary wine tasting
hours: Monday and Thursday through Saturday 9–5; Sunday 11–5
amenities: Online Store, Picnic Area, Private Events, Tours, Weddings, Wheelchair Accessible, Wine Club

Barrel Springs Winery 🔟

There's something about the quietude of agrarian Prosser. It's a town where hard work and an appreciation of American-cowboy ethics reign supreme. It's not by accident that the high school mascot is the Mustang. It's also where vineyards thrive and people can retire to live out their dreams.

Jim Madison and Shelly Belt, founders and owners of Barrel Springs Winery, are doing just that. Come by and enjoy an afternoon with the Belts; sample their fine cabernet franc and admire the vineyard, nestled against the winery. It's so tranquil and quiet, you can almost hear the vines groan as their tendrils reach for the trellis line.

It's a special treat when wine and art converge, as it does at Barrel Springs Winery, but this convergence has a decidedly Western bent. For those who love the American West portrayed in oils, sculpture and pottery, Barrel Springs Winery has corralled a fine collection of the genre, along with other art pieces, all available for purchase.

BARREL SPRINGS WINERY
opened: 2010
winemaker(s): Jim Brousseau
location: 46601 North Gap Road, Prosser, WA 99350
phone: 509-786-3166
web: www.barrelspringswinery.com
e-mail: 4madison@msn.com
hours: Thursday through Monday 10–5
amenities: Art Gallery, Picnic Area, RV/Bus Parking, Vineyard on Premise, Wheelchair Accessible

Jim Brousseau

Tucker Cellars

Located in Sunnyside, Tucker Cellars is just off I-82 at exit 69. This is the place to "enjoy a taste of Yakima Valley," as the Tucker family likes to say. And your taste buds likely will agree: You can sample and purchase Tucker farm products, from pickled asparagus spears to White Cloud popcorn to muscat canelli.

Randy Tucker and his wife, Debbie, own Tucker Cellars, and they rely on the fruit and vegetables of nearby Tucker Farm to produce a full array of red and white wines, as well as a variety of pickled and packaged produce. This is "one-stop shopping," Yakima Valley style. Don't pass up the opportunity to experience what Yakima Valley is famous for: great produce and down-home friendliness.

Most interesting to me is the fact that Randy and Debbie are third-generation grape farmers. That's nearly unheard of. In the 1930s, Randy's grandparents Melvin and Vera Tucker planted *Vitis vinifera* vines from cuttings taken from other early Yakima Valley grape farmers. The sons of Melvin and Vera continued in the wine industry, adding to the vineyard and working for William Bridgman's Upland Winery. (Note: If Walter Clore is the father of the Washington wine industry, then certainly William Bridgman is the industry's grandfather!)

The wines Tucker Cellars offer — and there are many — come courtesy of its 50-acre estate vineyard. Tucker Cellars doesn't stand on formality. That easygoing attitude makes it a fun place to visit, and to experience Yakima Valley's wines and produce. And the prices will leave money in the bank for your next generation.

TUCKER CELLARS
opened: 1981
winemaker(s): Randy Tucker
location: 70 Ray Road, Sunnyside, WA 98944
phone: 509-837-8701
web: www.tuckercellars.net
e-mail: wineman@televar.com
fee: Complimentary wine tasting
hours: Daily 10–5
amenities: Gift Shop, Newsletter/Blog, Picnic Area, RV/Bus Parking, Tours, Vineyard on Premise, Wheelchair Accessible

Prosser South
WineTrail

Following a WineTrail that takes Merlot Drive to Chardonnay Lane and enters Vintner's Village, you know you're on a turbo-charged wine excursion. On this WineTrail, you have the luxury of simply parking your vehicle and walking from winery to winery, all within a 32-acre winery "candy land." With the likes of Airfield Estates, Willow Crest, Thurston Wolfe and Milbrandt Vineyards wineries, you will need to budget a full day to experience these beauties. Of course, hunger may strike along the way, and to curb those pangs, check out the wood-fired pizza and other delights at Wine O'clock.

Prosser WineTrail South also features the grandeur of adobe-wrapped Desert Wind and its nearby neighbor, Snoqualmie Winery (one of the many properties of Ste. Michelle Wine Estates), which is strikingly beautiful in a Northwest rustic, timbered way. Finally, be sure you budget time to visit Yakima Cellars. There, you can sample premium wines and learn about the valley's winemaking history from a true pioneer.

Prosser WineTrail South

1 Airfield Estates Winery
2 Willow Crest Winery
3 Thurston Wolfe Winery
4 The Bunnell Family Cellar
— Wine O'clock

5 Milbrandt Vineyards
6 Gamache Vintners
7 Winemakers Loft
8 Canyon's Edge Winery

9 Yakima River Winery
10 Snoqualmie Vineyards
11 Desert Wind Winery

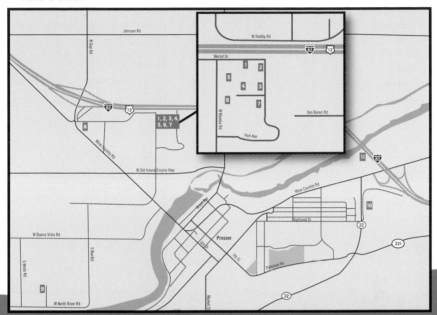

Region: **Yakima Valley Wine Country**

\# of tasting rooms on tour: **11**

Estimate # of days for tour: **3**

Getting around: **Car and foot**

Key Events: ❏ **Spring Barrel Tasting in the Yakima Valley (last weekend in April); Red Wine and Chocolate (mid-February); Catch the Crush (October) and Thanksgiving in Wine Country sponsored by Wine Yakima Valley. See www.wineyakimavalley.org.**

Tips: ❏ **Hungry? Check out Wine o'Clock at Prosser's Vintners Village for wine country cuisine.**

❏ **Consider hiring a limousine service (e.g., S.U.V. Tours 509- 783-7060, A+ Pacific Limousine 206-437-1298 or Sunset Coach Tours 800-941-2941 to name a few).**

Best: ❏ **Eats: The Bunnell Family Cellar — Wine o'Clock**

❏ **Views: Yakima River Winery**

❏ **Picnicking: Snoqualmie Vineyards**

❏ **Eats, gift shop: Desert Wind Winery**

Airfield Estates Winery

In his 30s, winemaker Marcus Miller's young age belies his long history in the wine business. You could say that winemaking is in his blood, not only because of his own achievements in the field, earning a degree from Walla Walla Community College's enology and viticulture program, and putting in stints at a variety of other wineries, but because the rest of the Miller family has been growing premium grapes in Washington since 1960. What's more, one of Marcus' grandfathers was friends with Walter Clore — the man generally credited as being the father of Washington's wine industry.

In the spring of 2007, the Millers launched Airfield Estates Winery in Prosser's Vintage Village. Visitors to the village will have no problem spotting Airfield Estates Winery. It's the winery with the tower that has "AIRFIELD" written on its sides. Since then, the family has opened a second tasting room in Woodinville, near the Hollywood Schoolhouse traffic circle.

Visitors to the Prosser location will arrive to find several hangar doors at the front of the winery, which is modeled after an old World War II aircraft hangar. The delightful interior features model airplanes, classic airfield photos, and a wacky dummy's head sporting an aviator's hat and goggles. It's fun and it works. But the airfield theme is no accident. It turns out that H. Lloyd Miller, Marcus Miller's grandfather, built a 1,200-acre airport ranch near Sunnyside for an air training station during World War II.

Of course, having taken wing with the airfield theme, the Millers continue to fly with it, coming up with some great names to go with some fabulous wines. Check out some of their red blends, with catchy names such as Mustang Red, Spitfire, and Runway Red, and some luscious whites, including Flygirl White. It should come as no surprise that their wine club bears the name "Officer's Wine Club." Roger that.

AIRFIELD ESTATES WINERY
opened: 2007
winemaker(s): Marcus Miller
location: 560 Merlot Drive, Prosser, WA 99350
phone: 509-786-7401
web: www.airfieldwines.com
e-mail: info@airfieldwines.com
fee: Tasting fee refunded with purchase
hours: Monday through Thursday 11–5, Friday through Sunday 10–6; Winter hours vary; call ahead
amenities: Gift Shop, Newsletter/Blog, Online Store, Picnic Area, RV/Bus Parking, Tours, Wheelchair Accessible, Wine Club, Wines by the Glass
connect:

Willow Crest Winery ❷

"A great wine starts in the vineyard!" exclaims the Willow Crest website. In this case, however, it really begins with Willow Crest founder David Minick. A viticulturist and winemaker, David developed the 200-acre Willow Crest Estate Vineyard in the Roza area north of Prosser, later launching the Willow Crest Winery. He invested years in the

vineyard, meticulously managing the vines and developing a reputation for producing outstanding pinot gris and syrah.

A few years later, in 2008, Precept Wine Brands partnered with Willow Crest. The Willow Crest label makes a nice addition to Precept Wines' portfolio, which includes other notables such as Apex, Waterbrook, and Charles Smith's wildly successful Magnificent Wine Company (House Wine). Willow Crest's loyal fans can breathe a sigh of relief; other than small changes to Willow Crest's label design, the winery remains essentially the same. Clearly, Precept knew a good thing when it acquired Willow Crest. Why fix what's not broken?

At an elevation of 1,300 feet, the winery and vineyard offer a commanding view of a rich patchwork quilt of growing flora. However, for the tasting room experience, wine tourists can enjoy Willow Crest wines at its Tuscan-style abode in the Prosser Vintner's Village, as well as its Bavarian-style tasting salon on Leavenworth's well-trafficked Front Street. In addition to Willow Crest's signature pinot gris (pinot grigio if you're feeling Italian) and syrah, there are a number of other reds and whites to experience. My first sample of the riesling led to another, but then, I'm a sucker for a riesling like this one: dry, fruit forward, balanced and crisp with a nice little lemon note at the end. Lovely!

WILLOW CREST WINERY
opened: 1995
winemaker(s): David J. Minick
location: 590 Merlot Drive, Prosser, WA 99350
phone: 509-786-7999
web: www.willowcrestwinery.com
e-mail: info@willowcrestwinery.com
fee: Complimentary wine tasting
hours: Daily 10–5 except major holidays
amenities: Gift Shop, Mailing List, Newsletter/Blog, Online Store, Picnic Area, Restaurant/Food Pairings, Tours, Wheelchair Accessible, Wine Club
connect: 🐦 📘

Thurston Wolfe Winery ③

You know you're entering "wine world" when you drive into a winery and spot roads with names such as Merlot Drive, Port Avenue, and Cabernet Court! That's what you'll see when you take a drive to the Thurston Wolfe winery.

Few winery owners can boast that their winery is "legendary," but with wine-industry roots that go back to the mid-1980s, Wade Wolfe and Becky Yeaman can make that claim. Both worked closely with other pioneers in the industry, such as Walter Clore (considered to be the father of Washington's modern premium wine grape industry), to create Thurston Wolfe. Along with a doctorate from the University of California-Davis, Wade's résumé includes stints at Ste. Michelle, Hogue, and Hyatt before he launched his own winery. Now he and Becky devote all of their time to their winery.

Thurston Wolfe's forte is making "non-mainstream" wines. Yes, you can find award-winning Bordeaux and Rhône-style wines at Thurston Wolfe, but don't pass up the opportunity to enjoy its JTW port (named after Wade and Becky's son), primitivo, petite sirah, sangiovese, lemberger, The Spaniard (a blend of tempranillo, grenache, and syrah), and pinot gris/viognier (PGV). Keep in mind, though, that with only 3,000 cases produced annually, the winery tends to sell out quickly. Don't expect all varietals to be available when you visit.

Located in the Vintner's Village just off I-82, the Thurston Wolfe winery features a contemporary design and a spacious tasting room. A large fireplace provides a warm and cozy environment during the winter, and the exceptionally long wine bar offers extra elbow room for weekend crowds. One of Becky's roles is that of tasting room manager, and she is there most days. With her wealth of knowledge about the wine industry in Yakima Valley, she entertains, informs, and pours, all in an engaging manner.

2006
ZEPHYR RIDGE
PETITE SIRAH
WASHINGTON STATE

THURSTON WOLFE WINERY
opened: 1987
winemaker(s): Wade Wolfe
location: 588 Cabernet Court, Prosser, WA 99350
phone: 509-786-3313
web: www.thurstonwolfe.com
e-mail: Beckyyeamon@earthlinnk.com
fee: Complimentary wine tasting
hours: Thursday through Sunday 11–5, April through November; Call or check website for other dates and times; Closed January
amenities: Gift Shop, Online Store, Picnic Area, RV/Bus Parking, Tours, Wheelchair Accessible, Wine Club

The Bunnell Family Cellar — Wine O'clock [4]

Located in Prosser's Vintner's Village, The Bunnell Family Cellar is a hop and a skip from nearby Thurston Wolfe Winery, Gamache Vintners, and Milbrandt Vineyards. However, many visitors end up coming to Bunnell's tasting room and never leaving. The reason? I

suspect the fusion of Rhône-style wines, good hospitality and yummy bistro food may have something to do with it.

Food-friendly wines such as viognier, syrah, petite sirah, Mourvèdre, and Rhône blends comprise a smorgasbord of tasting pleasure. The Bunnells' second-label wines, dubbed RiverAerie, are more wallet-friendly and honor the eponymous family home located on the banks of the Yakima River.

The contemporary home-like atmosphere invites you to make yourself comfortable and imbibe. Once there, the smell of fresh, hot pizza pairs wonderfully with the bouquet of the syrah, and before long, you may find yourself among the lucky ones ensconced in the Wine O'clock Wine Bar. There, you can order wines by the glass or by the bottle at retail prices, to go with some thin-crust pizza or the bistro's daily special.

The Bunnell Family Cellars reflects the winemaking talents of Ron Bunnell and the culinary flair of spouse Susan Bunnell. Like peas and carrots, peanut butter and jelly, the pairing of wine and fine food is one of life's givens. However, it all begins in the vineyard, and for this task, Ron and Susan have hooked up with a who's who of Washington grapes growers, including Dick Boushey, Rob Andrews, Mike Andrews, and the Milbrandt brothers. With names like those tending the wine, you've got to do some serious swirling and sipping. After all, it must be Wine O'clock somewhere!

THE BUNNELL FAMILY CELLAR — WINE O'CLOCK
opened: 2004
winemaker(s): Ron Bunnell
location: 548 Cabernet Court, Wine O'clock, Vintner's Village, Prosser, WA 99350
phone: 509-786-2197
web: www.bunnellfamilycellar.com
e-mail: info@bunnellfamilycellar.com
fee: Tasting fee
hours: Monday through Thursday 12–6; Friday and Sunday 12–8
amenities: Restaurant/Food Pairings, RV/Bus Parking, Wheelchair Accessible, Wine Club, Wines by the Glass
connect: ⬛

Milbrandt Vineyards

Milbrandt Vineyards' story is one of two brothers, each with a background in growing things, who, in 1997, decided to plant vines — lots of vines. Today, brothers Butch and Jerry Milbrandt command more than 2,000 acres of vineyards in eastern Washington,

focusing on the Wahluke Slope AVA and the soon-to-be-designated Ancient Lakes AVA. A laundry list of well-known vineyards are under their ownership, including such names as Evergreen, Northridge, Clifton Bluff, Clifton, Clifton Hill, Pheasant, Purple Sage, Sundance, Ancient Lakes, Don Talcott, and Katherine Leone.

Despite their empire of grapes and the emergence of Milbrandt Vineyards wines, these guys never forget their agriculture roots. They are farmers first, and the rich agricultural heritage instilled by their mom and dad courses through their blood.

A love of pairing food with wine also runs deep. This would explain the bistro-style restaurant at their Vintner's Village grand tasting room. Brother Butch is the self-confessed foodie, and I suspect he is responsible for the mouthwatering recipes on the Milbrandt website. As you sample Milbrandt's estate Malbec, just imagine garlic-crusted rib roast paired with this bold wine. Alternatively, picture paella with generous amounts of Northwest seafood paired with a Milbrandt grenache. Hungry yet?

MILBRANDT VINEYARDS
opened: 2008
winemaker(s): Joshua Maloney
location: 508 Cabernet Court, Vintner's Village, Prosser, WA 99350
phone: 509-788-0030
web: www.milbrandtvineyards.com
e-mail: wine@milbrandtvineyards.com
fee: Tasting fee refunded with purchase
hours: Daily 10–5 except Christmas and New Years Day
amenities: Gift Shop, Newsletter/Blog, Online Store, Picnic Area, Private Events, Restaurant/Food Pairings, RV/Bus Parking, Wheelchair Accessible, Wine Club, Winemaker Dinners
connect:

Gamache Vintners 6

Looking for a reason to visit the Vintner's Village in Prosser, Washington? How about this: "splendid, multidimensional bouquet of wood, smoke, olives, sage, violets, espresso, black currant and blackberry that soars from the glass … some racy acidity, a velvety texture, excellent volume and incipient complexity … impeccably balanced." Those glowing words are from a review of Gamache Vintners' 2006 Cabernet Sauvignon Reserve in Robert M. Parker's *Wine Advocate*, August 31, 2010; the cabernet earned a heady 92 points. And with the village (and Gamache Vintners' tasting room) a mere two minutes off Interstate 82, it's well worth it to stop in to swirl, sip, and appreciate.

Of note is the fact that brothers Bob and Roger Gamache planted their vineyard in the White Bluffs area, northwest of Richland, back in 1982. At the time, there were just a couple of dozen wineries in the state. However, the fourth-generation farming brothers foresaw a demand for premium wine grapes. The brothers worked the Gamache vineyard year after year and developed a keen awareness of varying soil types and microclimates within their vineyard. Finally, in 2002, they took the plunge with the creation of Gamache Vintners to brand their own estate wine, relying on the talents of famed winemaker Charlie Hoppes.

The Gamache tasting room is a beautiful, spacious, contemporary setting where the focus is clearly on experiencing Gamache wines. I could live there, especially with an address that includes "Cabernet Court." Everything about it is an expression of the Gamache family's rural roots; clean and authentic, there's nothing pretentious here. Even the estate wines are clear expressions of the grape variety, with little blending: viognier, riesling, cabernet franc, cabernet sauvignon, syrah, and merlot. Their one red blend, dubbed Boulder Red, is a perfect answer to the question "What should be served with the grilled burger?" especially when it sells for just $18 a bottle.

GAMACHE VINTNERS
opened: 1982
winemaker(s): Charlie Hoppes
location: 505 Cabernet Court, Vintner's Village, Prosser, WA 99350
phone: 509-786-7800
web: www.gamachevintners.com
e-mail: wine@gamachevintners.com
fee: Tasting fee refunded with purchase
hours: Daily 10–5; December and January open Friday through Sunday only
amenities: Mailing List, Online Store, Picnic Area, RV/Bus Parking, Wheelchair Accessible, Wine Club
connect: 🐦

Winemakers Loft 7

Situated in a courtyard setting in Vintner's Village in Prosser, the Winemaker's Loft provides "incubator" space for as many as seven wineries. These are small-lot, punch-down wineries

for which winemaking is more about art and less about industrial production. Here the winemakers can trace each bottle back to the hand-sorting of the harvested grapes — and in many cases, they grew that fruit!

At the time of this writing, the lineup of wineries included Apex Cellars, Martinez & Martinez Winery, Tasawik Vineyards, Coyote Canyon Winery, and Plaza Winery.

Friendly, well-trained staff does the pouring honors, and if your visit coincides with crush, you can check out the production area in the back. Once you see the area's limited space, you'll understand why the wineries are kept to about a 1,000 cases each (with the exception of Apex Cellars, which has other Precept Wine Brands–owned production facilities at its disposal).

Who knows, maybe the wine bug will hit you real bad and you'll get on the list to start your own label at Winemaker's Loft!

Apex tasting room

WINEMAKERS LOFT
winemaker(s): Various wineries and winemakers
location: 357 Port Avenue, Prosser, WA 99350
web: www.facebook.com/WinemakersLoft
fee: Tasting fees apply
hours: Varies
amenities: Gift Shop, Picnic Area, RV/Bus Parking, Wheelchair Accessible

Canyon's Edge Winery 🄼

Question: Maryhill Winery, Bookwalter, Barnard Griffin, Columbia Winery, Canoe Ridge, Gordon Brothers, and Apex Cellars are distinct wineries but they have one big thing in common. Can you guess it?

Answer: They have all sourced their grapes from Aldercreek Vineyard in the Horse Heaven Hills and these are just a few of more than 40 wineries in total that rely on this exceptional vineyard.

At nearly 300 acres, the Aldercreek Vineyard enjoys the moderating influence of the Columbia River, arid climate, and lots of wind. The result is amazingly intense fruit sought after by many of the state's top wineries.

Now Canyon's Edge Winery has become the estate winery for Aldercreek and wine enthusiasts can experience their wines at their tasting room on Merlot Drive in Prosser opened in June of 2007. Managing owners, Dave and Brian Groth (father and son respectively) turned to experienced winemaker John P. Haw for converting their fruit into premium wine that showcases the Horse Heaven Hill's *terroir*.

Despite its winemaking youth, the portfolio of Canyon's Edge estate wines is ambitious. Featured at the tasting room are their Sage Brush Red table wine, merlot, syrah, cabernet sauvignon, cabernet franc, and Jeremiah's Chocolate Port. With the tagline, "Where Quality, the Palate and Value Meet," the tasting room is a charming stop along the Prosser WineTrail South.

CANYON'S EDGE WINERY
opened: 1998
winemaker(s): John P. Haw
location: 10 Merlot Drive; Suite D, Prosser, WA 99350
phone: 509-786-3032
web: www.canyonsedgewinery.com
e-mail: info@canyonsedgewinery.com
fee: Complimentary wine tasting
hours: Sunday through Wednesday 10–6; Thursday through Saturday 10–8
amenities: RV/Bus Parking, Wheelchair Accessible
connect: f

Yakima River Winery 🄨

John and Louise Rauner have been focused on creating complex red Yakima wines for nearly 30 years. Beginning in 1977, John began making wine under the Yakima River Winery label. Since those early beginnings, John has become a huge proponent of the Yakima Valley appellation. Forget Napa — come to the Yakima Valley!

As a testament to his love of winemaking, he posted on his website an article nearly 2,000 words in length explaining his philosophy about winemaking. Now that's passion! But to enjoy his wine, you don't need to read his treatise in advance. All you have to do is head to the winery's North River Road location, near the Yakima River, and sample his big reds.

P.S. Be sure to try the John's Port. You don't need a cigar to enjoy this beauty, but such a combo would be sublime!

John Rauner

YAKIMA RIVER WINERY
opened: 1978
winemaker(s): John Rauner
location: 143302 West North River Road, Prosser, WA 99350
phone: 509-786-2805
web: www.yakimariverwinery.com
e-mail: redwine@yakimariverwinery.com
fee: Complimentary wine tasting
hours: Daily 10–5 closing at 4:30 during winter; closed Thanksgiving and Christmas Day
amenities: Picnic Area, Tours, Vineyard on Premise, Wheelchair Accessible

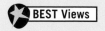 BEST Views

Snoqualmie Vineyards 🔟

Snoqualmie Vineyards, a subsidiary of Ste. Michelle Wine Estates, is conveniently located off Interstate 82 in Prosser. The Snoqualmie winery visitor center, with its rustic timbered facade and beautiful landscaping, features stylish deck chairs and tables set around a manmade waterfall. The tasting room itself reflects the "simplicity and uncomplicated goal

of making approachable, food-friendly wines." You might not expect to find a Cascade-style timber lodge situated in a farming community like Prosser, where pickup trucks outnumber cars, but somehow it works. Perhaps it's because of the friendliness of the pouring staff at Snoqualmie or the simple elegance of the building itself, but in the end, it is the wine that wins your heart. Snoqualmie's goal is to produce quality, approachable wines at an affordable price.

Be prepared to go *au naturel* at this tasting room. No, we're not talking about a nudist wine colony here (although that does conjure up an idea for a new business venture). Rather, "naked" refers to Snoqualmie's Naked line of organic wines, which includes riesling, gewürztraminer, merlot, and cabernet sauvignon. In addition to the Naked wine label, Snoqualmie also produces a Columbia Valley portfolio expressing the unique varietal character of Northwest wines. Priced at about $10 a bottle, these great value wines are the perfect solution for family picnics or tonight's chicken dinner.

But wait, there's more!

Winemaker Joy Andersen reserves the best of the best in terms of select grapes for Snoqualmie Vineyards Reserve Wines. More elegant, more complex but

still sporting an attractive price point (low to mid-20s) these Reserves showcase the *terroir* of the Columbia Valley's merlot, cabernet sauvignon and syrah. They also demonstrate that Joy is an accomplished winemaker with a skilled team in the background (it takes a village when it comes to Snoqualmie Vineyard's large-scale production). That's the naked truth.

SNOQUALMIE VINEYARDS
opened: 1983
winemaker(s): Joy Andersen
location: 660 Frontier Road, Prosser, WA 99350
phone: 509-786-5558
web: www.snoqualmie.com
e-mail: info@snoqualmie.com
fee: Complimentary wine tasting; $5 tasting fee for reserve wines
hours: Daily 10–5 except Thanksgiving, Christmas, New Year's Day, and Easter
amenities: Gift Shop, Online Store, Picnic Area, RV/Bus Parking, Wheelchair Accessible
connect: 🐦 📘

⭐ **BEST Picnicking**

Desert Wind Winery

Few wineries in Washington can boast that they offer a place for wine tasting, dining, lodging, attending a cooking seminar, and getting married, but the 34,000-square-foot Desert Wind Winery in Prosser offers just such amenities, and more. Designed by Tate Architects of Pasco, Washington, the pueblo-style building opened its doors in early 2007 and quickly distinguished itself from other wineries in the lower Yakima Valley with its sheer size and ambiance. Desert Wind sets the bar high with thoughtful touches such as flat-panel televisions in the suites, warm earth tones throughout, full-length mirrors in the bridal-party changing rooms, and a set of French doors that open to a magnificent view of the Yakima River.

Culinary arts and wine pairing

Desert Wind Winery is co-owned by the Fries and Jenkins families, which started Duck Pond Cellars in Dundee, Oregon, in 1993. After considerable study, they decided to locate Desert Wind Winery conveniently off I-82 in Prosser, in the heart of wine country. Next to the winery is the Walter Clore Wine & Culinary Center. With its location and an abundance of parking spaces (even for the family RV), Desert Wind's 4,755-square-foot tasting room easily accommodates plenty of thirsty visitors.

Son Greg Fries is the chief winemaker for Desert Wind Winery, as well as for Duck Pond Cellars. He enjoys the fact that this is a fully integrated approach to winemaking, and that sales rely on fruit from the family vineyards in both Washington and Oregon. In his role as winemaker, Greg strives to meet the desires of most palates at relatively low price points — check out Ruah which sells for $20.

Come hungry and enjoy some fine dining at the winery's 65-seat-capacity restaurant, Mojave at Desert Wind. The thoughtful menu uses fresh, local produce, fish, and meats served Southwestern style, along with select wine-pairing suggestions.

DESERT WIND WINERY
opened: 2001
winemaker(s): Greg Fries
location: 2256 Wine Country Road, Prosser, WA 99350
phone: 509-786-7277
web: www.desertwindvineyard.com
e-mail: info@desertwindwinery.com
fee: Complimentary wine tasting
hours: Daily 11–5 from October through April; daily 10–5 May through September
amenities: Gift Shop, Lodging, Online Store, Picnic Area, Restaurant/Food Pairings, RV/Bus Parking, Wheelchair Accessible, Wine Club
connect: 🐦 📘

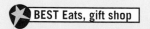
⭐ BEST Eats, gift shop

Other Wineries to Visit

ANTOLIN CELLARS
winemaker(s): Tony Haralson
location: 16 North 2nd Street, Unit C, Yakima, WA 98901
phone: 509-833-5765
web: www.antonlincellars.com
hours: Friday through Saturday 1–9, Sunday 1–5

COTE BONNEVILLE WINERY
winemaker(s): Kerry Shiels
location: 2841 Fordyce Road, Sunnyside, WA 98944-9771
phone: 509-840-4596
web: www.cotebonneville.com
hours: By appointment only

DINEEN VINEYARDS
winemaker(s): Scott Greer
location: 980 Gilbert Road, Zillah, WA 98953
phone: 206-276-4287
web: www.dineenvineyards.com
hours: Friday through Sunday 12–5 (April through October) or by appointment

CHRISTOPHER CELLARS
winemaker(s): Chris Hoon
location: 3601 Highland Drive, Zillah, WA 98953
phone: 509-945-0410
web: www.christophercellars.com
hours: Friday 12–5, Saturday 11–5, Sunday 12–5

DAVEN LORE WINERY
winemaker(s): Gordon Taylor
location: S 23103 1521 PRSW, Prosser, WA 99350-0000
phone: 509-786-1575
web: www.davenlore.com
hours: Saturday and Sunday 12–5 or by appointment

DOMANICO CELLARS
winemaker(s): Jason Domanico
location: 24901 North Crosby Road, Prosser, WA 99350
phone: 206-465-9406
web: www.domanicocellars.com
hours: Opening spring 2013 — see website

Other Wineries to Visit

FONTAINE ESTATES WINERY
winemaker(s): Marcus Robert
location: 151 Rowe Hill Drive,
Naches, WA 98937
phone: 509-972-8123
web: www.fontaineestateswinery.com
hours: April through October,
Friday Saturday and Sunday 10–5

LOOKOUT POINT WINERY
winemaker(s): George Petzinger
location: 16 North 2nd Street, Unit C,
Yakima, WA 98901
phone: 509-698-5040
web: www.lookoutpointwinery.com
hours: Friday and Saturday 1–9
or by appointment

NORTON ARNOLD VINTNERS
winemaker(s): Steven Arnold
location: 1680 Cherry Lane,
Grandview, WA 98930
phone: 206-784-0884
web: www.nortonarnoldvintners.com
hours: By appointment only

PAREJAS CELLARS
winemaker(s): Mark Wysling
location: 114 Grandridge Road,
Grandview, WA 98930
phone: 509-910-9844
web: www.parejascellars.com
hours: By appointment only

HINZERLING WINERY
winemaker(s): Mike Wallace
location: 1520 Sheridan Avenue,
Prosser, WA 99350-1140
phone: 800-727-6702
web: www.hinzerling.com
hours: Monday through Saturday
11–5, Sunday 11–4, from March to
Christmas and most holiday weekends;
Tuesday through Saturday 12–4 in the
winter; closed New Year's Day, Easter,
Christmas and St. Swithun's Marn;
open on event weekends

Other Wineries to Visit

RAMSEYER VINEYARDS
winemaker(s): John Ramseyer
location: 2255 Gilbert Road, Zillah, WA 98953
phone: 206-909-1548
web: www.ramseyervineyards.com
hours: By appointment only

SELAH HEIGHTS WINERY
winemaker(s): Mike Clark
location: 31 Katie Lane, Selah, WA 98942
phone: 509-910-1257
web: www.selahheights.com
hours: By appointment only

THORNY ROSE
location: 2800 Lee Road, Prosser, WA 99350
phone: 800-565-9779
web: www.thornyrosewines.com
hours: Daily 10–5

RUNNING SPRINGS WINE TASTING ROOM
winemaker(s): Tefft Cellars
location: 9950 US Highway 12, Thompson Fruit Stand, Naches, WA 98937
phone: 509-653-2848
web: None
hours: 10–5 weekends from April through May; daily 10–5 from June through October

SOUTHARD WINERY
location: 670 Tibbling Road, Selah, WA 98942
phone: 509-697-3003
web: www.southardwinery.com
hours: Saturday and Sunday 12–5 or by appointment

TIETON CIDER WORKS
location: 321 Humphrey Road, Tieton, WA 98947
phone: 509-673-2880
web: www.tietonciderworks.com
hours: Wednesday through Friday 11–4:30; call for Saturday and Sunday appointments

Other Wineries to Visit

UPLAND ESTATES
winemaker(s): Todd Newhouse
location: 6141 Gap Road,
Outlook, WA 98938
phone: 509-839-2606
web: www.uplandwinery.com
hours: By appointment only

WALTER CLORE WINE AND EVENT CENTER
location: 2140 Wine Country Road,
Prosser, WA 99350
phone: 509-786-1000
web: www.theclorecenter.org
hours: Opening fall 2013, check
website for times and dates

YAKIMA VALLEY VINTNERS-YVCC
TEACHING WINERY
winemaker(s): Various winemakers
location: 110 Grandridge,
Grandview, WA 98930
phone: 509-882-7069
web: www.yakimavalleyvintners.com
hours: Friday 3–6, Saturday 11–5:30
(Closed January)

Horse Heaven Hills
WINE COUNTRY

MCKINLEY SPRINGS

2008 SYRAH
HORSE HEAVEN HILLS

Coyote Canyon
W I N E R Y

2006
ESTATE CHARDONNAY
HORSE HEAVEN HILLS
14.0% ALC. BY VOL.

RIESLING

Champoux
Vineyards   1979

TWO VINES

MERLOT-CABERNET
75% MERLOT, 20% CABERNET FRANC, 5% CABERNET SAUVIGNON
WASHINGTON STATE 2006

14 HANDS
2008 RIESLING
WASHINGTON STATE
ALC 11.5% BY VOL

2005

RED DIAMOND

CHARDONNAY
WASHINGTON STATE
ALC 13.5% BY VOL

McKINLEY
SPRINGS
HORSE HEAVEN HILLS

2007
SYRAH

ALC. 15.2%
BY VOL

Horse Heaven
WineTrail

Bordered on the north by the Yakima Valley and on the south by the majestic Columbia River, this area is home to some of the state's most celebrated vineyards, including Champoux, Destiny Ridge, Andrew, Alder Ridge, Canoe Ridge, and Zephyr Ridge. The area's soil, wind (and lots of it), low moisture, gentle southern slopes, and proximity to the Columbia River all conspire to create intense wine grapes.

It is a required field trip for all WineTrail enthusiasts to visit Columbia Crest at Paterson. During the warm weather months, check out Chateau Ste. Michelle's Tasting Gallery highlighting the exceptional fruit of Canoe Ridge Vineyard. Close by is the family-owned McKinley Springs Winery. If you are urban dweller, you will be stunned by the scenery as you travel to these wineries. Don't forget your camera. Pack a good lunch and make sure you have plenty of gas, because those kinds of necessities are hard to come by in the Horse Heaven Hills. Besides, once you saw the picnic grounds at Columbia Crest, you would kick yourself if you forgot lunch.

Horse Heaven WineTrail

1 Columbia Crest Winery

2 Chateau Ste. Michelle
Tasting Gallery

3 McKinley Springs Winery

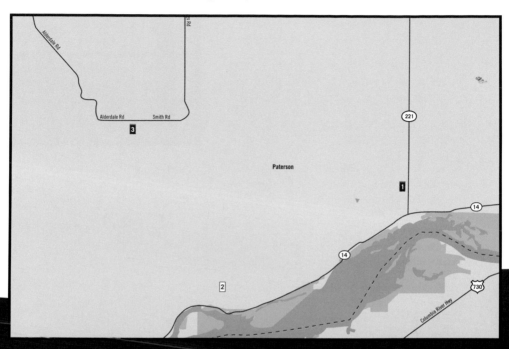

Region: **Horse Heaven Hills Wine Country**
# of tasting rooms on tour: **3**
# of satellite tasting rooms: **1**
Estimate # of days for tour: **1**
Getting around: **Car**
Key Events: ❑ **Columbia Crest sponsors events throughout the year — check website for details.**
Tips: ❑ **Pack a picnic and make sure you have plenty of gas — Horse Heaven Hills is about agriculture.**
❑ **Columbia Crest offers a self-guided tour taking you from vineyard to barrel room to tasting room.**
❑ **Don't have time to get to Woodinville? No problem, visit Ste. Michelle's Tasting Gallery at Canoe Ridge Estate.**
❑ **Check out Champoux Vineyards for wine tasting and vineyard tours. By appointment only — call 509-894-5005.**
Best: ❑ **Destination, views, music venue, gift shop and picnicking: Columbia Crest Winery**
❑ **Views and picnicking: Chateau Ste. Michelle Tasting Gallery**
❑ **Views and picnicking: McKinley Springs Winery**

Columbia Crest Winery

Can you name Washington's largest producer of wine? It's Columbia Crest, and it leaves its closest competitor in the dust. Owned by Chateau Ste. Michelle, Columbia Crest Winery bottles 1.7 million cases per year. How does Columbia Crest produce such volume without compromising quality? To find the answer, WineTrail trekkers need to visit Columbia Crest's Horse Heaven Hills production facility and take the self-guided tour.

Before you let that 1.7 million number jettison the word "artisan" from your vocabulary when describing this winery, realize that Columbia Crest is actually many wineries in one. The various Columbia Crest wines produced at its massive Paterson, Washington, facility sport labels such as Reserve, Grand Estate, H3 (Horse Heaven Hills), and Two Vines. Historically, Columbia Crest enjoyed a reputation as the state's value-priced leader. However, that title was blown away when, in 2009, *Wine Spectator* rated the 2005 Columbia Crest Reserve cabernet sauvignon as the best wine in the world. The world, mind you!

Now under the direction of 30-something chief winemaker Juan Muñoz-Oca, Columbia Crest's tradition of making world-class wines continues. Argentine-born, -bred, and -trained, Juan has an impressive résumé that reflects an advanced wine education and stints at premium wineries in Argentina, France, Australia and Spain, all of which ensure that he brings a wealth of knowledge. But perhaps more important is his passion for winemaking and his love of Washington wine.

Columbia Crest's spacious tasting room offers a wide variety of its wines — both of the red and the white persuasions. Featuring two tasting bars, the tasting room can readily accommodate the occasional onslaught of visitors disgorged from tour buses. As you would expect from any Ste. Michelle–owned asset, the staff is exceptionally well trained and affable. No wine snobbery here, despite its no. 1 ranking.

COLUMBIA CREST WINERY
opened: 1982
winemaker(s): Juan Munoz-Oca
location: Columbia Crest Drive, Paterson, WA 99345-0000
phone: 509-875-4227
web: www.columbiacrest.com
e-mail: info@columbia-crest.com
fee: Complimentary wine tasting except for reserve wines
hours: Daily 10–4:30 except for major holidays
amenities: Gift Shop, Live Music, Mailing List, Newsletter/Blog, Online Store, Picnic Area, Restaurant/Food Pairings, RV/Bus Parking, Tours, Vineyard on Premise, Wheelchair Accessible, Wine Club, Wines by the Glass
connect: 🐦 📷 f

⭐ **BEST Destination, views, music venue, gift shop and picnicking**

Chateau Ste. Michelle Tasting Gallery ②

CHATEAU STE. MICHELLE TASTING GALLERY
opened: 1934
winemaker(s): Bob Bertheau (Red) and Wendy Stuckey (White)
location: 239653 Canoe Ridge Road, Paterson, WA 99345
phone: 509-222-8570
web: www.ste-michelle.com
e-mail: creinfo@ste-michelle.com
fee: Tasting fee refunded with purchase
hours: Thursday through Sunday 11–4, May through September
amenities: Gift Shop, Mailing List, Newsletter/Blog, Online Store, Picnic Area, Tours, RV/Bus Parking, Vineyard on Premise, Wheelchair Accessible, Wine Club, Wines by the Glass, YouTube
connect: 🐦 f

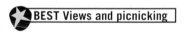

BEST Views and picnicking

www.winetrailsnw.com/wineries/chateau_ste_michelle_tasting_gallery

McKinley Springs Winery

Imagine selling your fruit for many years to well-established wineries and one day realizing that you, too, can turn grapes into fine wine. Such is the epiphany that occurred within the Andrews family regarding their McKinley Springs Vineyards in the Horse Heaven Hills American Viticultural Area.

After more than 25 years of growing premium grapes, the Andrews family made the decision to take the next step: to ferment their product into premium wine. Doug Rowell is the winemaker and is in the fortunate position of having plenty of fruit to work with, given that the Andrews Estate Vineyard comprises 2,000 acres composed of 20 different grape varieties. It's a small-lot winery with a huge vineyard: Guess who gets the "pick of the litter" from the grapes.

The McKinley Springs address indicates Prosser, but the vineyard and winery are many miles to the south in the Horse Heaven Hills. It's rural here; agriculture abounds, and from the McKinley Springs tasting room you can look south to Alder Ridge and Chateau Champoux vineyards. Surrounding the Andrews farm is row upon row of *Vitis vinifera*, which are the responsibility of grape grower Rob Andrews. Sadie, the resident Australian sheep dog, is a sort of symbol of the vineyard's history. A century ago, sheepherders would stop at McKinley Springs — the only watering hole between Prosser and the Columbia River — where the sheep were loaded onto trains and transported to Montana for the summer.

A stunning metal sculpture greets you at the entrance to the winery. Right away, you know that McKinley Springs is serious about its wines. The two-story post-and-beam building that houses the tasting room offers an airy space in which to sample its 10 different wine varietals. Fortunately for WineTrail enthusiasts, there are plenty of large picture windows to view the windswept vineyards and hillsides.

MCKINLEY SPRINGS WINERY
opened: 2002
winemaker(s): Doug Rowell
location: 1201 Alderdale Road, Prosser, WA 99350
phone: 509-894-4528
web: www.mckinleysprings.com
e-mail: rowell@mckinleysprings.com
fee: Complimentary wine tasting
hours: Friday through Sunday 11–5 Memorial Day Weekend through Labor Day Weekend; Closed September through May
amenities: Gift Shop, Picnic Area, RV/Bus Parking, Tours, Newsletter/Blog, Online Store, Vineyard on Premise, Wheelchair Accessible, Wine Club
connect: 🐦 f

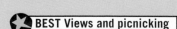 BEST Views and picnicking

Other Wineries to Visit

CHATEAU CHAMPOUX
winemaker(s): Various
location: 524 Alderdale Road, Prosser, WA 99350
phone: 509-894-5005
web: www.chateauchampoux.com
hours: June 1st through November 5th by appointment

Red Mountain

WINE COUNTRY

Chandler Reach
VINEYARDS

2008 CORELLA
YAKIMA VALLEY

PRODUCE OF THE USA   WASHINGTON STATE   BRENT AND SARAH GOEDHART, PROPRIETORS

Produced and Bottled at Bel' Villa Vineyard

TRADE **G** MARK

RED MOUNTAIN
AMERICAN VITICULTURAL AREA

Bel' Villa Vineyard

N°569 X 12 BTL CASES   20|10| Syrah

Goedhart ♥ family   750 ML 14% ALC/VOL

RM PROPRIETOR PRODUCED
RMAVA GRAND CLASS
AUTHENTIC PLACE OF ORIGIN RED WINE

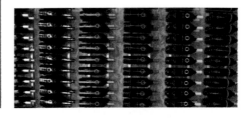

Red Mountain
WineTrail

Visitors to Red Mountain don't go for the overnight lodging or fabulous restaurants. You won't find these amenities on Red Mountain. Instead, what you will find are fields of grapes and a number of wineries dotting the landscape. Make no mistake, Red Mountain is zoned for agriculture. It is home to what many wine enthusiasts agree are incredibly intense cabernet sauvignon grapes. With prominent winery names like Hightower, Fidelitas, Tapteil, Col Solare, Terra Blanca, and Kiona, you're in for a great day (or two). In between tasting rooms, you will pass some of the state's most distinctive vineyards, including Ciel du Cheval, Klipsun, Hedges, Kiona, and Artz.

Red Mountain WineTrail is just a dot on the map lying between Prosser and Richland off I-82. Nevertheless, what a dot it is. In terms of places to stay and eat, nearby Prosser and the Tri-Cities offer plenty of choices.

Red Mountain WineTrail

1. Chandler Reach Vineyard
2. Terra Blanca Winery & Estate Vineyard
3. Cooper
4. Kiona Vineyards and Winery
5. Fidelitas Wines
6. Hedges Family Estate
7. Tapteil Vineyard and Winery
8. Hightower Cellars
9. Col Solare

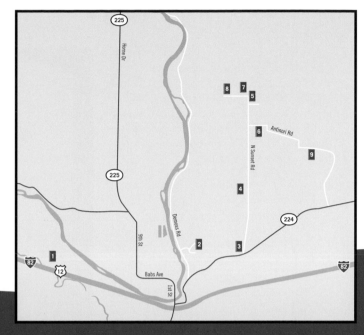

Region:	**Red Mountain Wine Country**
# of tasting rooms on tour:	**9**
Estimate # of days for tour:	**2**
Getting around:	**Car**
Key Events:	❏ **Spring Barrel Tasting in the Yakima Valley (last weekend in April); Red Wine and Chocolate (mid-February); Catch the Crush (October) and Thanksgiving in Wine Country sponsored by Wine Yakima Valley. See www.wineyakimavalley.org.**
Tips:	❏ **For good information about this region, see www.redmountainava.com.**
	❏ **Restaurants and lodging are found in nearby Prosser or the Tri-Cities.**
	❏ **Consider hiring a limousine service.**
Best:	❏ **Music venue and picnicking: Chandler Reach Vineyard**
	❏ **Views and picnicking: Terra Blanca Winery and Estate Vineyard**
	❏ **Views and picnicking: Kiona Vineyards and Winery**
	❏ **Views and picnicking: Fidelitas Wines**
	❏ **Views: Hedges Family Estate**
	❏ **Views and picnicking: Tapteil Vineyard and Winery**
	❏ **Views: Hightower Cellars**
	❏ **Destination, views and picnicking: Col Solare**

Chandler Reach Vineyard ❶

If you have ever traveled on Interstate 82 between Richland and Prosser, you may have wondered about the Tuscan-style villa near exit 93. Wonder no more. That, my wine-tasting friend, is the site of Chandler Reach Vineyards. Inspired by a trip to Tuscany in 1997, owner/winemaker Len Parris decided to create a Tuscan-style winery/tasting room at his Benton City location.

Located on a north-facing slope overlooking Red Mountain, the 42-acre Chandler Reach Vineyards supplies the fruit for a number of wineries. The heat index in this part of the state is high and these temperatures could be responsible for the intensity of Len's fruit. However, not all the ripe grapes leave the Chandler Reach Vineyards. Select lots become the fruit for 2,500 cases of Chandler Reach's own estate wines: cabernet sauvignon, cabernet franc, merlot, syrah, and sangiovese.

If your taste buds are seeking something other than intense, full-flavored wines, keep driving. However, if you are ready to try some serious reds, take exit 93 and head for the villa. The tasting room provides a warm environment for sampling the estate wines. After all, you are here to taste the *terroir*. Juxtaposed

against Red Mountain, in an area famous for its cabernet sauvignon, Chandler Reach is all about the "taste of the land." Bellissimo!

Check out the value-priced 36 Red. At around $13 a bottle this might be the best deal in the state!

CHANDLER REACH VINEYARD
opened: 2002
winemaker(s): Len Parris
location: 9506 West Chandler Road, Benton City, WA 99320-7852
phone: 509-588-8800
web: www.chandlerreach.com
e-mail: shelbey@chandlerreach.com
fee: Complimentary wine tasting
hours: Thusday through Sunday 11–5, call for winter hours
amenities: Live Music, Newsletter/Blog, Online Store, Picnic Area, Restaurant/Food Pairings, RV/Bus Parking, Vineyard on Premise, Wheelchair Accessible, Wine Club
connect: 🐦 ⓕ

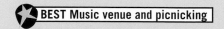
⭐ BEST Music venue and picnicking

Terra Blanca Winery & Estate Vineyard ②

Terra Blanca has it all, with the exception, perhaps, of communal jackets and sweaters. So, don't forget to bring your own when you visit, even if it's 100 degrees outside. Puzzled? The reason for the warm clothing is Terra Blanca's cave system, which retains a constant temperature of 57 degrees for housing barrel upon barrel of aging wine.

Inspired by the use of natural caves for wine storage in Europe, Terra Blanca's creators built two extensive cave systems to hold row after row of French oak barrels. Fabricated in 1997, the first cave houses 1,000 58-gallon barrels. In 2004, the construction of a second, larger cave system, with a capacity of 3,000 barrels, was completed.

Its Tuscan-inspired architecture includes a tasting room that includes a baby grand piano and is large enough to accommodate busloads of weekend visitors. Indoors, you will discover a wine library with shelving systems rising at least 15 feet high, a complete gourmet-style kitchen, and several banquet rooms. One banquet room seats as many as 180 guests and makes an excellent venue for a high school reunion, a corporate affair, or a wedding.

Outside, a cobblestone path leads to a waterfall, a recently completed amphitheater for summer concerts, and, of course, Terra Blanca's popular caves. From the patio, enjoy what WineTrails Northwest rates as one of its "Top 10 View." With the vineyards of Red Mountain behind you and the beautiful Horse Heaven Hills in front, you'll want to plant yourself for a nice, long stay. And, depending upon the weather outside, do take advantage of the guided vineyard tours to appreciate Terra Blanca's fruit source.

Winemaker Keith Pilgrim is in the enviable position of having access to Red Mountain fruit, state-of-the-art equipment, and those caves to produce a full range of reds and whites. Terra white and terra red for all palates!

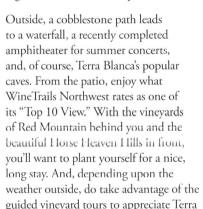

TERRA BLANCA WINERY & ESTATE VINEYARD
opened: 1993
winemaker(s): Keith Pilgrim
location: 34715 North Demoss Road, Benton City, WA 99320
phone: 509-588-6082
web: www.terrablanca.com
e-mail: info@terrablanca.com
fee: Tasting fee
hours: Daily 10–6 April through October; daily 11–6 November through March
amenities: Gift Shop, Newsletter/Blog, Online Store, Picnic Area, Private Events, Restaurant/Food Pairings, RV/Bus Parking, Tours, Vineyard on Premise, Weddings, Wheelchair Accessible, Wine Club
connect: 🐦 📘

⭐ **BEST Views and picnicking**

 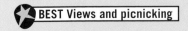

Cooper ⓷

Everything about this Sunset Road winery speaks authenticity. There's nothing pretentious about it. From the welcoming staff to the winery dog, every aspect invites visitors to relax and experience Cooper.

Check out the logo-adorned wine label with a weathered

"C" painted on a red barn door. If you find yourself thinking along the lines of the Old West, down-hominess, family, mom and apple pie, and hard work, you are not alone. That evocation is intentional, because with a gazillion wineries out there competing, you have to create a winery that breaks through the clutter.

Cooper succeeds because it is a reflection of its creator and owner — Neil Cooper. His agrarian roots and straightforward style are out there for all to see. What you see is what you get, and what you get are some extraordinary wines that show great promise for this young Red Mountain winery. Amazingly, despite its youth, Cooper offers a variety of wines to sample, including pinot gris, chardonnay, cabernet, and Bordeaux blends.

In keeping with Cooper's essence, these wines showcase the viticultural areas in which they grew — the Columbia Valley AVA. They're big, bold, and with just the right amount of acid to give them spark and balance out their flavor profiles.

Cooper's spacious tasting room provides comfortable shade from summer's heat and shelter from winter's cold. Year around, it is a welcoming space for tasting the *terroir* of Washington.

COOPER
opened: 2010
winemaker(s): Neil Cooper
location: 35306 North Sunset Road, Benton City, WA 99350
phone: 509-588-2667
web: www.cooperwinecompany.com
e-mail: coop@cooperwinecompany.com
fee: Tasting fee refunded with purchase
hours: Thursday through Monday 11–5 or by appointment
amenities: Mailing List, RV/Bus Parking, Vineyard on Premise, Wheelchair Accessible
connect: 🐦 f

Kiona Vineyards and Winery ▣

Before Red Mountain became vineyard green, it was dusty brown. In fact, local Native Americans referred to this area as "Kiona," which means "brown hills." An excellent name for a winery, don't you think?

It must have taken a lot of intestinal fortitude for the Williams and Holmes families to set roots down on this tract of land on Red Mountain in 1972. There were no roads, no electricity, and the nearest water was located more than 500 feet below solid rock. Talk about your Maalox moment; indeed, there must have been times when they questioned their sanity as they surveyed miles of sagebrush and dry,

crusty-looking land. However, there was water, and the roads and electric wires did come, and by 1975, through much hard work, the families succeeded in planting a small vineyard. They named it Kiona Vineyards.

We fast-forward some 30 years later to the present, and the Williams and their offspring continue to evolve their grape asset. Having grown from basement "garagiste" winemaking operation to its 20,000-square-foot tasting and banquet facility (equipped with a full kitchen), Kiona Vineyards and Winery is a must-stop along the Red Mountain WineTrail. The barrel room, built underground, is where wine is aged in oak at a constant temperature. In the contemporary tasting room, you can sample Kiona's full slate of red and white estate wines produced by second-generation winemaker Scott Williams.

In keeping with the Williams family's belief that wine should add to life's pleasures, Scott named his second label "Vivacious Vicky," after his wife. According to Scott, his spouse has "put up with long hours, busy harvests, lost weekends, strangers for dinner, and fruit flies for 25 years and counting." As you will discover, this Vivacious Vicky has legs. Give the red blend a swirl, then a taste, and imagine what this place must have been like over 35 years ago.

KIONA VINEYARDS AND WINERY
opened: 1972
winemaker(s): Scott Williams
location: 44612 North Sunset Road, Benton City, WA 99320-7500
phone: 509-588-6716
web: www.kionawine.com
e-mail: info@kionawine.com
fee: Complimentary wine tasting
hours: Daily 12–5
amenities: Gift Shop, Newsletter/Blog, Online Store, Picnic Area, Private Events, RV/Bus Parking, Tours, Vineyard on Premise, Wheelchair Accessible
connect: 🐦 f

★ **BEST Views and picnicking**

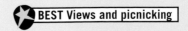

Fidelitas Wines 5

"I love using grapes from different regions of Washington. It's like being a chef and having access to a variety of spices that I can use to create amazing flavors," acclaimed winemaker/owner Charlie Hoppes once noted. Since 2001, Hoppes has produced wines under his

Fidelitas label, but many know Hoppes as the consultant winemaker for Gamache Family Vintners, Glencorrie, and other wineries. With his own label, Charlie is the author of his own vintages and recipient of numerous accolades, including five (count 'em) medals at the prestigious 2011 Seattle Wine Awards.

In his early career, Hoppes (pronounced hop-pas) cut his winemaking teeth working with Mike Januik (current winemaker for Woodinville-based Novelty Hill/Januik winery) and then gained experience at Ste. Michelle Wine Estates, first at Snoqualmie, and then at Chateau Ste. Michelle. But since the early 1980s, Hoppes had dreamed of establishing his own label. With his acquisition of a 5-acre plot of land in 2005, Hoppes finally had the chance to create his signature Bordeaux blends (including Optu white wine and Optu red wine, a red wine lover's dream) as well as pure cabernet sauvignon and merlot.

The eco-friendly winery and tasting room offers visitors plenty of space to sample wine and take in the views of Horse Heaven Hills in the distance. The outdoor patio invites visitors to purchase a bottle and uncork an afternoon of delectable decadence — with a capital D.

Fidelitas wine bottles wear the distinctive circle labels; the circle is reminiscent of a wedding ring and reflects a commitment to a long-lasting marriage. Also found on the label is the tagline "Faithful, Loyal, True." Certainly, fans of Fidelitas Wines have vowed those very same words.

FIDELITAS WINES
opened: 2001
winemaker(s): Charlie Hoppes
location: 51810 North Sunset Road, Benton City, WA 99320
phone: 509-588-3469
web: www.fidelitaswines.com
e-mail: info@fidelitaswines.com
fee: Tasting fee refunded with purchase
hours: Daily 11–5, closed Christmas and New Years weekends; Winter hours, Thursday through Monday 11–5, or by appointment
amenities: Online Store, Picnic Area, Private Events, Tours, Vineyard on Premise, Wheelchair Accessible, Wine Club
connect: 🐦 📘

⭐ BEST Views and picnicking

Hedges Family Estate 6

Talk about winning the vineyard lottery: In 1990, Tom Hedges and his French-born wife, Anne-Marie, purchased a parcel of land in an obscure area called Red Mountain. Today,

they are sitting on a viticultural "goldmine," and the price tag for land in this designated American Viticultural Area has gone up considerably. However, such are the spoils for those with vision, passion, and a willingness to take risks.

A destination winery, the Hedges chateau presents a visual landmark on Red Mountain and offers a commanding view of miles of vineyards, with numerous wineries dotting the landscape, including neighbors Col Solare, Tapteil Vineyard & Winery, and Kiona Vineyards Winery. The Horse Heaven Hills AVA is in the distance. Hedges Family Estate is the perfect place to enjoy one of its award-winning blends and soak in one of the top views in Washington as you lounge on some elegant outdoor furniture.

As you drive up to the winery, a sign directs you to the upscale chateau, where you can sample the winery's top-tier wines for a fee (refundable with purchase). The tasting room features Hedges' elegant blended and varietal whites and reds. The CMS white is a blend of white grapes with a sauvignon blanc backbone and is a perfect match for Northwest seafood. The CMS red blend combines cabernet, merlot, and syrah. Its price tag of $14 translates into a great value. The principal ingredient — cabernet sauvignon from Red Mountain grapes —

informs your palate that you are about to experience a wonderfully intense yet balanced wine. And the DLD syrah, with its spicy notes and hints of licorice on the midpalate, had me asking for a second pour. Delish!

HEDGES FAMILY ESTATE
opened: 1987
winemaker(s): Pete Hedges
location: 53511 North Sunset Road, Benton City, WA 99320
phone: 509-588-3155
web: www.hedgesfamilyestate.com
e-mail: info@hedgesfamilyestate.com
fee: Complimentary wine tasting
hours: Saturday and Sunday 11–5 from April through November or by appointment
amenities: Mailing List, Online Store, Picnic Area, RV/Bus Parking, Tours, Vineyard on Premise, Wheelchair Accessible, Wine Club
connect: 🐦 f

⭐ BEST Views

 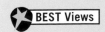

Tapteil Vineyard and Winery 🔢

It's interesting to contemplate what drives people to create businesses. For some, it is a drive to make lots of money. For others, it's a mission of the heart, and the money is secondary. Take one Lawrence "Larry" Pearson.

Equipped with a solid civil engineering background, Larry dreamed of growing cabernet sauvignon. Despite his very analytical nature, he set about satisfying that winegrowing itch without the benefit of a detailed business plan and financial projections. He, along with his spouse, Jane, took the big leap and purchased a parcel of land in a relatively obscure part of Washington called Red Mountain. Then, in 1985, Larry realized his dream of getting dirt under his fingernails by planting his first cabernet sauvignon vines. He named his vineyard Tapteil, after the lower portion of the Yakima River where the Tapteilmin, or "narrow river people," once lived.

Today, 25 acres later and endless days managing the vineyards, Larry and his vineyard team now grow merlot, syrah, and cabernet franc amongst the rows of cabernet sauvignon on the south slope of his property. Still learning, still reinventing, Larry continues to produce the intense, full-flavored cabernet sauvignon that has come to define Red Mountain.

Located at the north end of Sunset Road, Tapteil Vineyard Winery commands a sweeping view of the Red Mountain table and the panoramic Horse Heaven Hills in the distance. If you do decide to picnic, be sure to pack some fresh artisan bread to soak up the select virgin olive oil and balsamic vinegar that Jane sells in the tasting room. As you take in the wine, the food, the gorgeous view, don't be surprised if you catch yourself daydreaming about quitting that day job and planting vines.

TAPTEIL VINEYARD AND WINERY
opened: 1984
winemaker(s): Larry Pearson
location: 20206 East 583 PR NE, Benton City, WA 99320
phone: 509-588-4460
web: www.tapteil.com
e-mail: winery@tapteil.com
fee: Complimentary wine tasting
hours: Friday through Sunday 11–5 from April through November, or by appointment
amenities: Gift Shop, Lodging, Online Store, Picnic Area, RV/Bus Parking, Wheelchair Accessible
connect: ⬛f

⭐ **BEST Views and picnicking**

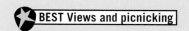

Hightower Cellars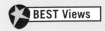

"Service only a smaller winery can provide.... A perfect example is Hightower Cellars, located in Eastern Washington's Red Mountain growing region. Tim and Kelly Hightower literally run the entire winemaking process from start to finish. They're also wonderful hosts, and you'll be hard pressed to find a nicer pair of people in the wine business. "
— Dan Radil, *The Bellingham Herald*

I couldn't have said it better … so I won't try. Tim and Kelly Hightower and their yellow Lab are the nicest family with a great story that involves the courage to leave their Western Washington comforts for the unknown tumbleweed-infested land of the Columbia Valley.

Tim and Kelly have the rare distinction of being a husband-and-wife winemaking duo. Beginning in the mid-'90s, they honed their winemaking skills in one of the Woodinville business parks that cater to suburban "garagiste." However, the temptation to own real estate in one of the world's most acclaimed grape-growing locations proved too much, and in 2002, the Hightowers decided to move to the agricultural land of Red Mountain. What cinched the deal for them was the fact that the land they purchased includes water rights to support a 10-acre vineyard.

While their vines mature, the Hightowers are reliant on other growers for their fruit, and fortunately they don't have far to go. The Hightowers source their grapes from nearby Artz and E. & E. Shaw vineyards, Alder Ridge Vineyard in Horse Heaven Hills and Pepper Bridge Vineyard in Walla Walla Valley. Even though their own vines produce cabernet sauvignon, cabernet franc, merlot, Malbec, and petit verdot, the Hightowers will continue to rely on other growers for their fruit. In the meantime, their yellow Lab will continue to guard the vineyard, pose for pictures, and refrain from barking while visitors sample the wine.

HIGHTOWER CELLARS
opened: 1997
winemaker(s): Tim and Kelly Hightower
location: 19418 East 583 PR NE, Benton City, WA 99320-8598
phone: 509-588-2867
web: www.hightowercellars.com
e-mail: handsorted@hightowercellars.com
fee: Complimentary wine tasting
hours: Thursday through Sunday 11–5
amenities: Mailing List, Online Store, Picnic Area, Vineyard on Premise, Wheelchair Accessible
connect: f

⭐ BEST Views

Hightower's resident yellow Lab

Col Solare 9

Col Solare is the result of a partnership between Washington's Chateau Ste. Michelle and one of Italy's great wine institutions, Marchesi Antinori. We're talking 26 generations, or more than 600 years, of winemaking by the Antinori family. Marchesi Piero Antinori, ever driven to push their winemaking boundaries, visited Washington state in 1992 at the urging of legendary Russian-born winemaker André Tchelistcheff, and he saw tremendous potential.

Col Solare's mission is to produce exceptional red blends with a cabernet sauvignon backbone. It may seem strange that a Tuscany-based wine institution would focus on cabernet and not sangiovese, until you realize that Marchesi Antinori's fame rose significantly with the use of international varieties to create the "Super Tuscans" in the 1970s. Beginning with the 1995 vintage, the Col Solare blend uses 75 percent cabernet and a mixture of other (primarily Bordeaux) varieties.

In 2006, Col Solare opened its grand winery and tasting room at its 40-acre site on Red Mountain. Driving along on nearby Interstate-82, you'll be able to spy the winery's 56-foot-tall campanile (bell tower). With its pinkish-brown stucco skin and contemporary lines, the Tuscan-inspired architecture mirrors the surrounding landscape. Radiating out over the southerly slope are 28 acres of grapes destined to be the estate wines of Col Solare.

Visitors to the winery enjoy ultrapremium vintages (paired with small plates of select cheeses and salami) and, on weekends, can tour the cellar rooms and production facilities below. Here, you'll learn how winemaker Marcus Notaro relies on the best of the best in terms of grapes, barrels, and winemaking equipment to create big, bold, delicious blends retailing for $75 a bottle. A more wallet-friendly second label called Shining Hill, at $40 a bottle, is also available for tasting and purchase.

COL SOLARE
opened: 2006
winemaker(s): Marcus Notaro
location: 50207 Antinori Road, Benton City, WA 99320
phone: 800-267-6793
web: www.colsolare.com
e-mail: info@colsolare.com
fee: Tasting fee
hours: Saturday and Sunday 1–5
amenities: Mailing List, Online Store, Picnic Area, RV/Bus Parking, Tours, Vineyard on Premise, Wheelchair Accessible, Wines by the Glass
connect: 🐦

⭐ **BEST Destination, views and picnicking**

Other Wineries to Visit

BUCKMASTER CELLARS
winemaker(s): Buckmaster Cellars
location: 35802 Sunset Road, Benton City, WA 99320
phone: 509-628-8474
web: www.buckmastercellars.com
hours: Yakima Valley Wine Association event weekends 10–5 and by appointment

GOEDHART FAMILY
winemaker(s): Sarah Goedhart
location: 50739 North Sunset Road, Benton City, WA 99320
phone: 509-554-6042
web: www.goedhartfamily.com
hours: Saturday 12–4 or by appointment

PORTRAIT CELLARS
winemaker(s): Ed Shaw
location: East 27318 Ambassador Private NE Rd, Benton City, WA 99320
phone: 509 588-453
web: www.portraitcellars.com
hours: By appointment only

SLEEPING DOG WINES
winemaker(s): Larry Oates
location: 45804 North Whitmore PR NW, Benton City, WA 98320
phone: 509-460-2886
web: www.sleepingdogwines.com
hours: By appointment only

STONECAP WINES
winemaker(s): Charlie Hoppes
location: 63615 East Jacobs Road, Benton City, WA 99352
phone: 509-627-6249
web: www.stonecapwines.com
hours: By appointment only

Tri-Cities

WINE COUNTRY

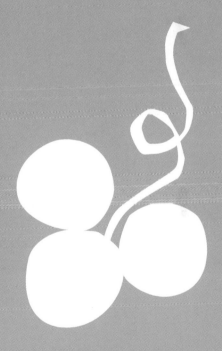

COUPLET
CHARDONNAY · VIOGNIER
2011
CONNER-LEE VINEYARD

Reserve Syrah

COLUMBIA VALLEY | WASHINGTON STATE
ARETÉ VINEYARDS

BARNARD
GRIFFIN

COLUMBIA VALLEY
Chardonnay
2011

Produced and Bottled by Barnard Griffin
Richland, Washington   Alcohol 13.2% by Volume

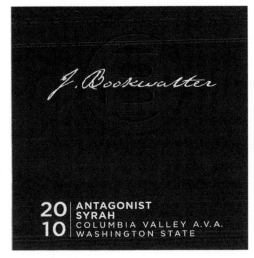

J. Bookwalter

20   ANTAGONIST
10   SYRAH
     COLUMBIA VALLEY A.V.A.
     WASHINGTON STATE

Tri-Cities
WineTrail

To fully appreciate the Tri-Cities WineTrail, take the time to understand its winemaking history.

Beginning in 1976, Bill and Joann Preston used the fruit from their own Pasco-based vineyard to create estate wines. At the time, there were only a handful of bonded wineries in the state, with consumers still drinking post-Prohibition fortified wines. In 1983, California transplants Rob Griffin and Deborah Barnard launched the highly successful Barnard Griffin Winery in Richland. At around the same time, father and son Bill and Greg Powers planted Badger Mountain Vineyard, with a focus on growing organic grapes. The well-known Powers Winery is the offshoot of that vineyard.

Now, a new generation of winemaking talent has entered the Tri-Cities scene, building on the success of the past. Experiencing the Tri-Cities WineTrail is a pleasurable history lesson that teaches why this area is the heart of Washington wine country — understand its past; taste its future.

Tri-Cities WineTrail

1. Thomas O'Neil Cellars
2. J. Bookwalter Winery
3. Barnard Griffin Winery
4. Tagaris Winery
   & Taverna Tagaris
5. Hamilton Cellars
6. Goose Ridge Winery
7. Badger Mountain
   Vineyard / Powers Winery
8. Smasne Cellars
9. Preston Premium Wines

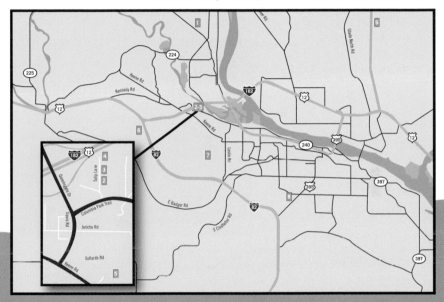

Region: **Tri-Cities Wine Country**
# of tasting rooms on tour: **9**
Estimate # of days for tour: **2**
Getting around: **Car and foot**
Key Events: ❑ **Tri-Cities Wine Festival.**
See www.tricitieswinefestival.com for details.
Tips: ❑ **If you like what glass does to light, take a glass class at Barnard Griffin.**
❑ **Bookwalter Winery provides bistro fare tailored to pair with the wine.**
❑ **Tagaris Winery & Taverna Tagaris offers both wine tasting and restaurant fare with a Mediterranean accent.**
❑ **Pack a picnic for Preston Premium Wines and enjoy the outdoor deck.**
❑ **Consider hiring a limousine service.**

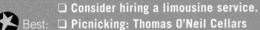

Best: ❑ **Picnicking: Thomas O'Neil Cellars**
❑ **Eats: J. Bookwalter Winery**
❑ **Gift shop, eats: Barnard Griffin Winery**
❑ **Eats: Tagaris Winery & Taverna Tagaris**
❑ **Eats: Smasne Cellars**
❑ **Gift shop: Preston Premium Wines**

Thomas O'Neil Cellars

Relatively new to the north end of Richland is Thomas O'Neil Cellars, offering premium wine, live music, and small-plate appetizers, is drawing crowds and creating a buzz. It also has free Wi-Fi and a place to play checkers and chess, so patrons could easily find themselves

settling in for an afternoon or an evening. On weekend nights, there's likely to be live music on the patio (weather permitting); check out its website's event section for the schedule of live music acts.

With a background that includes a degree in enology from Michigan State University, an internship with a little winery called Chateau Ste. Michelle, and an assistant winemaker stint at Milbrandt Vineyards, Thomas O'Neil had the requisite background to launch his own winery in early 2010. And it certainly doesn't hurt to have a spouse blessed with a customer-winning smile and a discerning palate. Such are the assets that Tricia O'Neil brings to the enterprise.

Visitors to the winery enjoy tableside service and have the option of experiencing wines from either the Thomas O'Neil label or the lower-priced Fahrenheit 100 label. If it's available, make a point of trying their flagship Fusion wine, a blend of syrah, petite sirah, and grenache, which has the most interesting dark eggplant purple color

in the glass. If you're feeling a little peckish, check out the Tuscan chicken flatbread with three cheeses, and see if you agree with me that this is the perfect accompaniment for Thomas O'Neil's Fusion.

THOMAS O'NEIL CELLARS
opened: 2010
winemaker(s): Tom O'Neil
location: 2323 Henderson Loop, Richland, WA 99354
phone: 509-371-1900
web: www.thomasoneilcellars.com
e-mail: info@thomasoneilcellars.com
fee: Tasting fee refunded with purchase
hours: Tuesday through Thursday 12–6; Friday and Saturday 12–10
amenities: Live Music, Online Store, Picnic Area, Restaurant/Food Pairings, Wheelchair Accessible, Wine Club, Wines by the Glass
connect: 🐦 f

⭐ BEST Picnicking

J. Bookwalter Winery

The Bookwalter Winery story began in 1983 with the establishment of the winery by John's dad, Jerry Bookwalter. The winery was the first in Washington to use a gold-embossed, full-color wine label. Early on, Jerry produced a number of "vineyard-designated vintages" before they became widely popular. Time marches on, and in 1997, John joined the family winery.

Every bit as innovative as his father, John secured the services of consulting winemaker Zelma Long. A number of prestigious awards and honors have followed, including the 2005 Winery of the Year award presented by Northwest Press. More recently, John has been benefiting from the advice of French vintner Claude Gros, who pays meticulous attention to detail, from vineyard to wine storage.

In 2003, Bookwalter Winery opened a trendy wine lounge, JBistro, next door to Barnard Griffin in Richland. The hip atmosphere succeeded in attracting a younger audience with a taste for premium wine, handcrafted cheeses, and artisan breads. The definition of a "tasting room" shifts in this contemporary ambiance. Here, you can order a glass of wine to pair with regional cheeses while listening to live music, which more often than not is the sound of jazz. During warm weather, the tasting room spills out on to a patio, giving the place a true bistro feel.

Bookwalter offers a full slate of reds and whites, which have captivating names such as Subplot, Foreshadow, Antagonist, and Conflict. My self-confessed weakness for merlot had me going for the Foreshadow merlot and while smacking my lips, I couldn't help but paraphrase the quote "every bottle tells a story" — in this case, a story with a great opening, a nice midpalate plot, wrapped up in a great finish.

J. BOOKWALTER WINERY
opened: 1983
winemaker(s): John Bookwalter and Zelma Long
location: 894 Tulip Lane, Richland, WA 99352-8588
phone: 509-627-5000
web: www.bookwalterwines.com
e-mail: info@bookwalterwines.com
fee: Tasting fee refunded with purchase
hours: Sunday through Tuesday 11–8; Wednesday through Saturday 11–11
amenities: Live Music, Online Store, Picnic Area, Private Events, RV/Bus Parking, Vineyard on Premise, Wheelchair Accessible, Wine Club
connect: 🐦 📘

 BEST Eats

Barnard Griffin Winery

With a production of more than 65,000 cases annually, Barnard Griffin is the state's largest family-owned winery. From its beginning, the winery's focus has doggedly remained on the quality in the bottle. It has also evolved itself with the latest remodel in 2012 now offering a restaurant section as well as glass studio where Deborah Barnard can ply her passion and teach eager students.

Winemaker Rob Griffin's boyhood home is in Napa Valley, where he grew up surrounded by the burgeoning wine industry. A graduate of the University of California-Davis' Department of Viticulture & Enology program, Rob understands the science of making wine. This scientific background is at the heart of Barnard Griffin's success. But you can draw this conclusion for yourself by conducting field research at Barnard Griffin's tasting room, sandwiched between the Bookwalter and Tagaris wineries on Tulip Lane.

A distinctive clock tower marks its location. There is often a small crowd to contend with in the tasting room, but the staff works the gathering efficiently and with genuine friendliness. Subject to supply, Barnard Griffin's popular "Tulip Label" wines include chardonnay, fumé blanc, riesling, semillon, merlot, syrah, and cabernet sauvignon. For port lovers, check out the syrah port (if available) — it's one of the most delectable ports in the Northwest.

This is an on-premise production facility and part of the joy of visiting the winery on event weekends is the chance to tour the facility complete with stacks of barrels and drunken fruit flies. Rob is often in attendance to answer questions. Given the plethora of wineries to visit in the Tri-Cities region, without question Barnard Griffin is at the top of the list in terms of must-see (and taste) wineries.

BARNARD GRIFFIN WINERY
opened: 1983
winemaker(s): Rob Griffin
location: 878 Tulip Lane, Richland, WA 99352-8588
phone: 509-627-0266
web: www.barnardgriffin.com
e-mail: info@barnardgriffin.com
fee: Complimentary wine tasting; Tasting fee for reserve wines
hours: Daily 10–5
amenities: Art Gallery, Gift Shop, Live Music, Online Store, Picnic Area, Restaurant/Food Pairings, RV/Bus Parking, Wheelchair Accessible, Wine Club

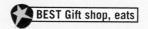 BEST Gift shop, eats

Tagaris Winery & Taverna Tagaris 4

Located on Tulip Lane in Richland, next to Barnard Griffin, both Tagaris Winery and Taverna Tagaris restaurant are the brainchild of Michael Taggares, who started the winery

in 1987. The spelling of the winery and the restaurant honors the correct spelling of the family's last name, Tagaris. The original name changed when Michael's grandfather, Pete, immigrated to America through Ellis Island. Eventually moving west and settling in Prosser, Pete Taggares became very successful in both farming and business. Today, the Taggares family is responsible for a number of successful enterprises, including Michael's 1,400-acre farm, with 700 of those acres dedicated to varietal grapes. The Taggares grow 18 different varieties, including petit verdot, counoise, Malbec, Mourvèdre, grenache, and tempranillo, to name a few. These grapes are the primary source of fruit used by Tagaris winemaker Frank Roth.

For centuries, Greek villages have had their *tavernas,* popular watering holes where friends gather to enjoy wine, hearty fare, and music. To that end, Michael established Taverna Tagaris restaurant at the winery. Elegance is the word that comes to mind upon entering the restaurant. A full Mediterranean-influenced menu offers small to large plates designed to match any appetite. In warmer weather, the 9,000-square-foot Patio Kouzina provides bistro-style fare and is a perfect accompaniment to cold wine served up sangría style. The young restaurant staff is smartly dressed and can readily suggest which wine would pair nicely with, for example, the goat cheese tortelli.

Taverna Tagaris also features live music from Northwest bands. During most summer weekends, visitors to the winery/ restaurant can enjoy contemporary-style music, jazz, and blues from a variety of popular bands. With its wine, food, and music, the taverna offers a trio of life's pleasures with a distinctive Mediterranean flair.

TAGARIS WINERY & TAVERNA TAGARIS
opened: 1986
winemaker(s): Frank Roth
location: 844 Tulip Lane, Richland, WA 99352
phone: 509-628-1619
web: www.tagariswines.com
e-mail: info@tagariswines.com
fee: Tasting fee refunded with purchase
hours: Daily 11–5; Extended hours for Taverna Tagaris Restaurant
amenities: Live Music, Mailing List, Online Store, Private Events, Restaurant/Food Pairings, Tours, Wheelchair Accessible, Wine Club, Wines by the Glass
connect: ▪️

⭐ BEST Eats

Hamilton Cellars 5

The birthing process was exceedingly long and arduous, but Stacie and Russ Hamilton refused to give up. Dealing with a host of building-permit issues and zoning laws, the couple finally got their dream off the ground in 2007 with the launch of Hamilton Cellars. With the opening of the winery's unique tasting room — which is really more of a wine bar than a simple tasting room — friends and business colleagues can gather, and actually relax and share a bottle of wine.

Stacie and Russ made several strategic moves at the beginning to position Hamilton Cellars as a serious newcomer to the wine industry. Key among those moves was choosing a celebrated winemaker — Charlie Hoppes — whose wines they'd enjoyed over the years. With Charlie's extensive portfolio, including his background at Chateau Ste. Michelle and his own label, Fidelitas, the Hamiltons nailed down the key ingredient needed for a successful winery.

Another vital decision involved setting aside a big chunk of the tasting room for club members only. So-called "Miltonaires Club" members imbibe in an exclusive area, complete with restaurant-style seating and an outdoor covered patio area with a fire pit. What's more, they can order small plates of nibblies to pair with their wine if hunger calls. (By the way, the name "Milton" refers to the Milton stick figure that adorns the Hamilton Cellars label.)

In terms of the wine, don't you dare leave the premises without trying the Hamilton Cellars Malbec. This raspberry-ripe, juicy wine with tamed tannins is wonderful. The combination of great fruit (Connor Lee Vineyard and Snipes Canyon Vineyard) and Charlie's winemaking prowess are responsible for this beauty. Priced at $30 a bottle (with a 15 percent discount for Miltonaires), this wine is the perfect accompaniment for the anything-grilled you have in mind.

HAMILTON CELLARS
opened: 2009
winemaker(s): Charlie Hoppes
location: 1950 Keene Road, Building I, Queensgate Village, Kennewick, WA 99352
phone: 509-628-8227
web: www.hamiltoncellars.com
e-mail: stacie@hamiltoncellars.com
fee: Tasting fee
hours: Wednesday through Sunday 12–5; Thursday 12–6; Friday and Saturday 12–9 or by appointment; Closed Christmas and New Years Day
amenities: Live Music, Mailing List, Online Store, Picnic Area, Restaurant/Food Pairings, Wheelchair Accessible, Wine Club, Wines by the Glass
connect: 🐦 📘

Goose Ridge Winery

What's in a name?

If it's the name Clore, as in Dr. Walter Clore, it refers to "the father of the Washington wine industry." In the 1990s, Dr. Clore consulted with the Monson family to help plan the 1,400-acre south-slope-facing Goose Ridge Estate Vineyards. (Note: That's not a typo. Goose Ridge Estate Vineyards consumes 1,400 acres of prime grape-growing real estate adjacent to Red Mountain.)

What's in a name? Well, does the name "Kendall Mix" ring a bell? He's the winemaker for Goose Ridge. Kendall's task is to create estate wines from a dozen Bordeaux and Rhône grape varieties. It's a challenge, but when you have more than 20 years of winemaking experience under your belt, you can take on the vagaries Mother Nature throws at you. Kendall's ability to blend cabernet, merlot, and syrah creates Goose Ridge's award-winning (and hugely popular) red blend Viero — a wine chock-full of black cherries and tobacco notes.

Located just four miles east of Benton City, on the "ridge" of Goose Hill, the winery's tasting room is situated adjacent to the expansive vineyards, and from its interior, you get a bird's-eye view of the well-groomed rows of grapes. It's a tastefully decorated room, with warm, neutral colors and little to distract you from enjoying Kendall's varietal and blended vintages.

What's in a name? If the name is "Sol Duc Meritage," it's a Bordeaux blend ready to take on a juicy steak. Named for the sparkling waters that nourish the sun-drenched Columbia Valley, the Sol Duc Meritage is, according to the winemaker's notes, "a concentrated classic red wine with nice integration of rich black cherry, cassis, and notes of vanilla and spice." By any other name, this wine would taste "as sweet."

GOOSE RIDGE WINERY
opened: 1999
winemaker(s): Kendall Mix
location: 16304 North Dallas Road, Richland, WA 99352-7750
phone: 509-628-3880
web: www.gooseridge.com
e-mail: info@gooseridge.com
fee: Complimentary wine tasting
hours: Monday through Saturday 11–6; Sunday 12–6 or by appointment
amenities: Mailing List, Online Store, Picnic Area, Private Events, RV/Bus Parking, Tours, Vineyard on Premise, Wheelchair Accessible, Wine Club, Wines by the Glass
connect: 🐦 📘

Badger Mountain Vineyard / Powers Winery 7

When you visit Badger Mountain Vineyard, you're in for a two-for-one treat. Not only do you have the opportunity to sample certified 100 percent organic Badger Mountain wine, but you can also taste wine bearing the Powers label, made from grapes grown in select Columbia Valley vineyards.

The 82-acre Badger Mountain Vineyard serves as the backdrop to its tasting room, located a few miles off Interstate 82 in Kennewick. The vineyard is

certified 100 percent organic, which means that no chemical herbicides, insecticides, fungicides, or synthetic fertilizers touch the vineyard. Only organic and naturally occurring substances are applied. What's more, there are no added sulfites in the production of Badger Mountain wine. These wines are referred to as NSA wines, as in "no sulfur added." (Readers should note that trace amounts of sulfite do occur naturally.)

Father and son, Bill and Greg Powers, established Badger Mountain Vineyard in 1982. From those early years, they have steadily ramped up production to nearly 50,000 cases annually. As testament to their success, Badger Mountain wines were featured on a segment of NBC's *Today* show that highlighted organic foods.

At Badger Mountain's tasting room, you are faced with the enviable challenge of choosing which wines to sample. Here's a thought: Give those synapses a rest and enjoy them all! Ever the innovator, Badger Mountain Winery also began offering wine in a box, under the names Pure White and Pure Red. This method of packaging essentially negates that annoying little oxidation problem, and there's no need to worry about cork failure either. In keeping with the winery's philosophy of offering affordable wines, these attractive 3-liter boxes sell for $22 for Pure White and $24 for Pure Red.

BADGER MOUNTAIN VINEYARD / POWERS WINERY
opened: 1982
winemaker(s): Greg Powers
location: 1106 South Jurupa Street, Kennewick, WA 99338-9392
phone: 800-643-9463
web: www.badgermtnvineyard.com
e-mail: info@badgermtnvineyard.com
fee: Complimentary wine tasting
hours: Daily 10–5
amenities: Gift Shop, Mailing List, Online Store, Picnic Area, Private Events, RV/Bus Parking, Weddings, Wheelchair Accessible
connect: f

Smasne Cellars

A consultant winemaker to more than a dozen Washington wineries, with a résumé that includes stints at Amavi Cellars, Pepper Bridge Winery, and Covey Run, Robert Smasne

uses his Woodinville tasting room to showcase his own six labels: Smasne Cellars, AlmaTerra, Farm Boy, Farm Girl, Smasne Reserve, and 1/2 Ass. These wines express the *terroir* of the 11 million acres that comprise the Columbia Valley AVA, including such respected vineyards as Uplands, Phinny Hill, and Lawrence. However, beyond the vineyards, these wines express five generations of a family's love affair with farming in the Yakima Valley.

Veteran winemaker Robert O. Smasne says it best, "Built on the foundation of family, farming heritage, love for the area and passion for wine, our mission is to handcraft limited-release, world-class artisan wines from specific vineyards that are noted for yielding the highest quality of wine grapes."

Farm Boy is the name given to his value-priced label. At $12 to $14 a bottle for red, white, or rosé wine, these table wines go great with tonight's burger, pizza, or a pink-hued sunset. Local artist Herb Leonhard executes the artistic image of Robert as a young farm boy. It's an expression of his agrarian roots and his love for the valley's *terroir*.

WineTrail Note: Enjoy Smasne Cellars wines in the Columbia Gorge at AlmaTerra tasting room in Bingen, Wash. on Highway 14.

SMASNE CELLARS
opened: 2010
winemaker(s): Robert O. Smasne
location: 3617 Plaza Way, Suite A, Kennewick, WA 99337
phone: 509-783-9915
web: www.smasnecellars.com
e-mail: via website
fee: Tasting fee
hours: Wednesday through Thursday 1–9; Friday and Saturday 10–10 and Sunday 12–6
amenities: Gift Shop, Live Music, Online Store, Private Events, Restaurant/Food Pairings, RV/Bus Parking, Wheelchair Accessible, Wine Club
connect: 🐦 📘

 BEST Eats

Preston Premium Wines

Preston Premium Wines became the third bonded winery in Washington state when it took root in 1976 — making it ancient by Washington wine standards. Bill and Joann Preston had a dream to establish a vineyard and put Washington on the map for premium wine production. That dream became reality and eventually mushroomed to 157 acres.

The Prestons have created a miniature museum at their winery, where visitors can get an overview of cork production in Portugal and examine Joann's extensive collection of corkscrews, among other items of note.

The elevated tasting room provides a commanding view of the Preston vineyard. Preston Premium Wines offers a full slate of estate wines, including a second label bearing the name Long Tail Lizard. For port fans, Preston produces Tenrebac port ("Tenrebac" is cabernet spelled backward). The winery's spacious tasting room also features a well-stocked gift shop and is the portal to the wine museum downstairs.

Of particular note is the large outdoor seating area used for picnicking and listening to live music. For those WineTrail trekkers seeking a winery for a corporate event, family hoedown, or wedding, take note of the winery's many amenities. From the deck outside the tasting room, you can see Preston's manicured park, which includes a gazebo, a pond, an amphitheater, and a waterfall.

PRESTON PREMIUM WINES
opened: 1976
winemaker(s): Dave Harvey
location: 502 East Vineyard Drive, Pasco, WA 99301
phone: 509-545-1990
web: www.prestonwines.com
e-mail: info@prestonwines.com
fee: Complimentary wine tasting for up to 4 wines; tasting fee for reserves
hours: Daily 10–5:30, closed major holidays
amenities: Gift Shop, Live Music, Online Store, Picnic Area, Private Events, Tours, Vineyard on Premise, Weddings, Wine Club
connect: f

 BEST Gift shop

Other Wineries to Visit

ANELARE
winemaker(s): Victor Cruz
location: 46415 East Badger Road, Benton City, WA 99320
phone: 509-521-8926
web: www.anelare.com
hours: By appointment only

ELISEO SILVA
winemaker(s): Frank Roth
location: 844 Tulip Lane, Richland, WA 99352
phone: 509-628-0020
web: www.eliseosilva.com
hours: Daily 11–5

KITZKE CELLARS WINERY
winemaker(s): The Kitzke's
location: 72308 E 260 PRNE, Richland, WA 99352
phone: 509-628-9442
web: www.kitzkecellars.com
hours: Monday, Thursday, Friday and Saturday 11–6, Sunday 12–5, or by appointment

MARKET VINEYARDS
location: 1950 Keene Road, Building S, Richland, WA 99352
phone: 509-396-4798
web: www.marketvineyards.com
hours: Thursday through Sunday 12–6 or by appointment

SUN RIVER VINTNERS
location: 9312 West 10th Avenue, Kennewick, WA 99336
phone: 509-627-3100
web: www.sunrivervintners.com
hours: By appointment only

Walla Walla
WINE COUNTRY

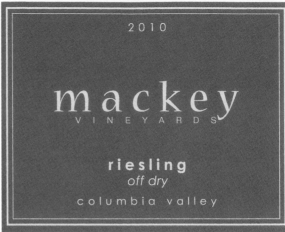

2010

mackey
VINEYARDS

riesling
off dry
columbia valley

WALLA WALLA VINEYARD
SPRING VALLEY VINEYARD
WASHINGTON

ESTATE GROWN 2006

Frederick
RED WINE

ALC 15.4% BY VOL.

W A L L A   W A L L A   V A L L E Y

Maddily

Rosè

ROBISON RANCH CELLARS

DINNER
BELL RED
2008

Vintage Red Wine

GRANTWOOD

CABERNET
SAUVIGNON

2008 WALLA WALLA VALLEY

MANNINA
CELLARS
M
2010
CABERNET SAUVIGNON
WALLA WALLA VALLEY

MANSION CREEK CELLARS
Columbia Valley
2008 WALDHEIM CUVÉE
Red Wine
14.8% ALC. BY VOL.   750ML

plumb
2007 CABERNET SAUVIGNON
COLUMBIA VALLEY

SLEIGHT OF HAND
CELLARS
Simply
Magical
Wines
THE ILLUSIONIST
2008
Columbia Valley Cabernet Sauvignon

TEMPUS
CELLARS
2009
RIESLING
COLUMBIA VALLEY

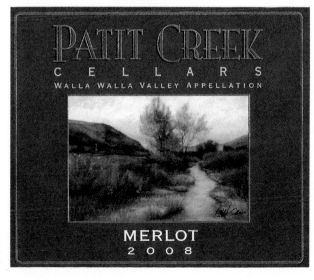

PATIT CREEK
CELLARS
WALLA WALLA VALLEY APPELLATION
MERLOT
2 0 0 8

WALLA WALLA
SPRING VALLEY VINEYARD
WASHINGTON
estate grown 2010
walla walla valley
DERBY
cabernet sauvignon
ALC. 14.9% BY VOL.

Walla Walla West
WineTrail

Whitman Mission

Be sure to slow down going through Lowden on Highway 12 and not just because of the speed limit. Lowden is the home of iconic L'Ecole No. 41 and Woodward Canyon wineries, and, with their side-by-side location, these wineries are a convenient stop traveling to or from Walla Walla.

However, these are but two among many splendid wineries on this WineTrail that offer a diversity of wines and tasting-room experiences. Many are well established, some are brand-new, but all possess a passionate desire to make great wine. At the end of the day, your biggest challenge could be identifying your favorite. All of these wineries are good and each offers some Kodak moments.

Walla Walla WineTrail West

1. Woodward Canyon Winery
2. L'Ecole No 41
3. Waterbrook Winery
4. Glencorrie
5. Cougar Crest Estate Winery
6. Reininger Winery
7. Three Rivers Winery
8. Bunchgrass Winery
9. Grantwood Winery
10. Skylite Cellars
11. Canoe Ridge Vineyard
12. Gramercy Cellars
13. Foundry Vineyards
14. Bergevin Lane Vineyards

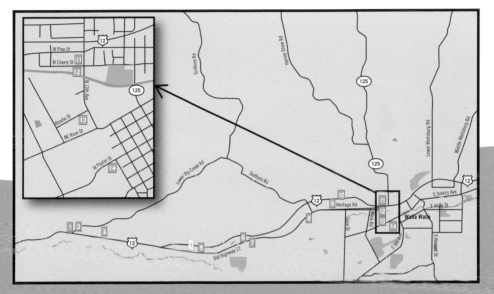

Region: **Walla Walla Wine Country**

\# of tasting rooms on tour: **14**

\# of satellite tasting rooms: **1**

Estimate # of days for tour: **3**

Getting around: **Car**

Key Events: ❑ **Events sponsored by Walla Walla Valley Wine Alliance: Spring Release Weekend (first full weekend of May); Balloon Stampede Weekend (second full weekend of May); Vintage Walla Walla (first full weekend of June); Entwine: An Auction to support Walla Walla Arts, Wine, and Education (mid-October); and Holiday Barrel Tasting (first full weekend of December). See www.wallawallawine.com/events for details and ticketing.**

Tips: ❑ **Three Rivers Winery offers a 3-hole golf course (free).**
❑ **Be sure and view the artwork at Woodward Canyon.**
❑ **Consider using a limousine service.**

 Best: ❑ **Gift shop: L'Ecole No 41**
❑ **Gift shop and picnicking: Waterbrook Winery**
❑ **Gift shop: Cougar Crest Estate Winery**
❑ **Gift shop and picnicking: Three Rivers Winery**

Woodward Canyon Winery

Located off Highway 12 in Lowden is the 1870s farmhouse that serves as Woodward Canyon's primary tasting room. Next to this charming room is the new Reserve House, built for private tastings and special events. If you get a chance to experience the Reserve

One of the original bonded wineries in the Walla Walla Valley

House, do so. It's lovely, especially when owner Rick Small is pouring and sharing his zeal. In fact, the Reserve House definitely makes my top 10 list of winemaker-dinner venues.

Started in 1981 by Rick and his wife, Darcey Fugman-Small, Woodward Canyon is among the group of original wineries that served as the "starter dough" for the whole Walla Walla Valley wine industry. Rick honed his self-taught winemaking skills in the mid-'70s by collaborating with Gary Figgins, who would go on to create famed Leonetti Cellar. Rick believes that "intensity is key," and he is passionate about Woodward Canyon's vineyard, spending a great deal of time there as well as working with select vineyards in Columbia Valley, Horse Heaven Hills and, of course, Walla Walla Valley. His philosophy remains the same: quality over quantity, and the numerous awards throughout the years speak volumes about Woodward Canyon's success.

Woodward Canyon's winemaker, Kevin Mott, produces about 15,000 cases annually. Its premium wines include cabernet sauvignon, merlot, Bordeaux blends, chardonnay, sauvignon blanc, and riesling. In addition, Woodward Canyon diverges from Bordeaux-only wines, to make dolcetto and barbera wines as well. Woodward Canyon also makes a second "declassified" label wine called Nelms Road, known for its excellent value.

Each year since 1992, Woodward Canyon has selected an original artwork to adorn the label of its top-quality cabernet sauvignon. At Woodward Canyon, art is for everyone. For WineTrail enthusiasts visiting this winery, art can be seen on a canvas and tasted from a bottle.

WOODWARD CANYON WINERY
opened: 1981
winemaker(s): Kevin Mott
location: 11920 West Highway 12, Lowden, WA 99360
phone: 509-525-4129
web: www.woodwardcanyon.com
e-mail: getthedirt@woodwardcanyon.com
fee: Tasting fee refunded with purchase
hours: Daily 10–5
amenities: Gift Shop, Online Store, Restaurant/Food Pairings, RV/Bus Parking, Tours, Vineyard on Premise, Wheelchair Accessible
connect: 🐦 f

L'Ecole No 41

Whatever you do, don't skip school whenever you pass through Lowden on old Highway 12. Specifically, be in attendance at the Walla Walla Valley's iconic L'Ecole No 41 winery, housed in a former "Frenchtown" schoolhouse. In the past, a rendering of this 1915 building adorned L'Ecole No 41's distinctive labels, drawn in 1983 by then-8-year-old Ryan Campbell when the winery was established. The new "sepia" label presents a much more classic image and feel for this old structure.

Established in 1983, L'Ecole No 41 is the Walla Walla Valley's third-oldest winery, with only Woodward Canyon and Leonetti Cellar being a little older. Today, L'Ecole No 41 produces about 35,000 cases annually, guided by a philosophy of traditional hands-on winemaking. Its owners, Megan and Martin Clubb, are clear about their goal: "To achieve clean, ripe, stylistically expressive and aromatic wines that let the individual site characteristics of our vineyards shine through." While Martin spends most of his time these days managing the vineyards, winemaker Mike Sharon is usually at the winery overseeing a mountain of chores.

This schoolhouse of bygone days will take you back in time; the sounds, the smells, and even the fine craftsmanship of the building itself will have you imagining the sounds of laughing children playing at recess. As you walk inside, check out the cast-iron school bell at the entrance. In the upstairs tasting room, you will notice an old chalkboard now used to list L'Ecole N° 41's wines and prices. A stained-glass replica of L'Ecole No 41 gracefully sits center stage behind the wine bar. The gift shop offers a variety of wine-related items and L'Ecole No 41 logo–bedecked clothing and gear. The tasting room staff field questions about L'Ecole No 41 and the winemaking process with patience and engaging smiles. They are, by all appearances, very well schooled.

L'ECOLE NO 41
opened: 1983
winemaker(s): Mike Sharon
location: 41 Lowden School Road, Lowden, WA 99360-0000
phone: 509-525-0940
web: www.lecole.com
e-mail: info@lecole.com
fee: Tasting fee refunded with purchase
hours: Daily 10–5; closed New Year's Day, Easter, 4th of July, Thanksgiving and Christmas; closed 1 p.m. December 24 and 31
amenities: Gift Shop, Mailing List, Online Store, Picnic Area, RV/Bus Parking, Tours, Wheelchair Accessible, Wine Club
connect: 🐦 f

⭐ **BEST Gift shop**

Waterbrook Winery

Opened in 2009 (coincidentally on its 25th anniversary), Waterbrook Winery's new tasting pavilion is much more than a simple tasting room. It's a statement — a statement about Waterbrook Winery's amazing success story as well as a commentary about the Washington wine industry as a whole. You can't help but be impressed by the contemporary Northwest-

style, 5,000-square-foot facility and more than a little curious about experiencing the award-winning wines that brought you here.

Situated on 75 acres, Waterbrook Winery's tasting center is where most visitors will come and linger. Expansive floor-to-ceiling windows provide a view of the 53,000-square-foot production facility beyond the pond. As you swirl and sip, try to imagine the 10,000 wine barrels resting in the production facility as they age wine for Waterbrook and other Precept Wine Brand labels. This is production on an advanced scale.

The friendly tasting room staff will guide visitors through a robust line-up of winemaker John Freeman's creations, which include dry whites, crisp rosés, and smooth but complex reds. My personal favorites are Waterbrook's varietally true chardonnay and its signature "Mélange Noir," which answers the age-old question "What do you get when you blend merlot, cabernet franc, cabernet sauvignon, and sangiovese?" Answer: liquid joy.

Inside the tasting room, there's plenty to marvel at, including the high ceiling with its huge beams, the natural earth tones, and the pleasing textures. The space mirrors the beauty of the surrounding Walla Walla Valley's rolling wheatfields and the Blue Mountains beyond. Lucky visitors on weekend nights can spring for a cheese plate and a glass (or two) of Waterbrook wines, and retreat to the outside patio and contemplate the meaning of life. Or, you can do what I do and relish the moment.

WATERBROOK WINERY
opened: 1984
winemaker(s): John Freeman
location: 10518 West Highway 12, Walla Walla, WA 99362
phone: 509-522-1262
web: www.waterbrook.com
e-mail: info@waterbrook.com
fee: Tasting fee
hours: Sunday through Thursday 10–6; Friday and Saturday 10–7
amenities: Gift Shop, Online Store, Picnic Area, Private Events, Tours, Weddings, Wheelchair Accessible, Wine Club
connect: ◼

BEST Gift shop and picnicking

Glencorrie ④

GLENCORRIE
opened: 2009
winemaker(s): Charlie Hoppes
location: 8052 Old Highway 12,
Walla Walla, WA 99362
phone: 509-525-2585
web: www.glencorrie.com
e-mail: MelanieLeathers@glencorrie.com
fee: Tasting fee refunded with purchase
hours: Thursday through Monday 10–6
amenities: Online Store, Picnic Area, Private Events,
RV/Bus Parking, Vineyard on Premise, Weddings,
Wheelchair Accessible, Wine Club, Winemaker Dinners
connect: 🐦 📘

www.winetrailsnw.com/wineries/glencorrie

Cougar Crest Estate Winery 5

The environmentally friendly, $3.2 million Walla Walla facility is downright sumptuous. There's plenty of space to sit, relax, marvel at fine art — which includes selected works by Jeffrey Hill and Karen Ehart — and, of course, taste award-winning wine. Inside the Prairie-style facility, visitors bask in natural light streaming from windows positioned in the dramatic cupola above. You can purchase a glass of wine, camp out in front of the stone fireplace, and take in peek-a-boo views of the production area.

Dave and Deborah Hansen, the owners of Cougar Crest Estate Winery, take pride in the fact that their labels bear the word "estate." Relying on earth-friendly, sustainable practices, Dave manages their vineyards, which are located just south of Walla Walla on the Oregon side of the state line. When most mortals would be sleeping, he might be turning on the wind machines to prevent a frosty cold snap from harming the vines. With fall's crush, it's then time for winemaker Deborah to take over. In this role, her scientific training as a pharmacist comes in very handy. Deborah's minimalist winemaking style calls for careful extraction of the tannins and judicious use of oak to preserve the varietal character of the fruit. It's in the blending of the wine that science is set aside in favor of an experienced palate to derive the best blends.

For me, Cougar Crest Estate Winery's Dedication red table wines reflect this art of blending. The Hansens chose the wines' name to honor the sacrifice and professionalism shown by Portland-based Doernbecher Children's Hospital staff when saving their daughter following a life-threatening injury. With their layered complexity and wonderful mouthfeel, Cougar Crest's Dedication wines never disappoint.

COUGAR CREST ESTATE WINERY
opened: 2001
winemaker(s): Deborah Hansen
location: 50 Frenchtown Road, Walla Walla, WA 99362
phone: 509-529-5980
web: www.cougarcrestwinery.com
e-mail: info@cougarcrestwinery.com
fee: Tasting fee refunded with purchase
hours: Daily 10–5
amenities: Art Gallery, Gift Shop, Newsletter/Blog, Online Store, Pet Friendly, Picnic Area, RV/Bus Parking, Tours, Wheelchair Accessible, Wine Club, Wines by the Glass
connect: 🐦 f

⭐ **BEST Gift shop**

Reininger Winery

Winemaking has a way of attracting people from different career fields. Washington's wine scene includes many lawyers, doctors, engineers, and accountants who pick up winemaking

as a second career. But how about those whose résumés include mountaineer and climbing guide? Such is the case with Charles Reininger of Reininger Winery.

After working as a mountain guide for many years, Charles hung up his ice axe, moved to the Walla Walla Valley, and married Tracy Tucker, a Walla Walla native. That was back in the early '90s. It was around this time that

Charles caught the wine bug and began assisting at Waterbrook Winery, dabbling in home winemaking on the side. For most mountain guides, their reward is in the journey itself. For winemakers, their reward is to create the ultimate expression of the grape, its true varietal character. As Charles notes on the winery's website, "Wine is the adventure of the soul." We submit, however, that the destination can be great, too, whether it is a mountain summit or recognition by *Wine & Spirits* as being one of America's top 40 wineries (2005).

Reininger Winery produces small lots of Walla Walla Valley merlot, cabernet sauvignon, and syrah, in addition to its Helix-labeled wines, which are made with fruit from the Columbia Valley. Much of the fruit for the Reininger label comes from nearby Ash Hollow Vineyard, owned in part by the Reiningers.

The Reiningers' tasting room is more of a tasting pavilion, featuring a fusion of basalt harvested from the Snake River in northern Walla Walla County; reclaimed potato-shed wood; zinc-covered countertops, and finely crafted cabinetry. One particularly aesthetic touch are the vines intertwined around the perimeter of the tasting bar. This is a grand tasting room that invites all who trek here to linger longer and enjoy the stellar line-up of wines.

REININGER WINERY
opened: 1997
winemaker(s): Chuck Reininger
location: 5858 Old Highway 12, Walla Walla, WA 99362
phone: 509-522-1994
web: www.reiningerwinery.com
e-mail: info@reiningerwinery.com
fee: Tasting fee refunded with purchase
hours: Daily 10–6; closed major holidays
amenities: Gift Shop, Mailing List, Newsletter/Blog, Online Store, Picnic Area, RV/Bus Parking, Tours, Wheelchair Accessible, Wine Club, Wines by the Glass
connect: ◼

Three Rivers Winery 7

Midway between Lowden and Walla Walla sits the 16-acre site of Three Rivers Winery — plenty of space to sample wine, shop for merchandise, and play golf. Golf? Yes, Three Rivers is unique among Washington wineries; it comes equipped with a short, three-hole golf course. What's more, the golfing is free.

This is a destination winery for a variety of reasons. Foremost is the sheer size of the complex, which is composed of a winery, tasting room, gift shop, conference room, and outdoor deck. At 18,000 square feet, there's plenty of room to host your next corporate event or join a swarm of other wine tasters at the generous tasting room bar. The gift shop is one of the largest in the state, with enough stock to cross everything off next year's Christmas list.

The structure itself is an inviting contemporary-style building with massive entrance doors, an interior with high-trussed ceilings, a huge stone-hearth fireplace, and an ample deck featuring one of the top views in Washington, courtesy of the Blue Mountains in the distance. It's an ideal wedding venue or corporate event space as well, all of which added to the allure of its current owner, William Foley, a California businessman who includes a number of other wineries in his portfolio, including Firestone.

The tasting fee varies depending upon what wines you sample, with a higher fee charged for reserve wines. We recommend that you indulge in the

reserves and experience why winemaker Holly Turner has garnered so many awards and high praise. A few sips will reveal why local readers of the Walla Walla *Union Bulletin Newspaper* voted Three Rivers Winery "Best Local Winery" five years in a row. Just remember to pack your 9-iron. Fore!

THREE RIVERS WINERY
opened: 1999
winemaker(s): Holly Turner
location: 5641 Old Highway 12, Walla Walla, WA 99362
phone: 509-526-9463
web: www.threeriverswinery.com
e-mail: info@threeriverswinery.com
fee: Tasting fee applies; more for reserve wines
hours: Daily 10–5; closed major holidays
amenities: Gift Shop, Online Store, Picnic Area, Private Events, RV/Bus Parking, Tours, Vineyard on Premise, Weddings, Wheelchair Accessible, Wine Club
connect: 🐦 📘

⭐ **BEST Gift shop and picnicking**

Bunchgrass Winery

Tom Olander, sales and marketing director for Bunchgrass Winery, uncorked a bottle of its Bordeaux blend with the intriguing name of "Triolet." Naturally, I had to ask my host from where the name Triolet was derived. It would seem all five owners of Bunchgrass Winery are well-read individuals equipped with college degrees, teaching credentials and a shelf full of books in the tasting room as tribute to their love affair with the English language. Pouring a deep purple sample of their red blend, Tom noted that a triolet is a one-stanza French poem of eight lines; the first, fourth and seventh lines are identical, as are the second and final lines. In a triolet, all the lines are in iambic tetrameter. Of course, I couldn't let this alone. So here's my attempt at a triolet which I call "Harvest Near":

Throughout the valley, the vines grow faster,
The warmth of summer sends tendrils twining
Among green grapes — each sun-lit cluster
Throughout the valley, the vines grow faster,
Swelling sugars turn pulp alabaster
Growers keep watch for weather's warning
Throughout the valley, the vines grow faster,
The warmth of summer sends tendrils twining.

Among Walla Walla Wineries, Bunchgrass Winery is a Lazarus of sorts. In 1997, Roger Cockerline began crafting small batches of premium wine with grapes from his now-dormant family vineyard. His plan was to eventually shut the winery down and enjoy his retirement. However, an unforeseen partnership came to pass to revitalize Bunchgrass Winery.

Situated in a 1943 restored dairy barn, Bunchgrass Winery is a tad small for moving barrels around, but just perfect

for those visitors who are into quaintness. Quality over quantity is the mantra here. Long in barrel, long in bottle, Bunchgrass wines aren't rushed to market. Let's just say the owners are exercising their own take on poetic license.

BUNCHGRASS WINERY
opened: 1997
winemaker(s): William vonMetzger
location: 151 Bunchgrass Lane, Walla Walla, WA 99362-9588
phone: 509-540-8963
web: www.bunchgrasswinery.com
e-mail: info@BunchgrassWinery.com
fee: Complimentary wine tasting
hours: Saturday 11–4 April through December or by appointment
amenities: Mailing List, Newsletter/Blog, Online Store, Picnic Area, RV/Bus Parking, Tours, Wheelchair Accessible, Wine Club
connect: ■

Grantwood Winery

 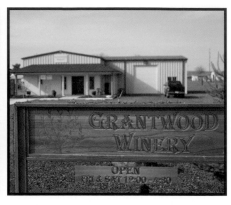

Joe Grant

Retirees Joe Grant and Doris Wood (get it...Grant-Wood) have been making wine for the past nine years using only Walla Walla grapes most notably the produce of Les Collines and Pepper Bridge. Albeit a small quantity — only 200 cases per year — it embodies the true definition of artisan winery. These are big wines and won't disappoint fans of full-bodied reds (which I count myself among them).

Although both have their roots in the Walla Walla Valley, Joe took a side trip for a few decades and worked in the space industry in Livermore, CA. In between sips, you can learn about his rich background and discover why he returned to Walla Walla. I suspect it had to do in large part to his life partner, Doris.

Be sure and pet the family dog — she's one of the stars featured in the Winery Dogs of Washington book!

GRANTWOOD WINERY
opened: 2010
winemaker(s): Joe Grant
location: 2428 Heritage Road, Walla Walla, WA 99362
phone: 509-301-9546
web: grantwoodwinery.com
e-mail: www.grantwood@charter.net
fee: Complimentary wine tasting
hours: Friday and Saturday 12:30–4:30 or by appointment
amenities: Picnic Area, RV/Bus Parking, Wheelchair Accessible
connect:

Skylite Cellars 🔟

Skylite Cellars produces wine under two different labels: the Skylite Cellars brand and the Hiney Wine label. Two labels — but one unifying theme: passion. A love story is behind the creation of Skylite Cellars, that of Tom Hodgins and his focus on growing a radio empire in Eastern Washington and his wife,

Cheryl, whose farming background included driving tractors and planting gardens. As divergent as their backgrounds may have, the couple has one vital interest in common, and that is wine.

Skylite Cellars' main tasting room, just west of town on Campbell Road, is a high-ceilinged space with a spiral staircase taking center stage. Upon walking into this tasting room, your

first reaction will likely be "Wow!" It is readily apparent that a lot of creative energy went into this space. There's ample parking, a peek-a-boo view of the barrel room from an upstairs window, and a terrific mural on an interior wall of the tasting room.

Consultant winemaker Robert Smasne and winemaker Robert Matiko produce small quantities of "distinctive tasting wines for the discerning wine lover." The 5-acre Skylite Vineyard supplies the fruit for cabernet sauvignon and merlot, and other varieties are sourced from select vineyards in the Walla Walla and Columbia valleys. But Hiney Wine, Skylite's second label, is the real attention getter. With its "world famous" red wine and slogans such as "You only go around once in life, so grab all the Hiney Wine you can get!" "Feel my Hiney," and "Uncork the Hiney," it's obvious that Tom and his cohorts don't take themselves too seriously. They're all about having a great time while making great wine. Bottoms up!

SKYLITE CELLARS
opened: 2005
winemaker(s): Robert Smasne and Robert Matiko
location: 25 South Campbell Road, Walla Walla, WA 99362
phone: 509-529-8000
web: www.skylitecellars.com
e-mail: info@skylitecellars.com
fee: Tasting fee refunded with purchase
hours: Monday through Saturday 12–5; Sunday 12–4
amenities: Online Store, Pet Friendly, RV/Bus Parking, Wheelchair Accessible, Wine Club
connect: 🐦 📘

Canoe Ridge Vineyard

Merlot is such an elegant wine, great by itself or paired with food. Rich and velvety, with flavors of chocolate, cherry, and raspberry — what's not to like? Merlot loves to grow in eastern Washington, particularly in the Horse Heaven Hills American Viticultural Area (AVA), which also happens to be the home of Canoe Ridge Vineyard. (**WineTrail Note**: Canoe Ridge was named by explorers Lewis and Clark on their historic journey west. From the Columbia River, the massive ridge looks like an upside-down canoe.) Here, the proximity to the weather-moderating Columbia River, hot summers, cool nights and dry conditions all conspire to create the perfect growing conditions for merlot, cabernet sauvignon and other European varieties.

A visit to the Canoe Ridge winery, on the outskirts of downtown Walla Walla, offers a study in merlot. True, Canoe Ridge Vineyard does produce a full line-up of elegant, easy-to-quaff red wines, but at the winery, you have the opportunity to sample merlot of different vintages and qualities. And while the winery focuses on red wines, it does make a limited quantity of whites, including chardonnay, gewürztraminer and riesling.

Owned by Seattle-based Precept brands, Canoe Ridge's winemaking philosophy begins in the vineyard, where the level and quality of ripeness become the foundation of every new vintage. Each winemaking effort aims to honor the uniqueness of the Canoe Ridge vineyard site, reflecting its individuality through the depth, nuance, concentration, and balance of Canoe Ridge wines. It's a winning formula that brings together a big wine conglomerate (by Washington standards), exceptional fruit and local talent to create wonderfully approachable wines.

CANOE RIDGE VINEYARD
opened: 1989
winemaker(s): Bill Murray
location: 1102 West Cherry Street, Walla Walla, WA 99362
phone: 509-525-1843
web: www.canoeridgevineyard.com
e-mail: info@canoeridgevineyard.com
fee: Tasting fee refunded with purchase
hours: Thursday through Monday 11–5
amenities: Gift Shop, Online Store, Pet Friendly, Tours, Wheelchair Accessible, Wine Club
connect:

Gramercy Cellars 🕛

"I have a great idea. I think we should quit our jobs, sell everything we own and move to Walla Walla to start a winery," states the goateed man in the short video. "That is the dumbest freaking thing I've ever heard," replies the finely attired woman to her partner. Such is the hilarious opening to a two-and-a-half minute portrayal of Greg and Pam Harrington's real-life leap into the winemaking business. New York–based sommelier Greg convinced Pam, his wife, to leave their already full (some would say "enviable") lives and relocate to rural Walla Walla, where "they think the subway is a sandwich shop." Their adventure into country living makes for a YouTube video; view it and more on the Gramercy Cellars website; it pretty much sums up their lives since 2005.

The tasting room resides in the same building where the Amavi winery got its start, but the similarity ends there. Instead, the interior has been transformed into a "man-cave", complete with stuffed leather chairs, bar stools, flat-screen television and requisite dartboard. Often, Steve Wells, Gramercy's "Director of Awesome," can be found there, regaling visitors with his over-the-top personality.

Greg has the distinction of achieving Master Sommelier status at age 26 — that's when most of us mortals were trying to figure out what we should do in life. But with his background, Greg experienced wines of the world at a young age and learned what makes Bordeaux great, why the pinots of Burgundy shine, and just how heavenly the flavors of Italy's Piedmont barolos are. The importance of "place" rings true with all of these wines, and in the wine world, we call that typicity. When it comes to Gramercy Cellars, we also call it damned good.

GRAMERCY CELLARS
opened: 2007
winemaker(s): Greg Harrington
location: 635 North 13th Avenue, Walla Walla, WA 99362
phone: 509-876-2427
web: www.gramercycellars.com
e-mail: info@gramercycellars.com
fee: Complimentary wine tasting
hours: Saturday 11–5 or by appointment
amenities: Newsletter/Blog, Online Store, Wheelchair Accessible, Wine Club
connect: 🐦 f

Foundry Vineyards 13

Imagine a "creative blending of fine wine and contemporary art" and you have Foundry Vineyards, or FV for short. It's true. At Foundry Vineyards, art takes many forms, from bronze sculpture and colorful glasswork to estate wines. Even the labels on the bottles reflect modern art, as exemplified on FV's 2006 Artisan Blend label, featuring Deborah Butterfield's horse-inspired sculpture (see Practical Stuff, "Decoding a Washington Wine Label").

Located a short drive west of downtown, FV's tasting room is Northwest contemporary in style, designed with lots of glass, steel, and concrete — a perfect space for showcasing the art within. The style also lends the room a sense of airiness and light. Here, visitors sampling Foundry Vineyard wines can't help but pause their sipping and gawk. Works of art hang on the wall or rest handsomely on pedestals. Of particular note are FV co-owner Squire Broel's works, which include imaginative paintings and sculpture (also celebrated on the Artisan Blend label, for the 2007 vintage). As Robert Mondavi stated in *Harvest of Joy*, "Making good wine is a skill. Fine wine is an art."

The brainchild of Walla Walla native Mark Anderson, Foundry Vineyards relies on grapes from the valley, including the fruit of his own 3.5-acre estate Stonemarker Vineyard, to produce premium wine. Mark and Squire's goal is to produce small lots of wine using traditional means, and to focus on a few select wines. This isn't the Baskin-Robbins of wineries, with 31 flavors to sample. I discovered a manageable sampling of their many-layered cabernet sauvignon, a Bordeaux blend called "Fire Red" and a white blend of chardonnay and viognier possessing just the right acidity. Mark makes fabulous wines, but then, it seems that all his projects turn into works of art.

FOUNDRY VINEYARDS
opened: 2006
winemaker(s): Ali Mayfield
location: 1111 Abadie Street, Walla Walla, WA 99362
phone: 509-529-0736
web: www.foundryvineyards.com
e-mail: info@foundryvineyards.com
fee: Tasting fee refunded with purchase
hours: Friday and Saturday 11–5
amenities: Art Gallery, Online Store, Pet Friendly, Picnic Area, Wheelchair Accessible, Wine Club
connect: 🐦 📘

Bergevin Lane Vineyards 14

If you spend any time in Walla Walla and dine at some of the city's finer restaurants, you may notice that one establishment serves a Bergevin Lane viognier. Another offers a Bergevin syrah. A trip to a nice bottle shop in town reveals a row of Bergevin wines. You might find yourself in the downtown Starbucks and overhear someone mention that they had Bergevin Lane's "Calico" White last night with their fresh halibut. By day three, you begin to detect a pattern and you ask, "'Where the hell is this Bergevin Lane Vineyard?'"

The Bergevin Lane facility comes fully equipped with a spacious winemaking/testing area and barrel storage area. Co-owner Gary Bergevin has learned from his experience with other wineries, including Canoe Ridge Vineyards, that size does matter.

Danish-born and -bred Steffan Jorgensen oversees the winemaking duties for Bergevin Lane Vineyards. With ample space and advanced equipment, Steffan plies his extensive experience gained from winemaking stints in France, Chile, and Sonoma. A peek into the production area often finds Steffan, with his shaved head and energetic smile, working his magic — perhaps close to achieving a final blend, with nose stuck in a just-swirled glass of red.

Amber Lane

Bergevin Lane's story is one of a collaborative effort between two women to produce premier wines. Gary's daughter, Annette Bergevin, and her partner, Amber Lane, have formed a hugely successful team to manage the sales and marketing, as well as the day-to-day operations, of Bergevin Lane. They must be doing something right. The emperor of wine himself, Robert M. Parker Jr., had this to say about Bergevin Lane's cabernet sauvignon, "Edge-free, fruit-driven decadence." Five simple words, but certainly just the right verbiage to convince WineTrail enthusiasts to stop in and take a swirl.

BERGEVIN LANE VINEYARDS
opened: 2001
winemaker(s): Dave Harvey
location: 1215 West Poplar Street, Walla Walla, WA 99362-2780
phone: 509-526-4300
web: www.bergevinlane.com
e-mail: info@bergevinlane.com
fee: Tasting fee refunded with purchase
hours: Spring-Summer, open daily Monday through Saturday 11–4:30 and Sunday 12–3; October through February Monday through Saturday 11–4:30 or by appointment
amenities: Gift Shop, Online Store, RV/Bus Parking, Tours, Wheelchair Accessible, Wine Club
connect: 🐦 f

Walla Walla
Downtown
WineTrail

Walla Walla Sweet Onions

Amazingly, you can drive to downtown Walla Walla, park your car, and visit more than 30 winery tasting rooms. With most of the area's hotels located downtown, it's the ultimate in wine-touring convenience. Don't forget to pack a good pair of walking shoes. And speaking of forgetting — after a day of wine tasting, good luck trying to remember where you parked your car!

Although devoid of vineyards, the Downtown WineTrail isn't lacking in any of the creature comforts. It has extraordinary restaurants, amazing shops, and friendly coffee bars offering a double-tall afternoon pick-me-up. Along the way, you will discover historic architecture and real estate offices featuring wine-country homes for sale. You may find yourself daydreaming of what it would be like to leave behind that dreary day job that handcuffs your soul and live in Walla Walla. Cabernet does have a way of enabling life-changing decisions!

Walla Walla Downtown WineTrail

1. Seven Hills Winery
2. Trio Vintners
3. Locati Cellars
4. Tero Estates
5. Flying Trout Wines
6. Lodmell Cellars
7. Don Carlo Vineyard
8. Glencorrie Tasting Room
9. Maison Bleue Family Winery
10. Spring Valley Vineyard
11. Kerloo Cellars
12. Sweet Valley Wines
13. Sapolil Cellars
14. Otis Kenyon Wine
15. Mark Ryan Winery
16. The Chocolate Shop
17. Rotie Cellars
18. Chateau Rollat Winery
19. DaMa Wines

20. Sinclair Estate Vineyard
21. Fort Walla Walla Cellars
22. Walla Faces
23. El Corazon Winery
24. Charles Smith Wines

25. Mansion Creek Cellars
26. Plumb Cellars
27. Forgeron Cellars
28. Walla Walla Village Winery
29. Morrison Lane Winery

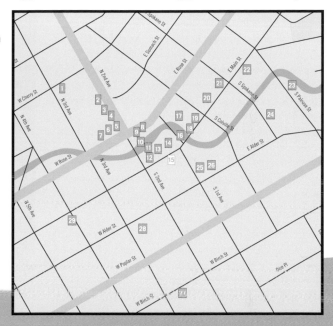

Region:	**Walla Walla Wine Country**
# of tasting rooms on tour:	**29**
# of satellite tasting rooms:	**1**
Estimate # of days for tour:	**6**
Getting around:	**Car and mostly foot**
Key Events:	❏ **Events sponsored by Walla Walla Valley Wine Alliance: Spring Release Weekend; Balloon Stampede Weekend; Vintage Walla Walla; Entwine: An Auction to support Walla Walla Arts, Wine, and Education; and Holiday Barrel Tasting. See www.wallawallawine.com/events for details and ticketing.**
Tips:	❏ **Saturdays are the best times to experience tasting rooms — most are open.**
	❏ **Great restaurants to choose from.**
	❏ **Consider using a limousine service.**
Best:	❏ **Best music venue and eats: Sapolil Cellars**
	❏ **Lodging: Walla Faces**
	❏ **Music venue: Charles Smith Wines**
	❏ **Gift shop: Forgeron Cellars**
	❏ **Music venue: Walla Walla Village Winery**

Seven Hills Winery

The Seven Hills Winery is located in the superbly restored Whitehouse-Crawford building in downtown Walla Walla. The award-winning restoration of this former lumber mill preserved the 100-year-old brick building, including its posts, its beams, and most importantly, its charm. You can find it listed in the National Historic Register. It turns out that this historic building is an excellent venue for making fine wine and tasting the finished product. You can view the sky-lit temperature- and humidity-controlled barrel room from the tasting room itself, thanks to a strategically placed picture window. The barrels themselves are the traditional Bordeaux-style 225-liter oak barrels that are prevalent throughout the industry. The barrels are also the source of the Seven Hills wine club's name, the Barrique Society. Nice touch.

Seven Hills Winery focuses on reds and enjoys a reputation for great balance, which it states is a "trinity of fruit, acidity, and tannin." This trinity of ingredients inspired the use of seven Irish trinity cross-knot symbols as part of the winery's logo — at least we at WineTrails Northwest choose to think so. Enjoy the wine right out of the bottle now or order it with your meal at the gourmet Whitehouse-Crawford Restaurant, also housed in the building. Alternatively, you can cellar this wine for years. Working closely with the grape growers of Red Mountain, Columbia Valley, and Walla Walla (especially the distinguished Seven Hills Vineyard), winemaker Casey McClellan makes single-vineyard wines and blends selectively to achieve, you guessed it, "harmony among fruit, acidity, and tannin."

I was just pondering … it's a good thing the winery doesn't use the 300-liter barrels often used in Australia to age its wines. Otherwise, the name of the wine club would have to be the "Hogshead Society."

SEVEN HILLS WINERY
opened: 1988
winemaker(s): Casey McClellan
location: 212 North 3rd Avenue, Walla Walla, WA 99362
phone: 509-529-7198
web: www.sevenhillswinery.com
e-mail: info@sevenhillswinery.com
fee: Tasting fee refunded with purchase
hours: Summer hours: Monday through Saturday 10–5, Sunday 10–2; Winter hours vary, call ahead
amenities: Newsletter/Blog, Online Store, Pet Friendly, Tours, Wheelchair Accessible, Wine Club
connect:

Trio Vintners ②

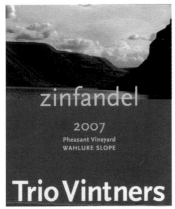

When it comes to tasting rooms, three key rules to follow are location, location, and location. With Trio Vintners' recent move to a ground-floor space in the historic Marcus Whitman Hotel, a floor it shares with Locati Cellars, Flying Trout Wines/Tero Estates, Lodmell Cellars, and Don Carlo Vineyard, it has accomplished two things. First, it is in a high-traffic location to which wine lovers seem to gravitate. Second, the Trio Vintners' tasting room benefits from the "co-opetition" found when wineries band together.

This is an ideal space for the relatively new owner of Trio Vintners, Karen LaBonte, to sell her non-Bordeaux wines. Not that her wine varietals are hard to find; it's just that you don't often see zinfandel, sangiovese, Mourvèdre, tempranillo, grenache, carménère, and rosé under one roof. The zinfandel, in particular,

got my attention, because I can count on just one finger the other wineries in Walla Walla that vinify zin: Forgeron Cellars. But the lineup of wines reflects Karen's penchant for unusual varietals, in particular, food-friendly wines that seem to shout to be paired with Mediterranean cuisine. Bearing that in mind, I thought the blend of sangio, Mourvèdre, and grenache called Riot (an anagram of Trio) was especially drinkable, and at $18 a bottle, a good buy. So I did.

You may be wondering how the name Trio Vintners came about, considering the fact that it has just one winemaker. It turns that out the original Trio Vintners was launched by three winemakers who had stained their hands purple at the Walla Walla Institute for Enology and Viticulture at Walla Walla Community College. Now under Karen's direction, the trio in Trio Vintners is represented by Washington's exceptional fruit, outstanding soils, and perfect climate for growing grapes. But by any other name, the zinfandel would taste just as delightful.

TRIO VINTNERS
opened: 2007
winemaker(s): Karen LaBonte
location: 6 West Rose Street, Suite 101, The Marcus Whitman, Walla Walla, WA 99362
phone: 509-529-8746
web: www.triovintners.com
e-mail: wine@triovintners.com
fee: Complimentary wine tasting
hours: Thursday through Sunday 11–5, or by appointment
amenities: Gift Shop, Mailing List, Online Store, Picnic Area, Wheelchair Accessible, Wine Club
connect: 🐦 📘

Locati Cellars

To those who have grown up in the valley, the name "Locati" is synonymous with Walla Walla sweet onions. The Locati family's roots (no pun intended) go back many generations to the pioneer settlers from Italy who made the Walla Walla Valley renowned for row crops — most famous of all, the illustrious Walla Walla sweet onion, which is harvested mid-June through September. The story goes that a French soldier stationed on the island of Corsica

(which is part of France, but geographically closer to Italy) pocketed a sweet onion seed and brought it to Walla Walla.

However, like many farming families in the valley, the Locatis have gone beyond row crops to grow premium wine grapes, and not just any ol' wine grapes, but varieties that come from their native land, such as sangiovese and barbera. Relying on the winemaking expertise of Matt Steiner (owner and winemaker for Stella Fino Winery), Michael Locati produces pasta-friendly wines, including pinot grigio, orange muscat, barbera, and sangiovese. Maybe it was because of the warm spring day, but my sample of their crisp, oh-so-refreshing pinot grigio had me tipping the glass to get the last drop.

Located in The Marcus Whitman, the Locati Cellars' tasting room features a small but inviting ambiance to taste wine. While tasting, you might just imagine a Walla Walla sweet onion recipe to pair with a juicy burger and a Locati Cellars' sangiovese. Drooling cups are optional.

LOCATI CELLARS
opened: 2009
winemaker(s): Michael Locati
location: 6 West Rose Street, Suite 102, The Marcus Whitman, Walla Walla, WA 99362
phone: 509-529-5871
web: www.locaticellars.com
e-mail: tastingroom@locaticellars.com
fee: Tasting fee refunded with purchase
hours: Monday through Thursday 1-5; Friday and Saturday 11–6; Sunday 11–4
amenities: Gift Shop, Online Store, Wheelchair Accessible, Wine Club

Tero Estates

Doug Roskelley

When visiting with Doug and Jan Roskelley at their winery/vineyard outside Milton-Freewater, one gets the sense that they have always lived there. But such is not the case. In 2007, they made the big leap from their home in Woodinville, Washington, trading a successful home-modeling business for a farm. However, if you're imagining a ramshackle farmhouse on a dusty plot of land, think again. No, their new life began with the purchase of the renowned 25-acre Windrow Vineyards, which had plenty of space to build a production facility and a new home. Needless to say, Doug's background as a remodeler has came in handy.

Of course, you have to come up with a memorable name when you launch a winery, and Doug worked and reworked various names, but came to a dead end. He was nearly ready to give it up, but then the idea hit him to combine the first two letters from his last name, Roskelley, with the first two letters of the last name of his winery partner and friend, Mike Tembreull. A little shuffling of letters and he came up with Tero Estates. The fact that "Tero" plays on the word *terroir* is a bonus.

At the Tero Estates tasting room, located at street level inside the Marcus Whitman Hotel, you can sample the wines of Tero Estates and Flying Trout. While Doug and Jan were getting started with their winery, they developed a strong friendship with Ashley Trout (winemaker for Flying Trout). Wanting to focus on winemaking and not be shackled with the business side of owning a winery, she's partnered with Doug and Jan.

WineTrail Tip: Don't miss Tero Estates' S.T. (Super Tuscan), a blend of cabernet with a sangiovese backbone. Bet you can't sample just one. It's pure Walla Walla heaven.

TERO ESTATES
opened: 2011
winemaker(s): Doug Roskelley
location: 6 West Rose Street, Suite 103, The Marcus Whitman, Walla Walla, WA 99362
phone: 541-203-0020
web: www.teroestates.com
e-mail: talk@teroestates.com
fee: Tasting fee refunded with purchase
hours: Sunday through Thursday 12–5; Friday and Saturday 10–6
amenities: Mailing List, Online Store, RV/Bus Parking, Tours, Wheelchair Accessible, Wine Club
connect: f

Flying Trout Wines

Ashley Trout, a transplant from Washington, D.C., somehow picked the Pacific Northwest to move to and, taking the "when in Rome, do as the Romans do" approach, found part-time work at a winery. Whereas most winemakers get into the business of making wine for their love of it, for Ashley, the reverse was the case. She discovered that she had a love for the work involved — the smell of the job, the labor in the vineyard, the mental exercise in terms of the biochemistry. It was the challenge of the unknown and the sensory bombardment that led to her to fall head over heels for wine.

A rock-climbing fall of 35 feet resulted in a long period of healing for Ashley, and it was during that period that she realized her career path really did center on making wine. Temporarily confined to a wheelchair, she couldn't participate in crush. However, because she spoke Spanish before she learned English, it wasn't long before Ashley came up with the idea of going to Argentina and working in a winery there. And so she became a bihemispheric winemaker, thanks to the diametric nature of the hemispheres' seasons. She also developed a deep affection for that noble Bordeaux grape variety Malbec.

Flying Trout (named such because Ashley has racked up considerable frequent flyer miles traveling all over the world) has a symbiotic relationship with Tero Estates and its owners, Doug and Jan Roskeller. Located on the Oregon side of Walla Walla Valley, Tero Estates' most noteworthy feature is its 25-acre Windrow Vineyard. It's the source of the fruit that Ashley uses for making Flying Trout wines, including that delectable Malbec!

FLYING TROUT WINES
opened: 2007
winemaker(s): Ashley Trout
location: 6 West Rose Street Suite 103, The Marcus Whitman, Walla Walla, WA 99362
phone: 541-203-0020
web: www.flyingtroutwines.com
e-mail: talk@flyingtroutwines.com
fee: Tasting fee refunded with purchase
hours: Sunday through Thursday 12–5; Friday and Saturday 10–6
amenities: Mailing List, Newsletter/Blog, Online Store, RV/Bus Parking, Tours, Wheelchair Accessible, Wine Club
connect: 🐦 f

Lodmell Cellars ⑥

I first met co-owner/winemaker Andrew Lodmell with his dogs Mazzy and Kimball, and although they were playing and romping around the winery during my visit, they kept a

close eye on their owner, Andrew Lodmell. In his mid-40s, with a tanned, whisker-stubbled face shaded under a well-worn baseball cap, Andrew has the look of an Eastern Washington farmer. Andrew pointed out that Mazzy and Kimball were once feral vineyard dogs, and they're still most comfortable playing among the 30 acres of Lodmell Vineyards wine grapes, located near the Snake River, 30 miles northwest of Walla Walla.

A few minutes with Andrew reveals his love of the land, and like other farmers-turned-winemakers in the valley, he's a farmer first, despite growing up in the shadow of Seattle and a winemaker second. A fourth-generation farmer, Andrew's great-grandfather established the family farm in the late 1800s. As it's often said, it all starts in the vineyard; you can't make good wine from bad grapes. Lodmell Vineyards' south-facing slope, high heat units, shallow soils, and arid conditions put plenty of stress on the grapes, and the result is intense flavor profiles. That's a good thing — a really good thing.

To allow Andrew the much-needed time to grow grapes, his sister Kristie Lodmell Kirin and her husband, Randy Kirin, focus on the business side of the winery. In addition to financing the operation, the Seattle-based couple (Kristie in particular) manages the Whitman Hotel-based tasting room, markets the wine, and handles the myriad piles of paperwork.

Before visiting a word of caution is needed here — budget a good half hour or more for your visit. The wines are just bloody good and time to savor them is required.

LODMELL CELLARS
opened: 2008
winemaker(s): Andrew Lodmell
location: 6 West Rose Street, Suite 104, The Marcus Whitman, Walla Walla, WA 99362
phone: 509-525-1285
web: www.lodmellcellars.com
e-mail: info@lodmellcellars.com
fee: Complimentary wine tasting
hours: Saturday 11–5, or by appointment
amenities: Mailing List, Online Store, Pet Friendly, Picnic Area, Wheelchair Accessible, Wine Club
connect: f

Don Carlo Vineyard

"We don't need no stinkin' wine glass," says a Don Carlo Vineyard devotee as he tipped the open bottle to his lips. Although done in jest, the urge to chug, rather than merely sip, is there. A wine glass is appropriate for sipping, but when you crave a big dose of cabernet, what's wrong with a little instant gratification?

Producing estate wines from — you guessed it — grapes grown in Don Carlo Vineyard, this relatively new winery to Walla Walla produces classic favorites such as chardonnay, merlot, and cabernet sauvignon. As you taste your way through this manageable portfolio, the word "expressive" may come to mind, because these wines convey the Walla Walla *terroir*. From the soft, round mouthfeel of the merlot to the layered, complex dark fruit flavors of the cabernet, these are nice wines to savor while enjoying the friendly chatter of owners Lori and Tim Kennedy as they work the tasting room.

Named in honor of Lori's Italian grandfather Carlo, the Kennedys opened a tasting room in a strategic location: a ground-floor retail space at the Marcus Whitman Hotel. Talk about a captive audience; most folks who flock to the hotel are on a mission to taste Walla Walla wines. Now, you don't even need to leave the hotel.

Here's an offbeat pairing to try at the Don Carlo tasting room: Don Carlo Vineyard wine with chocolate-dipped potato chips. It's like going to the Texas State Fair and noshing on doughnuts topped with chocolate-covered, deep-fried bacon. Forget the calories and enjoy the culinary journey! And that bowl of Tim's Cascade Style Potato Chips you spotted on the counter is no coincidence. Yes, dear reader, the "Tim" behind the counter pouring your sample is none other than Tim of Tim's Cascade Style Potato Chips, who has proven that barbecue-flavored chips really do pair well with merlot.

DON CARLO VINEYARD
opened: 2011
winemaker(s): Lori Kennedy
location: 6 West Rose Street, Suite 105, The Marcus Whitman, Walla Walla, WA 99362
phone: 509-540-5784
web: www.doncarlovineyard.com
e-mail: info@doncarlovineyard.com
fee: Tasting fee refunded with purchase
hours: Friday through Saturday 2–6
amenities: Online Store, RV/Bus Parking, Wheelchair Accessible, Wine Club
connect: 🐦 f

Glencorrie Tasting Room

As in life, finding the right balance in wine is the goal of all great winemakers; moderation is a good thing. Exceptional wines embody qualities of moderation: not too flabby, but not too sour either; just the right amount of oak; a fruit-forward taste on the front end and a long-lasting finish, perhaps with a lingering spice note (love that).

One evening in 2004, before they started Glencorrie winery,

brothers Ronn and Dean Coldiron were having dinner in Spokane, and the Walla Walla merlot they ordered just so happened to perfectly complement their meat dish. The flawless pairing and their subsequent "aha" moment gave definition to the wine style they were seeking: food-friendly wine to match a beef dish or a meal with rich sauces. We're talking opulent reds with layered flavors, tannins for structure, and strong acidity. This gave them the wine style they both loved and, like a compass, directed them to Walla Walla to start a winery.

It was a stroke of luck when 13 acres of prime real estate became available west of Walla Walla along old Highway 12. The choice acreage is south-facing, with excellent air drainage and the ideal soil for planting food-friendly Bordeaux varieties. The brothers contracted with family-owned, well-established vineyards in the Columbia Valley for their fruit (and continue to do so while waiting for their own vineyard to mature). Armed with the best fruit, they then secured the services of famed winemaker Charlie Hoppes.

That's an auspicious beginning, and it doesn't hurt that Ronn has a Ph.D. in geology and brother Dean's background is in finance. Like peas and carrots, peanut butter and jelly, the two complement one another.

GLENCORRIE TASTING ROOM
opened: 2009
winemaker(s): Charlie Hoppes
location: 6 East Rose Street, Walla Walla, WA 99362
phone: 509-525-2585
web: www.glencorrie.com
e-mail: MelanieLeathers@glencorrie.com
fee: Tasting fee refunded with purchase
hours: Thursday through Monday 10–6
amenities: Mailing List, Online Store, Private Events, Wheelchair Accessible, Wine Club
connect: 🐦 f

Maison Bleue Family Winery

> "Maison Bleue Family Winery may be the most compelling new producer uncovered in my 2010 trip to Washington." — Jay Miller, Robert Parker's *The Wine Advocate*

Seattle magazine seconded Jay Miller's sentiments when it named Maison Bleue Family Winery the Best Emerging Winery of 2011, describing Jon Meuret-Martinez's wines as "food friendly," being fruit-forward, soft, low in tannins, and possessing just the right acidity. Maison Bleue has joined the ranks of other Washington wineries with stellar reputations for Rhône-style wines.

Jon, in his thirties, is one of a handful of young winemakers who are members of a new generation taking Washington to the next level of quality wine. A transplant from Kansas City, Missouri, he left his profession as a dentist to pursue his winemaking passion. A trip to France sparked his deep love for Rhône-style wines, which led to intensive wine coursework at Missouri State, Virginia Tech, and University of California-Davis. (Note: Many of us wouldn't think of Missouri as a wine-producing state, but the first designated American Viticultural Area, or AVA, was in Missouri.)

Armed with some serious winemaking knowledge and a preferred style of wine, Jon then had to determine where to ply his newfound passion. He decided on Washington state because he believed the best Rhône grape varieties come from here. Ever the student, he picked up a certificate from Washington State University's (WSU) distinguished enology program along the way.

Jon was quick to develop relationships with established vineyards such as Alder Ridge, Boushey, French Creek, and Olsen — all within an hour's drive of each other. This gives him ready access to Rhône grape varieties such as syrah, grenache, Mourvèdre, Marsanne, and viognier. Maison Bleue sure beats pulling teeth.

MAISON BLEUE FAMILY WINERY
opened: 2008
winemaker(s): Jon Meuret-Martinez
location: 20 North 2nd Avenue, Walla Walla, WA 99362
phone: 509-786-2307
web: www.mbwinery.com
e-mail: info@mbwinery.com
fee: Tasting fee refunded with purchase
hours: Thursday through Sunday 12–5
amenities: Mailing List, Online Store, Wheelchair Accessible, Wine Club
connect: f

Spring Valley Vineyard 🔟

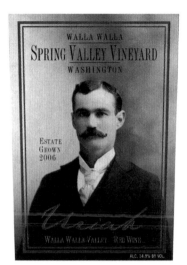

The tasting room of Spring Valley Vineyard is immersed in history. Spring Valley's story is one of a homesteading farm family, the Corkrums, who settled in Walla Walla Valley in 1865. Their offspring were later to marry and introduce the names of Derby and Elvin into the mix. On the tasting room walls, you see enlarged photos of the Spring Valley Vineyard, neatly kept rows of vineyards surrounded by golden wheatfields. Pictures of key family figures adorn the wine labels, as do their names, such as Uriah, Frederick, and Derby. Don't be surprised if one of the relatives is working the tasting room.

After the tragic death of winemaker/manager Devin Corkrum Derby in 2004, the Derbys turned to Ste. Michelle Wine Estates for assistance. In 2005, Ste. Michelle Wine Estates agreed to lease the vineyard and winery, and purchase the Spring Valley Vineyard wine brand. Ste. Michelle's decision to invest proved a smart business decision. Since that time, Spring Valley Vineyard has had four separate wines place on the prestigious *Wine Spectator* Top 100 list of the world's wines. Be sure to sample the "Uriah," a Bordeaux blend that The Wine Advocate described as "a complex fruitful mouth of blackberry, currant, and cherry with a hint of licorice and leather." Yum. And if you have the opportunity to sample them, the "Frederick," "Derby," "Katherine," "Nina Lee," and "Mule Skinner" vintages demonstrate the powerful and firm finish intensity of these 100 percent estate wines.

If time permits, take the short, 20-minute drive out of town and check out the 1,100-acre Spring Valley Vineyard and wheat farm. And take your camera. You may very well want to enlarge these pictures for one of your walls at home. Cheers to seven generations!

SPRING VALLEY VINEYARD
opened: 1999
winemaker(s): Serge Laville
location: 18 North 2nd Avenue, Walla Walla, WA 99362
phone: 509-525-1506
web: www.springvalleyvineyard.com
e-mail: info@springvalleyvineyard.com
fee: Tasting fee refunded with purchase
hours: Thursday through Monday 10–4:30, Sunday 11–4:30
amenities: Gift Shop, Mailing List, Online Store, Tours, Wheelchair Accessible, YouTube
connect: f

Kerloo Cellars

Photos by Tom Volk

I surveyed the wine list at one of my favorite Walla Walla restaurants, Saffron Mediterranean Kitchen, when proprietor Island Ainsworth came to my aid. "If you're looking for something to go with leg of lamb, I'd suggest the Kerloo tempranillo." Lately, I'd been enjoying Washington's version of this noble Spanish grape, and her recommendation was spot on.

As I relished the balanced complexity of Kerloo's tempranillo, I half-expected its winemaker, Ryan Crane, to walk into Saffron for dinner. Walla Walla is one of those towns that is small enough to bump into acquaintances with regularity. If he had, I would have ventured a compliment to him for showcasing an unusual red grape variety and adding to my already exceedingly long bucket list for when I visit Spain's Rioja region, home of tempranillo.

Listening to an inner voice, which sounded strangely like a whooping crane, "ker-loo, ker-loo," Ryan and Reneé Crane left behind their comfortable West Seattle urban life and moved to Walla Walla to follow a long-held dream of becoming vintners; to create something that has their signature on it and to create a legacy for their children. It takes guts, hard work, some luck, and a willingness to go without, for a brighter future. It also takes a friendly soul, and it wasn't long before members of the winemaking community came to Ryan's aid, most notably Va Piano Vineyards' Justin Wylie, who provided space, winemaking tools, and access to his vineyard's oh-so-beautiful estate syrah.

Now recognized as one of Walla Walla's up and coming young winemakers, Ryan can often be found welcoming guests and pouring samples for visitors to Kerloo's downtown tasting room. It's an experience that reinforces the overall vision of the winery — to create wine that expresses a "sense of place."

KERLOO CELLARS
winemaker(s): Ryan Crane
location: 16 North Second Avenue, Walla Walla, WA 99362
phone: 206-349-0641
web: www.kerloocellars.com
e-mail: info@kerloocellars.com
fee: Tasting fee refunded with purchase
hours: Friday and Saturday 11–4
amenities: Mailing List, Wheelchair Accessible, Wine Club
connect: f

Sweet Valley Wines 12

Tall, friendly, 20-something Josh McDaniels' youth belies his experience, which was gained growing up in Walla Walla, and working as a cellar rat for Don Redman at Mannina Cellars and then as an assistant winemaker at famed Leonetti Cellar. That working experience is in addition to the degree he earned from Walla Walla Community College's in-depth enology and viticulture program. Nevertheless, becoming a great winemaker is a lifelong endeavor, and to this end, at the time of my visit Josh was preparing to venture south to Argentina to work at Paul Hobbs' winery in Viña Cobos.

Josh isn't going solo in the Sweet Valley Wines venture. His parents and longtime family friends are partners in the business. They bring needed capital and complementary skills to the business of running a winery. What's more, Josh knows a host of key suppliers that provide essential ingredients for the winery, from the grape growers to the cork suppliers. Heck, he probably went to school with some of them.

My tasting at Sweet Valley Wines included a lineup of cabernet sauvignon, merlot, syrah and a red blend called "Double Barrel Red" (so named because Josh had only two barrels of wine to blend). Josh noted that this year's crop of wines included a viognier, which unfortunately wasn't available for tasting. It had sold out.

Murphy

While I was eyeballing the deep red merlot, Josh's yellow Lab, Murphy, plunked down next to my feet. The dog's youthful appearance matched Josh's. These signs of young blood reflect Sweet Valley Wines' future; the many vintages to come with Josh at the winemaking helm. My curiosity compelled me to ask Josh how he intended to distinguish himself in such a competitive market as Walla Walla. To this question, he gave a one-word response. "Quality," he said. "Oh, the promise of youth!" I thought to myself.

SWEET VALLEY WINES
opened: 2007
winemaker(s): Josh McDaniels
location: 12 North 2nd Street, Walla Walla, WA 99362
phone: 509-526-0002
web: www.sweetvalleywines.com
e-mail: info@sweetvalleywines.com
fee: Tasting fee refunded with purchase
hours: Fall and winter months, Thursday through Saturday 11–5; Spring and summer months, Tuesday through Saturday 11–5; also open on release and event weekends and by appointment
amenities: Pet Friendly, Wheelchair Accessible, Wine Club
connect:

Sapolil Cellars 13

Owner and winemaker Bill Scherwin, didn't have to venture far to come up with a name for his winery; the production winery is located on Sapolil Road about 10 miles east of Walla Walla. Sapolil was a Native American who served alongside Dr. Dorsey Syng Baker during the 1870s construction of the Walla Walla & Columbia River Railroad, from Wallula, on the Columbia River, to Walla Walla. One of its many railway stations, used for loading wheat and other merchandise, bore the name Sapolil Station to honor Sapolil.

Sapolil Cellars is truly a family-run business. While Bill is instrumental in making the wine, his wife, Linda Scherwin, manages the tasting room/piano bar. Marketing and other duties fall on the experienced shoulders of their daughter Abigail Scherwin, and she's done a remarkable job. In a competitive wine market like Walla Walla, creating an identity that fuses full-bodied red wines with the sounds of Philly KingB & The Stingers, Dr. Mark Brown, Papa Loves Mambo, and the like was pure genius.

Sapolil Cellars' red blend "Gandy Dancer" features Jeffrey's artwork on the label. While I stuck my nose into a freshly poured glass of this New World blend, Abigail explained to me that "gandy dancer" is a slang term for a worker who maintained the railroad tracks, an expression that originated in the late 1800s. Moving together in a rhythmic dance, gandy dancers used a "gandy tool" to move displaced track back into place to prevent train derailment. It occurred to me that the gandy-dancer sounds of the past might jive nicely with the rhythmic blues and jazzy notes pulsating from Sapolil Cellars. Find out for yourself by sampling some great syrah and getting into the beat.

SAPOLIL CELLARS
opened: 2004
winemaker(s): Bill Schwerin
location: 15 East Main Street, Walla Walla, WA 99362
phone: 509-520-5258
web: www.sapolilcellars.com
e-mail: abigail@sapolilcellars.com
fee: Complimentary wine tasting
hours: Monday through Friday 11–4, Saturday 10–4, Sunday 1–4
amenities: Live Music, Mailing List, Online Store, Private Events, Restaurant/Food Pairings, Wheelchair Accessible, Wine Club, Wines by the Glass
connect: 🐦 f

⭐ BEST Best music venue and eats

Abigail Scherwin

Otis Kenyon Wine

In the early 1900s, James Otis Kenyon was a struggling dentist in nearby Milton-Freewater when a new dentist moved into town and became instant competition. Having a wife and two kids to fend for, James came up with the harebrained idea to burn down his competitor's dental office. As I was imagining James striking a match to flambé his nemesis's practice, the pourer noted that the derby-capped silhouette on the bottle is an image of old James Otis Kenyon himself.

The authorities arrested James, but rather than serving time in jail, he was "sentenced" to practice dentistry at a nearby hospital. During this time, his wife abandoned him and gave their two young sons the distinct impression that their father was dead. The wife and kids relocated to Walla Walla. As an adult, one of the sons, Robert, never spoke of his father, even to his own son, Stephen Otis Kenyon. However, as a young adult, Stephen discovered that, in fact, his grandfather was alive and living on the Oregon coast. Nearly 50 years to the day of the torching incident, James Otis Kenyon got a call from his grandson. Understandably, James was hesitant to meet him, but Stephen succeeded in reconnecting with his grandfather, and happily, James became a significant member of a family he had never known existed. James lived to age 101 — long enough to witness the birth of his first great-grandchild, Muriel, who now runs the winery's tasting room in downtown Walla Walla.

Today, owners Stephen Otis Kenyon and Deborah Dunbar produce small-lot premium wines, relying primarily on fruit from the Walla Walla area (including their own 10-acre Stellar Vineyard). Local winemaker Dave Stephenson handcrafts the wines for Otis Kenyon Wines with a clear focus on Bordeaux and Rhône varietal wines. Even crazy dentists with a penchant for torching things would love these wines.

OTIS KENYON WINE
opened: 2004
winemaker(s): Dave Stephenson
location: 23 East Main Street, Walla Walla, WA 99362
phone: 509-525-3505
web: www.otiskenyonwine.com
e-mail: info@otiskenyonwine.com
fee: Tasting fee refunded with purchase
hours: Thursday through Monday 11–5
amenities: Mailing List, Online Store, Wheelchair Accessible, Wine Club
connect: 🐦 f

Mark Ryan Winery 15

MARK RYAN WINERY
opened: 1999
winemaker(s): Mark Ryan McNeilly
location: 26 East Main Street, Suite 1,
Walla Walla, WA 99362
phone: 509-876-4577
web: www.markryanwinery.com
e-mail: mark@markryanwinery.com
fee: Tasting fee
hours: Daily 11–5
amenities: Mailing List, Online Store,
Wheelchair Accessible
connect: f

www.winetrailsnw.com/wineries/mark_ryan_winery

The Chocolate Shop

The hot new category of wine consumption is chocolate wine, and you don't even have to wait until Valentine's Day to imbibe. We're not talking the cream sherry concoctions that grandma used to pour, the ones that have the consistency of Milk of Magnesia. No, these have a red-wine base (cabernet, syrah, merlot, for example) with chocolate extract and fruit flavors added. These fall into the red dessert wine category and garner serious attention at prestigious wine competitions.

My visit to Walla Walla's Chocolate Shop, across from the downtown Starbucks, stopped me in my tracks as I surveyed the room — a chocolate lover's fantasy. From gourmet chocolate confections to novelty apparel, the shop offers all things chocolate. But most important (to the WineTrekker, anyway), this Precept Brands-engineered company offers chocolate wine. As I surveyed the lineup of wines, I knew I was in for a sweet treat (pun intended).

I was surprised to learn from my informative tasting room pourer that their chocolate red wine (priced at $15 a bottle) is the number-one selling chocolate wine in the world. "Really?" I asked, and having no way to verify such a comment, I took it with a grain of salt. However, after one sip, I unabashedly became one of the consuming statistics and bought a bottle.

Many a wine connoisseur states that chocolate and red wine do not pair well, and yet the majority of wineries make Valentine's Day a special event, pairing the two. I must say that I agree with the critics and have found that only tawny port or sweet sherry works with chocolate. But the beauty of The Chocolate Shop's wines is that the debate ends here, because the flavor of the wine and the silky smooth texture of the chocolate essence result in a harmonious palate symphony. It delivers a high note of true decadence.

THE CHOCOLATE SHOP
opened: 2009
location: 31 East Main, Walla Walla, WA 99362
phone: 509-522-1261
web: www.chocolateshopwine.com
e-mail: info@chocolateshopwine.com
fee: Tasting fee
hours: Sunday, Monday, Thursday and Friday 11–5; Saturday 11–6
amenities: Gift Shop, Wheelchair Accessible
connect: 🐦 f

Rotie Cellars 🔟

I'm a big fan of the Winepeeps wine blog, because it lends a critical palate to the Northwest wine scene. So I took notice when Winepeeps co-blogger Kori Vorhees made the following

comment about a then new Walla Walla wine, after she attended the packed 2009 Rhône Rangers soiree in Seattle: "Our most exciting discovery was the 2007 Rôtie Cellars 'Northern' Red Blend. It is a bold wine, yet exhibits remarkable finesse at the same time. I was blown away by its purity of fruit."

The affable, 6-foot-plus proprietor/winemaker Sean Boyd poured a sample of his super-crisp southern Rhône white blend of roussanne and viognier. As I daydreamed of pairing this wine with pasta salad, Sean spoke of his days as a geologist, when he was deep into oil- and gas-exploration endeavors. The work was exciting, but the constant travel took him away from his wife, Annie, and their baby daughter, Bridget. Even as I savored the lingering notes of the white blend, it was clear to me that Sean is a family man to the core. But leaving a lucrative career and starting up a winery…now that takes guts.

Sean Boyd

Next up for the sampling were his two reds — a northern Rhône blend of syrah fermented together with viognier, which, by the way, has notes of floral and bacon (no kidding) reminiscent of the famed Côte-Rôtie in the northern Rhône; and a southern-Rhône-blend version featuring a backbone of grenache and smaller amounts of syrah and Mourvèdre. The southern blend, with its lighter, fruit-forward taste, provided an answer to that ever-troubling question: What to pair with chicken *à la Provençal?* I left that

day with a fine case of Rhône rage, having chanced upon one of the state's finest wineries for Rhône-style wines.

ROTIE CELLARS
opened: 2010
winemaker(s): Sean Boyd
location: 31 East Main Street, Suite 216, Walla Walla, WA 99362
phone: 253-312-5991
web: www.rotiecellars.com
e-mail: alicia@rotiecellars.com
fee: Tasting fee refunded with purchase
hours: Typically Fridays and Saturdays; call ahead for hours
amenities: Mailing List, Newsletter/Blog, Online Store, Wheelchair Accessible, Wine Club
connect: 🇫

Chateau Rollat Winery 🔢18

I came for the "Edouard de Rollat." Sometime ago, I read a review by noted *Seattle Times* wine columnist Paul Gregutt (October 17, 2007) in which he used the word "polished" to describe this Bordeaux blend; obviously relishing the wine, he noted that it was a *vin de garde* — a French term for wines that you can cellar for many years. Palate curiosity got the better of me and I decided to discover this wine for myself at the Chateau Rollat (pronounced ROLL-ah) tasting room in downtown Walla Walla.

Now, dear reader, it is not often that I splurge for a wine priced in the mid-$60s but maybe it was the intense fruitiness of the wine or the lasting finish that made me spring for a bottle of "Edouard de Rollat." Perhaps it was the friendliness of the pouring staff that encouraged my spendthriftiness as they wove a rich story about owner Bowin Lindgren and his great-grandfather Edouard.

If I could go back in time to early 1900s New York City, I would make a beeline for Café Martin, on 27th Street, and meet sommelier/wine steward Edouard Rollat in the flesh. Standing at more than 6 feet tall and sporting a neatly cropped mustache, the recent emigrant from France was an imposing figure of a man. It must have been disheartening to him when an amendment to the U.S. Constitution prohibited the manufacture and sale of wine during the 1920s. But he made the most of the dry spell and continued to teach and write about wine, and eventually the "Great Experiment" was repealed. Imagine the pride Rollat would have felt to learn that his great-grandson Bowin Lindgren would produce a highly acclaimed wine named after him.

CHATEAU ROLLAT WINERY
opened: 2007
winemaker(s): Bowin Lingren and Matt Loso — consulting winemaker
location: 43 East Main Street, Walla Walla, WA 99362
phone: 509-529-0143
web: www.chateaurollat.com
e-mail: information@chateaurollat.com
fee: Tasting fee
hours: Thursday, Friday, Sunday 11–4, Saturday 11–5, or by appointment
amenities: Wheelchair Accessible

DaMa Wines 19

I always try to balance the light with the heavy — a few tears of human spirit in with the sequins and the fringes. — Bette Midler

Perhaps the quotation above, one of several pithy sayings found on the DaMa Wines website, says it best about the winery's raison d'etre. After all, co-owners and co-winemakers Dawn Kammer and Mary Tuuri Derby (the "Da" and "Ma" of DaMa) are always in the middle of a balancing act, with their shared goals of creating strong yet graceful wines; seeing to the financial needs of their winemaking operation while still giving back to the community; and meeting the challenges of being a female-owned business in a male-dominated industry. Despite these hurdles, DaMa Wines succeeds.

Continuing the legacy of women winemakers in Washington, Dawn and Mary blend different backgrounds, training and ultimately different noses to create wines that are "full-bodied, true to the varietal taste with a smooth, rounded finish." Dawn grew up in Vacaville, California (near Napa Valley), and the "cowgirl" in her kept her out west, where she migrated from one prison town to another by random circumstance and eventually ended up in Walla Walla. She obtained a degree from the Institute of Enology and Viticulture at Walla Walla Community College before working at College Cellars and the iconic Marcus Whitman Hotel. Mary's route to DaMa included a long stint in the culinary arts working for renowned restaurants in San Francisco and Chicago. Eventually she, too, landed in Walla Walla, where she and her late husband, Devin Derby, launched Spring Valley Vineyard. Although their backgrounds and training are quite different, the two women possessed a common vision of the type of winery and wine style they sought to create.

Dawn Kammer

DAMA WINES
opened: 2007
winemaker(s): Dawn Kammer and Mary Tuuri Derby
location: 45 East Main Street, Walla Walla, WA 98362
phone: 509-525-2299
web: www.damawines.com
e-mail: info@damawines.com
fee: Tasting fee
hours: Monday 11–4; Thursday 11–5; Friday and Saturday 11–6; Sunday 11–2
amenities: Mailing List, Online Store, Wheelchair Accessible, Wine Club
connect: 🐦 📘

Sinclair Estate Vineyard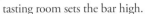

The wood flooring is lovely; the chandelier perfect. This isn't your average tasting room, with the typical Spartan accoutrements. No, indeed. With original artwork, a baby grand piano, and an inviting fireplace with comfy, strategically placed chairs, the Sinclair Estate Vineyards tasting room sets the bar high.

Sinclair Estate Vineyards is the brainchild of Tim and Cathy Sinclair, who, with their penchant for fine wine, moved from the Seattle area following Tim's retirement from Microsoft.

As they say, it all starts in the vineyard, and in this case, the Sinclairs put their wager on a 117-acre plot of wheat-filled land east of Walla Walla, near Walla Walla Vintners. The Sinclairs devoted 20 acres of their property to wine grapes.

However, rather than waiting for the vineyard to mature, they quickly moved to establish Sinclair Estate Vineyards, planting grapes sourced from a number of highly acclaimed vineyards throughout the Columbia Valley. The strategy was a success.

I had heard the buzz surrounding their chardonnay, so I was delighted that my first pour was of this signature white wine, which reflects winemaker Amy Alvarez-Wampfler's sur lie aging technique, imparting a creamy lemon-bar quality to the wine. Imagine creme brûlée in a luscious liquid form. It was oh so nice, but the surprise quaff for me was the bold yet silky-smooth Pentatonic red blend, which had me smacking my lips.

It was so amazingly good, I purchased a glass of the Pentatonic and retreated to one of the high-backed upholstered chairs by the fireplace. Once ensconced, I celebrated the fact that people like the Sinclairs don't retire. They reinvent.

SINCLAIR ESTATE VINEYARD
opened: 2010
winemaker(s): Amy Alvarez-Wampfler
location: 109-B East Main Street, Walla Walla, WA 99362
phone: 509-876-4300
web: www.sinclairestatevineyards.com
e-mail: info@sinclairestatevineyard.com
fee: Tasting fee
hours: Thursday and Friday 1–6, Saturday 10–6, Sunday 12–4
amenities: Art Gallery, Live Music, Lodging, Newsletter/Blog, Online Store, Private Events, Wheelchair Accessible, Wine Club, Wines by the Glass
connect:

Fort Walla Walla Cellars 21

Owners Jim Moyer and Cliff Kontos appreciate tradition. As Walla Walla natives, they know a thing or two about the area's history and, in particular, it's grape-growing past, which goes as far back as the mid-1800s, when the early settlers in the area planted vines for wine production. Many of these pioneers emigrated from France and Italy, where winemaking is a centuries-old tradition handed down from one generation to the next. So in 1998, when Jim and Cliff began making wine together, they thought it would be

fitting to name their winery to honor the past. They christened their new venture "Fort Walla Walla Cellars," paying homage to the landmark that helped establish Walla Walla.

Study Fort Walla Walla Cellars' wine labels and you'll see an illustration of Fort Walla Walla itself. The labels even have that "aged look," as if the bottles they adorn have been kept in a pioneer's wine cellar. With Jim and Cliff's penchant for history, it's not surprising that they stick to a traditional winemaking style, using tried-and-true techniques passed down from generations of winemakers. Using these methods, they produce approximately 2,000 cases per year.

Located in the heart of downtown Walla Walla, the winery's fort-like red brick tasting room enjoys a steady stream of visitors. WineTrail enthusiasts will have an opportunity to swirl and taste premium cabernet sauvignon, merlot, syrah, and, my personal favorite, their award-winning Bordeaux blend "Treaty." Even with a dozen visitors milling about, the amiable tasting room manager, Terry Farley, finds time to pour, chat, and work the cash register with ease. Yes, there is a spittoon on the wine bar, but Fort Walla Walla wines are too luscious to be wasted in a spittoon.

FORT WALLA WALLA CELLARS
opened: 1998
winemaker(s): Jim Moyer and Cliff Kontos
location: 127 East Main Street, Walla Walla, WA 99362
phone: 509-520-1095
web: www.fortwallawallacellars.com
e-mail: info@fortwallawallacellars.com
fee: Tasting fee refunded with purchase
hours: Thursday through Monday 10–4:30 or by appointment
amenities: Gift Shop, Online Store, Picnic Area, Tours, Wheelchair Accessible, Wine Club
connect: 🐦 📘

Walla Faces 22

Sometimes dreams do come true.

Such is the case of Rick and Debbie Johnson, who got married on December 31, 1999 and a month later, honeymooned on the Oregon coast at Manzanita. While walking on the beach, the Johnsons had one of those "What shall we do next in life?" discussions, and the answer they arrived at was growing premium wine grapes.

It would take five more years before Rick and Debbie stumbled onto vineyard property in Walla Walla that suited their tastes as well as their life's goals. Once it was found, however, the Johnsons moved from Seattle to their new home — Walla Walla — and never looked back.

Their "home" turns out to be a vineyard estate and luxurious inn east of town. It's the perfect place for realizing their dream — managing a 10-acre vineyard estate (8.5 acres of premium cabernet sauvignon and syrah under production) and running the elegant guesthouse, complete with outdoor pool. Here, Rick can apply his education and training in viticulture gained from Washington State University's viticulture program and his extensive coursework at the University of California-Davis. However, now that he's beyond the textbooks, Rick has real-world difficult decisions that come with the business of growing grapes.

JANICE
2006 Cabernet Sauvignon
Walla Walla Valley

Walla Walla Inns at the Vineyard

Stylish and chic (thanks in large part to Rick's urban planning and commercial real estate background), the tasting room décor includes walls replete with the celebrated artwork of Rick's sister, Candice Johnson. Her "Faces" series is a visual representation of the winery's name and takes center stage on the labels of its wines. As I studied the label, Debbie mentioned that they recently had a clairvoyant in the tasting room giving readings for folks eager to get a sneak peak of their future. Although I am no soothsayer, I can easily see a bright future for the Johnsons in their adopted home.

WALLA FACES
opened: 2009
winemaker(s): Rick Johnson
location: 216 East Main Street, Walla Walla, WA 98362
phone: 877-301-1181
web: www.wallafaces.com
e-mail: info@wallafaces.com
fee: Tasting fee refunded with purchase
hours: Daily 1–6
amenities: Lodging, Tours, Online Store, Wheelchair Accessible, Wine Club, YouTube
connect: 🐦 📘

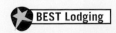
BEST Lodging

El Corazon Winery

"I want to be a volcanologist," said 6-year-old, Tiger, in answer to his mother's question about a future career. "How about being a winemaker?" his mom, Jennifer McKnight Sievers, asked. With a shrug of his shoulders, young Tiger gave a "Maybe, one day" response while eating a cup of yogurt and studying photos in a book he was perusing. Just like his mom and dad, Tiger has a can-do attitude.

Spencer Sievers

To say that Tiger's father, Spencer Sievers, has volcanic energy is the classic understatement. His fire instills a sense of *esprit de corps* in all those who are exposed to him. Tall and possessing a terrific smile, this lanky winemaker exudes great confidence, but not in a cocky way. Rather, it is a passion to try different things in life, such as moving to Kansas and opening a health food store in Lawrence (by the way, Jennifer owns Arizona Trading Co., a clothing reseller in Lawrence); living in Panama with Jennifer and toddler, Tiger; and, in a leap of faith, relocating to Walla Walla to make wine.

At El Corazon (which means "the heart" in Spanish), handcrafted wine comes alive with small-lot productions of cabernet franc, syrah, Malbec, carmenere, and red blends. With his winemaking partner, Raul Morfin, Spencer works to keep El Corazon small (with production at 1,000 cases) but true to the fruit found in the Walla Walla Valley.

With a tip of his wine glass toward his son, Spencer noted, "Tiger has a really good palate and picks up flavors that I don't." He was quick to add that Tiger tastes eyedropper-size samples. In this respect, it's only fitting that their 100 percent carménère wine bears the name "Tiger's Blood." At El Corazon Winery, the plan for succession is alive and well!

EL CORAZON WINERY
opened: 2008
winemaker(s): Spencer Sievers
location: 37 South Palouse Street, Walla Walla, WA 99362
phone: 509-240-5292
web: www.elcorazonwinery.com
e-mail: elcorazonwinery@gmail.com
fee: Complimentary wine tasting
hours: Friday and Saturday 12–7; Sunday 11–4, or by appointment
amenities: Online Store, Pet Friendly, Wheelchair Accessible, Wine Club, Wines by the Glass
connect: 🐦 f

Spencer Sievers

Charles Smith Wines

Boom-boom, this place rocks!

Walla Walla's iconic winemaker, Charles Smith (yes, the one pictured on the billboard as you drive into town), expanded his growing empire with the launch of Charles Smith Wines:

The Modernist Project. You know the label already — distinctive black and white designs bearing the names of Kung Fu Girl Riesling, Eve Chardonnay, The Velvet Devil Merlot, and Boom Boom Syrah. They stand out in the grocery wine aisle and carry a wallet-friendly price tag of $12–$14. Charles realized early on that most Americans purchase wine to have with that evening's dinner, not with the intent of cellaring them. (However, if you really want to age your wines, Charles Smith does offer his Royal City syrah and his King Coal cabernet-syrah, which retail for a mere $100 a bottle.)

Charles' South Spokane Street tasting venue is an architectural splendor to behold. Drawing on the design talents of Seattle's award-winning Olson Kundig Architects, he transformed an old auto repair shop into the alluring Charles Smith Wines downtown tasting room. While there, be sure to check out the movable platforms bearing chairs and tables that can readily be rearranged to accommodate the live music and other special events that happen with great regularity. (Charles does like to party, and with his trademark out-of-control cork-screw locks, he's easy to spot in the crowd.)

But my favorite architectural touch has to be the tasting room's doors. These aren't your ordinary doors, mind you. In an attempt to echo the past ambiance of the auto repair shop, the doors consist of two large, crank-operated steel swing windows that open onto sidewalk seating. Given the doors' massive weight, their installation must have required an industrial crane and 20 beefy men. Rock-on dear WineTrail trekker!

CHARLES SMITH WINES
opened: 2010
winemaker(s): Charles Smith; Andrew Latta (Assn't)
location: 35 South Spokane Street, Walla Walla, WA 99362
phone: 509-526-5230
web: www.charlessmithwines.com
e-mail: charles@charlessmithwines.com
fee: $5 for 6 core wines or $10 for any 6 wines refunded with purchase
hours: Open daily at 10 a.m.
amenities: Live Music, Mailing List, Online Store, Private Events, Wheelchair Accessible, Winemaker Dinners, Wines by the Glass
connect: 🐦 📘

⭐ **BEST Music venue**

Mansion Creek Cellars 25

Located in downtown Walla Walla, Mansion Creek Cellars shares space with Plumb Cellars at a nicely renovated spot dubbed Wine@NINE. In addition to sampling wines from two boutique wineries, visitors have the pleasure (we hope) of meeting Julia Russell, co-owner with hubby, Roger Russell, of Mansion Creek Cellars. Julia's friendly demeanor lights up the space as she waxes eloquently about their wines (and those of Plumb Cellars). Just a few minutes into a discussion with Julia and you realize that family, friends, nature, culture, and an appreciation for the good things in life all mesh to create a memorable visit.

Winemaker Jerry Myrick is the mastermind behind these delectable small-lot wines. Highly structured, complex, with long finishes, these wines sing the Walla Walla *terroir*.

The Colonial Revival house adorning the Mansion Creek Cellars wine label is the Waldheim mansion, of which the winery and several of the Russells' wines — including Waldheim syrah, Waldheim white wine, and Waldheim cuvée — are the namesakes. Built by German immigrants in the late 1800s, the mansion must be a lovely place to call home. Just ask Julia. While you're at it, you might also run the idea by her of releasing a wine called "Where in the World Is Waldheim?" Just an idea.

MANSION CREEK CELLARS
opened: 2011
winemaker(s): Jerry Myrick
location: 9 South 1st Avenue, Walla Walla, WA 99362
phone: 253-370-6107
web: www.mansioncreekcellars.com
e-mail: mansioncreekcellars@hotmail.com
fee: Tasting fee
hours: Wednesday through Saturday 11–5; Sunday 12–4
amenities: Wheelchair Accessible, Wine Club
connect: 🐦 f

Plumb Cellars

Plumb Cellars, which shares a space with Mansion Creek Cellars, is a nice find off Main Street. It's the home of Damn Straight, a Bordeaux blend and the collaborative effort of Crandall Kyle, Margo and Gary Kagels, and Edie and Dale Johnson. It may not require a committee to make wine, but hey, the more the merrier. At the end of crush, you have a ready-made party for celebrating the harvest.

With a plumb bob displayed on the label, you might guess that someone involved with Plumb Cellars has an architectural penchant for straight lines and level floors. That would be Gary, who is a custom homebuilder. While planting the Plumb Cellars vineyard in the Walla Walla Valley, Gary was the one with the plumb bob in hand, ensuring that the stakes stood straight. With the resulting straight rows and a vertical trellis system at perfect 90-degree angles to the ground, the name Plumb Cellars was, straight up, the right call.

For those looking for a bit of sustenance with their wine, I discovered a great pairing of Plumb Cellars' viognier with the seared scallop nigiri from nearby Aloha Sushi — a match made in heaven, or maybe nirvana in this case.

PLUMB CELLARS
opened: 2010
winemaker(s): Gary Kagels
location: 9 South 1st Avenue, Walla Walla, WA 99362
phone: 509-529-9463
web: www.plumbcellars.com
e-mail: info@plumbcellars.com
fee: Tasting fee
hours: Wednesday through Saturday 11–5; Sunday 12–4
amenities: Newsletter/Blog, Online Store, Wheelchair Accessible
connect: 🐦 📘

Forgeron Cellars

If you're a fan of chardonnay, your ship has come in — and docked at Forgeron Cellars. Early on, winemaker and co-owner Marie-Eve Gilla insisted that Forgeron Cellars make chardonnay. At the time, this decision was somewhat controversial; after all, Walla Walla is mecca for big, intense reds. Fortunately, for the other 50-plus investors in Forgeron, she got her way. Today, if you ask the locals where to find great chardonnay, they would steer you to Forgeron. With chardonnay production around 1,400 cases a year to meet demand, those same investors are celebrating Marie-Eve's success.

Forgeron's chardonnay is made from Columbia Valley grapes, using neutral French oak to create luscious "variety expressive" chardonnay. The fact is Marie-Eve happens to hail from the part of France that's famous for its chardonnay: Burgundy, where the white wines of Chablis and Côte de Beaune enjoy a bit of a reputation. When I taste her chardonnay, my mind immediately goes into "foodie" mode with thoughts of chicken, seafood and summer salads.

However, if you are a devotee of red wines, Forgeron Cellars will not disappoint. After all, three-quarters of the wines produced at Forgeron are red — bold, layered, fruit-forward explosions with lingering finishes. In fact, it's Marie-Eve's Bordeaux blends, her syrah and her barbera that get many a visitor to join the winery's Anvil Wine Club — that, and the fact that the wine club offers a number of primo benefits.

Forgeron's winery/tasting room was once the site of a blacksmith's workshop,

hence its name, which is French for "blacksmith." Rumor has it that horseshoes were discovered during the renovation of the former blacksmithy. As you are swirling, sipping, and yakking with the friendly staff, you might just ask to see one of the horseshoes. Some of the good luck it has brought Forgeron is bound to rub off.

FORGERON CELLARS
opened: 2001
winemaker(s): Marie-Eve Gilla
location: 33 West Birch Street, Walla Walla, WA 99362
phone: 509-522-9463
web: www.forgeroncellars.com
e-mail: tastingroom@forgeroncellars.com
fee: Complimentary wine tasting
hours: Daily 11–4 excluding major holidays
amenities: Gift Shop, Mailing List, Online Store, Pet Friendly, RV/Bus Parking, Tours, Wheelchair Accessible, Wine Club, YouTube
connect: 🐦 f

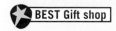 ⭐ **BEST Gift shop**

Walla Walla Village Winery 28

It was the summer of 1967. I was 15 at the time, and my dad and mom had thrown two of my three sisters and me into the two-tone blue Ford Fairlane 500 to drive from Spokane to the Bay Area. Our city tour included Haight-Ashbury, where I saw plenty of hippies and psychedelic posters announcing upcoming concerts. I was to learn later that Stanley Mouse was the artistic creator behind many of the posters. Today, serious collectors wage bidding battles on eBay for his work.

So imagine my delight nearly 40 years later when I walked into the Walla Walla Village Winery tasting room and saw that its labels were designed by none other than Stanley Mouse. The same guy whose art embodied quintessential '60s rock had loaned his talents to the creation of Walla Walla Village's wine labels.

Barb and Lynn Irish Clark, owners of Walla Walla Village Winery, had Mouse create the label for their first 2003 release of gewürztraminer. His label designs also capture the spirit of other wines they offer. I was to discover that the eye-popping sunburst label perfectly represented the spiciness of the gewürztraminer, as well as the luscious, rich flavor of their "Bordello Red." The Clarks' son, Joel, is their winemaker, and he has created a full sleight of wines using grapes from Washington's Columbia Valley.

Located in a renovated 1900 building, the Walla Walla Village Winery tasting room beautifully complements Walla Walla's downtown architecture. Inside, the high ceilings feature still-shiny copper tiles, and the refurbished tasting bar dates back to an era that honored artisanship. As you sample the delectable offerings and gaze through the arched windows, you can almost imagine a horse-drawn carriage passing by. It would be the perfect moment to hear "On a warm San Francisco night … "

WALLA WALLA VILLAGE WINERY
opened: 2003
winemaker(s): Joel Clark
location: 107 South 3rd Avenue, Walla Walla, WA 99362
phone: 509-525-9463
web: www.wallawallavillagewinery.com
e-mail: info@wallawallavillagewinery.com
fee: Tasting fee refunded with purchase
hours: Tuesday through Saturday 12–6, extended hours on Thursday evening 7–11 for live music; hours subject to seasonal change so call ahead
amenities: Gift Shop, Live Music, Online Store, Picnic Area, RV/Bus Parking, Tours, Wine Club, Wines by the Glass
connect: f

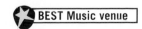
BEST Music venue

Morrison Lane Winery 29

Often, wineries are successful because owner and winemaker march together to the beat of a different drummer. When your lineup of wines includes such uncommon choices as cinsault, carmenere, barbera, nebbiolo, and counoise, you distinguish yourself immediately. Such is the case with Morrison Lane.

Since 1997, Dean and Verdie Morrison have supplied a number of wineries with premium grapes of Rhône and Italian origins from their 23-acre vineyard, located just south of Walla Walla. In 2002, the couple took the plunge themselves, not only growing the fruit, but also turning it into fine wine. Today, Morrison Lane wines are produced from the "Morrison family committee." Dean and Verdie manage their vineyards and winery, and sons Sean and Dan manage the winemaking tasks.

The Morrisons still use the winemaking facilities of other wineries and therefore technically can't label their wines as "estate." The fed's Alcohol and Tobacco Tax and Trade Bureau would slap their wrists. Nevertheless, by any other name, the Rhône varietal counoise (pronounced koon-WAHZ) would taste just as delicious. It actually tastes like the syrup from canned Bing cherries — very fruit forward, yet not sweet.

The Morrison Lane tasting room is situated downtown in the historic Dacres Building, on the corner of Main and Fourth streets. Wine pairs wonderfully with music, and it's no accident that a baby grand piano graces the tasting room. Because Morrison Lane is a small, family-owned and -operated winery, you will often find Verdie and Dean working the tasting room. When I asked Verdie if they had a wine club she noted, "We don't have a wine club per se, but we do have a baseball bat under the bar." We discovered that she wasn't kidding. Under the bar, there is a bat inscribed with the words "Wine Club" on its barrel.

MORRISON LANE WINERY
opened: 2002
winemaker(s): Verdie Morrison and son Sean Morrison
location: 201 West Main Street, The Library Tasting Room, Walla Walla, WA 99362
phone: 509-526-0229
web: www.morrisonlane.com
e-mail: sean@morrisonlane.com
fee: Complimentary wine tasting
hours: Friday through Sunday 12–5, or by appointment; Closed January and February
amenities: Tours, Art Gallery, RV/Bus Parking, Mailing List, Vineyard on Premise, Wheelchair Accessible
connect: f

Walla Walla South
WineTrail

Winter with Blue Mountain foothills in the distance

Many WineTrail enthusiasts head to the southern outskirts of Walla Walla, where excellent wineries abound. With more than 20 wineries to taste your way through, you'll want to budget a solid week (or several weekend forays, as I did) for this WineTrail.

For winery tourists who enjoy bicycling, the gentle hills of WineTrail South will get the heart pumping and work up an appetite. Whether you are in a car, on a bike, or sampling premier wines at one of the many tasting rooms, the views of the Blue Mountains' foothills in the distance and row upon row of cabernet sauvignon grapes provide a terrific backdrop. Be sure to pack a picnic. Along this WineTrail, you will experience one of Washington's top wine-country resorts, picturesque vineyards, great people, and some intense reds.

1. Basel Cellars Estate Winery
2. Zerba Cellars
3. Watermill Winery & Blue Mountain Cider Company
4. Amavi Cellars
5. Beresan Winery
6. Balboa Winery
7. Saviah Cellars
8. Sleight of Hand Cellars
9. Waters Winery
10. Va Piano Vineyards
11. Northstar Winery
12. Pepper Bridge Winery
13. Dusted Valley Vintners
14. Isenhower Cellars
15. Rulo Winery
16. Tertulia Cellars
17. Fjellene Cellars
18. Morrison Lane Winery
19. Gifford Hirlinger Winery
20. Castillo de Feliciana Vineyard and Winery
21. Spofford Station

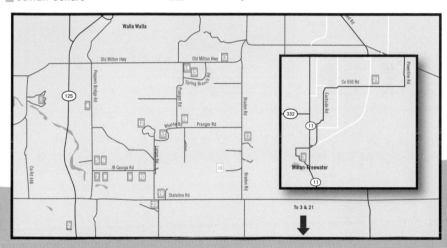

Region:	**Walla Walla Wine Country**
# of tasting rooms on tour:	**21**
# of satelite tasting rooms:	**1**
Estimate # of days for tour:	**6**
Getting around:	**Car or bike**
Key Events:	❏ **Spring Release Weekend; Balloon Stampede Weekend; Vintage Walla Walla; Entwine; and Holiday Barrel Tasting. See www.wallawallawine.com/events for details.**
Tips:	❏ **Consider using a limousine service.**
Best:	❏ **Destination, lodging, views and picnicking: Basel Cellars Estate Winery**
	❏ **Views and picnicking: Amavi Cellars**
	❏ **Views and picnicking: Waters Winery**
	❏ **Picnicking: Va Piano Vineyards**
	❏ **Gift shop, views and picnicking: Northstar Winery**
	❏ **Views and picnicking: Pepper Bridge Winery**
	❏ **Picnicking and views: Tertulia Cellars**
	❏ **Views: Fjellene Cellars**
	❏ **Picnicking: Gifford Hirlinger Winery**
	❏ **Views and picnicking: Castillo de Feliciana Vineyard and Winery**

Basel Cellars Estate Winery

One word: "Awesome."

Basel Cellars Estate Winery first burst onto the wine-tour scene in 2005–2006, when *Seattle* magazine bestowed on it the title of "Best Destination Winery." And it deserves those props.

Situated on 87 acres high on a bluff just south of Walla Walla, the winery proffers not just fine wine, but luxury accommodations, including spacious meeting rooms, a gourmet kitchen for private dinners, hot tubs, a sauna, an outdoor pool with poolside cabana, and much more. This is where well-heeled companies hold corporate retreats and loving partners get away from it all to create lasting memories. The winery's spacious 13,800-square-foot estate house is a fusion of elegant artisanship and rustic timbers, and if the hand-carved entrance doors don't grab your attention, the views of the valley and the surrounding Blue Mountains surely will.

Steve and Jo Marie Hansen joined Basel Cellars Estate Winery in 2004 as co-owners. Since that time, they have experienced the extremes of the winemaking business, enduring a brutal winter that killed the grape vines, but then enjoying a number of years when Mother Nature blessed them with exquisite fruit. Today, the Hansens are the winery's majority owners, and with a résumé that includes establishing and managing a number of successful business enterprises, they — and Basel Cellars — will reap the benefits.

The fact that the Hansens chose the highly acclaimed Ned Morris as their winemaker clearly communicates their desire to continue Basel Cellars' legacy of producing premium wines. Ned's background as the assistant winemaker to John Abbot at Abeja, as winemaker at àMaurice Cellars, and as winemaker and general manager at Canoe Ridge Vineyards promises many outstanding vintages to come.

BASEL CELLARS ESTATE WINERY
opened: 2002
winemaker(s): Ned Morris
location: 2901 Old Milton Highway, Walla Walla, WA 99362-7156
phone: 509-522-0200
web: www.baselcellars.com
e-mail: info@baselcellars.com
fee: Tasting fee refunded with purchase
hours: Daily 10–4
amenities: Gift Shop, Lodging, Mailing List, Newsletter/Blog, Online Store, Private Events, RV/Bus Parking, Tours, Vineyard on Premise, Weddings, Wheelchair Accessible, Wine Club, YouTube
connect: 🐦 f

 BEST Destination, lodging, views and picnicking

Zerba Cellars

Prior to launching their winery, Cecil and Marilyn Zerba had a successful nursery business that served the Walla Walla Valley. However, their love of wine and the economics of growing premium cabernet sauvignon and other varieties convinced the couple to plant

Zerba Cellars tasting room

grapes in three vineyards: Dad's Place, Cockburn Hills, and Winesap Road. In 2004, Cecil and Marilyn opened Zerba Cellars with their estate-bottled 2002 wines. It was a slow start — their 2004 release checked in at a paltry 200 cases. But production is on a roll now, with more than 7,500 cases being produced.

When I first met Marilyn at the tasting room, I made the same mistake that nine out of 10 visitors make. Dyslexia must have hit me, because I referred to her winery as "Zebra Cellars." The confusion is due, in part, to a drawing of a zebra prominently displayed on the label of Zerba's "Wild Z" red table wine. Marilyn explained that the zebra-adorned label was "tongue in cheek," because so many people make the mistake of referring to the Zerbas' winery as Zebra Cellars. I wasn't the first, and I won't be the last.

The winery's log-cabin-inspired tasting room was built with western juniper from central Oregon. This knotty tree consumes 40 to 50 gallons of water per day; consequently, vegetation is scarce surrounding a western juniper. The trees used to build the tasting room laid on the forest floor for years, allowing worms to attack and eat their way between bark and wood. The results are amazing patterns etched in the wood; as you sample Zerba's finest, study the wood to see nature's artwork. No two patterns are the same — just like the distinctive reds and whites of Zerba Cellars.

Marilyn Zebra

ZERBA CELLARS
opened: 2004
winemaker(s): Cecil Zerba
location: 85530 Hwy 11,
Milton-Freewater, OR 97862
phone: 541-938-9463
web: www.zerbacellars.com
e-mail: info@zerbacellars.com
fee: Tasting fee refunded with purchase
hours: Daily 12–5
amenities: Online Store, Pet Friendly, Picnic Area, RV/Bus Parking, Vineyard on Premise, Wheelchair Accessible, Wine Club
connect:

Watermill Winery & Blue Mountain Cider Company

Just like the old Doublemint gum jingle "Double your pleasure, Double your fun …," Watermill Winery & Blue Mountain Cider Company offers twice the tasting pleasure with two tasting rooms in one. Here, you can savor noble wine varietals while also sampling refreshing hard cider.

Watermill Winery is located just 10 miles south of Walla Walla in the historic town of Milton-Freewater. The tasting room is actually a diminutive structure near the front of the property with the many-storied Watermill Building dominating the property in the back. With plenty of space for wine production and storage, capacity is clearly not an issue here.

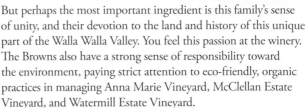

Watermill Winery's future looks promising, because it has the three essential ingredients for success: exceptional vineyards, advanced winemaking equipment and facilities, and a skilled and experienced winemaker in Noah Fox Reed.

But perhaps the most important ingredient is this family's sense of unity, and their devotion to the land and history of this unique part of the Walla Walla Valley. You feel this passion at the winery. The Browns also have a strong sense of responsibility toward the environment, paying strict attention to eco-friendly, organic practices in managing Anna Marie Vineyard, McClellan Estate Vineyard, and Watermill Estate Vineyard.

The Blue Mountain cidery was a surprise find when I visited on a hot August day. Though a hardship to walk the 6 feet from the wine-tasting bar to the cider-tasting bar, I somehow managed. The hard cider has less alcohol than its wine counterpart, but certainly delivers on taste and refreshment. It's perfect by itself or paired with a summer salad or barbecue. My favorite was the bubbly cherry apple hard cider, created from a blending of five types of local apples with a splash of tart cherry freshness. A sip of this and I was reaching for my wallet a second time!

WATERMILL WINERY & BLUE MOUNTAIN CIDER COMPANY
opened: 2005
winemaker(s): Noah Fox Reed
location: 235 E. Broadway Avenue, Milton-Freewater, OR 97862
phone: 541-938-5575
web: www.watermillwinery.com
e-mail: info@watermillwinery.com
fee: Complimentary wine tasting
hours: Monday through Saturday 11–4, or by appointment
amenities: Mailing List, Online Store, Picnic Area, RV/Bus Parking, Wheelchair Accessible, Wine Club
connect: 🐦 📘

Amavi Cellars

Inside the tasting room, visitors have a full frontal view of Pepper Bridge Winery, Amavi Cellars' sister winery, situated on a hilltop a little way in the distance. The view from a floor-to-ceiling wall of windows takes in the famous Pepper Bridge Vineyard (the source,

along with Les Collines and Seven Hills Vineyards, of Amavi's wine grapes) at a slightly higher elevation than the valley floor. Doors lead to a spacious outside deck, where I spied several visitors soaking in the view with freshly opened bottles of Amavi Cellars' wine. As I took more photos from the deck, I had that "six S's of wine tasting" mantra going through my mind: seeing, swirling, smelling, sipping (or swallowing), and savoring.

Back inside, Ray Goff (co-owner of Pepper Bridge Winery and Amavi Cellars) poured me a sample of their 2007 estate syrah, and I made a conscious decision to slow down and exercise the six S's. With a lean, athletic physique and sporting a Mad Hatter's hat, Ray gave me a generous pour and explained in his folksy Montana way that Amavi wines are one of the super values in the valley. Priced at less than $30, the creations of winemaker Jean-François Pellet are fruit forward and ready to enjoy with an evening's meal.

Recalling the six S's of wine tasting, I gave my glass a few brisk swirls before sticking my nose inside the glass to smell the 100 percent syrah. There followed a full mouth onslaught (no wimpy sip this time) with agitated swishing to all parts of the palate, followed by an audible gulp. Now came the savoring part, during which, with a satisfied grin, I looked up to see Ray's expectant eyes on me. That's when I exclaimed, "Ahhhh."

Amavi Cellars truck

AMAVI CELLARS
opened: 2001
winemaker(s): Jean-François Pellet
location: 3796 Peppers Bridge Road, Walla Walla, WA 99362-1769
phone: 509-525-3541
web: www.amavicellars.com
e-mail: info@amavicellars.com
fee: Tasting fee refunded with purchase
hours: Daily 10–4 or by appointment
amenities: Mailing List, Online Store, Pet Friendly, Picnic Area, Private Events, RV/Bus Parking, Tours, Vineyard on Premise, Wheelchair Accessible, Wine Club
connect: 🐦 📘

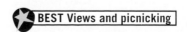 **BEST Views and picnicking**

Beresan Winery 5

Located about four miles south of Walla Walla, Beresan Winery occupies a lovingly restored 1926 red barn. The barn is a distinctive landmark and one of our favorite stops along Walla Walla WineTrail South. Tom and Debbie Waliser, owners of Beresan Winery, meticulously

renovated the old barn to serve the dual purpose of making and tasting wine. When you walk into the barn's tasting room, at its south end, you are struck by the attention to detail. The barn's high ceilings, rustic colors, quality woodwork, and turn-of-the-century furnishings create an ambiance that speaks volumes about the Walisers' passion for making great wine.

By the way, the greeting committee of tail-wagging, friendly dogs is composed of strays that have found a home at Beresan Winery. They are just a few members of the menagerie of animals at this former horse farm, as you will discover.

Tom Waliser is a quintessential "wine grower." He manages his own 20-plus acres of estate vineyards — Yellow Jacket Vineyard, Beresan Estate Vineyard, and Waliser Vineyard — the source for Beresan Winery's estate wines. He's also the vineyard manager for some of the region's most prestigious vineyards, including Pepper Bridge Vineyard, Seven Hills West, Candy Mountain Vineyard (love that name) and Mirage Vineyard. Evidently, farming is in Tom's genes. The Waliser family history includes many generations of farmers whose origins go back to the Beresan area of the Ukraine.

However, growing premium wine grapes is one thing. Converting the fruit to fine wine is another. For this, Tom turned to another Tom — Tom Glase, who also makes wine under his own wine label, Balboa. Together, the two Toms collaborate from vineyard to bottle to produce a portfolio of predominantly red estate wines, including syrah, merlot, cabernet sauvignon, carménère, and several red blends. It's tail-wagging good!

BERESAN WINERY
opened: 2003
winemaker(s): Tom Glase
location: 4169 Peppers Bridge Road, Walla Walla, WA 99362
phone: 509-522-2395
web: www.beresanwines.com
e-mail: info@beresanwines.com
fee: Tasting fee
hours: Friday and Saturday 11–5, or by appointment
amenities: Newsletter/Blog, Picnic Area, RV/Bus Parking, Tours, Vineyard on Premise, Wheelchair Accessible, Wine Club
connect: f

Balboa Winery

"Hey, what happened to the screw caps?" I asked, eyeing the bottle closure for a Balboa bottle of wine. In response, our tasting-room host said, "We went with a more environmentally sound closure. A conglomerate cork that uses sustainable cork products that are biodegradable." I should have seen this coming. After all, Balboa is known for its environmentally sound practices. From the vineyards it chooses to work with to its decision not to use decorative foil around bottle necks, Balboa Winery is all about sustainability. Guiding this endeavor is owner, winemaker and "go green" advocate Tom Glase.

There's a certain breed of person who feels compelled to roll the dice and leave the comforts of home to resettle in a new place. These are adventurous souls, willing to take a risk and try something new. Tom is just such a person, giving up a comfortable existence on Bainbridge Island and moving to Walla Walla in 1997. Tom was volunteering at Walla Walla's L'Ecole No 41 Winery when its owner/winemaker, Martin Clubb, asked him if he knew of anyone available to work at the winery. In fact, Tom did know of someone — himself.

There followed a three-year stint at L'Ecole No 41, during which Tom learned to make wine — very good wine. He then left L'Ecole No 41 to become winemaker for Tom Waliser at Beresan Winery. With a winemaking facility and premium grapes at his disposal, it wasn't long before Tom had created his own wine under the Balboa label. With fruit sourced from vineyards managed by Waliser's Premiere Vineyard Management company, Tom focuses on single-vineyard wines such as Balboa Merlot from Pepper Bridge block 64 and Balboa Syrah from their estate Eidolon Vineyard.

BALBOA WINERY
opened: 2006
winemaker(s): Tom Glase
location: 4169 Peppers Bridge Road, Walla Walla, WA 99362
phone: 509-529-0461
web: www.balboawinery.com
e-mail: info@balboawinery.com
fee: Tasting fee
hours: Thursday through Monday 10–4
amenities: Mailing List, Online Store, Picnic Area, RV/Bus Parking, Vineyard on Premise, Wheelchair Accessible, Wine Club
connect: 🐦 f

Saviah Cellars

Saviah Cellars celebrates tradition. Perhaps that is why an old wine press rests in its tasting room/winery located just south of Walla Walla. Reflecting winery owners Richard and Anita

Funk's roots in Montana, the wines have names that pay tribute to their heritage: a white wine called "Star Meadows" is the location of the original family homestead; its "Une Vallée" red wine derives its name from their current family homestead; and its "Big Sky" cuvée gets its name from ... well, you guessed it, Montana's official nickname. The Funks also produce a delicious blend of Columbia Valley merlot and cabernet sauvignon that they have dubbed "The Jack," named in honor of Anita's grandfather. The Saviah name itself comes from Anita's side of the family — it was her grandmother's middle name.

Richard and Anita moved from Montana in 1991 and, armed with a background in environmental science, Richard focused on water-quality programs. His work with the Walla Walla Health Department brought him in close contact with many of the local winemakers. He also found time to get his fingernails dirty by analyzing the soil around the valley. It wasn't long before the artistic side of winemaking captured his scientific mind. In 2000, his father and mother, Mike and Kay Funk, joined forces with Richard and Anita and launched Saviah Cellars.

With all winemaking, you have the rhythm of cycles, from harvest through crush, fermenting, and bottling. States Richard, "The winemaker's cycle repeats itself over and over, year after year. Always the same and always different ... and the winemaker is always hopeful." It's all about appreciating these cycles and understanding your role in them, whether it is making premium wine or keeping the family legacy alive.

SAVIAH CELLARS
opened: 2000
winemaker(s): Richard Funk
location: 1979 JB George Road, Walla Walla, WA 99362
phone: 509-522-2181
web: www.saviahcellars.com
e-mail: info@saviahcellars.com
fee: Complimentary wine tasting
hours: Daily 10–5, or by appointment
amenities: Mailing List, Picnic Area, RV/Bus Parking, Tours, Vineyard on Premise, Wheelchair Accessible, Wine Club
connect: 🐦 f

Sleight of Hand Cellars 8

Any new realizations would have to wait

'Til he had more time

More time

A time to dream

To himself

He waves goodbye

To himself

I'll see you on the other side

Another man moved by sleight of hand

— "Sleight of Hand," Pearl Jam

To say that co-owner and winemaker Trey Busch is a fan of Pearl Jam is an understatement. Pearl Jam holds cult status in Trey's mind and is the inspiration for Sleight of Hand's branding. With names and amazing label graphics for such wines as "The Magician" gewürztraminer, "Spellbinder" red blend, and "Levitation" syrah, you half expect the tasting room staff to pull a rabbit out of a hat. But there are no tricks up their sleeves. The real magic visitors experience are the premium small-lot wines.

Trey Busch

It was Trey's chance encounter with Jerry and Sandy Solomon at a Sun Valley auction in 2002 that eventually led to the creation of Sleight of Hand Cellars. As the winemaker for Basel Cellars Estate Winery, Trey had established himself as one of Washington's up-and-coming young winemakers. Given his résumé, it was only natural for Trey to consider launching his own winery, with a focus on showcasing Washington *Vitis vinifera* fruit. He approached Jerry and Susan with the idea of a joint venture à la Walla Walla and the rest is Washington winemaking history.

Sleight of Hand's relatively new tasting room and winery on JB George Road in south Walla Walla is a comfortable abode to explore the senses of the tasteful kind. It's not an illusion — the price and the taste you experience are indeed a great value. It's little wonder that Trey Busch is hailed as one of Washington's up-and-coming winemakers to watch. It's wine of the magical kind.

SLEIGHT OF HAND CELLARS
opened: 2007
winemaker(s): Trey Busch
location: 1959 JB George Road, Walla Walla, WA 99362
phone: 509-525-3661
web: www.SofHCellars.com
e-mail: info@SofHCellars.com
fee: Tasting fee refunded with purchase
hours: April through November, Thursday through Saturday 11–5, or by appointment
amenities: Mailing List, Online Store, RV/Bus Parking, Vineyard on Premise, Wheelchair Accessible, Wine Club
connect: 🐦 📘

Waters Winery

When I first visited Waters Winery's tasting room in 2006, a sign on the door greeted visitors with "Sold Out — See You Next Vintage." The space was a postage-stamp-size room at the Train Depot building in downtown Walla Walla. Even though founder Jason

Huntley and winemaker Jamie Brown were producing fewer than 1,000 cases of wine, I figured that these native Walla Wallans must have been doing something right.

Fast-forward to a few years later and now their tasting room has morphed into a beautiful state-of-the-art winemaking and tasting facility south of town on J.B. George Road. It's so beautiful I stopped my car to snap pictures of the contemporary-style complex from the vineyard covered hillside.

At the heart of Waters Winery's collection of wines is syrah. However, you won't find a blend of syrah from various vineyards in the Columbia Valley. Rather, you'll discover vineyard-designated syrah from Leonetti Cellar's Loess Vineyard, Pepper Bridge Vineyard, or the winery's own estate vineyard, Forgotten Hills. Why is this? I suspect it's because syrah is such a *terroir* expressive grape it allows Waters Winery to showcase a multitude of flavor profiles.

As I studied the calligraphy on the Waters label, wondering how the hell anyone could write so beautifully, the pourer reminded me that Waters Winery is behind the production of two other brands. In a brilliant move, Jason teamed with Gramercy Cellars' Greg Harrington to create their exclusive 100-case 21 Grams cabernet sauvignon as well as wallet-friendly Substance wines. With its periodic-table theme, Substance would allow me to easily "tweet" 140

characters of praise — if I had time to tweet. Waters wines, 21 Grams, and Substance are all reminders that the Washington wine scene is forever evolving.

WATERS WINERY
opened: 2006
winemaker(s): Jamie Brown
location: 1825 JB George Road, Walla Walla, WA 99362
phone: 509-525-1590
web: www.waterswinery.com
e-mail: via website
fee: Tasting fee refunded with purchase
hours: Friday and Saturday 10–5, or by appointment
amenities: Online Store, Picnic Area, RV/Bus Parking, Vineyard on Premise, Wheelchair Accessible, YouTube
connect: 🐦 f

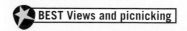

BEST Views and picnicking

Va Piano Vineyards

Imagine drinking superb wine and contributing to a good cause while under the roof of a Tuscan-inspired estate. You can, simply by experiencing Va Piano Vineyards. Upon buying

a bottle of Va Piano's "Bruno's Blend" at the vineyards, a portion of your purchase goes to a charitable organization, such as an African-based charity that supports children orphaned by AIDS. But how does a medium-priced wine get the name of "Bruno," and why an African-based charity?

The answers have their roots in the mid-'90s, when Va Piano's proprietor and winemaker, Justin Wylie, attended Gonzaga University's Florence campus during his senior year. There, Justin met and befriended the Rev. Bruno Segatta, a Catholic priest and assistant dean of the Florence program. Bruno, as students and friends alike know him, is also an avid painter and ardent contributor to a variety of charities for developing countries. Routinely, he contributes half the proceeds of his art sales to such causes.

The 7,500-square-foot, Tuscan-inspired winery and tasting room features timber-beamed ceilings, a red-tile roof, earth-toned stucco, and distressed alder doors. The colors, textures, and quality of materials hark back to Justin's time in Tuscany. Inside the tasting room, Bruno's artwork graces Va Piano's walls, and the décor's warm earth tones and the staff's relaxed style make you feel right at home. However, to savor the moment (and the wine), you need to keep Va Piano Vineyards' motto in mind: *Chi va piano, va sano e va lantano*, which translates to "He who goes slowly,

goes safely and goes far." Thus the name "Va Piano," or "go slowly," reminds us to swirl, observe the dark red color, take in the aroma, and concentrate on some amazing tastes.

VA PIANO VINEYARDS
opened: 2003
winemaker(s): Justin Wylie
location: 1793 JB George Road, Walla Walla, WA 99362
phone: 509-529-0900
web: www.vapianovineyards.com
e-mail: info@vapianovineyards.com
fee: Tasting fee refunded with purchase
hours: Friday and Saturday 11–5, or by appointment; Winter hours by appointment only
amenities: Gift Shop, Mailing List, Online Store, Picnic Area, RV/Bus Parking, Vineyard on Premise, Wheelchair Accessible, Wine Club
connect:

BEST Picnicking

Northstar Winery 11

Northstar's focus is on merlot. Not just your garden-variety merlot, but ultrapremium merlot sourced from the best vineyards in Washington using their finest grapes. Merlot, a black-skinned grape that originated in France back in the 1700s, is often called Bordeaux's other red-wine grape, cabernet sauvignon being the signature grape of the region.

Sporting tinted glasses and a hair style reminiscent of U2's Bono, winemaker David "Merf" Merfeld meets the challenge of blending the best-of-the-best merlot grapes with other Bordeaux-derived varieties, including cabernet sauvignon, petit verdot, and cabernet franc, to produce 90+ point award winners. Words such as "intense," "muscular," "chocolate," and "licorice" come to mind when I taste Northstar's prized merlots. It's all in the blending, and Merf draws upon what he dubs a "spice rack" of varieties to create merlot-based wines.

Located just south of Walla Walla, within a stone's throw of Pepper Bridge Winery and Tertulia Cellars, Northstar offers a commanding view of the distant Blue Mountains. These mountains provide most of the water for the valley's 1,200 acres of *Vitis vinifera*, including the 14 acres of grapes growing next to the winery (take a wild guess at the variety). Ste. Michelle Wine Estates, the parent company of Northstar, is all about elegance, and this is in evidence in Northstar's stylish tasting room and state-of-the-art production facility.

Be sure to ask a staff person if you can take a peek at Northstar's production area. From a side door, you look down into the winemaking area. By most standards, the facility is huge, with mammoth stainless steel tanks lining the walls like sentinel soldiers. From this vantage point, it's easy to imagine Merf and his production team blending great wines from their industrial-size spice racks.

NORTHSTAR WINERY
opened: 1992
winemaker(s): David 'Merf' Merfeld
location: 1736 JB George Road, Walla Walla, WA 99362
phone: 509-529-0948
web: www.northstarmerlot.com
e-mail: info@northstarmerlot.com
fee: Tasting fee refunded with purchase
hours: Monday through Saturday 10–4, Sunday 11–4, or by appointment
amenities: Gift Shop, Online Store, Pet Friendly, Picnic Area, Private Events, Restaurant/Food Pairings, RV/Bus Parking, Tours, Vineyard on Premise, Wheelchair Accessible, Wine Club, YouTube
connect: 🐦 📘

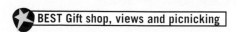
★ BEST Gift shop, views and picnicking

Pepper Bridge Winery 12

As you approach Pepper Bridge Winery, you are likely to spot a Swiss flag flying above this handsome tri-level estate and winery. No, you haven't left the U.S.; the flag honors the home country of Pepper Bridge winemaker Jean-François Pellet. It was in Switzerland that Jean-François honed his winemaking skills, beginning at his family's winery/vineyard and later working in Spain.

The wonderful thing about Pepper Bridge is the team of people who have come together to create an integrated winery, working cohesively from "grape buds to bottle." This team is composed of managing partners, viticulturists, winemakers, marketing and sales staff, and tasting-room hosts. Whomever you visit with, you are struck by their professionalism and dedication to Pepper Bridge Winery. You come to understand that the winery is more than the personality of one individual — it is about an organization.

The winery/tasting room sits on a hill on the southern edge of Walla Walla, with Northstar Winery within view to the northeast. The hill provides a panoramic vista of the Blue Mountains, but the location was chosen to take advantage of gravity's force. The three-story production facility allows harvested grapes to gently flow from top to bottom, from destemming to fermentation.

WineTrails Northwest rarely advocates joining a particular winery's wine club, but we make an exception with the Pepper Bridge Vine Club. Using an innovative approach, Pepper Bridge Winery sells vines to its Vine Club members at the cost of $150 per year. For that fee, members receive a bottle of wine, a certificate of ownership, and a "hands-on" day in the Pepper Bridge Vineyard, where they learn pruning, thinning, and harvesting techniques. What's more, your name is prominently displayed on your vine. Now that's a different kind of wine club … *vive la différence!*

PEPPER BRIDGE WINERY
opened: 2000
winemaker(s): Jean-Francois Pellet
location: 1704 JB George Road, Walla Walla, WA 99362
phone: 509-525-6502
web: www.pepperbridge.com
e-mail: info@pepperbridge.com
fee: Tasting fee refunded with purchase
hours: Daily 10–4
amenities: Online Store, Picnic Area, RV/Bus Parking, Tours, Vineyard on Premise, Wheelchair Accessible, Wine Club, YouTube
connect: 🐦 f

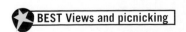 **BEST Views and picnicking**

Dusted Valley Vintners 🔟

Named by *Wine Press Northwest* as 2010 Washington Winery of the Year, Dusted Valley Vintners is the story of two families from Wisconsin — the Johnsons and the Braunels. In 2003, they moved to Walla Walla, driven by a love affair with Northwest wines. Chad Johnson's background includes a degree in food science; Corey Braunel grew up on a ginseng farm in northern Wisconsin. In addition to sharing a passion for making wine, it turns out that Chad and Corey also share a familial connection. Chad is married to Janet, and Corey is married to her sister Cindy.

Given their Badger background, it may come as no surprise that Corey and Chad use white oak (Quercus alba; aka American oak) from Wisconsin to barrel-age some of their wines. Although other well-established wineries outside Walla Walla rely on American oak (e.g., the renowned Silver Oak Winery in California uses American oak exclusively), it is rare to find a winery in the valley venturing beyond the standard French oak. But Corey and Chad must be on to something with this American oak thing. Their 2006 Reserve Cabernet Sauvignon, which features oak from Wisconsin, grabbed a gold medal at the 2009 Seattle Wine Awards.

In addition to the winery, the families own 90 acres of vineyards in the Walla Walla Valley, giving them control over their growing portfolio of wines, from bud break to bottling. The fact that the 90 acres of vineyards are scattered among four different locations provides distinct flavor profiles for their fundamental ingredient — the grapes.

With a wide assortment of Dusted Valley Vintners wines to sample — including my personal favorite, the "Stained Tooth" syrah — you'll want to budget plenty of time to taste. If time permits, you can retreat to the outside patio and enjoy a bottle of wine with the Blue Mountains in the background.

DUSTED VALLEY VINTNERS
opened: 2003
winemaker(s): Chad Johnson and Corey Braunel
location: 1248 Old Milton Highway, Walla Walla, WA 99362-8174
phone: 509-525-1337
web: www.dustedvalley.com
e-mail: info@dustedvalley.com
fee: Tasting fee refunded with purchase
hours: February 15th through March, Saturday and Sunday 12–5; April through November, Thursday through Monday 12–5; Closed December to February 15th
amenities: Online Store, Picnic Area, Private Events, RV/Bus Parking, Tours, Wheelchair Accessible Wine Club, YouTube
connect: 🐦 f

Isenhower Cellars 🟦14

"Go, Butler!" exclaimed Olivia, one of the Isenhowers' three daughters. The little blond-haired girl was dressed in a Butler Bulldog cheerleading outfit and she, along with friends and family, was gearing up for the 2010 Final Four match-up with Michigan State. It turns

out that her mom, Denise Isenhower, graduated from Butler University, hence the Bulldog shout-out.

While Olivia doodled with crayons, her dad, Brett Isenhower, described the family's 1998 move from Colorado to make wine, equating it to "diving head first into shallow water." But the couple came armed with backgrounds in chemistry (both Denise and Brett were pharmacists) as well as Brett's successful business experience in concocting homemade beer. An exhaustive review of wine-growing areas (Brett is very analytical) found Walla Walla to be more than just a dot on the map. As Brett put it, "Walla Walla is the most attractive town in Eastern Washington," referring not just to its climate and soil, but to the town's general culture, architecture and school system. At that, Olivia rattled off something in Spanish, to which 40-something Brett smiled and explained that she attends a bilingual grade school. Proof positive that they had chosen wisely.

With 15+ years of winemaking experience, Brett continues to evolve — and experiment with — his chosen craft. His current releases feature Bordeaux and Rhône varietal wines that grow exceptionally well in the Columbia Valley. Many of his wines have been christened after flowers, for example, "Wild Alfalfa" (syrah), "Batchelor's Button" (cabernet sauvignon), and "Red Paintbrush" (Bordeaux blend). However, there's nothing "garden variety" about these wines. Grabbing my attention was the wonderfully balanced white Rhône blend of roussanne and viognier called "Snapdragon," bearing a stunning label. Brett proudly pointed out that the label is the creation of local artist Squire Broel.

P.S. Butler won!

Brett Isenhower

ISENHOWER CELLARS
opened: 1998
winemaker(s): Brett Isenhower
location: 3471 Pranger Road, Walla Walla, WA 99362-7307
phone: 509-526-7896
web: www.isenhowercellars.com
e-mail: info@isenhowercellars.com
fee: Tasting fee refunded with purchase
hours: Thursday and Friday 12–4, Saturday 11–5 or by appointment
amenities: Gift Shop, Mailing List, Online Store, Tours, Vineyard on Premise, Wheelchair Accessible, Wine Club, YouTube
connect: 🐦 📘

Rulo Winery 15

The sign above the front door states: "Relive a memory; realize a dream." Realizing a dream, though, often requires hard work and some serious intestinal fortitude. Such is the case for

Rulo Winery owners Kurt and Vicki Schlicker, who launched their winery in 2000. By day, Kurt shares an anesthesia practice and is typically on duty at Providence St. Mary Medical Center in Walla Walla. At crush, Kurt's focus switches from gases that are inhaled to gas that's released by fermenting grapes, CO_2, along with ethyl alcohol — a different form of anesthetic.

Unlike many of its big-bucks winery neighbors, Rulo Winery embodies America's heritage of hard-working, do-it-yourself individuals. You won't find tasting room staff bedecked in logo-emblazoned casual wear here. Instead, you find Kurt and Vicki working the tasting room, pouring and explaining their winemaking process to loyal fans and newly converted Rulo disciples.

The name "Rulo" harks to the Schlickers' family farm, located close to the Rulo grain elevator on the Washington side of the state line. That grain elevator was the inspiration for

Kurt Schlicker

Rulo's nice logo: a simple line drawing of the elevator's silos. There are many grain-elevator stations strewn about the valley, and each one has a name. Locals know your location by your proximity to the nearest grain elevator. Kurt and Vicki refer to this as "farmer GPS." Like other community members, the Schlickers embody a work ethic that is so much a part of our heritage. As I exited through the door, I again looked up at the sign posted above it and thought of another quotation, an anonymous scribbler's words of wisdom I once read, that would be every bit as apropos for Rulo Winery: "There is no elevator to success. You have to take the stairs."

RULO WINERY
opened: 2000
winemaker(s): Kurt J. Schlicker
location: 3525 Pranger Road, Walla Walla, WA 99362
phone: 509-525-7856
web: www.rulowinery.com
e-mail: schlick@pocketinet.com
fee: Complimentary wine tasting
hours: Typically open Saturdays 12–3; call ahead
amenities: Mailing List, RV/Bus Parking, Tours, Wheelchair Accessible
connect:

Tertulia Cellars 16

Tertulia — a word of Spanish origin describing a social gathering with literary or artistic overtones, especially in Iberia or Latin America. — *Wikipedia.com*

Jim O'Connell, the Arizona-based owner of Tertulia Cellars, envisioned the creation of a winery that serves as a place of "social gathering of friends" — and that vision is realized in

this architecturally pleasing space (which includes state-of-the-art winemaking equipment, including an indoor crush pad). The facility and tasting room are downright beautiful, and the Mediterranean orange and red colors only add to the venue's warmth. Moreover, although it was winter during my visit, I could easily imagine the outdoor patio filled with folks enjoying a summer evening, complete with good food, background music, and Tertulia Cellars wine to enjoy.

The dazzling wines I sampled during my visit are of a decided southern Rhône persuasion, with viognier, syrah, grenache, and Mourvèdre varietals on offer. The harmonious, full-bodied Les Collines syrah (I relish that midpalate taste explosion followed by a long finish) had me reading the label's fine print to appreciate this wine's pedigree. But there are also wonderfully rich Bordeaux varietals, including a sumptuous cabernet sauvignon.

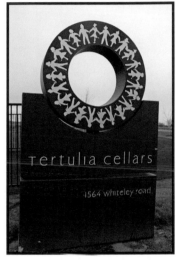

Winemaker Ryan Raber has the enviable challenge of producing more than 4,000 cases of wine per year for the growing number of Tertulia Cellars' fans. Armed with an enology and viticulture degree from nearby Walla Walla Community College, Ryan is expected to rely more on Tertulia Cellars' estate fruit to craft an increasing mix of Rhône-style wines. I'm sure that to celebrate the release of his wines, there will be a gathering each spring in Walla Walla, complete with laughter, food, and wine — a tertulia in the truest sense.

TERTULIA CELLARS
opened: 2007
winemaker(s): Ryan Raber
location: 1564 Whiteley Road, Walla Walla, WA 99362
phone: 509-525-5700
web: www.tertuliacellars.com
e-mail: info@tertuliacellars.com
fee: Tasting fee refunded with purchase
hours: Thursday through Saturday 11–6, Sunday 11–5, or by appointment
amenities: Mailing List, Newsletter/Blog, Online Store, Picnic Area, RV/Bus Parking, Vineyard on Premise, Wheelchair Accessible, Wine Club, Wines by the Glass, YouTube

⭐ **BEST Picnicking and views**

Fjellene Cellars 17

I've known river-rafting and mountain-climbing guides, and they all possess good planning skills. They have to. They organize their equipment, study the weather, and think of contingencies. Some people think that outdoor guides are creative people, but I would add a caveat. They may be creative, but really good guides anticipate the unexpected and under duress, make panic-free decisions.

Such is the case with winemaker/proprietor Matthew Erlandson of Fjellene Cellars. Fjellene is pronounced "fyell-lay-nuh" and means "mountains" in Norwegian, reflecting his family heritage. Matthew had worked as an outdoor guide and educator for about 15 years, leading climbing expeditions in various locations with a special focus on South America. While completing his studies at the University of Idaho, Matthew made a number of forays to Walla Walla and discovered the joy of wine. Eventually, he worked crush and learned the winemaking craft (even creating his own brand) at Balboa Winery before venturing out on his own.

Located on Merlot Drive (apropos, don't you think?), the Fjellene Cellars tasting room and winery is a relaxed and, judging from the countenance of other visitors, fun place to spend an afternoon. Matthew's distinctive label features his favorite Peruvian mountain and one that he's ascended on numerous occasions. As you sip and swirl Fjellene Cellars' wines (possessing modest alcohol levels and a nice spark of acidity), be sure to ask Matthew about his worm-derived tea compost for the vineyard.

Perhaps it was the hot summer sun beaming down that day, but the watermelon-colored rosé made my knees buckle with its balanced juiciness. Looking at this rather tall winemaker with his shoulder-length locks, I thought if I were seeking an outdoor guide, I'd hire Matthew in a second, especially if he brought his wine along on the journey. *Skål!*

FJELLENE CELLARS
opened: 2010
winemaker(s): Matthew Erlandson
location: 1050 Merlot Drive, Walla Walla, WA 99362
phone: 541-861-9359
web: www.fjellenecellars.com
e-mail: via website
fee: Tasting fee refunded with purchase
hours: Friday and Saturday 11–4, or by appointment
amenities: Online Store, Private Events, RV/Bus Parking, Vineyard on Premise, Weddings, Wheelchair Accessible, Wine Club
connect: 🐦 📘

★ BEST Views

Morrison Lane Winery [18]

MORRISON LANE WINERY
opened: 2002
winemaker(s): Verdie Morrison and son Sean Morrison
location: 1249 Lyday Lane,
Walla Walla, WA 99362
phone: 509-526-0229 or 888-541-5532
web: www.morrisonlane.com
e-mail: sean@morrisonlane.com
fee: Complimentary wine tasting
hours: Friday through Sunday 12–5, or by
appointment; Closed January and February
amenities: Art Gallery, Mailing List,
Wheelchair Accessible
connect: f

www.winetrailsnw.com/wineries/morrison_lane_winery

Gifford Hirlinger Winery 🔟9️

Located on Stateline Road on the south side of Walla Walla, Gifford Hirlinger Winery is literally a stone's throw — or a mere lob — from Oregon. Housed in an ultramodern building, the winery is the domain of to winemaker and co-owner Mike Berghan. The architecture is stunning and offers ample patio space to enjoy a bottle of wine with a front-row seat for viewing Mike's now-matured vineyard.

This is a family affair, complete with Mike's parents, his wife, Melissa, and assorted laughing children pitching in to assist. Resident border collies Chewy and Charlie also contribute to the process. I suspect that, besides looking adorable, the dogs keep the local deer from munching on the ripening grapes.

Mike Berghan

In early 2000, Mike made his mark on the Walla Walla wine scene with a red blend he appropriately named "Stateline Red," a Bordeaux marriage of estate cabernet and merlot. Berghan Vineyard also produces cabernet sauvignon, tempranillo, merlot, Malbec, petit verdot, and pinot gris. Visitors can choose from a variety of wines — primarily reds — to swirl and sip, but personally, I went straight for Mike's cabernet sauvignon, because I believe it showcases Walla Walla Valley black fruit so nicely.

Originally from Sandpoint, Idaho, Mike became incredibly bored while chasing the American dream at Smith Barney in San Francisco. He did what many of us only daydream of doing: He quit his high-paying job to get his hands dirty (literally) working for a vineyard management company in California. Eventually, he landed in Walla Walla, but that wasn't by chance; his ancestors homesteaded in the Walla Walla Valley. In fact, the name Gifford Hirlinger (GH for short) derives from his not-too-distant relatives. Yes, it's true that the name twists the tongue a bit, but my opinion of GH wines is not at all difficult to pronounce: liquid decadence.

GIFFORD HIRLINGER WINERY
opened: 2001
winemaker(s): Mike Berghan
location: 1450 Stateline Road, Walla Walla, WA 99362
phone: 509-529-2075
web: www.giffordhirlinger.com
e-mail: wine@GiffordHirlinger.com
fee: Complimentary wine tasting
hours: Friday through Sunday 11–5, or by appointment
amenities: Mailing List, Online Store, Pet Friendly, Picnic Area, RV/Bus Parking, Vineyard on Premise, Wheelchair Accessible Wine Club, YouTube
connect: 🐦 f

BEST Picnicking

Castillo de Feliciana Vineyard and Winery 🔳20

Rarely does the WineTrail Guy gush over a particular winery. After all, my motto is to leave it up to my readers to discover their own preferences. However, in the case of upstart Castillo de Feliciana Vineyard and Winery, I will make an exception to the rule and strongly recommend that you allow time for this gem. Here's why.

First, owners Sam and Deborah Castillo made one brilliant move in getting their new winery off the ground. They appreciated the wines of the Iberian Peninsula and in particular, Spain's noble black grape, tempranillo. This then gave them the varietal compass to go with juicy food-friendly wines and the architecture to match emphasizing outdoor living areas.

The winery itself lies just over the state line south of Walla Walla and features a Mediterranean style that brings to mind the red-tile-roofed abodes in southern Spain overlooking the blue Atlantic. In this case, however, the view from the house features a maturing vineyard surrounding the property. In keeping with the Castillos' Spanish heritage, their wines lean toward the varieties of the Iberian Peninsula with wines such as tempranillo, albariño, and red blends made in a style suggestive of Spain's Priorat region and comprising a healthy dose of grenache (*garnacha*).

Let me suggest that you make Castillo de Feliciana the last stop on your day's tour. Just outside the tasting room are an open fire pit, inviting chairs, and a view of the Blue Mountains in the distance, reminding one of the mountains found in Spain's Rioja region. Sitting there, soaking in the moment and sampling their tempranillo, I found myself wanting to suggest to Sam or Deb that they start serving paella — it would be the ultimate dish to pair with this wine!

CASTILLO DE FELICIANA VINEYARD AND WINERY
opened: 2009
winemaker(s): Chris Castillo
location: 85728 Telephone Pole Road, Milton-Freewater, OR 97862
phone: 541-558-3656
web: www.castillodefeliciana.com
e-mail: info@castillodefeliciana.com
fee: Tasting fee refunded with purchase
hours: Friday, Saturday and Sunday 11–5
amenities: Online Store, Picnic Area, Private Events, Receptions, RV/Bus Parking, Tours, Weddings, Wheelchair Accessible, Wine Club
connect: ⬛f

⭐ **BEST Views and picnicking**

Spofford Station 21

To appreciate JLC Winery is to know that Lynne Chamberlain is a farm girl at heart. Following a prolonged sojourn in Washington, D.C., she returned home to her family's 500-acre farm, located on the Oregon side of the Walla Walla Valley. It's where she grew

up and it also is home to her celebrated 40-acre Spofford Station Vineyard. Along with the grapes, other crops such as mint and wheat are grown at the station. You might even find a few cases of uncorked Angus milling around.

WineTrail Note: The word "station" refers to locations where trains would stop and load farm produce for transport. Known as "stations" on the Oregon side, they are referred to as "grain elevators" in Washington. Built in the 1800s, the "grain train" still makes daily stops at the stations to load soft white wheat for transport to Portland and eventually on to markets in Asia.

JLC produces premium red wines, including Lynne's exclusive Spofford Station estate syrah and merlot wines. The label of her popular red table wine "Palette" features an angel enjoying her "angels' share" of wine. The original painting used for the label sold for $3,500 in a Portland benefit auction. As their own Angels Share Club member pamphlet explains, "In the days of old, before science grabbed attention, the winemaker left the cellar at evensong. His cellar rats continued to care for the precious elixirs as he rested.

On returning, he noted that the juice in the barrel had been lowered. 'You have stolen my precious nectar!' The reply, 'No master, a mere sip is promised the Angels.' What is now called evaporation was known as 'Angels' Share.'"

Lynne Chamberlain

SPOFFORD STATION
opened: 2002
winemaker(s): Lynne Chamberlain
location: 85131 Elliot Road, Milton-Freewater, OR 97862
phone: 509-529-1398
web: www.spoffordstation.com
e-mail: spoffordstation@gmail.com
fee: Tasting fee refunded with purchase
hours: Friday 12–4, Saturday 11–4, or by appointment
amenities: Picnic Area, RV/Bus Parking, Vineyard on Premise, Wheelchair Accessible, Wine Club
connect: f

Walla Walla East
WineTrail

Airport Incubator Buildings

During World War II, the regional airport near Walla Walla housed more than 10,000 military personnel. After the war, most of these properties sat idle, and the Port of Walla Walla had a major problem deciding what to do with all the buildings left behind, including barracks, mess halls, and fire stations. The answer was a low-cost solution, allowing start-up businesses to rent space in the buildings. Today, more than a dozen wineries make and sell wine at the Walla Walla Regional Airport and Industrial Park, including such well-known labels as Dunham Cellars, Five Star Cellars, Tamarack Cellars, SYZYGY, and Buty Winery. You can easily spend several weekends trekking the Airport WineTrail, and unless you bring a bike or a good pair of hiking boots, plan to use your car to get from one tasting room to the next.

Walla Walla WineTrail East

1. College Cellars of Walla Walla
2. K Vintners
3. àMaurice Cellars
4. Walla Walla Vintners
5. Russell Creek Winery
6. Trust Cellars
7. Dunham Cellars
8. Tempus Cellars
9. Patit Creek Cellars
10. SYZYGY
11. Adamant Cellars
12. Buty Winery
13. Tamarack Cellars
14. Revelry Vintners
15. Mannina Cellars
16. Five Star Cellars
17. Eleganté Cellars
18. Kontos Cellars
19. Corvus Cellars
20. Walla Faces
21. CAVU Cellars
22. Ash Hollow Winery

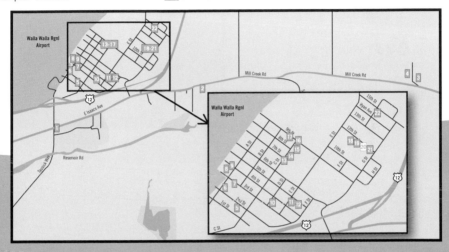

Region:	**Walla Walla Wine Country**
# of tasting rooms on tour:	**22**
# of satellite tasting rooms:	**1**
Estimate # of days for tour:	**4**
Getting around:	**Car and foot**
Key Events:	❏ **Events sponsored by Walla Walla Valley Wine Alliance: Spring Release Weekend; Balloon Stampede Weekend; Vintage Walla Walla; Entwine: An Auction to support Walla Walla Arts, Wine, and Education; and Holiday Barrel Tasting. See www.wallawallawine.com/events for details.**
Tips:	❏ **Purchase one or two inexpensive Styrofoam chests to store your wine purchases. In the summer, interior car temperatures easily get over 100ºF.**
	❏ **Saturdays are the best times to experience tasting rooms — most are open.**
	❏ **Great restaurants to choose from.**
	❏ **Consider using a limousine service.**
	❏ **Looking for a gift? Check out Dunham Cellars gift shop.**
Best:	❏ **Picnicking: àMaurice Cellars**
	❏ **Picnicking: Walla Walla Vintners**
	❏ **Gift shop and picnicking: Dunham Cellars**

College Cellars of Walla Walla

"What do you hope to do with your degree?" I asked as my pourer offered me a sample of cabernet sauvignon. She was a second-year student at the Institute for Enology and Viticulture at Walla Walla Community College and with graduation on the horizon, she had some choices to make. I suspect she will have many opportunities to choose from.

When you visit Walla Walla's wineries, I encourage you to make a point of chatting with the tasting room staff and discovering their backgrounds. Chances are that many pourers you encounter are students at the institute. In addition, many other members of local winemaking staffs are graduates of the program, including Matt Huse of Five Star Cellars, Ryan Raber of Tertulia, and Denise Slattery and Steve Michener, who began Trio Vintners, to name a few.

College Cellars of Walla Walla offers students of all ages and backgrounds an intensive hands-on experience in crafting wines, with most of their first year devoted to fieldwork in the vineyards. During their second year, students round out their education with additional exposure to the science associated with winemaking. One-quarter of the students come from outside the state of Washington, and many end up finding work in Walla Walla, attracted to its small-town feel and the opportunity to apply their freshly gained knowledge.

During my visit at College Cellars, I particularly enjoyed my sample of "Governor's White," a Bordeaux blend of sémillon and sauvignon blanc, in part because the grapes came from

the college's Stan Clarke Teaching Vineyard. Stan Clarke was a founding member of the viticulture program and a key instructor at the school before his premature death in 2007. As I swirled and sipped, I couldn't help but glance heavenward in appreciation.

COLLEGE CELLARS OF WALLA WALLA
opened: 2003
winemaker(s): Tim Donahue and students
location: 500 Tausick Way,
Walla Walla, WA 99362-9270
phone: 509-524-5170
web: www.collegecellarsofwallawalla.com
e-mail: info@collegecellars.com
fee: Complimentary wine tasting
hours: Friday 1–5, Saturday 12–4,
or by appointment
amenities: Mailing List, Online Store,
Pet Friendly, Private Events, Tours, Weddings,
Wheelchair Accessible
connect: 🐦 📘

K Vintners

Call him an edgy rock 'n' roll aficionado, and any-reason-to-ride motorcyclist, or a wine-loving freak — just don't call him lucky, because it's not by luck that Charles Smith has

succeeded in the wine business. We're not talking about successful small-lot wine production. No, we're talking over-the-top production under such labels as K Vintners, Charles Smith Wines and Charles and Charles. To succeed, you must have a good product, yes. Equally important, however, is a business vision and the wherewithal to market your product — which Charles has in spades. His rare combination of amazing palate fused with focused energy has garnered the man and his wines a cult-like following.

Originally from northern California, Charles managed rock 'n' roll bands in Scandinavia for 11 years before moving back to the U.S. and launching K Vintners. He also is the creator and winemaker for The Magnificent Wine Company, whose bottles sport his boldly lettered label "House Wine" (see Walla Walla Wine Works). The wines themselves go easy on the wallet, with price points in the teens. Another point in their favor: They are ready to drink with an evening's meal, and truth be told, that is why most Americans buy wine — for the dinner table, not for the cellar.

Charles Smith

The K Vintners winery and main tasting room are located a few miles east of Walla Walla on Mill Creek Road. A second tasting venue, completely different in design with an urban feel, is in downtown Walla Walla. Unless your eyes happen to be glued to the Blue Mountains ahead of you, you can't miss the giant K looming in front of the small vineyard and a big, old farmhouse, a massive tree ensconced next to it. Once you arrive, be prepared to party. This isn't one of those genteel, reverential, church-quiet establishments; it's a house of kick-ass wines. Party on, dudes!

K VINTNERS
opened: 2001
winemaker(s): Charles Smith; Andrew Latta (Assistant)
location: 820 Mill Creek Road, Walla Walla, WA 99362-8415
phone: 509-526-5230
web: www.kvintners.com
e-mail: charles@kvintners.com
fee: Tasting fee may apply
hours: Friday 12–5; Saturday 10–5, or by appointment; Closed in winter
amenities: Mailing List, Online Store, Picnic Area, RV/Bus Parking, Tours, Vineyard on Premise, Wheelchair Accessible, YouTube
connect: 🐦 f

àMaurice Cellars [3]

Malbec originated in France where it is one of the five great grapes of the Bordeaux region. In France, Malbec is often blended with other Bordeaux varieties such as cabernet sauvignon or merlot to create some of the world's great classic wines. After working the fall harvest at Paul Hobbs' celebrated Viña Cobos winery in Argentina's Mendoza wine-growing region, àMaurice winemaker/partner Anna Schafer knows a thing or two about Malbec.

Although àMaurice isn't the only winery in the valley to produce this varietal, it certainly enjoys a reputation for creating top-notch Malbec, and this may be what attracts most visitors to àMaurice. But Anna's other creations also shine; critically acclaimed syrah, viognier, chardonnay and a Bordeaux blend that honors a different Northwest artist each year serve to showcase the talents of this dual-hemisphere winemaker.

The Schafer family, including parents Tom and Kathleen Schafer, planted 13 acres of *Vitis vinifera* grapes in the Mill Creek area east of Walla Walla in 2006. At 1,200 feet and with good air drainage, the location is reminiscent of Mendoza's high-altitude vineyards. Now that the vineyards are mature, the family adheres to sustainable methods in maintaining them.

The notion of sustainable crops is nothing new to the Schafers, given their family heritage. Tom's father, Maurice Schafer, was responsible for developing a self-sustaining 20,000-acre evergreen tree farm. Because of Maurice's vision, and his kindness toward others, the Schafers paid homage to him by naming the winery after him; in the French language, à Maurice means "to Maurice."

ÀMAURICE CELLARS
opened: 2006
winemaker(s): Anna Schafer
location: 178 Vineyard Lane, Walla Walla, WA 99362
phone: 509-522-5444
web: www.amaurice.com
e-mail: info@amaurice.com
fee: Tasting fee refunded with purchase
hours: Friday 10:30–4:30; Saturday 10:30–4:30, or by appointment
amenities: Online Store, Pet Friendly, Picnic Area, RV/Bus Parking, Vineyard on Premise, Wheelchair Accessible, YouTube
connect: 🐦 f

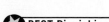
BEST Picnicking

Walla Walla Vintners 4

Started by Dr. Myles Anderson and Gordon Venneri, Walla Walla Vintners was a "hobby business" that morphed into a very successful venture. Both men come from well-ordered,

structured backgrounds. Myles Anderson was the founding director of Walla Walla Community College's Institute for Enology and Viticulture. Gordon is a retired accountant and a retired agent for Knights of Columbus Insurance. You would expect, with these backgrounds, that the two men would operate from a detailed business plan, complete with financial projections that would warm a banker's heart. Nope, no plan. Nada. Zilch.

Before launching Walla Walla Vintners in 1995 (and becoming the eighth bonded winery in Walla Walla Valley), Myles and Gordon experimented. The winery grew out of a labor of love for handcrafting premium wine. It also grew out of much failure experimenting with used oak barrels, beer kegs, food-grade plastic buckets, and glass carboys. The yeast and chemicals came from a local drug store that specialized in stocking such items for beer and winemakers. Now, that is passion!

Myles and Gordon have also gained a reputation for being exceptionally generous with their time, expertise, and winemaking equipment. They provide the training ground for the enology and viticulture program's interns, educate other would-be winemakers, and lend their production facility and equipment to start-ups such as nearby àMaurice Winery. Their winemaker, William vonMetzger, graduated from the enology and viticulture program.

However, Miles and Gordon's real claim to fame is their wine — premium red wine. The buzz surrounding the release of their 2003 sangiovese was loud, and the wine earned top honors at the Seattle Wine Awards. Their other reds, including cabernet sauvignon, cabernet franc, and a red-blend cuvée, have also garnered high marks.

WALLA WALLA VINTNERS
opened: 1999
winemaker(s): William vonMetzger, Myles Anderson and Gordon Venneri
location: 225 Vineyard Lane, Walla Walla, WA 99362
phone: 509-525-4724
web: www.wallawallavintners.com
e-mail: info@wallawallavintners.com
fee: Complimentary wine tasting
hours: Friday 1–5; Saturday 10:30–4:30; Monday through Thursday by appointment; closed Sunday
amenities: Online Store, Pet Friendly, Picnic Area, RV/Bus Parking, Tours, Vineyard on Premise, Wheelchair Accessible Wine Club, YouTube
connect: f

★ **BEST Picnicking**

Russell Creek Winery

When I first met Larry Krivoshein in 2007, he was both owner and winemaker of Russell Creek, having launched the winery in the early days of the Walla Walla wine boom back in 1998. Fast-forward to 2010, and Larry is back at the helm following a brief detour.

You see, there was a point when Larry had sold the winery, but evidently things didn't work out. In October 2010, Larry took back control of Russell Creek, and loyal fans of the winery

are now breathing a collective sigh of relief. They can still find his ever-popular sangiovese, as well as the winery's number-one seller, Tributary, a blend of cabernet sauvignon, merlot, and syrah. That's reassuring.

Regarding the aforementioned sangiovese, Russell Creek's tasting notes read, "Sangiovese is the closest thing in America to a Tuscan wine. 100% Sangiovese, our lightest-bodied red boasts bright aromas of crushed blackberry easing into cranberry and lemon peel on the palate...." I understand the part about sangio being the closest thing we have to Italian sangiovese (aka Chianti), but Larry's sangiovese packs power and boatloads of blackberry flavor, quite unlike Italian sangio-based wines, which often come across as thin and tomatoey. Perhaps his secret is the use of new American oak, perhaps it is the fruit itself, which comes from older vines, or maybe it is the fact that Larry doesn't cut corners.

Testament to his remarkably good wine is the Best in Show award Russell Creek Winery took home from the Tri-Cities Wine Festival in 2010, outscoring more than 400 other wine entries. Congratulations to Larry and the whole Krivoshein family!

Larry Krivoshein

RUSSELL CREEK WINERY
opened: 1998
winemaker(s): Larry Krivoshein
location: 301 Aeronca Avenue, Walla Walla, WA 99362
phone: 509-522-6515
web: www.russellcreek-winery.com
e-mail: russellcreekwinery@gmail.com
fee: Tasting fee refunded with purchase
hours: Daily 11–4; special events 10–5
amenities: Online Store, RV/Bus Parking, Tours, Wine Club
connect: f

Trust Cellars 6

Working in Atlanta for 19 years at CNN as a TV producer brought Steve little joy. At the age of 40, he had proven to himself and others that he had mastered his job, but the gloom of the news business and the constant travel were taking a toll. He sought a career that would allow him to spend more time with his two young girls and give him and his

wife Lori, a television director also working at CNN, an opportunity to exercise their passion for food and wine. After all, this couple would plan tummy-tantalizing vacation itineraries focusing on the restaurants and foods they wanted to experience.

Steve Brooks

Steve knew he wanted to make wine, and by announcing to his coworkers and friends that he was quitting his executive job to become a winemaker, he was forced to make good on his promise. So in late 2001, spurred by a review of the American wine scene that included a *New York Times* article highlighting the winemaking virtues of Walla Walla, Steve and family packed their Volvo and headed west.

Upon arrival in Walla Walla, he discovered a community of winemakers willing to help by lending advice and equipment. He enrolled in the local Walla Walla Community College Institute for Enology and Viticulture and learned from the best. Not having the deep pockets to buy his own vineyards, Steve developed collaborative relationships with the region's premium grape growers. He notes that in exchange for him picking up the lunch tab, a local winemaker he admires told him the secrets of making rosé.

Uprooting your family from Atlanta, moving them to Walla Walla, and launching a new career takes a lot of guts. To do it, Steve had to place his trust in his family, his friends, and, ultimately, the one person he knows best — himself.

TRUST CELLARS
opened: 2007
winemaker(s): Steve Brooks
location: 202 A Street,
Walla Walla Regional Airport,
Walla Walla, WA 99362
phone: 509-529-4511
web: www.trustcellars.com
e-mail: Trust.Cellars@facebook.com
fee: Tasting fee
hours: Thursday through Friday 11–4,
Saturday 11–5, Sunday 11–4
amenities: Mailing List, Online Store, Picnic Area, RV/Bus Parking, Wheelchair Accessible, Wine Club
connect: 🐦 📘

Dunham Cellars

Dunham Cellars is dog friendly — just as friendly as co-owner and winemaker extraordinaire Eric Dunham, but we'll get to him in a bit. This is border collie heaven, with angelic canines Konnie and Maysy circling underfoot. While Maysy is pictured on the "Four Legged White" label, Eric's dog Port, now deceased, still graces the label of his delectable "Three Legged Red." All these dogs share something special: They are rescue dogs and they won the lottery by being taken into this loving home.

Located at the Walla Walla Airport Complex, Dunham Cellars' tasting room is one of my favorite wine stops along the Walla Walla Airport WineTrail. Named by *Sunset* magazine in 2009 as one of the top tasting rooms in the West, Dunham Cellars' provides relaxed comfort inside its oh so nicely decorated Hangar Lounge or, weather permitting, outside at one of many picnic tables. Eric is often at the winery, tending to the never-ending duties of winemaking, but he still manages to find time to visit with guests, whether they are novice wine drinkers or experienced connoisseurs.

In addition to the "Three Legged Red," you have an opportunity to sample their renowned syrah, cabernet sauvignon, sémillon, "Shirley Mays" chardonnay, a crisp rosé, as well as a Bordeaux blend called "Trutina" (the Latin word for "balance"). By the way, the vivid artwork that graces the single-vineyard-designated wines is the work of Eric himself. In addition, the staff at Dunham Cellars vouch that Eric is also a fabulous cook. Culinary artist, fine-arts painter, celebrated winemaker — the guy is multitalented. Does he ever sleep? I'm dog-tired just thinking about it.

DUNHAM CELLARS
opened: 1999
winemaker(s): Eric Dunham
location: 150 East Boeing Avenue, Walla Walla, WA 99362-7400
phone: 509-529-4685
web: www.dunhamcellars.com
e-mail: wine@dunhamcellars.com
fee: Tasting fee refunded with purchase
hours: Daily 11–4
amenities: Gift Shop, Online Store, Pet Friendly, Picnic Area, RV/Bus Parking, Tours, Wheelchair Accessible, Wine Club, YouTube
connect: 🐦 f

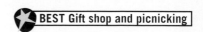 ⭐ **BEST Gift shop and picnicking**

Dunham Cellars' Three-Legged Red was named after owner Eric Dunham's dog, Port

Tempus Cellars

Joe Forest

As Joe Forest (co-owner/winemaker) for Tempus Cellars points out, "Tempus has a Latin root meaning "time." We went with that name because within an 18-month period my fiancé (now Mollie Delaney Forest) got married, bought a house, got a dog, had a baby and started a winery." A handsome photo of the Forest family sans dog but with child number two, graces their airport tasting room.

For aficionados of neighbor winery Patit Creek Cellars and Dunham Cellars, the name Joe Forest might have a familiar ring. Joe's resumé includes assistant winemaker at Dunham Cellars and he's head winemaker for Patit Creek. His wines reflect the personality of Joe — friendly, approachable, take-home-for-dinner-tonight wine. A few sips of his wine may convince you why in August 2010 *Seattle* magazine named Tempus Cellars among 10 Up-And-Coming Washington Wineries.

My favorite turned out to be his 2008 Cabernet Sauvignon with loads of blackberry and chocolate notes. Knowing the supply was limited, I bought a bottle and informed him that I would let it rest in my cellar for many moons. However, even as I signed for my purchase I knew I was telling a lie. The bottle didn't last a fortnight in my cellar. One more dead soldier for the bottle cemetery.

A last look at the handsome family photo on my way out the door made me think that if they accomplished all that they have done in 18 months, what will they do over the next 10 years. Well, Tempus ... er...time will tell.

TEMPUS CELLARS
opened: 2010
winemaker(s): Joe Forest
location: 124 West Boeing Avenue, Suite 3, Walla Walla, WA 98362
web: www.tempuscellars.com
e-mail: joe@tempuscellars.com
fee: Tasting fee refunded with purchase
hours: Saturday 11–5, or by appointment
amenities: Newsletter/Blog, RV/Bus Parking, Wheelchair Accessible, Wine Club
connect: ⬜

Patit Creek Cellars

"Sure!" I blurted to the question "Would you like to try our 2008 Semillon Ice Wine?" As I watched Ed Dudley pour a golden sample of Patit Creek Cellars' dessert wine, I reflected that at one time Patit Creek Cellars had produced just two wines — cabernet sauvignon and merlot. But that was the focus of the former ownership group, before Ed and his business partner, Karen La Bonté, purchased the winery in 2007.

Prior to acquiring Patit Creek Cellars, Ed and Karen worked in the communications industry: he in Virginia, and she in California. Both had more than a mere interest in wine; they shared something closer to a fervor. They studied all aspects of the wine industry, read books, volunteered at crush, and bent the ears of winemakers from coast to coast. Their desire to purchase an existing winery eventually led to the purchase of Patit Creek Cellars. Papers were signed, dollars transferred, and Ed and Karen were the proud parents of a Walla Walla winery.

Once the ink had dried on the sales contract, one of Ed and Karen's first moves was to relocate the downtown Walla Walla tasting room and the Dayton, Washington-based production facility into a common 6,000-square-foot facility at the Walla Walla Region Airport wine incubator complex. Visitors will ooh and ah at the Tuscan-style interior, with its warm colors and an inviting fireplace, where you can enjoy a glass of wine.

With winemaker Joe Forest in charge of wine production, all the Patit Creek Cellars wines are a pure pleasure to taste. However, the semillon ice wine buckled my knees with its silky smooth finish and satisfying sweetness. With a final gulp, I felt a smile growing across my face, happy in the knowledge that Patit Creek Cellars is under good stewardship.

PATIT CREEK CELLARS
opened: 1999
winemaker(s): Joe Forest
location: 325 A Street, Walla Walla, WA 99362
phone: 509-522-4684
web: www.patitcreekcellars.com
e-mail: info@patitcreekcellars.com
fee: Complimentary wine tasting
hours: Tuesday through Saturday 11–5; Sunday 11–4; Closed Monday
amenities: Gift Shop, Online Store, Picnic Area, Private Events, RV/Bus Parking, Tours, Weddings, Wheelchair Accessible, Wine Club
connect:

SYZYGY

The word "syzygy" is defined as the alignment of earth, moon, and sun. Such was the inspiration of winemaker Zach Brettler when he launched SYZYGY in 2002 — the convergence of different Walla Walla and Columbia Valley vineyards and varieties to create the perfect blend of red wine. It's also in keeping with Zach's other passion — he's an astronomy buff.

Zach gets his grapes from select growers in Walla Walla, Horse Heaven Hills and the Wahluke Slope. Of note is the fact that he purchases his grapes by the acre and not by the ton. That's a little unusual. By purchasing his grapes by the acre, Zach is clearly communicating his focus on high-quality grapes, sacrificing tonnage for quality. Grape growers "green prune" to leave fewer clusters on the vine, thus ensuring the remaining grapes get the vine's attention. Although this lowers the yield per acre, what remains are intensely flavored grapes.

SYZYGY's distinctive orange-and-blue bottle label may indicate that the wine inside is 100 percent syrah or 100 percent cabernet sauvignon, and that it is, but it's actually a blend of the same grape variety but from various vineyards. The goal is syzygy — an optimal blend of grapes from different sources to achieve just the right balance, taste, and finish. And it's more than a wine style that Zach brings to his craft; it's also a philosophy that speaks to a cosmic harmony of sorts. Something seems to be in alignment, because Zach's blends have gone on to receive high acclaim from wine connoisseurs.

The tasting room at SYZYGY still has the original golden-colored hardwood floors and it complements the orange walls giving the room a light airy feel. It's a pleasurable space meant to be shared with friends, family, and lovers — it feels like syzygy.

SYZYGY
opened: 2002
winemaker(s): Zach Brettler
location: 405 East Boeing Avenue, Walla Walla, WA 99362
phone: 509-522-0484
web: www.syzygywines.com
e-mail: info@syzygywines.com
fee: Complimentary wine tasting
hours: Friday through Sunday 11–4, or by appointment
amenities: Mailing List, Newsletter/Blog, Online Store, Picnic Area, Tours, Wine Club, Wines by the Glass
connect: ⓕ

Adamant Cellars

When I first met Devin and Debra Stinger, they were part of the initial group of nascent wineries at the Walla Walla Airport incubator complex. The rental situation at the complex involves a lease with an expiration date, with the cost of rent escalating during the lease period. Under these circumstances, wineries are forced to sink or swim. In this case, the Stingers and their baby, Adamant Cellars, not only swam, they rode the wave.

On my next visit to Adamant Cellars, I found Devin working the tasting room at their stand-alone facility at the Port of Walla Walla Airport facility, on East Cessna. The Stingers continue to evolve their working partnership. Devin manages the winemaking duties, from working with select growers

Devin Stinger

in the Walla Walla AVA through vinification and bottling. He even takes care of the unglamorous paperwork duties demanded by ever-watchful federal and state regulators and tax collectors. Meanwhile, Debra performs "everything else," which essentially means she's kept busy full time managing the tasting room, marketing their wines, crushing grapes, and mopping floors. It's all hard work.

The couple began their winemaking adventure in 2000 in the basement of their Portland home, where they produced their first wine. Taking the name "Adamant" (a substance of impenetrable hardness; the word shares the same etymology with the word "diamond") for their venture, the Stingers embarked on their winemaking business in late 2006.

While still focusing on Bordeaux reds, Adamant Cellars has increased its portfolio to include an unusual nonvintage sparkling tempranillo rosé, dubbed Scintillate, as well as an estate albariño white wine, which is hard to find outside its native northwest coastal region of Spain. It will be interesting to follow what the Stingers do with this diamond in the rough.

ADAMANT CELLARS
opened: 2006
winemaker(s): Devin Stinger
location: 525 East Cessna Avenue, Walla Walla, WA 99362
phone: 509-529-4161
web: www.adamantcellars.com
e-mail: devin@adamantcellars.com
fee: Tasting fee refunded with purchase
hours: Daily 11–5 from February through December; Friday through Sunday 11–4 during January
amenities: Art Gallery, Mailing List, Online Store, Picnic Area, Wheelchair Accessible, Wine Club
connect: 🐦 📘

Buty Winery

The story goes that Frank Buty gave his future son-in-law, Caleb Foster, this warning: "Any man who marries one of my 'beauties' will become the beast." The beauty Frank was referring to was one of his three daughters, Nina Buty, but fortunately for everyone involved, Nina and Caleb didn't heed her dad's admonition. And behold, their marriage begot Buty Winery.

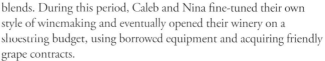

The winery wasn't born of a whim, however. Before launching Buty Winery in 2000, winemaker Caleb Foster cut his teeth as an apprentice at Woodward Canyon Winery, working for Rick Small; did a stint at Mount Baker Winery; and spent time overseas in New Zealand and South Africa, where he cultivated his predilection for blends. During this period, Caleb and Nina fine-tuned their own style of winemaking and eventually opened their winery on a shoestring budget, using borrowed equipment and acquiring friendly grape contracts.

Caleb Foster and son

Well aware that great wine starts in the vineyard, Caleb and Nina collaborate with a who's who of well-known growers, including Champoux, Lonesome Spring Ranch, Conner Lee, and Phinney Hill. However, in 2006 they realized a long-held dream of owning a 10-acre plot in the prized cobblestone-populated land located on the Oregon side of the Walla Walla Valley. The singular goal for this vineyard — planted in syrah, Mourvèdre, grenache, cabernet sauvignon, Marsanne, and roussanne — is to grow fruit for the production of their prized "Rediviva of the Stones" red blend.

Buty's portfolio includes chardonnay, red and white Bordeaux blends, and a southern Rhône blend with the captivating name Rediviva. Their bottles bear the distinctive "buty mark" logo on the label — a clever touch. Along with the Buty label, the couple now has a second — dubbed Beast — which offers wallet-friendlier prices yet delivers stunning fruit-forward flavors.

BUTY WINERY
opened: 2000
winemaker(s): Caleb Foster and Nina Buty Foster
location: 535 East Cessna Avenue, Walla Walla, WA 99362-7412
phone: 509-527-0901
web: www.butywinery.com
e-mail: info@butywinery.com
fee: Tasting fee
hours: Daily 11–4, winter hours by appointment
amenities: Mailing List, Online Store, RV/Bus Parking, Wheelchair Accessible, Wine Club

Tamarack Cellars

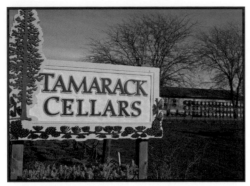

Ron Coleman has the nicest smile, and he's not fazed by visitors to this winery who turn up their noses at the thought of trying his chardonnay or wince when they sample his "Firehouse Red." He just smiles and conveys a "to each his or her own" attitude. Ironically, his *c'est la vie* approach wins a lot of converts. Behind his friendly demeanor is a quiet confidence honed by years of experience in the wine trade. With winemaking stints at Canoe Ridge and Waterbrook as well as working as a wine sales representative and sommelier, Ron's wine background runs deep. These past experiences and his creative talents converge with Tamarack Cellars.

Established in 1998 by Ron and his wife, Jamie, the winery is located in a restored World War II fire station and barracks at the Airport. The winery is named after the tamarack, a coniferous North American larch tree (*Larix laricina*) that has needles borne on short spur shoots. Ron and co-winemaker Danny Gorgon are dedicated to making handcrafted wines using varieties from select vineyards in several Washington appellations, including Walla Walla Valley, Horse Heaven Hills, Rattlesnake Hills, Yakima Valley, and Red Mountain. By doing so, they can focus on a single-vineyard reserve wine or blend varieties from a number of different vineyards.

Tamarack Cellars' current production is approximately 20,000 cases a year, give or take a few pallets. His hugely popular "Firehouse Red" blends a number of black grape varieties that corresponds with the vintage year. For example, his 2011 Firehouse Red features eleven grape varieties, including cabernet sauvignon, syrah, merlot, cabernet franc, and four others. It's a symphony of flavors with no one variety dominating the flavor profile. At $18 a bottle, it's a steal.

TAMARACK CELLARS
opened: 1998
winemaker(s): Ron Coleman and Danny Gordon
location: 700 C Street, Walla Walla, WA 99362
phone: 509-526-3533
web: www.tamarackcellars.com
e-mail: info@tamarackcellars.com
fee: Tasting fee refunded with purchase
hours: March through December, Thursday and Friday 12–4, Saturday and Sunday 10–4; January and February, Thursday and Friday 12–4, Saturday 10–4
amenities: Online Store, Pet Friendly, RV/Bus Parking, Tours, Wheelchair Accessible, Wine Club, YouTube
connect: 🐦 📘

Revelry Vintners

Prior to visiting a winery, I try to do a fair amount of online research in preparation. It gives me some idea of what to expect. Such was the case as I pulled up to the Revelry winery at the Walla Walla airport location. I knew from Googling that winemaker/owner Jared Burns was the son of Dennis Burns, the founder of Pro-Tec helmets, Gargoyles sunglasses, and

the inventor of the synthetic wine cork. (I bet Jared beamed with pride at "Bring Your Dad to School" Day.) I figured that with this pedigree, Jared, too, would have a large streak of creative drive and entrepreneurial spirit. But beyond that, I knew little of Revelry Vintners and what would unfold as I walked through the door.

First impressions matter. In this case, the woman greeting me from the bar made me feel welcome from the get-go. It's surprising how many wineries fail to extend that basic courtesy. I felt open to discovery, to uncovering the "story in the bottle" in terms of what makes Revelry Vintners tick. Through tasting and Q&A, a picture began to emerge of a winemaker who is truly in touch with select grape growers and renowned vineyards in Walla Walla, Red Mountain and Horse Heaven Hills. He lets the Columbia Valley speak for itself, giving you a "sense of place" with every sip.

I later met Jared in the barrel room of his winery and had a chance to visit with him. Within a few minutes all my conceptions about Revelry Vintners — its unpretentious nature, its celebration of life, its reverence for Washington's appellations — were confirmed. Young, energetic, and equipped with a vision for his winery, Jared elicited the following

comment in my notepad, "This guy is a great ambassador for Washington wine." I still revel in that knowledge.

REVELRY VINTNERS
opened: 2006
winemaker(s): Jared Burns
location: 720 C Street,
Walla Walla, WA 98362
phone: 509-540-5761
web: www.revelrywines.com
e-mail: info@revelrywines.com
fee: Complimentary wine tasting
hours: Wednesday through Saturday 10 to 5,
Sunday 10–3, or by appointment
amenities: Online Store, Newsletter/Blog, RV/
Bus Parking, Wheelchair Accessible, Wine Club
connect:

Mannina Cellars

To know Mannina Cellars is to appreciate the winegrowing family behind it — not just a lone winemaker, mind you, but an entire cast of family members, including a black Lab named Lucy. Although Don Redman is owner and winemaker, his wife, Nicole, and their three children are often found pruning the vines at their Cali Vineyard or assisting at their Walla Walla Airport winery. Don is ever grateful for his family's involvement and for his family heritage, so it's no accident that many Mannina Cellars wines bear the names of family members. There is the red blend "Cali," named after his grandmother Rose Cali, and "RoseAnne's Red," named for his mother. Even the winery's name, "Mannina," comes from Don's maternal grandmother, who emigrated from Italy. A photograph of Mannina graces the wall behind the tasting room.

Don Redman

Speaking of Cali, I would be remiss if I didn't disclose one of the reasons for my sojourn to Mannina Cellars. At the time, this cabernet dominant blend sold for only $17 a bottle and was a steal. With my purchase I began to imagine a rib-eye steak with a red wine reduction paired with Cali. Egads, I realized I was drooling.

As a side note, the other thing that drew my attention during my visit was the artwork of local artist Squire Broel on Mannina Cellars labels. Squire's watercolor of vineyard rows adorns the labels of the winery's merlot, cabernet sauvignon, "RoseAnne's Red" and sangiovese. For me, this imagery is a beautiful reminder that Don relies exclusively on Walla Walla Valley fruit, including that from such notable vineyards as Pepper Bridge, Seven Hills, and Les Collines. As Don's own, 28-acre Cali Vineyard matures, look for his increasing reliance on his own fruit.

MANNINA CELLARS
opened: 2006
winemaker(s): Don Redman
location: 760 C Street,
Walla Walla, WA 99362
phone: 509-200-2366
web: www.manninacellars.com
e-mail: info@manninacellars.com
fee: Complimentary wine tasting
hours: Friday 11:30–4:30 Saturday 11–4:30, or by appointment
amenities: Online Store, Pet Friendly, RV/Bus Parking, Wheelchair Accessible, Wine Club
connect: 🐦 f

Five Star Cellars

"It is a wise father that knows his own child." — William Shakespeare, *The Merchant of Venice*

Along the WineTrails of Washington, you come across a number of retirees who traded in the tedium of retirement to create fine wines. Such is the story of David Huse. He didn't have to launch Five Star Cellars, but his passion won out. In 2000, following his career as a farm equipment provider and a few stints assisting at other wineries, David started Five Star Cellars. He hasn't looked back.

Of course, when you name a winery "Five Star," you'd better deliver wines worthy of that premier rating. To achieve this level of quality, David needed a helping hand. He didn't have far to look. In 2002, his son Matt signed on to assist with winemaking, and Matt's timing couldn't have been better: Production had doubled to more than 1,000 cases per year. He enrolled in the enology and viticulture program at Walla Walla Community College and was a member of the program's first graduating class. Today, Matt is Five Star's chief winemaker, and current production is around 5,000 cases. This has freed David to assume the duties of operations manager, marketing director, and chief bottle-washer.

Located at the Walla Walla Airport Complex, across from Eleganté Cellars, Five Star Cellars offers an inviting space to sample its ultrapremium wines: merlot, syrah, cabernet sauvignon as well as some serious red blends. Be sure to check out their "Quinque Astrum" (Latin for "five star") a super Tuscan blend with a sangiovese backbone. Matt and David have made significant improvements to the leased space. For example, as part of this renovation, they've added a wood stove. Imagine visiting on a cold winter day with the stove blazing, keeping you toasty warm with bright stars in the night sky.

FIVE STAR CELLARS
opened: 2000
winemaker(s): Matt Huse
location: 840 C Street,
Walla Walla, WA 99362-7423
phone: 509-527-8400
web: www.fivestarcellars.com
e-mail: info@fivestarcellars.com
fee: Tasting fee
hours: Saturday 10–4, or by appointment
amenities: Gift Shop, Mailing List, Online Store, Pet Friendly, RV/Bus Parking, Tours, Wheelchair Accessible, Wine Club
connect:

Elegante Cellars

Doug Simmons, a native Walla Wallan, had a problem. In 2002 when he retired from teaching, Doug still had his health, an inquisitive mind, and a desire to start his own business. What's more, after 30 years of teaching chemistry in the Walla Walla School District, he was left with a sense of emptiness, and he realized he wasn't finished being a scientist. He clearly needed a lab in which to mix and match potions.

Doug's résumé also includes a long stint of farming. For 49 summers, Doug stained his fingers red while working at a local Walla Walla institution, Klicker's Strawberry Acres.

Thus, when Doug retired from teaching high school, becoming a winemaker was a no-brainer solution to his life's dilemma. The fact that Walla Walla Community College just happens to offer a superb enology and viticulture

Doug Simmons

program helped to cement his career decision. He graduated from Walla Walla Community College with an A.A. degree in enology and viticulture. Soon thereafter, in 2007, he created Elegante Cellars, following a practicum at Five Star Cellars. Now he just needed a name for his winery. Recalling that a fellow teacher in Walla Walla always said "elegant" when asked how his day was going, Doug added the "é" on the end of that word to give it a Euro feel. Thus, Elegante Cellars was christened.

I met Doug in late January 2010 at his winery, located in the Walla Walla Airport Complex. His faithful Boston terrier, Bing, was at his side (it's hard to find such loyal help these days!). Trim, with graying temples, Doug possesses a youthful look belying his 60-some years. By the way, following a sampling of his premium red wines, save room to sample his slightly sweet but lovely strawberry wine. There's no doubt about the source of his strawberries — Klicker's, of course.

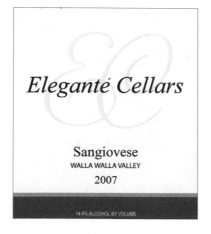

Elegante Cellars

Sangiovese
WALLA WALLA VALLEY
2007

14.4% ALCOHOL BY VOLUME

ELEGANTE CELLARS
opened: 2007
winemaker(s): Doug Simmons
location: 839 C Street,
Walla Walla, WA 99362
phone: 509-525-9129
web: www.elegantecellars.com
e-mail: simmondl@yahoo.com
fee: Tasting fee refunded with purchase
hours: Daily 11–4
amenities: Online Store, RV/Bus Parking, Wheelchair Accessible, Wine Club

Kontos Cellars

Hot tubs and a seemingly genetic desire to make great wine began the journey for brothers Cameron and Chris Kontos. While stargazing from their family's hot tub on cold winter nights, the brothers talked of starting a winery. However, lest you think this was a pipe dream, please note that winemaking is in their blood. People familiar with the Walla Walla wine industry appreciate the premium wines of Fort Walla Walla Cellars, where the brothers' father, Cliff Kontos, is co-owner and winemaker. Yes, pedigree does have certain bennies.

Located on "Incubator Block" (Piper Avenue) in the Walla Walla Regional Airport complex is the charming yellow structure that Kontos Cellars calls home — at least temporarily. The modern building stands in stark contrast to nearby World War II-constructed housing. As the "incubator" nickname implies, building leases here have a limited time span, six years to be exact.

A distinctive identity is key for all new start-ups. To this end, the brothers fused their Greek-derived name (actually the name Kontos is the Americanized version of a much longer Greek name) with the Washington state official insect — the green darner dragonfly. As they were dreaming of launching the winery, the brothers would notice dragonflies landing on wine barrels or buzzing around their wheat field and saw this as good omen for Kontos Cellars.

Chris and Cameron Kontos (l to r)

When it comes to winemaking, Cameron is in charge, and he had the good fortune to learn from one of the best winemakers of Walla Walla: Forgeron Cellars' Marie-Eve Gilla. For seven years, Cameron worked as Forgeron's assistant winemaker learning from renowned winemaker Marie-Eve. After a few samples, Cameron's comments were scribbled haphazardly on my notepad. Later, I had a difficult time discerning what I had written. It was all Greek to me.

KONTOS CELLARS
opened: 2008
winemaker(s): Cameron Kontos
location: 594 Piper Avenue, Walla Walla, WA 99362
phone: 509-386-4471
web: www.kontoscellars.com
e-mail: info@kontoscellars.com
fee: Complimentary wine tasting
hours: Saturday and Sunday 10–4
amenities: Online Store, Pet Friendly, Picnic Area, RV/Bus Parking, Wheelchair Accessible, Wine Club
connect: 🐦 📘

Corvus Cellars

When Trio Vintners vacated the "incubator" complex at the Port of Walla Walla airport in 2010, an opportunity arose for Randall and Jennifer Hopkins to move their Corvus Cellars winery from Benton City to Walla Walla. Randall and Jennifer, together with winemaker/

partner Steve Lessard, opened their tasting room doors in October 2010.

Their motto reads, "Balanced wines ... from the earth — to the vine — to the wine." With that as a mantra and production limited to 1,200 cases annually, they have the opportunity to know each block of wine grapes from harvest through bottling. Certainly this is very different for winemaker Steve, whose prior stints at Stag's Leap Wine Cellars in Napa, Hedges Family Estate on Red Mountain and the now defunct Whitman Cellars in Walla Walla involved wine production on a much larger scale. At Corvus, punch-down translates into some tired arms by day's end, and the trio can eyeball barrel of wine and know that each will produce 25 cases of wine. Thus, in doing the math, their 1,200 cases require about 48 barrels, give or take a few carboys. That level of production is a gnat's eyebrow compared to that of big-time producers like Columbia Crest, but the Corvus people wouldn't have it any other way.

The Walla Walla airport location allows Corvus to market its wine directly to consumers. Given the steady stream of tourists — especially during the summer — anticipate inventory of each vintage to go quickly. With legendary Red Mountain fruit from its vineyard and solid relationships with Walla Walla Valley growers, Corvus Cellars will continue its focus on cabernet sauvignon and Bordeaux blends.

Incidentally, for WineTrail trekkers looking to lodge among the vineyards and have ready access to the grand wineries of Red Mountain, consider staying at Corvus Casa. See vrbo.com/400323 for rates and availability.

CORVUS CELLARS
opened: 2008
winemaker(s): Stephen Lessard
location: 602 Piper Avenue, Walla Walla, WA 99362
phone: 509-241-0318
web: www.corvuscellars.com
e-mail: info@corvuscellars.com
fee: Complimentary wine tasting
hours: Saturday 11–5 and Sunday 11–3; Friday by appointment or special event weekend
amenities: Mailing List, Online Store, RV/Bus Parking, Wheelchair Accessible, Wine Club
connect: 🐦 f

Walla Faces 20

WALLA FACES
opened: 2009
winemaker(s): Rick Johnson
location: 598 Piper Way,
Walla Walla, WA 99362
phone: 877-301-1181
web: www.wallafaces.com
e-mail: info@wallafaces.com
fee: Tasting fee refunded with purchase
hours: Call for times
amenities: Online Store, RV/Bus Parking, Wheelchair
Accessible, Wine Club, YouTube
connect: 🐦 📘

www.winetrailsnw.com/wineries/walla_faces

CAVU Cellars 21

Aviation enthusiasts will delight in discovering a winery bearing the name CAVU — an acronym for "ceiling and visibility unlimited." And how appropriate that CAVU Cellars is located at the Walla Walla Regional Airport's "incubator complex" on Piper Avenue. But it wasn't a case of kismet that brought CAVU to the complex. A flyover would reveal the location's ready access to the most treasured crop: its vineyards.

The winery's name pays homage to winemaker/owner Joel Waite's airline-pilot father, Jim Waite. It's befitting because Joel's parents (Jim and Karen Waite) are business partners and active participants in all aspects of the winery. The day of my visit found Joel and his dad racking barrels of wine in the production area.

Joel's winemaking style leans toward creating food-friendly wines and relies in part on atypical varieties such as barbera and Malbec. It turns out that his background includes considerable experience in the culinary arts as owner and chef of Catered Affairs, a Washington, D.C.-based enterprise that provided high-end private dinners. A later training stint at V. Sattui Winery, through the Napa Valley Cooking School, ignited his desire to pursue a winemaking career.

Joel Waite

As Joel notes, it was during a trip to WallaWalla to attend a family wedding that he was struck with the notion of moving to the valley and immersing himself in winemaking and owning a winery. Once relocated, Joel traded his chef's apron for textbooks at Walla Walla Community College's respected Institute for Enology and Viticulture. Following some hands-on experience at Maryhill Winery, Joel opened CAVU Cellars' doors in the spring of 2009, together with Jim and Karen. With clear skies ahead, CAVU Cellars is prepared for take-off with many vintages to come.

CAVU CELLARS
opened: 2009
winemaker(s): Joel Waite
location: 175 Aeronca Avenue, Walla Walla, WA 99362
phone: 509-540-6352
web: www.cavucellars.com
e-mail: info@cavucellars.com
fee: Complimentary wine tasting
hours: Daily 11–5
amenities: Online Store, Picnic Area, RV/Bus Parking, Wheelchair Accessible, Wine Club
connect: 🐦 📘

Ash Hollow Winery

You know that old adage "The more things change, the more they remain the same." Well, that isn't the case at Ash Hollow Winery. True, the name is the same as the original winery, which began in 2002, but gone are John Turner (managing partner) and Steve Clifton (consultant winemaker and partner). Currently, John Turner is running for Walla Walla County sheriff, having returned from Iraq, where he was embedded with the U.S. military as a investigator for counterterrorism; and Steve Clifton is making wine in southern California. But that's another story....

When I asked our affable tasting-room host, "What about the Ash Hollow motto, 'Family, friends, food, fun, and great wine' — is that still in play?" She replied, "We're revisiting that line. The family-and-friends theme has become overused by other wineries and it doesn't differentiate us." While scribbling my notes, I glanced over at the new wine labels the winery is using for its Legends series of red blends: "Four Horsemen" and "Headless Red." These new labels are stunningly bold, in stark contrast to the rather staid and traditional Ash Hollow Winery labels, which bear the ink drawing of a lone tree. Turning the music down a bit, my youthful pourer explained, "We're about having fun, and the new wine labels reflect that."

I applaud the ownership group and managing partners (including the likes of Jay Tucker of Reininger Winery fame) for evolving the winery in this direction. Perhaps it was serendipity, but they managed to hire employees who possess turbo-charged creative drive, potentially positioning Ash Hollow to connect with the often-overlooked but fastest-growing

demographic of wine drinkers — the 21- to 30-year-olds. Led by sales and marketing director Jennifer Gregory and talented winemaker Spencer Sievers, the winery's future looks anything but ashen.

ASH HOLLOW WINERY
opened: 2002
winemaker(s): Spencer Sievers
location: 1460 F Street, Walla Walla Airport Complex, Walla Walla, WA 99362
phone: 509-529-7565
web: www.ashhollow.com
e-mail: info@ashhollow.com
fee: Tasting fee refunded with purchase
hours: Sunday and Monday 12–4; Thursday 11–4; Friday and Saturday 11–5
amenities: Gift Shop, Online Store, Pet Friendly, RV/Bus Parking, Tours, Wheelchair Accessible, Wine Club, YouTube
connect: f

ABEJA

winemaker(s): John Abbott
location: 2014 Mill Creek Road,
Walla Walla, WA 99362-8424
phone: Winery 509-526-7400
web: www.abeja.net
hours: Wine tasting for
overnight guests

CADARETTA

winemaker(s): Brian Rudin and Virginie
Bourgue (consultant)
location: 1120 Dell Avenue, Suite B,
Walla Walla, WA 99632
phone: 509-525-1352
web: www.cadaretta.com
hours: By appointment only

CADARETTA

chardonnay | columbia valley | 2007

CORLISS ESTATES

location: 511 North Second Avenue,
Walla Walla, WA 99362
phone: 509 526-4400
web: www.corlissvineyard.com
hours: By appointment only

CHESTER-KIDDER

winemaker(s): Allen Shoup
& Gilles Nicault
location: 1604 Frenchtown Road,
Walla Walla, WA 99362
phone: 509-526-0905
web: www.longshadows.com
hours: By appointment only

COUVILLION WINERY

winemaker(s): Jill Noble
location: 86 Corkrum Road,
Walla Walla, WA 99362
phone: 509-337-6133
web: www.couvillionwinery.com
hours: For special events 10–4

DOUBLEBACK
winemaker(s): Chris Figgins
(consulting winemaker)
location: 229 East Main Street,
Walla Walla, WA 99362
phone: 509-301-3477
web: www.doubleback.com
hours: By appointment only

DOWSETT FAMILY WINERY
winemaker(s): Chris Dowsett
location: 315 East Cessna,
Walla Walla, WA 99362
phone: 509-520-8215
web: www.dowsettwines.com
hours: By appointment only

DUMAS STATION WINES
winemaker(s): Jay and Doug
location: 36229 Highway 12,
Dayton, WA 99328
phone: 509-382-8933
web: www.dumasstation.com
hours: Saturday 1–5 p.m.

ENSEMBLE CELLARS
winemaker(s): Craig Nelsen
location: 145 East Curtis Avenue,
Walla Walla, WA 99362
phone: 509-525-0231
web: www.ensemblecellars.com
hours: Saturday 11–3 or
by appointment

FEATHER WINERY
winemaker(s): Randy Dunn
location: 1604 Frenchtown Road,
Walla Walla, WA 99362
phone: 509-526-0905
web: www.longshadows.com
hours: By appointment only

FIGGINS ESTATE
winemaker(s): Chris Figgins
location: 2900 Melrose Street,
Figgins Wine Studio,
Walla Walla, WA 99362
phone: 509-522-7808
web: www.figginswine.com
hours: By appointment, Friday and
Saturday 11–5, May through August

GARRISON CREEK CELLARS
winemaker(s): David March
location: 4153 Hood Road,
Walla Walla, WA 99362-1860
phone: 509-386-4841
web: www.garrisoncreekcellars.com
hours: By appointment only

GOLDEN RIDGE CELLARS
location: 153 Wheat Ridge Lane,
Walla Walla, WA 99362
phone: 509-301-1192
web: www.facebook.com/goldenridge
hours: By appointment only

LONG SHADOWS VINTNERS
winemaker(s): Allen Shoup et al
location: 1604 Frenchtown Road,
Walla Walla, WA 99362
phone: 509-526-0905
web: www.longshadows.com
hours: By appointment only

MACKEY VINEYARDS
winemaker(s): Brothers Roger and
Philip Mackey
location: 4122 Powerline Road,
Walla Walla, WA 99362
phone: 509-240-9226
web: www.mackeyvineyards.com
hours: By appointment and
special events

PEDESTAL
winemaker(s): Michael Rolland

PIROUETTE
winemaker(s): Augustin Huneeus Sr.
& Philippe Melka

co-location: 1604 Frenchtown Road,
Walla Walla, WA 99362
phone: 509-526-0905
web: www.longshadows.com
hours: By appointment only

POET'S LEAP WINERY
winemaker(s): Armin Diel

SAGGI
winemaker(s): Ambrogio and
Giovanni Folonari

SEQUEL
winemaker(s): John Duval

co-location: 1604 Frenchtown Road,
Walla Walla, WA 99362
phone: 509-526-0905
web: www.longshadows.com
hours: By appointment only

ROBISON RANCH CELLARS
winemaker(s): Brad Riordan
location: 2839 Robison Ranch Road,
Walla Walla, WA 99362
phone: 509-301-3480
web: www.robisonranchcellars.com
hours: By appointment only

SULEI CELLARS
winemaker(s): Tanya Woodley
location: 1509 Beet Road,
Walla Walla, WA 99362
phone: 509-529-0840
web: www.suleicellars.com
hours: Friday through Sunday 11–5

TRANCHE CELLARS
winemaker(s): Kendall Mix
location: 705 Berney Drive,
Walla Walla, WA 99362
phone: 509-526-3500
web: www.tranchecellars.com
hours: By appointment only

Spokane
WINE COUNTRY

MOUNTAIN DOME

B R U T

WASHINGTON STATE SPARKLING WINE
FERMENTED IN THIS BOTTLE BY
MOUNTAIN DOME WINERY, SPOKANE, WASHINGTON USA
ALCOHOL 12% BY VOLUME 750 ML

OVERBLUFF CELLARS

LSD

LATOUR :: SPOFFORD :: DINEEN
VINEYARDS

CABERNET · SAUVIGNON

WALLA WALLA VALLEY

2008

ALC. 14.3% BY VOL.

2005

GRANDE RONDE

CABERNET SAUVIGNON
PEPPERBRIDGE VINEYARD

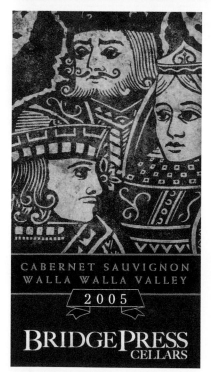

CABERNET SAUVIGNON
WALLA WALLA VALLEY

2005

BRIDGEPRESS
CELLARS

WHITESTONE

Haig Family Estate Wine
Lake Roosevelt Shores Vineyard

Cabernet Sauvignon
2005

COLUMBIA VALLEY
WASHINGTON STATE

ALCOHOL BY VOLUME 14.01%

Pieces of RED

red wine
v.6.022
WHITESTONE WINERY
COLUMBIA VALLEY • WASHINGTON STATE

ALCOHOL BY VOLUME 14.6%

BARRISTER

Bacchus Vineyard
SYRAH
Columbia Valley

2006

ALCOHOL 14.5% BY VOLUME

Spokane
WineTrail

The Spokane WineTrail gives you the chance to put on a pair of sneakers and visit most of the wineries on foot. But that's only part of the adventure on this WineTrail, as there are additional wineries to explore heading east on I-90 toward Coeur d'Alene, Idaho. While in downtown Spokane, you can experience rich architectural history, a rushing river and wonderful eateries. Don't pass up the opportunity to stroll through the restored Davenport Hotel, where you can linger over the photographs of turn-of-the-century Spokane. In downtown Spokane, you can stop in at the tasting rooms of Barrister Winery, Robert Karl Cellars, Whitestone Winery, and Caterina Winery to savor their wines. There are also several secondary tasting rooms, including one belonging to Cougar Crest.

Don't forget to throw in a picnic basket and head north to Colbert to Townshend Cellars, where bucolic views and Don Townshend's delectable T3 red blend await you.

Spokane WineTrail
1. Barrister Winery
2. Patit Creek Cellars
3. Cougar Crest Tasting Room
4. Whitestone Winery & Vineyard Tasting Room
5. Arbor Crest River Park Square Tasting Room
6. Caterina, Lone Canary and Mountain Dome Winery
7. Nectar Tasting Room
8. Robert Karl Cellars
9. Market Place Wine Bar
10. Vintage Hill Cellars
11. Grande Ronde Cellars
12. Overbluff Cellars

13. Townshend Cellar
14. Arbor Crest Wine Cellars
15. Knipprath Cellars

16. Nodland Cellars
17. Latah Creek Wine Cellars
18. China Bend Winery

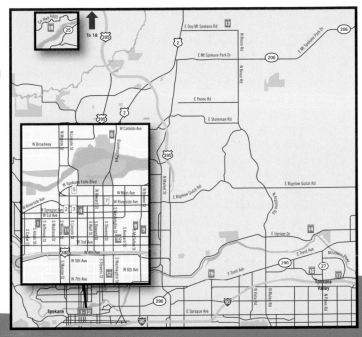

Region:	**Spokane Wine Country**
# of tasting rooms on tour:	**18**
# of satellite tasting rooms:	**4**
Estimate # of days for tour:	**6**
Getting around:	**Car and foot**
Key Events:	❑ **The Spokane Winery Association features three key events: Spring Release (mid-May), Holiday Wine (mid-November) and ValenWine (February). See www.spokanewineries.net for more information.**
Tips:	❑ **Downtown Spokane wineries can be visited on foot with good walking shoes.**
	❑ **Many area restaurants feature local wines and honor a no corkage policy if it's a Washington wine purchased the day of your visit and you can show a receipt.**
Best:	❑ **Views: Townshend Cellar**
	❑ **Destination, views, gift shop, picnicking and weddings: Arbor Crest Wine Cellars**
	❑ **Gift shop: Latah Creek Wine Cellars**
	❑ **Views, picnicking: China Bend Winery**

Barrister Winery

Who doesn't love a success story about two guys who toil in their garage making wine only to have their passion take them beyond "garagiste"? Such is the tale of Barrister Winery. Launched in a garage by attorneys Greg Lipsker and Michael White, the winery produces wonderfully full-bodied, supple reds. As Greg and Michael tell it on the winery website, "In the fall of 1997, we bought our first 5-gallon home winemaking kit. Since then, winemaking has become the 'little hobby' that got out of control."

Barrister Winery inhabits a 100-year-old brick building in the historic Davenport Arts District of downtown Spokane. Its alley entrance may cause you to wonder what you have gotten yourself into. However, all worries fade once you enter to its spacious environment, which features exposed brick, plenty of beckoning tables and chairs, and friendly pourers. In fact, don't be surprised if Greg or Michael is there to greet you and help pour.

Greg Lipsker tending bar

Periodically, one of them will lead tours of the barrel room, which is located in the basement of the building. As you descend the stairs, your nose tells you that you are entering the barrel room, detecting the distinct musty, damp smell hints of cabernet. Here in the low light of the room, you can see row upon row of French and American oak barrels, which nurture the wine for 16 to 24 months. In the dimness and dampness of the barrel room, the wine tourists pepper their guide with questions about the winemaking process. Every question is answered with care, much like that taken by Greg and Michael in crafting their premium wines. Although the winery has grown into a full-blown business, it is still a labor of love. Greg and Michael's primary goals are to remain small and to focus on producing top-notch reds.

WineTrail jury members, I rest my case.

BARRISTER WINERY
opened: 2001
winemaker(s): Greg Lipsker and Michael White
location: 1213 West Railroad Avenue, Spokane, WA 99201
phone: 509-465-3591
web: www.barristerwinery.com
e-mail: info@barristerwinery.com
fee: Tasting fee refunded with purchase
hours: Monday through Saturday 12–5; First Fridays 5–10
amenities: Online Store, Private Events, Tours, Weddings, Wine Club
connect:

Patit Creek Cellars ②

PATIT CREEK CELLARS
opened: 1999
winemaker(s): Joe Forest
location: 822 West Sprague Avenue,
Spokane, WA 99201
phone: 509-868-4045
web: www.patitcreekcellars.com
e-mail: info@patitcreekcellars.com
fee: Complimentary wine tasting
hours: Sunday, Monday and Thursday 12–6;
Friday and Saturday 12–8
amenities: Online Store, Private Events, RV/Bus
Parking, Wheelchair Accessible, Wine Club
connect: 🐦 📘

www.winetrailsnw.com/wineries/patit_creek_cellars

Cougar Crest Tasting Room ③

COUGAR CREST TASTING ROOM
opened: 2001
winemaker(s): Deborah Hansen
location: 8 North Post Street, Suite 8, Peyton Building,
Spokane, WA 99201
phone: 509-241-3850
web: www.cougarcrestwinery.com
e-mail: info@cougarcrestwinery.com
fee: Tasting fee refunded with purchase
hours: Monday 12–6; Wednesday and Thursday 12–6;
Friday and Saturday 12–8; Sunday 12–6
amenities: Newsletter/Blog, Online Store,
Wheelchair Accessible, Wine Club, Wines by the Glass
connect: 🐦 📘

www.winetrailsnw.com/wineries/cougar_crest_tasting_room

Whitestone Winery & Vineyard Tasting Room 4

Washington state is full of surprises when it comes to wine. Take, for example, Whitestone Winery. Who would have guessed that you could find a winery in the wee town of Wilbur, let alone a winery with its own estate vineyard? If you're straining your brain trying to figure out where Wilbur is, it's located just south of Roosevelt Lake and about halfway between Coulee City and Davenport, along U.S. 2. Wilbur is the home of Wild Goose Bill Days, held the second Saturday in June. What do you mean you haven't experienced Wild Goose Bill Days?

Walter and Judy Haig planted Whitestone Winery's vineyard in 1992 with the help of Washington State University. WSU researchers knew the area was the perfect combination of climate and soil for growing premium wine grapes. Historically, nearby Whitestone Rock had been the site of one of the largest vineyards in eastern Washington. Then, in 1941, the newly built Grand Coulee Dam put the vineyard underwater and created Roosevelt Lake. Nearly 50 years later, the Haigs have turned back the clock by planting of merlot, cabernet sauvignon, and syrah.

In 2005, Whitestone Winery opened in a renovated gas station in the heart of Wilbur. Here, you can experience Whitestone's big red wines and visit with one of the Haig family members pouring and providing background about their estate wines. Walter and Judy's son, Michael Haig, is the winemaker and vineyard manager, and he welcomes the opportunity to showcase the Whitestone flavor profile.

Fortunately for most WineTrail trekkers that don't have an opportunity to visit Wilbur, Whitestone Winery's primary tasting room is located in downtown Spokane on North Post Street. A convenient spot to enjoy a glass of wine before dinner or a movie. It's also a convenient spot to relish a glass of wine after dinner or a movie!

WHITESTONE WINERY & VINEYARD TASTING ROOM
opened: 2005
winemaker(s): Walter Haig and Michael Haig
location: 8 North Post Street; Suite 8, Spokane, WA 99201
phone: 509-838-2427
web: www.whitestonewinery.com
e-mail: info@whitestonewinery.com
fee: Complimentary wine tasting
hours: Tuesday and Wednesday 12–6; Thursday and Friday 12–7; Saturday 12–5
amenities: Live Music, Newsletter/Blog, Online Store, Wheelchair Accessible, Wine Club, Wines by the Glass
connect: 🐦 📘

Arbor Crest River Park Square Tasting Room ⑤

ARBOR CREST RIVER PARK SQUARE TASTING ROOM
opened: 1982
winemaker(s): Kristina Mielke van Loben Sels
location: 808 West Main Street, 3rd Floor,
River Park Square, Spokane, WA 99201
phone: 509-747-3903
web: www.arborcrest.com
e-mail: info@arborcrest.com
fee: Tasting fee
hours: Monday through Thursday 11–9; Friday and
Saturday 11–10; Sunday 12–5
amenities: Online Store, Restaurant/Food Pairings,
Wheelchair Accessible, Wine Club, Wines by the Glass
connect: 🐦 📘

www.winetrailsnw.com/wineries/arbor_crest_river_park_square_tasting_room

Caterina, Lone Canary and Mountain Dome Winery 6

Question: What do T3, C4, and LC5 have in common? To begin your quest for the answer, you'll want to head to Caterina Winery for a little one-on-one research.

Located in the historic Broadview Dairy Building, adjacent to Riverfront Park, the charming Caterina Winery provides a nice venue for tasting wine (and for listening to live music occasionally performed on First Fridays). Named after the beloved Italian grandmother of one of the founders, Caterina Winery has been producing a wide range of affordable varietals since 1993, under the original winemaking direction of Mike Scott.

Now that Caterina is under the ownership of Don Townshend (of Townshend Cellars), visitors can taste a wide portfolio of wines, including its non-vintage C4 red blend. Also noteworthy are its critically acclaimed cabernet sauvignon (Willard Vineyards-sourced fruit), and a surprisingly crisp and floral-noted viognier. A sip of the cabernet reminded me of the Italian adage "One barrel of wine can work more miracles than a church full of saints."

But wait, there's more! Visitors also can taste wines under Townshend's other label, Lone Canary. Recently acquired from Mike, the remaining inventory of Lone Canary is at Caterina Winery. Make a point of sampling the Lone Canary barbera as well as its Bird House Red, both packed with wonderful fruit flavors and priced for less than 20 bones. If it's available, be sure to taste the LC5, which is another of Don's non-vintage red blends.

Alas, visitors to Caterina Winery will not have the opportunity to sample any of Townshend Cellars' wine, such as Don's ever-popular T3 red blend. For that, they'll need to motor to the nearby burg of Colbert to visit the source itself, Townshend Cellars. Don is often on hand, and he'd be happy to answer that perplexing question of what T3, C4, and LC5 have in common.

CATERINA, LONE CANARY AND MOUNTAIN DOME WINERY
opened: 1993
winemaker(s): Don Townshend
location: 905 North Washington Street, Broadview Dairy Building, Spokane, WA 99201-3210
phone: 509-328-5069
web: www.caterina.com
e-mail: info@caterina.com
fee: Tasting fee
hours: Thursday through Sunday 12–6; First Fridays 6–9
amenities: RV/Bus Parking, Tours, Wheelchair Accessible, Wine Club, Wines by the Glass
connect: f

Nectar Tasting Room ⑦

NECTAR TASTING ROOM
wineries represented: Anelare Winery, Hard Ron to Hoe Vinyards, Northwest Cellars, Skylite Cellars, and Terra Blanca Winery
location: 120 North Stevens, Spokane, WA 99201
phone: 509-869-1572
web: www.drinknectar.com
e-mail: info@nectartastingroom.com
fee: Tasting fee
hours: Thursday 2–8; Friday 2–10; Saturday 12–10
amenities: Live Music, Private Events, Restaurant/Food Pairings, Wheelchair Accessible, Wine Club, Wines by the Glass
connect: 🐦 📘

www.winetrailsnw.com/wineries/nectar_tasting_room

Robert Karl Cellars 8

In the mid-'90s, Joseph and Rebecca Gunselman decided to cure their recently acquired wine bug and head west from Virginia. That's quite a prescription, considering that many physicians are terrible at self-diagnosing and treating their own ailments. Joseph Gunselman is a practicing anesthesiologist and continues his day job at Sacred Heart Hospital in Spokane. However, his real passion is making wine, and to this end, he and Rebecca have created Robert Karl (a combination of family names).

Robert Karl has hit a home run in his choice of grapes from the Horse Heaven Hills AVA, home to vineyards such as McKinley Springs, Andrews Horse Heaven Ranch, and Phinny Hill, as well as its own estate vineyard, Gunselman Bench Vineyard. Joe collaborates closely with the growers and tracks vineyard data regarding temperature, precipitation, sugar content, and more. He's intimate with this windswept land.

Rebecca assists with winemaking, manages the tasting room, and is charge of marketing. Making it a true family affair, their three sons have lent a hand during crush, racking, and bottling. Together, this family produces about 2,500 cases annually of cabernet sauvignon, claret (their flagship wine), merlot, sauvignon blanc, syrah, and a dry cabernet franc rosé. As a consequence of remaining "boutique," Robert Karl Cellars often has to inform its visitors that a particular label is sold out. We had the good fortune of tasting a recent vintage of its claret before loyal fans snapped it up. As we learned, the word "claret" originates from the French clairet, meaning light red wine that is composed of varietals from Bordeaux. We promise to get no more cork dorky than that.

They may be transplants, but the Gunselmans are bullish about the wine industry in their adopted state, because "Washington grapes are the best."

ROBERT KARL CELLARS
opened: 1999
winemaker(s): Joe Gunselman
location: 115 West Pacific Avenue, Spokane, WA 99201
phone: 888-4CLARET (425-2738)
web: www.robertkarl.com
e-mail: info@robertkarl.com
fee: Complimentary wine tasting
hours: Thursday and Friday 2–5; Saturday 12–4; First Friday Art Walk
amenities: Wheelchair Accessible, Wine Club
connect: 🐦 📘

Market Place Wine Bar

This makes for an attractive space to hang out with friends, or your trusty laptop, and enjoy some wine and friendly staff. A collaboration of Spokane natives Brian and Melody Padrta and Mark and Valerie Wilkerson, the Market Place Wine Bar features the wines of Bridge Press Cellars and Emvy Cellars. The founding couples rely on the winemaking talents of John Mueller and Dave Westfall of Grande Ronde Cellars and Mountain Dome Winery to vinify their grapes.

Owned by the Padrtas, Bridge Press Cellars has the distinction of being Washington's 600th bonded winery. While Melody manages the Market Place Wine Bar, Mike focuses on the winemaking tasks, in addition to working his day job.

They've collaborated with their friends the Wilkersons of Emvy Cellars to create Market Place Wine Bar. In case you're wondering, the name "Emvy" is a contraction of sorts of Mark's and Valerie's first initials: M-V. Get it? By working closely with Grande Ronde Cellars, they created their first wine, dubbed Devotion, a Bordeaux blend of Walla Walla AVA grapes. More recently, Emvy Cellars released a white blend called Veba Blanc, a nonvintage red blend called Veba Rouge, and a viognier.

MARKET PLACE WINE BAR
opened: 2011
winemaker(s): Consultants Dave Westfall and John Mueller
location: 32 West Second Avenue, Spokane, WA 99201
phone: 509-474-1070
web: www.marketplacewinebar.com
e-mail: marketplacewinebar@gmail.com
fee: Tasting fee
hours: Thursday 3–Close; Friday and Saturday 12–9; First Friday Art Walk
amenities: Gift Shop, Live Music, Private Events, Restaurant/Food Pairings, Wheelchair Accessible, Wines by the Glass
connect: 🐦 📘

Vintage Hill Cellars 🔟

Winemakers Cody George and Brian Murray have something that many winemakers either don't have or it takes them years to accomplish. They have a distinct wine style. I say distinct because with one sip you realize that you are experiencing a unique creation of wine that pleases their palates — and I suspect will please your palate too.

How is it possible that Vintage Hill is unlike other Spokane wine creations or for that matter different from the other 700 plus Washington wineries? The answer to the mystery lies in the barrel or rather, the length of time in the barrel.

Reminiscent of Italian Barolo Riservas that are required by Piedmont regulations to age five years before consumers can purchase, Vintage Hill Cellars matures many of their wines between 39 and 55 months in the barrel before bottling. Residing for 55 months in neutral oak with with regular "topping off" to mitigate the impact of evaporation, results in wine with a very different flavor profile. It gives it depth of character with a caramel to nutty component on the palate adding to the zing of intense black fruit notes. Imagine a mouthful of blueberries and black cherries followed by a dose of cashews and you get what I mean.

But the wine is only part of the story when visiting Vintage Hill Cellars because while "the boys" are busy producing wine or pursuing other endeavors, Cody's parents (Mark and Paula George) work the tasting room and often lead visitors through a wine and food tasting sensory evaluation exercise. Seriously. Here the combination of spices, chocolates and herbs bring out the flavor components in the wine heretofore hidden from the retro-nasal passage that leads most visitors slack-jawed and reaching for their wallet. *Vive la différence!*

VINTAGE HILL CELLARS
opened: 2007
winemaker(s): Cody George and Brian Murray
location: 319 West 2nd Avenue, Spokane, WA 99201-4309
phone: 509-994-0878
web: www.vintagehillcellars.com
e-mail: info@vintagehillcellars.com
fee: Tasting fee refunded with purchase
hours: Wednesday through Saturday 1:30–5:30; First Friday Art Walk
amenities: Art Gallery, Gift Shop, Mailing List, Online Store
connect: 🐦

Grande Ronde Cellars

Started in 1997, Grande Ronde Cellars was the inspiration of four partners: Dave Westfall, Michael Manz, John Mueller, and J. David Page. It was Michael Manz, however, that

became the winemaking heart and soul for Grande Ronde Cellars and moonlighted as the vintner for Mountain Dome. Unfortunately, Michael's premature death in 2006 resulted in a huge loss for Grande Ronde Cellars.

It was also a turning point for Grande Ronde and a renewed commitment to move forward with equal passion.

Now at the helm of winemaking is Michael's brother, John Mueller (bearing a different last name). With Dave Westfall focusing on their vineyard sources (most notably Pepper Bridge and Seven Hills) the two make a dynamic duo.

At the friendly confines of their downstairs tasting room digs, visitors experience a wine style that expresses quintessential Washington *terroir* — big, full-flavored good to the last drop Columbia Valley reds. Also available are second label wines including Kibitzer and Bridge Press.

"Kibitzer" is a Yiddish term often associated with a bridge or board games and refers to a non-participant who hangs around a game, offering (often-unwanted) advice or commentary. This tells you that the partners involved in this venture play a lot of bridge (Dave Westfall is a professional bridge player). It can also refer to the fact that the wine is a bridge to Walla Walla where they source grapes from such premiere vineyards as Pepper Bridge and Seven Hills in their quest to make single vineyard designated award-winners.

GRANDE RONDE CELLARS
opened: 1999
winemaker(s): John Mueller and Dave Westfall
location: 906 West Second Avenue, Spokane, WA 99201
phone: 509-455-8161
web: www.granderondecellars.com
e-mail: grcellars@hotmail.com
fee: Tasting fee refunded with purchase
hours: Wednesday and Thursday 4–7; Friday and Saturday 12–7; and First Friday Art Walk until 9
amenities: Art Gallery, Gift Shop, Live Music, Online Store, Restaurant/Food Pairings, RV/Bus Parking, Wheelchair Accessible, Wines by the Glass
connect: 🐦 f

Overbluff Cellars

I found myself quite taken with the names Duality, Occult, LSD Siren, and Oh Jerry. But what do they all mean? For that, dear WineTrail trekker, you will need to make a beeline to Overbluff Cellars, located very near downtown Spokane. Its garage-like entrance may

have ivy blanketing the outside, but it actually has an inviting effect. Once inside, you're likely to find winemaker and co-owner John Caudill doing the pouring honors. With those pours, you can experience the "full-bodied" (read big) flavors of Overbluff's lineup of wines, including the aforementioned Duality and Occult.

John Caudill

It's not often that a small winery achieves financial success. I think that many winery owner wannabes too often see the "Sommelier starts a winery" video that's catching a lot of hits on YouTube. They follow their heart and launch a winery, but neglect to listen to their common sense in the process (such as coming up with a well-conceived business plan). However, a few minutes with John and you sense he's not one of those wannabes. He's a smart dude and knows that making wine is just half the battle; the other half is marketing.

The tasting room itself is a nice venue; add the charm of the proprietors and throw in the aforementioned Oh Jerry wine, and by golly, they (John, his wife Lynnelle Caudill and their business partner, Jerry Gibson) just may succeed. That's my humble opinion, anyway. After visiting more than 500 wineries throughout the Pacific Northwest since 2006, I've developed a sense about these things. It's a little like tasting wine: You know when a wine is a clunker, and you know when a wine strikes a chord (causing your taste buds to sing). In the case of Overbluff Cellars, it's perfectly tuned.

OVERBLUFF CELLARS
opened: 2010
winemaker(s): John Caudill
location: 620 South Washington Street, Spokane, WA 99204
phone: 509-991-4781
web: www.overbluffcellars.com
e-mail: john@overbluffcellars.com
fee: Tasting fee refunded with purchase
hours: Friday 2–6 and Saturday 12–5 or by appointment
amenities: Mailing List, Online Store, Wheelchair Accessible, Wine Club
connect: 🐦 f

Townshend Cellar

Don Townshend is the mad scientist of winemaking. He's constantly tinkering to find the right blend, best grapes, and optimum oak for aging. His portfolio of table wines, dessert wines, and port-style wines is extensive, offering about 20 different reds, whites, and specialty beverages. When he's not mixing and matching in the winery, he sheds the lab coat and is occasionally seen at events wearing a tux as he introduces his wine to guests, pouring and getting feedback from soon-to-be-loyal fans.

Inside Townshend's comfortable tasting room, you're struck by the number of wines to sample, and it occurs to you that you're going to be here for a while. Let your taste buds work their way through the Townshend Cellar whites, which feature chardonnay and dry riesling, and then onto the reds, which are highlighted by syrah, cabernet franc, and merlot. While in the red zone, be sure you sample Don's special red blends, such as "T3". The "T3" may strike a familiar note; there's a chance you imbibed this wine at one of the select Northwest restaurants where it is often served. Also, be sure to save room for Don's very popular huckleberry port wine, made from wild huckleberries picked in northern Idaho.

By the end of your visit, you realize that Don Townshend lives and breathes wine, 24/7, from purchasing grapes to putting the labels on the bottle. You imagine him racing from one event to another and meeting with his distributors. Then add to the equation the Caterina, Lone Canary and Mountain Dome labels (which you can savor at Broadview Dairy Building in downtown Spokane) and you realize Don has solved the need for sleep. He doesn't.

TOWNSHEND CELLAR
opened: 2001
winemaker(s): Don Townshend
location: 16112 North Greenbluff Road, Colbert, WA 99005
phone: 509-238-1400
web: www.townshendcellar.com
e-mail: info@townshendcellar.com
fee: Complimentary wine tasting
hours: Friday through Sunday 12–6
amenities: Gift Shop, Newsletter/Blog, Online Store, Picnic Area, Private Events, Tours, Wheelchair Accessible, Wine Club, Winemaker Dinners
connect: [f]

★ BEST Views

Arbor Crest Wine Cellars 🔢

Arbor Crest Wine Cellars is a labor of love from a family with a shared vision of producing high-quality wines at affordable prices. The winery's spectacular view overlooking the Spokane Valley is, in itself, reason to visit, but equally gratifying at this stop are some serious wines certain to brighten anyone's day. It's no wonder *Wine Spectator* named Arbor Crest

one of the "50 Great Producers Every Wine Lover Should Know" for quality and price. To give you an example, Arbor Crest's merlot sells for $20 a bottle.

Keeping it all in the family, winemaker Kristina Mielke–van Löben Sels is the daughter of one of the winery's founders, and her husband, Jim van Löben Sels, is its viticulturist and chief operations manager. It makes for a nice marriage. Together, they produce about 20,000 cases of wine annually.

Back in 1985, the Mielke brothers purchased the Cliff House, a designated national historic site that sits 450 feet above the Spokane River. The mansion, which was built in 1924 by inventor Royal Newton Riblet (honest, that was his name), houses Arbor Crest's tasting room. (The actual wine production facility is located about a mile down the road.) The tasting room staff is well versed in the nuances of the wines and equally adept at making WineTrails adventurers feel at ease. There is a small 5-acre vineyard at the site, which provides the fruit used to produce an estate-bottled sparkling wine. All other Arbor Crest wines are made from grapes grown in the Columbia Valley AVA.

The estate grounds feature gardens, picnic areas, scenic views, and a manmade waterfall. It's perfect for weddings, summer concerts, and just relaxing with a bottle of wine.

ARBOR CREST WINE CELLARS
opened: 1982
winemaker(s): Kristina Mielke van Loben Sels
location: 4705 North Fruithill Road, Spokane, WA 99217
phone: 509-927-9463
web: www.arborcrest.com
e-mail: info@arborcrest.com
fee: Tasting fee
hours: Daily 12–5
amenities: Gift Shop, Picnic Area, Private Events, Online Store, Tours, Vineyard on Premise, Weddings, Wheelchair Accessible, Wine Club
connect: 🐦 📘

 BEST Destination, views, gift shop, picnicking and weddings

Knipprath Cellars 15

Knipprath's winery/tasting room

Knipprath Cellars, housed in the old 1913 Parkwater Schoolhouse in Spokane Valley, is the offspring of a family's love affair with wine.

Knipprath Cellars serves as many as seven different port-style wines inoculated with an extra dose of neutral alcohol, which makes the wines 20 percent alcohol by volume. So a sip here and a sip there can add up, and the tasting room can become a pretty lively place!

Offering vanilla- and chocolate-flavored port, Knipprath can satisfy a sweet tooth. Its ports include Northwest Positron, Au Chocolat! Lagrima white port, LaV! dessert wine (V is for vanilla), Matrix ruby port, a pink port, and (my favorite) Spanish Nudge, a coffee port.

Knipprath produces a number of wines in addition to its port wine series. Another personal favorite is the Alpine wine, served warm and made from a family recipe for Glühwein, which calls for steeping the wine with assorted holiday spices. You can definitely taste notes of clove and other spices in this full-bodied red wine. Après-ski anyone?

KNIPPRATH CELLARS
opened: 1991
winemaker(s): Henning Knipprath
location: 5634 East Commerce Avenue, Spokane, WA 99212-1307
phone: 509-534-5121
web: www.knipprath-cellars.com
e-mail: grapesoknipprath@aol.com
fee: Complimentary wine tasting
hours: Wednesday through Sunday 12–5, or by appointment
amenities: Gift Shop, Picnic Area, Tours, Wine Club

Nodland Cellars 16

Owner/winemaker Tim Nodland knows a thing or two about both making wine and playing jazz. In the case of Nodland Cellars, the two come together to offer liquid art in a 750-milliliter bottle. Drop by on a Friday evening and you are likely to encounter live music as accompaniment to your Bebop (an off-dry riesling) or Bad Attitude (a merlot-based Bordeaux blend).

While taking in the tunes, be sure to experience Nodland's signature wine, Private Blend. This red beauty is a juicy mix of all six Bordeaux grapes (merlot, cabernet sauvignon, cabernet franc, petit verdot, carménère, and Malbec). Made with grapes from various Columbia Valley AVAs, Private Blend is a wine that truly expresses the *terroir* of Washington, and it's no secret what Tim's palate grooves to.

His winemaking methods include the use of open-top, punch-down fermentation tanks, which produce very small batches of handcrafted wine. Which means that if a particular bottle tickles your fancy, buy it then and there, while it's in stock. It's little wonder Tim adds a note of caution to his posted hours: "Open Saturdays 12–4 p.m. until sold out." So you'd better bebop over to Nodland and pick up your own bottle of Private Blend.

NODLAND CELLARS
opened: 2006
winemaker(s): Tim Nodland
location: 11616 East Montgomery Drive, Suite 70, Spokane Valley, WA 99206
phone: 509-927-7770
web: www.nodlandcellars.com
e-mail: Tim@nodlandcellars.com
fee: Tasting fee refunded with purchase
hours: Saturday 12–4 until sold out or by appointment
amenities: Art Gallery, Live Music, RV/Bus Parking, Wheelchair Accessible
connect: f

Latah Creek Wine Cellars

Latah Creek Wine Cellars has everything going for it: history, innovative wines, great location, and a gift shop to die for. Since 1982, when they started Latah Creek, Mike and Ellena Conway have been on a rather exclusive list of Washington wine industry founders. Keeping it in the family, their daughter Natalie is part of the venture and shares the title of winemaker with her dad.

To appreciate Latah Creek is to understand the philosophy that guides Mike Conway. Essentially, he believes in giving his customers the best value for their wine dollar. Consequently, the Conways sell many of their wines at a low price point (around $10 a bottle) and rely on grapes from the same region of the state that so-called higher-end wineries use. Don't be surprised if you see loyal customers carting away cases from their tasting-room visit. Judging by Latah Creek's ample selection of wines, Mike also believes that the consuming public has a wide variety of taste preferences. In other words, you're sure to find a Latah Creek wine you like.

You won't need a GPS device to find this winery. Located just off the I-90 freeway a few miles east of downtown Spokane, Latah Creek boasts ample parking and a generously sized tasting room. A gift shop within the tasting room spills into the wine production area. Ellena has an eye for wine merchandise, and there is a good chance that all of your holiday gift buying for the wine lovers on your list can be done with a visit to Latah Creek.

LATAH CREEK WINE CELLARS
opened: 1982
winemaker(s): Mike Conway
(Natalie Conway-Barnes, assistant)
location: 13030 East Indiana Avenue,
Spokane, WA 99216-1118
phone: 509-926-0164
web: www.latahcreek.com
e-mail: info@latahcreek.com
fee: Complimentary wine tasting
hours: Daily 9–5
amenities: Gift Shop, Online Store, Picnic Area, Tours, Wheelchair Accessible, Wine Club
connect: 🐦 f

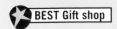
⭐ BEST Gift shop

China Bend Winery

Some believe it's the journey that matters, and the destination, not so much. However, when it comes to China Bend Vineyards and Winery, we beg to differ. The journey's fine, but the real reward is in the destination. China Bend Vineyards and Winery is located a couple

of hours north of Spokane, near the Canadian border. Situated on the banks of the beautiful Columbia River, China Bend offers a host of delightful surprises, not to mention stunning views of the surrounding hills and Lake Roosevelt.

China Bend Vineyards and Winery is the dream of owners/winemakers Bart and Victory Alexander. They had the foresight to realize that grapes would grow surprisingly well in this area's harsh winter environment. In their case, they have French oenophiles to thank for a hardy Alsatian grape varietal with the unlikely name of Marechal Foch. (Foch was a famous French general who ran the Germans out of France in World War I.) If you are from upstate New York or Québec, you may already be familiar with this varietal, but in Washington's Bordeaux-dominated landscape, Marechal Foch is a rare find. The grape produces a soft, full-bodied wine and, not surprisingly, is China Bend's no. 1 seller.

China Bend Winery

On your way to the tasting room, you will also go by the China Bend Bed and Breakfast. Guests wake up each morning to a full breakfast made from the bounty of Victory's organic garden. (We told you that this was a destination winery.) The attractive red-roofed tasting room is your WineTrail destination, where you can choose from Bart's portfolio of red and white wines. Another highlight of the tasting room is the assortment of organic products Victory makes and sells. Check out her attractively packaged jams, pickled garlic, dill pickles, and salsas.

CHINA BEND WINERY
opened: 1995
winemaker(s): Bart Alexander
location: 3751 Vineyard Way, Kettle Falls, WA 99141-8852
phone: 800-700-6123
web: www.chinabend.com
e-mail: winery@chinabend.com
fee: Complimentary wine tasting
hours: Monday through Saturday 12–5 April through October, or by appointment
amenities: Art Gallery, Gift Shop, Lodging, Picnic Area, Private Events, Restaurant/Food Pairings, RV/Bus Parking, Tours, Vineyard on Premise, Wheelchair Accessible, Wine Club
connect: ▉

⭐ **BEST Views, picnicking**

Tournament quality croquet grounds

  www.winetrailsnw.com/wineries/china_bend_winery

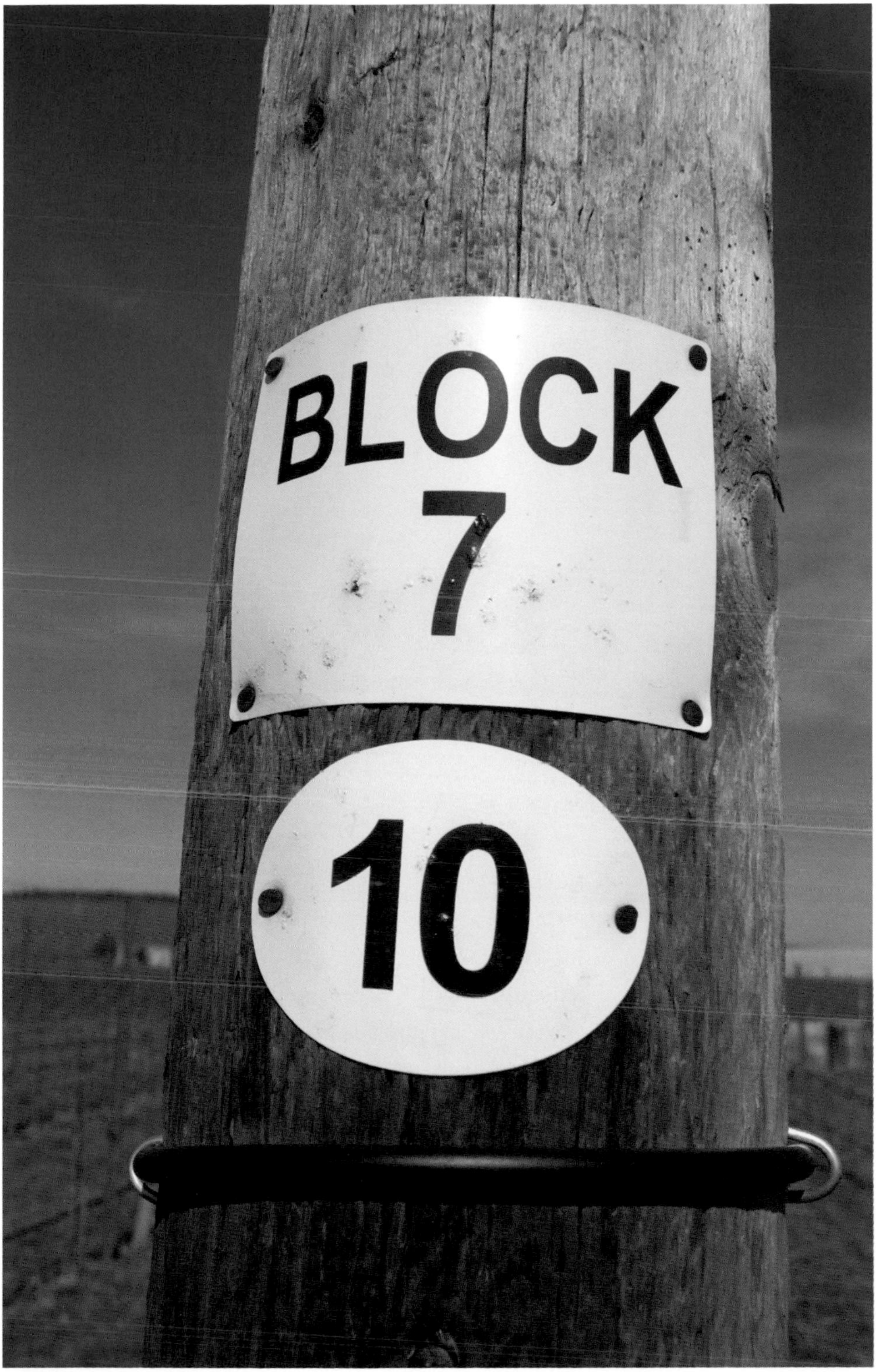
BLOCK
7
10

Pullman
WineTrail

Perhaps the most surprising aspect of the Pullman WineTrail is that there isn't a plethora of wineries to visit. After all, Washington State University's enology and viticulture program is located here and regularly produces exceptionally trained vintners. What's more, this land has viticultural history on its side: Nearly 100 acres of *Vitis vinifera* was planted near the geologic wonderland of Lewiston, Idaho, in the early 1900s. That was before Prohibition forced grape growers to yank out the vines. Today, most Pullman-area wineries source their fruit from the Walla Walla Valley, but look for local grapes to become the norm as the nearby vineyards mature. Go, Cougs!

Pullman WineTrail
1 Merry Cellars   **3** Clearwater Canyon Cellars   **4** Basalt Cellars
2 Wawawai Canyon

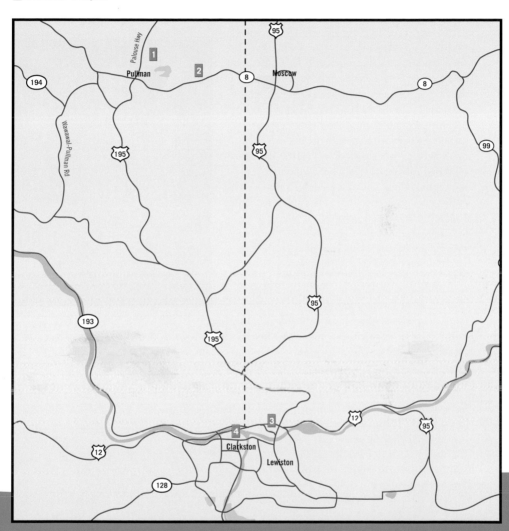

Region: **Spokane Wine Country**
# of tasting rooms on tour: **4**
Estimate # of days for tour: **1**
Getting around: **Car**
Tips: ❏ **Pack your camera and get ready for surprising vistas**
❏ **Visit Wawawai Canyon's vineyard or Clearwater Canyon Cellars' Umiker Vineyard to see the viticulture potential of this region**
❏ **Take in the original artwork at Wawawai Canyon winery**

Merry Cellars ❶

"Wine is sunlight, held together by water!" — Galileo Galilei

I believe if Galileo were a Coug he would have reworked his poetic line to read, "Wheat is sunlight, held together by undulating hills." When I think of the Palouse, I see fields of gold and green, I feel dry heat, and I hear the crickets at night. However, until the emergence of Merry Cellars, wine imagery wasn't used in the same sentence with the Palouse. But that was before one sip of Merry Cellar's "Twilight Hills Red" shook my world, and I learned that the taste of the Palouse comes in a bottle. It's true. As its tasting notes make clear, Merry Cellars creates wines "comfortable and approachable, and maybe just a little rugged around the edges." For me, that brings to mind my eastern Washington roots.

Patrick Merry - photo courtesy of Merry Cellars

Winemaker and owner Patrick Merry is a transplanted Montanan who grew up in a family that appreciated wine. I am envious of that. My own family's experience with wine was a bottle of cold duck left in the refrigerator for eons after some family event. Patrick's goal is to create wines for different occasions, from backyard barbecues to elegant weddings. He respects the fruit's origin and applies a minimalist approach to his hand-picked and hand-sorted grapes in order to bring out the *terroir* of each vintage.

Located on the outskirts of Pullman in the Port of Whitman County, and surrounded by rolling wheatfields, Merry Cellars is a joy to visit any time of the year. When Merry Cellars hosts wine-

tasting and food-pairing events, there is no need for you to stop by The Coug bar to pick up Cougar Gold. Merry Cellars will supply the perfect wine to accompany delectable cheeses.

Photo courtesy of Merry Cellars

MERRY CELLARS
opened: 2004
winemaker(s): Patrick Merry
location: 1300 NE Henley Court, Port of Whitman County, Pullman, WA 99163
phone: 509-338-4699
web: www.merrycellars.com
e-mail: bemerry@merrycellars.com
fee: Tasting fee refunded with purchase
hours: Tuesday through Saturday 12–6; Sunday 11–4
amenities: Live Music, Online Store, Picnic Area, RV/Bus Parking, Wheelchair Accessible, Wine Club
connect: 🐦 f

Wawawai Canyon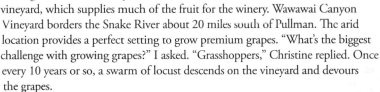

When it comes to winemaking, "My husband, Ben [Moffett], is the pilot and I'm the copilot," noted Christine Havens as she poured me a healthy dose of their cabernet sauvignon. No doubt Christine was being modest in terms of her winemaking involvement. After all, she met Ben while both were attending Walla Walla Community College's enology and viticulture program. This was before they came home to Ben's native Pullman and established Wawawai (pronounced wah-WOW-ee) Canyon Winery.

The couple brought with them the technical expertise to make fine wine and an inherent desire to add their own unique touch. As testament to their creative license, they released an unfiltered pinot noir using the Old World sur lies technique for aging the wine. The result is a wine that has a very different flavor profile compared to a traditional "light" pinot noir.

Ben's parents, David and Stacia Moffett, both teach at nearby Washington State University and work their vineyard, which supplies much of the fruit for the winery. Wawawai Canyon Vineyard borders the Snake River about 20 miles south of Pullman. The arid location provides a perfect setting to grow premium grapes. "What's the biggest challenge with growing grapes?" I asked. "Grasshoppers," Christine replied. Once every 10 years or so, a swarm of locust descends on the vineyard and devours the grapes.

Check out the winery's gorgeous logo created by Christine, which also serves as the image on Wawawai Canyon wine labels. In fact, the family celebrates artistic inclinations by hosting rotating art exhibits in the tasting room. Clearly the entire family (and this is a family affair from the vineyard to the tasting room) has many other endeavors that intrigue its members. Along with teaching, painting, consulting, and cooking, producing signature wines is one of many passions they pursue.

WAWAWAI CANYON
opened: 2004
winemaker(s): Ben Moffett and Christine Havens
location: 5602 State Route 270, Pullman, WA 99163
phone: 509-338-4916
web: www.wawawaicanyon.com
e-mail: wine@wawawaicanyon.com
fee: Complimentary wine tasting
hours: Friday and Saturday 12–6, Sunday 12–4 or by appointment
amenities: Art Gallery, Live Music, Mailing List, Online Store, Picnic Area, Private Events, RV/Bus Parking, Wheelchair Accessible, Wine Club
connect: 🐦 f

Clearwater Canyon Cellars 3

"It may not be too visionary to dream of the slopes and hillsides of the Snake and Clearwater rivers being covered with vineyards." These are the words of award-winning vintner Robert Schleicher in 1906 when the Clearwater Canyon area was emerging as premium wine grape country. Then Prohibition came, and the fledging wine industry died a quick death.

Thus, it seems only fitting that in 2005, Clearwater Canyon Cellars released its first vintage under the name Renaissance Red and under the direction of their youthful winemaker Coco Umiker. Even in her 20s, Coco possessed considerable experience in winemaking from a stint in Walla Walla as well as an advanced degree in winemaking from Washington State University.

Starting out in 2004 the winery had to rely in large part upon grapes from Washington's Horse Heaven Hills AVA and other Columbia Valley vineyards. However, with each vintage, an increasing percentage of the grapes are locally grown and now compose approximately 85% of Clearwater Canyon's total production. As part-owner Patty Switzer pointed out, "Our goal is to use local fruit. Increasingly, our grapes will come from growers here in the Lewiston Clarkston Valley."

Coco Umiker

During my visit to the winery, Patty, with thief and wine glass in hand, created a blend of locally sourced syrah and merlot for my tasting pleasure. As I stuck my nose into the wine glass and took a whiff, I couldn't help but think of how those early winemaking pioneers would have slapped high fives at seeing the reemergence of the Idaho wine industry in the Clearwater Canyon area. It's clear that Clearwater Canyon Cellars honors the past but looks resolutely to a bright future.

CLEARWATER CANYON CELLARS
opened: 2004
winemaker(s): Coco and Karl Umiker
location: 1708 6th Avenue North, Suite A, Lewiston, ID 83501
phone: 208-816-4679
web: www.clearwatercanyoncellars.com
e-mail: kcumiker@cccellars.com
fee: Complimentary wine tasting
hours: Saturday 1–5
amenities: Newsletter/Blog, Online Store, Wheelchair Accessible
connect: 🐦 f

Basalt Cellars 4

If you live in the Pacific Northwest and haven't had the pleasure of visiting the twin cities of Lewiston-Clarkston, you need to put them on your "top 10 local places to visit" list. Why? How about history? This is where Lewis and Clark camped in 1805 as guests of the Nez Perce Tribe. How about beauty? The scenic Lewis-Clark Valley will compel you to pull the car over and get out to soak in the view. How about wine? At one time in the late 1800s, this area harbored a bounty of vineyards that produced premium wine grapes. But with Prohibition, the fledgling wine industry came to a halt. Now, however, a reemergence of vineyards and wineries is in the offing, beginning with Clarkston's Basalt Cellars.

Founders Rick Wasem, Don McQuary, and Lynn DeVleming took enology classes at the Clarkston campus of Walla Walla Community College and there, discovered in one another a kindred passion for crafting wine. It wasn't long before they bonded the winery, and Basalt Cellars was born in 2004. From just 200 cases produced in their first year, they have enjoyed phenomenal growth, using local grapes as well as fruit from the Columbia Valley. By the way, if you are wondering how they came up with the name Basalt Cellars, simply take your nose out of the glass and look around.

Rick Wasem is Basalt Cellars' chief winemaker and also one of a half-dozen Washington winemakers who have backgrounds as pharmacists. Rick has garnered medals at wine-tasting competitions in San Francisco, the Tri-Cities and a number of other cities. In addition to Bordeaux and Rhône-style wines, Basalt Cellars produces rosé and dessert wines.

Clarkston may be known to many as the "Gateway to Hells Canyon," but for WineTrail enthusiasts, it serves as the entrance to a heavenly selection of Basalt Cellars wines.

BASALT CELLARS
opened: 2004
winemaker(s): Rick Wasem
location: 906 Port Drive, Clarkston, WA 99403-1805
phone: 509-758-6442
web: www.basaltcellars.com
e-mail: info@basaltcellars.com
fee: Complimentary wine tasting
hours: Monday through Saturday 12–5:30, or by appointment
amenities: Mailing List, Online Store, RV/Bus Parking, Wheelchair Accessible, Wine Club
connect: 🐦 📘

Other Wineries to Visit

BARILI CELLARS
winemaker(s): Russ Feist and
Steve Trabun
location: 608 West 2nd Avenue,
Spokane, WA 99201
phone: 509-995-4077
web: www.barilicellars.com
hours: First Friday Art Walks;
Event Weekends or by appointment

LIBERTY LAKE WINE CELLARS
winemaker(s): Douglas Rupert Smith
location: 1018 South Garry Road,
Liberty Lake, WA 99019-9771
phone: 509-255-9205
web: www.libertylakewinecellars.com
hours: Select Saturdays throughout the
year; Call for tasting room hours

WHITESTONE WINERY & VINEYARD
winemaker(s): Walter Haig and
Michael Haig
location: 115 NE Main Street,
Wilbur, WA 99185
phone: 509-838-2427
web: www.whitestonewinery.com
hours: Open select dates;
check website

COEUR D'ALENE CELLARS
winemaker(s): Warren Schutz
location: 3890 North Schreiber Way,
Coeur d'Alene, ID 83815
phone: 208-664-2336
web: www.cdacellars.com
hours: Monday through Saturday 11–5

PEND D'OREILLE WINERY
winemaker(s): Julie and
Stephen Meyer; James Bopp
location: 220 Cedar Street,
Sandpoint, ID 83864
phone: 208-265-8545
web: www.powine.com
hours: Monday through Thursday
10–6:30; Friday and Saturday 10–8;
Sunday 11–6

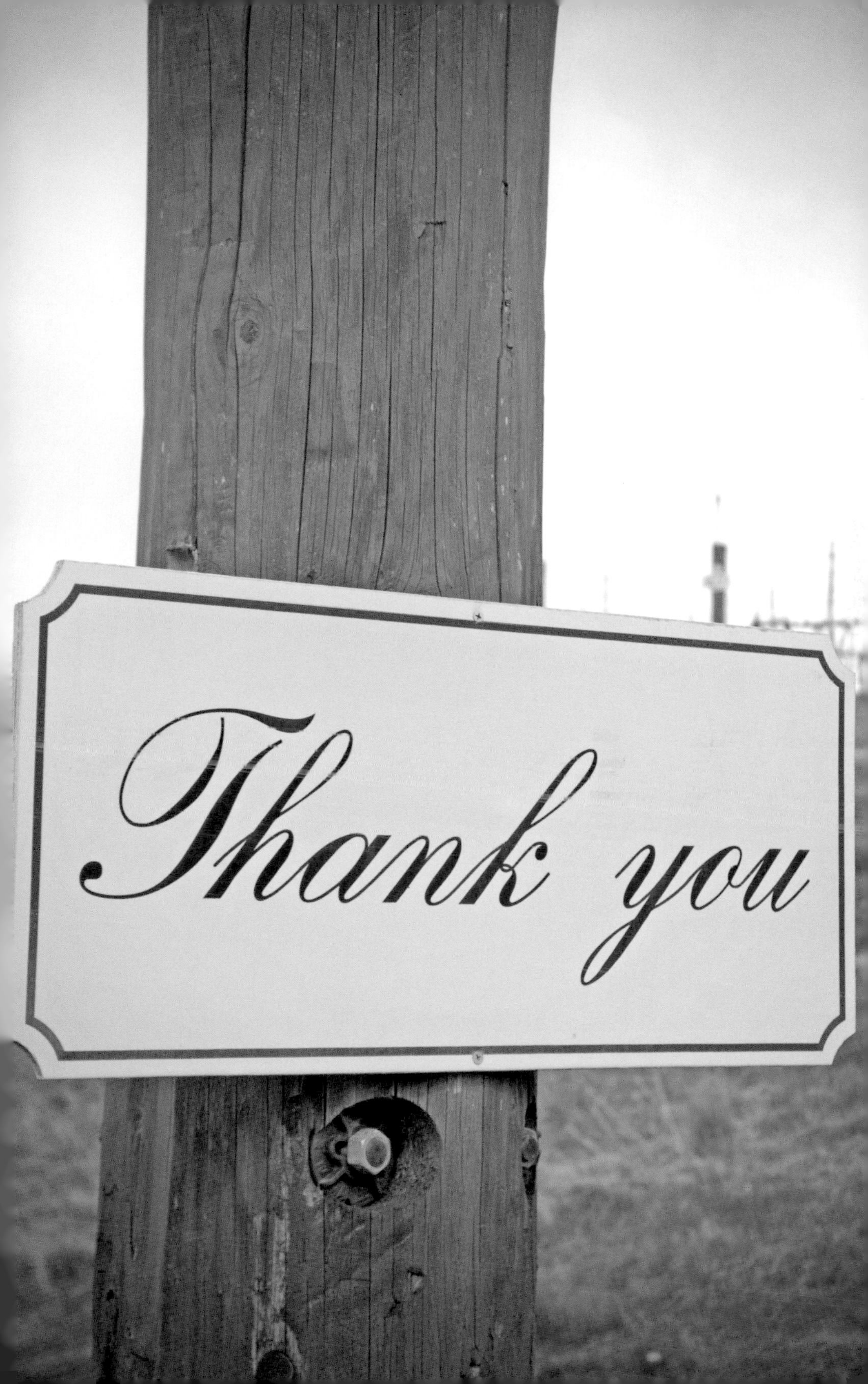
Thank you

Zin and the Art of Wine Tasting

The key to tasting wine is to take it slow and concentrate.

All that's required of you is to swirl, sniff, and taste. A visual check of the wine informs you of the basic type of wine you are about to taste — red or white. Red wine ranges in color from purple to ruby red, deep red, red brown, and mahogany. White wine hues range from yellow green to straw, gold, yellow-brown, and amber brown. To judge the true color of a wine, hold your glass up to a white background (or wall or napkin). Where the wine falls in the color spectrum prepares your taste buds for what they are about to experience.

Once a wine has been poured, some folks like to tilt the wine glass and observe how the wine flows down the inside of the glass. However, there is no correlation between the "legs," or "tears," of wine on the inside of the glass and the taste of the wine itself.

Swirling

A wine just poured needs to stretch its legs and aerate. Swirling allows the wine to open up and release aromas. Up to this point in the wine's existence, oxygen has been a bad thing; now, oxygen is the wine's best friend. It allows the wine to create a bouquet. Most

Robert Ramsay Cellars — Woodinville

tasting rooms provide wine glasses roomy enough to swirl the wine without spillage. You need that space between the wine and your nose to smell the aroma. If you chance upon a winery that uses little plastic cups or tiny "orange juice glasses," you may want to consider shortening your visit and moving on to the next winery.

Sniffing

The aroma given off by a wine is its "nose." Right after a vigorous swirl, quickly stick your nose as far down into the glass as possible and sniff. Concentrate and give your imagination free rein as you attempt to describe what you smell. In time, descriptions such as sweaty saddle, cat pee (no kidding), tar, kerosene, burnt match, and asparagus may enter your sniffing lexicon. Researchers say that flavor is 75 percent smell and 25 percent taste. (This explains why food tastes bland when you have a cold — you can't smell it.) Merlot, pinot noir, and cabernet sauvignon are known for their distinctive smells.

Tasting

Most of us were taught in science class that the tongue has certain regions that taste salt, bitter, sweet, and sour. Have you ever seen those drawings of the tongue that depict which part of the tongue tastes what? But according to the latest research, all taste buds can taste salt, bitter, sweet, and sour to varying degrees. Taste buds cover the entire top of the tongue, front and back, which explains why you see sommeliers and wine connoisseurs vigorously swishing

the wine around their mouth; they are getting the maximum exposure throughout their mouth to taste the wine. While you are swishing, your brain is also registering other sensations, such as heaviness, roundness, finish, and astringency from the tannins found in the wine. While the wine is in your mouth, focus on it for a few seconds. Swirl it around in your mouth and attempt to suck in a little air — without committing the *faux pas* of gagging — to pick up the full flavors of the wine.

Remember, take it slow and concentrate.

Tasting Room Etiquette

There are definite rules of the road when it comes to visiting tasting rooms, and most involve common sense. Moderation is a good thing. Those innocent little ounces add up. So have a strategy ahead of time and try to stick to it. Here's some WineTrail do's and don'ts:

Do:

- Drink responsibly — Designate a driver or hire a limo.
- Spit or dump as much as you want — That's what those buckets are for!
- Have patience with the wine pourer — Don't elbow your way forward with outstretched hand begging for another fill; they'll get to you.
- Have a tasting strategy — Choose which wines you would like to sample. If you are only interested in the reds, let your pourer know that.
- Ask questions — Tasting-room pourers are passionate about their wines and anxious to tell you why.
- Purchase wine if you want to — Assuming it is in your budget and you like it, spring for it.

- Be open to wines you believe you won't like — Reds, whites, port wines, late-harvest dessert wines, rosés — go on, try them! You might be surprised to learn how delicious, say, a dessert wine made from frozen grapes can taste. Open your mind when you open your mouth.

- Let them know if you like their wine — There's a reason the pourer is staring at you with an expectant look. If you like the wine, tell them. Winemakers live for such moments.

Don't:

- Generally, ask for a second helping — Unless you are contemplating purchasing a bottle or you need a second helping to clarify what you just tasted.

- Feel that you have to purchase a bottle of wine — The winery's primary goal is to give you a positive experience, so you tell your friends and family about it.

- Wear perfumes or colognes — Your nose needs to smell the wine.

- Attempt to engage the tasting-room staff in esoteric debates — Save the Hungarian vs. American oak debate for a conversation with the winemaker, not the poor pourer.

- Take anything — The wine glasses are theirs, not yours (unless the tasting fee includes a glass).

- Drink excessively — Keep your wits; spit/dump often and pace yourself.

Rolling Bay Winery — Bainbridge Island

Resources for Washington Wine Touring

Wine Country Links

WineTrails Northwest
Companion website to this guidebook; provides fresh winery and event information
www.winetrailsnw.com

> **Smartphone Apps for WineTrails**
> Get the latest on winery hours, tasting fees, turn-by-turn directions and more:
>
> - For **Android** users, go to Google Play and search Google Play for WineTrails of Washington and WineTrails of Walla Walla
>
> - For **iPhone and iPad** users, go to App Store and search for WineTrails of Washington and WineTrails of Walla Walla

AAA
800-829-5448, www.aaa.com

Alaska Airlines—City Guides
800-ALASKAAIR,
www.alaskaair.com/Destinations

Amtrak
800-USA-RAIL, www.amtrak.com

Columbia Gorge Winegrowers Association
www.woodinvillewinecountry.com

Columbia Cascade Winery Association
www.columbiacascadewines.com

Go Taste Wine
www.gotastewine.com

Lake Chelan Wine Valley Association
www.lakechelanwinevalley.com

Leavenworth Wineries
www.leavenworthwineries.org or www.leavenworth.org

LocalWineEvents.com
www.localwineevents.com

Olympic Peninsula Wineries
www.olympicpeninsulawineries.org

Prosser Chamber of Commerce
800-408-1517,
www.prosserchamber.org

Prosser
www.prosservintnersvillage.com

Rattlesnake Hills Wine Trail
www.rattlesnakehills.org

Skagit Valley Wine Association
www.skagitvalleywineries.com

Spokane Winery Association
www.spokanewineries.net

South Seattle Artisan Wineries
www.ssaw.info

The Washington State Hotel & Lodging Association (WSH&LA)
877-906-1001,
www.stayinwashington.com

Tourism Walla Walla
877-WW-VISIT, www.wallawalla.org

Tri-Cities Visitor & Convention Bureau
800-254-5824,
www.visittri-cities.com/visitors/wine

Virtual Tourist
www.virtualtourist.com

Washington State Travel Counselor
800-544-1800,
www.experiencewa.com

Walla Walla Valley
www.wallawallawine.com

Washington Wine Commission
206-667-9463,
www.washingtonwine.org

Washington Wine Highway
www.washingtonwinehighway.com

Wine Press Northwest
509-582-1564,
www.winepressnw.com

Whatcom Wineries Association
www.whatcomwineries.com

Wenatchee Wine Country
www.wenatcheewines.com

Winery Alliance of Bainbridge Island
www.bainbridgewineries.com

Wines Northwest
www.winesnw.com

**Woodinville Warehouse District /
Tasting Woodinville**
www.woodwarewine.com

Woodinville Wine Country
www.woodinvillewinecountry.com

Yakima Valley Wine Country
www.wineyakimavalley.org

Road Conditions
www.wsdot.wa.gov/traffic or call 511

Touring and Limousine Services — Getting Around

Washington Wine Tours
Serving multiple regions

A+ Pacific Limousine Tours
Serving Yakima Valley, Tri-Cities and
Walla Walla Valley. 509-585-7717,
www.limo01.com/winetours.html

All Points Charters & Tours
Serving Olympic Peninsula, Yakima
Valley, Leavenworth and Woodinville.
360-582-3736, www.goallpoints.com

Bon Vivant Wine Tours
Serving Seattle, Woodinville,
Bainbridge Island, Yakima Valley/
Rattlesnake Hills, Leavenworth/
Wenatchee. 206-524-8687,
www.bonvivanttours.com

DeVine Limousine
Serving Walla Walla, Red Mountain,
Benton City, Sunnyside, Prosser and
Yakima Valley. 509-531-7999,
www.devinelimos.com

Elegant Wine Country Limousine
Serving Yakima Valley, Red Mountain,
and Walla Walla. 509-781-0360,
www.elegantwinelimo.com

Four Star Limos
Serving Yakima Valley, Tri-Cities and
Walla Walla. 509-521-7849,
www.fourstarlimos.com

Sacco Tours
Serving Yakima Valley, Tri-Cities and
Red Mountain. 509-783-7060,
www.saccotours.com

Sunset Coach Tours
Serving Yakima, Walla Walla &
Columbia Valleys, Red Mountain and
Horse Heaven Hills. 800-941-2941,
www.sunsetcoachtours.com

Columbia Gorge Wine Tours
Columbia Wine Tours
541-380-1410,
www.columbiawinetours.com

Explore the Gorge
800-899-5676,
www.explorethegorge.com

Lake Chelan Wine Tours
Chelan Valley Tours
509-682-2386,
www.chelanvalleytours.com

Lakeside Limousine Tours
509-470-0333, www.chelanlimo.com

Leavenworth Wine Tours
Le Tours'
509-548-8687,
www.leavenworthenchantedtours.com

Spokane Wine Tours
Spokane Winery Tours
509-280-2560,
www.spokanewinerytours.com

Tri-Cities & Red Mountain Wine Tours
Fruit of the Vine Tours
509-546-1044,
www.fruitofthevinetours.com

Genie Tours
509-946-1400, www.genietours.com

Walla Walla Wine Tours
Bella Fortuna Event and Tours
509-540-9109,
bellafortunaevents.squarespace.com

Black Tie Limousines
509-585-8585, www.blacktielimos.net

Caveman Coach Wine Tours
509-529-7170,
www.thecavemancoach.com

Dream Ride Charters & Tours
509-337-0100,
www.dreamridecharters.com

Imbibe Wine Tours
800-605-3765,
www.imbibewinetours.com

Winery Tours Walla Walla
509-540-9518,
www.winerytourswallawalla.com

Whatcom County Wine Tours
Whatcom Wine Tours
360-224-0734,
www.whatcomwineries.com

Woodinville & Seattle Wine Tours
Barrel Wine Tours
425-273-5156,
www.barrelwinetours.com

Bayview Limousine Service
800-606-7880,
www.bayviewlimo.com

Butler Seattle
206-233-9233 or 425-883-0850,
www.butlerseattle.com

EverGreen Escapes
206-650-5796 or 866-203-7603,
www.evergreenescapes.com

Winery Bus
425-481-8860, www.winerybus.com

Wine Touring and Wheelchair Access

An increasing number of tasting rooms throughout the Pacific Northwest have become accessible by wheelchair. This accessibility is gained through designated special parking spaces for cars bearing wheelchair placards, the absence of stairs to impede access, wide doors, and restrooms meeting ADA standards.

Many Washington wineries — particularly the newer ones that meet stiffer building codes — reflect a sensitivity to this issue and have been designed or redesigned to accommodate disabled travelers.

That said, even if the winery indicates that it is wheelchair accessible, we believe it's a good idea to call ahead if you have concerns. For example, if you have a van that is specially equipped for wheelchair loading and unloading, you may have questions about the winery's parking lot being large enough to accommodate the vehicle. Another possible problem for  disabled visitors is access to areas outside designated-accessible spaces. Say you are attending a special event, such as a winemaker dinner or a wedding; you may have wheelchair access to the tasting room, but what about the rest of the winery, the bathroom facilities, and outdoors among the vineyards? Call or email the winery ahead of time to get the lowdown on the layout.

For general information to assist disabled travelers, check out these websites:

- Access-Able Travel Source (access-able.com).
- Global Access Disabled Travel Network (globalaccessnews.com).
- Mobility International (miusa.org).

Wine Touring with Pets

"Pets welcome" is a sign that you don't often see at wineries. In fact, quite the opposite. Wineries don't often welcome dogs into their tasting rooms. Too many things can go wrong, such as a counter-surfing dog snarfing crackers and cheese trays or scrapping with the winery cat.

That said, the wineries of Walla Walla deserve special mention for accommodating dogs. Many of them have gone out of their way to let visitors know that it is fine to bring their dogs. If you are planning a Walla Walla wine tour with your four-legged family member, check out each winery's website or call ahead. They may ask you to bring a leash, but including the family pet may be just fine.

Ironically, a large percentage of wineries do have a winery dog, which has led to an explosion of coffee-table books featuring mug shots of winery pooches. However, even though the winery owners might be dog-friendly regarding their own pooch, introducing your own dog into the tasting room is bound to create territorial issues.

However, should Fido accompany you on your next wine tour, you will find a number of hotels and quaint country inns that welcome pets. Some may charge an additional fee, but it's typically a nominal amount.

If you do bring along your dog, pack doggy snacks and water, and allow for pit stops along the way. Always keep the window open and park in the shade, especially in hot weather, to avoid baking your dog. In the summertime, particularly in eastern Washington, it's downright dangerous to keep a dog in a car — even with windows open. Bottom line: Take your dog to the park, but not to the winery, unless otherwise indicated.

Wine Touring with Kids

As a general rule, wineries are not set up to handle little tykes — after all, these establishments are "no whining zones." The stacked bottles of wine and Riedel crystal are easy targets for a wandering 3-year-old. Few wineries offer a play area as part of the tasting room or a playground for kids to enjoy — although the former schoolhouse serving as the L'Ecole No 41 winery is a nice exception; check out its backyard playground. In Woodinville, check out the play area behind the tasting room's curtain at Two Vintners in Woodinville.

When play areas are included, they are often more a means of distracting the kids in order to allow parents to swirl, sip, and experience the wine. However, if you do have your children along and insist on checking out a winery or two, here are a few tips to make it a family-friendly experience.

First, make it informational and choose wineries that feature a wine tour. Treat it like a field trip and discover how wine is made. At harvest time, it is not unusual to see kids stomping grapes (talk about cheap labor). The smiles on their faces says it all.

Try to combine wine tasting with family activities, such as picnicking at the winery, checking out a hands-on museum, or going on a nature hike. Involve the kids in the planning. Sure, you're picking up the tab, but if you cater to their needs, it's easier for them to accommodate you.

Two Vinters Winery — Woodinville

Don't attempt more than a couple of wineries in a day. Dragging kids to more than one or two wineries is a surefire way to ruin the day.

Finally, if your focus really is on wine tasting throughout the day, consider splitting up. Dad takes the kids the first day and enjoys kid-friendly activities, while mom checks out three or four must-see wineries. On day two, it's dad's turn to sample his favorite wineries, while mom entertains the kids. Divide and conquer!

There's plenty to do in Washington wine country for families. However, to make it truly memorable, you need to plan ahead and create a win-win situation for both kids and parents.

Bicycling in Wine Country

Looking to minimize your carbon footprint in wine country? How about foregoing the car in favor of your bike! Sipping and cycling in wine country is more than wishful thinking. Choices abound in the Pacific Northwest to ride alongside lush vineyards and sample amazing wines. What better way to work off some calories while taking in some much needed refreshment in the form of reds and whites. It's the ol' input and output equation — by the end of the day you break even calorie-wise but gain immeasurably in life's pleasures.

An exceptional regional resource for planning your bike tours is found at **www.bicyclepaper.com**. Here "everything biking" abounds with respect to news and event information including a number of rides that take you through the heart of wine country. If you're looking for an experienced touring company that provides fully supported bike touring (i.e., from boxed lunches to overnight accommodations) check out **www.bicycleadventures.com**.

Washington is a bicycler's paradise for weekend getaway wine touring. Think Walla Walla, Lake Chelan, Yakima Valley, San Juan Island and Columbia Gorge and pairing biking with wine touring gets the heart pumping. Throughout the year, you can find bicycling events to combine sipping and cycling. For example, Skagit Valley's Tulip Pedal in April takes you through miles of tulips and nearby wineries; the Walla Walla Wine Tour in June combines rolling hills and vineyards; and Yakima Valley's Wine Country Trek in September are great opportunities to pair pedaling with amazing wines.

Cycling in wine country

If you are planning a Washington state bike tour combined with swirling and sipping, here are some online resources:

The state's Department of Transportation's website at **www.wsdot.wa.gov/Bike/** for tour and map information

The Bicycle Alliance of Washington's site at **www.bicyclealliance.org** for events, clubs, and resources

A word of caution is in order here. Riding a bicycle is potentially dangerous. It's often not the cyclist's riding behavior but the car driver's inability to either see or exercise caution while negotiating around cyclists. Adding alcohol only compounds the danger. Riders need to have a tasting strategy – either sip and spit with great frequency or sample one or two wines at each wineries and limit the number of tasting rooms you visit. Alternatively, plan your biking for the morning and leave the wine tasting for the afternoon. Drink responsibly; ride responsibly.

Weddings — Getting Married in Wine Country

"I do."

With those two words, you can finally relax knowing that all those months of planning are over. The flowers you chose, the colors selected for the dresses, and the vows you wrote (and rewrote) are behind you. Now you can undo your tie or shed those 4-inch heels and let lose — after all, you're in the heart of wine country and there is cabernet sauvignon awaiting your pleasure.

Getting hitched at a winery is gaining in popularity throughout the Northwest and a number of Washington wineries welcome on premise weddings (see Winery Amenities Chart in the Introduction on page 6). Many wineries offer a quiet retreat for couples to share a special day with friends and family. What's more, an increasing number have become "destination wineries" for weddings, complete with creature comforts

The WineTrails Guy and new Bride (Kathleen) at Vista Hills Vineyard & Winery (Dayton, OR) 9/20/2009.

such as a spa for working out those nuptial-day tension, overnight lodging with smelly soaps, ponds stocked with koi and, of course a cellar full of wines.

A word to the wise is in order if you wish to exchange vows in wine country: Once you have established your criteria (i.e., budget and size), nail down the winery setting as soon as possible — a year prior to the big day is key for booking popular wineries!

To reduce your risk of things going wrong, I offer this three step process that guarantees success.

1. **Choose the location** — Wineries can accommodate wedding parties of varying sizes, from just two (can you say "elope"?) to several hundred well-wishers. It really depends on you, the couple. This is your day, and you get to choose what fits your personality, not to mention budget. For couples who are getting married the second time around or renewing their marriage vows, a big wedding may not be in the cards. When it comes to weddings, size matters. If you want a wedding that has a guest list approaching 250, most wineries can't accommodate that an event of that size — they lack the parking facilities, the lawn space for chairs, or they have postage-stamp-size dance floors that are just too small for Uncle Willy's sprinkler dance steps.

If you are looking at a destination winery, consider the number of out-of-town guests and whether or not the winery and nearby inns/resorts can accommodate them all.

Once you have selected potential wineries for your wedding, plan on visiting each one and speaking to its wedding/event coordinator. These folks have a wealth of information and can readily answer your questions concerning costs and availability for your ceremony. Imagine what the winery may look (or feel) like months away, during the morning or evening; think in terms of the chances of rain, sunlight for photography (best in the morning or early evening), and wind. You may decide to bag the idea of a "unity" candle for an outdoor event, being at the mercy of the wind. There's nothing like a candle that refuses to light or stay lit for a couple just starting out — an inauspicious beginning!

2. **Know thy wedding planner** — Many wineries have a person on staff responsible for planning weddings, or they can refer you to a preferred wedding planner if you need one. My advice — embrace their service.

Bring your planner a latte and befriend that person. The fact is these people have tons of experience and know the pitfalls associated with putting on a wedding. They can suggest caterers, photographers, florists, transportation services, wedding officiants, and more. You don't have to use them, but through their experience, they have identified the most reliable and best-qualified companies in the area for these one-time services.

Once you have met with a wedding planner, plan to reconnect several months in advance of the wedding to go through the myriad details associated with the event. By this time, you might have a special request that you didn't address the first time. For example, if you want champagne at each table for a toast, but

Future bride for wine country wedding?

the winery doesn't make sparkling wine, how do you handle that? Is the winery copasetic with the two of you exchanging vows while stomping grapes in a tub at harvest? This is your special day and it should reflect your personalities, but be sure you and the winery are on the same page.

As the big day approaches, it is a good idea to visit the winery during the time of day you have reserved for your wedding. Note the light and wind conditions. Review the other "little things" that you didn't think about earlier, such as:

- Does the bride's dressing room have full-length mirrors?
- Will the musicians be located where they can be heard?
- Does the area where the wedding will take place have wheelchair access?
- Will non-wedding guests wander into the event *à la Wedding Crashers*?
- What happens in the event of bad weather? Is the interior space large enough? Will you need to rent a tent as a backup?

3. **Day of event: Arrive early and expect the unexpected.** I understand that you think you have thought through all contingencies. But remember Murphy's Law: "Whatever can go wrong will go wrong," and be prepared for the unexpected. On the big day, emotions will be running high, and if the

Over 45,000 acres of premium wine grapes in Washington

caterer should fail to deliver the ginger-peanut sauce for the fire-grilled, spiced chicken skewers, don't freak out. Life will go on and your guests won't mind. In fact, they might not even notice.

4. **Plan to arrive early.** This is the time to review and change the setup. If Aunt Bertha forgot the special guest book, you can call your best friend and ask her to stop by the mall and pick one up. If the power cord isn't long enough to reach the AV equipment, there's time to dash to ACE Hardware for a new one. No worries, mate. Just relax and realize that these things will happen and add to your special day. Friends of mine related that on their special day, their linens had been mixed up with those of a nearby hotel and they received form-fitting sheets for queen-size beds instead of regular tablecloths. After the bride's mother had a conniption, the groom and his friends draped the outdoor tables with the sheets, and after a few rounds of wine, the assembled crowd had a good laugh!

Now, one more piece of advice, which is probably the most important tip I can give: Have fun!

The Washington AVAs

Washington is the nation's second-largest producer of premium wines, with more than 45,000 acres under cultivation. Currently, Washington has 13 American Viticultural Areas (AVAs) as designated by the federal government's Alcohol and Tobacco Tax and Trade Bureau (TTB). Unlike other winemaking countries, such as France and Italy, where it is their countries' agricultural departments that regulate grape-growing regions, the U.S. relies on the TTB with its roots (pun intended) in the post-Prohibition, post–Al Capone era. Below are snapshots of Washington's 13 AVAs described from western to eastern Washington:

1. Puget Sound
Established: 1995

Size: 69 vineyard acres under production

Varieties: Madeleine Angevine, siegerrebe, and Müller-Thurgau predominate. Pinot noir and pinot gris show promise.

Climate: Maritime climate that rarely results in prolonged freezes in winter and brings mild and dry summers. Precipitation averages 15–60 inches per year. Growing season (the period generally between May and October in the northern hemisphere that is frost free) is about 210 days per year. Long-term average of 1,542 cumulative growing degree days (GDDs); the coolest AVA in the state.

Soil: Semipermeable cemented subsoil allows deep-rooted vinifera vines to survive the late-summer soil water deficit.

2. Columbia Gorge
Established: 2004

Size: 4,432 acres with about 350 acres under production ("a world of wine in 40 miles")

Varieties: Main varieties include barbera, cabernet sauvignon, chardonnay, chenin blanc, gewürztraminer, merlot, pinot blanc, pinot noir, sangiovese, sauvignon blanc, syrah, tempranillo, viognier, and zinfandel.

Climate: Maritime climate on western end becoming continental climate moving east. Annual precipitation ranges from 36 inches at the western end of the range to only 10 inches in the eastern part. Strong winds reduce mildew impact. Has a cumulative average of 3,000 GDDs.

Soil: Generally silty loam collected over time from floods, volcanic activity, and landslides.

3. Lake Chelan
Established: 2009

Size: 24,040 acres with 227 acres of planted grapes in 2007

Varieties: Leading grape varieties are syrah, merlot, Malbec, riesling, pinot gris, gewürztraminer, chardonnay, and pinot noir.

Climate: Lake Chelan has a moderating effect on the temperatures during both winter and summer, and its higher elevation, relative to the Columbia Valley, results in slightly cooler temperatures. This AVA averages 2,682 GGDs. Annual rainfall averages 11 inches, with 39 inches of average annual snowfall.

Soil: Due to the ice age glaciers that formed Lake Chelan, the soil profile is coarse, sandy sediment with notable amounts of quartz and mica.

4. Columbia Valley
Established: 1984

Size: At 11 million acres, the state's largest AVA representing more than one-third of Washington's land mass with more than 40,000 acres planted in wine grapes. Contains 10 other AVAs, with only the Puget Sound and Columbia Gorge AVAs located outside the Columbia Valley AVA.

Varieties: About 40 different grape varieties are commercially grown, with riesling, chardonnay, merlot, syrah, and cabernet sauvignon being the predominant grapes grown.

Climate: Continental climate featuring cold winters (dormant period) and hot, dry summers (long hang time into the fall) with relatively long daylight hours, given the northern latitude location above 46 degrees north. Growing season of 180–200 days with annual average precipitation of 6–8 inches. GGDs range between 2,600 and 3,100.

Soil: Volcanic and sandy loam soil is poor in nutrients, making it ideal for growing *Vitis vinifera.*

5. Ancient Lakes (newest)
Established: 2012

Size: 162,762 acres in Grant, Douglas, and Kittitas counties, all entirely within the Columbia Valley AVA. As of late 2012, 1,399 acres were under production.

Varieties: Most wine grapes grown are white varieties, with riesling, chardonnay, pinot gris, and gewürztraminer leading the way, although a number of red grapes are also under cultivation.

Climate: Continental climate featuring cold winters (dormant) and hot, dry summers (long hang time into the fall) with relatively long daylight hours, given the northern latitude. Growing season of 180–200 days, with an annual average precipitation of 6–8 inches. Has an average of 2,570 GGDs annually.

Soil: Volcanic and sandy wind-blown silt (loess) is poor in nutrients (aka scabland), ideal for growing *Vitis vinifera.*

6. Wahluke Slope
Established: 2006

Size: 81,000 acres, all within Grant County, with about 5,600 acres of wine grapes planted. The Wahluke Slope AVA provides 20 percent of the grapes for the state's wine production.

Varieties: Top grape varieties are merlot, syrah, cabernet sauvignon, riesling, chardonnay, and chenin blanc.

Climate: With an average of 3,009 GGDs annually, Wahluke Slope is one of the hotter viticultural regions in the state and is also one of the driest appellations, with only 8 inches of annual rainfall. The Columbia River moderates the temperature of the nearby vineyards.

Soil: Volcanic and sandy wind-blown silt (loess) is poor in nutrients (aka scabland), ideal for growing wine grapes.

7. Naches Heights
Established: 2012

Size: 13,254 acres in Yakima County with 37.5 acres under production in 2012

Varieties: A wide range of grapes grow in the vineyards, including Bordeaux, Rhône, Italian, and Portuguese varieties.

Climate: Continental climate, giving cold winters and hot summers. It is located northwest of Yakima at elevations ranging between 1,200 and 2,100 feet, and receives about 10–13 inches of rainfall annually. With an average of 2,158 GGDs, it is one of the cooler wine appellations in the state.

Soil: Ancient volcanic bedrock with wind-blown silt (loess) and heavy in clay, helping the soil retain moisture.

8. Yakima Valley (oldest)
Established: 1983

Size: 600,000 acres in Yakima County, with 37.5 acres under production in 2012

Varieties: With a number of different mesoclimates making up this viticultural area, all popular wine grapes are grown in the valley, with chardonnay, merlot, cabernet sauvignon, riesling, and syrah representing a significant percentage of the plantings.

Climate: Continental, with an average 190-day growing season and low precipitation of 8 inches per year (thanks to the Cascade Range's rain shadow effect). The AVA's annual average is 2,628 GGDs.

Soil: Silt-loam soils predominate, and with few nutrients to feed the vines, the plants' vigor is held in check.

9. Rattlesnake Hills
Established: 2006

Size: Located in the Rattlesnake Hills of the Yakima Valley, this region has 68,500 acres with 1,566 in grape production. The appellation is centered around the town of Zillah.

Varieties: Primary grapes include cabernet sauvignon, Malbec, merlot, syrah, chardonnay, and riesling. However, with a wide range of mesoclimates at varying elevations and unique soil profiles, the Rattlesnake Hills AVA grows a large number of European-derived grape varieties.

Climate: Continental with a 190-day growing season (typically) and low precipitation of 7 inches per year. It has an average of 2,627 GGDs a year, mirroring the Yakima Valley AVA, of which it is a part. Vineyards are usually planted on ridges and terraces, resulting in good air drainage, which reduces the risk of frost and cools down the vineyard at night during summer's heat.

Soil: Silt-loam soils predominate, possessing little organic matter, which forces the vines to focus energy on the grape clusters rather than the vines' foliage.

10. Snipes Mountain
Established: 2009

Size: 4,145 acres, of which 759 acres are planted with commercial grapes, making it the second-smallest AVA in the state, with Red Mountain being the smallest. It is located entirely within the Yakima Valley AVA, but its topography and soils set it apart from a viticultural perspective.

Varieties: Leading grapes are cabernet sauvignon, pinot noir, semillon, and syrah. Its vineyards produce more than 30 different grape varieties, supplying the winemaking needs of more than 25 wineries. The Harrison Hill Vineyard features cabernet sauvignon vines planted in 1962, the grapes of which are used by the renowned DeLille Cellars in Woodinville.

Climate: Continental, but the higher elevations of Snipes Mountain and Harrison Hill make it slightly cooler than its AVA neighbors, such as Red Mountain and Horse Heaven Hills. Annual precipitation is only 7 inches per year, with a cumulative average of 2,493 GDDs.

Soil: Aridisols (desert soils) featuring very low organic matter, ideal for growing premium wine grapes.

11. Horse Heaven Hills
Established: 2005

Size: 570,000 acres, of which about 10,130 are planted in wine grapes. It's bounded on the north by the Yakima Valley and on the south by the Columbia River. Horse Heaven Hills is home to the state's largest winery, Columbia Crest, and features a number of Washington's famed vineyards, such as Alder Ridge, Champoux, Canoe Ridge, Andrews Vineyard, and Wallula Gap.

Varieties: Primary grapes are cabernet sauvignon, merlot, chardonnay, riesling, and syrah, with nearly 40 grape varieties planted. About 25 percent of the state's wine production relies on grapes from Horse Heaven Hills.

Climate: Proximity to the Columbia River creates significant wind, while moderating continental climate temperature extremes. The average number of GGDs is 2,982.

Soil: Sandy soils offer excellent drainage.

12. Red Mountain
Established: 2001

Size: Red Mountain is more of a large hill than a mountain, and at only 4,040 acres, it is the smallest AVA in the state, with only 600 acres under cultivation. Despite its diminutive size, Red Mountain enjoys a world-class reputation for its cabernet sauvignon. It is the home of celebrated vineyards Ciel Du Cheval, Klipsun, Kiona, Ranch at the End of the Road, Col Solare, Tapteil, Corvus, and Terra Blanca.

Varieties: The leading grapes are cabernet sauvignon, merlot, cabernet franc, syrah, sangiovese, Malbec, and petit verdot.

Climate: The hottest AVA in the state in terms of growing degree days with a cumulative average of 3,110 GGDs. Its growing season is about 180 days. Annual precipitation checks in at a paltry 6–8 inches.

Soil: Wind-blown loess at varying depths throughout Red Mountain.

13. Walla Walla Valley
Established: 1984

Size: Composed of 300,000 acres of land entirely within the Columbia Valley AVA, stretching from the foothills of the Blue Mountains westward toward the Columbia River. The Walla Walla Valley AVA dips into Oregon, where much of the planting is syrah.

Varieties: While cabernet sauvignon is the leading grape variety (41 percent), merlot, chardonnay, and syrah comprise a large percentage of the other varieties under cultivation, most of which are red grapes.

Climate: The growing season varies between 190 and 220 days, with annual rainfall averaging 12.5 inches per year. It has an average of 2,769 GGDs. Because of the proximity to the Blue Mountains and the tendency for cold air to flow to the floor of the valley and remain there, frost is a major concern for the grape growers of the valley.

Soil: Wind-blown soil and floodwater deposits gave rise to the loess soil that dominates the valley's floor.

Decoding a Washington Wine Label

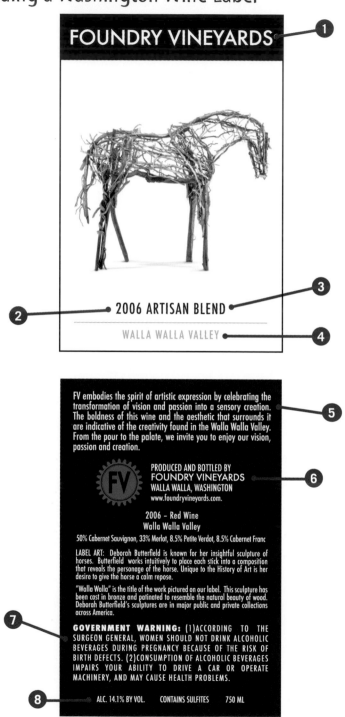

FOUNDRY VINEYARDS

1

2 2006 ARTISAN BLEND **3**

WALLA WALLA VALLEY **4**

FV embodies the spirit of artistic expression by celebrating the transformation of vision and passion into a sensory creation. The boldness of this wine and the aesthetic that surrounds it are indicative of the creativity found in the Walla Walla Valley. From the pour to the palate, we invite you to enjoy our vision, passion and creation. **5**

FV PRODUCED AND BOTTLED BY
FOUNDRY VINEYARDS
WALLA WALLA, WASHINGTON
www.foundryvineyards.com. **6**

2006 - Red Wine
Walla Walla Valley

50% Cabernet Sauvignon, 33% Merlot, 8.5% Petite Verdot, 8.5% Cabernet Franc

LABEL ART: Deborah Butterfield is known for her insightful sculpture of horses. Butterfield works intuitively to place each stick into a composition that reveals the personage of the horse. Unique to the History of Art is her desire to give the horse a calm repose.

"Walla Walla" is the title of the work pictured on our label. This sculpture has been cast in bronze and patinated to resemble the natural beauty of wood. Deborah Butterfield's sculptures are in major public and private collections across America.

7 **GOVERNMENT WARNING:** (1)ACCORDING TO THE SURGEON GENERAL, WOMEN SHOULD NOT DRINK ALCOHOLIC BEVERAGES DURING PREGNANCY BECAUSE OF THE RISK OF BIRTH DEFECTS. (2)CONSUMPTION OF ALCOHOLIC BEVERAGES IMPAIRS YOUR ABILITY TO DRIVE A CAR OR OPERATE MACHINERY, AND MAY CAUSE HEALTH PROBLEMS.

8 ALC. 14.1% BY VOL.   CONTAINS SULFITES   750 ML

Front

1 **Winery Name**

2 **Vintage:** At least 95 percent of the grapes were harvested in the year shown on the label — if the fruit is from a designated viticultural area, such as the Walla Walla Valley AVA. The requirement lowers to 85 percent if the grapes come from a state or county appellation.

3 **Varietal:** At least 75 percent of the grapes come from a specific variety, such as cabernet franc, cabernet sauvignon, merlot, syrah, carménère, petite sirah, and chardonnay. In this case, "2006 Artisan Blend" means that there was no dominant grape variety used to produce this wine. The back of the label indicates that it is a Bordeaux blend of 50 percent cabernet sauvignon, 33 percent merlot, 8.5 percent petit verdot, and 8.5 percent cabernet franc.

4 **Appellation or American Viticultural Area:** Washington state law requires that any wine with a label claiming or implying that its contents are from "Washington" must contain at least 95 percent Washington-grown grapes. Thus, a label that specifies it is a "Walla Walla Valley" wine will have at least 95 percent of the grapes from the Walla Walla Valley AVA, even though, ironically, all the grapes may come from the Oregon side of the AVA.

Back

5 **Descriptive information:** Gives consumers additional information, albeit for marketing purposes.

6 **Produced and bottled by:** Denotes the winery that actually made and bottled the wine, and the winery's location.

7 **Government warning:** Cautions pregnant women that wine may cause health problems for their unborn babies; and that those driving a car or operating machinery may be impaired by drinking alcohol.

8 **Contents:** Indicates the presence of sulfites, volume (e.g., 750 ml), and alcohol content by volume. **Note:** Federal law requires wine bottles to be of specific sizes: 50 ml, 100 ml, 187 ml, 375 ml, 500 ml, 750 ml, 1 L, 1.5 L, or 3 L. Containers of more than 3 L must be whole liters in capacity. No other bottle sizes are permitted.

Additional Terms:

Vineyard designation: Identifies in which vineyard the grapes were grown. At least 95 percent of the wine must come from the designated vineyard.

Estate wine: Denotes that the winery and the vineyards are in the same appellation, the vineyards are controlled or owned by the winery, and the wine was created entirely at that winery.

Reserve wine: Implies the wine is of a higher quality than usual, or has been aged before sold, or both. Traditionally, winemakers would "reserve" some of their best wine rather than sell it immediately, hence the term.

"Growing green" designations (optional): Certifies wine is "organic" as designated by a seal of a USDA-accredited certifying agent placed on the label. Examples include Salmon Safe and LIVE (Low Input Viticulture and Enology) designations.

UPC/EAN Barcode (optional): Although not a regulatory requirement, a significant percentage of wineries place the UPC/EAN barcodes on back labels for retailer scanners.

Common Washington Grape Varieties - Whites

Ch_{ardonnay}

Burgundy origins, vigorous and adaptable to many soils. Cool climate grape. Typically aged in oak but trend toward un-oaked. Fruity with terms such as apple, peach, citrus and pineapple used to describe. Very food friendly.

Ch_{enin Blanc}

With origins from the Loire Valley in France this grape variety is also called Steen in South Africa and Pineau de la Loire in France. Vouvray is chenin blanc. Considered a terroir specific grape, chenin blanc expresses the place of origin as well as winemaker's treatment in vintage.

Ge_{würztraminer}

German-Alsatian grape variety reddish-brown thick skinned grape with typical spicy flavor. One of the earliest to mature. Prefers cool climate. Spicy, floral, fruity, lychee, honey and jasmine tea are terms often used to describe. Dry to sweet.

Mü_{ller-Thurgau}

Hermann Müller of Thurgau, Switzerland created this white wine grape. In 1882 he crossed riesling and Madeleine Royale to create a hybrid. Straw yellow in color, fruity with distinctive peach notes, the Puget Sound AVA is the number one producer of Müller Thurgau in the state.

Mu_{scat}

World's oldest known grape variety. Classic rich nose of dried fruits, raisins, oranges and intense ripe fruit characteristics. Pronounced sweet floral aroma.

Pi_{not gris}

Grayish-hue fruit (gris is French for gray) is called pinot grigio in Italy. Originating in Burgundy, the wine is very terroir dependent ranging in style from crisp, light and dry (Italy) to rich, fat, and honeyed (France's Alsace region and Western U.S.).

Ri_{esling}

German white grape originating in the Rhine River Valley. Very terroir expressive, rieslings balance on a fine line between acidity an delicacy. Flavor descriptors include peach, apple, quince and citrus. Riesling pairs wonderfully with grilled fish, chicken, Thai food and summer salads.

Ro_{ussanne}

Derived from the northern portion of France's Rhône region, often used for blending. The berries are russet colored when ripe — roux is French for the reddish brown color russet, the root for the variety's name. Full-bodied, with flavors of honey and pear.

Sa_{uvignon Blanc}

Green skinned grape originating in Bordeaux where it is often blended with semillon. Vigorous with tender skin, produces crisp, dry and refreshing wines. Fruity to grassy depending upon origin and viticulture methods.

Sé_{millon}

Bordeaux derived grape vinified as a single variety or blended – often with sauvignon blanc. Vigorous, found world-wide. By itself, sémillon produces wines that are not well-rounded and very light in color. Blended with sauvignon blanc, the resulting wines can be extraordinary.

Vi_{ognier}

Golden colored wine with significant cultivation in the northern Rhône region of France. Often blended with other white grapes and syrah. Very fruity bouquet with pronounced floral notes.

Common Washington Grape Varieties - Reds

Barbera

Italy's third most popular grape grown principally in the Piedmont area, vary significantly from medium body wines to powerful intense wines capable of cellaring. Deep ruby color, pink rim, noticeable levels of tannins and pronounced acidity.

Cabernet Franc

Black-skinned Bordeaux grape often blended with cabernet sauvignon and merlot. Increasingly, it is vinified by itself. It prefers cooler climate relative to cabernet sauvignon. Aromas include raspberries, cassis, tobacco and floral.

Cabernet Sauvignon

Blue-black berries with Bordeaux origins, cabernet sauvignon is the most important grape in the world. Vigorous, the grape prefers warm weather climates. Full-bodied, rich and tannic, it is often blended with merlot and cabernet franc to soften it.

Carménère

Smooth, full, rich, dark fruits with good color. Once widely grown in Bordeaux but now principally grown in Chile where it was mistakenly thought to be merlot.

Dolcetto

Meaning "little sweet one" in Italian, this Piedmont deep colored variety has notes of almonds, plums and blackberries. Best drunk young.

Grenache

Grenache grape does well in hot, dry regions and strong stalk makes it well suited for windy conditions. Grenache wines are sweet, fruity, and very low in tannins. Often exhibits high alcohol levels (15 to 16%). Widely planted in southern France with origins in Spain.

Lemberger

Called Blaufränkisch in Germany, Lemberger has nuances of merlot and cabernet but with a hard to define spicy note. Mildly tannic with moderate alcohol. Characterized as fruity, light, and lively.

Malbec

Ink-dark with robust tannins, malbec is a Bordeaux grape. It's put Argentina on the wine world map. Often blended with other Bordeaux grapes to produce clarets. Characterized by dark fruit notes and herbal aromas.

Me_{rlot}

Popular Bordeaux grape often blended with cabernet sauvignon. Merlot is medium body ("fleshy") noble grape with hints of berry, plum and currant. Consistently described as smooth, it is lighter in color, acid and tannins than cabernet sauvignon.

Mo_{urvèdre}

From southern France's Rhône region, mourvèdre grapes produce garnet-colored wines with spicy, peppery characteristics. Due to high tannins and alcohol levels, it is often blended with grenache. The grapes are thick-skinned exhibiting blue-black colors.

Ne_{bbiolo}

Considered Italy's most noble grape, Nebbiolo has notes of roses, cherries and tar. Grown widely throughout Piedmont, it is the variety in Barolo, Barbaresco, Gattinara, Ghemme and Langhe.

Pe_{tit Verdot}

A high quality Bordeaux grape used primarily as a blending "seasoning" wine. Full-bodied, deep-colored with peppery, spicy flavor characteristics. High in tannins and alcohol. Increasing popularity as a standalone variety wine in new world.

Pi_{not Noir}

Described as the most finicky of grapes, this Burgundy grape is small, blue-black and thin-skinned in pinecone shaped clusters. Light ruby red, the flavors are often characterized as fresh strawberry to berry jam, spicy, black pepper and cherry.

Sa_{ngiovese}

Considered by many to be Italy's "aristocratic" variety, sangiovese has notes of black cherries, spice, smoke, herbs and nuts. Chianti, Brunello di Montalcino, Super Tuscans and VinoNobile di Montalcino are all sangiovese-based wines.

Sy_{rah}

Vigorous and performs well in different soil types. Rhône derived variety, syrah is big-bodied and capable of aging for many years. Often blended with grenache and mouvrèdre in Rhône. In Australia, syrah is called shiraz.

Te_{mpranillo}

Spain's noble grape, tempranillo is a full-bodied wine ruby red in color. Aromas of berries, plum, tobacco, vanilla, leather and herb describe this wine. Tempranillo prefers mild to hot weather continental climate zones.

Zi_{nfandel}

Identical with southern Italy's Primitivo grape, zinfandel is vinified in many styles including slightly sweet blush wine, red table wine, late harvest dessert wine, sparkling wine and port-style wines. Zinfandel is often characterized as hearty and spicy.

Winery	Chardonnay	Chenin blanc	Gewürztraminer	Pinot gris	Riesling	Roussanne	Sauvignon blanc	Sémillon	Viognier
21 Cellars								●	
509 Wine Company									●
Adamant Cellars									
Adytum Cellars									
Agate Field Vineyard								●	
Airfield Estates Winery	●		●	●	●		●		●
Alexandria Nicole Cellars			●		●		●		●
Almquist Family Vintners	●								
Alta Cellars Winery									
àMaurice Cellars	●								●
Amavi Cellars							●		
Amelia Bleu				●					
AniChe Cellars			●						
Anton Ville Winery									
Arbor Crest Wine Cellars	●			●			●		
Ash Hollow Winery		●							●
Aspenwood Cellars									
Atam Winery		●		●					
Auclair Winery						●			
Badger Mountain / Powers	●			●					
Baer Winery									
Balboa Winery	●								
Barnard Griffin Winery	●			●			●		●
Baroness, Bergdorf & Mannina								●	
Barons Winery						●			
Barrage Cellars	●			●					
Barrel Springs Winery									
Barrister Winery						●			
Bartholomew Winery				●					●
Basalt Cellars							●	●	
Basel Cellars Estate Winery	●						●		
Bella Terrazza Vineyards	●	●	●	●					
Benson Vineyards Estate	●	●	●				●		●
Beresan Winery				●				●	
Bergevin Lane Vineyards	●								●
Bethany Vineyard & Winery	●		●	●					
Black Diamond Winery									

WHITES

Barbera	Bordeaux red blend	Cabernet franc	Cabernet sauvignon	Grenache	Malbec	Merlot	Mourvedre	Pinot noir	Sangiovese	Syrah	Tempranillo	Rhône red blend	Pg #
			•	•							•		108
			•			•				•			77
	•	•	•			•				•		•	532
	•					•							149
	•					•				•			358
•	•		•		•	•	•	•	•	•	•	•	386
			•	•	•	•				•	•		375
•	•	•	•	•						•			78
	•	•	•							•			177
			•		•	•				•			524
			•										501
•													188
	•									•			244
			•										186
	•		•		•					•			567
			•		•	•				•	•		543
	•	•											213
•													286
	•					•							214
			•			•				•			440
		•	•	•		•							196
			•	•		•		•		•	•		503
•			•	•		•				•			436
	•		•	•		•	•			•			304
	•		•										219
	•		•			•				•			195
	•	•				•				•			381
	•	•				•				•			554
	•		•		•						•		84
	•		•					•					577
	•	•	•		•	•				•	•		498
	•												319
	•	•				•		•	•				277
	•	•	•		•	•				•			502
	•		•	•				•		•			463
	•		•			•		•		•			235
								•					65

WineTrail	Winery	Chardonnay	Chenin blanc	Gewürztraminer	Pinot gris	Riesling	Roussanne	Sauvignon blanc	Sémillon	Viognier
	Blooms Winery			•					•	
	Bonair Winery	•		•	•					
	Boudreaux Cellars	•			•					
	Brian Carter Cellars									
	Bunchgrass Winery									
	Buty Winery	•			•					
	C.R. Sandidge Wines									•
	Cairdeas Winery					•				
	Camaraderie Cellars									
	Canoe Ridge Vineyard	•		•	•					
	Canon de Sol Winery									
	Canyon's Edge Winery						•			
	Carpenter Creek Winery	•			•		•			
	Cascade Cliffs Winery									
	Cascadia Winery	•			•					
	Castillo de Feliciana			•						•
	Caterina & Lone Canary	•	•	•		•				
	Cave B Estate Winery	•		•				•		•
	CAVU Cellars						•			
	Celaeno Winery									•
	Challenger Ridge Vineyard	•		•						•
	Chandler Reach Vineyard									
	Charles Smith Wines	•		•	•					•
	Chateau Faire Le Pont	•		•	•		•			•
	Chateau Rollat Winery							•		
	Chateau Ste. Michelle	•	•	•	•	•		•	•	
	Chatter Creek Winery			•						•
	Chelan Estate Winery									
	Chelan Ridge Winery	•			•					
	China Bend Winery									
	Chinook Wines	•					•	•		
	Claar Cellars	•			•		•			
	Clearwater Canyon Cellars									
	Cloudlift Cellars	•								
	Col Solare									
	College Cellars				•		•		•	•
	Columbia Crest Winery	•		•	•		•			

Barbera	Bordeaux red blend	Cabernet franc	Cabernet sauvignon	Grenache	Malbec	Merlot	Mourvedre	Pinot noir	Sangiovese	Syrah	Tempranillo	Rhône red blend	Pg #
			•							•			49
	•		•	•		•	•			•			352
			•			•				•			301
													164
	•		•	•									457
	•		•	•						•			533
										•			282
		•				•				•			283
	•	•	•	•		•							66
		•								•			460
			•			•							166
			•			•		•		•			393
		•				•	•			•			39
•			•			•				•			253
			•			•							310
	•			•							•		517
		•				•		•		•			558
•			•	•		•		•		•	•		328
•			•	•									542
							•			•			138
							•			•			41
	•		•					•		•			418
			•	•		•				•			489
			•			•	•			•			321
	•		•										483
			•	•		•				•			132
	•	•	•							•			215
	•		•			•	•						293
•	•					•				•			278
						•							571
	•		•			•				•			372
			•			•		•		•			364
	•			•		•							576
•						•							85
•													426
	•		•	•		•	•			•			522
	•		•			•				•			408

WineTrail / Winery	Chardonnay	Chenin blanc	Gewürztraminer	Pinot gris	Riesling	Roussanne	Sauvignon blanc	Sémillon	Viognier
Columbia Winery	●	●	●	●					●
Comforts of Whidbey									
Confluence Winery									
Convergence Zone Cellars		●	●	●					
Cooper	●		●						
Copper Mountain Vineyards	●	●							
Cor Cellars					●				
Corvus Cellars									
Cougar Crest Estate Winery	●								●
Covington Cellars								●	●
Cowan Vineyards		●							
Crayelle Cellars				●					
Cuillin Hills Winery									
Cultura Wine									
Dakota Creek Winery	●		●	●					●
DaMa Wines	●								●
Darby Winery									●
Davenport Cellars									
DeLille Cellars						●			
Des Voigne Cellars									
Desert Wind Winery	●			●		●	●		●
DiStefano Winery						●	●		●
Domaine Pouillon		●			●				●
Domanico Cellars				●					
Don Carlo Vineyard	●								
Dunham Cellars	●			●					
Dusted Valley Vintners	●			●					●
Dusty Cellars Winery	●	●		●					
Dutch John's Wines	●								
Dynasty Cellars									
Eagle Creek Winery	●	●	●	●					
Eagle Harbor Wine Co.	●								●
Eagle Haven Winery									●
Eaglemount Wine and Cider									
East Fork Cellars	●		●				●		●
Efesté				●			●		
Eight Bells Winery	●		●						

REDS

Barbera	Bordeaux red blend	Cabernet franc	Cabernet sauvignon	Grenache	Malbec	Merlot	Mourvedre	Pinot noir	Sangiovese	Syrah	Tempranillo	Rhône red blend	Pg #
●		●	●		●	●			●	●			135
													46
			●		●					●			239
	●											●	211
	●		●			●							420
			●			●				●			266
	●	●	●		●								248
	●		●							●			540
		●	●	●		●				●			454
●		●	●		●				●	●			218
	●	●	●			●							376
								●		●			313
	●	●								●		●	198
	●	●	●										361
		●	●		●	●			●	●	●		25
			●			●			●	●			484
	●	●		●						●		●	168
	●									●			181
	●		●							●			163
						●			●	●			180
●			●			●			●	●			396
	●	●	●	●		●				●			144
												●	249
	●		●			●				●			76
		●	●			●							472
		●	●			●				●			528
	●	●	●	●	●	●	●		●	●			510
	●	●				●				●			51
			●			●				●			315
	●		●			●							29
			●			●				●			306
			●						●	●			98
								●	●	●			40
	●		●			●				●			62
	●	●						●		●			237
			●							●			176
			●			●			●	●			81

Winery	Chardonnay	Chenin blanc	Gewürztraminer	Pinot gris	Riesling	Roussanne	Sauvignon blanc	Sémillon	Viognier
El Corazon Winery									●
Eleganté Cellars		●							
Elevation Cellars				●					
Eleven Winery			●				●		
Elsom Cellars									
English Estate Winery	●								
Esther Bricques Winery	●	●						●	
Eye of the Needle Winery	●		●				●		
Facelli Winery	●								
FairWinds Winery		●							
Fidelitas Wines							●		
Finn Hill Winery	●								
Finnriver Farm & Cidery									
Five Star Cellars									
Fjellene Cellars							●		
Flying Dreams Winery							●		
Flying Trout Wines									
Forgeron Cellars	●					●			
Fort Walla Walla Cellars									
Foundry Vineyards	●								
Four Lakes Winery	●		●	●			●		
Gamache Vintners				●					●
Gård Vintners			●	●	●				●
Gifford Hirlinger Winery				●					
Gilbert Cellars	●			●					
Glacial Lake Missoula									
Glacier Peak Winery									
Glencorrie Tasting Room									
Goose Ridge Winery	●			●	●				
Gordon Brothers Cellars	●	●					●		
Gorman Winery	●								
Gougér Cellars Winery									
Gramercy Cellars									
Grande Ronde Cellars	●			●			●		
Grantwood Winery									
Guardian Cellars							●		
Hamilton Cellars		●							

WHITES

Barbera	Bordeaux red blend	Cabernet franc	Cabernet sauvignon	Grenache	Malbec	Merlot	Mourvedre	Pinot noir	Sangiovese	Syrah	Tempranillo	Rhône red blend	Pg #
	•			•					•				488
		•		•	•			•	•				538
		•											199
		•		•		•							99
		•											139
		•					•		•				241
		•					•						269
					•			•	•			•	191
•	•	•			•			•	•				143
		•											61
	•	•			•				•				422
	•	•			•								210
													60
		•		•				•	•				537
	•	•		•					•				514
			•						•	•			201
	•	•		•				•	•				470
•		•							•				492
	•	•			•				•				486
		•			•				•				462
		•			•				•				284
	•	•		•					•				391
		•		•					•				329
		•			•						•		516
•				•					•			•	342
•		•							•				24
		•					•		•				42
•		•			•				•				453
		•		•	•				•				439
•									•				178
		•							•				156
	•			•	•								240
			•			•			•		•	•	461
	•	•			•								563
		•			•				•	•			458
•		•							•				193
•				•	•								438

Winery	Chardonnay	Chenin blanc	Gewürztraminer	Pinot gris	Riesling	Roussanne	Sauvignon blanc	Sémillon	Viognier
Harbinger Winery	●							●	
Hard Row to Hoe Vineyards			●				●		
Heaven's Cave Cellars	●			●					
Hedges Family Estate	●						●		
Hestia Cellars		●							
Heymann Whinery	●			●			●		
Hightower Cellars									
Hollywood Hill Vineyards									
Holmes Harbor Cellars	●		●	●	●				
Hoodsport Winery	●						●		
Horan Estates Winery									●
Horizon's Edge Winery	●		●						
Hyatt Vineyards				●	●				
Icicle Ridge Winery	●		●	●	●		●		
Illusion Winery	●			●	●				
Isenhower Cellars									
Island Vintners	●			●	●		●		
J. Bookwalter Winery	●				●				
Jacob Williams Winery	●						●		
Januik Winery	●								
JM Cellars	●						●		
Jones of Washington Estate	●		●		●				●
K Vintners	●				●				●
Kaella Winery									
Kalamar Winery									
Kana Winery					●				
Karma Vineyards	●	●							
Kerloo Cellars									
Kestrel Vintners	●								●
Kiona Vineyards and Winery	●	●			●				
Knight Hill Winery	●				●	●			
Knipprath Cellars	●					●			
Kontos Cellars	●								
L'Ecole No 41	●	●					●		
Lachini Vineyards	●		●						
Lake Chelan Winery	●		●	●					
Latah Creek Wine Cellars	●				●		●		

Barbera	Bordeaux red blend	Cabernet franc	Cabernet sauvignon	Grenache	Malbec	Merlot	Mourvedre	Pinot noir	Sangiovese	Syrah	Tempranillo	Rhône red blend	Pg #
	•					•				•			67
•	•	•				•				•			279
	•	•	•	•						•			373
	•	•				•				•			423
	•	•		•		•							183
		•				•				•			233
•		•				•				•			425
			•	•		•					•		169
		•				•	•			•			50
	•					•				•			116
		•				•				•			314
		•				•	•						366
		•				•							357
		•	•			•				•			309
		•				•							251
	•	•		•				•		•			511
•	•	•		•				•					97
		•				•							435
		•				•				•			254
		•				•							136
		•				•							134
		•				•		•					327
		•	•			•		•	•	•			523
	•					•		•		•			212
		•				•		•					106
•										•	•	•	343
		•		•			•			•		•	294
			•	•						•	•		476
		•			•			•		•			377
		•	•	•				•					421
	•				•								355
	•				•			•		•			568
	•	•		•	•					•			539
	•	•			•					•			451
		•				•		•					162
		•	•			•		•		•			276
						•		•					570

REDS

Winery	Chardonnay	Chenin blanc	Gewürztraminer	Pinot gris	Riesling	Roussanne	Sauvignon blanc	Sémillon	Viognier
Laurelhurst Cellars									
Locati Cellars			•						
Lodmell Cellars	•						•	•	
Lopez Island Winery	•			•					
Lost River Winery			•					•	
Madsen Family Cellars	•		•	•					
Maison Bleue Family Winery						•			•
Maison de Padgett Winery	•		•						
Malaga Springs Winery		•					•		•
Mannina Cellars									
Mansion Creek Cellars	•								
Mark Ryan Winery	•								•
Market Place Wine Bar									•
Marshal's Winery									
Martin-Scott Winery	•		•	•					•
Maryhill Winery	•		•	•		•			•
Masset Winery	•								
Matthews Estate						•			
McCrea Cellars						•			•
McKinley Springs Winery		•							•
Medicine Creek Winery									
Memaloose McCormick									
Mercer Estates	•		•	•			•		
Merry Cellars							•	•	
Michael Florentino Cellars			•						
Milbrandt Vineyards	•	•	•	•	•	•		•	•
Morrison Lane Winery						•			•
Mount Baker Winery			•						
Naches Heights Vineyard		•	•	•					
Napeequa Vintners									•
Nefarious Cellars				•			•		•
Nodland Cellars				•					
Northstar Winery							•		
Northwest Cellars	•								
Northwest Mountain Winery	•			•					
Northwest Totem Cellars									
Northwest Wine Academy	•		•						

WHITES

Barbera	Bordeaux red blend	Cabernet franc	Cabernet sauvignon	Grenache	Malbec	Merlot	Mourvedre	Pinot noir	Sangiovese	Syrah	Tempranillo	Rhône red blend	Pg #
	•	•	•			•			•				86
•								•					468
						•			•				471
		•			•	•		•	•				32
	•		•			•							270
	•	•	•			•		•					113
			•						•		•		474
				•		•							359
		•	•	•				•	•				325
	•		•			•		•					536
	•		•			•							490
	•		•				•		•				151
	•					•							561
•	•		•			•			•				252
			•			•	•	•	•				323
•		•	•	•	•	•		•	•				255
			•			•			•				347
	•	•	•										148
				•		•			•			•	114
			•	•					•				410
	•	•	•			•		•	•				110
•	•	•						•				•	250
			•			•		•	•			•	378
			•			•			•			•	574
	•	•	•	•	•	•		•	•	•			185
	•		•	•				•	•	•			390
•			•					•	•	•			494
			•			•	•		•	•			27
	•								•	•	•		340
•	•		•										307
	•	•	•		•				•				292
		•	•										569
	•	•	•			•			•				508
						•	•						95
	•		•						•				112
	•	•	•	•		•			•				173
•	•	•	•	•		•	•		•				90

Winery	Chardonnay	Chenin blanc	Gewürztraminer	Pinot gris	Riesling	Roussanne	Sauvignon blanc	Sémillon	Viognier
:Nota Bene Cellars									
O·S Winery				•					
Obelisco Estate									
Okanogan Estate	•		•	•	•				
Olympic Cellars	•				•				
Otis Kenyon Wine					•				
Ott & Murphy Wines									•
Overbluff Cellars								•	•
Page Cellars						•			
Palouse Winery					•				•
Paradisos del Sol		•			•		•		
Pasek Cellars Winery	•								
Patit Creek Cellars	•				•				
Patterson Cellars	•								
Pepper Bridge Winery									
Piccola Cellars	•			•					
Piety Flats Winery	•	•	•		•				
Plumb Cellars									•
Pomum Cellars					•				
Pondera Winery									
Pontin del Roza Winery		•		•	•				
Portteus Vineyards & Winery	•								•
Preston Premium Wines	•				•		•		
Red Sky Winery								•	
Reininger Winery								•	
Revelry Vintners	•				•				
Rio Vista Wines	•				•				
Robert Karl Cellars							•		
Robert Ramsay Cellars								•	•
RockWall Cellars	•		•		•				•
Rolling Bay Winery	•		•						
Ross Andrew Winery			•						
Rotie Cellars									
Rulo Winery	•								•
Russell Creek Winery									
Rusty Grape Vineyard			•						
Ryan Patrick Vineyards	•								

WHITES

Barbera	Bordeaux red blend	Cabernet franc	Cabernet sauvignon	Grenache	Malbec	Merlot	Mourvedre	Pinot noir	Sangiovese	Syrah	Tempranillo	Rhône red blend	Pg #
	•	•		•		•				•		•	88
	•	•				•				•			87
			•		•	•				•			204
			•			•	•			•			267
		•	•							•			64
			•		•	•				•			479
	•			•						•	•	•	48
	•		•							•			564
			•										202
	•	•	•							•			102
			•										360
													38
			•			•				•	•	•	530
	•		•							•			157
	•		•			•							509
	•		•							•			190
			•			•				•			248
	•		•			•		•		•			491
	•		•							•	•		220
	•		•		•					•			179
			•			•		•					379
		•	•			•		•					363
			•			•				•			442
	•		•							•			203
			•			•		•		•			455
		•	•							•			535
•			•							•			274
	•		•			•				•			560
						•				•			205
		•	•					•		•			269
	•		•	•						•			100
			•							•			152
		•					•			•		•	482
			•			•				•			512
			•			•		•		•			526
			•		•	•	•	•		•			238
•	•		•			•				•			299

WineTrail Winery	Chardonnay	Chenin blanc	Gewürztraminer	Pinot gris	Riesling	Roussanne	Sauvignon blanc	Sémillon	Viognier
Saint Laurent Winery	•				•				
Samson Estates Winery	•				•		•		
San Juan Vineyards	•				•				
Sapolil Cellars	•								
Saviah Cellars	•						•	•	
Seven Hills Winery			•		•				•
Severino Cellars					•				•
Sheridan Vineyard									
Silvara Vineyards	•			•	•				
Silver Lake Winery	•	•	•		•		•		
Sinclair Estate Vineyard	•								
Sky River Meadery									
Skylite Cellars	•		•						•
Sleight of Hand Cellars	•	•							
Smasne Cellars	•	•			•				•
Snoqualmie Vineyards	•	•	•		•		•		
Sparkman Cellars	•						•		
Spofford Station								•	•
Spring Valley Vineyard									
Stemilt Creek Winery									
Steppe Cellars			•		•			•	
Stevens Winery							•		•
Stina's Cellars	•				•	•	•		•
Stomani Cellars Falling Rain			•						
Stottle Winery									•
Swakane Winery					•		•		
Sweet Valley Wines									•
Swiftwater Cellars	•				•			•	
Syncline Wine Cellars						•			•
SYZYGY									
Tagaris Winery & Taverna	•		•	•	•		•		
Tamarack Cellars	•								
Tanjuli Winery			•						•
Tapteil Vineyard and Winery	•				•				
Tefft Cellars Winery	•	•							•
Tempus Cellars					•				
Tero Estates									

WHITES

Barbera	Bordeaux red blend	Cabernet franc	Cabernet sauvignon	Grenache	Malbec	Merlot	Mourvedre	Pinot noir	Sangiovese	Syrah	Tempranillo	Rhône red blend	Pg #
			•			•			•				324
	•		•			•			•				26
			•			•		•	•				33
			•			•		•	•				478
		•		•		•			•				504
	•			•		•			•		•		466
									•				365
	•	•	•						•				216
						•			•			•	308
	•	•				•			•				362
	•							•	•				485
									•				172
			•		•	•			•				459
		•				•			•				505
			•	•					•				441
			•			•			•				395
			•				•		•				159
			•			•			•		•		518
		•	•			•			•				475
			•			•			•				322
			•			•			•				368
			•	•		•			•				221
	•	•	•			•		•	•				109
•	•		•			•		•	•				79
•			•	•		•		•	•		•		111
	•	•	•			•							320
			•						•		•		477
							•		•				318
		•				•	•		•			•	247
			•						•		•		531
•	•	•	•		•	•		•	•	•			437
	•	•	•			•	•	•	•				534
			•	•		•		•					353
			•			•			•				424
	•		•			•			•				367
	•		•	•	•	•			•				529
	•	•	•	•		•							469

WineTrails NW 619

WineTrail / Winery	Chardonnay	Chenin blanc	Gewürztraminer	Pinot gris	Riesling	Roussanne	Sauvignon blanc	Sémillon	Viognier
Terra Blanca Winery	●				●	●		●	
Tertulia Cellars								●	
The Blending Room	●	●							
The Bunnell Family Cellar	●	●	●	●		●		●	
The Chocolate Shop									
The Hogue Cellars	●	●	●	●	●				
The Tasting Room — Seattle	●								
The Tasting Room — Yakima	●		●	●			●		●
The Woodhouse Wine Estates	●			●					
Thomas O'Neil Cellars	●			●					
Three Brothers Winery	●	●	●	●		●			
Three Rivers Winery	●		●	●		●			
Thurston Wolfe Winery									
Tildio Winery				●					
Townshend Cellar	●			●		●		●	
Treveri Cellars									
Trillium Creek Winery	●			●		●			
Trio Vintners	●								
Trust Cellars				●					
Tsillan Cellars	●		●	●					
Tucker Cellars	●	●		●					●
Tunnel Hill Winery				●					●
Two Mountain Winery	●			●					
Two Vintners Winery									
Va Piano Vineyards							●	●	
Vartanyan Estate Winery	●								
Vashon Winery							●		
Vin du Lac Winery	●		●	●			●		●
VineHeart Winery				●					
Vintage Hill Cellars				●			●	●	
Vortex Cellars									●
Walla Faces									
Walla Walla Village Winery	●		●	●					
Walla Walla Vintners									
Walter Dacon Wines						●			●
Wapato Point Cellars			●	●		●			
Ward Johnson Winery	●								

WHITES

REDS

Barbera	Bordeaux red blend	Cabernet franc	Cabernet sauvignon	Grenache	Malbec	Merlot	Mourvedre	Pinot noir	Sangiovese	Syrah	Tempranillo	Rhône red blend	Pg #
	●	●	●		●	●				●			419
			●	●	●	●				●	●		513
	●	●	●		●	●							281
●				●	●	●	●		●	●		●	389
													481
			●			●				●			374
	●	●	●			●				●	●		83
		●	●		●	●			●	●			341
	●	●	●		●	●				●	●		141
			●			●				●		●	434
	●		●			●		●		●			236
		●	●	●	●	●				●	●		456
			●							●	●		388
		●			●					●	●		285
		●	●			●			●	●			565
													345
			●			●				●			107
●				●			●		●		●	●	467
			●							●			527
					●	●				●			290
		●	●			●			●	●			382
								●		●			291
		●	●			●				●			356
	●					●				●			217
		●	●			●				●			507
			●			●				●			28
		●	●	●	●	●		●					103
			●			●				●			275
			●						●				380
	●	●	●			●				●			562
										●	●	●	197
	●		●							●			487
		●	●			●				●			493
		●	●		●	●			●	●			525
					●	●				●			115
									●	●			280
			●			●				●			80

Winery	Chardonnay	Chenin blanc	Gewürztraminer	Pinot gris	Riesling	Roussanne	Sauvignon blanc	Sémillon	Viognier
Waterbrook Winery	●		●		●		●		
Watermill & Blue Mountain		●							●
Waters Winery									●
Waterville Winery	●				●				
Waving Tree Winery									
Wawawai Canyon							●	●	●
Wedge Mountain Winery	●			●	●				
Westport Winery	●		●		●				
Whidbey Island Winery	●			●		●			
White Heron Cellars						●			●
Whitestone Winery				●					
Widgeon Hill Winery	●	●					●		
William Church Winery				●					●
Willow Crest Winery				●	●				
Wind River Cellars	●		●	●	●				
Wind Rose Cellars				●					
Windy Point Vineyards			●		●				
Wineglass Cellars	●								
Winemakers Loft	●				●		●		●
Woodinville Wine Cellars							●		
Woodward Canyon Winery	●				●		●		
XSV Wines	●								
Yakima River Winery									
Zerba Cellars	●			●		●		●	●

WHITES

Barbera	Bordeaux red blend	Cabernet franc	Cabernet sauvignon	Grenache	Malbec	Merlot	Mourvedre	Pinot noir	Sangiovese	Syrah	Tempranillo	Rhône red blend	Pg #
			•	•		•		•	•	•			452
	•	•	•			•	•	•	•	•			500
			•						•				506
			•						•				312
•			•	•				•				•	256
													575
	•	•				•			•				311
		•				•			•				232
	•	•			•	•		•					47
	•		•		•		•						326
	•		•			•			•				556
			•			•			•				234
	•		•		•				•				161
		•							•				387
		•				•	•		•	•			245
•	•					•			•				63
	•		•			•	•		•				346
	•		•			•		•	•				354
	•	•	•		•				•	•	•		392
		•				•			•				145
•			•			•			•				450
			•			•			•				182
			•			•			•				394
•	•		•			•	•	•	•		•		499

ORDER PAGE

WineTrails OF WASHINGTON, 2nd Edition

Great gift for your wine loving friend or loved one, get autographed copy and enjoy the convenience of online shopping.
Only $24.95 plus S&H

WineTrails OF WASHINGTON - The App

The perfect companion to the book with regular updates.
Published for the iPhone/iPad and Android platforms
Only $2.99 at Google Play or the iTunes Store

WineTrails OF WALLA WALLA

First Edition
Go beyond the tasting rooms and discover why Walla Walla is one of the world's great wine destinations.
Only $19.95 plus S&H

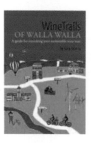

WineTrails OF WALLA WALLA - The App

All things Walla Walla when it comes to wine including where to stay, eat and play. Published for the iPhone/iPad and Android platforms.
Only $2.99 at Google Play or the iTunes Store

WineTrailsNW Shop

Call **800-533-6165** or order online at
www.winetrailsnw.com/shop

VISIT. TASTE. EXPERIENCE.

Index

This index lists wineries alphabetically and by city. Both primary and secondary tasting room locations are specified.

S

Woodinville